BRITISH FREEMASONRY, 1717–1813

CONTENTS OF THE EDITION

VOLUME 1
General Introduction
Institutions

VOLUME 2
Rituals I – English, Irish and Scottish Craft Rituals

VOLUME 3
Rituals II – Harodim Material and Higher Degrees

VOLUME 4
Debates

VOLUME 5
Representations
Index

BRITISH FREEMASONRY, 1717–1813

GENERAL EDITOR
Róbert Péter

Volume 4
Debates

Edited by
Róbert Péter

Routledge
Taylor & Francis Group
LONDON AND NEW YORK

First published 2016
by Routledge
2 Park Square, Milton Park, Abingdon, Oxon OX14 4RN

and by Routledge
52 Vanderbilt Avenue, New York, NY 10017

Routledge is an imprint of the Taylor & Francis Group, an informa business

Copyright © Editorial material Róbert Péter 2016

The right of Róbert Péter to be identified as author of the editorial material, and the contributors for their individual contributions, has been asserted in accordance with sections 77 and 78 of the Copyright, Designs and Patents Act 1988.

To the best of the Publisher's knowledge every effort has been made to contact relevant copyright holders and to clear any relevant copyright issues. Any omissions that come to their attention will be remedied in future editions.

British Library Cataloguing-in-Publication Data
A catalogue record for this book is available from the British Library

Library of Congress Cataloging-in-Publication Data
A catalog record for this book has been requested.

Set ISBN: 978-1-84893-377-4
Volume 1 ISBN: 978-1-138-10017-6 (hbk)
Volume 1 ISBN: 978-1-315-63986-4 (ebk)
Volume 2 ISBN: 978-1-138-10018-3 (hbk)
Volume 2 ISBN: 978-1-315-63985-7 (ebk)
Volume 3 ISBN: 978-1-138-10019-0 (hbk)
Volume 3 ISBN: 978-1-315-63984-0 (ebk)
Volume 4 ISBN: 978-1-138-10020-6 (hbk)
Volume 4 ISBN: 978-1-315-63983-3 (ebk)
Volume 5 ISBN: 978-1-138-10021-3 (hbk)
Volume 5 ISBN: 978-1-315-63981-9 (ebk)

CONTENTS

Acknowledgements   vii

Abbreviations   ix

Introduction   xi

Bibliography   xxiii

Anon. [signed Philo Lapidarius], *An Answer to the Pope's Bull, with the Character of a Freemason* (1738)   1

Bernard Clarke, *An Answer to the Pope's Bull, with a Vindication of the Real Principles of Free-Masonry* (1751)   9

William Imbrie and William Geddes, *The Poor Man's Complaint against the Whole Unwarrantable Procedure of the Associate Session in Glasgow, Anent him and Others in Seeking a Confession of the Mason and Chapman Oaths* (1754)   43

James Steven, *Blind Zeal Detected: or, A True Representation of the Conduct of the Meeting I was a Member of, and of the Kirk-Session of the Associate Congregation, at Glasgow* (1755)   67

[Associate Synod], 'An Act of the Associate Synod Concerning the Mason-Oath' and A, R, 'An Impartial Examination of the Act against Freemasons' (1757) in the Appendix of *The Free Masons Pocket Companion* (1761)   81

Richard Lewis, *The Free-Masons Advocate. Or, Falsehood Detected* (1760)   99

Laurence Dermott, *Ahiman Rezon*, 2nd edn, excerpt containing polemic against Moderns Freemasons and in praise of Antients Freemasonry (1764)   117

[Anon.], *A Defence of Free-Masonry, as Practiced in the Regular Lodges, both Foreign and Domestic under the Constitution of the English Grand Master* (1765)   129

[Anon.], *Masonry the Way to Hell, a Sermon* (1768)   151

[Anon.], *Masonry Vindicated: a Sermon. Wherein is Clearly and Demonstratively Proved, that a Sermon, Lately Published, 'Intitled Masonry the Way to Hell', is an Intire Piece of the Utmost Weakness, and Absurdity* (1768)   169

George Smith, 'Ancient and Modern Reasons Why the Ladies
Have Never Been Admitted into the Society of Freemasons',
in *The Use and Abuse of Free-Masonry* (1783)   181

[A Friend to Truth], *A Defence of Free Masons etc., in Answer
to Professor John Robison's Proofs of a Conspiracy* (1797)   195

[Anon.], *The Indictment and Trial of John Andrew, Shoemaker in
Maybole, Sometime Teacher of a Private School There, and Robert Ramsay,
Cart Wright There, Both Members of a Masonic Lodge at Maybole:
Charged with the Crime of Sedition, and Administering
Unlawful Oaths* (1800)   217

[Anon.], *Petition and Complaint at Brother Gibson's Instance
Against Brother Mitchell, and His Answers Thereto; With the
Procedure of the Grand Lodge Thereon and Proof Adduced* (1808)   229

[Anon.], *An Exposition of the Causes which Have Produced the
Late Dissensions Among the Free Masons of Scotland* (1808)   301

[Anon.] *An Enquiry into the Late Disputes among the Free-Masons
of Ireland; Wherein is Detailed a Free and Important Account
of the Different Transactions which Gave Rise to, and Continued
the Controversy, from the Commencement to the Establishment
of the Grand Lodge of Ulster* (1812)   351

Editorial Notes   387
Silent Corrections   427
List of Sources   429

ACKNOWLEDGEMENTS

I am indebted to Ric Berman, David Stevenson and Mark Wallace for their valuable contributions to this volume. I am also very grateful to Jan Snoek, who, apart from the last Irish text, thoroughly read and commented upon all my editorial work. I wish to thank the following scholars for replying to my specific questions concerning the texts reproduced in this volume: Rebecca Hayes, Claus Oberhauser, Reinhard Markner, Petri Mirala, Christopher Powell, Andrew Prescott, Marsha Keith Schuchard and Mark Wallace. Thanks are also due to Éva Horváth for assistance in correcting numerous OCR errors in the texts after they were keyed. My warm thanks go to Christopher Powell and Edward Kelly for proofreading the texts.

ABBREVIATIONS

AQC	*Ars Quatuor Coronatorum*, the transactions of Quatuor Coronati Lodge, No. 2076
CMN	*Crossle Masonic Notes*, Library of Freemasons' Hall, Dublin
Constitutions 1738	J. Anderson, *The New Book of Constitutions of the Antient and Honourable Fraternity of Free and Accepted Masons: Containing their History, Charges, Regulations, &c. Collected and Digested by Order of the Grand Lodge from their Old Records, Faithful Traditions and Lodge-Books, for the Use of the Lodges* (London: Printed for Brothers Cæsar Ward and Richard Chandler, 1738)
EB	*Encyclopaedia Britannica Online Academic Edition* (2013), available at http://www.britannica.com [accessed 5 July 2014]
EMC	D. Knoop, G. P. Jones and D. Hamer (eds), *Early Masonic Catechisms*, 2nd edn (1943; London: Quatuor Coronati Lodge, 1975)
Foundations	R. Berman, *The Foundations of Modern Freemasonry. The Grand Architects. Political Change and the Scientific Enlightenment, 1714–1740* (Brighton: Sussex Academic Press, 2012)
FRS	Fellow of the Royal Society
GL of S	Grand Lodge of Scotland Minutes
GLFI	J. H. Lepper and P. Crossle, *History of the Grand Lodge of Freemasons of Ireland*, 2 vols (Dublin: Lodge of Research, CC., 1925) vol. 1
Handbook	H. Bogdan and J. A. M. Snoek, *Handbook of Freemasonry* (Leiden and Boston, MA: Brill, 2014)
HPO	*History of Parliament Online,* Maintained by the Institute of Historical Research, available at http://www.historyofparliamentonline.org/ [accessed 10 July 2014]
IMR	K. Cochrane (ed.), *Irish Masonic Records*, third CD edition (2009). Originally Published by P. Crossle and the Grand Lodge of Ireland (Dublin, 1973)
Lane	J. Lane's Masonic Records 1717–1894 version 1.0 available at http://www.hrionline.ac.uk/lane/ (HRI Online Publications, October 2011).
LMFL	Library and Museum of Freemasonry, London

Mirala	P. Mirala, *Freemasonry in Ulster, 1733–1813: A Social and Political History of the Masonic Brotherhood in the North of Ireland* (Dublin: Four Courts Press, 2007)
MMLDP	C. Porset and C. Revauger (eds), *Le Monde Maçonnique des Lumières. Europe-Amérique et colonies. Dictionnaire prosopographique*, 3 vols (Paris: Champion, 2013)
NRS	National Records of Scotland
ODNB	*Oxford Dictionary of National Biography* (Oxford: Oxford University Press, 2014), available at www.odnb.com [accessed 15 July 2014]
OED	*Oxford English Dictionary* (Oxford: Oxford University, 2014), available at www.oed.com [accessed 15 June 2014]
Schism	R. Berman, *Schism: The Battle that Forged Freemasonry* (Brighton: Sussex Academic Press, 2013)

INTRODUCTION

Róbert Péter

This volume concerns attacks, vindications, debates and feuds related to Free-masonry in England, Scotland and Ireland. When a work is not widely available, and if space allows, the arguments of both sides of a given conflict have been included in order to give a balanced picture.

Debates related to Freemasonry can be grouped under three main headings: religious disputes, social conflicts and political, financial and legal feuds. Of course this is an artificial categorization – these quarrels were not one-dimensional since social, religious and political factors all played a role in many of these masonic struggles. As for the last group, three conflicts narrated in this collection indicate that political or financial disputes between lodges could lead to legal battles. Richard Lewis's pamphlet, which aims to refute an alleged ritual exposure, cannot be clearly associated with any of the above categories, although it touches upon social conflicts and religious disputes. The debates in this volume are not only concerned with Freemasonry *per se* but can be seen as manifesting contemporary religious, political and social tensions and anxieties.

The single reference to Freemasonry in Roy Porter's *magnum opus* well illus-trates the root of the conflicts contained in this volume: 'masonry was also riddled with typically British ideological tensions, combining deference to hierarchy with a measure of egalitarianism, acceptance of distinction with social exclusiv-ity and commitment to rationality with a taste for mysteries and ritual.'[1] These tensions were manifested in a variety of conflicts surrounding Freemasonry. For example, lodges fiercely debated lodge precedence and the pre-eminence of (Grand) lodges, the presence of operative (stone) masons, ritual practice, the ways of distributing the charity fund, and which lodges could be regarded as regular. They even accused one another of sedition and the organization itself of illicit meetings and expelled lodge members for such reasons.

Freemasonry was attacked and ridiculed by the state, ecclesiastical authorities and ex-Freemasons in official edicts, laws, sermons, pamphlets and in the columns of newspapers. Hitherto research has primarily focused on the history of anti-Masonry. Masonic historians often overlooked, belittled or misinterpreted the feuds and conflicts within Freemasonry, be they between Grand Lodges and independent lodges, or between the (Grand) Lodge(s) and individual Freemasons. The old lodges sometimes disagreed with the innovations of the Grand Lodges and did not obey them, which led to rivalries and rifts.

The vindications of Freemasonry are not only important as attempts to refute accusations regarding the fraternity, but they are significant in highlighting the self-perceptions of Freemasonry from the perspectives of individual Freemasons. They reveal what motivated so many people to join lodges in this period, how they functioned in people's lives, and what Freemasonry actually meant to them. Several defences admit that some 'unworthy' Freemasons caused great damage to the fraternity, but emphasize that corrupt members can join any society and one should not condemn the whole organisation as a consequence.

Both the attacks and the defences contain illogicalities, exaggerations and distortion of facts, which the reviewers of these works often pointed out in the press. Sometimes they remain silent when replying to a particular charge mentioned in the accuser's writings. A common method in these polemics is to point out the inconsistencies and fallacies in the opponent's argument, often in the light of reason and revelation.

Religious Disputes

This volume contains two Irish, three Scottish and two English documents that are primarily concerned with religious quarrels about Freemasonry, though they dispute social aspects of the fraternity too.

The earliest documented attacks against Freemasonry appeared in the seventeenth century. In 1637, John Stewart, Earl of Traquair, who was affiliated with those opposed to Charles I, was criticized for having the 'Masone word', which seems to have referred to some secret bond that connected men for sinister purposes.[2] In 1649, the General Assembly of the Church of Scotland also expressed concerns about the Mason Word. In 1652, James Ainslie, a Scottish Presbyterian minister of Kelso, also faced problems for the same reason before his new appointment. In 1698, a London leaflet warned the 'Christian Generation' and attacked

the Mischiefs and Evils practised in the Sight of God by those called Freed [*sic*] Masons... their Ceremonies and Secret Swearings... For this devvlish Sect of Men are Masters in secret which swear against all without their Following. They are the Anti Christ... [who] meet in secret Places and with secret Signs... Mingle not among this corrupt People.[3]

Such charges were repeated in both state and church condemnations from the eighteenth-century onwards.

The first bans on masonic meetings were announced by governmental rather than church authorities in the mid-1730s. The States of Holland and the Republic of Geneva prohibited masonic meetings because of the potentially subversive activities of the sovereign lodges, whose members took a clandestine oath and selected their Grand Masters democratically during secret gatherings that the authorities were unable to control. The fears of the Catholic Church seem to have been confirmed by the activities of some Italian lodges, especially the one in Florence, which had several English and Irish members. Without examining fundamental masonic texts, the Holy See issued papal bulls against Freemasonry in 1738 and 1751, which reiterated, *inter alia*, the arguments of the aforementioned governmental interdicts. Apart from confirming the validity of the bull of 1738, the 1751 decree added an inconsistent argument relying on Roman law. As José A. Ferrer Benimeli points out, 'paradoxically, the Masons were accused of the same crime for which the pagans impugned the first Christians.'[4]

Irish Freemasons such as the schoolmaster Bernard Clarke, the author of the 1751 pamphlet, felt it important to react immediately to both papal bulls, even though they were not announced in Ireland because it was under Protestant British rule. In 1760, the cardinal protector of Ireland expressed his serious concern to Irish metropolitans that many Irish priests had joined masonic lodges. His anger increased when he was informed that though some of these priests confessed this misdeed to their bishops, others defended themselves by pointing out that the decree was not implemented in France either.[5] Despite clear-cut warnings, the number of Catholics in Irish lodges, in many of which they mixed with Protestants, grew in the 1760s.[6] Patrick Fagan stresses that in this ecumenical environment, the fact that 'protestants were prepared to accept the necessity of relief measures for catholics, has never been adequately studied, much less sufficiently recognized, by historians.'[7] This does not mean that there was no tension between Catholicism and Freemasonry, nor between Catholic and Protestant Freemasons in Ireland. In some towns there were separate lodges for Catholics and Protestants. Some lodges explicitly barred Catholics from membership.[8] Following the direction of his bishop in 1779, a Catholic priest in Sligo threatened the Freemasons of his congregation belonging to Lodge No. 355, with not administering 'the Rights and privileges of his Church' to them in order that they would denounce Freemasonry.[9] In the late 1790s the Irish Catholic dioceses promulgated the papal bull, which resulted in a decrease in the number of Catholics in lodges.

As in Ireland, certain Scottish Presbyterian communities were split because of their different attitudes to Freemasonry. The conflicts lasted from 1739 to the 1760s. The 1730s and 1740s saw schisms in the Presbyterian Church of Scotland, as a result of which the breakaway Secession Church was split into 'Burgher' and 'Antiburgher' churches in 1747 because of a dispute over the 'burgess oath' regarded as sinful by the antiburghers. In 1753, the Glasgow Antiburgher Associate Kirk Session started examining the Mason oath. William Imbrie's and James Steven's pamphlets give an account of this local religious controversy about swearing the Mason oath, which was discussed in the lowest court in the Presbyterian court hierarchy. They were involved in building a house for a company of Freemasons. Relying on the authority of the Bible and numerous theologians they rejected the accusations and their exclusion from the communion service. They did not accept the right of the Kirk Session to question them and provocatively compared the attitude of the session to the attitude of the Catholic Church. Unlike John Coustos during his Portuguese inquisition trial, they did not reveal masonic secrets and rituals. Because of the anxieties of the Glasgow presbytery, in 1755 the Antiburgher Synod investigated the issue and passed an act condemning the mason oath and disciplining Freemasons in congregations in 1755. Both the Act as well as a more informal, provocative and harsh masonic response, where the author relies on secular authorities in this religious dispute, are printed in this volume.

The tensions between Catholics and Protestants in the 1760s manifested themselves in a hitherto overlooked pamphlet war, which was launched by the publication of *Masonry: The Way to Hell* in 1768.[10] This anti-masonic sermon with a strong anti-Protestant sentiment and its five responses, not devoid of staunch anti-Catholic remarks, support their arguments with reason and revelation, which their authors considered compatible. One of the responses argues that the author of *Masonry: The Way to Hell* was a Jesuit and does not conceal a dislike of the Jesuit order. These reprinted documents reinforce John Pocock's thesis that 'Enlightenment was a product of religious debate and not merely a rebellion against it.'[11]

In his refutation of the authenticity of a ritual in 1760, Richard Lewis argues that religion and Freemasonry are intertwined, 'they have a close connection with each other ... Masonry may be looked on as a wholesome supplement to religion'. This simultaneously universal and sectarian masonic religiosity was exported to the British Empire.[12]

Social Conflicts

In spite of masonic idealism popularized in the constitutions and the press reports of masonic meetings, Freemasonry in the British Isles was torn apart in the establishment of several long-standing or ephemeral Grand Lodges in the period. The most influential of these, which had major international impact, was the founding of the Grand Lodge of the Antients in 1751. For a long time, English masonic historians claimed that a split had occurred in Freemasonry in the late 1740s within the Grand Lodge of England. This account was based upon the writings of William Preston, who in his *Illustrations of Masonry* claimed that certain Freemasons had seceded from the regular lodges and declared independence.[13] Henry Sadler's *Masonic Fact and Fiction* (1887) and recently Ric Berman's *Schism: The Battle that Forged Freemasonry* (2013) have demythologized this false explanation. What happened in 1751 was not a split: most Antient Masons never belonged to the Grand Lodge of England since many of them were of Irish origin and initiated in the Grand Lodge of Ireland or independent lodges before 1751. The most important reason for the creation of this rival masonic body was that Irish immigrants of low social standing working in London were not allowed to join the lodges of English gentlemen Freemasons in the capital. Though the Antients objected to the de-Christianizing policy of the 'Moderns'[14], manifested in the rituals, they seemed to be more tolerant towards men of other faiths.[15] A chapter from *Ahiman Rezon* (1764), the constitution of the Antients, is reprinted, in which Laurence Dermott, the editor and the prime mover of the new organization, demonstrates the pre-eminence of the Antients and makes ironic comments about those he nicknames 'Moderns'. The arrogant and superior attitude of the socially exclusive Grand Lodge of the Moderns towards the Antients is revealed in their official response to Dermott, which has been overlooked in the scholarly literature on the subject, but which is reprinted here.

By the end of the century, the joint defence of Freemasonry in the parliamentary debates over the Unlawful Societies Act of 1799 helped the two Grand Lodges draw together.[16] Eventually it was realized that the rivalry was in the interest of neither and in December 1813 the two were united to form the present United Grand Lodge of England.

Another form of exclusiveness, which characterizes British Freemasonry till the present day, is related to the constitutional prohibition of women from masonic membership. However, there were individual Freemasons such as George Smith who did not seem to share the official policy of the Grand Lodges. Having elaborated on the reasons for the non-admission of women, he argues that this ancient practice should be abandoned and encourages them to create female lodges. His radical masonic essay, which contributes to the polemic over women's intellectual role and capabilities of the period, shows how male attitude towards women evolved in the last decades of the century.

Although the constitutions warned Freemasons to avoid excessive drinking and eating during lodge nights, according to lodge minutes, the application of this rule caused problems, which was more or less admitted by the authors of the masonic defences. This is also illustrated by the sanctioning of drinking in lodges, in contemporary paintings and in the bawdy masonic drinking songs.[17] For example, Isaac Head, who wrote one of the replies to *Masonry: The Way to Hell*, encouraged the brethren 'to avoid the Shameful sin of drunkenness'.[18] The author of the last text in this volume asks his fellow Freemasons 'not [to] go to the meetings of their Lodges with the sole intention of drinking to excess ... [since] refreshment should not extend to inebriation'. Epicurean lodge meetings were frequent themes in masonic attacks and vindications.

Political, Financial and Legal Feuds

British Freemasonry was predominantly loyalist and pro-Hanoverian in the eighteenth century. These pro-establishment facets of British Freemasonry were crucial to its success. In the first half of the eighteenth century many influential English Freemasons, who had close associations with the government, were involved in a pro-Whig masonic nexus. In the early decades of organized Freemasonry, the Whig–Jacobite struggle caused conflicts in some lodges.[19]

As David Stevenson points out, some Scottish people considered Freemasonry to be conspiratorial in the seventeenth century.[20] In the first half of the eighteenth century perhaps the most vehement press attack on British Freemasonry with reference to conspiracy was published in the *Craftsman* in April 1737.[21] Although English Freemasons were reluctant to publish a defence, the French issued a reply to this attack.[22] However, in the 1790s they became much more pro-active and defensive.

In the wake of the French Revolution, Freemasons emphasized their loyalty and patriotism in several public forums and the Grand Lodges, when they noticed them, made every effort to suppress radical activities in lodges. However, masonic conspiracy theories associating Freemasonry with Jacobinism and radicalism, became increasingly widespread in the last decade of the century.[23] In 1797, the scientist and former Freemason John Robison warned the British people of the subversive activities of British masonic lodges in his highly influential and popular *Proofs of a Conspiracy*,[24] the arguments of which are still quoted in some present-day conspiracy theories.[25] It is highly unlikely that Robison himself was aware of any radical or subversive activity in lodges in England, Scotland or Ireland in the 1790s, although recent research has shown that some existed.[26] An anonymous masonic response to Robison's work, in which the author attempts to deconstruct his 'proofs' and argues that they draw on gossip and unsubstantiated allegations, is reproduced in this volume.

At the height of the French revolutionary war and with the emergence of republican and seditious organizations such as the United Irishmen, among whose leaders we can find Freemasons,[27] secret societies were seen as possible threats to church and state in Britain. Consequently, societies requiring secret oaths were banned by the Unlawful Societies Act in 1799, during the parliamentary debates of which there were references to Robison's work. The Maybole Trial of Sedition in 1800, a transcription of which is published here, clearly demonstrates the aura of anxiety and suspicion concerning clandestine and illicit meetings both within and outside Freemasonry.[28] Two irregular members of a lodge in Maybole, Ayrshire, Scotland, were accused of collaborating with radical Irish societies to carry out subversive, Illuminati-like activities and of taking seditious oaths at this court battle.

The masonic historian W. J. Chetwode Crawley provides an account of a conflict between Dr John Mitchell, Master of an Edinburgh lodge, and the Grand Lodge of Scotland. Crawley claims that Mitchell and the lodges that supported him were 'charged with illegality under the Secret Societies Act of 1799'[29] and focuses on the legal aspects of the dispute. However, as is typical in masonic historiography, he fails to mention the real reasons for the feud, which were political *par excellence* as the *Petition and Complaint at Brother Gibson's Instance against Brother Mitchell, and His Answers Thereto; with the Procedure of the Grand Lodge Thereon and Proof Adduced* (1808) clearly reveals. It depicts a quarrel between the Whig-dominated Grand Lodge, represented by James Gibson, and the Tory John Mitchell, who proposed in 1807 that the Grand Lodge should send a masonic address to the King. The Grand Lodge did not approve Mitchell's request backed by a Tory minority. The political rivalry resulted in a trial, where the Tory masonic faction was accused of a conspiracy to destroy the Grand Lodge.[30] In June 1808, all Freemasons who were associated with Mitchell were expelled from the Grand Lodge. In response, they formed a separate organization called 'The Associated Lodges Seceding from the Present Grand Lodge of Scotland'. *An Exposition of the Causes Which Have Produced the Late Dissensions among the Free Masons of Scotland* sheds fresh and new light on how the forceful Grand Lodge of Scotland violated basic masonic tenets concerning democratic voting and equal representation of lodges in the conduct of masonic business, and imposed its own political agenda on all lodges in which, at least in theory according to the constitutions, the discussion of politics was not allowed.

The last Irish pamphlet of the volume offers novel insights into how certain members of the Grand Lodge of Ireland breached fundamental masonic – and Enlightenment – ideals and principles, for example, by 'the gross misapplication of a charitable fund', and by ignoring the decision of the majority during the election of Grand Officers, which eventually resulted in the temporary establishment of the Grand Lodge of Ulster (1808–13). The author provides a unique account of this major contest within Irish Freemasonry from the perspective of this new organization. Even though masonic historians of Irish Freemasonry were aware of the arguments and evidence presented in this rare pamphlet, they do not even make a mention of its existence in their accounts of the conflict, yet it is the only work which provides a detailed narrative of this financial and legal contest from its early days to almost its very end.

As we have seen, this kind of misinterpretation is not unprecedented in masonic historiography. As in the case of the history of the Antients Grand Lodge (1751–1813), it was again Henry Sadler who deconstructed the accepted narrative and pointed out the shortcomings of Francis C. Crossle's account by examining 'the Ulster version of the episode'.[31] However, Philip Crossle and J. H. Lepper – largely ignoring Sadler's arguments and presented evidence – relied on Crossle's father in the most elaborate account of the dispute. Their chapter title, 'The Seton Secession', is telling.[32] Like the members of the Antients Grand Lodge in the middle of the eighteenth century, the Ulster Masons were also dubbed as 'seceders'. These often ahistorical – but for the Grand Lodge of England and the Grand Lodge of Ireland – convenient interpretations were created not only to find scapegoats but to conceal the real failures and weaknesses of the Grand Lodges at the time, which this overlooked pamphlet demonstrates. Most masonic historians do not admit this. For instance, William James Hughan argued that 'the Seceders from the Grand Lodge of Ireland did wrong, as also did the "Ancients" of England.'[33]

This volume demonstrates that despite masonic idealism, in practice Freemasonry was affected by the political, social and religious divisions of real life. The tension between masonic rhetoric and practice is not surprising since it is natural that there are inconsistencies between the different layers of experience in every society, be they secular or religious.[34] That is how Freemasonry in action, as a lived experience of individual lodges and Freemasons working rituals, could differ from the grandiose proclamations of the books of constitutions or the teachings of masonic sermons and charges.[35] Although one can also understand the biases of masonic historians defending their own Grand Lodges and often demonizing their critics, their accounts need to be replaced by scholarly works on the subject which place these debates in context and relate the findings to current scholarly concerns in eighteenth-century studies.

Editorial Principles

The texts are reproduced *ad litteram*. Original capitalization and punctuation have been retained and only the significant typographical errors have been amended. The texts have been proofread against a single original source, even if they were printed in different editions. It must be noted that there cannot only be differences between different editions of texts, but also between individual extant copies. Any differences between the printed text and other original texts have to be considered in this light. Where we could consult more editions of a given text, further information, such as alternative readings, is provided in notes. We indicate the details of the sources from which the documents were reprinted in the List of Sources at the end of the volume. Footnotes of the original documents are indicated by asterisks or other signs. The original pagination of the text is signified by the inclusion of / within the text at the point of the page break. Any sections omitted from the text are indicated by [...]. Any other editorial interventions are also contained within square brackets.

Notes

1. R. Porter, *Enlightenment: Britain and the Creation of the Modern World* (London: Allen Lane, 2000), p. 38.

2. D. Stevenson, *The Origins of Freemasonry: Scotland's Century, 1590–1710* (Cambridge: Cambridge University Press, 1988), p. 127.

3. D. Knoop and G. P. Jones, 'An Anti-Masonic Leaflet of 1698', *AQC*, 55 (1942), p. 153. For the different types of masonic secrets, see R. Péter, 'Unio Mystica in the Dramatic Revelation of Masonic Secrecy?' in K. E. Dubs (ed.), *Now You See It, Now You Don't: Hiding and Revealing in Text and Performance* (Piliscsaba: Pázmány Péter Catholic University, 2006), pp. 166–78.

4. J. A. F. Benimeli, 'Freemasonry and the Catholic Church' in *Handbook* p. 141. Another example of the inconsistent attitude of the Catholic Church towards Freemasonry is that in 1789 Bartholomew Ruspini, a prominent Anglican Freemason at that time, received the papal order of the Golden Spur for his benevolence and hospitality to the Italian community in London.

5. P. Fagan, *Catholics in a Protestant Country: The Papist Constituency in Eighteenth-Century Dublin* (Dublin: Four Courts Press, 1998), p. 129.

6. For the Christian members of these lodges, 'the religious Enlightenment represented a renunciation of Reformation and Counter-Reformation militance, an express alternative to two centuries of dogmatism and fanaticism, intolerance and religious warfare.' D. Sorkin, *The Religious Enlightenment. Protestants, Jews and Catholics from London to Vienna* (Princeton, NJ: Princeton University Press, 2008), p. 5.

7. Fagan, *Catholics in a Protestant Country*, p. 130.

8. P. Mirala, *Freemasonry in Ulster, 1733–1813: A Social and Political History of the Masonic Brotherhood in the North of Ireland* (Dublin: Four Courts Press, 2007), pp. 132–44.

9. S. F. Sweetnam, 'Two Hundred Years of Freemasonry in Sligo', *Transactions of the Lodge of Research No. 200 (1996–1998)*, 24 (2000), pp. 179–81. According to the minutes of the lodge, the real reason was that Freemasons assembled in a house whose owner, according to the priest, committed a sin of adultery because he had married a Protestant.

10. '[I]t is likely that in the first seventy years of the century the English Catholic community moved from over 60, 000 to under 80,000 ... The number of Catholics in London seems to have been about 20, 000 and to have increased steadily throughout the century.' G. E. Rupp, *Religion in England, 1688–1791: Oxford History of the Christian Church* (Oxford: Clarendon Press, 1986), p. 190.

11. J. G. A. Pocock, *Barbarism and Religion: The Enlightenments of Edward Gibbon, 1737–1764* (Cambridge: Cambridge University Press, 1999), p. 5

12. V. Fozdar, 'That Grand Primeval and Fundamental Religion': The Transformation of Freemasonry into a British Imperial Cult', *Journal of World History*, 22:3 (2011), pp. 493–525. D. G. Hackett, *That Religion in which All Men Agree: Freemasonry in American Culture* (Berkeley, CA: University of California Press, 2014).

13.	W. Preston, *Illustrations of Masonry* (London: Printed for G. Wilkie, 1781), pp. 259–61.

14.	It is important to note that the term 'de-Christianization' does not imply an anti-religious or anti-clerical activity carried out by irreligious infidels in this context.

15.	For the attitude of Antient lodges towards Jews, see R. Péter, 'The Mysteries of English Freemasonry. Janus-Faced Masonic Ideology and Practice between 1696–1815' (PhD thesis, University of Szeged, 2006), pp. 141–4.

16.	Parliament passed this Act at the height of the French Revolutionary wars. However, as a result of the efforts of the Duke of Atholl, the Grand Master of the Antients, and the Earl of Moira, the Grand Master of the Moderns, Freemasonry was exempted. The only requirement was that lodge secretaries were to make an annual return of names, addresses and descriptions of members to the local Clerk of the Peace. After the Criminal Law Act of 1967 this was no longer required. For a detailed analysis of the 1799 Act and its masonic consequences see A. Prescott, 'The Unlawful Societies Act of 1799', in M. D. J. Scanlan (ed.), *The Social Impact of Freemasonry on the Modern World* (London: Canonbury Masonic Research Centre, 2002), Canonbury Papers, vol. 1, pp. 116–34.

17.	P. Clark, *British Clubs and Societies, 1580–1800: The Origins of an Associational World* (Oxford: Clarendon Press, 2000), pp. 325–6.

18.	I. Head, 'A Charge Delivered to a Constituted Lodge of Free and Accepted Masons at the King's Arm, Helston, Cornwall on Tuesday April 21, 1752', in *The Pocket Companion and History of Free-Masons* (London: Printed for J. Scott; and sold by R. Baldwin, 1754), pp. 300–7, 303. M. M. Roberts, 'Masonics, Metaphor and Misogyny: A Discourse of Marginality', in P. Burke and R. Porter (eds), *Languages and Jargons* (Cambridge: Polity 1998), pp. 133–55. M. M. Roberts, 'Hogarth on the Square: Framing the Freemasons', *British Journal for Eighteenth-Century Studies*, 26:2 (2003), pp. 251–70.

19.	J. P. Jenkins, 'Jacobites and Freemasons in 18th-Century Wales.' *Welsh History Review* 9.4 (1979) pp. 391–406. Sean Murphy, 'Irish Jacobitism and Freemasonry.' *Eighteenth-Century Ireland* 9 (1994) pp. 79–82. M. K Schuchard, 'The Young Pretender and Jacobite Freemasonry: New Light From Sweden on His Role as Hidden Grand Master.' in R. Caldwell *et al.* eds., *The Selected Papers of Consortium on Revolutionary Europe, 1750–1850* (Tallahassee: Institute on Napoleon and the French Revolution, Florida State University, 1994), pp. 363–75.

20.	Stevenson, *The Origins of Freemasonry: Scotland's Century, 1590–1710*, p. 7.

21.	See vol. 2, pp. 12–15.

22.	*Le Pour et Contre*, 12 (May 1737), pp. 282–8. R. Péter, 'Representations of Anti-Masonry in Eighteenth-Century London Newspapers', paper presented at the 12th International Canonbury Conference on the Study of Freemasonry (London, 28–30 October 2010).

23.	For example, see J. M., 'The French Revolution Caused by Free-Masonry', *Walker's Hibernian Magazine* (July 1794), pp. 37–40. P. R. Campbell, *Conspiracy in the French Revolution* (Manchester: Manchester University Press, 2010).

24.	J. Robison, *Proofs of a Conspiracy Against all the Religions and Governments of Europe, Carried on in the Secret Meetings of Free Masons, Illuminati, and Reading Societies. Collected from good authorities by John Robison, A. M. Professor of Natural Philosophy, and Secretary to the Royal Society of Edinburgh* (Edinburgh: printed for William Creech, 1797).

25.	Several of Robison's arguments mirror typical Counter- or Anti-Enlightenment tenets. Although he partially supported the views of Mary Wollstoncraft, he rejected the atheism and religiosity of French *philosophes*. He also played the anti-Catholic card. Robison also attempted to link the dangerous and subversive Illuminati Order with the Jesuits, with which the ex-Jesuit Abbé Baurrel, the author of the most influential *Mémoires pour servir à l'Histoire du Jacobinisme*, did not agree.

26. A. Prescott. 'Freemasonry and Radicalism in Northern England 1789–1799: Some Sidelights', in *Lumières, 7 (Franc-maçonnerie et Politique au Siècle des Lumières: Europe-Amériques)* (2006), pp. 123–142. J. Money, 'Freemasonry and the Fabric of Loyalism in Hanoverian England.' in Hellmuth Eckhart ed., *The Transformation of Political Culture: England and Germany in the Late Eighteenth Century* (Oxford, 1990), pp. 235–269 p. 256. M. D. J. Scanlan, 'John Wilkes. Freemasonry and the Emergence of Popular Radicalism.' in M. D. J. Scanlan (ed.), *The Social Impact of Freemasonry on the Modern World* (London: Canonbury Masonic Research Centre, 2002), Canonbury Papers, vol. 1, pp. 36–59. Mirala, pp. 141–234. J. Woods, 'The British View of Freemasonry during the Emergence of Conspiracy Theories, c.1795 to 1815' (BA dissertation, University of Leeds, 2010).

27. Mirala, pp. 189–208.

28. For example, some Scottish lodges accused one another of accepting irregular Freemasons and permitting them to organize illegal meetings.

29. W. J. C. Crawley, 'Legal Episodes in the History of Freemasonry' (London: George Kenning, 1899), p. 5.

30. The continuing close association of Freemasonry with politics is illustrated by the fact that senior members of the St Luke Lodge No. 44 were the leaders of the Scottish Whig party between 1807 and 1860. R. S. Lindsay, *A History of the Mason Lodge of Holyrood House (St Luke's) No. 44.* (Edinburgh, 1935), p. 299 quoted in M. Wallace, 'Scottish Freemasonry, 1725–1810: Progress, Power, and Politics' (PhD thesis, University of St Andrews, 2007), pp. 234–235.

31. H. Sadler, 'The Grand Lodge of Ulster', LMFL. This is a 24-page reprint of Sadler's article appearing in *The Freemason* between 21 January and 18 March, 1893.

32. *GLFI*, pp. 321–406.

33. W. J. Hughan, 'Freemasonry in Ireland' *The Freemason* (25 March, 1871), p. 179.

34. For the inconsistencies between masonic idealism and practice in England, see R. Péter, 'The Mysteries of English Freemasonry. Janus-faced Masonic Ideology and Practice between 1696–1815' (PhD thesis, University of Szeged, 2006).

35. R. Péter, 'Masonic Religious Rhetoric in England during the Long Eighteenth Century' in T. Stewart (ed.), *Freemasonry and Religion: Many faiths – One Brotherhood* (London: Canonbury Masonic Research Centre, 2006), Canonbury Papers, vol. 3, pp. 167–204.

BIBLIOGRAPHY

Primary Sources

A Free-Mason's Answer to the Suspected Author of a Pamphlet Entitled Jachin and Boaz, or an Authentic Key to Freemasonry. Addressed to All Masons, as well as to the Public in General (London: Printed for J. Cooke, 1762).

A letter from the Grand Mistress of the Female Free Masons to Mr Harding the Printer (Dublin, 1724).

Associate Presbytery of Edinburgh Minutes, 1744–60, MS CH3/111/1, National Records of Scotland, Edinburgh.

Barruel, A., *Memoirs, Illustrating the History of Jacobinism. A Translation from the French of the Abbé Barruel. vol. 3. The Antisocial Conspiracy* (London: printed for the author, by T. Burton and Co. No. 11, Gate Street, Lincoln's-Inn Fields, 1798).

Brewster, D. [often attributed to A. Lawrie who wrote the dedication and printed the book], *The History of Freemasonry, Drawn from Authentic Sources of Information, with an Account of the Grand Lodge of Scotland* (Edinburgh: A. Lawrie, 1804).

Burke, W., *A Defence of Free-Masonry: Containing the Censures Passed upon it by Six Doctors of Sorbonne and two Popes with an Answer to them* (Dublin: Printed for the Author by T. Butler, 1787).

Calcott, W., *A Candid Disquisition of the Principles and Practices of the most Ancient and Honourable Society of Free and Accepted Masons; together with some Strictures on the Origin, Nature, and Design of that Institution. Dedicated, By Permission, To the most Noble and most Worshipful Henry Duke of Beaufort, &c. &c. Grand Master. By Wellins Calcott, P.M.* (London: printed for the author, by Brother James Dixwell, in St. Martins Lane. A. L. 5769. A. D., 1769).

Clifford, R., *Barruel's Memoirs of Jacobinism, to the Secret Societies of Ireland and Great Britain. By the translator of that work* (London: sold by E. Booker, No. 56, New Bond-Street, [1798]).

Cockburn, H., *Memorials of His Time* (1856; Edinburgh: Mercat Press, 1971).

Common Place Book, Containing Copies of Circulars, Extracts from Accounts, Reports, Proceedings, Lists of Lodges, Addresses, &c., Grand Lodge of Ireland: includes material on the Grand Lodge of Ulster, 1775 – 1812, manuscript by P. Crossle, LMFL BR 50 CRO fol...

Constitutions of the Antient Fraternity of Free and Accepted Masons, Containing their History, Charges, Regulations, &c. First Compiled by Order of the Grand Lodge, From their Old Records, and Traditions, by James Anderson, D.D. A new edition revised, enlarged, and brought down to the year 1784, under the direction of the Hall Committee, by John Noorthouck. (London: printed by J. Rozea, printer to the Society, No. 91, Wardour Street, Soho, [1784]).

Coustos, J., *The Sufferings of John Coustos, for Free-Masonry, and for His Refusing to Turn Roman Catholic, in the Inquisition at Lisbon; Where He Was Sentenc'd, During Four Years to the Galley; and Afterwards Releas'd ... To Which Is Annex'd, the Origin of the Inquisition, ... Extracted from a Great Variety of the Most Approved Authors* (London: printed by W. Strahan, for the author, 1746).

D'Assigny, F., *An Impartial Answer to the Enemies of Free-masonry wherein their Unjust Suspicions, and Idle Reproaches of that Honourable Craft, Are Briefly Rehearsed, and Clearly Confused. To which Are Added, Several Serious Admonitions Necessary to Be Observed by the Fraternity* (Dublin: Printed by Edward Waters in Dames' Street, 1741).

—, *A Serious and Impartial Enquiry into the Cause of the Present Decay of Freemasonry in Ireland* (Dublin: Printed by Edward Bate, 1744).

Dermott, L., *Ahiman Rezon or, A Help to a Brother; Shewing the Excellency of Secrecy ... The Ancient Manner of Constituting new Lodges ... Also the Old and New Regulations ... To which is added, the Greatest Collection of Masons Songs ... Together with Solomon's Temple an Oratorio ...* (London: printed for the editor; sold by Brother James Bedford, 1756).

Die Freimäurerei der gerade Weg zur Glückseligkeit: zur Beantwortung der Schrift: "Die Freimäurerei der Weg zur Hölle": aus dem Englischen übersetzt (Frankfurt und Leipzig, 1769).

Die Freimäurerei, der Weg zu Hölle: ein Predigt, worinn deutlich aus Schrift und Vernunft gezeiget wird, dass alle, die zu diesem Orden gehören, in einem der Verdammniss sind (Braunschweig, 1768).

Finch, W., *An Appeal to the Officers and Members of the Grand Lodge of the Ancient and Honourable Society of Freemasons: Likewise to Those who are not Masons* (London: J. Hayes, [1807?]).

General Associate Synod Minutes, 1741–79, 1752–63, MS CH3/28/1, CH3/144/5, National Records of Scotland, Edinburgh.

Grand Lodge of Ireland Membership Register, Library of Freemasons' Hall, Dublin.

Grand Lodge of Ireland Minute Books, Library of Freemasons' Hall, Dublin.

Grand Lodge of Scotland Minutes, Museum and Library of the Grand Lodge of Scotland, Edinburgh.

Head, I., 'A Charge Delivered at the Kings-Arms, in Helston, Cornwall, on Tuesday, April 21, 1752', in J. Entick (ed.), *The Pocket Companion and History of Free-Masons: Containing their Origine, Progress, and Present State: An Abstract of their Laws, ... A Confutation of Dr. Plot's False Insinuations: ... and a Collection of Songs. The second edition. Revised, corrected and greatly enlarged throughout, and continued down to this time in all its parts* (London: Printed for R. Baldwin, ... P. Davey and B. Law, ... and J. Scott, ..., 1759), pp. 325–31.

Inwood, J. *Sermons in Which are Explained and Enforced the Religious Moral and Political Virtues of Freemasonry* ([Deptford]: Printed for the author by J. Delahoy, Deptford-Bridge, [1799]).

J. G. D. M. F. M., *Relation Apologique et historique de la Société des Francs-Maçons* (Dublin: Odonoko, 1738).

James, T., *Bellum papale, siue, Concordia discors Sixti quinti et Clementis octaui, circa Hieronymianam editionem* (London: G. Bishop R. Newberie & R. Barker, 1600).

La Franche-Maçonnerie n'est que le chemin de l'enfer, trad. de l'allemand de Meyer (Frankfurt, 1769).

Leslie, C., *A Vindication of Masonry, and its Excellency Demonstrated in a Discourse at the Consecration of the Lodge of Vernon Kilwinning, on Friday, May 15 1741* (Edinburgh: Printed by Drummond and Company, 1741).

Les Vrais jugemens sur la société des francs-maçons où l'on raporte un détail abrégé de leurs statuts, où l'on fait voir combien ces maximes sont contraires à celles de la religion (Bruxelles: chés Pierre de Hondt, 1752).

M. J., 'The French Revolution caused by Free-Masonry', *Walker's Hibernian Magazine*, July 1794, pp. 37–40.

Magistracy Settled upon its only True Scriptural Basis ... With an Appendix containing a few Questions, & a Protestation etc. against the Mason-Word ([s.n.], 1747).

Magnum Bullarium Romanum seu eiusdem continuatio (Luxembourg: Henrici-Alberti Gosse, 1727–54).

Mounier, J. J., *On the Influence Attributed to Philosophers, Freemasons, and the Illuminati on the Revolution in France* (1801; Scholars Facsimiles and Reprints, Delmar, New York, 1974).

Preston, W., *Illustrations of Masonry,* 2nd edn (London: J. Wilkie, 1775).

Prichard, S., *Masonry Dissected, being a universal and genuine description of all its branches from the original to this present time. As it is deliver'd in the constituted regular lodges Both in City and Country, According to the Several Degrees of Admission. Giving an Impartial Account of their Regular Proceeding in Initiating their New Members in the whole Three Degrees of Masonry. Viz. I. Enter'd Prentice, II. Fellow Craft. III. Master. To which is added, the author's vindication of himself* (London : printed for J. Wilford, at the Three Flower-de Luces behind the Chapter-House near St. Paul's, [1730]).

Robison, J. *Proofs of a Conspiracy against all the Religions and Governments of Europe, Carried on in the Secret Meetings of Free Masons, Illuminati, and Reading Societies. Collected from Good Authorities by John Robison, A. M. Professor of Natural Philosophy, and Secretary to the Royal Society of Edinburgh* (Edinburgh: printed for William Creech; and T. Cadell, junior, and W. Davies, London, 1797).

Select Orations on Various Subjects; Viz. I. The Divinity and Sublime of Masonry, as Display'd in the Sacred Oracles [...] (London: Printed for John Tillotson, [1737]).

Stevenson, A., *History of the Church and State of Scotland,* 4 vols (Edinburgh: [n.p.], 1753–7).

Supplément aux Vrais jugemens sur la société maçonne en réfutation de l'Intitulé: Le Secret des francs-maçons, avec un Recueil des leurs chansons (Bruxelles: chez Pierre de Hondt, 1754).

The Constitutions of the Free Masons, Containing the History, Charges, Regulations, &c. of that Most Ancient and Right Worshipful Fraternity, For the Use of the Lodges (Dublin: Printed by J. Watts, at the Lord Carteret's Head in Dames-Street, for J. Pennell, at the three Blue Bonnets in St Patrick-Street, 1730).

The Freemasons Vindication, Being an Answer to a Scandalous Libel, Entituled the Grand Mystery of the Free Masons Discovered &c. wherein is Plainly Prov'd the Falsity of that Discovery, and how Great an Imposition It Is on the Publick (Dublin[?], 1725).

The Pocket Companion and History of Free-Masons, Containing their Origine, Progress, and Present State: an Abstract of their Laws, Constitutions, Customs, Charges, Orders and Regulations, for the Instruction and Conduct of the Brethren: a Confutation of Dr. Plot's False Insinuations: an Apology Occasioned by their Persecution in the Canton of Berne, and in the Pope's Dominions: and a Select Number of Songs, and Other Particulars, for the Use of the Society (London: Printed for J. Scott, at the Black-Swan, in Duck Land, near West Smithfield; and sold by R. Baldwin, at the Rose in Pater-Noster-Row, [1754]).

Thompson, J., *Remarks on a Sermon Lately Published; Entitled, Masonry the Way to Hell. Being a Defence of that Antient and Honourable Order, against the Jesuitical Sophistry and False Calumny of the Author* (London: Printed by S. Axtell and H. Hardy, for T. Evans, at No. 20, in Pater-noster Row, 1768).

Thorp, J. T. (ed.), *A Master-Key to Free-Masonry* (1760; Leicester: Johnson, Wykes & Paine, 1925).

Watkins, J., 'An Impartial Examination of a Book Entitled Proofs of a Conspiracy against All the Religions and Governments of Europe', *The Scientific Magazine and Freemasons' Repository*, 9 (October 1797), pp. 242–9; 9 (November 1797), pp. 324–7; 10 (January 1798), pp. 36–8; 10 (April 1798), pp. 255–8.

Williams, W., *Masonry Founded on Scripture in a Sermon Preached Before Lodges of Gravesend on New Year's Day, 1752* (Aberdeen, 1771).

Wilson, T., *Solomon in all His Glory: Or, the Master-Mason. Being a True Guide to the Inmost Recesses of Free-Masonry, both Ancient and Modern. ... by T. W. ... Translated from the French Original Published at Berlin* (London: printed for G. Robinson and J. Roberts, 1766).

Wilson, T., *Solomon in all His Glory: Or, the Master-Mason. being a True Guide to the Inmost Recesses of Free-Masonry, both Ancient and Modern. ... Illustrated with several Elegant Copper-Plates, Exhibiting the Different Lodges, Free-Masons Cyphers, &c. to which is Added, a Complete List of all the English Regular Lodges in the World, ... by T. W. ... the Second Edition, with the Addition of Two Beautiful Copper-Plates. Translated from the French Original Published at Berlin* (London: printed for Robinson and Roberts, 1768).

Secondary Sources

Adams, C., 'Ahiman Rezon, the Book of Constitutions', *AQC*, 46, (1937), pp. 239–306.

Adams, J. R. R., 'Belfast Almanacs and Directories of Joseph Smyth', *Linen Hall Review*, 8 (1991), pp. 14–15.

Ars Quatuor Coronatorum, the transactions of Quatuor Coronati Lodge, No. 2076.

Baldi, M., 'Nature and Man Restored: Mysticism and Millenarianism in Andrew Michael Ramsey', *Anglophonia*, 3 (1998), pp. 89–102.

Beattie, K., 'The Freemasons of Ballymoney and the 1798 Rebellion', *The Glynns: Journal of the Glens of Antrim Historical Society*, 29 (2001), pp. 93–102.

Beck, G. L., 'Celestial Lodge Above: The Temple of Solomon in Jerusalem as a Religious Symbol in Freemasonry', *Nova Religio*, 4:1 (2000), pp. 28–51.

Begemann, G. E. W., *Vorgeschichte und Anfänge der Freimaurerei in Irland* (Berlin: E.S. Mittler und Sohn, 1911).

Belton, J., *The English Masonic Union of 1813* (Suffolk: Arima, 2012).

Benimeli, J. A. F., *Masoneria, iglesia e ilustración: un conflicto ideológico-político-religioso*. Vol. 1. *Las bases de un conflict, 1700–1739* (Madrid: Fundación Universitaria Española, 1976).

—, *Masoneria, iglesia e ilustración: un conflicto ideológico-político-religioso*. Vol. 2 *Inquisición: procesos historícos (1739–1750)* (Madrid: Fundación Universitaria Española, 1977).

—, 'The Catholic Church and Freemasonry: An Historical Perspective', *AQC*, 119 (2006), pp. 234–55.

—, 'La Présence De La Franc-Maçonnerie Stuartiste à Madrid Et à Rome', *Politica Hermetica*, 24 (2010), pp. 68–88.

—, 'Freemasonry and the Catholic Church', in H. Bogdan and J. A. M. Snoek (eds), *Handbook of Freemasonry* (Leiden-Boston: Brill, 2014), pp. 139–54.

Berman, R., *The Foundations of Modern Freemasonry: The Grand Architects: Political Change and the Scientific Enlightenment, 1714–1740* (Brighton: Sussex Academic Press, 2012).

—, *Schism: The Battle that Forged Freemasonry* (Brighton: Sussex Academic Press, 2013).

—, 'The London Irish and the Antients Grand Lodge', *Eighteenth-Century Life*, 39:1 (2015), pp. 103–30.

Bogdan, H. and J. A. M. Snoek, *Handbook of Freemasonry* (Leiden–Boston: Brill, 2014).

—, 'The History of Freemasonry: An Overview', in H. Bogdan, and J. A. M. Snoek (eds), *Handbook of Freemasonry* (Leiden-Boston: Brill, 2014), pp. 13–32.

Buckley, A. D., 'Royal Arch, Royal Arch Purple and "Raiders of the Lost Ark": Secrecy in Orange and Masonic Ritual', in T. M. Owen (ed.), *From Corrib to Cultra: Folklife Essays in Honour of Alan Gailey* (Belfast: Institute of Irish Studies, 2000), pp 163–80.

Campbell, P. R., *Conspiracy in the French Revolution* (Manchester: Manchester University Press, 2010).

Chakmakjian, P., 'Theological Lying and Religious Radicalism in Anderson's Constitutions', *Aries*, 8:2 (2008), pp. 167–90.

Clark, P., *British Clubs and Societies 1580–1800: The Origins of an Associational World* (Oxford and New York: Oxford University Press, 2000).

Conlon, L., 'The Influence of Freemasonry in East Cavan during the Rebellion of 1798', *Breifne: Journal of Cumann Seanchais Bhréifne*, 8:33 (1997), pp. 782–807.

—, 'The Influence of Freemasonry in Meath and Westmeath in the Eighteenth Century', *Ríocht Na Mídhe [Journal of the County Meath Historical Society]*, 9:3 (1997), pp. 128–57.

—, 'Dissension, Radicalism, and Republicanism in Monaghan and the Role of Freemasonry up to and during the 1798 Rebellion', *Clogher Record: Journal of the Clogher Historical Society*, 16:3 (1999), pp. 86–111.

Crawley, W. J. C., 'Notes on Dr Barlow's Paper, "A Curious Historical Error"', *AQC*, 10 (1897), pp. 58–9.

—, *Legal Episodes in the History of Freemasonry* (London: George Kenning, 1899).

—, 'The Old Charges and the Papal Bulls', *AQC*, 24 (1911), pp. 110–15.

Crossle, F. C., 'The Grand East of Ulster', *The Freemason*, 21 December 1892, pp. 9–13.

Dashwood, J. R., 'Trial of John Coustos by the Inquisition', *AQC*, 66 (1953), pp. 107–23.

—, 'Notes on the Early Records of the Grand Lodge of the Antients', *AQC*, 70 (1957), pp. 63–78.

Eijnatten, J., 'Reaching Audiences: Sermons and Oratory in Europe', in S. J. Brown and T. Tackett (eds), *Enlightenment, Reawakening and Revolution 1660–1815*. Vol. 7 (Cambridge: Cambridge University Press, 2006), pp. 128–46.

Elias, A. C. (ed.), *Memoirs of Laetitia Pilkington* (London: University of Georgia Press, 1997).

Fagan, P., *Catholics in a Protestant Country. The Papist Constituency in Eighteenth-century Dublin* (Dublin: Four Courts Press, 1998), ch. 5 (pp. 144–55).

—, 'Infiltration of Dublin Freemason Lodges by United Irishmen and Other Republican Groups', *Eighteenth-Century Ireland: Iris an dá Chultúr*, 13 (1998), pp. 65–85.

Ferguson, W., *Scotland, 1689 to the Present* (Edinburgh: Oliver & Boyd, 1968).

Förster, O. W. (ed.), *Matrikel der Freimaurerloge 'Minerva zu den drei Palmen' 1741–1932* (Leipzig, 2004).

Fozdar, V., '"That Grand Primeval and Fundamental Religion": The Transformation of Freemasonry into a British Imperial Cult', *Journal of World History*, 22:3 (2011), pp. 493–525.

Gould, R. F., *Gould's History of Freemasonry Throughout the World, revised by Dudley Wright*, 6 vols (New York: C. Scribner Son's, 1936).

Hackett, D. G., *That Religion in which All Men Agree: Freemasonry in American Culture* (Berkeley, CA: University of California Press, 2014).

Hammond, W., 'Two Pamphlets [Notes & Queries]', *AQC*, 10 (1897), p. 158.

Harris, B., 'Print Culture', in H. T. Dickinson (ed.), *A Companion to Eighteenth-Century Britain* (Oxford: Blackwell, 2002), pp. 283–93.

Haunch, T. O., 'English Craft Certificates', *AQC*, 82 (1969), pp. 169–253.

Haydon, C., 'Religious Minorities in England', in H. T. Dickinson (ed.), *A Companion to Eighteenth-Century Britain* (Oxford: Blackwell Publishing, 2002), pp. 241–51.

History of Parliament Online, maintained by the Institute of Historical Research, at http://www.historyofparliamentonline.org/ [accessed 10 July 2014].

Hughan, W. J., 'Freemasonry in Ireland', *The Freemason*, 25 March 1871, pp. 179–81.

Jackson, A. C. F., *English Masonic Exposures, 1760–69* (London: Lewis Masonic, 1986).

Jacob, M., *Living the Enlightenment* (New York, NY: Oxford University Press, 1991).

Jenkins, J. P., 'Jacobites and Freemasons in 18th-Century Wales', *Welsh History Review*, 9:4 (1979), pp. 391–406.

Kantorowicz, E. H., *The King's Two Bodies: A Study in Mediaeval Political Theology* (1957; Princeton, NJ: Princeton University Press, 1997).

Kelly, J. and M. J. Powell, (eds), *Clubs and Societies in Eighteenth-Century Ireland* (Dublin: Four Courts Press, 2010).

Knoop, D. and G. P. Jones, 'An Anti-Masonic Leaflet of 1698', *AQC*, 55 (1942), pp. 152–4.

— and D. Hamer (eds), *Early Masonic Catechisms*, 2nd edn (1943; London: Quatuor Coronati Lodge, 1975).

Lane, J., *A Handy Book to the Study of the Engraved, Printed, and Manuscript Lists of Lodges of Ancient Free & Accepted Masons of England, from 1728 to 1814* (London: George Kenning, 1889).

Lepper, J. H., 'The Earl of Middlesex and the English Lodge in Florence', *AQC*, 58 (1947), pp. 4–77.

Lepper, J. H. and P. Crossle, *History of the Grand Lodge of Freemasons of Ireland*, 2 vols (Dublin: Lodge of Research, CC, 1925), vol. 1.

Lindsay, R. S., *A History of the Mason Lodge of Holyrood House (St Luke's No. 44)* (Edinburgh: T and A Constable, Ltd, 1935).

Loiselle, K., *Brotherly Love: Freemasonry and Male Friendship in Enlightenment France* (Ithaca, NY: Cornell University Press, 2014).

Luckert, S. 'Jesuits, Freemasons, Illuminati, and Jacobins: Conspiracy Theories, Secret Societies, and Politics in Late Eighteenth-Century Germany' (PhD thesis, State University of New York at Binghamton, 1993).

Lyon, D. M., *History of the Lodge of Edinburgh (Mary's Chapel), No. 1, Embracing An Account of the Rise and Progress of Freemasonry in Scotland Mary's Chapel* (London: Gresham Publishing Company, 1900).

Lyttle, C. H., 'Historical Bases of Rome's Conflict with Freemasonry', *Church History*, 9:1 (1940), pp. 3–23.

McFarland, E., *Ireland and Scotland in the Age of Revolution: Planting the Green Bough* (Edinburgh: Edinburgh University Press, 1994).

McIntosh, M. K., *Working Women in English Society, 1300–1620* (Cambridge: Cambridge University Press, 2005).

Mirala, P., 'Conservative and Revolutionaries: Freemasonry in Eighteenth-Century Ireland', in M. D. J. Scanlan (ed.), *The Social Impact of Freemasonary on the Modern Western World* (London: Canonbury Masonic Research Centre, 2002), pp. 107–15.

—, 'Freemasonry, Conservatism and Loyalism in Ulster, 1792–9', in R. Gillespie (ed.) *The Remaking of Modern Ireland, 1750–1950* (Dublin: Four Courts, 2004), pp. 14–48.

—, *Freemasonry in Ulster, 1733–1813. A Social and Political History of the Masonic Brotherhood in the North of Ireland* (Dublin: Four Courts Press, 2007).

—, 'Masonic Sociability and its Limitations: The Case of Ireland', in J. Kelly and M. J. Powell (eds), *Clubs and Societies in Eighteenth-Century Ireland* (Dublin: Four Courts Press, 2010), pp. 315–31.

Mollier, P., 'The Masonic Degree of Rose Croix and Christianity: The Complex Links Between Religion and Freemasonry during the Enlightenment', *Ritual, Secrecy and Civil Society*, 1:2 (2013), pp. 15–24.

Money, J., 'Freemasonry and the Fabric of Loyalism in Hanoverian England', in H. Eckhart (ed.), *The Transformation of Political Culture: England and Germany in the Late Eighteenth Century* (Oxford: Oxford University Press, 1990), pp. 235–69.

Monod, P. K., *Jacobitism and the English People, 1688–1788* (Cambridge: Cambridge University Press, 1989).

Morrell, J. B. 'Professors Robison and Playfair and the Theophobia Gallica: Natural Philosophy, Religion and Politics in Edinburgh, 1789–1815', *Notes and Records of the Royal Society*, 26 (1971), pp. 43–63.

Murdoch, S., *Network North: Scottish Kin, Commercial and Covert Associations in Northern Europe 1603–1746* (Leiden: Brill, 2006).

Murphy, S., 'Irish Jacobitism and Freemasonry', *Eighteenth-Century Ireland*, 9 (1994), pp. 79–82.

Oberhauser, C., *Die verschwörungstheoretische Trias: Barruel-Robison-Starck* (Innsbruck: Studien Verlag, 2013).

Olsen, K., *Daily Life in 18th-Century England* (Westport: Greenwood, 1999).

Önnerfors, A., 'Secret Savants, Savants Secrets: The Concept of Science in the Imagination of European Freemasonry', in A. Holenstein, H. Steinke and M. Stuber (eds), *The Practice of Knowledge and the Figure of the Savant in the 18th Century* (Leiden: Brill, 2013), pp. 433–57.

Outram, D., 'Enlightenment Thinking About Gender', in D. Outram, *The Enlightenment* (Cambridge: Cambridge University Press, 2005), pp. 84–98.

Oxford Dictionary of National Biography (Oxford: Oxford University Press, 2014), available at http://www.oxforddnb.com/ [accessed 15 July 2014].

Pellizi, C. M., 'The English Lodge in Florence 1732–38', *AQC*, 105 (1992), pp. 129–37.

Péter, R., 'Masonic Religious Rhetoric in England during the Long Eighteenth Century', in T. Stewart (ed.), *Freemasonry and Religion: Many Faiths – One Brotherhood*. (London: Canonbury Masonic Research Centre, 2006), Canonbury Papers, vol. 3, pp. 167–204.

—, 'The Mysteries of English Freemasonry. Janus-faced Masonic Ideology and Practice between 1696–1815' (PhD thesis, University of Szeged, 2006).

—, 'Unio Mystica in the Dramatic Revelation of Masonic Secrecy?', in Kathleen E. Dubs (ed.), *Now You See It, Now You Don't: Hiding and Revealing in Text and Performance* (Piliscsaba: Péter Pázmány Catholic University, 2006), pp. 166–78.

—, '"The Fair Sex" in a "Male Sect". Gendering the Role of Women in Eighteenth-Century English Freemasonry', in M. Cross (ed.), *Gender and Fraternal Orders in Europe from 1200 until the Present* (Basingstoke: Palgrave, 2010), pp. 133–55.

—, 'Religion and Enlightenment in Thomas Dunckerley's Neglected Writings', in A. Önnerfors and R. Péter (eds), *Researching British Freemasonry, 1717–2017* (Sheffield: University of Sheffield, 2010), pp. 127–57.

—, 'Representations of Anti-masonry in Eighteenth-century London Newspapers', paper presented at the 12th International Canonbury Conference on the Study of Freemasonry (London, 28–30 October 2010).

Pick, F. L. and G. N. Knight, *The Pocket History of Freemasonry* (London: Muller, 1954).

Plomer, H. R., G. H. Bushnell and McC. Dix (eds), *A Dictionary of the Printers and Booksellers who were at Work in England, Scotland and Ireland from 1726 to 1775* (n. p.: Oxford University Press for the Bibliographical Society, 1932).

Pocock, J. G. A., *Barbarism and Religion: The Enlightenments of Edward Gibbon, 1737–1764* (Cambridge: Cambridge University Press, 1999).

Pollard, M., *A Dictionary of Members of the Dublin Book Trade 1550–1800* (Oxford: Oxford University Press, 2000).

Pope, S., 'Military Lodges and Military Masons in East Kent during the 18th and Early 19th Centuries', *AQC*, 61 (1948), pp. 77–113.

Porset, C. and M.-C. Révauger, *Franc-Maçonnerie et Religions Dans l'Europe des Lumières* (Paris: Champion, 2006).

Porset, C. and C. Révauger (eds), *Le Monde Maçonnique des Lumières. Europe-Amérique et colonies. Dictionnaire prosopographique*, 3 vols (Paris: Champion, 2013).

Porter, R., *Enlightenment: Britain and the Creation of the Modern World* (London: Allen Lane, 2000).

Prescott, A., 'The Unlawful Societies Act of 1799', in D. J. S. Matthew (ed.), *The Social Impact of Freemasonry on the Modern World* (London: Canonbury Masonic Research Centre, 2002), Canonbury Papers, vol. 1, pp. 116–34.

—, 'Freemasonry and Radicalism in Northern England 1789–1799: Some Sidelights', *Lumières (Franc-maçonnerie et Politique au Siècle des Lumières: Europe-Amériques)*, 7 (2006), pp. 123–42.

Read, W., 'Let a Man's Religion ... Be What It May...', *AQC*, 98 (1985), pp. 69–89.

Révauger, C., 'Women Barred from Masonic "Work": A British Phenomenon', in I. Baudino, J. Carré and C. Révauger (eds), *The Invisible Woman: Aspects of Women's Work in Eighteenth-Century Britain* (Aldershot: Ashgate, 2005), pp. 117–27.

Roberts, M. M., 'Masonics, Metaphor and Misogyny: A Discourse of Marginality', in P. Burke and R. Porter (eds), *Languages and Jargons* (Cambridge: Polity, 1998), pp. 133–54.

Ronny E. J., 'The Evolution of the Church's Prohibition against Catholic Membership in Freemasonry', *The Jurist*, 56:2 (1996), pp. 735–55.

Rupp, G. E., *Religion in England, 1688–1791* (Oxford: Clarendon Press, 1986).

Sadler, H., 'The Grand Lodge of Ulster' (1893), LMFL BRN 105 SAD.

Scanlan, M. D. J., 'John Wilkes. Freemasonry and the Emergence of Popular Radicalism', in M. D. J. Scanlan (ed.), *The Social Impact of Freemasonry on the Modern World* (London: Canonbury Masonic Research Centre, 2002), Canonbury Papers, vol. 1, pp. 36–59.

Schuchard, M. K., 'Swedenborg, Jacobitism, and Freemasonry', in E. J. Brock (ed.), *Swedenborg and His Influence* (Bryn Athun, PA: The Academy of the New Church, 1988), pp. 359–79.

—, 'The Young Pretender and Jacobite Freemasonry: New Light From Sweden On His Role As Hidden Grand Master', in R. Caldwell et al. (eds), *The Selected Papers of Consortium on Revolutionary Europe, 1750–1850* (Tallahassee, FL: Institute on Napoleon and the French Revolution, Florida State University, 1994), pp. 363–75.

—, 'Lord George Gordon and Cabalistic Freemasonry: Beating Jacobite Swords and Jacobin Ploughshares', in M. Mulsow and R. H. Popkin (eds), *Secret Conversions to Judaism in Early Modern Europe* (Leiden: Brill, 2004), pp. 183–231.

—, 'Les rivalites maconniques et la *Bulle in Eminenti*', *La Regle d'Abraham*, 25 (June 2008), pp. 3–48.

Small, R., *History of the Congregations of the United Presbyterian Church from 1733 to 1900*, 2 vols (Edinburgh: David M Small, 1904).

Smyth, J. 'Freemasonry and the United Irishmen' in D. Dickson, D. Keogh and K. Whelan (eds), *The United Irishmen: Republicanism, Radicalism and Rebellion* (Dublin: Lilliput Press, 1993), pp. 167–75.

—, 'Wolfe Tone's Library: The United Irishmen and "Enlightenment"', *Eighteenth-Century Studies*, 45:3 (2012), pp. 423–35.

Snoek, J. A. M., 'Freemasonry and Women' in H. Bogdan and J. A. M. Snoek (eds), *Handbook of Freemasonry* (Leiden-Boston: Brill, 2014), pp. 407–21.

Songhurst, W. J., *The Minutes of the Grand Lodge of England of Freemasons of England, 1723–1739. Quatuor Coronatorum Antigrapha*, Vol. 10 (London: Quatuor Coronati Lodge, 1913).

Sorkin, D., *The Religious Enlightenment. Protestants, Jews and Catholics from London to Vienna* (Princeton, NJ: Princeton University Press, 2008).

Stauffer, V., *New England and the Bavarian Illuminati* (New York, NY: Russell and Russell, 1918).

Stevenson, D., *The Origins of Freemasonry. Scotland's Century, 1590–1710* (Cambridge: Cambridge University Press, 1988).

—, *The First Freemasons. Scotland's Early Lodges and their Members*, 2nd edn (Edinburgh: Grand Lodge of Scotland, 2001).

Stokes, J. 'Masonic Teachers of the Eighteenth Century (The Prestonian Lecture for 1928)' in H. Carr (ed.), *The Collected 'Prestonian Lectures' 1925–1960* (London, 1967), pp. 63–94.

Sweetnam, S. F., 'Two Hundred Years of Freemasonry in Sligo', *Transactions of the Lodge of Research No. 200 (1996–1998)*, 24 (2000), pp. 175–83.

Thorne, R. G., *House of Commons: History of the House of Parliament*, 5 vols (London: Haynes Publishing Company, 1986).

Wallace, M., 'Scottish Freemasonry, 1725–1810: Progress, Power, and Politics' (PhD thesis, University of St Andrews, 2007).

—, 'Threats of Illuminism: 18th-Century Scottish Masonic Conspiracy Theories', *History Scotland*, 10:3 (2010), pp. 20–4.

Wartski, L. D., 'Freemasonry and the Early Secret Societies Act', monograph compiled and presented by the author for private circulation by the District Grand Lodge of Natal of Antient Free and Accepted Masons of Scotland.

Wood, T., 'A Great English Casuist', *Church Quarterly Review*, 147 (1948), pp. 29–45.

Woods, J., 'The British View of Freemasonry during the Emergence of Conspiracy Theories, c.1795 to 1815' (BA dissertation, University of Leeds, 2010).

ANON. [SIGNED PHILO LAPIDARIUS], *AN ANSWER TO THE POPE'S BULL, WITH THE CHARACTER OF A FREEMASON* (1738)

Anon. [signed Philo-Lapidarius], *An Answer to the Pope's Bull, with the Character of a Freemason. In an Epistle to the Right Honorable and Right Worshipful Lord Mountjoy, Grand Master of Ireland* (Dublin: Edward Waters, in Dames' Street, 1738).[1]

As the following Irish anonymous pamphlet states, the Catholic Church was not the first enemy of Freemasonry. From 1735 onwards European governments began to forbid masonic meetings. The first official bans on Freemasonry were issued by Protestant countries, including the states of Holland and West Friesland (1735), and the Republic of Geneva (1736).[2] In 1737 the French government imposed a ban on masonic assemblies and those noblemen who joined lodges were threatened with exclusion from court. These governmental attacks criticized masonic secrecy and the oath taken during the rituals under severe penalty and suggested that the lodges could become subversive and dangerous to public order.[3]

It is not surprising that the Holy See soon followed in the footsteps of lay governments that banned masonic meetings. The activities of a lodge in Florence contributed considerably to the publication of the first papal condemnation. This lodge was founded around 1732 and contained a number of English residents, various Italians including three abbots, and two Irish Augustinian friars – namely, Fathers Denhey and Flood.[4] Among the members, the most influential were Baron Philipp von Stosch, a spy for Sir Robert Walpole, and Tomasso Crudeli, who had earlier written satirical verses against the church. The multi-religious background of this lodge, including Protestants, Jews and Catholics, also gave impetus to the charges of heresy brought by Paolo Antonio Ambrogi of the Holy Office.[5] Until the twentieth century the Church of Rome forbade meetings of Catholics with non-Catholics under the penalty of excommunication. During the last days of the Medicean Grand Duke in 1737 the lodge was closed because of quietism, Molinism and epicureanism, and several Freemasons were jailed.[6] The bans of the secular governments and the activities of the Florentine lodge paved the way for the first official papal statement on Freemasonry.

On 28 April 1738, Clement XII issued a papal bull condemning 'the Society or Conventicles De Liberi Muratori, or of the Freemasons under the Penalty of ipso facto excommunication'.[7] It starts with the words 'In eminenti apostolatus specula' and was published, *inter alia*, in the *History of the Works of the Learned* with an English translation in November 1738.[8] It was also reprinted in several *Pocket Companions* of Freemasonry.[9] In what follows, the four main reasons why it banned masonic meetings are summarized, and why Catholic Freemasons were excommunicated *ipso facto*: 1. Freemasons admitted men of 'whatsoever religion and sect'; 2. during their private ceremonies they took an oath 'on the Sacred Volume, as by the imposition of heavy penalties, to conceal under inviolable silence'; 3. 'the very serious injuries which are in the highest degree inflicted by such societies, or conventicles not merely on the tranquility of the temporal state, but also on the spiritual welfare of souls'; 4. 'they are inconsistent alike with civil and canonical sanctions'.

The first papal condemnation had both political and religious motives. Like the European Protestant governments of the period, the Catholic Church was concerned with the security of the state and public order, which, as Benimeli notes, is confirmed by Cardinal Firrao's decree (14 January 1739). It claims that masonic meetings could be suspected of heresy as well as being dangerous to the security of the ecclesiastical state and the public peace. This was the reason why the edict condemned anyone attending lodges to death, the confiscation of their property and the destruction of their meeting places.[10] As for the religious motives, there were religiously mixed lodges including Protestants and Catholics. Among the Catholics one can find Grand Masters such as Thomas Howard, Eighth Duke of Norfolk, Anthony Browne, Sixth Viscount Montagu and Henry Barnewall, Fourth Viscount Kingsland from the 1730s in Great Britain and Ireland.[11] However, it is questionable whether the Holy See was aware of their existence in the British Isles. Unlike the authors of the Holland ban, even James Anderson's *Constitutions* (1723) was unknown to the Holy Office before the publication of the bull.[12]

Being in Protestant hands, the bull was not announced in Ireland, where Catholics were the majority of the population. However, there were barriers to them joining masonic lodges. Non-Anglicans such as Catholics and Jews were second-class citizens in Ireland and excluded from political power, as well as several societies in whose meetings English rather than Irish (Gaelic) was used.[13] Further research is needed to calculate the proportion of Irish Catholics in lodges in the 1730s. Living in a Protestant country, they did not have to worry about the consequences of the papal condemnations. As the epistle shows, there was a need to issue a defence in which some, but not all, of the charges of the bull were questioned. The anonymous author also protests against charges such as devil worship and necromancy that are not mentioned in the bull. It is dedicated to Lord Mountjoy, William Stewart (1709–69), an Anglo-Irish peer who was Grand Master of Ireland between 1738 and 1740.[14]

Another influential and widely translated defence of Freemasonry reflecting on the papal bull, entitled *Relation Apologique et Historique de la Société des Francs-maçons*, was also published in Dublin in 1738.[15]

The reproduction of this very rare epistle is based on a photocopy, available in the Library and Museum of Freemasonry in London, the original of which can be found in the Library of Queen's University, Belfast. Edward Waters, the publisher, printed books including some by Jonathan Swift and John Arbuthnot, from 1708 to the early 1740s. He also published the *Dublin Journal*.[16]

Notes

1. This headnote was written by Róbert Péter.
2. H. Bogdan and J. A. M. Snoek, 'The History of Freemasonry: An Overview', in H. Bogdan, and J. A. M. Snoek, *Handbook of Freemasonry* (Leiden-Boston: Brill, 2014), pp. 13–32, on p. 20.
3. J. A. F. Benimeli, 'Freemasonry and the Catholic Church' in *Handbook*, pp. 139–54, on p. 139. J. A. F. Benimeli, 'The Catholic Church and Freemasonry: an Historical Perspective', *AQC*, 119 (2006), pp. 234–55, on p. 234. J. A. F. Benimeli, *Masoneria, iglesia e ilustración: un conflicto ideológico-político-religioso. Las bases de un conflict, 1700–1739* (Madrid: Fundación Universitaria Española, 1976).
4. C. M. Pellizi, 'The English Lodge in Florence 1732–38', *AQC*, 105 (1992), pp. 129–37. J. H. Lepper, 'The Earl of Middlesex and the English Lodge in Florence', *AQC*, 58 (1947), pp. 4–77.
5. C. H. Lyttle, 'Historical Bases of Rome's Conflict with Freemasonry', *Church History*, 9:1 (1940), pp. 3–23, on p. 16.
6. Benimeli, *Masoneria, iglesia e ilustración: un conflicto ideológico-político-religioso. Las bases de un conflict, 1700–1739*, p. 174. See also vol. 5, p. 152. Marsha Keith Schuchard examined the political-masonic background to the first papal bull in the light of hitherto unknown documents in several papers. My thanks go to Professor Schuchard for sending me her revised version of an earlier French paper entitled. 'Jacobite versus Hanoverian Rivalries: the Political-Masonic Background to the Papal Bull *In Eminenti* (1738)'. 'Les rivalites maconniques et la *Bulle in Eminenti*', *La Regle d'Abraham*, 25 (June 2008), pp. 3–48. On 12 December 1739 the Grand Lodge of England voted for funds to support 'The Petition of Bro: Thomas Crudeli a Prisoner in the Inquisition in Florence on Account of Masonry', in W. J. Songhurst, *The Minutes of the Grand Lodge of England of Freemasons of England, 1723–1739. Quatuor Coronatorum Antigrapha*, Vol. 10 (London: Quatuor Coronati Lodge, 1913), p. 323.
7. It is available in *Magnum Bullarium Romanum seu eiusdem continuatio* (Luxembourg: Henrici-Alberti Gosse, 1727–54), vol. 18. p. 184; 'The Bull of Pope Clement XII', *AQC*, 24 (1911), pp. 62–3. The citations above rely on the latter. On 4 July 1738 *The Leeds Mercury* and *The York Courant* reported the earliest news about the papal bull. See vol. 5, pp. 152–3.
8. *History of the Works of the Learned* (November 1738), pp. 384–6. See vol. 5, pp. 153–5.
9. For example, *The Pocket Companion and History of Free-Masons, Containing their Origine, Progress, and Present State: an Abstract of their Laws, Constitutions, Customs, Charges,*

Orders and Regulations, for the Instruction and Conduct of the Brethren: a Confutation of dr. Plot's False Insinuations: an Apology Occasioned by their Persecution in the Canton of Berne, and in the Pope's Dominions: and a Select Number of Songs, and Other Particulars, for the Use of the Society (London: Printed for J. Scott, at the Black-Swan, in Duck Land, near West Smithfield; and sold by R. Baldwin, at the Rose in Pater-Noster-Row, [1754]), pp. 247–51 and subsequent editions.

10. Benimeli, 'The Catholic Church and Freemasonry', p. 235.

11. Thomas Howard, Eighth Duke of Norfolk (1663–1732), who was brought up as a Catholic, was Grand Master of the Premier Grand Lodge between 1729 and 1730. After his death, Anthony Browne, Sixth Viscount Montagu (1686–1767), from a traditional Roman Catholic family, led the Grand Lodge of England for a year. Henry Benedict Barnewall, Fourth Viscount Kingsland was Deputy Grand Master of Ireland in 1732 and Grand Master of Ireland in 1733 and 1734. He came from an Anglo-Norman Catholic family that long settled in Ireland. In 1740 he refused to take the anti-Catholic English oath of allegiance, so he did not take his seat in the House of Lords. *GLFI*, p. 150. *Schism*, p. 229. W. Read, 'Let a Man's Religion ... Be What It May ...', *AQC*, 98 (1985), pp. 69–89. P. Fagan, *Catholics in a Protestant Country. The Papist Constituency in Eighteenth-century Dublin* (Dublin: Four Courts Press, 1998), pp. 144–55 (Catholic Involvement in Freemasonry).

12. Benimeli, 'The Catholic Church and Freemasonry', p. 235.

13. P. Mirala, 'Masonic Sociability and its Limitations: the Case of Ireland', in J. Kelly, M. J. Powell (eds), *Clubs and Societies in Eighteenth-Century Ireland* (Dublin: Four Courts Press, 2010), pp. 315–31.

14. See *Schism*, pp. 213–35 (Appendix V, An Introduction to Eighteenth-Century Irish Freemasonry).

15. J. G. D. M. F. M., *Relation Apologique et Historique de la Société des Francs-maçons* (Dublin: Odonoko, 1738), the authorship of which is debated. The book was placed on the Index and burnt in Rome by the Inquisition. Andreas Önnerfors notes that considerable parts of this French text were translated into German and Swedish in 1738. A. Önnerfors, 'Secret Savants, Savants Secrets: the Concept of Science in the Imagination of European Freemasonry', in A. Holenstein, H. Steinke and M. Stuber (eds), *The Practice of Knowledge and the Figure of the Savant in the 18th Century* (Leiden: Brill, 2013), pp. 433–57. I am grateful to Andreas Önnerfors for sharing his paper with me before its publication.

16. H. R. Plomer, G. H. Bushnell and McC. Dix (eds), *A Dictionary of the Printers and Booksellers Who Were at Work in England, Scotland and Ireland from 1726 to 1775* (n. p.: Oxford University Press for the Bibliographical Society 1932), p. 404.

Anon. [signed Philo Lapidarius], *An Answer to the Pope's Bull, with the Character of a Freemason* (1738)

AN
ANSWER
TO THE
Pope's BULL;

WITH THE
Character of a Free Mason.
In an EPISTLE to the
Rt. Honourable and Rt. Worshipful
Lord *MOUNTJOY.* [1]
Grand MASTER of *IRELAND.*
Dublin: Printed and Sold by *Edward Waters* in *Dames'-street*, 1738. /

AN
ANSWER
To the Pope's *BULL*, &c.

My LORD;

AS the Fraternity of FREE MASONS have made such a Noise in the World, and have not only became dreadful to the Ignorant part of Mankind, but even suspicious to *some certain Powers*; I hope it will not be taken amiss, if I endeavour to paint their *Folly*, who blame that with which they cannot possibly be acquainted: And I must imagine, that it will appear as ridiculous in any of Them, as it wou'd in a Man, (altho' he had never been in *China*, and an entire Stranger to its Inhabitants, Laws, Constitutions, and Government;) who would confidently report, *That the People of that Nation were the most Disloyal, Rebellious*[i]*, and wicked Subjects throughout the World*: And, that this is the Case with the *Enemies of Masonry* will plainly appear, when we consider of the insignificant Methods, with which They endeavour[ii] to persuade People against it; and because that they Themselves cannot arrive at the *Secret* in / an illegal manner, are resolv'd to put others quite out of Humour with it, which they strive to do in the subsequent manner, by informing the World, *that* MASONS *in their private Assemblies draw such*

– 5 –

Circles, and other strange Lines,[2] *that causes the Devil to pop up, and take his Place amongst Them,* which some say *is under the Table,* and others *as a Door-keeper.*

NOW, if the MASONS are such *Conjurers* as to raise the Devil,[3] and sit with calm and pleasant ease in his Company, I must boldly affirm, that I look upon Them to be Most Heroick, if not most Religious Men; for, as the Divines inform us, he is the general Enemy of Mankind, we cannot set him too much at defiance, and sure no greater can be, than that of face to face; but I cannot think it reasonable to believe that he is ever Employ'd as a *Door-keeper,* for as the Scripture describes him, to be so assiduous in grasping all that might come into his Reach, he would not be at all fit for that Office: But to be more serious, I suppose the World takes a distaste at MASONS, because they are true to their Words, and will not disclose the *least Secret* that is repos'd in their Breasts, altho' the breaking of the *One,* or the divulging of the *other,* seems to me an Argument of a most dishonest and treacherous Disposition: And I wou'd not have the World imagine, that they can ever arrive at the Perfection of the Art of *Masonry,* without first undergoing *a certain Operation,* which will entirely remove that Film that at present hangs over their visionary *Orb;* for, altho' they may be of Opinion that they see already very well, I durst venture to say, that they are as much in darkness at this time, as an unfortunate Prisoner, who is confin'd in such a Dungeon, that the least glimmering Ray of Light cannot possibly creep into him. /

BUT among the many Enemies of *Masonry,* there hath lately started up a most formidable *One,* (and by some Reckon'd Infallible) I mean the *Pope;*[4] who, as he tells us, judging that Fraternity highly to deserve *Ecclesiastical Censures,* hath issu'd out his *Bull of Excommunication,* which strictly forbids any *Catholick, to enter into, Countenance, or Defend Them:* His Holiness begins in the following Formal and Solemn Manner.

'IN the midst of the Cares of the Apostleship, and the continual Attention we have to extirpate *Heresies,* and maintain the Lord's Vineyard in its utmost Purity; We have heard with grief and bitterness of Soul, that a certain Society, who stile Themselves, *The Fraternity of* Free Masons, after making progress in several States in *Europe,* have likewise spread into *Italy,* and even there had some Increase. We have consider'd, that the Impenetrable Secret of this so Mysterious Society is the essential Part, and as it were the Basis of its Institution; and that being thereby become suspitious to the Temporal Powers, several of Them have proscribed it in their Dominions. We have likewise consider'd, that by such stronger Reasons it ought to be suspitious to the Spiritual Power, whose Charge is to have an ever-watchful Eye over every Thing which may concern the Salvation of Souls. For these Reasons, and animated by our Pastoral Care, we have Condemned, and do Condemn, by the present *Bull, &c. &c.'*

THERE is no one that doubts but the Care of the Apostleship will ever be defended by his Holiness, or at least so long as there are Advantages attending it; but that he shou'd stile the Society of FREE MASONS, or any other parcel of

Men, by the Name of *Hereticks*, convinces me both of his Ignorance and Fallibility: And if the Truth was sufficiently / known, *that grief and bitterness of Soul*, with which he seems so greatly to be oppress'd, does not proceed from any Spirit of Virtue animated by his *Pastoral Care*, or from an Opinion, that the Society of FREE MASONS commit Actions *either Base or Impure*, but rather from that part of his *Holiness's Wisdom*, which will not permit him to Approve of any, *but those who do Contribute towards the Increase of his Revenue and Treasures*: For, as he very prudently observes, *The Lord's Vineyard wou'd be in Danger of Starving*, or at least cou'd not be maintain'd in all its Purity without *those Benefices*; And I do not question, if the *Fraternity* wou'd allow him an *Annual Stipend,* to be disposed off, according to the *charitable Discretion of his Holiness*, (which agreeable to an old Maxim, *often begins at Home*) but that he wou'd Approve of Them, nay, Condemn and brand with *Heresy*, all those who wou'd not come into the same way of thinking, and instead of declaring Them *suspitious to the Spiritual or Temporal Powers*, his Holiness wou'd insist on in the most strenuous manner, *That the Secret of Free Masonry was the very Basis of Religion, and so greatly conducing to the Welfare of Mankind, as to be even essential to the Salvation of their Souls.*

AND that this *Change* might be wrought in his Holiness will not seem improbable, when we take into our view the many *Brothel Houses* which are supported by his Protection in the Dominions of *Italy*; for which Favour a valuable Income yearly arises to him. Now in those Assemblies Vice generally appears in its various and most deformed Shapes, and I need not acquaint the Publick, that they have been ever found to debauch our Principles, as well as to destroy the peace and quiet of our Families, by dissolving Conjugal / Love and Affection; Nay, they have been the cause of the greatest Evils which have happen'd to Mankind: These Iniquitous Practices his Holiness can pass over with an Eye of Approbation, without determining Them either pernicious to the Principles of State, or the Merit of Souls; but Those of the Fraternity of FREE MASONS (to which he is an absolute Stranger) cannot by any means be digested by him; wherefore his Holiness must excuse Us, if we believe that a *golden Key is sufficient to blind a* Pope, *and lock up all his Senses*; tho' God forbid that any of the *Fraternity* shou'd pay that Obedience to his *Supremacy, as to trample Reason under their Feet*; and methinks 'tis the Duty of every moral Man to shake off the Yoke of *Arbitrary Power* when leading to Destruction.

IF his Holiness and the Amazed Croud wou'd require to know, *what a strange and secret Man a* MASON *is*, I will describe him in the following manner.

THAT is, *One* who pays a due Reverence to his *Great Creator*, free from the *gross errors of Superstition*, or blind *Arrogance of Atheism and Deism;*[5] *One* who is ever true and loyal to his Prince, dutiful and obedient to all higher Powers, provided they do not exceed the limited Bounds of Religion and Reason: *One* who is ever dispos'd to Contribute to the Welfare and Peace of his Country, utterly *abhorring any wicked Plots or dark Designs against the State*:[6] *One* who never shuts his Ear unkindly to the Complaints of *wretched Poverty*, but with Patience hears, pitys, and relieves the *Distressed*: *One* who never gives the least Umbrage to Animosities and Contentions, but strives to promote a cordial Love and Friendship amongst the *Brethren*. In short, a MASON is *One* who / strictly pursues the Religion of *Nature*,[7] ever making that grand Precept of *doing unto others, as he would they should do unto him*; the main Center and Guide of all his Actions.

THESE are the Qualifications which every *true* MASON hath, and such as, in my Opinion, no Christian need to be asham'd to profess and Practise.

NOW, if his Holiness is not Content with this *Character* of a MASON, I wou'd advise him to send some of his Cardinals amongst them, who will perhaps return with the same Answer, as the Ministers of the Scotish Assembly did to their *Elders*,[8] when dispatched on that *Errand*:

You may go yourself, and then you'll be satisfy'd.

I am, My Lord,

Your Most devoted humble Servant.

Philo-Lapidarius.[9]

BERNARD CLARKE, *AN ANSWER TO THE POPE'S BULL, WITH A VINDICATION OF THE REAL PRINCIPLES OF FREE-MASONRY* (1751)

Bernard Clarke, *An Answer to the Pope's Bull. With a Vindication of the Real Principles of Free-Masonry. Publish'd by the Consent and Approbation of the Grand-Lodge of Ireland. By Bernard Clarke* (Dublin: printed by John Butler, for the author, 1751).[1]

Despite the publication of the decrees against Freemasonry in the 1730s, the number of lodges increased rapidly in many European countries in the 1740s. Following in the footsteps of the Netherlands, the Canton of Geneva and the Catholic Church, several states issued bans against Freemasonry. The monarchs of Sweden and Poland banned masonic lodges in 1739.[2] In 1740 the papal bull was approved in Spain and the lodges were suppressed. In 1744 the authorities of Avignon and Paris banned masonic meetings, as did the Council of Berne, the electorate of the city of Hanover and the chief of the Paris police in 1745. Three years later the Grand Sultan of Constantinople followed their example.[3] *An Apology for the Free and Accepted Masons, Occasioned by their Persecution in the Canton of Berne, with the Present State of Masonry in Germany, Italy, France, Flanders and Holland* (Frankfurt, 1748), reproduced in volume 1 (pp. 51–70), well summarizes the state of continental Freemasonry, the prohibitions and the masonic reactions in the 1740s.

As for the reactions to the Catholic ban in the British Isles, in 1741 Fifield D'Assigny published a detailed refutation of the papal condemnation entitled *An Impartial Answer to the Enemies of Free-masonry* with the approbation of the Grand Lodge of Ireland.[4] John Coustos, a Swiss Protestant diamond cutter, published the story of his trial on account of his masonic membership before the court of the Portuguese inquisition in 1744 in a popular book printed several times in London and Dublin as *The Sufferings of John Coustos, for Free-Masonry, and for His Refusing to Turn Roman Catholic, in the Inquisition at Lisbon; Where He Was Sentenc'd, During Four Years to the Galley; and Afterwards Releas'd*.[5]

On 18 May 1751, Pope Benedict XIV (1740–58) issued a new bull, *Providas Romanorum Pontificum*, in order to dispel rumours that Clement XII's bull was no longer effective, and to confirm and renew his predecessor's condemnation.[6]

It elaborated on some of the points of the first bull. The author of the following pamphlet was supposed to reply to the following accusations of the Holy See: 1. men of every religion and sect attend these meetings, which causes great injury to the purity of Catholic religion; 2. the impenetrable bond of secrecy; 3. the secret oath, which can be used to protect a member of these societies from confessing when questioned by legitimate authority, whether anything contrary to religion and state is done during those secret meetings; 4. these societies are opposed to both civil and canonical sanctions; 5. the said societies were already proscribed and banished by laws of secular princes; 6. these societies were of ill repute among wise and virtuous men: in their judgement anyone who joined them incurred a stigma of depravity and perversion. Following this second bull, Charles VII of Naples and his brother Ferdinand VI of Spain banned masonic meetings.

The new bull was published in Irish newspapers. As in the case of the first papal condemnation, an Irish Freemason replied to the charges almost immediately, that is, on 19 September, little more than four months after the promulgation of the bull in Rome.

The author of this pamphlet is Bernard Clarke. At the time of the publication he was a poet and young schoolmaster in Navan, Co. Meath. In 1751 Clarke also published the four-part *Collections of Poems upon Various Occasions*.[7] According to Chetwode Crawley, he is said to have been the uncle and teacher of Adam Clarke, the famous dissenting scholar.[8] Patrick Fagan notes that he was apparently a Protestant writer.[9] John Butler, the publisher of the pamphlet, worked as a bookseller and printer in Dublin on 'Cork Hill' between 1751 and 1754.[10]

The new papal bull generated a religious dispute in Europe. The responses to this second Catholic condemnation include Baron Theodore H. Tschoudy's *Etrenne au Pape ou les Franc-Maçons: response a la bulle, Pape Benedoit XIV, 1751* (The Hague, 1752) and a pamphlet entitled *Les Vrais jugemens sur la société des francs-maçons où l'on raporte un détail abrégé de leurs statuts, où l'on fait voir combien ces maximes sont contraires à celles de la religion* (Brussels, 1752).[11] The latter came to the opposite conclusions of Bernard Clarke with regard to the papal bull. In 1782 Karl Michaeler, a Jesuit professor at Innsbruck University, also published a response to Benedict XIV's decree, which highlights some illogicality in its argument. Freemasons continued to issue defences in the second half of the eighteenth century. These apologies include George Smith's *Defence of Masonry in General, but in Particular against Edicts, Bulls, Decrees, Condemnations, &c by Several Powers in Europe* (1783) and Walter Burke's *A Defence of Free-Masonry: Containing the Censures Passed upon it by Six Doctors of Sorbonne and Two Popes with an Answer to Them* (1787).[12]

The reproduction of this very rare pamphlet is based on a copy in the Library and Museum of Freemasonry in London.[13] It is also available in volume 236 of the Haliday pamphlets in the Royal Irish Academy, but the end of that copy is imperfect.

Notes

1. This headnote was written by Róbert Péter.
2. C. H. Lyttle, 'Historical Bases of Rome's Conflict with Freemasonry', *Church History*, 9:1 (1940), pp. 3–23, on pp. 20–1. In 1739 the Grand Master of the Knights of Malta announced the bull and sent several masons into exile.
3. J. A. F. Benimeli, 'Freemasonry and the Catholic Church', in H. Bogdan and J. A. M. Snoek, *Handbook of Freemasonry* (Leiden-Boston: Brill, 2014), pp. 139–54, on p. 139. J. A. F. Benimeli, 'The Catholic Church and Freemasonry: an Historical Perspective', *AQC*, 119 (2006), pp. 234–55, on p. 234. J. A. F. Benimeli, *Masoneria, iglesia e ilustración: un conflicto ideológico-político-religioso. vol. 2. Inquisición: procesos históricos (1739–1750)* (Madrid: Fundación Universitaria Española, 1977).
4. F. D'Assigny, *An Impartial Answer to the Enemies of Free-masonry wherein their Unjust Suspicions, and Idle Reproaches of that Honourable Craft, are Briefly Rehearsed, and Clearly Confuted. To which are Added, Several Serious Admonitions Necessary to be Observed by the Fraternity* (Dublin: Printed by Edward Waters in Dames' Street, and are to be sold at his Shop, 1741). It is reproduced in *AQC*, 77 (1964), pp. 156–68.
5. J. Coustos, *The Sufferings of John Coustos, for Free-Masonry, and for His Refusing to Turn Roman Catholic, in the Inquisition at Lisbon; Where He Was Sentenc'd, During Four Years to the Galley; and Afterwards Releas'd ... To Which Is Annex'd, the Origin of the Inquisition, ... Extracted from a Great Variety of the Most Approved Authors* (London. printed by W. Strahan, for the author, 1746). It was also translated into French (1746) and German (1756).
6. It is available in *Magnum Bullarium Romanum seu eiusdem continuatio* (Luxembourg: Henrici-Alberti Gosse, 1727–54), vol. 18, pp. 212–14. It can also be found with an English translation in W. J. C. Crawley, 'The Old Charges and the Papal Bulls', *AQC*, 24 (1911), pp. 110–15. The above citations rely on the latter.
7. A. C. Elias (ed.), *Memoirs of Laetitia Pilkington* (London: University of Georgia Press, 1997), pp. xxxii–xxxiii, 505.
8. Crawley, 'The Old Charges and the Papal Bulls', p. 109.
9. P. Fagan, *Catholics in a Protestant Country. The Papist Constituency in Eighteenth-Century Dublin* (Dublin: Four Courts Press, 1998), 129.
10. H. R. Plomer, G. H. Bushnell and McC. Dix (eds), *A Dictionary of the Printers and Booksellers who were at Work in England, Scotland and Ireland from 1726 to 1775* (n. p.: Oxford University Press for the Bibliographical Society 1932), p. 377.
11. *Les Vrais jugemens sur la société des francs-maçons où l'on raporte un détail abrégé de leurs statuts, où l'on fait voir combien ces maximes sont contraires à celles de la religion* (Bruxelles: chés Pierre de Hondt, 1752). In two years time a supplement was published to this book: *Supplément aux Vrais jugemens sur la société maçonne en réfutation de l'Intitulé: Le Secret des francs-maçons, avec un Recueil des leurs chansons* (Bruxelles: chez Pierre de Hondt, 1754).
12. G. Smith, *The Use and Abuse of Free-Masonry; a Work of the Greatest Utility to the Brethren of the Society, to Mankind in General, and to the Ladies in Particular. by Capt. George Smith* (London: printed for the author; and sold by G. Kearsley, 1783), pp. 245–63. W. Burke, *A Defence of Free-Masonry: Containing the Censures Passed upon it by Six Doctors of Sorbonne and Two Popes with an Answer to them* (Dublin: Printed for the Author by T. Butler, 1787).
13. It is republished in *AQC*, 77 (1964), pp. 157–68.

Bernard Clarke, *An Answer to the Pope's Bull, with a Vindication of the Real Principles of Free-Masonry* (1751)

AN
ANSWER
TO THE
POPE's BULL.
WITH A
VINDICATION
OF THE
REAL PRINCIPLES
OF
FREE-MASONRY.

Publish'd by the Consent and Approbation of the GRAND-LODGE of
Ireland.
By BERNARD CLARKE.
Magna est Veritas, et prævalebit.
DUBLIN:
Printed by JOHN BUTLER, on *Cork-hill,*
For the AUTHOR, 1751. /

TO THE
Right Worshipful *and* Right Honourable
Lord *GEORGE SACKVILLE,*[1]
GRAND MASTER of the *Antient* and *Honourable Fraternity*
of FREE and ACCEPTED MASONS in *IRELAND.*

My LORD,

ON Account of the *Pope's Bull* against FREE-MASONRY, lately publish'd
in our News-Papers /, and some Aspersions thrown upon it by Enemies to the
Craft, I was prevailed on, by several Worthy *Brethren*, to Publish a Vindication
of the Principles of FREE-MASONRY, and an Answer to the *Pope's Bull.*

It would be vain in Me, My Lord, to endeavour to assign any Reason why the
Fraternity did me this Honour: If I can obtain your Lordship's Patronage, and
Answer their Expectations, my Trouble will be amply rewarded.

However, I think it absolutely requisite to Apologize for my Presumption in
Dedicating the following Sheets to Your Lordship, as I have not the Honour of
being known to You.

It is Natural and Common for Men who exhibit their Writings / to the Publick, to seek the Patronage of great Men, particularly of those, whose Fortunes
are only subservient to the Humanity and happy Dispositions of their Minds.

Power without Humanity and good Nature, was ever distasteful, and often
hated; but great are its Charms when repos'd in one, whose inherent Honour, Virtue and Sweetness of Temper, render it amiable to all Ranks and Degrees of Men.

That This is Your Lordship's Characteristick is Universally Granted; For,

In you fair Virtue bids the Flame aspire;
The People feel the Warmth and catch the Fire.

When Affability is accompanied with good Sense, it guards it / from Extremes, and teaches the great Man to shine, and at the same time shew the World they have an Interest in his Virtues.

Nature and Fortune, My Lord, seem Spontaneously to join in their Choice of You, and the impartial Distribution of their Favours.

Your Lordship is equally Respected for Your Private, as well as Publick Virtues: And That Knowledge and Love of the Art Military, in which You so much excel, have gain'd You the Approbation of an Old, experienced General, and the Universal Esteem of the Army. And I am certain, My Lord, wherever you Command, You are obey'd as much thro' Inclination as Duty. /

As a Demonstration of Your Lordship's Abilities and Merit, You are now Chosen to Act an Important and Pleasing Part under your illustrious Father, whose Titles of Honour are inferior to the innate Dignity of his Mind.

I could here, as usual in Addresses of this Kind, Indulge the high Respect I have for Your Lordship, by relating your many Acts of Humanity and Generosity, to which our Country is no Stranger. However, I am better pleas'd to hear this General Happy Character of You, than to offend your Modesty by a Recital of it.

Yet as an entire Silence in this Point would be so high an Injustice to Your Merit, I am constrain'd to declare some further / Reasons for chusing your Lordship a Patron to this Work.

That Love of Mankind, which always appear'd in Your Lordship's Actions, with your Steady Attachment to MASONRY, induced me to place this Treatise under Your Patronage; and that the FREE MASONS of *Ireland* owe Your Lordship the highest Compliments for Reasons not (perhaps) proper to Insert here, is Irrefragable, and to do any thing less, than chuse Your LORDSHIP for their GRAND MASTER, would be injudicious, and ungrateful.

As this Work is published by Approbation of the GRAND LODGE, it would give the *Fraternity* extreme Pleasure to have it patronised by Your LORDSHIP. /

Therefore I take Leave to hope Your LORDSHIP's Acceptance of this Dedication, from him, who is,

MY LORD,
With highest Duty and Respect,
Your LORDSHIP's
Most Humble,
Most Obedient,
And Devoted

DUBLIN: *Sept. 19th*, 1751.

Bernard Clarke. /

AN
ANSWER
TO THE
Pope's BULL, &c.

AS Society, and an amicable Intercourse with Mankind are highly grateful to every generous Mind; That *Fraternity*, whose Laws and wise Regulations best tend to the Support of each of these, claims a superior Dignity above any other.

It has been often said, that all human Institutions, tho' never so wisely founded, may be liable to Corruption; but it must, however be granted, that the Institution is still the same, tho' some of the Members may basely prostitute it.

Notwithstanding, a *Fraternity* founded upon Secrecy, Morality, brotherly Love and every social Virtue, crown'd, and improv'd, by the Wisest, and greatest Earthly King, and known to have acted, from / Time immemorial, pursuant to the Laws and wise Regulations of their most *amiable Institution, which is to this Day, and will be, till all Nature expires, the same it was in the Beginning*: Yet the Members of this *Fraternity*, as well as the rest of Mankind, have a free Will, and may, or may not, adhere to the wise and prudent Dictates upon which their real Principles are founded. Their degenerating can never in Effect injure the Foundation more than by being a Disgrace to it.

This Infelicity attends many other Institutions as well as FREE-MASONRY, (which is the Subject of the following Sheets;) nor is the Church free from bad Members, yet the Law and the Gospel are the same they were at their first Promulgation.

Hence it naturally follows, that the Irregularity and Immorality of particular Members, ought not to put an Institution, or a whole Fraternity under Disrepute.

Before I presume to take the POPE's *formidable* BULL *by the Horns*, I beg leave to inform my Readers that I have / no View in, nor desire for Controversy, but in a clear moderate and impartial Manner, to invalidate His Holiness's ANATHEMA against a *Mystery* he is entirely unacquainted with.

The *Pope's* BULL runs thus.

'IN the midst of the Cares of the Apostleship, and the continual Attention we have to extirpate *Heresies*, and maintain the Lord's Vineyard in its utmost Purity We have heard with Grief and Bitterness of Soul, that a certain Society, who stile themselves, *the Fraternity of Free Masons*, after making Progress in several States in *Europe*, have likewise spread into *Italy*, and even there had some Increase. We have consider'd, that the Impenetrable Secret of this so *Mysterious Society* is the essential Part, and as it were the Basis of its Institution; and that being thereby become suspicious to the Temporal Powers, several of them have proscribed it in their Dominions. We have likewise consider'd, that by such stronger Reasons it ought to be suspicious to the Spiritual Power, whose Charge is to have an / ever-watchful Eye over every Thing which may concern the Salvation of Souls. For these Reasons, and animated by our Pastoral Care, we have Condemned, and do Condemn, by the present BULL, *&c. &c.*'

I cannot avoid stiling this Declaration a *Bull indeed.* The POPE is Anathematizing; What? An impregnable Secret, he says. However, the first thing to be consider'd is, where the Infallibility of the *Church of Rome* lies, and whether, according to the Usage and Practice of the *Church of Rome*, it is in the *Pope*'s Power or not, to condemn FREE-MASONRY under the Title of *Heresy, Mystery, Impregnable Secret,* &c. which last I am certain gives him the most Uneasiness, as it has above all other Secrets stood the Test of the Inquisition.

The *French Catholicks*, and many eminent Doctors of the *Church of Rome*, (as BELLARMINE[3] confesses,) and among the Rest *Pope* ADRIAN[4], and others, who were no Enemies to Papal Authority, declare it no Crime to deny the *Infallibility of the Pope.* /

The *Pope* and all the *Italian Jesuits* and *Catholicks* allow the Council alone no *Infallibility*, but all *Roman Catholicks* agree that the *Infallibility* consists of a *Pope*, and general Council assembled, and agreeing together. Without entering into any Debate about the Word general Council, I hope his Holiness will permit me to ask a few reasonable Questions. Is he more Infallible than other *Popes* were? The general Belief of the *Church of Rome* must make him confess he is not.

Hence it follows, that *Infallibility* is not in him, which can be prov'd by the Writings of *Pope* SIXTUS VI.[5] who tells us in the Preface to his Translation of the Bible.

'That he picked out of the Cardinals, and almost out of all Nations, a College of the most learned Men who advised him in that Work; they (saith he,) consulted, and I chose that which was best.'
And he adds these remarkable Words.

'It is most evident that there is no surer nor stronger Argument, than the comparing of Antient and approv'd Copies, / and (he tells us) that he carefully corrected it with his own Hands.'

In two Years after, CLEMENT VIII.[6] put forth another Edition and Translation of the Bible, different from the former in two thousand Places, as Doctor JAMES proves from his *Bellum Papale*, and Defence of it.[7]

And which is more than all this, we have these Words in his Preface to this Edition.

'Receive, Christian Reader, this Vulgar Edition of the Scripture, corrected with all possible Diligence, which, tho' in Respect, of human Weakness it be hard to affirm that it is compleat, yet is not to be doubted but it is more pure and correct than all that hath gone before it.'

These two Quotations from the Writings of the Popes themselves, may satisfy any reasonable Person that he must be a meer Dupe to Superstition and blind Obedience, who would ascribe Infallibility to Men who did not perceive it in themselves; nor had they Arrogance enough to assume it. /

Suppose we were to admit the Infallibility of a *Pope* and general Council assembled together, I would be glad to know, before what *Pope* or general Council were the Principles and Mysteries of FREE-MASONRY laid open and reveal'd? Or what *Pope* and general Council ever condemn'd that Institution, or these Principles, of which they were intirely Ignorant.

Some Deeds, the *Church* of *Rome* saith render Men excommunicated by the Fact itself, but that Sentence can never be pass'd by the Church, until the Facts are represented, try'd, and prov'd. Those are particular Offences with Regard to Individuals, but the *Pope* cannot Anathematize any Sect, or their Principles, if they do not stand Condemn'd by some *Pope* and general Council assembled, and agreeing together, until he calls a General Council upon that Occasion. Who then is the Prosecutor? How can that *Pope* or that Council condemn what they know nothing of? What do they hold a Council upon? A Secret. *Risum teneatis.*[8] Now I presume the *Pope's* late *Bull* must / appear ridiculous and inconsistent to any Person, even of the Church of *Rome*, who is capable of the least Reflection, as it is contrary to the receiv'd Opinion of the most Learned Doctors of his own Church. This Invasion would soon bring all *Roman Catholicks* under an intollerable Restraint, and deprive them of the Freedom of Thought.

If Thousands should condemn our *Art* on Account of its Secrecy, we stand acquitted in our own* Conscience, and inform them our Gates are open to all who are willing to receive it Lawfully.

The Curiosity of the Church of *Rome* is greatly offended, because the Art of *Free Masonry* is not reveal'd in Auricular Confession. But why should Professors of that Religion reveal what is not in itself Criminal? are they to give a Detail of their good, as well as bad Actions? If his Holiness enquires of a *Free Mason* what the Principles of his Art are, he will solemnly assure him, there is nothing in them contrary to Religion, / Morality, Decency, brotherly Love or any Social Virtue. Nor did he ever see or hear any thing in *Free Masonry* but what tended to Mens Welfare upon Earth, and Happiness in a future State.

This Confession I think ought to be highly satisfactory to any Religious Power in the World.

If any Number of *Free Masons* in the *Pope's* Dominion, act contrary to Religion, Virtue, and Morality, let him excommunicate those particular *Free Masons* but not judge the whole Fraternity by the Misbehaviour of a few. If *Christianity*

---

*   Accusent nos mille licet, Mens conscia recti, Stat tamen, et nunquam judicis ora timet. Au.[9]

itself was to be judg'd by the Conduct of some of its Professors, who would believe its *Divine Beauties*? When *Free Masons* act irregular[10], we admonish them; when they are intirely refractory to our Laws, and will not reform, we exclude them, which is all in our Power to do.

If the Apostles were to be under Disrepute on Account of the fall of *Judas*, the *Pope* would lose one of his darling Arguments to support his Supremacy. Perhaps the Pope may alledge, that to / bind Men by Oath to conceal, is iniquitous, as there appears no Necessity to him for such an Obligation. Admit this Sacred Tye among *Free Masons*, where is the Impiety, Immorality, or Folly in a set of Men to form themselves into a civilized Society, in order to be improved in commendable Skill and Knowledge, to promote Universal Benificence and the social Virtues of human Life, under the Penalty of an *Obligation*, and this with whatever innocent *Ceremonies* they think proper. This Privilege every incorporate Society enjoys without the least Impeachment.

An *Apprentice* is bound by Articles to keep his *Masters Secrets*, a Freeman is obliged to Consult the Interest of his Corporation, and not to promulgate in Common the Mystery of his Trade. Secret *Committees* and *Privy Councils* are solemnly enjoined not to divulge abroad their Debates and Resolutions. Admit, I say, *Free Masonry* under these Restrictions, there appears to be something like it in all regular Societies. /

The Question now to be ask'd is, Are Obligations in *Free Masonry* Lawful? To solve this Difficulty I shall produce the Opinion of the learned *Bishop Sanderson*[11] upon that of Oaths, who treated that Subject with more Judgment than any Man who went before him.

'† When a thing (says that Prelate) is not by any Precept, or Interdict Divine or Human, so determined but every Man *pro hic et nunc*,[12] may at his Choice do, or not do, as he sees convenient, *let him do what he will, he Sinneth not. I Cor. vii. 36.* As if *Caius* should Swear to Sell his Land to *Titius*, or to lend him an hundred Crowns, the Answer is brief, an Oath in this Case is both lawful and binding.'[13]

Now if the general Design of *Free Masonry* is not of more Importance and Benefit to Mankind than the lending a private Man an hundred Crowns, no wise Man would embark that way. From the above Quotation it appears, (admitting there were Obligations in Masonry,) an Oath is justifiable, and Lawful. /

If *Free-Masons* are bound by Obligations, they are certainly coersive, tho' the Pope, to satisfy his Curiosity, should promise his Dispensation; 'For tho' a Matter is so trivial,[iii] that it signifies not a Straw whether it is done or not, as to reach up a Chip, or to rub one's Beard, or for the Slightness of the Matter, is not much to be esteem'd, as to give a Boy an Apple, or lend him a Pin, yet an Oath is binding in a Matter of the least Consequence, because weighty and trivial Things have a like Respect unto Truth and Falshood, and further, because every Party swearing is bound to perform all he promises, as far as he is able, and it is lawful. To give a Boy an Apple is both possible, and lawful, he is therefore bound to fulfil his Oath.'

'One *Hipparchus*,[14] of the old Pythagorean Discipline, out of Spleen and Malice broke through the Bond of his Oath, and committed the Secrets of the Society to Writing, in order to bring it into Disrepute, he was immediately expell'd the School as a most infamous Wretch, as one dead to all Sense of Honour, Fidelity, / and Virtue: The *Pythagoreans*, according to their Custom, made a Tomb for him as if he had been actually dead.'

'The Shame and Disgrace that justly attended the Violation of his Oath, threw the poor Wretch into Despair, and Madness, he cut his Throat, and his Memory was so abhored after Death, that his dead Body lay upon the Shore of the Island *Samos*, and had no other Burial than the Sands of the Sea*.'

'The *Essenes*, among the *Jews*, were of the *Pythagorean* Discipline, who when they received a Person into their Society, he was to pass two Degrees of Probation before he could be Master of their Mysteries, but before he was receiv'd as an establish'd Member, he first voluntarily bound himself by an Oath to do Justice, to do no wrong, to embrace the Faith, and keep it with all Men, to keep his Hands from Pollution, Theft, and fraudulent Dealing, not to conceal from his fellow Professors any of the Mysteries, nor communicate any of them to the Prophane, tho' it would be to save his Life, to deliver / nothing but what he received, and endeavour to preserve the Principles of what he professed. They Eat and Drank at one common Table, and the *Fraternity* that came from any other Place, were sure to be received, and cherish'd [†].'

After what has been say'd, I believe no wise Man will expect that a *Free Mason*, if he has taken any O[b]ligations of Secrecy, should communicate his Art to any, except to those who receive it lawfully as he did.

Every Man has, or ought to have a Respect to his own Conscience, and if any one is to blame for concealing *Free Masonry* from those who seek it but thro' Curiosity, it must be the first Institutor, and to blame him for any of his wise Institutions, would be a Presumption I should be sorry any Christian could be guilty of. Let no one thro' wilful Ignorance or invincible Stupidity blame *Free Masonry* on Account of its Secrecy: He who seeks it in his Heart, asks it as he ought, and knocks as he should, our Gates will instantly become open to him, and all our Secrets fairly unbosom'd. /

If the *Pope* should affirm, (tho' he never had been in *Ireland*, nor heard any of the Laws or Regulations of that Country,) that the Inhabitants thereof were the most irreligious, infamous, and prophane People upon Earth, and through his

---

*   De obligatione Juramenti, Prælectio 3d; Lect. 15th[15]

†   Clem: Alexand. Strom. 5.[16]

own Caprice, condemn, unheard, and unacquainted, a People, and their Laws, Principles, and Tenets of which he was intirely ignorant, what Man of Understanding would notice the *roaring of so blind a Bull, poking in the Dark, and endeavouring to strike at, he knew not what*? Then, since no Precept, Divine or Human, has any way determined upon the Principles of *Free-Masonry*, which in all human Probability will ever prove an *impregnable Secret* to the *Pope*, it is plain that his condemning it is a similar Case.

But Perhaps, he may say, if there be any thing sacred, religious or holy in it, it should be revealed to him (who is the Grand Repository of Secrets,) that he might divulge it for the Good of the Church, and that it argues a sufficient cause of Suspicion to his Holiness, because / *Free-Masons*, (Stubborn Fellows!) will not lead him into that Secret, without receiving it as they did. His Holiness perhaps is in dread of some *Jewish Practice*, or that he would be obliged to go through some *ordeal Tryal*. But to be serious, would it not be unreasonable for a Great Man's Son to say, 'My Father has Interest for me to be a Bishop, I will not go through the usual Ceremony, tell me I am a Bishop without any further intervening; I am a great Man, and should not receive things in the Ordinary way with the rest of Mankind.' This Arrogance would certainly be spurn'd by the Church, and were he the Son of a King, he must receive *Episcopal Orders* like other Men.

To close this Answer to his Holiness, I will inform him that *Free-Masonry*, (whatever Irregularities some of its Members may commit) directs to pay a due Reverence to the *Mighty Architect* of the World.

To be free from *Superstition, Idolatry, blind Obedience, Atheism, Deism* and *Enthusiasm*, to be ever true and loyal to / our King and Country; dutiful and obedient to all higher Powers, not exceeding the limits of Reason, and national Liberty; to be chearfully disposed to contribute to the Welfare and Peace of Mankind, to detest all Plots and Conspiracies, private or publick Contentions, or disagreeable Debates about Religion, to have their Ears ever attentive to the Complaints of the *poor* and *afflicted*, to avoid all Animosities, Malice, Spleen, Envy, and Hatred. To be foremost in promoting *Social Love, Friendship, Charity*, good *Fellowship* and every Scheme which tends to the Utility or Emolument of the Community: to forgive Injuries, and do good for Evil, to encourage Arts and Sciences, to live in *Faith, Hope* and *Charity* with all the World, which is the Centre, and main Guide of a true *Free-Mason's* Action's.

'*To vindicate the ways of God to Man*,'[17] is one of the noblest of the *Free-Mason's* Principles, he does it by his Example, and by a ready Submission to the little Evils of Life, as well as the Great, he pities the Tattle of the Ignorant, and / the Misrepresentations of Men, who might know better, give him little Pain.

The Free Mason who is the generous, brave, free disinterested Man, laughs and contemns the Censures of the Thoughtless, who know not what they despise; he is comforted by the Innocence of his Conscience, Quaffs the Bowl of Reason, *and chearfully Sings*.'

TO all who MASONRY despise,[18]
This Counsel I bestow,
Don't ridicule, if you are wise,
A *Secret* you don't know;
Yourselves you banter, but not it,
You shew your Spleen's quite void of Wit.
With my fal. &c.

Some of our Rules I may impart,
But must conceal the Rest,
Thy're safely lodg'd in Mason's Heart,
Of Secresy possess'd;
We Love our Country and our King,
We Toast the Ladies, laugh and sing.
With my fal. &c.

If *Union and Sincerity*
Have a Pretence to please,
We *Brothers* of FREE-MASONRY,
Lay justest claim to these,
To State Disputes we ne'er give Birth,
Our Motto Friendship is, and Mirth.
With my fal. &c. /

The Social Virtues of our Rules
Which we preserve secure,
Inspire *Compassion for those Fools*,
Who think our acts impure;
From Ignorance we know proceeds
Such mean Opinion of our Deeds.
With my fal. &c.

Let Men of Sense our Witness be,
Who know our *Secret Art*,
Such think they're bless'd in MASONRY,
Proud to espouse our Part.
Let *Rome* or *Naples* then despise,
A Secret hid from both their Eyes.
With my fal. &c. /
[blank page]

A
VINDICATION
OF THE
REAL PRINCIPLES
OF
FREE-MASONRY.

IT may be expected that I should give a History of *Masonry* in this *Treatise*, but as that has been so well done before, and particularly in Brother *Edward Spratt's New Book of Constitutions*,[19] collected from the Writings of the learned *Doctor Anderson*, I must refer my Readers to that Performance, which will certainly both edify, and entertain. However as an Introduction, I will give a Sketch of the Progress of *Free-Masonry* in England, where, some of the most illustrious *Kings, Princes*, and Noble Men encouraged the *Royal Art*; and also recite such *Lodges* in other Nations, as sat under the Sanction of the *Grand Masters* of *England.*

We are informed by *Records written in the Reign of King Edward* II. of the Norman Line, about A.D. 1362. 'That *King Athelstan (Grandson of King Alfred the Great*, an ingenious *Architect,)* the first anointed King of / *England*, who Translated the *Holy Bible* into the *Saxon Tongue*, when he had brought the Land to Rest and Peace, built many great Works, and encouraged *Masons* from *France*, who brought with them the *Charges* and Regulations of *Lodges*, preserved since the *Roman Time*, who also prevailed with the *King* to improve the *Constitution* of the English Lodges, and to encrease the Wages of *working Masons*. And that the said *Kings* youngest Son *Prince Edwin*, being instructed in *Masonry*, and assuming the Charges of a *Master-Mason* thro' the Love he had for the *Craft*, and the *Honourable Principles* whereon it is Grounded, purchased a *Free Charter* of King *Athelstan* his Father, for Masons to have a Power to regulate themselves, to amend what might happen amiss, and to hold a Yearly *Communication* and general Assembly.'[20]

'That Accordingly Prince *Edwin* Summoned all the Masons in the Realm to meet at York, who came and composed a general Lodge, of which he was *Grand Master*, and having brought with him all the Writings and Records that could be found in *Greek, Latin, French* and other Languages, from the Contents thereof, that Assembly framed the Constitution and Charges of an English Lodge; and made a Law to preserve, and observe the same in all Time to come, and Ordained good Pay for working *Masons*, &c.' HAL.

'In Process of Time when Lodges were more frequent, the Right worshipful the Master and Fellows, with Consent of the Lords of the Realm, (for most of the Great Men were / then *Free-Masons*) Ordained that for the future at the *Making* or *Admission* of a Brother, the Constitution and Charges of Lodges should be read by the *Master* or *Wardens*, and that such as were to be admitted, should be examined, whether they were able and skilful to serve their respective Lords, as well the highest, as the lowest, to the Honour of their *Art*, and Profit of their Employers. And, exclusive of many other things, the said Records add, that those *Charges*, and *Laws* of *Free-Masons*, have been seen, and perused by our late Sovereign Lord King *Henry* VI. and by the Lords of his Honourable Council, who allow'd them to be good and reasonable to be holden, as they have been drawn and collected from the Records of Antient Times.'

'In the third Year of said King *Henry* VI. while an Infant, the Parliament made an Act entitled *Masons shall not Confederate themselves into Chapters and Congregations*.*'

'This Act only affected *working Masons*, who, contrary to the *Statute for Labourers*, had confederated not to work, but at their own Price and Wages; and because such Agreements were supposed to be made at the general Lodges, it was then thought expedient to level the said Act against the said Congregations. Yet when the said King *Henry* arriv'd to Man's Estate, the *Free-Masons* laid before him and his Lords the above mentioned Records and Charges, who reviewed them, and solemnly approved of them as good and reasonable to be holden. And Masons were encouraged / all his Reign. But as there was not a single Instance of the Acts being put into Execution in that, or any other Reign, the Brethren continued to hold their Lodges, and thought it unnecessary, to employ their noble and eminent Brethern to have it repealed; because working *Masons* who are free of a Lodge, scorn to be guilty of any Combination, and *Free* and *Accepted Masons* have no Concern in Trespass against Statutes.'

'This Act was formed when Ignorance prevailed, when Learning was deem'd a Crime, and *Geometry* condemn'd for Conspiration,'

'Antient Records inform us that the Parliament were influenced by the illiterate Clergy, who neither understood the Secrets of the Craft, nor true *Architecture*, but, apprehending that they had an *indefeasable Right* to the *Secrets* of the People by *Auricular Confession*, they were jealous with *Free Masons*, and represented them as dangerous to the *State*, in order to reflect a Dishonour upon the whole Fraternity.

'But the Opinion of the great Judge *Cooke* clears all our doubts in regard to the Statute against *Masons.*   For

Cessante ratione legis, cessat ipsa Lex[†].[21]

'The Kings of *Scotland* very much encouraged the *Royal Art*, from the earliest of Times, down to the *Union* of the *Crowns*, where *Lodges* were kept up without Interruption many Hundred Years. The *Scotch* always gave undeniable Evidences of their Love and Loyalty, whence came the old Toast among the *Scots Masons: God bless the King, and the Craft*. /

*   Tertio Henrici Sexto, Chap. 1. A. D. 1425.

†   Vide Co: Par: 3 Fol. 99.

'And to this Day they are as knowing *Free-Masons* as any in Europe.'

'The learned and Magnanimous Queen *Elizabeth* beginning her Reign, A. D. 1558. in troublesome Times, was diffident of her Subjects holding private Assemblies, and therefore attempted to dissolve the Annual Communication of *Free-Masons*.'

'She sent some Noble Persons to pay a Visit to the Lodge at *York*, where being admitted, they delivered up their Swords, *heard the Fraternity*, and returned the Queen a most honourable Account of them, whereby her political Fears and Doubts were remov'd, and she look'd upon them afterwards as a People no ways suspicious, since they were respected by the Noble and Wise of all polite Nations.'

'Upon her Demise, King *James* the VI. of Scotland, and first of England, a *Mason King*, reviv'd the English Lodges, and as he was the first King of *Great-Britain*, he was also the first Prince in the World that recovered the *Roman Architecture* from the *Ruins* of *Gothick Ignorance*. Ever since that King's Reign *Free-Masonry* has supported itself in England, and shed its Influence upon all Nations in Europe'

'The Knights of *Malta*, and many other *Religious Orders* and *Societies*, borrowed their Solemn *Usuages* from our *Antient Fraternity*, who can most justly affirm, that no Sect of Men are better instituted, more decently instaled, or whose Laws and Charges in general have been more Sacredly observ'd.' /

DEPUTATIONS *granted beyond Sea.*[22]

'*Inchiquin, Grand Master*, granted a Deputation to some Brothers in Spain, to hold a Lodge at Gibralter.'

'*Coleraine*, G. M. granted a Deputation for constituting a *Lodge* at *Madrid*.'

'*Kingston*, G. M. granted one to Brother *George Pomfret*, to constitute a *Lodge* at *Bengal*, in *East India*.'

'*Norfolk*, G. M. granted one to Capt. *Ralph Farwinter*,[iv] to be *Provincial* G. M. of *East-India*.'

'And another to Monsieur *Du Thom*, to[v] be *Provincial* G. M. of the Circle of lower Saxony. Another to Mr. *Daniel Cox* to be *Provincial* G. M. of New Jersey in America.'

'*Lovel*, G. M. granted one to Noble Brother *Chesterfield*, Embassador at the Hague, for holding a Lodge there, that made his *Royal Highness Francis Duke of Lorrain*, now our *Royal Brother, Emperor* of *Germany*.'

'Another to Captain *John Philips*, to be *Provincial* G. M. of Russia.'

'Another to Captain *James Cummerford*, to be *Provincial* G. M. of *Andalousia* in *Spain*.'

'Viscount *Montagu*,[vi] G. M. granted one for constituting a Lodge at *Valenciennes*.'

'Another to a *Lodge* at *Hotel de Bussy*, Paris.'

'*Strathmore*,[vii] G. M. granted one to hold a Lodge at *Hamburg*.'

'*Weymouth*, G. M. to Noble Brother *Richmond*, for holding a *Lodge* at his Castle *D'Aubigny* in France.'

'Another to *Randolph Tooke*, Esq; to be *Provincial* G. M. of *South America*.' /

'Another to Brother *George Gordon*, for constituting a Lodge at *Lisbon* in *Portugal*.'

'Another to Brother *Roger Lacy*, Merchant of *Georgia in America*.'

'Another to *Richard Hull*, Esq; to be *Provincial* G. M. of *Gambray* in *West-Africa*.'

'*Loudon*, G. M. to *Robert Tomlinson* Esq; to be *Provincial* G. M. of *New-England* in *America*.'

'Another to *John Hammerton*, Esq; *Provincial* G. M. of South *Carolina* in *America*.'

'Another to *David Creighton*, M. D. to be *Provincial* G. M. at *Cape-Coast-Castle* in *Africa*.'

'*Darnley* G. M. to *James Watson*, Esq; to be *Provincial* G. M. of the Island of *Montserrat* in *America*.'

'Another to *George Hamilton*, Esq; to be *Provincial* G. M. of *Geneva*.'

'Another to *Henry William Marshalch*, Esq; Hereditary Marshal of *Turingia*, to be *Provincial* G. M. of the Circle of Upper *Saxony*.'

'Another to Captain *William Douglas*, to be *Provincial* G. M. on the Coast of *Africa*, and in the Islands of *America*, except in such places where a Provincial is already Deputed.'

'Another to Captain *Richard Riggs*, to be *Provincial* G. M. of *New-York*,'

'*Caernarvon*, G. M. to his Excellency *William Matthews* Esq; Captain General, and Governor in Chief of his Majesty's Leeward and Carribbee Islands, Vice Admiral, and Chancellor of the same, to be *Provincial* G. M. there. All these Lodges are under the G. M. of England; but the old Lodge at *York* City, / and the Lodges of *Scotland, Ireland*, France,* and *Italy* are under their own *Grand Masters*, tho' they have the same Constitutions, Charges and Regulations for Substance with their Brethren of England.'   *Anderson's Con.*[23]

---

*   The Right Honourable Lord *Kingston*,[24]
      The Right Honourable Lord *Netterville*.[25]
      The Rt. Hon. *Henry Barnewall*[viii], Lord *Kingsland*[ix].[26]
      The Rt. Hon. Sir *Marcus Beresford*[x], Earl of *Tyrone*.[27]
      The Rt. Hon. the Earl of *Blessington*[28]:
      The Rt. Hon. Lord *Donerayle*,[29]
      The Rt. Hon. Lord *Tullamore*,[30]
      The Rt. Hon. Lord *Southwell*[xi].[31]
      The Rt. Hon. Lord *Allen*,[32]
      Sir *Marmaduke Wywill*[xii],[33]
      Right Honourable Lord *Kingsborough*,[34] were Grand Masters of *Ireland*.

By the foregoing Account of the Progress of *Free-Masonry* in so many different Nations, and the Honours pay'd it by so many Kings, Princes and Noblemen, every reasonable Person may infer, that if there was not some thing in *Free-Masonry* worth the Attention of a Wise and learned Man, it would never support itself against the many Misrepresentations, whimsical Conjectures, and ignorant Attacks it has met with from those who knew nothing of it.

Were Men to consider thro' what Obscurity and Darkness the Mystery of *Free-Masonry* has been handed down to Us, the many Centuries it has surviv'd, the different Countries, Languages, / Sects, and Parties it has ran thro', it is surprising how it retain'd its Perfection under so many Disadvantages, or indeed how it ever arriv'd to the present Age. The Interposition of Providence in its behalf is evident, for if Religion or History, were to be transmitted to Posterity under the Restrictions of *Free-Masonry*, it is a Question whether both would not be crowded with so many Fables, Innovations and Superstitions, that they would rather confuse, than improve the Faith or Understanding of Mankind.

'It has long run in muddy Streams, and as it were under Ground, and notwithstanding it might have contracted some Rust the *old Fabrick* is still remaining, and the Essential *Pillars* of the *Temple* appear above the Rubbish'.[38]

'The *Bust* of an old Hero is of great value among the curious, tho' it has lost an Eye, the Nose, or the right Hand'.

Thus *Free-Masonry* even under some Disadvantages on account of the Singular manner of its Propagation, (in my humble opinion) should be receiv'd with Candor and Esteem from a Veneration to its Antiquity.

Free-Masons form themselves into Societies founded on the wisest Laws to devote their Labour, Application, and Industry to the Service of that Supreme Architect, who is the direct Author of Harmony, and true Proportion. To imbibe the best Principles, to serve their Fellow Creatures, to render their Minds harmoniz'd by Virtue, Morality and a perfect Resignation to the Will of God, to subdue their Passions, and attune them to the Ear of Reason. In a word, to / devote their Soul and every Faculty to the Noblest Purposes.

In this School of Reason,[39] The good *Mason* feels his Heart warm'd by the Blessings his Art bestows. Friendship, Benevolence, and mutual Love exclude

---

June the 24th 1751. The Right Honourable Lord GEORGE SACKVILLE,[35] was unanimously chosen *Grand-Master* in *Ireland*, the Honourable *Thomas Southwel*, Esq; Deputy G. M. the Hon. *Roderick Mackenzie*[xiii],[36] Esq; Senior Grand Warden, and the Honourable *Brinsley Butler*,[37] Esq; Junior Grand Warden. *January* the 3d. 1749, the *Grand Master's* Lodge commenced.

the Anxiety of Care, and every selfish Design, whilst all act in one common Interest there.

Lectures upon *Free Masonry* and useful Knowledge are given by a proper Person among us chosen for that Purpose.

By our Art the distant *Chinese* are able to converse with Ease and Freedom with their British Brethren.[40]

In *Lodges* they admit no religious, political or factious Debates, they wisely consider that Debates and dark intricate Questions rather tend to corrupt and bewilder the Understanding, than to rectify Doubts, and promote mutual Friendship.

They strictly follow that Rule, which orders us *to be subject to higher Powers*. They are dutiful and obedient to their King and Country, or to the reigning Power of whatever State they reside in. They are ever ready to defend a Prince, or that Power which supports the Subjects in the Natural Rights of Mankind; for him, or them, they will, and ought to sacrifice all that is valuable, even Life.

Their Art teaches them to dispense that Mercy they would willingly obtain. They feel the sufferings of an honest afflicted Brother, and according to his Necessity, and their Ability, they chearfully contribute to his Relief. The Practice of Virtue, Knowledge of Geometry, and / the rest of the Liberal Arts and Sciences, are, or ought to be the Entertainments of every private *Lodge*, nor can any Man obtain a satisfactory Knowledge of *Free-Masonry*, who is unacquainted with Scripture,[41] History, and the Arts and Sciences.

But when, by the Imprudence of some of the *Fraternity*, illiterate, immoral, low-bred Men are receiv'd, tho' they are admitted into Lodges, it is not to be expected they can behave as *Free and Accepted Masons* should do, nor can such Men in any particular, be an Honour or Ornament to the *Craft*. Their Pursuit after this Knowledge, which, they have not Abilities to comprehend, leads them into Expence and Inconveniences, by running (as some Phrase it,) *Mason Mad*, which prejudices several People against the *Craft* in general.

I most solemnly assure all my Readers, that by the Laws of *Free-Masonry*, no Man is, or ought to injure himself or Family by it, nor will any prudent Man find it more expensive or inconvenient than any other civiliz'd Society.

Their Expences at their usual Meetings are limited by the Rules of Sobriety and Reason, and he who transcends either, is liable to a Reprimand.

To unbend the Mind with moderate Refreshment is highly allowable, but to debase the Character of a rational Being by Ebriety, is strictly prohibited by the Master of every *Lodge*.

If any one, thro' a malevolent Disposition, should object against the general Character I have given the *Fraternity*, by his Knowledge of the ill Conduct of some particular *Free-Masons*, I / can with Safety answer, that if all the *Fraternity* are not what I describe them to be, they at least ought to be so, as their *Rules*,

Regulations, and *By-Laws* tend to the present, and future Happiness of the *Craft*; and I will therefore endeavour to answer such Objections as are generally made against *Free-Masonry*, by those (who tho' they are in the Dark) enveigh against, they know not what, and by an affected Carriage of Wisdom, draw Inferences from the ill Behaviour of a few, without considering the many wise, virtuous, and learned Noblemen who thought themselves honoured by being Members of that Antient, and Honourable *Fraternity*, which give a seasonable Lecture to Kings not to be Arbitrary, that Virtue alone makes a true Distinction between *Man* and *Man*; and while they converse with their Brethren, they consider it is not a long *Race* of illustrious *Heroes* that enobles Men, but the Abilities and real Virtues they possess. The Monarch sees and knows that all good Men are to be valued alike, and by *Free Masonry* he is taught that wise and Noble Lesson, *To know himself.*

As to the Idle Whims, Giddy Fancies, and ridiculous Fables spread abroad concerning our *Art*, I shall think them entirely unworthy of Notice or Examination, as they are believed by none who could be any Honour or Emolument to Society. It is to the wise and discreet Part of Mankind I direct my Discourse, those I would willingly satisfy, but despise and pity the ill judging Crowd, nor can the virtuous and wise be ever kept at a distance from Us, but by false Informations, / which, when their Eyes are opened, they will heartily contemn, and laugh at their own Credulity.

The first Objection against *Free Masonry* is,

'If it be such a good, and Divine Science, productive of so much Virtue, Harmony and Happiness, why is it concealed from any one'?. Or why should not all be equally happy by its Dictates'?. To which I answer, it is by no means a fault in *Free Masons* to observe the invariable Rules handed down to them for many thousand Years, and from which they ought not to deviate.

The greatest Earthly King and Prince of Wisdom founded our *Laws*, and whoever makes this Objection, if he be a Person of Virtue and Probity, he is welcome to enter into our *Fraternity* as other Brothers did, and then he will be sensible of the just Reason for our keeping the Art of *Free-Masonry* a Secret from those who are not inclin'd to prepare themselves for it, and receive it in *Righteousness*.

It is not an Art consisting only of a few Words and secret Signs, (as some imagine) it requires Time to make a Progress in it, and were it to be indifferently revealed to every Person who thro' an Idle Curiosity sought it, he would find little Satisfaction in what he would be able to learn after such a superficial Manner.

The Mysteries of Trade are only revealed to those who serve a lawful Apprenticeship. *An Act of Grace*, tho' it is serviceable to a great many Men, yet the Government have prudent Reasons not to reveal it immediately, nor allow any Person / the Benefit thereof, until he is properly prepared for it, by proving he us'd no sinister Methods to obtain it.

Many Salutary Decrees are kept secret by *Council*, until it is thought proper to reveal them, nor should the Curiosity of the Publick be offended, because the private Conference of the *Council* is not promulgated in Common.

The *Great Creator* of the *World*, who intends the good of all his *Creatures*, did not communicate his *Will* at *all Times*, in all *Places* and to all *Persons alike*: The *true Rule* of a *Free Masons Faith** proves, that Virtue was taught to *a few*, the *Means of Happiness* not to *many*: Some adored Stocks and Stones, the *Mighty Architect* neglected; God distinguish'd Nations, *by his great Love to a peculiar one*; to this Day some parts of the World are depriv'd of the Knowledge of Christianity, and must we find Fault because the same God, who permits Man to Sin, could (if it appeared just in his Supreme Wisdom) destroy his Free-Will, and communicate himself alike to the Righteous, and unrighteous?

The second Objection may be, 'Is a Man more wise, virtuous, or learned by being a *Free Mason* than he was before? Will *Free Masonry* make him serve God better than the Church directs, or go further to serve a Friend, than that natural Portion of Humanity and good Nature he is indued with, inclines him to? Or what good are their *Lodges* or Meetings productive of'.

To prove a Man may be more learned by *Free Masonry*, would be to reveal the Mysteries of our / Art; Therefore, in this Point I can only tell my Readers, there is a great part of Knowledge slip'd over in a Course of Reading of History, Divine and Human, which *Free Masonry* particularly points out and explains.

There are some Traditions peculiar to our Art, which illustrate several Passages in Scripture and History, and these Traditions by their Antiquity and Connexion, deserve equal Belief with many things transmited to us in Writing from Age, to Age. So far, a Man might be more learned.

As to his being more virtuous, it may with equal justice be say'd, 'Since we have the *Bible*, which is the Rule of our Faith, what need we go to Church to hear a Sermon?'. But the oftner we hear Lessons of *Morality, Brotherly Love*, and Social Virtue, either in a Church, or a private Room, the deeper those Principles must be inculcated, as Custom has a Mechanical Operation upon the Mind, as well as the Body.[42]

In Lodges, *Lectures* are given adapted to the Capacity and Reason of the Hearers, which demonstrate that *unbyass'd Zeal* which always warms an honest Heart, and inclines it to every Act of Humanity, Charity and Friendship.

Free-Masons, in their *Grand* and *private Lodges*, consult the Happiness and Benefit of their *Fraternity*, when a Brother of a good Character is in want, *if he asks, he shall have*, if Debt confines him from his Family, the Fraternity chearfully contribute to set him Free.

---

*   The Bible.

If contingent Disorders fall upon an honest Brother, he is allowed a Weekly Subsistance untill / he is able to provide for himself and Family. The Profligate and Immoral are excluded, not only from these Benefits, but even from the Society of every regular Lodge.

The third Objection is, 'Can a Man be a *Free Mason* with a safe Conscience?' To presume he may not, is to brand some of the wisest Kings and Princes with Infamy. Is it to be imagined that so many Noblemen would publickly patronize a System of Immorality? He who puts a specious Colour of Virtue on Vice, and gilds Falshood with an Appearance of Truth, is a Seducer of the People; And would any good Man recommend *that* to his Friend, for which he might afterwards upbraid him with Infidelity?.

It may be objected 'If Virtue be the End of *Free Masonry*, why are so many of the *Fraternity* addicted to Vice?' It is too true that some of them degenerate from the Principles of the Craft, yet, that ought not to alarm any wise Man, since no Fraternity, no Sect upon Earth, but have some bad Members among them.

If a Clergyman is degraded, must the Church be degraded too. Hence it evidently follows, that to condemn a Fraternity for the Irregularity of some of the Members thereof, would be as ridiculous, as uncharitable.

Some have objected, 'Why is the most agreeable half of Man, the *Porcelain* of Human Nature, a fine Woman, excluded from our Art'?[43]

In Answer to this Objection I must inform the Ladies, that we are so far from doing them an Injury, that our Principles direct us to admire them / for their Excellence and Virtue. Perhaps if *Free Masons* introduc'd *Ladies into Lodges*, the Natural Superiority of Man would be lost, which might rob our *Principle Guide* of some of that Adoration, our Craft religiously pays so Divine a *Being*, at their Solemn Meetings.

If Women were permitted to enter *Lodges*, by our Rules they must have a Voice there, of which they were ever debar'd in all Religious Assemblies. St. *Paul* hinted at the Necessity of this, when he say'd, *the Women must be covered because of the Angels.*[44] Women, as they are the weaker Sex, should not be invested with important Secrets, which would draw on them the artful Applications of Men, who so often make them reveal one Secret, for another.

Some ill-natur'd, ignorant Persons say, 'That Our Art makes Men Idle, fond of Drink and Company, and consequently negligent of their Families'. Whereas *Free-Masonry* points out the opposite Virtues, and People who are guilty of these Practices, would be the same Men in any *Club or Society*. Men of such a base Turn of Mind, are not permitted to sit in regular *Lodges*, if the Members are made acquainted with their evil Practices. In Lodges no Indecency, Swearing, Lying or Debauchery of any kind are permitted, but the Fraternity are no more accountable for the Behaviour of any of the Members out of a *Lodge*, than a School-Master is for his Scholars out of School. If a dull, illiterate Man is made a *Free-Mason*, he burns in Pursuit (as I hinted before) of what he has not Abilities to comprehend. This may make him ambitious to / sit with every Person who is able to instruct him; by such means he may neglect his Business, and be no wiser in the End, for every good *Free-Mason* will avoid the Company of those ignorant *refreshing Seekers*, Others may be vain of their imaginary* Abilities in that way, and commence Casuists and Lecturers in *Free Masonry*; this Vanity may lead them into Inconveniencies, which every prudent Man carefully avoids.

The admitting such People, make some Men affirm 'there is no Secret in *Free-Masonry*, if there was, it would some time or other be revealed by the Indiscretion of those Imprudent Men.' But as there needs no Argument to prove what is so generally granted, I think it is an Honour to the *Craft*, that even the meanest of its Professors, and those, who perhaps have no other Virtue, are endowed with Secrecy to conceal, what they received with so much *Reverence* and *Solemnity*.

After what has been said in Vindication of the real Principles of *Free Masonry*, tho' the stubborn Part of Mankind should continue in invincible Ignorance and Disbelief, the generous *Free-Mason* glories in his *Art*, which directs him to the Practice of every thing that is agreeable to the *Author* of *Light*.

Free-Masons borrow their Light from the true I *am*,[45] as the Moon, from that bright Orb, that illumines the boundless Space. In Imitation of / those great Luminaries; the good *Free-Mason*, in his Sphere, dispenses Virtue, Morality and Universal Benevolence, as *Light* among Men. Let Fools then despise our laudable Pursuits, while Dogs bark with Spleen and Envy at the Moon, impotent and silly are the Attacks of the one, and the other. The Moon will continue her invariable Course, and the *Craft* support the *Light of Reason*, tho' Myriads of inveterate Foes should endeavour to eclipse it.

No Society can be expected to flourish, if there is not a prudent Choice of the Members who are to compose it, as it is well known, one bad Member is sufficient to disconcert a whole Company. He who understands the Laws and Duties of *Free-Masonry*, and what the Conduct of its Professors should be, will always be cautious whom he admits. When a Person is reported to be made in any regular Lodge, his Character is inspected into by all the Brethren, and if any one of them can make a reasonable Objection against him, he is rejected.[46] This

---

*   A little Learning is a dangerous thing,
    Drink deep or taste not the *Pierian Spring*,
    There *shallow Draughts* intoxicate the Brain,
    And drinking largely sobers us again. POPE.[47]

prudent Method deters Men of ill Fame to attempt to come among us, and to be one of the *Fraternity* of a regular well governed Lodge, is irrefragably to be an honest Man, for no other is admitted.

Some People may say 'There were several low-lived, and perhaps immoral Persons admitted among the *Fraternity* in this Kingdom'. This Assertion I am constrain'd partly to grant, there was some Years ago an *Interreign* of *Grand-Masters*, which reduced *Free-Masonry* in this Kingdom to a very low *Ebb*.[48] /

In this declining State some Persons crept in, who were afterwards a Disgrace to the *Craft*, and the Admission of three or four evil Members opened a Road for many more of the same Disposition.

But now, to the Honour of the *Craft*, they have a Grand Master, whose publick and private Virtues are so well known, it would be endless to expatiate upon them.

The Honourable *Thomas Southwell*,[49] Esq; Deputy Grand Master, is a real Ornament to Society; his Mind and Heart are suitable to the Noblest Purposes, nor need any doubt his Humanity and Goodness, while he displays so much of both in his happy Countenance. The Hon. *Roderick Mackenzie*, Esq;[50] Senior Grand Warden, for his Modesty and happy Character in publick, his Love and Attachment to the *Craft* in private, his Deliberation, and prudent Dictates from the *Chair*, has gain'd the general Affection and Esteem of the *Craft*. The Honourable *Brinsley Butler*, Esq;[51] gave the *Fraternity* such early Proofs of that growing Virtue, and these great Abilities which will one day make him an Honour and Ornament to his Country, that they chearfully demonstrated their Approbation of him, by electing him their Junior Grand Warden.

Their Treasurer *Edward Martin*,[52] Esq; is justly esteemed by the *Craft* for his Singular Attachment to it these eighteen Years past; when *Free-Masonry* was in the lowest Ebb in Ireland, he countenanc'd it with a friendly Zeal, and contributed very much to bring it, not only to its primitive Strength and Honour, but also to that Harmony so peculiarly its own, for this End, his Labours have / been indefatigable, and happily crown'd with Success.

Tho' the Fraternity take prudent Methods to prevent bad Men to enter among them, yet I shall humbly beg leave to offer one further Scheme to the Grand Lodge, and if that August Body do not think proper to coincide with me, I shall readily submit to their Superior Judgment.

If every Person who is reported to be made in any private Lodge, was to be reported in the Grand Lodge the next Monthly Night, and if, upon Enquiry, he was found to be a Man of good Conduct and Morality, the said private Lodge might then receive him the next *Lodge Night*. By this Precaution it would be scarce possible that any unworthy Person could be received among us.[53]

The *Grand Lodge*, which is composed of the *Masters* and *Wardens* of *private Lodges*, would scorn to traduce any Person, nor give a favourable Report of the undeserving, and as the *Grand-Lodge* is so numerous a *Body*, few Persons (if any) could be reported, that some Member had not a personal Knowledge of.

To admit a Person into that Antient Fraternity should not be a work of Expedition, every *Postulant* should be well known and his Conduct vouch'd by Men of Probity and Virtue.

Some Men figure to themselves an Inconvenience in *Free-Masonry*, by being (as they imagine) Subject to the *Beck* of every troublesome indiscreet Brother, but this Notion is false. *Despicable Traders* in *Free Masonry* are despised by the *Craft*, we follow the Advice of St. *Paul* in his Second Epistle to the *Thessalonians* Chap. iii.[54] /

> Now we command you, Brethren, in the Name of our Lord Jesus Christ, that ye withdraw yourselves from every Brother that walketh disorderly, and not after the Tradition which he received of us.
>
> For yourselves know how ye ought to follow us: for we behaved not ourselves disorderly among you.
>
> Neither did we eat any Man's Bread for nought; but wrought with Labour and Travel Night and Day, that we might not be chargeable to any of you:
>
> Not because we have not Power, but to make ourselves an Ensample[55] unto you to follow us.
>
> For even when we were with you, this we commanded you, that if any would not work, neither should he eat.
>
> For we hear that there are some which walk among you disorderly, working not at all, but are Busy-Bodies.
>
> Now them that are such we command, and exhort by our Lord Jesus Christ, that with Quietness they Work, and eat their own Bread.
>
> But ye Brethren, be not weary in well-doing.
>
> And if any Man obey not our Word by this Epistle, note that Man, and have no Company with him, that he may be ashamed.
>
> Yet count him not as an Enemy, but admonish him as a Brother.

The Master of every Lodge should be particularly assiduous in having the Members of his Lodge well skill'd in all the Points and Mysteries of *Free-Masonry*, some, I am sorry to say it, content themselves with that Portion of Knowledge, / which is sufficient to make them *known*; but is it not inglorious to neglect the Cultivation of our Understanding in useful Sciences?

How amiable is it to see a *Lodge* so well instructed, that any Brother who is called upon, can give a Lecture in a pleasing agreeable manner, carry on the Discourse from one Degree to another, with Propriety and due Connection.

The Noblest Science upon Earth, may appear with disadvantage when ill described, and I will venture to say, that *Free-Masonry* well Lectur'd upon, would afford as agreeable an Entertainment, as any man could desire to hear. The Choice of prudent, knowing Officers is highly conducive to the Honour of the *Craft*, and nothing should introduce a Man into an Office in a *Lodge*, but his Merit.

In the Grand Lodge there is Business of Consequence to the Fraternity transacted; young Masons are fond of Office, and desirous to sit in that August Assembly, some of them may be a little vain and fond of their own Opinions, this may carry them strenuously on the wrong Side, and spirit them up to Petulance, and Opposition. Therefore, none but discreet, knowing Men should be returned to the Grand Lodge, least there should be Opposition, where the *true Centre of Harmony* ought to reside.

The Respect due to the Grand Master in the *Chair*, is, and ought to be unlimited.[xiv] For it is evident any Person who is called to that *high Station*, can not be led astray by Interest or Partiality. When a Man of a cholerick, warm Temper appears before a Judge in Law, tho' he / imagines himself *in the Right*, yet he submits, because he knows he must acquiesce to the Sentence pass'd. Who is the Person then, that styles himself a *Free Mason*, that could presume to pay less Respect to the Grand Master, or his Representative in the *Chair*, than to a Judge on the Bench.

The Offices in particular Lodges, should be committed to those alone who might improve the Fraternity, and inhance their Value. No Person should be intrusted with such Charges, but those, whose Prudence and good Conduct were well known, and in some Measure experienced. If a County or Borough send bad Representatives to Parliament, they may expect to be represented accordingly, it is a similar Case in *Free-Masonry*; three Officers represent the whole Body of every particular Lodge, which indeed in a great measure, may be judg'd of by their *Representatives*.

All Persons admitted Members of a *Lodge*, should have the Character of being *Free from Bonds*, or *Servile Ties of any Kind*.[56] They should at least be of that Age which qualifies them for Inheritance by Law. Juvenile Years are judged incapable to manage their own, or the Affairs of the Publick, much less are they therefore capable to promote the Welfare of the *Craft*. *Free Masons* ought to be free from Maim or Defect in Body or Mind, and he or they who introduce any Person under these Disadvantages, sells his *Birth Right for a Mess of Pottage*.[57] Every Member of a particular Lodge should be in due Subjection to the Master and presiding Officers, for he who is not / a dutiful and loyal Subject, will never contribute to the Harmony and Peace of a Lodge. Factious, dissatisfied People will be uneasy in any State or Society, and therefore are carefully to be avoided.

'A *Lodge* is a Place where Masons assemble and Work, hence that duly organiz'd Society of *Free Masons* is call'd a *Lodge*, every Brother ought to belong to one and be subject to the By-Laws and general Regulations thereof. A Lodge is either particular or general, and will be best understood by attending it. Persons admitted Members of a Lodge must be good and true Men, Free-born and of mature and discreet Age, *no Bondmen*, no Women, no immoral or scandalous Men, but of good Report.'[58]

'All Preferment among *Masons* is grounded upon real Worth, and personal Merit only, that the *Lords* may be well served, the Brethren not shamed, nor the Royal *Craft* despised.'

'No Master shall take an Apprentice unless he be a perfect Youth, having no Maim or Defect in his Body or Mind that may render him incapable of Learning the *Art*, of serving his *Lord*, of being made a *Brother*, and a[xv] *Fellow Craft*, and in due time a Master; and when qualified, he may arrive to the Honour of being *Warden*, then Master of a *Lodge*, then *Grand Warden*, and at length *Grand-Master* of all the Lodges, according to Merit.'

'In a Lodge, while constituted, you are not to hold separate Conversation, without leave from the Master, nor talk of any thing impertinent or unseemly, nor interrupt the Master or / Wardens, or any Brother speaking to the Master, nor behave ludicrously or jestingly while the Lodge is engag'd in what is *Serious* and *Solemn*, nor use any unbecoming Language upon any account, but to pay due Reverence to the *Master, Wardens*, and *Fellows*.'

'If any Complaint be brought, the Brother found Guilty shall stand to the Award and Determination of the *Lodge*, for no common Law must intervene among *Free Masons* without an absolute Necessity apparent to the Lodge.'

'When the Lodge is over you may enjoy yourselves with Innocent Mirth, treating one another according to Ability; but avoiding all Excess, or forcing a Brother to eat or drink beyond his Inclination, or hindering him from going when his Occasions call him, or doing or saying any thing offensive, or that may hinder an easy and free Conversation, for that would interrupt our Harmony and defeat our laudable Purposes. No private Piques or Quarrels must be brought within the Door of a *Lodge*, far less any Quarrels about Religion, Nations, or Policy of State, for we are *Masons* of the *Catholick* Religion, we are also of all Nations, Tongues, Kindred and Languages, and are resolved against all Politicks, which never conduced to the Welfare of any *Lodge*, nor ever will.'

'Out of a Lodge you are to Salute one another in a courteous manner, calling each other *Brother*, freely giving mutual Instruction as shall be thought convenient, without being overseen or overheard, and without encroaching upon each other, or derogating from that / Respect which is due to any Brother, were he not a Mason: For tho' all Masons are Brethren upon the same *Level*, yet Masonry takes no Honour from a Man that he had before, it rather adds to his Honour, especially if he has deserv'd well of the *Brotherhood*, who must give Honour to whom it is due, and avoid ill Manners.'

'Before Strangers, who are not Masons, you are to behave circumspect and cautious, and manage in an exemplary Manner, for the Honour of the *worshipful Fraternity*.

'At home you are to act as a moral wise Man, particularly not to let your Family, Friends, *& c.* know the Business of the Lodge; you must wisely consult your own Honour, and that of the *Antient Brotherhood*, for Reasons not here to be mentioned.'

'You must also consult your Health, by not continuing together too late, or too long from home after Lodge hours are past; you must avoid Drunkenness, *& c.* that your Family be not neglected, or injur'd, nor you disabled from work or other Business. You are likewise honestly to pay your Debts, and not to contract any, but such as in your Conscience you know yourself able and inclined to pay, and that in a reasonable Time, that the *Craft* be not despis'd, nor the Brotherhood evil spoken of on your Account.'

'You are cautiously to examine a strange *Brother*, in such a Method as Prudence will direct that you may not be impos'd on, by an ignorant false *Pretender*, whom you are to reject with / Contempt and Derision, and beware of giving him any hints of Knowledge. But if you discover him to be a *true* and *genuine Brother*, you are to respect him accordingly, and if he is in *want*, you must relieve him, if you can, or else direct him how he may be reliev'd: or recommend him to be employ'd; but you are not to do beyond your Ability, nor prejudice yourself in any Respect, only to prefer a poor Brother that is a *good Man*, and *true*, before any other Person in the same Circumstances'.

Pennel's Const.[59]

These Charges are read to every Person when he is admitted a Member of a Lodge, and many more which are communicated to him in *another way*; The Fraternity are particularly directed to cultivate *Brotherly Love*, which is the Foundation and Glory of the Royal *Craft*.

Free Masons are strictly to avoid Quarreling, Slander, and Defamation, they are also directed not to permit others to defame an honest absent Brother, but to defend his Character, and do him any friendly Office conveniently in their Power. If a Brother imagines one of the Fraternity does him an Injury, he should apply to his own *particular Lodge*, and if the Affair cannot be determin'd there, they may have a Hearing at the Grand Lodge the next monthly Night. Tho' it would be more recommendable, that all Debates (if possible) should be decided in private Lodges, or by a *Committee* of the *Grand Officers*, as no Disturbance should intervene among so August a Body, who meet to consult the good, and welfare of the *Craft*, and by their Example animate / the rest of the *Fraternity*, to every Act of Charity, Humanity and Virtue.

Every Member in all the *regular Lodges* in Ireland, pay quarterly *Dues* to the *Grand Lodge*, those *Dues* with a Monthly Collection in the Grand Lodge, are

Deposited in the *Treasurer's* Hands, who answers such Draughts as are drawn upon him by the Fraternity for Charitable Uses, *&c.*

That those are real Benefits arising from *particular Lodges,* and the Assembly of the *Grand-Lodge*, will readily be granted by any Person in his Senses, and as the Fraternity are ever ready to promote all Schemes, which tend to the Honour of the *Craft*, and Relief of honest indigent Brethren; they have now opened a Subscription for erecting a *Grand Lodge Hall* in the City of Dublin,[60] for the Fraternity to assemble in on their *Solemn Meetings*, and occasionally to have Concerts or other Performances; and the profit thereof to be laid out in the Support of distressed and indigent Brethren, and other charitable Uses. As this Scheme is founded upon so laudable a Design, no doubt several worthy humane Persons exclusive of the *Craft*, will encourage so beneficent an undertaking, which is purely calculated to dissipate the Sorrows and Afflictions of the Distress'd.

Tho' I am perhaps the most inconsiderable Author that ever writ in defence of Masonry*, yet I presume to hope I have in some measure prov'd (what I shall always solemnly declare) / that no Institution upon Earth can be better calculated to preserve Charity and mutual Love among Mankind, nor is there any Society who have *wiser Laws*, or more prudent *Charges* and *Regulations*. Upon the whole, if *Free Masonry* had nothing else to recommend it than the Fraternity's Love to one another, and uninterrupted Harmony at their Solemn *Meetings*, where Pleasure and Social Joy dwell on every Brow, these Felicities alone might render it desirable to all who have a Taste for the Sweets of Society, and a Desire to contribute to the Happiness of their *Fellow Creatures*.

May the Father of Light therefore illumine the Minds and Hearts of the Fraternity (wherever dispersed all over the Globe,) with his divine Grace, and inspire them to act agreeable to his *blessed Will*, to render their Lives exemplary to the rest of Mankind, and to give the World a Demonstration of the happy Effects of their *ever glorious Institution*. May the whole Fraternity in this, as well as in all succeeding Ages, flourish with unsully'd Glory.

Whose lofty *Fabrick* never will expire,
Till ev'ry human thing's dissolv'd by Fire. /

A PRAYER[61] to be said at the opening of a *Lodge*, or making of a *Brother*.

MOST Holy and glorious Lord God, *thou great Architect of Heaven and Earth, who art the Giver of all good Gifts and Graces; and hast promised that where*

---

*   The Quotations mark'd in this Work are principally from the following Authors *viz.* M. *Pool,* Author of the Annotations on the Bible;[62] *Joseph.* Antiq.[63] Doctor *Anderson*[64] and Doctor *Leslie,* F.R.S.[65]

two or three are gathered together in thy Name, thou wilt be in the midst of them; in thy Name we assemble and meet together, most humbly beseeching thee to bless us in all our undertakings, to give Us thy Holy Spirit, to enlighten our Minds with Wisdom and Understanding, that we may know, and serve thee aright, that all our doings may tend to thy Glory and the Salvation of our Souls.

And we beseech thee, O Lord God, *to bless this*, our presen[t] Undertaking, and Grant that this, our new Brother, *may Dedicate his Life to thy Service, and be a true and faithful* Brother among Us; *imbue* xvi *him with divine Wisdom, that he may, with the Secrets of Masonry, be able to unfold the Mysteries of Godliness and Christianity.*

To be added when any Man is made

This we humbly beg in the Name, and for the sake of JESUS CHRIST *our* LORD *and* SAVIOUR *Amen.* /

THE
PROGRESS
OF
FREE-MASONRY.
A SONG.[66]
[Tune *Derry-Down.*]

WHOEVER wants Wisdom, must with some Delight,
Read ponder, and pore, Noon morning and Night,
Must turn over Volumes of Gygantick Size,
Enlighten his Mind, tho' he puts out his Eyes.

Derry down.

If a General would know how to Muster his Men,
By Hundreds, by Thousands by Fifties by Ten,
Or level by Seige, an high Castle, or Town,
He must borrow his Precepts from Men of Renown.

Derry down.

Would a wry-fac'd Physician or Parson excell,
In preaching or giving a Sanative Spell,
They first must read *Galen* or *Tillotson* through,
Ee'r they get Credentials, or Business to do.

Derry down.

But these are all Folly, Free Masons can prove,
In a Lodge they find Knowledge, fair Virtue and Love,
Without deaf'ning their Ears, without blinding their Eyes,
They teach the Compendious way to be Wise.

Derry down.

While all in Confusion the *Chaos* yet lay,
E'er Evening and Morning had made the first Day,
Th' unform'd Materials lay jumbl'd together,
Like so many Dutchmen in thick foggy Weather.

Derry down. /

When to this Confusion no end there appear'd,
The *Sovereign Mason's Word* sudden was heard,
Then teem'd Mother *Chaos* with *maternal Throws*,
And this beauteous *Lodge* of the World then arose.

Derry down.

The Earth and all Heav'n with *Jubile* rung,
And all the *Creation of Masonry* Sung,
When Lo! to compleat and adorn the gay Ball,
Old Adam was made the *Grand Master of All*.

Derry down.

But Satan met Eve as she was a gadding,
And set her, like some of her Daughters, a madding;
To find out the Secrets of *Free-Masonry*,
She eat of the Fruit *of the Life-giving Tree*.

Derry down.

Then Adam astonish'd like one struck with Thunder,
When seduc'd, he beheld her all over with *Wonder*,
'And since you have done this thing, Madam, says he,
For your sake no Woman Free Mason shall be.'

Derry down.

Now as she lamented in sorrowful Ditty,
The good Man he blush'd, and on her took Pity,
Free Masons are tender, so to the sad Dame,
He bestow'd a Green Apron to hide her from shame.

Derry down.

Then old Father *Enoch*, he mounts on the Stage,
In Manners severe but in Masonry Sage,
He built two fam'd *Pillars* full large and full thick,
The one was of Stone, and the other of Brick.

Derry down.

On these he engrav'd with wonderful skill,
Each Liberal Science with *adamant Quill*,
Proportion and Rule he formed by the Square,
And directed the use of all *Masonry There*.

Derry down.

At length all Mankind became past enduring,
'T was wenching, 'twas drinking, 'twas fighting and roaring,
Untill *Great Jehova* impatient with Anger,
Said that he would suffer such Wretches no longer.

Derry down.

Then from their high Windows the Heavens did pour,
For Days, and for Nights one continual Show'r,
'Till nought could be seen but the Waters around,
And in this great Deluge all Mortals were drown'd.

Derry down. /

But *Noah*, the wisest, who therefore judg'd right,
He built him an *Ark*, so stout and so tight,
Tho' Heaven and Earth were coming together,
He kept safe in his *Lodge*, and stood Bluff to the Weather.

Derry down.

Then after the Flood like a Mason so true,
Who still has the good of the Craft in his view,
He delved the *Ground* and he planted the *Vine*,
He *founded* his *Lodge*, and he gave his *Lodge* Wine.

Derry down.

Let Statesmen toss tumble, or jumble the *Ball*,
We sit safe in our Lodge, and we laugh at them all,
Let Bishops wear Lawn-Sleeves, and Lawyers their Gown,
Free Masons have *Jewels* of far more Renown.

Derry down.

Now charge my dear Brethren to Sackville's[xvii] *great Name*,
Our Noble Grand Master, whose Virtues and Fame,
Shall through the wide *Globe*, eternally ring,
While we in full *Chorus*, most joyfully sing.

Derry down.

FINIS.

WILLIAM IMBRIE AND WILLIAM GEDDES, *THE POOR MAN'S COMPLAINT AGAINST THE WHOLE UNWARRANTABLE PROCEDURE OF THE ASSOCIATE SESSION IN GLASGOW, ANENT HIM AND OTHERS IN SEEKING A CONFESSION OF THE MASON AND CHAPMAN OATHS* (1754)

William Imbrie and William Geddes, *The Poor Man's Complaint Against the Whole Unwarrantable Procedure of the Associate Session in Glasgow, Anent him and Others in Seeking a Confession of the Mason and Chapman Oaths, as also Several Objections Answered Thereanent. Together with a Comparison betwixt a Letter said to come from Mr. Gibb, to a Member of said Session, and an Epigram on Masonry done by the Reverend Mr. William Geddes Minister of the Gospel at Urquhart. By William Imbrie Mason in Glasgow, and Well-wisher to every one therein Concerned* (Glasgow, 1754).[1]

William Imbrie's pamphlet[2] is a contribution by a Glasgow stonemason to a controversy that had emerged following secessions from the established Presbyterian Church of Scotland in the mid-eighteenth century. In 1733 what became known as the Secession Church split from the established Church of Scotland, denouncing it for allowing the civil powers to control the appointment of parish ministers. The existence of masonic secrets and oaths had been widely known in Scotland for more than a century under the name of the 'Mason Word'. The term, though in the singular form, covered much more than one word, just as the term the 'Word of God' was used to refer to the whole of the Bible. However, in the Secession Church controversy the term 'mason word' is generally avoided, 'mason oath' being preferred. The term 'the word' was, it seems, to be reserved for the Bible, and the masons' use of it to describe their secrets seen to verge on blasphemy.

The earliest known reference to disagreements about this in the Secession Church may possibly be a passage in an Irish pamphlet of 1738 which denounced the papal bull against Freemasonry issued in April of that year, and included a challenge to the pope:

NOW, if his Holiness is not Content with this Character of a MASON, I wou'd advise him to send some of his Cardinals amongst them, who will perhaps return with the same Answer, as the Ministers of the Scottish Assembly did to their Elders, when dispatched on that Errand: You may go yourself, and then you'll be satisfy'd.[3]

However, there is no direct evidence that the word was debated in any eighteenth-century 'Scottish Assembly' before the 1740s, and it may well be that the pamphlet was not referring to the nascent seceder controversy, but to events in 1649–52 when the mason oath had been discussed in the General Assembly and other Church of Scotland courts.[4]

If this is the case, the earliest hint of worries about the mason oath among seceders dates from 1739, when a 'protestation and declinature' was signed by four operative members of the Lodge of Torphichen. They denounced the oath or oaths that they had taken on admission as Freemasons as containing 'dreadful Wickedness, Superstition, Idolatry, Blasphemy, and Profanation' of the name of God. The rituals contained ridiculous nonsense and superstition only fit for 'Amusement for children in a Winter-evening'. Moreover the lodge's observation of St John's day involved idleness, profane jests and drunkenness. All this was likely to bring God's wrath down on the country. The four masons concerned were led by James Chrystie (who was a member of the Secession Church), and they all renounced their masonic oaths and membership of the lodge.[5]

This 1739 protest against the mason oath was not printed until 1747, but circulation of it in manuscript may have helped raise wider concerns about the oath. In 1745 the moderator (chairman) of the Associate (Secession) Kirk Session[6] in Edinburgh raised the matter of some members of his congregation being 'of the Mason Craft'. He was 'much scrupled' about them being supposed to have 'Mysteries' taken from the Lord's Word (the Bible) and swearing secret oaths under pain of death. Should masons, in the light of such suspicions, be admitted to 'the sealing ordinances' (be allowed to take holy communion), he asked? The matter was referred to the Associate Synod.[7] The Edinburgh minister who thus brought the issue of the mason word to the attention of the church courts was Adam Gib,[8] who was a dominant figure in Secession Church affairs for many years, famous (or notorious) for his severity. 'No one in the secession churches ever wielded half the power that he did', but that was 'not all for good' for 'when matters of dispute arose worthy of his powers he came down on them like a battle-axe, clear weighty, and decisive'.[9] His rigidity led some to call him 'Pope Adam'.[10]

In September 1745 the synod ruled that it had no time to consider the mason oath but that it should be investigated by individual kirk sessions.[11] By this time the Secession Church was on the verge of breaking in two over arguments as to whether another oath, the 'burgess oath' imposed in some Scottish towns was sinful. Controversy had raged since 1741, and finally in 1747 rival 'Burgher' and 'Antiburgher' churches emerged. Not surprisingly, when worries over the mason oath reappeared some years later, it was the latter faction, already denouncing the burgess oath, that took the initiative.

In 1753 the Glasgow Antiburgher Associate Kirk Session began to investigate, under the 1745 act, whether some of it members had sworn the mason oath, and if so whether they had acted lawfully. The controversy evidently began when James Steven (author of the next text in this collection, *Blind Zeal Detected*) revealed that he had acted as 'collector' involved in building a house for a 'company' of Freemasons. Moreover, he said that another member of the congregation, William Imbrie, had earlier acted in a similar capacity.

The Poor Man's Complaint is Imbrie's account of his treatment by the session, which he was called before in June 1753, charged with being 'concerned in' the mason oath. His responses to questioning were evasive. It was clear, he stated, that the session's suspicion of him having taken the oath was so strong that, even if he denied it, he would not be believed, so he refused to answer. Moreover, asking him about the oath was a breach of the legitimate processes of church discipline. Eventually the exasperated session asked Imbrie outright: had he taken the burgess oath, the chapman[12] oath or the mason oath. Imbrie replied that he was not 'concerned' in the first two, but he continued to refuse to answer as to the third, and complained that no proof had been produced against him. After a brisk exchange of rival references to biblical texts, one piece of evidence against the lawfulness of the oath was revealed: a letter from Adam Gib, the Edinburgh Antiburgher minister who nine years before had first raised the mason oath issue. Gib now denounced the mason oath as 'most atheistical', describing some of the masons' 'superstitious ceremonies' and how they swore 'to be one anothers butchers'.[13]

Imbrie remained stubborn, citing the Bible and theologians about the nature of oaths, sin and confession. As to masons swearing to be 'mutual murtherers', Imbrie consulted a number of masons who all denied it, and Imbrie himself testified that he had seen 'much love among them' and that they were 'beneficial in sustaining the poor'. He also cited the case of William Templeton, a deacon of the Glasgow Antiburgher congregation who had already been suspended from office for refusing (like Imbrie) to say whether or not he has sworn the mason oath.[14] Finally, after repeating asserting that 'these oaths cannot altogether be condemned', Imbrie's tract ends abruptly at the end of page thirty-one, with the catchwords[15] 'I come'. However, the first words of page thirty-two are '*I should*'. Possibly this is simply an error, but it may be that the end of Imbrie's text has been omitted. A likely reason is that the printer had realized that he was committed to ending the thirty-two- page pamphlet he was producing with Geddes's *Epigram* and he was running out of space, so he cut off Imbrie's rhetoric in mid-flow and sought to cram the epigram into the last page – unsucessfully, as its last four lines are omitted.

William Geddes's verse had first appeared in 1690, as *An Ecomiastick*[16] *Epigram upon the Most Antient and Honourable Trade of Masons*.[17] However, there are verbal differences between the 1690 and 1755 texts, and the last four lines of the earlier text, and the explanatory marginal notes that had accompanied it are omitted in the later one. Its author, William Geddes, had resigned from the parish ministry of Urquhart in 1682 rather than take the Test Act Oath, which many believed threatened the future of Protestantism in Britain. He was restored to the ministry (at Wick) in 1692, and died two years later. He had written copiously on a number of subjects, but almost all his works remained unprinted. His little verse praising the masons draws on the legendary history of masonry found in copies of the 'old charges' (or 'old constitutions')[18] and contributes nothing directly to the mason oath debate.

William Imbrie portrays himself in his pamphlet as a poor man who lacked a 'liberal education'. Yet he clearly knew his Bible well, had access to works by a number of authors, and was able to present his case forcefully – if not always coherently or consistently. It seems clear that the session was justified in its suspicion that he had taken the mason oath. Whether he was, in the end, disciplined for this is unknown.

Imbrie was in many ways typical of Secession Church members in his obsession with minute examination of points of conscience, sometimes taking with great seriousness matters that to others might seem trifling or perverse. He was confident of his ultimate right to decide such matters as an individual, based on his interpretation of the Bible and other teachings, even if this meant defying the authority of his minister and kirk session. But though convinced of his own righteousness his complaints against his opponents are fairly restrained. There is no resort to crude abuse, though Imbrie complains that the session was impertinent, misguided and acting unlawfully.

The reactions of the three masons known to have been investigated by the Antiburgher Session of Glasgow in the 1750s – Imbrie, Steven and Templeton – have a great deal in common. They were evasive, dodging questions, trying to shift debate to other issues (of morality, theology, law or procedure) and determined not to reveal masonic secrets. It seems likely that Glasgow's masons had agreed among themselves on these as strategies to be used if questioned.

Nothing is known of Imbrie beyond what the pamphlet reveals. He was a stonemason by trade and, in spite of his prevarications (or, indeed, because of them) he may be assumed to have been a Freemason who had sworn the mason word.

Notes

1. This headnote was written by David Stevenson.
2. Only one copy of *The Poor Man's Guide* (Glasgow: [s.n.], 1754 [31 pp]) is known to survive: University of Edinburgh, New College Library, Special Collections, A.c.4.4/2.
3. See the first text in this volume, where the entire pamphlet is reproduced. Anon. [signed Philo Lapidarius], *An Answer to the Pope's Bull* (1738).

4. See D. Stevenson, *The Origins of Freemasonry: Scotland's Century, 1590–1710* (Cambridge: Cambridge University Press, 1988), pp. 127–9.

5. *Magistracy Settled upon its Only True Scriptural Basis ... With an Appendix containing a Few Questions, & a Protestation etc. Against the Mason-Word* ([s.n.], 1747), pp. 238–41. The protestation is summarized in the *Scots Magazine*, 17 (1755), pp. 136–7.

6. The kirk (church) session was the lowest court in the hierarchical Presbyterian court structure, operating at the parish level. Above it (ideally) were district courts (presbyteries), regional courts (synods) and a national or general assembly. But the Secession Church had only one synod, which served as its highest court.

7. CH3/111/1, Associate Presbytery of Edinburgh Minutes, 1744–60, MS National Records of Scotland, Edinburgh (hereafter NRS), pp. 36–7.

8. Adam Gib, 1714–88. In a later (1766) intervention in Glasgow antiburger affairs, Gib urged severity in a disciplinary dispute, helping to provoke a secession to yet another sect, the Relief Church, founded in 1761, R. Small, *History of the Congregations of the United Presbyterian Church from 1733 to 1900*, 2 vols (Edinburgh: David M. Small, 1904), vol. 1, pp. 36–7.

9. Small, *History of the Congregations*, vol. 1, p. 427.

10. W. Ferguson, *Scotland, 1689 to the Present* (Edinburgh: Oliver & Boyd, 1968), p. 229.

11. CH3/28/1, Associate Synod Minutes, 1741–79, MS NRS, pp. 886, 888, 897, 903. *Scots Magazine*, 19 (1757), p. 432. The synod's lack of time to consider the oath was probably related to the fact that the debate took place during a major political crisis. Just days before, Edinburgh had been occupied by the Jacobite army of Prince Charles Edward, seeking to restore the Stuart dynasty and (many feared) re-establish Roman Catholicism.

12. Chapmen were itinerant merchants or pedlars. Three men had revealed to the Glasgow session that they had taken an oath on admission to an organization of chapmen in Sirlingshire, but had come to feel 'uneasiness of mind' about it. The Antiburgher Synod ruled in August 1754 that the oath was sinful, CH3/144/5, General Associate Synod Scroll Minutes, 1752–63, (hereafter CH3/144/5), MS NRS, p. 68.

13. This is a reference to the threat in the masonic catechisms (the earliest dating from 1696), that anyone who revealed masonic secrets would have his 'tongue cut out under my chin', that is, have his throat cut. D. Knoop, G. P. Jones and D. Hamer (eds), *Early Masonic Catechisms*, 2nd edn (London: Quatuor Coronati Lodge, 1975), p. 33.

14. Templeton's case was discussed by the Antiburgher Synod in the following years, 1755–6, CH3/144/5, pp. 77–8, 79–80, 107–8, 110.

15. Catchwords were words set by the printer under the last line of each page and consist of the first words of the following page, a practice designed to help ensure that pages got printed and bound in the correct order.

16. Praising or flattering.

17. Only one copy of this edition (1690) survives: National Library of Scotland, Edinburgh, APS. 4. 83 24. It is reprinted in D. Stevenson, *The First Freemasons: Scotland's Early Lodges and their Members*, 2nd edn (Edinburgh: Grand Lodge of Scotland, 2001), pp. 207–8.

18. Stevenson, *The First Freemasons*, pp. 206–7.

William Imbrie and William Geddes, *The Poor Man's Complaint against the Whole Unwarrantable Procedure of the Associate Session in Glasgow, Anent him and Others in Seeking a Confession of the Mason and Chapman Oaths* (1754)

THE

POOR MAN'S

COMPLAINT

Against the unwarrantable Procedure of the ASSOCIATE SESSION in *Glasgow*, anent[1] him and others in seeking a Confession of the MASON and CHAPMEN OATHS,

AS ALSO

Several objections answered thereanent.

Together with a Comparison betwixt a Letter said to come from Mr. GIBB,[2] to a Member of said SESSION, and an Epigram on Masonry done by the Reverend Mr. WILLIAM GEDDES Minister of the Gospel at Urquhart.

By WILLIAM IMBRIE Mason in Glasgow, and well-wisher to every one therein Concerned.

GLASGOW,

Printed in the Year M DCC LIV. /

THE

POOR MAN'S

COMPLAINT

Against the unwarrantable Procedure of the ASSOCIATE SESSION, in *Glasgow*, &c.

Before entering upon this subject, it is necessary that the reader should understand, that the Composure hereof got not a liberal education, and therefore craves to be excused as to its stile, but judgeth that the matter contained in this pamphlet, will *be useful to the publick, in order to prevent mistakes therefore, I refer them to the thing itself. viz.*

UPON the twelfth day of June 1754, I being called before the associate
session in Glasgow, it was told me by them at my compearance,[3] that two of
their number had informed them that I was concerned in the Mason oath; upon
hearing of which I desired the minute of synod.[4] thereanent might be read over
to me; for I alledged that it was not reasonable for them to ask that question,
nor yet me to answer it blindfoldly, wherepon it was referred, in regard they had
not the minute present, till to morrownight, and I ordered to attend the session,
and likewise upon their part the minute was to be produced. Which accordingly
came to pass, only the minute / was still wanting; notwithstanding thereof, they
put the aforesaid question to me whether or not I was concerned in the Mason
oath, to which I answered, the session had more freedom to put that question to
me, than I had to answer it, yet they put it again and I said it was impertinent
in them to put, and no less in me to answer, seeing they had not the minute of
synod thereanent, and I said, altho' I would deny, they would not believe me,
their suspicion of my being concerned was so strong, to which I understood they
acquiesced, because they gave me no return, yet they alledged that I needed not
be afraid to confess, for it was not to be brought to the publick, nor yet any
censure inflicted upon me, my reply was, I was not afraid either of publishing,
nor yet of censure, but I looked upon their procedure to be contrary to church
discipline to give blind obedience, and further as they declared it was not to be
censured, now I alledge according to the rules of discipline, no process is to be
commenced,[5] unless the libel (or complaint) be relevant to infer censure, when
either confessed or proven; other confessions belongeth to God, or private brethren whom we have actually offended, and not under suspicion: howbeit after
some reasoning the session agreed to an overture, whether it should be dismissed,
or delayed to another meeting of session; and it was unanimously agreed to dismiss it, upon my acquiescing with the minute of synod thereanent, and also to
attend the session when called, which I agreed unto, upon condition they would
prove farther against me, which may be seen in Perdiven's collection of church
discipline[6] page 267, where he says, "Yea even tho' a party hath been dismissed
for a time through want of probation,[7] if it shall afterwards emerge, the process
may therepon be / wakened." Which plainly infers, cannot without probation.

My next compearance before the session was near the beginning of October,
and warning was given from the pulpit not only to me but to all in general who
had any intention to join in the bond.[8]

I was asked if I had a view to join the same, whereupon I answered, that ever
since I acceded to the testimony, I looked, upon myself materialy engaged in the
bond; and that I have been desirous of an opportunity of doing it formerly, but
declared at this time, I was under as many difficulties as ever, and I judged if I
offered these to the session now, it would not tend to edification, and likewise
they could not relieve me of my difficulties.

Notwithstanding of this answer they put the same questions to me, that they put to these who entered in the bond and who professed no such difficulties, such as, whether I was concerned in Burgess Chapmen or Mason oaths: to which I answered, I was not concerned in the two former, but refused to answer the latter; alledging that I was dealt with contrary to rules, they replyed I was no otherwise dealt with than the rest, I answered in regard the question was dismissed before unless of further proof, that I was dealt with in a quite contrary manner, for it was never put to any of the rest and dismised, and further reviving left to proof, which was plainly my case, so this was owned by the session to be truth seeing I view'd it in that light. Now tho' it be aserted that severals gave information of my being concerned in the Mason oath, none of these severals have compeared to prove it as yet; altho' I desired earnestly that the session should do it: as to this I got no answer, only they insisted I should confess, which obliged me to demand of them whither it could be / made appear from the scriptures of truth, or our subordinate standards,[9] alledging I was not to bring out an accusation against another man unless at the mouth of two or three witnesses, and far less against my self: for I said if they made me clear in this, I had several other things to bring out with respect to trade and other ways: whereupon one of the members rose up and said, I was at liberty, but I answered I was not, being bound by the word of God to the contrary; so they quoted several scriptures to me, for confessing particularly Josh. vii. 19. I replyed it was not applicable with my case, in regard that Achan was found guilty by the lot, and then desired to confess, and for that reason it did not answer my affair, then Jeremiah xxxiii. 17, 18, was cited to me; I referred the applicableness of the same to the session; but it appeared they did not approve thereof; and I believe who will read Henry thereon[10] will as little; for he says, "it was a needless question put to Baruch; for they wanted to know whether he had what he read by extraordinary revelation, or from Jeremiah's own mouth." Now whether of the ways he had it, it was the word of the Lord to them, and therefore no ways applicable, in regard he was not called to confess sin or guilt.

After they heard this I was dismised, and in a little called back again, the moderator intimate to me, that the further consideration of my affair was delayed until they got some advice from their brethren the ministers, which satisfied me, in regard I thought to have been made privy to the advice when given, or at least intimate to me before any sentence or agreement of session to seclude me from privileges formerly granted me.[11]

But contrary to the rule of Gods word (and my expectation) that there is no censure inflicted upon / suspicion, but upon real deeds, as Paul testifyeth 1 Cor. v. 2. *That he that hath done this deed may be taken away from among you;* he saith not, he that is supposed to have done this deed, and 1 Tim v. 20. *Them that sin, rebuke before all,* not them that is supposed to have sinned. True it is, I had the benefit of a letter said to come from Mr. Gibb sent to John Marshal, a member of session; read openly in session to me, and this was done in order to pave the way for my confession; this letter affirms the Mason oath to be most atheistical, and that their is several superstious ceremonies used therein; such as the entrants being stript of all metal, and put upon one of their knees on the ground, their elbow on the Bible, the compass and square to their breast, and sworn to secrecy under the name of concealing, and that they shall have their heart, or liver or some such thing, burnt within the sea mark, and he further says that this is to be performed by the society of Masons, and that they swear mutually to be one anothers butchers, (so I refer the truth of Mr. Gibbs letter to such as are seen therein) he further asserts in his letter that he is fully satisfyed with the motion of renewing our covenants, and signifieth to his friend the method that is taken with Masons there; such as to put the question to them, when and were they were entered, and in what company? how many degrees they have got, for he says there are three, and that the affair with them is dismissed with a sessional rebuke, so when he comes to give an account of the synod he says they were so thronged with other business that they could not overtake the affair of the Mason oath at that time; but that they referred it to kirk sessions; he further affirms to refuse the question put by the session is both sin and scandal, and to prove his assertion he quotes 1 Pet. / iii. 15. which he alledgeth intimates that we should be ready to give a reason of the hope that is in us to every brother that asketh it, and much more to a judicatory, for swearing is a solemn act of worship.

After reading of which I was asked if I would now acknowledge; I answered, as to the body of that letter I had nothing to do with it, only the scripture quoted was no ways applicable as to the confession of sin, otherwise I behoved to confess to every one who asked, whether I was a fornicator with my wife or others before marriage, and if I had not a liberty to deny, I behoved to be holden as confest. But however useful this letter was thought by the receiver and reader, in order to bring me or others to acquiesce in the question: yet considering the entertainment given to another letter of the same author's, to a different member in a difficult affair which was before the session, and part of the members, and some in the congregation wanted to be cleared therein who was present at said sederunt. This member said he had a letter from M. Gibb thereanent, which he would read if they would hear it, but it was answered by the receiver and reader of the other letter, that it was now unseasonable. It was answered by the other side, that he himself had agreed to refer it to Mr. Gibb's advice, and he owned it to be truth; but in regard it was too late and the thing over; and Mr. Gibb knowing that Mr. Jameson's[12] honour was therein engaged, he was obliged to maintain the same. But had it come in season before the action was commenced, he would have said two tales that he will not say now, yea ten. And this was seconded by other members of session, and several of the congregation, declared Mr. Gibb to say what he would, they would pay no regard to it, yea the synod, or assembly, or all the / men in the world, for they were sure the scriptures said otherwise; for every thing behoved to be established at the mouth of two or three witnesses, not at the mouth of one: whereupon the receiver of last letter, said it was needless to read it then. Upon the whole, how could it be expected I should pay any regard to Mr. Gibb's advice in the letter read, seeing that the receiver and reader of said letter of advice, with his concurrence, represents Mr. Gibb as a truckler, or one who has more regard to the honour of men, than to the honour of God, in not speaking the truth. Now what could I expect, or they themselves, who had thus represented the author by his advice, but this; that Mr. Gibb was to maintain his own honour, and the honour of those who had joined the bond, and this session who was about to do it. But I may say the less in regard the session seemed to pay no regard to this letter of advice.

It was motioned by the receiver and reader of said letter with respect to my affair, that it should be minuted what I said, which was but justice done me, and the honour of truth, which I agreed to, providing the session would minute theirs also: But it was answered that the session wanted no minute of that kind; for the moderator alledged it was a conference by the by, and so it was, seeing the affair was under delay. So I offered to go away, but they desired me to stay, which I did. Then a motion was made by the receiver and reader of said letter of Mr. Gibb's, to refer the affair to the reverend the presbytery, but some of the rest of the members said it was too late: to which he said it would not hinder long, it was only marking the word refer, but it was agreed by the majority of them, alledging they would have an opportunity of a meeting of session betwixt and / the occasion; whereby they would meet with some ministers to give them their advice, which would enable them to proceed or refer it to the presbytery, and so it was delayed that night. Now it evidences a keenness of spirit in the receiver and reader of the letter, with his accomplices, to have me denuded from my privilege, in regard that the presbytery was not to commence till after the solemn occasion was over; and the reference imputed me scandalous, and therefore I could not be admitted. And it plainly appears by this motion of reference, that they paid no regard to what they called Mr. Gibb's letter; and also that they were still in the dark anent the procedure with me and others. However I was told it was not referred, for the session was waiting for advice, which satisfied me, still thinking of hearing it when given.

Upon the Friday before the sacrament they having a session, I asked the elder of my proportion[13] if they had got that advice yet, to which he replied they had not, but desired me to attend, for the session was to hold at three o'clock in the afternoon said day, and Mr. Clarkson[14] and some other ministers were to be there, from whom they expected the advice.

Sermon being at six o'clock at night, I meeting with another of the members a little before sermon, asked him if the session had got any advice with respect to my affair: he said he believed they had not, the session being wholly taken up about William Templeton's affair[15] (which was the same with mine) and was not yet ended. So I thought I could get nothing done then, therefore I went in to hear sermon.

The next day I made it my business to enquire about it at the elder of my proportion, and another then present with him. The question I put to him, / was what answer they would give me now, for this was the last day before the sacrament: he answered that the other then present would tell me, but the other seemed as if he would not; then he himself said that Mr. Clarkson had given his advice that none concerned in forsaid oath was to be admitted. Upon hearing of this I made reply, but how did ye know that I was concerned therein? he said because I refused to answer the question: I said they should be debarred themselves because they had not answered my question: he replied, what question of mine? to which I said, that it was requiring the session to shew me from the scriptures of truth, and our subordinate standard, that I was obliged to answer them; and I added, that they had dealt with me as Job's three friends did in condemning him, and yet they found no answer, as is testified, Job xxxii. 3. and so we ended this conference.

At the close of the sermon the minister[16] intimated from the pulpit the order to be observed in going to and from the tables,[17] and how any in the congregation, and those that were to join them in the neighbourhood might be served with tokens.[18] He also intimated, that such as were suspected in the burgess, chapman, and mason oaths, who had not given satisfaction, the session had agreed that none of them were to be admitted; (affirming that the synod had condemned all these oaths.) Which intimation was further strengthened in the debarring upon the next day, not only those who were suspected of foresaid oaths; but likewise those who did not take hold of the opportunity of joining in the bond for renewing our solemn covenants offered at this time. Yet for all that, none were refused the sacrament, as being either negligent or wilful neglecters of the opportunity, excepting such as were / suspected in the foresaid oaths. By which it appears that the session was more keen in maintaining their new scheme of agreement, than the former made by the presbytery.

I being yet unsatisfied with the session's conduct, made it my business to attend the next publick sederunt, which held the beginning of November, in order to see if the session would resume the advice of their brethren the ministers. They answered they would, and told me that it was as follows; That it was the practice of most part of the cecession, which they said they believed I would pay little regard unto. I asked if they gave any scripture to prove that practice agreeable. It was answered they had, and read to me Leviticus v. 1, 5. I said I would consider this scripture, and asked if they had any thing from our standards; they said no. Then I told them that I looked upon their conduct towards me and others to be most disagreeable to our standards; and that it would serve all the ceceders in Britain to prove their practice agreeable to rule: (and my reason for so saying was) because they had neither found me guilty of what they alledged, nor yet admonished or rebuked me; but to the contrary, dismissed my affair, as may be seen in their minutes. Neither can it be said that I was obstinate, when I was seeking the law at their mouth. Their answer to this was, that they were under no promise to me in making me privy to the advice, nor yet to hinder them to act as they saw cause. I said they were not only under a promise to me, but to others like unto me, and this they had solemnly sworn before God, angels and men, which they acknowledged to be truth. I further asked them if they would reverse the former sentence or not, (there being present the minister, five elders, and two deacons)[19] / of which three of the elders said reverse, and two with the two deacons said not: and then in a little they came to say it was agreed by the session not to reverse; which obliged me to make the following declaration to this purpose. That suppose I understood that in ordinary cases wherein the party concerned did not acquiesce in a sentence, was to appeal to a superior judicatory; but for several reasons I did not look upon it to be expedient: for appealing supposed relief by redress of grievance. But this I cannot expect, in regard that this session now would not reverse their own sentence, and as little will they do it in another judicatory, as I was now informed that the most part of the cecession had agreed thereunto; therefore I could not expect relief either from presbytery or synod, for appeals behoves to be to a free court, and not to such as are already practisers of the thing complained of. And I added that the presbytery gave it as one of their main reasons for constituting, to relieve the oppressed heritage of God through the land, and that they were to maintain doctrine, worship, discipline and government in the church of Scotland; to the which testimony I acceded, and promised subjection to the presbytery in the Lord. But seeing this session had fallen upon new terms of communion, I declared they had broken through the stipulation between the presbytery and me, therefore the obligation was taken off. And took this opportunity to decline said session, ay and while they freed themselves of the imputation laid by me against them. And further declared, that my after walk and conversation should not be under their inspection; but that I still adhered to foresaid testimony, and that I looked upon it as lawful for one in my place and station, to testify against this step of defection in this session, / and all other judicatories whatsoever: which declaration they ordered me to dictate and they minuted what I said, (contrary to my expectation) and I believe it will be among the first declinatures that ever was received by a judicatory,

Having considered the text quoted to me by said session Lev. v. 1, 5. but sees nothing applicable therein for whatever confession was to be made, or offering to the priest in order to make atonement, for his sin, yet this he was to do without either being called or questioned. And therefore not agreeable to the scheme of session, and Mr. Henry on said place. "The offence here spoken of, are, 1st a mans concealing the truth when he was sworn as a witness to speak the truth; the whole truth, and nothing but the truth: judges among the Jews had power to adjure not only the witnesses as with us; but the person suspected, contrary to the rule of our law, that no man is bound to accuse himself" so much for the first verse, and on the fifth verse, he saith, "Now in this case, first the offender must confess his sin, verse 5. 6. and the offering was not accepted unless it was accompanied with a penitential confession, the confession must be particular, that he hath sinned in that thing as Davids confession *Ps.* li. 4. I have done this evil, and Achans *Josh.* vii. 20. thus and thus have I done, deceit lies in generals, many will own in generals they have sinned, for that all must own so that it is not any reproach to them. But that they have sinned in this thing, they stand too much upon their own honour to acknowledge, but the way to be well assured of pardon, and to be well armed against sin for the future, is to be particular in our penitent confessions, (2) the priest must make an atonement, for the atonement was not accepted without his repentance, so his repentance could not justify him / without the atonement, thus in our reconciliation to God; Christs part and ours are both needed, and the English annotations agreeth with Henry as to the scope, but has this different observe," that the confession here spoken, is no ground for papist priests, (and I think far less for a judicatory) for the priest was to eat the remainder of the sacrifice alone, least his family should get notice of the sin." Now this is the foundation for full agreement of session, together with the practice of some other sessions, whoever shall be satisfyed in this agreement yet I cannot, as it is so far inconsistant to both rule and reason, and this occasioned me to say in session, that where their was nothing but the practice, this was the way that all defection was carried on, and that the papists to this day, gives the fathers for so doing.

Now having given a short hint of the sessions proceeding in this affair, I come to shew wherein I cannot miss but be grieved and stumbled thereanent as follows.

First, In the first place, whether I was concerned therein or not nothing appeared in my walk and conversation offensive to any of the congregation, and as little anent my principles, either with respect to will-worship, or superstition, but none of these being proven, or offered to be proven, I look upon it to be will-worship in them, for whatever is not of faith, is sin, and I see not where faith can be grounded on a suspicion, in secluding me and others from the inestimable benefit of the gospel upon mere suspicion, which I believe cannot be instanced in any church that deserves the name of reformation, and more especially since our valuable delivery from popery, wherein, it is agreed in our standards, that none shall be secluded from sealing / ordinances, but upon clear proof, or confession, and that after admonution, as appears to be the practice of our reforming church, who was more careful to cast up the stumbling stones, and so to prepare the way to the people, rather than to involve them with insnaring questions, which rather tend to scattering, than gathering, as is evident from what is said in the directory for church discipline and further confirmed by Mr. Durham[20] upon the second command[21] page 99 and 100. "Says when such scandals, cannot be made out judically, tho' possibly they may be true in themselves, they may, tho' against the inclination and affection of the admitters, be admitted, yet not against their conscience, because that being a high censure in Christs house, his servants are not to walk arbitrary, for that would bring confusion with it, but by rules given them, whereof this is one, not to receive an accusation, but under two or three witnesses." Which plainly intimates whatever inquisition church judicatorys may make in order to find out suspected guilt, yet they can come to no sentence except it be either confessed or proven, and therefore such sentences that is founded upon suspicion can never bind the conscience, and this is further confirmed by the apostle Paul who says "he can do all things for the truth; but nothing against the truth."

2. Secondly I cannot miss but be grieved when I consider, the session, affirming, that the synod hath already condemned the Mason oath; if it be so, why did thy not rest in the dismission, upon my acquiescing with said minute, as they were then satisfyed with my so doing, but it seems they come to have other views of the minute, and therefore not being satisfyed, came to place this insnaring question in order catch the simple and unwary in confessing, and also / that they might get others debarred whom they knew had refused to answer that question; contrary to the law of God and man, and all well governed realms, and no where to be found but among papists and the like, who maintain that besides confessing of sin unto God, and seeking pardon thereof, there must be a confession to the priest; which is contrary to Proverbs xxviii. 13. *He that covereth his sin shall not prosper, but whose confesseth and forsaketh them shall have mercy.* and 1 John i. 9. *If we confess our sins, he is faithful and just to forgive us our sins; and to cleanse us from all unrighteousness,* from which scriptures it is clear, that there is no occasion for any further confession of secret sins but to God only, and that neither priest nor judicatory has any right to call for it, or we warranted to give it, for it is a piece of spiritual pride in the one to seek it, and voluntary humility, in worshiping of angels in the other to give it, which we are forbidden Col. ii. 18. and John when about to do it, was rejected by the angel saying, *See thou do it not, for I am thy fellow-servant – worship God.* Rev. xxii. 9.

3. I cannot miss but be further grieved, when I find myself and others debarred from church privileges, for that which was never a term of communion neither ministerial nor Christian. For suppose the synod had condemned the foresaid Mason oath, which is not truth, yet they never gave it out that the not answering the question, was a term of communion, but suppose they had, they never did when the party refusing put the question to the session to shew its agreeableness to the word of God, and our subordinate standards, and I acquiescing with the minute of synod thereanent, and they dismissing it, and the session under a delay till they got further advice from their brethren the ministers. / But it may be said,

it was not because we refused to confess, but because we refused also to deny, and so did not give the session satisfaction, therefore we were contumacious, for the law faith, that he who will not purge himself, is holden confessed; upon which account it was reasonable in the session to seclude us.

True, in ordinary causes, where confessing and denying brings neither sin, guilt nor disgrace along with it; but in this affair, either confessing or denying brought both: as would have been the case with Jonathan, if Saul his father had framed the question and put it to him, If he had any agreement or covenant with David? which to have confessed would have brought danger to himself; and to have denied, a plain lie. Yet no body can deny I think, but Saul had a strong suspicious of the thing being true, which plainly appears from the text, in his calling Jonathan, *the son of a perverse woman*; and as to denial if free, it exposed us not only to the mock and ridicule of our brethren the masons, but gave them just ground to look upon us as deceivers of them all along. Now besides, it was looked upon in time of the persecuting periods, to be a tyrannical way, in putting categorical questions to make them their own accusers. Such as, did they own the Bishop's death to be murder: or did they own Bothwell- Bridge to be rebellion, or if they were at such a conventicle, or when and where they saw such and such a person, or the like? which if they refused to answer, they threatened some, and others they tortured.[22] But this ye say ye abhor, therefore how come any to impute it to us? for we neither intend, nor threaten to inflict any thing upon mens bodies: but being a court of Christ, we only deal / with the conscience, to give men an opportunity to disburden their conscience of sin.

However it may appear to the natural eye, inflicting corporal punishment on mens bodies; yet in our Lord's account, the inflicting punishment upon the conscience, is the worst of punishments, it being more precious than the body; according to that saying, "He that offendeth one of the least of you, it were better for him he had never been born."[23] Therefore such as know no other way of disburdening their consciences of sin which is secret, let them take it. But I desire to be thankful there is another way pointed out by our Lord in Matt. xi. 28. "To cast all our burdens on him." And in I John ii, I. "If any man sin, we have an advocate with the Father, even Jesus Christ the righteous, and his blood cleanseth us from all sin."

Now having shown the unwarrantableness of the session's procedure, both from scripture, and the rules of reason and discipline, I come now to answer the objections really made to me and others, viz.

Obj. 1. *In regard that so many in the world know of this oath, and severals have confessed it, therefore it becomes publick, and ought to be confessed.*

Ans. Suppose severals know of it, yet it never becomes scandalous, except those who knew were offended, and used means to have satisfaction; and these means failing them, then they were to table their complaint, and prove the same, according to the rule prescribed in Matt, xviii. 15, 16, 17. Likewise such as have confessed, it makes it publick sin in themselves, and scandal to the church, and a scandalizing of their absent brethren, without taking the due means in shewing to them the sin in it, in / order of recovering them out of it, or endeavouring its reformation; for the future, according to Prov. xxv. 9, 10. *Debate thy cause with thy neighbour himself: and discover not a secret to another; Left he that heareth it, put thee to shame, and thine infamy turn not away.* But it makes it not a publick sin, in others who have not confessed, as in Prov. xi. 13. *A tale-bearer revealeth secrets, but he that is of a faithful spirit concealeth the matter.* It only lays a just foundation for censuring these confessors, not only for their wrong swearing, but also for not performing their oath.

Obj. 2. *Seeing the session says the synod hath condemned the Mason oath, as being contrary to our known principles, therefore it should be confessed.*

Ans. Granting the synod have done it, or should do it, yet it is no ground for confessing, but this they have not done, otherwise they would have sent down their act, with just reasons for condemning, and the warrantableness for the people to confess, but this they have not done, neither hath the session, but has led the people blindfoldy to a confession, without shewing them any reason for so doing, only telling them that it was sinful: and by this means made them their own accusers of guilt which the session knew nothing about, and others whom they had no suspicious off, by barely putting the question to them, confessed, which imboldned the session to say, they knew more about the Mason oath now, than they did before, which is evident they had not a sufficient knowledge at the beginning when they framed that question; and therefore could not be proper judges in either framing or putting of it, which is further manifested in their not censuring these confessors, but has left them in their sin and scandal, worse than they got them, and for all that, they / admitted them to swear the bond and sealing ordinances: from which circumstances it appears, that the synod did not condemn this oath, else they would have ordered the way of purging the scandal, and not have left it to inferior judicatories to do in it as they see cause. For here they were dismissed by confession, and at Edinburgh Mr. Gibb says, it was by a sessional rebuke. Obj. 3. *The session says it is sinfull, in regard that the entrant swears, before he knows what he swears to, in not doing it in truth and judgment, which renders it a sinful oath, and dangerous to keep, therefore should be confessed.*

Ans. It is truth he that did so sinned, but supposing it be so, yet it doth not become duty in him to confess, for the obligation of the oath stands, in regard this being but the manner not the matter of his oath, otherwise it may be said, the oath made to the Gibeonites was to be broken, in regard it was rashly made; and not in judgment, and contrary to God's command; but we find it was lawful to be kept, in as much as the Lord punished the breach of it in the house of Saul.

Obj. 4. *The matter is also sinful. For Mr. Gibb says it is a most Atheistical oath, and sundry superstitious ceremonies and other triffling things used thereat.*

Ans. Whatever sin is in the matter, was never obligatory to the swearer, but laid a foundation for humility and confession before God; but other things however indifferent in themselves, they are binding in regard of the oath, which is plain in Durham on the third commandment p. 129. "That our engagement by oath is to some thing of its own nature indifferent, well not lose us, tho' there be here no other tie upon us to the thing, and that without we were free; / yet the oath once engaged in, will tie us, as is clear in the 15 Psalm, for an oath is of its own nature obligatory, and according to Num. xxx 2. persons at their own dispose must do even in such cases as they have bound their souls." Therefore because it is not said that any is forced to take this oath, a voluntary oath is the more binding, because it is voluntary, fortheir can be no obligation more binding than that which we take willingly upon ourselves, as may be seen in the covenant between Jonathan and David. Now these confessors being bound as Mr. Gibb says to secrecy under the name of concealing, so their revealing that secret, cannot miss but be a breach of their oath. And Solomon saith Prov. xvii. 9. *He that covereth a transgression seeketh love, but he that repeateth a matter, separateth very friends.* Likewise those who get a secret intrusted to them and reveals it altho' their be no oath, is looked upon as unfit for society, and much more those who reveals one under an oath, especially as its not said to be to the hurt of other men.

Obj. 5. *It is to the hurt of themselves, in swearing to be one anothers mutual murtherers, and therefore it is sinful.*

Ans. The truth of this is yet unknown to me, altho' I have enquired at sundry Masons, all of them denyed it, so I cannot believe it to be true, in regard I never heard an instance of that kind (but to the contrary), for I see as much love among them as any other sect of men, and as beneficial for sustaining the poor, and were it as is alledged, they would be in a terror of each other, not knowing but some of them might be so zealous as perform that part of their oath, so I think their is no ground to believe Mr. Gibb's assertion till once we see the Masons at variance; but tho' it should be true that some were / so foolish as take this oath, let them be humbled for it, and amend it, but how comes Mr. Gibb to impute it to all, when himself says, that two of them scarce agrees in their confesing, for what the one says, the other gainsays, neither doth it lave any open, for publick confessing, seeing the party confessed to, cannot free them from their obligations, nor yet pardon them.

Obj. 6. *Some may say the whole of this oath is sinfull, and therefore ought to be confessed, in order to prevent its transmission to posterity.*

Ans. Its being wholly sinful, is more than is made appear, or yet can be made, in regard of their liberality to the poor, but granting it were, we are not *to do evil that good may come of it*, in perjuring ourselves to prevent it from posterity, neither doth it appear, tho' all the Masons belonging to the seceders should confess, how they can prevent it, seeing what is under their inspection are but a very few, in comparison of what are not, who neither are called to confess, nor yet likely to be. Obj.

7. *Such as are professing to bear witness to the testimony, ought to confess, for the good of the land, in order to keep off the wrath of the Lord.*

Ans. Saul had the same intent, not only for his own private good, but for the good of Israel and Judah, according to 2 Samnel 21. where we find that the Lord punished the whole land with sore famine for three years successively, for the breach of the covenant with the Gibeonites, although it might be looked upon in some case not lawful, seeing it was contrary to the command of God, which may deter against inconsiderate confessors to avoid perjuring of themselves.

Obj. 8. *According to this method, it takes away the power from the church, in searching into reports, / some of which cannot be easily proven, but by confession.*

Ans. I take no power from the church that ever was given her, which is for edification, and not for destruction, for Perdiven faith page 258. "Offences which the church may find, cannot be proven, ought not to be prosecute, for thus her authority is much weakened, and neither is the offender edifyed." I am not against making enquiry into such reports as has been the practice of the reforming periods, but I am against papists and their high commission courts,[24] which is testified by Samuel Rutherford[25] (in putting such questions as this one put by the session to me etc. in regard they knew themselves, the thing they wanted us to confess was secret) in his preface to Lex Rex p. 6.[26] he saith. "Its a lie that all sins, even all civil business come under the cognisance of the church, for only sins as publickly scandalous fall under their power, Matth. xviii. 15, 16, 17. etc. 2 Thess. iii. II. and I Tim. v. 20. Its a calumny that they search out secret crimes, or that ever they disgraced the innocent, or divided families, where there be flagrant scandals, or pregnant suspicions of scandalous crimes, they search out these, as the insest[27] of Spotswood the P. P. of St. Andrews, with his own daughter, the adulteries of Whitefoord P.P. of Brechen, whose bastard came weeping to the assembly of Glasgow in the arms of the whore,[28] these they searched out, but not with the damnable oath *ex officio*, that the high commission, put upon innocents to cause them accuse themselves, against the law of nature."

Now I see not how the session disagrees with any thing here complained by Rutherford, save only in putting the oath.

It is almost needless to say any thing concerning the CHAPMEN, for it may be fitly applied to what is said before, anent the MASONS, in regard of its secrecy, but I shall answer some objections made to me, and then the reader may compare and apply them himself.

Obj. 1. *But the sin thereof was laid open by William Graham &c. to the judicatories which they found just cause for condemning it as sinful, therefore no wise applicable to the Masons.*

Ans. Whatever William Graham might represent to the judicatories, yet I am credibly informed he keeped something to himself, unconfessed concerning that affair, and upon his representation, the judicatory condemned Stirling oath, and it is to be believed that the Chapman oath is not condemned yet, only William Grahams representation, but whatever the superior judicatory have done with respect to the Chapmen in Stirling shire, yet they have been nothing represented to them concerning the shire of Lanark, except what the session hath done of their own authority, in agreeing to suspend suspected Chapmen therein who gave not satisfaction in confessing the sinfulness thereof.

Obj. 2. *And ought not kirk-sessions to condemn it, and suspend those, whom they suspected to be concerned therein.*

Ans. How came the session to know of it, seeing they had nothing but the information of one man, when they could not judge upon the testimony of three or four, on the Chapman oath in the shire of / Stirling, but referred it to the presbytery for judgment thereanent.

Obj. 3. *That of the Lanark oath is equally sinfull with Stirling, and besides the session is more ripe now, to give judgment concerning oaths than before, was just ground for them to proceed.*

Ans. I am informed that their is nothing in Lanark, worthy of condemnation by the session, however mistaken some may have been in giving information against them, yet it was no ground nor authority in the session to suspend, and however ripe they may be in judging of the nature of oaths, yet they have mistaken themselves in this, seeing the synod got no information against them, and likewise, they had but the information of one man, who possibly misconstructed the nature of that oath, and this was no foundation for suspending others, upon his information.

Obj. 4. *This society have assumed the power of taking oaths, and have no authority for so doing, therefore they should be discouraged.*

Ans. They have the authority of the justices of the peace, for making them a society; and seeing they are a society, they are allowed to make what regulations they see best for the society's good, and if any were to quarrel them for so doing, it behoves to be those who impowered them, and not kirk-sessions, therefore I think their authority is good, unless it be said, that justice of peace have not authority to constitute them; which is not said yet.

Obj. 5. *This oath is not absolutely necessary, and therefore it is a profaning the name of God, which makes it sinfull.*

Ans. True, neither society nor oath is absolutely necessary, but both may be useful and simply necessary, as well here as in other society's; the regulations /

thereof being lawful, the want of its absoluteness, will not make it sinful, for whatever the society have agreed upon for the safe guard of this society, then it becomes necessary.

Obj. 6. *But this society hath agreed to meet once a year, in order to choose office-bearers, which is hurtful to the members thereof.*

Ans. This objection pointeth at the overthrow of every society, and that under the consideration of personal loss, but seeing there is nothing in the articles sinful, or they bound unto, except what is agreeable to the law civil and sacred, therefore they are bound by their oath, and I think none would have made this objection that could read the 15 psalm.

Obj. 7. *But it is sinful in regard young boys are admitted and sworn therein.*

Ans. However sinful it is in the overseers to admit young boys to an oath, who has not a competent judgment of an oath, yet it in no ways makes it sinful to men of understanding, therefore the objection is nothing.

Obj. 8. *By your charging the confessors with perjury, you own they have confessed these oaths;*

Ans. It is only supposition, for I own no such thing, for whether it was the Chapman word, the Mason word, or the Barrowman word. &c. Seeing some of these confessors owns they were under secrecy, they are perjured, and therefore have rendered themselves infamous in law, and their word cannot be regarded, especially what they have said with respect to their absent brethren, therefore their names ought to be made publick in order to prevent people from being imposed upon by them; but this I could not overtake at present, in regard some who are said to confess, refuse they did so, and others are said to be repenting, which leaves me in an uncertainty / as to their names, in case I should accuse the innocent, but if they continue obstinate, I shall endeavour to furnish the publick with their names the first opportunity.

Obj. 9. *The session never sought any confession of the secrecy, only the confession that these oaths was sinful*

Ans. True some they passed this way, but as for some others they did not, for William Graham and John Marshal etc. refused to be satisfied unless they would discover what they called the abominations, which for ought they knew was the secret; likewise before the session could make any such demand, it was requisite they had a just knowledge of what was sin in it, and that the party accused, was concerned therein, but this they had not, which makes it the more unjust in them to require any such thing, for confessing the oath sinful under this general, supposes the whole sinful: from which it may be thought very strange in William Graham, to press others, especially when he himself keeped something of the Chapman oath, (which probably was the secret), and confessed that which was not in the articles of the said oath, and that only took place sometimes in practice.

Obj. 10. *How come ye to blame William Graham and John Marshal &c. seeing that they could do nothing in session, without the concurrence of the rest of the members.*

Ans. In regard that they were the first movers of this affair as is well known, and after moved, pushed it all alongst. But severals of the rest of the members, never agreed with this scheme, for the following reasons *viz.* 1*stly*, because they knew nothing concerning some of these oaths. 2*dly*, when the question was agreed to be put, they declared their dissatisfaction, / in regard that it was not agreed to, whether it was to be made a term of communion to those that refused to answer, or not 3*dly*, altho' they agreed to the minute of synod to make inquiry, or travel therein, yet they did not see this scheme agreeable to the rules of our known principles, nor the law of the Lords words, nor the rules of right reason.

Obj. 11. *How come ye to free any in session, and blame others, seeing they neither discented nor protested against the procedure, which is the only document of their being disatisfied.*

Ans. Suppose they offered no descent at time of full agreement, there may be several reasons assigned therefore 1*stly*, They might be difficultate by the advice given by the ministers, 2*dly*, the occasion was so near, they might be afraid of disturbance, not only in session, but also in the congregation, and so marred the beauty of the solemnity. 3*dly* Some of which members was not present at the agreement, so their not descenting or protesting might be for peace sake: the truth of which is evidenced in my after compearance, near the beginning of November, where I heard William Templeton enquiring if he was yet in office (for he was suspended for not answering the question) and the session declared he was, whereon he replyed, if he had known at the time of framing and putting this question, he would have then marked his not consenting, but seeing he now knew it was a term of communion, he craved liberty to mark it, (which was granted him, being a member of court,) and further, when I petition the session to reverse the sentence, they framed an overture, reverse, or not, and the moderator asking the mind of the members, thereanent, Robert Ingles said, he was always against putting of / that question, and said reverse, John Bryce said the same; John Selkirk was always against making, the not answering the question a term of communion. From which it is evident, William Graham and John Marshal and some few more, carried on this unregular procedure.

So as I have freed severals of the members of session as being active in this affair, I likewise am obliged to free the synod, and I can do it no better than insert the minute itself, which is to this purpose, "In regard we have not time as yet to overtake that of the Mason oath, therefore we transmit the same unto kirk sessions, to travel therein, as far as is agreeable unto our known principles, rules of the Lords word, and right reason, and that they do nothing contrary to the foresaid rules, but if any difficulty shall arise thereanent, that they refer it to their respective presbyteries, and if the presbyteries cannot clear it, that it be referred to the synod."[29]

Now I have furnished the reader with the minute that I and others acquiesced in, spoken of in the beginning of this pamphlet, which the session gave out, that from this minute, the synod had condemned the Mason oath, therefore I leave the reader to judge, the justness of their conclusion.

Obj. 12. *Granting that the general design of the Mason society &c. may be commendable, or at least innocent, yet it may be carried on to the same advantage without the solemnity of an oath, especially, pressed under such dreadfull penalties as is represented by Mr. Gibb.*

Ans. I observe that the question is not whether the purpose of societies may as well be served without an oath, but whether an oath in the present case be lawful, and may be taken with a good conscience, / and to solve this difficulty I shall introduce the following opinion of bishop Sanderson,[30] who is said to be the most judicious Casuist that ever treated upon the nature of oaths. "when a thing is not by any precept or interdict, divine or human, so determined, but every man *pro hic et nunc*,[31] may at his choice do or not do, as he sees expedient, let him do what he will, he sinneth not I Cor. vii. 36. As if Caius should swear to sell his land to Titus, or to lend him an hundred crowns; the answer is brief, an oath in this case, is both lawful and binding," and granting it be as Mr. Gibb says with respect to the dreadfulness of the penalties, the world may be mistaken; for the solemnity of the oath does not in the least add to the obligation; or more expresly, the oath is equally binding without any penalty at all, the same Casuist says, "A solemn oath of itself, and in its own nature, is not more obligatory than a simple one; because the obligation of an oath, ariseth precisely from this, that God is invoked as a witness and revenger, no less in a simple oath, than in the solemn and corporal (for the invocation is made precisely by the pronunciation of the words) which is the same both in the simple and solemn, and not by any corporal motion, in which the solemnity of the oath consists." From which I think these oaths cannot altogether be condemned, because tho' every one cannot have a particular and distinct uptaking of all the particulars; yet they may understand the scope of the oath as bindeth to all necessary and lawful things, as the general condition requireth, likewise he taketh the oath for the end, and in the sense that it is commonly taken, to all the essentials pertaining to the benefit of that society, but taketh it not in every particular strectly, for no society can frame an oath to answer all particulars. / *I should now compare Mr. Gibb's letter and an Epigram on the most ancient and Honourable trade of Masonry; done by the Reverend Mr. William Geddes minister at Urquhart. But the reader may compare them himself, and he will find, that the learned have differed greatly in their opinions, which is no wonder what the vulgar do.*

AMONG mehanicks, Masons I extol,
and with the best I doubt not to enrol;
Before the flood, antiquity they claim,
the Masons then must have an ancient name
When godly Enoch by his divine art,
he did foretel how that the world should smart.
By fire and water: he two pillars made
the one with brick; the other with stone was laid,
He wrote thereon, all sciences and arts
which such defusion put to all mens hearts.
If water came, the stone might it endure,
the brick the fire; so all continued sure;
The moral law in write none could it have,
till God himself on stone must it engrave,
For hewing stone, none can put you to shame
the corner stone to Jesus is a name,
For this I think the Masons most be blest,
from ancient times they have a Divine crest:
A character, whereby they know each other,
and yet so secret none knows it but a brother;
All temples, forts, and palaces of Kings:
all castles, steeples, and such other things;
Strong holds, and houses, which so long endure,
do owe all what they have, from Masons sure
All pomp, grandeur, and magnifick state,
whate'er they have, from Masons they do get.

FINIS.

JAMES STEVEN, *BLIND ZEAL DETECTED: OR, A TRUE REPRESENTATION OF THE CONDUCT OF THE MEETING I WAS A MEMBER OF, AND OF THE KIRK-SESSION OF THE ASSOCIATE CONGREGATION, AT GLASGOW* (1755)

James Steven, *Blind Zeal Detected: or, A True Representation of the Conduct of the Meeting I was a Member of, and of the Kirk-Session of the Associate Congregation, at Glasgow, Anent some Oaths, especially the Mason's Oath* (Glasgow, 1755).[1]

The author of this pamphlet,[2] James Steven, describes himself as a merchant in Glasgow, though he was not a merchant burgess and therefore would have had only limited rights to trade in the city. He was a member of the Antiburgher congregation in Glasgow[3] and a regular attender at a 'fellowship meeting' at which members discussed worship and beliefs. He was absent from the meetings for two months in 1753, and on his return he explained that he had been away as he had been 'concerned in building a house belonging to a company of free *masons*, being collector'. Steven claims that he did not expect this to be controversial, but his colleagues at the meeting expressed their horror at him being involved in that 'abominable thing' – Freemasonry. The Kirk Session was informed of the matter, and declared his association with the masons devilish. He was then questioned as to whether he had 'sworn' (an oath) when made collector, and the money he had collected was declared abominable and unlawful. Steven argued that the session was wrong to question him, and pointed out that William Imbrie – who was present at the session meeting – had previously been the masons' collector and had not been denounced. It was presumably at this point that the questioning of Imbrie (author of the previous text, *The Poor Man's Complaint*) began.

At a later meeting of the Kirk Session Steven was again interrogated, and urged with threats and flattery to 'make a discovery of the mason oath'. He refused to do this, and in the end it was agreed that all those present should discuss the matter with their elders.[4] However, Steven was barred from attending further fellowship meetings, which he denounced as 'contrary to all rule', especially as he had not admitted to the Kirk Session that he was a mason. He now turns to the theme indicated by the title of his pamphlet. 'Blind zeal' had long been a pejorative term used by Protestants to denounce the belief of Roman Catholics, which was held to be based on unreasoning acceptance of the authority of the church, rather than on rational interpretation of the Word of God.[5] The Kirk Session's treatment of him resembled 'jesuitism' and the conduct of the Roman Catholic Church in three respects. Blind obedience was asked of him; he was urged to make 'auricular' (spoken) confession, and he was subject to 'extortion' (threats to force him to answer questions). If there was one matter that all factions of Presbyterians in Scotland were agreed upon, it was that the Pope and the Roman Catholic Church represented antichrist, the source of all evil. Thus to accuse Secession Church members of acting like them was highly provocative.

At this point Steven evidently admitted that he had taken the mason oath, but he still refused to accept that anyone had the right to question him on the matter without providing proof that being a mason was unlawful. There the matter rested for six months or so, but then one of the members of the fellowship meeting decided to refer the matter to the Kirk Session again, and Steven was repeatedly summoned before both the session and a special committee. He refused to cooperate, and was banned from admission to a forthcoming holy communion service.

Steven's reaction was furious. The session's treatment of him was 'without foundation in the divine law or human compositions, civil or ecclesiastic'. He had previously been admitted to communion even though it had been well known that he was a mason.[6] Other known masons in the congregation had not been disciplined, so the session was acting hypocritically and inconsistently. Moreover, though he had issued a formal complaint against the conduct of Tobias Lundie,[7] a member of the session, he had scandalously been admitted to communion. That Steven and Lundie were also quarrelling in a case before a civil court complicated matters. Carried away with righteous indignation, Steven rhetorically declared that for 1754 years (that is, since the birth of Christ) no one had ever questioned the mason oath. Neither Christ nor his apostles had mentioned it. Nowhere in the Word of God was it said that being a mason was a justification for exclusion from communion. Thus his exclusion was unscriptural and 'consequently irrational'.

Steven had converted his squabble with the session into a matter of universal truths and principles. However, he briefly toned down his heated language to assure 'the world' (was the world really interested?) that his 'minister was calm through the whole process'.[8] It was the other members of the session who were to blame for its 'great sin'. In particular, he blamed two individuals, Lundie and

Robert Todd, branding the former as the 'cause and promoter of the scandal which he spread thro' the city'.

Like William Imbrie, James Steven is only known through a pamphlet written in response to accusations against him. The two men are also similar in the resources they used to back up their arguments – the Bible and the works of a number of eminent theologians. Neither, however, managed to be entirely consistent or convincing. And in neither case is the outcome of their disputes with their church known.

Notes

1. This headnote was written by David Stevenson.
2. Only one copy of *Blind Zeal Detected* (Glasgow: [s.n.], 1755 [20 pp]) is known to survive: University of Edinburgh, New College Library, Special Collections, A.C.4.4/3.
3. See headnote to *The Poor Man's Complaint*, pp. 43–6.
4. Member of the congregation were assigned to individual elders to supervise their conduct and advise them.
5. See, for example, J. Milton, *Paradise Lost* (1667), 3.452 ('painful superstition and blind zeal').
6. Previously Steven stated that he had delayed admitting to the session that he was a mason. Now he claims that the session had known he was a mason all along.
7. 'Tobias Lundie merchant-staymaker in Glasgow' is named in the list of subscribers prefixed to the first volume in A. Stevenson, *History of the Church and State of Scotland*, 4 vols (Edinburgh: [s.n.], 1753–7).
8. John Jamieson (*c.* 1726–93) was the first minister of the Antiburgher congregation in Glasgow, having been ordained in 1753. D. Small, *History of the Congregations of the United Presbyterian Church from 1733 to 1900*, 2 vols (Edinburgh: David M. Small, 1904), vol. 2, pp. 27–8.

James Steven, *Blind Zeal Detected: or, A True Representation of the Conduct of the Meeting I was a Member of, and of the Kirk-Session of the Associate Congregation, at Glasgow* (1755)

BLIND ZEAL DETECTED:
OR, A TRUE
REPRESENTATION
OF THE

Conduct of the Meeting I was a Member of,[1] and of the Kirk-session of the Associate Congregation, at Glasgow, anent some Oaths, especially the Mason's Oath.

By JAMES STEVEN, Merchant in Glasgow.

GLASGOW:
Printed in the Year MDCCLV. /

BLIND ZEAL DETECTED:
OR, A TRUE
REPRESENTATION
OF THE

Conduct of the Meeting I was a Member of, and of the Kirk-session of the Associate Congregation at Glasgow, anent some Oaths, especially the Mason's Oath.

THOUGH it gives me no pleasure to make an appearance of this nature, against a society for whom I have always, since a member, payed the greatest regard, yet, as all my other appearances seemed fruitless, and my sincere travelling[2] with my brethren of no effect; my character, which is the dearest thing to me in life, being by some of them deeply wounded, and, as self-defence is the law of nature and nations, this is the inevitable method I am necessarily obliged to choose for vindication of my character, MY ALL! *A good name is rather to be chosen, than great riches*, Prov. xxii. I. (Put ceremony of preface apart).[3] To come to the point in view, which is an upstart late created thing, and to the procedure of the meeting and session, of a-piece with it.

They have raised a scandal where sure there was none, and I am persuaded will be made evident, which will free me from the crime of charging unjustly.

I was a member of a fellowship-meeting for several years without the least objection, except in the months of October and November, 1753; at which time I was concerned in building a house belonging to a company of free *masons*, being collector, whereby I was detained for several weeks from the meeting; and when I returned, as formerly, they were greatly displeased.

I told them, as above, what detained me, which greatly incensed them against me: they said but little as to my absence, but exclaimed greatly against me for being concerned with that abominable thing, as, I think, they called it: to which I made little return; but told them, I was sorry I had given them any ground of reflection from my absence: they were more displeased, and their rooted prejudice gathered strength.

I went to next meeting, expecting my fellow-worshippers would be more calm; for it will always be a rule with me to persist in being reconciled to those who have done me an injury: but, to my grief, found them more exasperated than before: and I cannot well account for it, that the party which does an injury is generally more hard to be reconciled, than the one which has received it. They then asserted that it was devilish, every thing about it was odious, and interrogated me about many things; such as, Was I sworn when I was made collector? *etc.* said that the money which was gathered was abominable and unlawful. I answered, they had wrong notions of these matters.

I remember little more which passed that night, / only, William Imrie being present, I told them he had been collector before me.

I went to the meeting the third night, expecting they might have dropt it, but found myself disagreeably deceived; indeed they did not insist so much about circumstances as formerly, tho' they asked several questions, I refused to answer: they insisted both by flattery and force to extort them from me, telling me it would be a piece of honourable generation-work to make a discovery of the mason oath, and that it would be a stop towards others doing so likewise; this, be sure, I refused, then they charged me with obstinacy, and threatened me with the consequences of it, especially John Marshall, and Tobias Lundie; for there were only five in the meeting, *viz.* John Marshall, James Watson, John Jameson, Tobias Lundie, and I.

At parting it was moved I should speak with my elder.[4] I told them they should do so also. They agreed that each of us should inform our respective elder; but notwithstanding this our mutual consent, and the affair in dependence, surprizing! they debarred me their meeting after that night. This to me appears to be a material excluding from Christian communion, contrary to all rule I ever had access to know; and that ere I had owned before the session I was a mason; which I was neither afraid nor ashamed to do: a conduct this too much resembling jesuitism in three things; I mean, articles of the Roman hierarchy, *viz. Blind Obedience, Auricular Confession*, and, if there is not simple compliance, *Extortion*. There is indeed this difference from the last article, the papists have / a material wheel, an awful degree of torture indeed, and too many in our days a spiritual wheel called *Anathema*, too indiscriminately used.

But tho' I did own I was a mason, I did not see that that could lay me under the remotest obligation on to make the least discovery of the matter itself; and it cannot be, that any court can pass sentence upon circumstances concerning any one thing, until that thing upon which they depend be proven unlawful, and the illegality of it be laid open in so many words and syllables.

All sin is against the law of God in general, yet every particular sin hath a particular reference either to the first or second tables of the law, and to one of them in particular; and till it be shown against which this is, I do not see how any court, or society of men can proceed in judgment against any one; for a mere supposition can never be a rational foundation for legal procedure, too much the present case tho', for which see I Tim. ii. 6, 7. *From which some having swerved, have turned aside unto vain jangling,*[5] *desiring to be teachers of the law, understanding neither what they say, nor whereof they affirm.* Gal. iv. 16, 17. *Am I therefore become your enemy because I tell you the truth? They zealously affect, but not well; yea, they would exclude you, that you might affect them.* From which, to me at least, it plainly appears, that blind zeal hath led on my brethren to proceed against me, from which rash judgment frequently springs: and I have known that confused notions arising from misplaced passions, have been the cause of blind zeal, and consequently of rash judgment.

As to my agreement with the meeting about conversing with my elder, I spoke both with minister[6] and elder; the elder said we might put it up, it was not come to be a scandal; the minister said I might give it him in writing, which I took to consideration, then told him I would write none at that time.

The members of the meeting continued silent, so far as I know, six or seven months: at last John Marshall spoke to Robert Todd about it, to bring it before this session: Robert told me to attend the session, which I did, the minute of the session was spoke of, and read; I owned I said I was a mason; but that there were some articles in said minute I could not acknowledge; for it is the rule of courts, whatever one may be charged with, real or supposed, the minute of court is read in the person's hearing that sederunt,[7] especially in ecclesiastic courts, which was not done to me; I told John Marshall afterwards, I would make him prove the libel contained therein. No more happened at this time worth the mentioning: I was dismissed till the session might get further information, for none of the meeting appeared but John Marshall.

Some time after I was again called to attend the session, I went, and was by them interrogated as formerly; was teazed[8] about my being collector, was asked if I attended any meetings, if I was at any entries; at some of which I owned I had been, but they seemed to be indifferent about this, and pressed me hard to discover the matter itself, which I absolutely refused.

John Marshall quoted the xvth Psalm, 4th ver. in prose, *He that sweareth to his own hurt, and changeth not:* upon which he insisted as an argument to make me yield! but I refused it belonged to the case in hand; for I find Mr. Durham[9] takes it in the quite opposite sense, when on the third command,[10] p. 113 and 114, at large.

It was insisted upon as a duty, and as an example to others.

I was desired to withdraw 'till called for: this I did, was again desired in, strong attempts made upon me to open upon the oath: I refused all attempts, told them I neither could nor would. Thus they dismissed me, and appointed a committee to labour with me.

Several weeks passed by; how many were appointed I know not, Robert Todd and John Marshall, were they who held the committee: they interrogated me close, and, as they said, repeated many gross expressions, which had been told by masons was the oath; such as, they were naked, that their throat was to be cut, that they were to be buried in the sea mark,[11] and were to murder one another, that it was odious and hellish: and John Marshall represented that a mason should have said, that tho' hell had been ransacked, there could not have been a more devilish oath contrived; and many such gross expressions they thundered out.

I told them tho' they should utter such language for hours together, I would not hear them, so as to give any answer; they invented all methods to / bring me to comply, but were answered by me, I call it neither good nor ill; so they desisted.

Last time I was with the session, was the Tuesday night immediately preceding the communion sabbath, I indeed went uncalled, expected to get the affair ended, but found them in the same temper they were in before: they asked the two men who had conversed me, what length they had brought me; they answered, that after all due pains with me, I only said, I would call it neither good nor bad, but it would stand as it was.

They went through several things we had been on before: they read the synod's minute, which I had never heard before, tho' I had desired a fight of it several times; neither knew I of it 'till the difference happened. They did not ask me whether I agreed to it: they seemed to pass by all that had happened before, except that of making a full discovery, which they pressed with as much eagerness as ever; but I told, as formerly, I could not.

They asked me my reason for it: I would not give any reason. I was desired to retire; which I did: after being called I was told, by the moderator, that the session had delayed it 'till another time.

That same night I tabled a complaint against Tobias Lundie, in the matter of an oath, before the town-court: [12] I told I had gone to him, and he appeared obstinate. The session desired me to go to him again, and take two with me; I went the next day, being Wednesday before the sacrament, / and carried with me Robert Todd and James Furlong; but found him still in the same mind he was in when I spoke to him myself. I asked him if he would acknowledge he was in the wrong in appearing so boldly before the court, and saying I had sworn wrong; and to back it, said I told him that I had hired a mare from widow Winning to an Edinburgh man: he said he would not. I asked him if he owned that clerk M'Gilchrist charged him to silence in the mean time: he owned it. I asked him why he came to the clerk's chamber at the time of my examination? He said he was desired. I told him I was come to make up the difference betwixt us: he said he would do no such thing. Robert Todd told him, that was wrong; for he was to leave his gift at the altar, and be reconciled with his brother.[13] Thus we parted.

From his conduct, it appears that he is the cause and promoter of the scandal which he spread thro' the city; a plain proof, is his coming to the chamber in a furious manner, and expressing himself as above; also his saying he was desired, makes it evident, that he, with some of his adherents, had agreed upon what he was to do; which was to dash and confuse me, that they might get an advantage of me in contempt of law, seeing they could not get the better of me according to law. A proof of its being grosly false and absurd; nay, wholly so, is, that the affair depending two months before the town-court, sure he would have witnessed against me, what he then was induced to say.

I have reason to suspect him of being both the raiser and publisher of the calumny which ensued / contrary to the apostle's advice, Eph. iv. 31. *Let all bitterness, and wrath, and anger, and clamour, and evil-speaking, be put away from you, with all malice.*

But true it is, that the very day following this, on which the above-mentioned men and I conversed him, the session allowed him to swear the bond,[14] with others that joined, not according to that rule laid down by our divine teacher and guide, Mat. v. 23, 24. *Therefore, if thou bring thy gift to the altar, and go thy way, first be reconciled to thy brother, and then come and offer thy gift.*

The reader may judge whether his zeal be according to knowledge, it being only his own bare assertion, which can never overturn a legal oath; hence it is evident, it is of a piece with that zeal Paul charges the Romans with, Rom. x. 2. *For I bear them record they have a zeal of God, but not according to knowledge.*

Now come we to the sessions conduct anent this affair.

Tho' I had observed the rule of the word, as already hinted, with Tobias, and entered a complaint before the session and two witnesses, as above observed, choosing to make reconciliation, yet this session received Tobias into full communion, both to bond and sacrament, and rejected me; for I went to my elder and asked a token, upon Saturday, which he refused, tho' I insisted: thus it appears they accepted of him as accuser, witness and / judge, contrary to all rule, both civil and ecclesiastic, nay, and the word itself, Luke vi. 37. *Judge not.* And verse 39. *And he spake a parable unto them, Can the blind lead the blind? Shall they not both fall into the ditch?* Agreeable to this, see Rutherford's[15] *due Right of Presbytery*,[16] p. 45 and 46. Speaking particularly concerning witness-bearing, and particularly condemns any one's being allowed to be accuser, witness, and judge. Also concerning scandal, see the learned Gillespie,[17] *Aaron's Rod blossoming*,[18] 553 and 554 pages. Nay, it is the greatest trespass which is committed against the soul of our neighbour, scandal is so soul murdering; it is a breach of the law of love, not only by omission, but commission; he that is commanded to edify his brother, and then giveth scandal, does he not trespass against his brother? See Matth. xviii. 7. *Wo unto the world because of offences, for it must needs be that offences come, but wo be to that man by whom the offence cometh.* Also the said Mr. Gillespie, concerning scandal in the foresaid book, p. 558. I appeal to the ordinance of parliament, dated October 20th, 1645. *The eldership of every congregation shall judge the matter of scandal aforesaid, being not capital, upon the testimony of two credible witnesses at the least.*[19] Deut. xix. 15. *One witness shall not rise up against a man for any iniquity, or for any sin, in any sin that he sinneth: at the mouth of two witnesses, or at the mouth of three witnesses shall the matter be established.* From the divine rule and our approven standards, nay, our whole constitution, it is evident, that all the proceedings of meeting and session about this affair, are founded upon some late framed principles of conduct, repugnant to our civil / and ecclesiastical laws, a kin to blind zeal, and perhaps spring from an itch of curiosity, which when they cannot satisfy, are prompted rashly to pass judgment against me, concerning a matter they cannot, at least have not clothed with words and syllables. It is further evident, from their partial dealing in admitting some, said to be masons; nay, who acknowledged no less to the session; with what they said the session were satisfied, whether it was a part, or the whole, or none of it: the pardon behoved to be according to the then present notion the session had of it.

I beg leave to say, that unless a court know the crime and nature of it, whether aggravated in a higher or lesser degree, and can challenge the person or persons to speak to the point in hand, they can never properly condemn nor absolve in judgment.

However, true it is, that the session freed some and condemned others, tho' they for a long time before admitted me to full communion, when known, by my confession, to be a mason.

According to the opinion of some, it might not have been amiss to have assembled at once all who were masons in their congregation, and dealt fairly with them, passed sentence, receive or reject; but to make divisions and subdivisions, and to have respect of persons, will by no means be judged by the world fair dealing. To take a man by surprize, it may make him timorous, and easy to be imposed / upon by interrogations and extortions, so inconsistent with primitive candour and ingenuity. Another bad effect attending this affair, is, passing different sentences on the same supposed crime, called by some of my pursuers, the devil's club, Satan's invisible world, hellish, and the like: too much is said, and nothing proven, and so may be applied to Matth. vii. I. *Judge not, and ye shall not be judged.* Verse 3. *And why beholdest thou the mote that is in thy brother's eye, but considerest not the beam that is in thine own eye.* Verse 4. *Or how wilt thou say to thy brother, Let me pull out the mote out of thine eye, and, behold, a beam is in thine own eye.* Agreeable thereto, Ecclef. vii. 26. *Be not righteous over much, neither make thyself over wise, why shouldst thou destroy thyself?* These I refer to the judgment of the reader.

Upon the whole, the reader will see my necessity of writing, contrary to my original design.

Had the session candidly told me, last time I was with them, which was the Tuesday before the sament,[20] that I was to be debarred from sealing ordinances, and that if I imagined myself wrong'd, I might have an opportunity of appealing to the presbytery, this had been using me well, like a man, like a Christian. But not one syllable of all this was I told; however, was debarred, while other masons were admitted; upon what grounds they know best.

As to the matter betwixt Tobias Lundie and myself, having entered a complaint, and expected a fair hearing before the session, he being received, / and I debarred, I cannot expect impartiality; they will contradict themselves: thus am I obliged to give a tacit assent in homologating their proceedings as above, which I cannot, yea, dare not do, seeing I am clear as to both affairs.

I consider the session's conduct towards me anent the mason's oath, as a new broached tradition, without foundation in the divine law or human compositions, civil or ecclesiastic in Scotland; and I may add, any other kingdom in Europe, so far as ever I heard.

Our Saviour, the apostles, and all the antient fathers, Ante-nicene and Postnicene,[21] or Athanasius his creed,[22] for these seventeen hundred and fifty four years, emitted not one syllable about the mason oath. Had it been truly a necessary term of communion, would our Saviour have passed over so important a point in silence? Would he not in his own doctrine, if it were sinful, have either inveighed against it, or left commands with his disciples to do so? But neither Christ, nor his apostles, nor the antient fathers, nor any of the learned world have mentioned one word about it; hence I presume it to be a fondling topic set on foot by busy spirits, to amuse the imagination, and lead the minds of the people of God from the substantial to the shadowy parts of religion: unbecoming rational creatures, and much more those who set up for teachers of mankind: far from the laudable practice of the primitive church, who never anticipated knowledge of things in examining causes, but allowed their unprejudiced understandings to byass their minds to the one side or the other

If it be, or can be a term of communion, why was it not introduced, as such, at the original establishment of this society; perhaps it may be said, it was not proper it should in its infancy, O absurdity! not proper then, and now judged proper! or it may be was not adverted to so early, at this rate you must own, your constitution, at the then present time, was imperfect, that the founders of it were ignorant what ought, and what ought not to be terms of communion.

Were your eyes opened from the word of God? Did it give foundation to its being thus introduced, or did it not? If the first, I would be greatly obliged to any man who would lead me to the passage: if the last, I mean, that it was not the word of God, I reject its being a term of communion, because unscriptural, and if unscriptural, consequently irrational.

Or was it a right founded in the society itself? if so, farewel rational religion, manly liberty, common-sense, all our standards, church discipline, and uniform regularity, the great bonds of human society.

But be it as it is, I never heard it was troublesome either to church or state.

For minute of synod see *the poor Man's Complaint*, p. 30.

My desiring to adhere to the principles of the presbyterian church in doctrine, discipline, worship and government, is one strong motive of my / present conduct; and tho' I write not with that pointed connection, with that purity of stile, and justness of period, which might be expected from an essay of this kind, I hope the candid reader will make proper allowances, and catch at the sentiment more than the language.

As a farther proof against rash judging, is, what a learned divine hath on Matth. vii. 1. *Judge not*, quoteth Gen. xi. 6, 7. he is said to come down to see the fact: and, Gen. xviii. 21. he is said to come down from heaven to see whether they had done according to the cry that was come up to the Lord. His inference is, *Whereby the Lord would teach us, that before we enter into judgment with any man, or any people, we first maturely consider the facts. Secondly, it gives as a taste and view of our own natural pride and self-love, so that what is not according to Isa.* viii. 20. To the law and to the testimony: if they speak not according to this word, it is because there is no light in them.

Gillespie in his epistle to the reader says, *What I speak of this divine ordinance of church-government, my meaning is not to allow mutables to animate any in the too severe and over strict exercise of ecclesiastical discipline and censures.*

It was observed by Hierom[23] as one of the errors of the Montanists,[24] *Illi ad omne pene delictum ecclesiae obserant fores;* [25] that is, *they excommunicate and shut out of the church almost at every offence.*

The best things, whether in church or state, have been actually abused, and may be so again, through the errors and corruptions of mankind. / The holy scriptures have been abused to the greatest mischiefs in the world, tho' subservient to the greatest good in the world.

I take this opportunity of acquainting the world that the minister was calm through the whole process; but as for the session, in *cumulo*,[26] I beg leave to inform them, that, according to their proceeding, they punish supposed sin with real sin; for, by their pressing and extorting, if any comply, in less or more, they are guilty of perjury: so it is a committing of a gross visible sin, in pretending to confess a supposed sin; how either the imposers or the imposed will account for it, I know not. I hope it will be granted that God is alone lord of the conscience, and knows heart-secrets; but this new way of going to work puts me in mind of what Matth. says, *Let them alone, they be blind leaders of the blind.*

I and others are said to have created schism in the congregation, to have exposed the session to the mockery of many, *etc.* If other congregations imitate this one, there must be schisms in most of them; nay, if masons were to be thrown out of Christian societies, through Britain, there would be many pulpits empty, places of civil judgment desolate; many incorporations and societies thin; nay, many thrones, courts, and commonwealths would be in disorder through the known world.

Being fully persuaded that many of the associate congregation in this place, will condemn this my undertaking, as bold and precipitant, I take this opportunity to acquaint them, that however it / may appear to them, yet I have done it not with a view to displease any one party, or to ingratiate myself into the favour of any other; but from a principle of love to truth, regularity and decorum, so very necessary to the support of religious societies; and from motives I have formerly mentioned: and if I have any knowledge of my own heart, this production never proceeded from pride, neither thirst after applause, or from a love of appearing singular. And I hoped that my humble mite thrown in, might perhaps do some service to the rescinding these arbitrary laws of late creation, and to be bold for the truth, was, and always will be a principle of my conduct, tho' with humility, and according to Durham on the fifth command,[27] p. 263.

This humility is not opposite to magnanimity, boldness and zeal, but is well consistent with these, as is clear in Christ, the apostles and others of the saints; for boldness and magnanimity is an adventuring in Christ's strength upon what one is called to according to warrantable grounds; and humility, although it leadeth us to entertain due thoughts of our own infirmities, yet it moderateth us in that also according to right reason, so that the exercise of both being to be ordered according to this rule of reason, as the call, occasion, object, and particular circumstances shall require, it is evident, that there is no inconsistency betwixt the two, but that they may very well be in one and the same person, and at one and the same time.

But to say no more.

Is it consistent with the character of a teacher of christianity, either to condemn or approve what / his understanding does not perceive or to bring over the people under his care, to consent to any one thing's being sinful, or the contrary, of which thing they, for the most part, are entirely ignorant. Have not men all the reason in the world to say, that it's building them on a principle purely popish, tho' under thumb, viz. implicite faith.[28]

Reject this as ye will, it carries in it neither less nor more in the eye of the thinking and unprejudiced world; and thus to act, is to offer an affront to the understandings of your stocks, to lead them from the infallible rule of faith and manners, to the fallible dictates, and opinionative reasonings of erring mortals, a mighty handle this, sure, to the enemies of the rational religion of Jesus Christ; for this purpose I recommend to this reader's perusal a passage, cited by Durham on scandal, p. 32. 33.

Ames in his Cases of Conscience,[29] lib. 5. cap II. *and Gillespie in his* Dispute of Ceremonies,[30] chap. 7. sect. 5. *observe, no man can command either our charity or our consciences; or make up the hazard of a given offence;*[31] *and therefore none command us warrantably to hurt the spiritual good of our neighbour, that being contrary to the command of love that God hath laid on.*

To conclude, If what I have said have no weight with my teachers and brethren, I own I must leave them in the quiet and unenvied posession of their favourite fondling, 'till conviction of a stronger kind shall inform either of us, which are in the right, and which in the wrong.[32]

THE END

[ASSOCIATE SYNOD], 'AN ACT OF THE ASSOCIATE SYNOD CONCERNING THE MASON-OATH' AND A, R, 'AN IMPARTIAL EXAMINATION OF THE ACT AGAINST FREEMASONS' (1757) IN THE APPENDIX OF *THE FREE MASONS POCKET COMPANION* (1761)

[Associate Synod], 'An Act of the Associate Synod Concerning the Mason-Oath', in *The Free Masons Pocket Companion* (Edinburgh: Printed by Ruddiman, Auld, and Company: and sold by William Auld, at the Printing House, Morocco's Close, Lawn-Market, MDCCLXI [1761]), pp. 3–8 (from the Appendix).[1]

A, R, 'An Impartial Examination of the Act of the Associate Synod against the Free-Masons', in *The Free Masons Pocket Companion* (Edinburgh: Printed by Ruddiman, Auld, and Company: and sold by William Auld, at the Printing House, Morocco's Close, Lawn-Market, MDCCLXI [1761]), pp. 8–24 (from the Appendix).[2]

The two preceding texts, by William Imbrie and James Steven, have traced the emergence into print of accounts of disputes between the Antiburgher Kirk Session of Glasgow and a number of members of the congregation who had sworn (or were suspected of having sworn) an oath or oaths on being initiated as Freemasons. The upper courts of the antiburgher hierarchy seemed at first reluctant to get involved in new controversies involving oaths of any sort, but in August 1754 they began to turn their attention to such matters. Their Glasgow presbytery expressed worries about the 'superstitious form of swearing' of the constable oath – at Newcastle in England![2] In the same month the synod decided that the chapman oath found in Stirlingshire was sinful.[3] Finally, in March 1755, the synod reconsidered the mason oath – under pressure from below. Three deacons and two elders from the Glasgow session had given in a 'protest and appeal' to the presbytery asking that the session be ordered to give them access to documents relating to the case of William Templeton, a deacon on the Kirk Session who had been suspended from 'sealing ordinances' (holy communion) for refusing to tell it 'whether he was concerned in certain Oaths, particularly the Mason

Oath'. The presbytery refused to give access to these records, whereupon the deacons and elders appealed to the synod, and gave in a document supporting their
case signed by three elders, one deacon and thirty-seven other members of the
Glasgow Congregation – evidence of how deeply divided the congregation was.
The synod 'heard at great length' evidence from representatives of the two sides,
and then passed an act ordering the Glasgow session to insist on a clear answer
from Templeton as to whether or not he has ever been 'engaged in the Mason-
oath'. If he refused, he was to be suspended from office as deacon and banned
from communion. If he still remained 'obstinate', he was to be referred to the
presbytery for deposition from office and placed under 'lesser excommunication'
(banned from all worship). Further, all other Kirk Sessions were to deal with
similar cases in this way.[4]

In the same month (March 1755) there was published in Edinburgh 'A
mason's confession of the oath, word, and other secrets of his craft', by an old
Freemason who had come to think the oath 'profane and abominable.'[5] This
may have been a coincidence, but it could be a sign that knowledge of the Antiburgher controversy about oaths was spreading outside that church and arousing
public interest.

The Templeton case dragged on. He remained contumacious, and in October 1755 he was summoned to appear before the synod the following April. He
failed to appear, refusing to accept that the synod had jurisdiction in the matter.
It was therefore agreed to delay the case until the next meeting,[6] at the same
time a synod committee was set up to consider procedures regarding the mason
oath. In August the committee's work became the basis for an act concerning
the mason oath, [7] Its text was soon available in print,[8] and a masonic response
quickly followed, written in October 1757 and published in November.[9]

The Act and the Impartial Examination are printed below, from the appendix to *The Free-Mason's Pocket Companion* (1761).[10] The Act is self-explanatory,
with thundering denunciations of masonic oaths and rituals and instructions on
how Freemasons in congregations were to be made to confess and what disciplinary action was to be taken against them.

As to the Impartial Examination, the most obvious comment to be made
on it is that completely fails to live up to its title. Impartiality was not its intention, but rather the destruction of the arguments of those opposed to the mason
oath, with much citation of biblical and other authorities. Within the first few
lines the masons' opponents are accused of malevolence, hypocrisy and 'bigot
zeal'. A main theme of the attack is then developed, denouncing the Antiburgher
Synod ('this Holy Association') for being in its principles and practices like the
Roman Catholic Church. Indeed the 1757 Act is compared to the 1738 papal
bull which had denounced Freemasonry. Much is made of equating (as Protestants usually did) Catholicism with tyranny in both church and state.

The synod's Act had stuck to the language of ecclesiastical dispute, harsh but measured. The Examination is in many places much less formal, descending at times to crude abuse. It is also much more secular than the act. Though sometimes arguing from the authority of the Bible, it also quotes from the satirical writings of Samuel Butler, Jonathan Swift and Alexander Pope. In the eyes of seceders (and indeed all Presbyterians), treating such writers as authorities in religious debate must have seemed scandalous. Indeed, many would have thought it sinful even to read such frivolous works. The Examination at one point almost seems to hint at religious scepticism. 'Mankind is so prone to religion, that it requires only confidence enough, for any persons, however unqualified, to assume the character of spiritual guides, and they will not fail to obtain votaries'.

In a final verbal flourish, the Examination's author announces that in future antiburgher attacks on the mason oath will be ignored – masons 'for the future will disdain to enter the lists with champions so weak and ignorant, so deluded and deluding'.

In 1757 the Antiburgher Synod had at last, twelve years after the Associate Synod had passed the first ineffectual act questioning the oath, seemed to have taken decisive action. And the Freemasons had fought back publicly and forcefully with the Impartial Examination. The battle lines had been set – but no battle followed. Instead the controversy almost vanishes from view. Only a single further dispute has been identified. In 1766 a member of the Alloa Antiburgher congregation was rebuked by the Antiburgher Presbytery of Stirling for having taken the mason oath. However, he was not ordered to be publicly rebuked before his own congregation, as was usually required in disciplinary cases, which may suggest that the presbytery was reluctant to publicise the case.[11]

Doubtless worries about the mason oath continued to trouble some Antiburghers, but it may be that realization of how divisive the issue could be, as congregations contained significant numbers of Freemasons led those opposing this and other oaths to avoid further conflict. In a criticism of the mason oath published in Edinburgh in 1769 the author only referred to the Antiburgher attack on it indirectly, by denouncing the belief that only 'fanatics' had scruples about the oath.[12] The implication is that the Antiburgher offensive had failed and should be regarded as irrelevant.

Notes

1. This headnote was written by David Stevenson.
2. These two texts are printed in *The Free Masons Pocket Companion* (1761), appendix, pp. 3–24. The appendix is paginated separately from the *Companion* and has its own title page, and thus could be sold as a separate work. The two texts were reprinted in the appendix to the second edition of the *Pocket Companion* (Edinburgh: Alexander Donaldson, 1763), pp. 149–60. The 'Act concerning the Mason Oath' was also printed in Associate Synod, *The Formula of Questions: Which Are Put To Ministers at their Or-*

dination, to Probationers at Receiving their Licence, and to Elders at their Ordination; by the Presbyteries and Sessions in Subordination to the Associate Synod. To which Is Annexed a Collection of Several Acts Passed by the Associate Synod (Edinburgh: printed by A. Donaldson and J. Reid, [1760]), pp. 30–5.

3. CH3/111/1, Associate Presbytery of Edinburgh Minutes, 1744–60, MS National Records of Scotland, Edinburgh (hereafter NRS), pp. 372–3.

4. CH3/144/5, General Associate Synod Minutes, 1752–62 (hereafter CH3/144/5), MS NRS, p. 68.

5. CH3/144/5, pp. 77–9.

6. *Scots Magazine*, 17 (1755), pp. 132–7. D. Knoop, G. P. Jones and D. Hamer (eds), *The Early Masonic Catechisms*, 2nd edn (London: Quatuor Coronati Lodge, 1975), pp. 99–107.

7. CH3/144/5, pp. 107–8, 110.

8. CH3/144/5, pp. 139, 144.

9. *Scots Magazine*, 19 (1767), pp. 432–3.

10. *Edinburgh Magazine*, 1 (1757); 'Extracts of a Paper Published in the EDINBURGH MAGAZINE, intitled, An Impartial Examination of the Act of the Associate Synod against the FREE-MASONS, Aug. 25, 1757', *Scots Magazine*, 19 (1757), pp, 583–5.

11. See note 1 above.

12. CH3/286/1, Associate Presbytery of Stirling Minutes, 1760–81, MS, NRS. I am most grateful to Professor Callum Brown for this reference.

13. 'A Disquisition into the Principles of Masonry, and the Mason-oath', *Weekly Magazine, or Edinburgh Amusement*, 6 (12 October and 19 October 1769), pp. 33–6, 69–71. These newspaper articles are reprinted in vol. 5, pp. 163–8.

Associate Synod, 'An Act of the Associate Synod Concerning the Mason-Oath'

[*First published in the* Scots Magazine, *for* August 1757.]

Edinburgh August 25. 1757.

WHEREAS an oath is one of the most solemn acts of religious worship, which ought to be taken only upon important and necessary occasions; and to be sworn in truth, in judgment, and in righteousness, without any mixture of sinful, profane, or superstitious devices:

And whereas the synod had laid before them, in their meeting at Stirling, on the 7th of March 1745, an overture concerning the MASON-OATH,[1] bearing, That there were very strong presumptions, that among MASONS an oath of secrecy is administered to intrants into their society, even under a capital penalty, and before any of those things which they swear to keep secret be revealed to them; and that they pretend to take some of these secrets from the BIBLE; beside other / things, which are ground of scruple, in the manner of swearing the said oath: and therefore overturing,[2] that the synod would consider the whole affair, and give directions with respect to the admission of persons engaged in that oath to sealing ordinances:

And whereas the synod, in their meeting at Stirling, on the 26th of September 1745, remitted the overture concerning the MASON-OATH to the several sessions subordinate to them, for their proceeding therein, as far as they should find practicable, according to our received and known principles, and the plain rules of the Lord's word, and sound reason:

And whereas the synod, in their meeting at Edinburgh, on the 6th of March 1755, when a particular cause about the MASON-OATH was before them,[3] – did appoint all the sessions under their inspection, to require all persons in their respective congregations, who are presumed or suspected to have been engaged in that oath, to make a plain acknowledgement, whether or not they have ever been so; and to require that such as they may find to have been engaged therein, should give ingenuous answers to what further inquiry the sessions may see cause to make, concerning the tenor and administration of the said oath to them; – and that the sessions should proceed to the purging of what scandal they may thus find those persons convicted of, according to / the directions of the above mentioned act of synod in September 1745.

And whereas the generality of the sessions have, since the aforementioned periods, dealt with several persons under their inspection about the MASON OATH; in the course of which procedure, by the confessions made to them, they have found others, beside those of the mason craft, to be involved in that oath:[4] And the synod finding it proper and necessary to give more particular directions to the several sessions, for having the hainous[5] profanation of the Lord's name by that oath purged out of all the congregations under their inspection:

Therefore the synod did, and hereby do appoint, that the several sessions subordinate to them, in dealing with persons about the MASON OATH, shall particularly interrogate them, – If they have taken that oath, and when and where they did so? If they have taken the said oath, or declared their approbation of it, oftener than once, upon being admitted to a higher degree in a Mason-lodge? If that oath was not administered to them, without letting them know the terms of it, till in the act of administering the same to them? If it was not an oath binding them to keep a number of secrets, none of which they were allowed to know before swearing the oath? If, beside a solemn invocation of the Lord's name in that oath, it did not contain a capital penalty about having their tongues / and hearts taken out in case of breaking the same? If the said oath was not administered to them with several superstitious ceremonies; such as, the stripping them of, or requiring them to deliver up, any thing of metal which they had upon them, – and making them kneel upon their right knee bare, holding up their right arm bare, with their elbow upon the Bible, or with the Bible laid before them, – or having the Bible, as also the square and compasses, in some particular way applied to their bodies? and, If among the secrets which the were bound by that oath to keep, there was not a passage of scripture read to them, particularly 1 Kings vii. 21.[6] with or without some explication put upon the same, for being concealed?

Moreover, the synod appoint, that the several sessions shall call before them all persons in their congregation who are of the mason-craft, and others whom they have a particular suspicion of, as being involved in the MASON OATH, except such as have been already dealt with, and have given satisfaction upon that head; and that, upon their answering the first of the foregoing questions in the affirmative, the sessions shall proceed to put the other interrogatories before appointed; As also, that all persons of the mason-craft, applying for sealing ordinances,[7] and likewise others concerning whom there may be any presumption of their having been involved in the MASON OATH, / shall be examined by the ministers if they have been so: and upon their acknowledging the same, or declining to answer whether or not, the ministers shall refer them to be dealt with by the sessions, before admitting them to these ordinances: And that all such persons offering themselves to the sessions for joining in covenanting-work,[8] shall be then examined by the sessions as to their concern in the aforesaid oath.

And the synod further appoint, that when persons are found to be involved in the MASON-OATH, according to their confessions in giving plain and particular answers to the foregoing questions, and professing their sorrow for the same; the said scandal shall be purged by a sectional rebuke and admonition, – with a strict charge to abstain from all concern afterwards in administering the said oath to any, or enticing any into that snare, and from all practices of amusing people about the pretended mysteries of their signs and secrets: But that persons who shall refuse or shift to give plain and particular answers to the foregoing questions, shall be reputed under scandal, incapable of admission to sealing ordinances, till they answer and give satisfaction as before appointed.

And the synod refer to the several sessions to proceed unto higher censure as they shall see cause, in the case of persons whom they may find involved in the said oath with special aggravation, as / taking or relapsing into the same, in opposition to warnings against doing so.

And the synod appoint, that each of the sessions under their inspection shall have an extract of this act, to be inserted in their books, for executing the same accordingly.

A, R, 'An Impartial Examination of the Act against Freemasons' (1757)

[*First published in the* Edinburgh Magazine *for* October 1757.]

THE SOCIETY of FREE-MASONS, which, notwithstanding the opposition of human power, civil and ecclesiastic, has now subsisted for many ages, and always maintained its inseparable character of SECRECY, PRUDENCE, and good MANNERS, stands at this day in such high repute, that an apology in its behalf is certainly unnecessary.

PUBLIC ESTEEM has always been reputed a crime in the eyes of Malevolence; and VIRTUE and GOODNESS have always been held as declared enemies, by Hypocritical Sanctity and Bigot Zeal. To such impure sources alone can be attributed a very extraordinary Act, lately pronounced against this Venerable Society, by the Synod of the Associate / Brethren, and published in the *Scots Magazine* for August 1757.

From this act the practices of this Holy Association appear so agreeable to those of the Roman Catholic Church, that they afford a shrewd suspicion, that the Principles from which such practices result, are of the same nature, and have the same dangerous tendency, with those professed by the Roman See.

In the year 1738, his Holiness at Rome, by the Plenitude of the Apostolic Power, issued a declaration[9] condemnatory of the Society of FREE-MASONS; with an absolute Prohibition to all the FAITHFUL IN CHRIST, to enter into, promote, or favour that Society, under no less penalty than an *ipso facto*[10] Excommunication; and the help of the secular arm is commanded to enforce the execution of this declaration. By an edict, consequent to this declaration, informations are commanded, under the severest corporal punishments; and encouraged by an assurance from the INFALLIBLE CHAIR, "That Oaths of Secrecy in matters already condemned, are thereby rendered void, and lose their obligation." Let it be recorded in history, to the honour of THEIR HOLINESSES THE ASSOCIATE SYNOD IN SCOTLAND, That, in the year 1757, they also thundered out their TREMENDUOUS BULL[11] against FREE-MASONS: Whereby all their votaries are enjoined to reveal every thing which under the sanction / of a solemn oath they are obliged to conceal; they are thereafter to abstain from such societies themselves: nor are they to entice others to enter into them, under the terrible certification of being reputed under SCANDAL, debarred from SEALING ORDINANCES, and subjected to HIGHER CENSURE, as there should appear cause.

The professed reasons which brought the Fraternity under the Papal Displeasure, were, That they confederated persons of all religions and sects, under a shew of natural honesty, in a close and inscrutable bond, and under certain ceremonies, which, by an oath taken on the Bible, they obliged them, by the imprecation of heavy punishments, to preserve with inviolable secrecy.

These urged by the Seceders as the motive of their proceedings, are, That the MASONS administered their Oath of Secrecy, under a capital penalty, without first declaring what the matters to be concealed are; and that some of these things are taken from the Bible. And the Publishers of the *Scots Magazine* very quaintly insinuate another reason, That the whole matters thus communicated under the strictest ties of secrecy, are a bundle of trifles and inconsistencies, unworthy of the solemnity of an oath: This they do by a reference made to a pretended Discovery of the Secrets of Masonry, published in their Magazine 1755, p. 133. and communicated to them, it may be presumed, by the same correspondents.[12] /

The great conformity betwixt these two Bulls leave small room to doubt but the last, as well as the first, would have had the sanction of corporal punishments, if God, for the curse of mankind, had strengthened the hands, and seconded the intolerating views of its authors with secular power. They have not, however, omitted what was within their grasp; but have attempted to erect a Dominion over the Consciences of Mankind, by assuming a power of dispensing with human obligations. This is a privilege, which, however envied, the Reformed Clergy have hitherto left, together with his pretended infallibility, in the possession of their Elder Brother at Rome; till, in this more enlightened age, these bold asserters of the Christian Rights have dared to reclaim and vindicate it as their own: for, should Antichrist enjoy any benefit which the Saints are not better intitled to?

This is not the least engine which has been successfully employed to rear up and support the enormous fabric of the Roman Hierarchy. The must[13] solemn treaties betwixt princes and states, the allegiance of subjects to their sovereigns, the obligations of private contracts, the marriage-vow, and every other the most sacred bond of human society, are dissolved, and fly off at the breath of this dispensing power, like chaff before the wind: and to this, as to their native source, / may be ascribed those many wars and devastations, rebellions, massacres, and assassinations, with which every page of the history of the Christian world is defiled. Is it possible that a doctrine attended with such a train of dreadful consequences can have any foundation either in Reason or Revelation?

The nature of an oath, particularly of a promissory oath, which this pretended power only respects, comprehends a solemn invocation of the Name of GOD, the Supreme and Omniscient Being, the Searcher of the hearts and the Trier of the reins of the children of men,[14] not only as an impartial witness* of what is promised, but likeways as the Judge, and certain Avenger of Perjury, Falsehood and Deceit. The performance of the oath becomes thereby cognoscible by the Omniscience of the Divine Tribunal†; and his Justice and Omnipotence will not fail to pour out the phial of his threatened vengeance upon that execrated head which has dared to invocate the name of the Lord in vain‡.

Such are the conclusions of sound Reason, warranted by Scripture. Can it then be imagined, that God has left it in the power of man to alter / these established rules of his judgments and procedure? Would not this be, as the poet says, to

Snatch from his hand the balance and the rod,
Rejudge his justice, be the God of GOD?
POPE.[15]

There arises likeways from an oath a requisitorial right to the person in whose behalf it is conceived. The thing promised becomes his property; of which, so far as the acquisition does not infringe any anterior obligation, he cannot be defrauded by any dispensing power, without manifest injustice, and the exercise of an arbitrary and despotic authority.

The cause of introducing oaths into civil society affords another forcible argument against this dispensing power. The natural and indispensable obligations to justice and equity, even assisted by the fear of civil punishments, were found insufficient to correct the depravity of the human mind, and prevent a bias to apparent self-interest in the performance of mutual contracts. It was found necessary to assume the aid of Religion, and upon the faith of an oath to establish a mutual trust. This arises from a confidence, that he who swears, will never violate that promise to which he called God to be his witness, and of the breach whereof he has obtested him to be the judge and avenger. But, if there is any where on earth lodged a power of absolving from these obligations, mutual terror / and dissidence must take place of the happiness and tranquillity expected from civil society, of which the utter subversion must ensue.

---

*   Jer. xlii 5.

†   Jer. xxix. 23.

‡   Zech. v. 4. Jurisjurandi contempta religio satis Deum ultorem habet.[Quoted from the Corpus Juris Civilis, or Code of Civil Law, indicating that God punishes the breakers of oaths (Latin).] *Pand. l. 2. c. de Reb. cred. et Jurejur.*

However extraordinary this claim may appear, his Holiness the Pope arrogates it to himself very consistently with his other high attributes. He is the Viceroy of God, and under him the Spiritual Lord of the Universe. All mankind are his subjects, and every oath, every contract, is with a reversion of its being to him well-pleasing.

But upon what consistent bottom their Holinesses the Brethren of the Association found their ABSOLVING POWER, is not so evident. Perhaps, like the Jesuits, those expert casuists,[16] and subtle divines, they will distinguish, and resolve it into a declaratory power; whereby, from their profound knowledge, they only shew that certain oaths, from the particular circumstances that attend them, are unjust or wicked; and the performance of them will not therefore be expected by God; nor is it eligible by man, or obligatory on the conscience.

In this view let us examine their conduct towards the FREE-MASONS; and endeavour to explore on which side the imputation of Blasphemy and Impiety will fall. In this conflict the match is very unequal. A FREE-MASON, while he defends the Mysteries of the Craft, is at every step under the awe and reverence of his oath. He cannot therefore exhibit those mysteries to view, / or subject them to examination. He must then, like the lion in the fable, suppose the picture such as it is represented by his antagonists.

Untainted Probity frequently meets with strong opposition from Villainy supported by Fraud. Experience has taught her to oppose Prudence to Cunning, and Secrecy and Resolution to the dark Designs and dire Machinations of her Foes. But the depravity or facility of mankind soon discovered the difficulty of attaining that degree of secrecy, upon which the success of enterprize must often depend; and from a confidence of which resolution and activity result. To remedy this defect, Religion opportunely interposes, and affords the sanction of an Oath; under the security of which, the schemes suggested, and maturely planned by judgement, are entrusted to Prudence and Resolution for their execution. Hence Oaths of Secrecy have become one of the necessary hinges of government; they have been adopted by every civil state; and every branch of administration requires them. To them must be ascribed the success of the greatest enterprizes. Under their influence the noble the generous plan of British Liberty was matured into execution, and the purposes of Popish Tyranny rendered abortive by the Revolution:[17] and to them the FREE MASON owns his grateful acknowledgements, for the unrestrained liberty of defending his Craft, and of detecting the damnable principles and black practices / of the pretended messengers of CHRIST, without the dread of a merciless Inquisition. The innocence of such oaths cannot then be doubted; and their necessity sufficiently sanctifies their use.

But it seems the Seceders hold it a crime to exact an Oath of Secrecy, before the things required to be kept secret are revealed. Can any thing be more ridiculous than this objection? The purposes of such oaths would thereby be disappointed: for the Secret would be communicated without any security or obligation to preserve it; and it would then become optional to grant it or not. Cromwel, that Arch-politician, when he imagined his secretary's clerk, who was fast asleep, had overheard him deliver some important orders, would not trust to the security of a subsequent oath, and thought that secrecy could be assured only by his immediate death.[18] The common practice of the world refutes the objection, which could only proceed from those whose want of modesty equals that of their honesty.

Mankind is so prone to religion, that it requires only confidence enough, for any persons, however unqualified, to assume the character of spiritual guides, and they will not fail to obtain votaries. These, from that same tendency, soon yield up their judgement and consciences to the direction of their teachers; and their affections or antipathies, which become no longer their own, / are pointed at particular objects, as the zeal or private interest of their priests shall dictate.

One distinguishing characteristic of the Associate Brethren seems to be, an abhorrence of every oath not devised by themselves, and framed to promote the interests of Faction, Rebellion, and Schism*. They have not as yet, however, perverted the morals of all their followers; some of them, notwithstanding all their endeavours, still retain a regard for an oath as the sacred and inviolable bond of society, This, they perceived, was a check to their ambitious views of an unlimited obedience from their people. It was therefore necessary to diminish that reverence, in hopes that when their deluded flock had learned to overleap the fence in one instance, they would not be scrupulous to do it in any other. And for this end the nature of an Oath of Secrecy is deliberately misrepresented, and rashness and profanity ascribed to it.

As I am obliged to SUPPOSE the Secrets of MASONRY such as they are represented by the Associate Bretheren, I shall follow the order laid down for their interrogatories in their act.

They object, That the Mason-Oath is administered by an invocation of the name of God, attended with certain rites and ceremonies of a superstitious nature, and under a capital penalty. /

By attending to the nature of an oath, it will appear, that the obtesting God[19] as a witness and avenger, necessarily implies an imprecation of his wrath; which, if the doctrine of Providence is believed, must imply all temporal, as well as eternal punishments: it matters not whether any penalty is

---

* They have in their synods condemned as unlawful, the clauses, in Burgess oaths, with respect to religion and allegiance to the King.

expressed; nor does the the doing so, in in any degree, alter the nature of the obligation*.

As to the Ceremonies pretended to be adhibited[20] to this oath, they appear to be innocent in themselves: and if the Masons use any such, instead of ascribing these to a superstitious regard, Charity would conclude they were not without an emphatic and allegorical meaning.

Oaths have almost universally had some rite or ceremony annexed, which, however insignificant in themselves, were originally expressive of something that tended to increase the awe and respect due to that solemn act. The Casuists all agree, that tho' the Oath is equally obligatory without them, the Perjury is however increased by the Solemnity. All nations have adopted them: The Hebrews, by putting their hand below the thigh / of the person to whom they swore†; the Pagans, by taking hold of the altar‡; and both, protending their hands to heaven§: in which last, they have been followed by all Christian nations; some of whom, particularly our sister kingdom, when they take an oath, touch or kiss the holy Gospels: and not only so, but every private society, every court of justice have forms of administering oaths, peculiar to themselves. Shall not then the Society of FREE-MASONS be allowed that privilege, without the imputation of Superstition and Idolatry?

---

*   Illud videtur esse certum, omne juramentum promissorium, quacunque forma concipiatur, explicatione vel contractione, utramque virtualiter conti ere attestationem, sc. et execrationem Nam in juramento, et excretatio supponit attestationem, ut quid sibi prius; et attestatio subinfert exceraionem ut suum necessarium consequens. [Quotation (not entirely accurate) from R. Sanderson, *Garamendi Promissory Re-elections Septum* (London: O. Pullen & S. Crook, 1647), pp. 16–17 (Latin). 'This in the mean time seemeth certain, that every promissory oath under what forme soever conceived, brief, or large, so it be an oath, and no mere Asseveration or Obtestation, virtually containeth both, that is to say, Attestation, and Execration. For in an oath both Execration supposeth Attestation as a thing before it in nature, and Attestation interreth Execration as its necessary consequen.' Translation from *De Juramento Seven Lectures Concerning the Obligation of Promissory Oathes* (London: Humphrey Moseley, Octavian Pulleyn & Andrew Crook, 1655), pp. 22.] *Saunderson, de oblig. juram. pral. I. §. x.*

†   Gen. xxiv. 2. – xlvii. 29.

‡   Et, ut mos Graecorum est, Jurandi causa, ad aras accederet. ['and, as is the custom of the Greeks, to take the oath he came near to the altar'. Quotation from Marcus Tullius Cicero's speech *Pro Balbo*, 56 BC (Latin).] *Cic. pro Balbo.*

§   Gen. xiv. 22. Suspiciens coelum, tenditque ad sidera dextram, Haec eadem, Ænea, terram, mare, sidera jure. ['[Latinus,] raising his eyes to heaven, followed [Aeneas], and stretches out his right hand to the stars [and swears] by these same powers, Aeneas, by the earth, the seas, the stars I swear ....' (Latin). Quotation from Virgil, *The Aeneid*, xii.] VIRG. I. 12. v. 196.

The MATTER of the oath comes next under consideration. The Free-Masons pretend to take some of their Secrets from the BIBLE. A grievous accusation truly! "Jack," in the Tale of a Tub, could "work his father's will into any shape he pleased; so that it served him for a night-cap when he went to bed, or an umbrella in rainy weather. He would lap a piece of it about a sore toe; or, when he had fits, burn two inches under his nose; or, if any thing lay heavy on his stomach, scrape off and swallow as much of the powder / as would lie on a silver penny: They were all infallible remedies." But it seems Knocking Jack of the North will not allow these pearls to be cast before swine, and reserves them only for his special favourites.[21] What magical virtue there can be in the words of the sacred passage mentioned in the act*, the world will be at a loss to discover; and the holy brethren, so well versed in mysteries, are the most proper to explain.

But there are *other things which are ground of Scruple in the manner of swearing of the said oath*. This the Synod have not thought fit to mention: But their Publisher has supplied the defect, by a reference to *A Mason's Confession of the Oath, Word, and other Secrets of his Craft*†; which indeed contains variety of matters insignificant, and ridiculous in themselves, and only fit for the amusement of such persons as the ignorance and incoherence of the author display him to be.

The FREE MASON[22] does not think himself at all concerned to defend and support whatever nonsense shall be fathered upon the Craft by the ignorant and malevolent. The honour of the Fraternity is not in the least tarnished by it.

The whole narrative, particularly the method of discovering a Mason, the Prentice's shirt, and the Monday's lesson, cannot fail to move laughter even in gravity itself. But absurd and ridiculous as the whole of this matter must appear, a / passion of another nature is thereby excited, which respects the discoverer himself; and that is an honest indignation of the perjury he has committed. For if this person, scrupulously conscientious as he is represented, was actually under the oath he pretends, however trifling and insignificant the thing itself might be; yet, in the opinion of the most eminent casuists, he was obliged to keep his oath; the respect due to truth and falsehood being the same in trivial matters as in those of greater importance; otherwise God must be invoked as witness to a lie‡.

---

*   1 Kings vii. 21.
†   Vide Scots Mag. 1755. P. 133.
‡   Saunderson, de obl. jur. prael. 3. § 15.

But, if Ignorance or Imbecility, deluded by hypocritical Sanctity, or head-strong Zeal, can afford any alleviation, (for an absolute acquittance it cannot) the charge must fall with redoubled weight upon those who induced him, and would induce others, over whom this influence extends, to put such an affront upon the honour of God, and to habituate themselves to the practice of Insincerity and Injustice towards man. Is not this to adopt the practices and opinions of their religious predecessors, in Hypocrisy, Sedition, and Rebellion? who held, That

Oaths were not purpos'd, more than Law,
To keep the good and just in awe;
But to confine the bad and sinful,
Like moral cattle, in a pinfold. *Butler.*[23]

The natural curiosity of mankind, always eager and impetuous in the pursuit of knowledge, / when disappointed of a rational account of things, is apt to rest upon conjecture, and often embraces a cloud in place of the Goddess of Truth. So has it fared with the Secrets of MASONRY. That Society, tho' venerable for its antiquity, and respectable for its good behaviour, has, thro' falsehood and misrepresentation, groundlessly awakened the jealousy of states, and the obloquy of malicious tongues. Their Silence and Secrecy, as they gave ample room for the most extravagant conjectures, so they likewise afforded an opportunity for the grossest imputations, without fear of a refutation. They have been traduced as Atheists and Blasphemers, branded as Idolaters, and ridiculed as the dupes of nonsense. The hard names liberally bestowed on their Secrets by the Seceders, partake of all these*; but their proof relates only to the last: and indeed, it seems rather like the delirious ravings of a brain sick head, inflamed with the fumes of Enthusiasm,[24] than a rational design to expose them. Its publication is an affront upon the judgment of the world; no less than inserting it in the Scots MAGA-ZINE, is an impeachment upon the taste of the Readers of that collection.

To remove such prejudices, and in some degree to satisfy the world and inquisitive cavillers, MASONS have condescended to publish what opinions they maintained, with respect to the great principles of human action. Their Belief in / GOD is founded upon the justest notion of his Being and Attributes, drawn from the Light of Nature assisted by Revelation. They never enter into the speculative regions, so much cultivated by Divines: What cannot be comprehended in his nature, they leave as incomprehensible. They adore his Infinite Being, and reckon it the perfection of mankind to imitate his communicable perfections. Their duty to their Superiors, to their neighbours, and to themselves, are all expressed in a manner the most agreeable to the foundest morality.

---

*   Vid. Scots Magazine 1755. p. 137.

And when their actions and behaviour, which alone are subject to human obser-vation, and affect human society, are conformable to such principles, no power on earth has a right to enquire farther.

The FREE MASON professes a particular regard to the liberal Arts; and he makes no scruple to own, that many of his secrets have a reference to them. From these, just notions of order and proportion are attained, and a true taste of symmetry and beauty

is formed. And as the transition from the beauties of the natural to those of the moral species are so easy and apparent; if there is any virtue, if there is any praise, instead of slander and defamation, protection and encouragement ought to be his reward. Men of the greatest power and dignity, the divine and the philosopher, have not been ashamed, in all ages, to own their relation to this / Society, and to encourage and protect it by their power and influence. But, should this combination terminate in nothing but wickedness and folly, can it be imagined, either that men of honour, wisdom, and integrity, would lend their countenance to fraud, and encourage folly, merely to make the world stare? or that an assocation, resting on so unstable a foundation, could so long have sub-sisted, without the cement of mutual trust and confidence, which result from virtue and consistency alone?

The FREE MASON, conscious of his integrity, and persuaded of the good tendency of his principles to promote the purposes of Virtue and human Hap-piness, beholds with contempt the impotent efforts of Envy and Ignorance, however sanctified the garb, or dignified the title they may assume. In his LODGE, which he considers as the School of Justice, Love, and Benevolence, he is taught to oppose Truth to Misrepresentation, good Humour and innocent Mirth to Sourness and Grimace, the certain signs of Malice and Imposture. – To attend the importunate calls of his enemies, would be to interrupt his tranquil-lity; and therefore, wrapt in his own innocence, he despises their impotent attacks, and for the future will disdain to enter the lists with champions so weak and ignorant, so deluded and deluding.

Edin. Oct. 25.[25]   R.A.   M.T.L.[26]
1757.

RICHARD LEWIS, *THE FREE-MASONS ADVOCATE. OR, FALSEHOOD DETECTED* (1760)

Richard Lewis, corrector of the press. *The Free-Masons Advocate. Or, Falsehood Detected. being a Full Refutation of a Scandalous Libel, Entitled, A Master-Key to Free-Masonry. with a Defence of the Brotherhood and the Craft, against all the Calumnies and Aspersions, that ever have been, or can be Thrown on them, by the Weakness of some, and the Wickedness of Others. by Richard Lewis. Corrector of the Press* (Dublin: printed for J. Hunter and sold by all the booksellers, 1760).[1]

The author of this apology was Richard Lewis, who was a bookseller, press collector and author. According to his own account in 1787, he was born in England and lived there for thirty-three years. Around 1754 he moved to Ireland and regarded himself as an Anglo-Irishman. Apart from writing poems and revising works for the press he translated French and Latin.[2] In the pamphlet he claims that he read the *Ahiman Rezon* rather than any of the revised editions of James Anderson's *Constitutions*, from which we may infer that the author belonged to the Antients and/or the Grand Lodge of Ireland.[3]

On the surface the purpose of this pamphlet is to demolish the authenticity of a masonic ritual exposure entitled *A Master-Key to Free-Masonry* (1760), the first edition of which is reproduced in volume 2. As Jan Snoek notes in his headnote, *A Master-Key to Free-Masonry* exposure, being the first English one in the 1760s, was a shortened and free translation of French exposures, in particular *L'Ordre des Francs-Maçons Trahi* [The Order of Free Masons Betrayed] of 1745. All the sections of the former can be found together in the latter in the same order. As the early French rituals were created by English Freemasons who established the first lodges in France from 1726 onwards, *A Master-Key to Free-Masonry* must fairly represent the English rituals of the period. In masonic historiography, this ritual is regarded as the earliest English publication which contains an important alteration in the ceremony made around 1739, that is, the reversal of the first and second degree words (Jachin and Boaz), in order to exclude 'imposters' from the lodges.[4] However, as Jan Snoek points out, there is no evidence for this statement made by the Premier Grand Lodge in 1809.

It is clear from Lewis's page references to the text of *A Master-Key to Free-Masonry* that the author had the second edition of the exposure in his hand, which apart from the pagination is identical to the first edition.

When interpreting the real purpose and arguments of Lewis's work, we need to consider the following. *A Master-Key to Free-Masonry* 'introduced the much more descriptive style of the French "exposures"',[5] which had been unknown to English and Irish Freemasons before.[6] It is possible that the Irish rituals of 1760 could greatly differ from the English and French rituals of the early 1740s, which is also suggested by the members of the Antients Grand Lodge.[7] *A Master-Key to Free-Masonry* contains some translation errors of typical French masonic jargon (e.g. 'Assistants' for 'Wardens', 'profane' for the non-initiated or 'touch' for the 'grip'), which must have been disturbing for the masonic readers in the British Isles. From these mistakes, Lewis seemed to come to the conclusion that the ritual was not authentic and regarded it as a 'scandalous libel', without realizing that it was merely a pseudo-exposure. To strengthen his argument, he dedicated his tract to Charles Moore, the Earl of Drogheda, who was Grand Master of Ireland between 1758 and 1760.

However, we cannot exclude the possibility that, like the masonic authors of most 'exposures' of the era, Lewis was playing a game with the readers in this apologetic writing. In other words he was aware that *A Master-Key to Free-Masonry* mirrored, at least partially, contemporary masonic ritual practice.[8] Therefore, his real objective was to mislead the public so that they should not know the real 'secrets' of the brotherhood.[9] That is one of the reasons why his apparent target audience was not Freemasons who could judge the authenticity of the exposure in question but "some honest, yet mistaken men, who, not belonging to the Craft, cannot be so assured of its excellency as its Brethren are".[10] To achieve his goal, he considerably exaggerated the inconsistencies and contradictions, as well as the criticisms of Freemasonry found in the exposure. As Thorp correctly argues,

> the author of *A Master-Key to Free-Masonry* has nothing to say against the Order; he may think it silly and childish, but he candidly confesses that there is much in it that is admirable, and defends it vigorously against the unjust attacks of calumniators.[11]

Such tricky argumentation was typical of the pseudo-exposures that were actually rituals published by and for Freemasons.

As he translated French works, he must have realized that the 'translation errors' of the exposure were systematic and clearly reflected French usage. However, belonging to the Antient/Irish tradition, he may well also have disliked *A Master-Key to Free-Masonry*, which was closer to the ritual of the Moderns.

Lewis's pamphlet can be compared to an anonymous refutation of the *Jachin and Boaz* (1762) exposure, which contained parts from the text of *A Master-*

Key. It was published in London under the following title: *A Free-Mason's Answer to the Suspected Author of a Pamphlet, Entitled, Jachin and Boaz; or, an Authentic Key to Free-masonry. Addressed to All Masons, as well as to the Public in General* (London: printed for J. Cooke, at Shakespeare's-Head, in Pater-Noster-Row, 1762).

The pamphlet was published by James Hunter, who was a printer and bookseller in Dublin 'in Sycamore Alley' between 1760 and 1788.[12] This work was one of his earliest publications.

This pamphlet is a rarity. Only two copies are known to exist: one in the Library of St Patrick College, Maynooth, and the other in the Library and Museum of Freemasonry in London. The following reproduction is based on the latter.

Notes

1. This headnote was written by Róbert Péter.
2. M. Pollard, *A Dictionary of Members of the Dublin Book Trade 1550-1800* (Oxford: Oxford University Press, 2000), pp. 365–6.
3. Two years before the publication of Lewis's defence, the Grand Lodge of Ireland ceased to have fraternal communications with the original Grand Lodge of England – dubbed 'Moderns' – and formally acknowledged the rival Antients Grand Lodge as the one and only grand lodge in England. *Schism*, p. 6.
4. J. T. Thorp, *A Master-Key to Free-Masonry, 1760. Masonic Reprints*, Vol. 8 (Leicester: Johnson, Wykes & Paine, 1925), p. 9.
5. See the headnote of *A Master-Key to Free-Masonry* in volume 2.
6. I am grateful to Jan Snoek for his assistance in contextualizing Lewis's claims about masonic rituals. Jan Snoek, email correspondence (2 May 2014).
7. The argument of the Antients is difficult to prove due to the lack of original Irish rituals from this period.
8. As Snoek notes in his headnote, the author of *A Master-Key* omitted some information about the third degree that can be found in the *L'Ordre des Francs-Maçons Trahi*. See vol. 2, p. 45.
9. This strategy was used by the author of *A Defence of Masonry* (1730), which was a response to the *Masonry Dissected* (1730). Andrew Prescott argues that the authorship of the former was incorrectly attributed to Martin Clare (1688–1751). *MMLDP*, vol. 1, pp. 808–16.
10. Another motivation for addressing the book to outsiders could be to reach the widest audience – being a bookseller, Lewis wanted to make a profit.
11. Thorp, *A Master-Key to Free-Masonry*, p. 10.
12. H. R. Plomer, G. H. Bushnell and McC. Dix (eds), *A Dictionary of the Printers and Booksellers who were at Work in England, Scotland and Ireland from 1726 to 1775* (n. p.: Oxford University Press for the Bibliographical Society 1932), p. 390.

Richard Lewis, *The Free-Masons Advocate. Or, Falsehood Detected* (1760)

...

THE

FREE-MASONS

ADVOCATE.

OR,

FALSEHOOD DETECTED.

BEING

A full REFUTATION of a scandalous LIBEL,

ENTITLED,

A MASTER-KEY to FREE-MASONRY.

WITH

A Defence of the BROTHERHOOD and the CRAFT, against all the CALUMNIES and ASPERSIONS, that ever *have* been, or *can* be thrown on them, by the Weakness of some, and the Wickedness of others.

By RICHARD LEWIS.

CORRECTOR of the PRESS.

He that is first in his own Cause seemeth just; but his Neighbour cometh and searcheth him. Proverbs xviii. 17.

A false Witness shall not be unpunished; and he that speaketh Lies shall not escape. Prov. xix. 5.

DUBLIN:

Printed for J. HUNTER, in *Sycamore-alley*. And sold

by all the Booksellers.

M,DCC,LX. /

TO THE
Right Honourable and Right Worshipful,
THE
EARL of *Drogheda.*

My Lord!

THE honourable Title you bear, of Grand-Master of the Worshipful Fraternity of Free and Accepted Masons in Ireland, naturally points you out as their great Advocate, as well as the proper Patron of those who engage in the same generous Cause: And I doubt not, but it would be thought as great an Impropriety, to dedicate a System of Divinity to a Lawyer, a Casuistical Essay to a Lady, or a Military Treatise to a Bishop, as to consecrate a Defence of Masonry at any other Shrine than your Lordship's. Yet, I must own, that if your Lordship had nothing but the mere Title, to cause you to be / considered as the Friend of Truth and Masonry, I had not once thought of inscribing my small Piece to your Lordship, or have sollicited the Lord, if I could not have found the Man. But when in the Earl of DROGHEDA, I view Greatness with Humanity, Judgment with Candor, and public Spirit with private Virtue, then all Doubt gives Way to Certainty, and Timidity flies before Resolution.

I am,

My Lord,

With the greatest Respect,

Your Lordship's

Most humble, and

Most obedient Servant,

Dublin, March
20, 1760.

R. LEWIS. /

THE

FREE-MASONS

ADVOCATE.

IT is a too melancholy truth, observed by moralists, and confirmed by expe-rience, that, such is the depravity of human nature, it more delights in giving pain, than administering pleasure. It hears with rapture, and devours with avid-ity, those insidious tales, which, begot by iniquity, and nursed by falshood, come flying on the wings of scandal. – But this must be understood only / of human nature, in its depraved, not its exalted, state.

It is observable, that low minds, never attempt to correct their natural deprav-ity, but still brood in one continued state of supine indolence, and unpardonable neglect. Like untilled soil, which without wholesome manure, only produces fertile crops of noxious weeds, they spontaneously shoot forth the blossoms of original depravation, which, in time, ripen to the baneful fruits of iniquity.

Perhaps, the best reason that can be assigned for the sin of omission, which too many are guilty of, in not duly cultivating their rational faculties, is the truest; – lest by rousing their sleeping powers, from a state of lazy apathy, they should forego the dear delights of happy ignorance and soothing dullness, and deprive themselves of those exquisite pleasures they taste in detraction: for it may be laid / down as self-evident, that enlarged minds, and noble souls, so far from reaping the least satisfaction, in degrading the excellencies of others, are ever studious of calling forth merit from the shade of retirement, to the glorious theatre of action; and taste more solid, more home-felt joy in displaying latent virtues, than in ransacking, with villainous industry, the human frame, for the discovery of vices.

When viewing superior abilities, the minds of these, glow with generous emulation; but those, on the contrary, do not attempt to rise to the perfections of others, but to bring others down to a level with themselves.

From hence it arises, that when falshood plans, and wickedness propagates, any malicious report, to the disadvantage of individuals or a society, there are never wanting a number / of ignorant, credulous people, who listen with the utmost attention, to the artful, pleasing tale. Nor is this to be wondered at. The pleasures of kindred minds are always mutual; and since knaves and fools compose three fourths of the world, it is not surprising, that at the propagation of wickedness, or folly, three fourths of the world should be highly pleased.

Did mankind indeed, act up to the dignity of their cultivated natures, they would feel no joy in deceiving or being deceived; in propagating scandal, or listening to it; in writing libels, or reading them. But as the case is quite the reverse; as vice erects its head, and falshood reigns triumphant; as virtue is near expiring, and religion, standing on tiptoe, is ready to wing its flight; I apprehend it to be a duty incumbent on every one, to detect the former, and defend the latter. /

If this opinion of mine be just, it will not appear strange, that I should take upon me to vindicate the noble art of Free-Masonry, against all the calumnies and objections, that ever have been, or can be thrown on it; and expose the malignity of a certain writer, who, in a late libellous pamphlet, attempts, not only to cast an odium on its professors, but, like the practice of infidels in their tracts against the clergy, to bring the profession itself into contempt.

And let not this be deemed an useless, or unnecessary work. It is of more service than it may at first sight appear to be. For though I would advise the Brotherhood, to regard their feeble, snarling adversaries, with the same silent indignation, and noble scorn, as the generous horse surveys the yelping cur at his heels; yet as there may be some honest, yet mistaken men, who, not belonging to the Craft, / cannot be so assured of its excellency as its Brethren are, it may be proper to inform such of the real intention of Free-Masonry, instead of suffering them to be misled by the defective and erroneous accounts given of it by many writers. Such a work, will at the same time demonstrate, that it is worthy that best of monarchs, who now reigns over a free and united people, and, who being a Free-Mason,[1] and convinced of its utility, honours and loves the Craft, and who reflects honour on the profession, as the profession reflects honour on so great and good a king.

Another reason for my undertaking the present performance, is a thorough conviction of the great excellence of Free-Masonry; the principles it teaches, tending to the glory of GOD, and the good of mankind. Were any of its tenets repugnant to the interests of religion or virtue, so far from engaging in its defence, I would / employ my small powers against it. But since I am confident of the reverse; since I am certain both of its tendency and efficacy, in mending the morals, informing the judgment, and refining the taste, it were unpardonable to suffer the pen to sleep in inactivity, when it might be employed in vindicating truth and worth, confuting error, and scourging falshood.

I know indeed, some weak Brothers, who, on first hearing that an answer was to be given to the Master-Key, without once reflecting seriously on the subject, have confidently pronounced it to be needless; and yet these very men have allowed, as indeed every Mason must allow, that it is replete with error, calumny, and falshood. For my part, I always thought, error, calumny and falshood, deserved to be exposed; and that the fully shewing them in their true lights, was the only way to impede their progress, and prevent their / influence. Let it be considered too, that when insects only buzz, to regard them were ridiculous; but when they attempt to sting, it is fit they should be crushed.

Such are my reasons for this essay, which, I doubt not, will be thought cogent by those with whom it is an honour to coincide in sentiments. I am indeed, not a little sorry, that I am to enter the lists with such contemptible antagonists; to combat with whom is no honour, and to conquer whom no victory; yet I ought to reflect, that to rout an army of deers, may become him, who is unable to beard the lion.

The author of the Master-Key, as he calls it, (though by the bye, it is but a very bungling one,) has even in his title page, given his readers a specimen of what they are to expect, and has not scrupled to assert the most notorious falsities, and the most palpable / contradictions: falsities so evident, that even those that are not Masons, may be capable of discovering them; and contradictions so manifest, that the most illiterate reader must discern them.

He says, that the Master-Key lays open all the secrets of the society; and that the public may depend upon its being a genuine account of their whole secrets. He assures them, that he has given an accurate account of the examination of the Apprentice, Fellow-Craft, and Master; and declares, that by virtue of such account, a person (that is not a Free-Mason, I suppose he means,) may gain admittance into a Lodge.

Agreeable to this representation, and consistent with this conduct, is his motto chosen. I would be the last man in the world, to cavil at trifling inaccuracies proceeding from a weakness of judgment; but when I view / glaring falshoods proceeding from a depravity of heart boldly asserted, I would be the first to detect them. His motto is a quotation –

– 'Your secrets, Sirs, will rise, Though all the earth o'erwhelm them, to mens' eyes.'[2]

Now I would fain know, what connection this motto has to his work, or how he proves the verity of the assertion? If the assertion be false, he must be a very weak man to introduce it: if it be true, what occasion was there for his taking so much pains, to write so many pages of unintelligible jargon? But,

Let us now enquire into the veracity of his several other assertions; bring them to the touch-stone of a due examination; and see, how far they are conformable to truth, and consistent with his own relation in other places. /

The difficulty of writing on a subject like the present, wherein I am not warranted to confute the anonymous writer, by irrefragable[3] arguments drawn from facts in Free-Masonry, and displaying those facts to the eyes of the world, is very visible; and will at the same time, prove the more eligible method I shall take, in condemning him from his own mouth.

And first, let us see, whether according to his own account, he has fulfilled in his book what he has promised in its title-page; when he assures the public, that his Master-Key unlocks all the mysteries of the society, and discloses their whole secrets.

And that he has not, appears in his 17th page, where he says; 'that when a candidate is admitted a Mason, the speaker, after telling him in general terms, that the society admits of nothing contrary to / law, religion or morality, adds, that the Grand-Master will tell him the rest.'[4]

If this representation be just, for I shall argue from his own assertions, and that there are more secrets to be learnt from the Grand-Master, as is implied by the word rest, why does not this writer inform us, what the rest of those secrets are? – If he does not inform us of these, and that he does not is very evident, how are all the secrets of the society disclosed?

Further; in page 24th, he says, 'that the reception of a Master is little more than a ceremony; scarce any thing new being learned at it.'[5] Supposing what is learnt ever so little, yet, as he acknowledges something new is learnt, if he does not communicate these additional secrets, he has not revealed them all.

But in his 26th page, he undermines / his own credibility in the most express terms possible. There he says, 'tis unnecessary to enter into a longer detail concerning the subjects, upon which the instructions or conversations of the Free-Masons generally turn; they are generally much of the same nature with those I have just mentioned.'[6]

If it was indeed unnecessary to enter into a longer detail, why did he promise to reveal all the secrets of the society? And how could he perform his promise, without entering into such longer detail? If likewise, he supposed the secrets were of the same nature with those he had revealed, why did he not mention them, that his readers might be enabled to judge whether they really were so or not? And how has he discharged his engagement to disclose all the secrets of the Craft, when he confesses, that he could reveal more, and enter into a longer detail, but that he conceived it unnecessary? /

Let us now see in other particulars, how the assertions of this writer correspond; and from thence learn, what degree of credit may be given to the assurances of a person, who declares, that every thing he says, is true; and that his pamphlet is a genuine account, of the whole secrets, &c.

In page 2nd, he declares, 'that whoever is invested with the dignity of Grand-Master,[7] is always stiled Right Worshipful;'[8] yet in pages 17, 18, 19, 25, 26, 29 and 30, in his imaginary descriptions, he makes his imaginary Free-Masons address him without the title of Right Worshipful.

So likewise, in his 4th page, he says, 'that when a Brother is fined, the fine must be paid directly, and is always set apart to relieve the poor.'[9] This assertion he iterates in his 28th page, saying, 'it is always applied / to the relief of the poor.'[10] And immediately after he pronounces, 'this has been always the practice among Free-Masons.'[11] One would imagine from these positive assertions, that the fact represented was true; or, at least, that the writer believed it to be so: but that he is absolutely assured of the contrary, is plain by his declaring, in the very next sentence, (page 28,) that 'some keep the Money to spend it in merry meetings.'[12]

Contradictions not less flagrant than these, are, that in his 10th page, he affects to speak well of the Fraternity, and says, 'that they are very reserved with regard to women; for in their assemblies, as well solemn as particular, they speak of them in very decent and concise terms; and that decency and sobriety, are always observed at their entertainments.'[13]

So in his 27th page, he observes, 'that the pleasures they enjoy, have / nothing of an impure nature in them: that there is nothing but what is perfectly innocent and harmless, in the conversations which they hold at their assemblies; and that the purity of their sentiments, distinguishes them from all others.'[14]

From these accounts, might it not be inferred, that the writer had not so mean an opinion of Free-Masonry, as he has elsewhere declared, himself to have? He has, 'tis true, in those places, done justice to the conduct of the Brethren; but to meet the applause of such writers, is, in effect, to be satirized with praise.

But let us observe, whether this favourable account of Free-Masons, was dictated by truth and sincerity, or the product only of carelessness and ignorance.

And that he is equally regardless of censure and praise, and considers himself / under no obligation to adhere to justice, or take truth for his guide, appears in pages 27 and 28, where he falsifies every thing he had before advanced. He does not say there, that the Free-Masons pleasures are of a pure nature; that their conversations are perfectly innocent, and even their sentiments chaste; but intrepidly asserts, 'that they think they may dispense with the laws of decency, and indulge themselves in the greatest obscenity.'[15]

Consistent with these flagrant contradictions, and iniquitous behaviour, is his assurance in page 25, 'that the Masters have no words to distinguish them from the Fellow-Crafts.'[16] But forgetting this assertion by the time he had scribbled nineteen pages further, which indeed, I don't wonder at, as such writers have generally bad memories, whereas, according to the trite proverb, 'they ought to have good ones;'[17] in page 44th, he / roundly asserts, 'that the Masters have not only a word, but a touch and a sign, peculiar to themselves.'[18]

Such are the blunders and inconsistencies which this anonymous writer has run into; and the accounts he has given of Free-Masonry, are not less ridiculous than his contradictions are unpardonable. I don't at all wonder that he has put invention to the stretch to describe what never existed, because it was impossible for him to describe what Masonry truly is, and he himself owns in his dedication, that he is not a Free-Mason;[19] yet he surely might have been uniform in his descriptions, and consistent with himself; but by the few contradictions I have proved in him, it will appear that even in falshood he has not been so. I would willingly point out his several other absurdities, but it would be an endless work, for almost every page abounds with them. /

His notion of Free-Masonry seems to me, to partake of the nature of Don Quixote's notion of giants, when he imagined a wind-mill to be one of those huge beings; or rather, like the blind-man's idea of colours, who conceived scarlet to be like the sound of a trumpet – In short, as the song says, he thinks that Free-Masonry,

'Is this, and is that, and he cannot tell what;'

And in consequence of such his opinion, he has given one of the strangest representations, and unaccountable pictures, that ever was drawn by any man. He may comfort himself, however, with this reflection, that he has not been guilty of a breach of the second commandment; for his description resembles neither any thing in heaven above, the earth beneath, or waters under the earth. /

From the several falshoods I have proved in this writer, even from his own words, may I not exclaim? – 'Out of thine own mouth will I condemn thee, thou wicked liar!'[20] And may not those, who are not so convinced of the falsity of his descriptions of Free-Masonry, as all the Brethren are, draw these just and natural inferences? That a Man who is capable of imposing on the world in some respects, is so in others? And that where there are abundance of known errors, it may be concluded, there are a great many latent ones, which yet, none but those that understand the subject can possibly discover? – In a word, the whole intent of this bungling performance, seems to me to be no other, than to draw the money out of the pockets of those, who have more curiosity than prudence, and more money than wit.

But as there is no sect without its followers, nor any doctrine without its / admirers, so there can be no report or description, how absurd or ridiculous soever, but will find some people credulous enough to believe it. I should not therefore be surprized, that those of weak heads and bad hearts, should, from the mere Ipse Dixits[21] of an anonymous writer, ashamed to set his name to his falshoods, entertain a mean idea of Free-Masonry. It is true, indeed, that the smallest reflection would shew them the inconsistency of such a conduct; but if we attend to the characters of such I have been describing, we shall find, they will not take the trouble of enquiring into the verity of any report, lest such enquiry, by shewing them the folly of their credulity, should also arraign them for their ignorance, and deprive them of the pleasure they take in possessing both.

Such persons as these, who, I will venture to affirm, are the only ones that think ill of Masonry, are always / more ready to believe what is to the disadvantage, than to the advantage of any one: but let us observe, that this very circumstance, reflects no small honour on Free-Masons, and no inconsiderable lustre on their Art; for to meet the censure of such, is to merit the esteem of the virtuous and intelligent.

Having sufficiently refuted the accounts given of Masonry, by the Author of the Master-Key; detected some notorious falshoods, by making him turn evidence against himself; and proved him to be as bad a writer as he is a man; I shall now endeavour to perform what I have promised in my Title-page; – defend the Brotherhood and the Craft, against all the calumnies and aspersions, that ever have been, or can be thrown on them, by the weakness of some, and the wickedness of others. /

It must be observed, that the author of the Master-Key, is not the only person that has wrote against Free-Masonry. Numbers have drawn their quills on the same subject; and have treated the subject much in the same manner. I know not to which of those treatises to give the preference; but think they are all equally entertaining, equally instructive, and what is still more, equally romantic. The reason of their thus employing their pens, (I will not say their abilities, for I can see none in any of them) on a topic they are all equally qualified for, is not so mysterious as the topic itself. Nay, I think it must be evident to every one; for, alas! if they do not write, they must not eat.

Among these several Quixotes in authorship, one only has been hardy enough to appear in propria persona,[22] by inserting his name in the title-page. Samuel Prichard[23] as much adorns the / title of Masonry Dissected, as the bloom-creating Rouge adorns the countenance of miss Wishfor't,[24] or the evidence of Jack Hackney,[25] the famous, or rather, infamous knight of the post, preponderates the ballanced scales of even-handed justice.

But though it is certain, that the artifices of the enemies to Masonry, have been ineffectual, and they have been unable with their feeble armour to penetrate its celestial shield; yet let us not be so bigotted, as to affirm, that the efforts of its advocates have always been successful.

Perfection is not the lot of mortality. In all professions, in all callings, in all trades, there are some unworthy members. Perhaps Masonry has as many as any other; nor is it surprizing; for it has twenty times more members than any profession, trade, or calling whatever. /

Yet as weak men, and bad members, are frequently the strongest advocates for the honour of their several callings, (as the most abandoned outlaw, is frequently the greatest stickler for his country's superiority,) it has happened, that when Masonry has been attacked with the blunted spears of pale-eyed malice, or conscious dulness, it has been defended, with all the impotence of disappointed rage, or with the more ponderous armour of conceited ignorance. Thus have men sometimes betrayed the cause they should have defended; and thus the ignorant, furious zealot, is discovered from the rational, sober advocate.

Now though I have admitted, there are as great a number of unworthy members in Masonry, as in any other profession; yet this is by no means, an argument against Masonry itself. It has been a known / maxim, and is now become a trite expression, that the abuse of any thing proves not its inutility; and it is as certain, that an honourable profession, receives no disgrace from the ignorance, or wickedness of its professors. There is no profession, perhaps, that has more unworthy members than religion. While they tear and divide the world, with their nonsensical disputes; this church contending for a multiplicity of Gods, and the other, that there is but one Supreme; this man insisting, that no person can perform a good action, and that our virtues require forgiveness; and that, that no one can act either virtuously or viciously, all our actions being foreknown, and in consequence of such fore-knowledge, bound fast in fate; yet let us not conclude, that therefore, religion is itself useless, or the functions of its professors contemptible. /

If the design, indeed, of religion, were to set its members together by the ears, and pilot them to destruction, instead of being the chart to guide them to happiness; or the office of its ministers to deal forth damnation, and brand as heretics, all those whose mental optics do not view objects in the same light with themselves; then indeed, we might reasonably detest the one, and despise the other.

But since its intention is quite different; since religion is the only cordial to a drooping, despairing soul, and all its ways are peace; and since the office of its professors, is to administer that sovereign balsam, which all the cobweb systems of the heathen could not dispense; let us thankfully receive the one in its purity, and honour and revere the other, when they prove worthy that reverence and honour. /

This comparison, and these reflections, may be looked on by some, as foreign to my subject; but those who are acquainted with the principles Free-Masonry teaches, know better. Religion and Masonry have a close connection with each other.[26] There is nothing in the former that the latter disproves: so far from it, it strengthens and confirms every thing that the other advances. As satire then, may be justly considered as a wholesome supplement to law, so Masonry may be looked on as a wholesome supplement to religion. In this light, which, I am convinced, is a just one, how amiable does it appear! how worthy the reception and practice of mankind! and what an honour does it reflect, on those who bear its title, if their title and practice correspond!

As it is then with religion, so is it with Free-Masonry. No function can be more honourable than that of a / clergyman; no character more venerable than that of a worthy clergyman. Yet, if it should unhappily be found, that among the clergy, two parts in five should prove faithless shepherds; are we on that account, to entertain a bad opinion of the remaining three parts? Or, are we to look on the profession as useless, if its professors do not live up to its rules?

In like manner, we are not to despise good Masons, if in so numerous a body, we should discover some bad ones: nor are we to imagine, when we see such, that Free-Masonry is the cause of their being so. The principles which Masonry teaches, are laudable, are just, are noble; and it is not improbable, that those bad men who belong to the Fraternity, would have been much worse if they had not belonged to it.

Was there any thing in Free-Masonry injurious to religion or morality, / we may rest assured, it would not have been patronized by the greatest and wisest men in all ages. Nay, not to content ourselves with giving it this negative kind of excellence, we may go further, and boldly assert, because it is strictly true; that had not the principles it inculcated, and the precepts it taught, been of the highest service to the community in general, emperors and monarchs would not have suffered it in their dominions, nor have walked in its train. And if it was not eminently serviceable to the great and glorious cause of religion, archbishops and bishops would not have belonged to the Fraternity, nor recommend it in their discourses. But since Masonry is both a supplement to religion, and an aid to virtue, it is no wonder that it should have the friends of religion and virtue for its ablest advocates, and be transmitted down from age to age with increasing lustre; for the wiser and better mankind / are, so much higher do they hold it in estimation.

It is no small evidence of the intrinsic excellence of Free-Masonry, that time in its recording tablets, does not produce an instance of any real Mason having been the promoter of, or assistant in, any insidious plots against the government under whose protection he lived. This may be looked on as a bold assertion, or a strange truth; yet if considered seriously, will appear to be neither. It is not a bold assertion, because it is an uncontrovertible fact: it is not a strange truth, because from the principles taught by Masonry, and solemnly enforced to its Brethren, nothing less could be expected.

Every Mason, is, in the true sense of the word, a Christian; and if a man arrogates the Title of Mason, without having the principles and practice of a Christian, I boldly pronounce / that man is not a Mason. He may indeed, be looked on as such by those who are ignorant of the design and extent of Masonry; and who may falsely imagine, that to pass through a few matters of form, and to have a pretty knack at answering a few common-place questions, constitute a Mason. But such are egregiously mistaken. Free-Masonry has a deeper design than their narrow capacities can fathom; and its extent is more unlimited than their feeble optics can discern.

He whose soul, borne on the wings of genius, can emerge from the dark cavern wherein it is immured, and soar to the illimitable sphere; whose mind greatly eminent, and incomprehensibly capacious, can, of the works of the Deity, see how confusion is order; chance, direction; discord, harmony; and partial evil, universal good; may be a Free-Mason: but he whose soul is low and groveling; whose understanding / is mean and superficial; and whose actions are iniquitous and base; cannot be made a real Mason by all the Lodges in the world.

'Tis in vain for useless forms, and idle ceremonies, to be passed through and observed, if the life and soul of Masonry be disregarded. Nor let the pretended, nominal Mason, boast the title, if he lives not the man. A parrot might be taught to answer questions by rote; but 'tis the mind's eye that must discern their meaning, and the heart's conviction that must influence the practice.

We see multitudes in the world, that assume the name of Christians, and who would take it as a great affront to be called infidels: but things, not names, we ought to prize; and the nominal christian that lives the heathen, is an infidel in Deed.

So we see numbers who glory in the / title of Free-Masons, but who are not such in reality. Unhappy fools! to suppose that Masonry resides in mere sound; and that religion and morality are empty names!

If we should denominate gold, iron, our mistake would not change the thing itself; and if we should nickname religion, bigottry, it would not alter its quality. Religion, like virtue, is a substantial good; and though the opinions of mankind differ much in regard to both, yet they both remain invariably the same, and will bestow immortal rewards on their friends.

I doubt not but many of my readers are surprized at finding Free-Masonry considered in this strange, yet true Light. A strange light I may well call it, since all the books which I have ever read on the subject, excepting only a judicious one, entitled, Ahiman Reson,[27] contain nothing more / than wretched accounts of the designing and erecting of temples, pyramids, castles, palaces, theatres, monuments, bridges, and a long string of &c. equally ridiculous; and all this Persiflage, delivered with a poverty of style, and inanity of sentiment, that would disgrace a school-boy. And a true light I am authorized to call it, since experience has fully evinced, that such is its force and virtue, the learned and pious grow wiser and better by its precepts; the brave, more heroic; and the benevolent, more humane.

I am aware that this last assertion may create surprize, and require evidence. Lawful evidence I am ready to give: farther ought not to be demanded. As religion (for the parallel holds in every respect,) has its mysteries, so has Free-Masonry. The former are incomprehensible; the latter, inscrutable. The former can only be understood, when, divested of our corporeal / forms, our beings are suited to receive them: the latter can only be known, when we are regularly made Masons, and admitted into a constituted Lodge, there to learn the secrets of the Craft. To know either these celestial, or terrestrial mysteries before we are duly prepared, would be highly improper; and therefore, the Deity has wisely concealed the one, and the universal practice of all Lodges, the other.

But notwithstanding I profess myself a great lover of Free-Masonry in its purity, yet I must confess, that, like all other good things, it has been vilely abused. Now, though our places of public worship, are open for the male and female, the sinner and the saint, the old and young, rich and poor, wise and otherwise; yet I see not, why this should be the case with Masonry. The abandoned miscreant, the thoughtless coxcomb, and the illiterate blockhead, ought never to enter / a Lodge: but according to the abused state of Masonry now prevailing, we find all three admitted; and, perhaps, it were not hazardous to assert, that in many Lodges, these characters form the majority. Nay, so very ill conducted are some of them, that they admit fools and asses who can neither read nor write, and whose understandings are so prodigiously shallow, that they can talk on no one subject. Such a perversion of Free-Masonry, tends more to discredit it, than the open hostilities, and close-contrived artifices of all its enemies in the world.

As it is with kingdoms, so is it, generally speaking, with societies. There is no foe so dangerous to a commonwealth as a domestic foe; and the worst enemy a society can have, is a corrupted member. It should, therefore, be the care of government, to restrain the natural licentiousness and impetuosity of human / nature within their proper bounds, and make mankind amenable to those laws, enacted both for the well-being and dignity of a state, and for the ease and happiness of a people. And it should be the care of every head of a society, to frame such rules and orders, as observed, reflect honour on their institution, and give felicity to its members.

But in vain are wise laws enacted, and excellent orders framed, if the judgment and vigilance of magistracy, do not correspond with the intention of the legislature. As the strings of two violins, wound up to an equal pitch, vibrate responsive to each other's note; so ought also the legislative and the executive power, to agree in harmony, and act in concert.

The body politic, and the body natural,[28] bear so close an analogy in their several operations, as well as those distinct bodies in the community, under / the denomination of lesser societies, that it were no unpleasing talk to run the parallel throughout. Nor would it be entirely useless; since from the methods we take to preserve the one in health and vigour, we should likewise learn how to manage and dispose the other. – But here, Apollo[29] plucks me by the ear, and bids presumption give way to modesty, and inclination submit to prudence. Perhaps, however, at some future time, and in a proper place, some hints may be thrown out, as, improved by men of more judgment, and greater experience, may tend to the honour of the Craft, and the good of the Brethren.

FINIS. /

TO THE
NOBILITY AND GENTRY.

AS there are many *Ladies* and *Gentlemen*, of sound Judgment and fine Sentiments, who are, nevertheless, at a Loss to display the one, or express the other, before the awful Tribunal of the Public; the Author of this Piece begs Leave to acquaint them, that he will, on a proper Application, write Original Pieces, in Verse or Prose, and correct *for* and *at* Press, any Pamphlet, Essay, or Petition, that may be of public or private Utility.

Letters directed to Mr. Lewis, at Mr. Hunter's, in *Sycamore-Alley*, will be duly attended to.

LAURENCE DERMOTT, *AHIMAN REZON*, 2ND EDN, EXCERPT CONTAINING POLEMIC AGAINST MODERNS FREEMASONS AND IN PRAISE OF ANTIENTS FREEMASONRY (1764)

Laurence Dermott, *Ahiman Rezon, or A Help to All that are, (or would be) Free and Accepted Masons*, 2nd edn (Printed for the author and sold by Br. Robert Black. London, 1764), pp. xxiv–xxxiii.[1]

First published in 1756, Laurence Dermott's *Ahiman Rezon* codified and publicized Antients Freemasonry, arguing in favour of its greater antiquity and superior ritual as compared to the (not dissimilar) masonic practices of the now disparagingly named 'Moderns'. Dermott's later editions of his book extended the argument, highlighting the Antients' relationship with the Grand Lodges of Ireland and Scotland and emphasizing a claim of masonic pre-eminence.

The Antients Grand Lodge had been established in London in 1751 and the Freemasonry it represented was shaped and supported by London's Irish diaspora. The organization provided an accessible social space as well as a focal point for the Irish in London and a home to members of previously independent 'St John's' lodges and those estranged from the original and now rival Grand Lodge of England. In doing so, the Antients opened Freemasonry to a more diverse membership, offering mutual financial assistance and a support structure available both to the expatriate Irish community and more broadly to the aspirational working class. From a relatively small base, Antients Freemasonry grew rapidly. By 1756 there were over a thousand members across more than forty lodges and two decades later over two hundred lodges spread across London, the provinces and overseas.[2] In 1773, when the third Duke of Atholl became Grand Master of the Antients and was simultaneously Grand Master elect in Scotland, the Grand Lodge of Scotland entered into a formal masonic pact with Ireland under which both grand lodges recognized the Antients Grand Lodge to the exclusion of the Moderns.

Much of the success of Antients Freemasonry was due to Dermott's leadership and management of the organization's public image. Under his guidance the Antients traded successfully on a combination of inclusivity and notionally superior antiquity. Underlining this, in the second edition of *Ahiman Rezon*, Dermott's 'Philacteria for such gentlemen as may be inclined to become Free-Masons'[3] accentuated the pre-eminence of Antients Freemasonry through a catechism, repeated below. Probably more than any other element, it captured and cemented the perception of the Antients as superior masonic beings. The image was instrumental in attracting and retaining new members. Of course, what Dermott held out to be facts were either untrue or opinions. Nevertheless, *Ahiman Rezon* comprised a powerful encouragement to join Antients Freemasonry whether as a new entrant or via conversion from the Moderns. The extract emphasizes that Dermott's polemic was directed to prospective Masons both at home and overseas, especially British and Irish colonists in the Americas whose 'right worshipful and very worthy gentlemen'[4] were singled out for particular flattery.

Notwithstanding his achievements – and perhaps because of them – some four decades after the 1813 union and six decades after his death, it had become commonplace to vilify Dermott. Laurie in his *History* commented that

> much injury has been done to the cause of the Antients ... by Laurence Dermott
> ... the unfairness with which he has stated the proceedings of the Moderns, the
> bitterness with which he treats them and the quackery and vainglory with which he
> displays his superior knowledge, deserve to be reprobated by every class of Masons
> who are anxious for the purity of their Order and the preservation of the clarity and
> mildness which ought to characterise all their proceedings.[5]

Mackey wrote of Dermott in a similar vein: 'as a polemic, he was sarcastic bitter, uncompromising and not altogether sincere or veracious'.[6] Nonetheless he acknowledged that Dermott was 'in intellectual attainments ... inferior to none ... [and] in advance of the spirit of his age'.[7] Gould's view was of an 'unscrupulous writer [but] a matchless administrator'.[8] Hughan called his works 'absurd and ridiculous'.[9] And Sadler commented variously on Dermott's writings as 'comical', 'ridiculous' and 'scarcely worth a moment's thought'.[10] Antipathy towards Dermott dated back a century and Gould's observation that 'in masonic circles, Dermott was probably the best abused man of his time' was accurate, if one was a Modern.

Dermott used subsequent editions of *Ahiman Rezon* to retaliate with satire. He joked that the rival Moderns had given up the study of geometry in favour of dining,[11] and that their debate over whether or not to continue to wear aprons had led to a decision to wear them upside down 'in order to avoid appearing mechanical'.[12]

Although the schism between the Moderns and Antients is often interpreted as formalizing existing masonic divisions and rivalries, it was more a product of less visible but more significant factors. There were two key drivers: England's increasingly calamitous relationship with the Irish on both sides of the Irish Sea; and the changing composition of British society, in particular, the development of an aspirational lower middle class. Under Dermott, Antients Freemasonry reflected and sometimes led changes then in progress elsewhere in British society. Antients lodges extended sociability beyond the professional classes and in doing so created an organization whose economic and social welfare function was as important as its ritual.

Notes

1. This headnote was written by Ric Berman.
2. *Schism*, p. 5.
3. See Dermott, *Ahiman Rezon*, 2nd edn, pp. xxiv–xxvii.
4. See Dermott, *Ahiman Rezon*, 2nd edn, p. xxvii.
5. W. A. Laurie, *The History of Free Masonry and the Grand Lodge of Scotland* (Edinburgh: Seton & MacKenzie, 1859), fn. p. 60. The comment is a virtual repeat of that made in the 1804 edition of *The History of Free Masonry* (Edinburgh, 1804), fn. pp. 117–18.
6. A. G. Mackey, *An Encyclopaedia of Freemasonry and its Kindred Sciences* (Philadelphia, PA: Moss & Co., 1874), p. 214.
7. Mackey, *An Encyclopaedia of Freemasonry and its Kindred Sciences*, p. 214.
8. R. F. Gould, *Gould's Freemasonry Throughout the World*, rev. D. Wright, 6 vols (New York: Charles Scribener's Sons, 1936), vol. 2, p. 151.
9. W. J. Hughan, *Memorials of the Masonic Union*, rev. edn (Leicester: Johnson, Wykes & Paine, 1913), p. 8.
10. H. Sadler, *Masonic Facts and Fictions* (London, 1887; Whitefish, MT: Kessinger, 2003), pp 110–2.
11. Dermott, *Ahiman Rezon*, 2nd edn, pp. xxix–xxxi.
12. Dermott, *Ahiman Rezon*, 2nd edn, pp. xxix–xxxi.

Laurence Dermott, *Ahiman Rezon*, 2nd edn, excerpt containing polemic against Moderns Freemasons and in praise of Antients Freemasonry (1764)

AHIMAN REZON[1]
Or a help to all that are.
(or would be)
FREE *and* ACCEPTED MASONS,
Containing
The Quintessence of all that has been Publish'd on the Subject of
Free Masonry

With many additions, which Renders this Work more Usefull. than any other
Book of Constitution, now Extant.
the Second Edition
By LAU. DERMOTT.[2] Secretary

Printed for the Author
and Sold by BR. ROBERT BLACK.[3]
Book-binder & Stationer
in George Yard. Tower Hill.
LONDON, 1764. / [...]

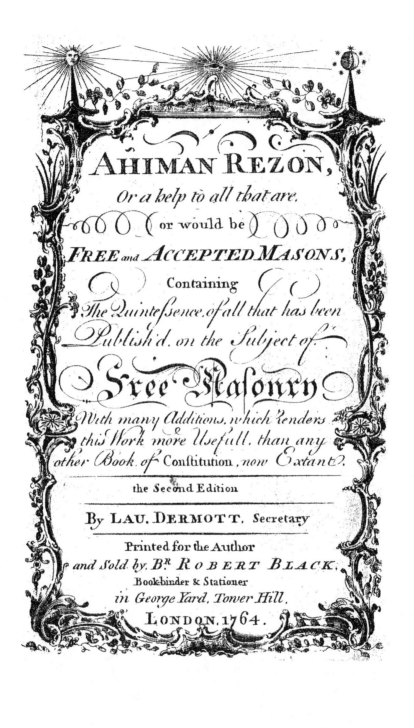

AHIMAN REZON,

Or a help to all that are,
or would be

FREE *and* ACCEPTED MASONS,

Containing

The Quinteſſence, of all that has been
Publiſh'd, on the Subject of

Free Maſonry

With many Additions, which Renders
this Work more Uſefull, than any
other Book, of Conſtitution, *now* Extant.

the Second Edition

By LAU. DERMOTT, Secretary

Printed for the Author
and Sold by, Bᴿ ROBERT BLACK,
Bookbinder & Stationer
in George Yard, Tower Hill,
LONDON, 1764.

Having taken my leave of the strangers, I now beg leave to address myself to the GENTLEMEN OF THE MOST ANTIENT AND HONOURABLE FRATERNITY.

GENTLEMEN and BRETHREN,

SEVERAL eminent craftsmen residing in Scotland, Ireland, America and other parts both abroad and at home, have greatly importuned me, to give them some account of what is called modern masonry in London. I cannot be displeased with such importunities, because I had the like curiosity myself, about sixteen or seventeen years ago, when I was first introduced into that society. However, before I proceed any farther concerning the difference between antient and modern, I think it my duty, to declare solemnly before God and man, that I have not the least antipathy against the gentlemen members of the modern society; but, on the contrary, love and respect them, because I have found the generality of them to be hearty cocks and good fellows (as the bacchanalian phrase is) and many of them I believe to be worthy of receiving every blessing that good men can ask or heaven bestow. I hope that this declaration will acquit me of any design of giving offence, especially if the following queries and answers be rightly considered. /

Quere 1st. Whether free masonry, as practised in antient lodges, is universal?
Answer. Yes.

2d. *Whether what is called modern masonry is universal?*
Answer. No.

3d. *Whether there is any material difference between the antient and modern?*
Ans. A great deal, because an antient mason can not only make himself known to his brother, but in case of necessity can discover his very thoughts to him, in the presence of a modern, without being able to distinguish that either of them are free masons.

4th. *Whether a modern mason may, with safety, communicate all his secrets to an antient mason?*
Ans. Yes.

5th. *Whether an antient mason may, with the like safety, communicate all his secrets, to a modern mason, without further ceremony?*
Ans. No. For as a Science comprehends an Art, (though an art cannot comprehend a science) even so antient masonry contains every thing valuable amongst the moderns, as well as many / other things that cannot be revealed without additional ceremonies.

6th. *Whether a person, made in the modern manner, and not after the antient custom of the craft, has a right to be called free and accepted, according to the intent and meaning of the words?*
Ans. His being unqualified to appear in a master's lodge, according to the universal system of masonry, renders the appellation improper.

7th. *Whether it is possible to initiate or introduce a modern mason into a royal arch lodge (the very Essence of masonry) without making him go through the antient ceremonies.*

Ans. No.

8th. *What Art or Science has been introduced and practised in London without receiving the least improvement?*

Ans. Free masonry.

9th. *Whether the present members of modern lodges are blameable for deviating so much from the old land marks?*

Ans. No. Because the innovation was made in the reign of king George the first, and the new form was delivered as orthodox to the present members. /

10th. *Therefore as it is natural for each party, to maintain the orthodoxy of their masonical preceptors. How shall we distinguish the original and most useful system?*

Ans. The number of antient masons, compared with the moderns, being as ninety-nine to one, proves the universality of the old order, and the utility thereof appears by the love and respect shewn to the brethren, in consequence of their superior abilities in conversing with, and distinguishing the masons of all countries and denominations, a circumstance, peculiar to antient masons.

I am so well acquainted with the truth of what I have just now inserted, that I am not in the least apprehensive of being contradicted. But if any person should hereafter labour under the spirit of opposition, I shall (even then) be contented, as I am sure of having the majority upon my side.

Therefore, In order to satisfy the importunities of my good Brethren (particularly the Right worshipful and very worthy Gentlemen of America, who for their charitable disposition, prudent choice of members and good conduct in general, deserve the unanimous thanks and applause of the masonical world) be it known, that the innovation, already mentioned, arose upon the fall of a GRAND MASTER, namely Sir Christopher Wren,[4] who (as Doctor / Anderson says) neglected the lodges. The Doctor's assertion is certainly true, and I will endeavour to do justice unto the memory of Sir Christopher, by relating the real cause of such neglect. The famous Sir Christopher Wren, Knight, (Master of Arts formerly of Wadham college, Professor of astronomy at Gresham and Oxford, Doctor of the civil law, President of the royal society, grand master of the most antient and honourable fraternity of free and accepted masons, architect to the crown, who built most of the churches in London, laid the first stone of the glorious cathedral of St. Paul, and lived to finish it.) having served the crown upwards of fifty years, was (at the age of ninety) displaced from employment, in favour of Mr. William B–ns–n,[5] who was made surveyor of the buildings &c. to his Majesty King George the first. The first specimen of Mr. B–ns–n's skill in architecture was a report made to the house of Lords, that their house and the painted chamber adjoining were in immediate danger of falling; whereupon the Lords met in a committee, to appoint some other place to sit in, while the house should be taken down. But it being proposed to cause some other builders first to inspect it, they found it in very good condition. The Lords, upon this, were going upon an address to the king, against the modern architect, for such a misrepresentation, but the Earl of Sunderland, then secretary, gave them an assurance that his majesty would remove him. /

Such usage, added to Sir Christopher's great age, was more than enough to make him decline all public assemblies. And the master masons then in London were so much disgusted at the treatment of their old and excellent grand master, that they would not meet nor hold any communication under the sanction of his successor Mr. B-ns-n, in short, the brethren were struck with a Lethargy which seemed to threaten the London lodges with a final dissolution.[6]

Notwithstanding this state of inactivity in London, the lodges in the country, particularly in Scotland and at York, kept up their antient formalities, customs and usages, without alteration, adding or diminishing, to this hour, from whence they may justly be called the most antient &c.

About the year 1717 some joyous companions, who had passed the degree of a craft, (though very rusty) resolved to form a lodge for themselves, in order (by conversation) to recollect what had been formerly dictated to them, or if that should be found impracticable, to substitute something new, which might for the future pass for masonry amongst themselves.[7] At this meeting the question was asked, whether any person in the assembly knew the Master's part, and being answered in the negative, it was resolved, *nem. con.* that the deficiency should be made up with a new composition, and what fragments of the old order found / amongst them, should be immediately reformed and made more pliable to the humours of the people. Hence it was ordered, that every person (during the time of his initiation) should wear boots, spurs, a sword and spectacles. That every apprentice (going and coming from work) should carry the plumb rule upon his right side, contrary to be antients. That every fellow craft should carry the level upon his left side, and not upon his right side, as the antients did. And that every person, dignified with the title of a *master mason*, should wear a square pendant to his right leg. It was also thought expedient to abolish the old custom of studying Geometry in the lodge, and some of the young brethren made it appear, that a good knife and fork in the hands of a dexterous brother (over proper materials) would give greater satisfaction, and add more to the rotundity of the lodge, than the best scale and compass in Europe, and farthermore added, that a line, a square, a parallelogram, a rhombus, a rhomboides, a triangle, a trapezium, a circle, a semicircle, a quadrant, a parabola, a cube, a parallelopipedon, a prism, a pyramid, a cylinder, a cone, a prismoid, a cylindroid, a sphere, a spheroid, a parabolick, frustrums, segments, polygons, ellipsis and irregular figures of all sorts might be drawn and represented upon Bread, Beef, Mutton, Fowls, Pies &c. as demonstratively as upon slates or sheets of paper; and that the use of the globes might be taught and explained as clearly and briefly upon two bottles, as upon Mr. Senex's[8] globes of 28 inches / diameter; and we are told, that from this improvement proceeded the laudable custom of charging to a public health at every third sentence that is spoke in the lodge. There was another old custom that gave umbrage to the young architects, i.e. the wearing of aprons, which made the gentlemen look like so many mechanicks, therefore it was proposed, that no brother (for the future) should wear an apron. This proposal was rejected by the oldest members, who declared, that the aprons were all the signs of masonry then remaining amongst them, and for that reason they would keep and wear them. It was then proposed, that (as they were resolved to wear aprons) they should be turned upside down, in order to avoid appearing mechanical. This proposal took place and answered the design, for that, which was formerly the lower part, was now fastened round the abdomen, and the bib and strings hung downwards, dangling in such manner as might convince the spectators, that there was not a working mason amongst them.

Agreeable as this alteration might seem to the gentlemen, nevertheless it was attended with an ugly circumstance: for, in taversing the lodge, the brethren were subject to tread upon the strings, which often caused them to fall with great violence, so that it was thought necessary, to invent several methods of walking, in order to avoid treading upon the strings. In brief, every meeting produced an addition or a palinody. Amongst other / things they seized on the stone masons Arms,* which that good natured company has permitted them to wear to this day, for which reason several of the brethren have turned their aprons in the old fashion, and affect to immitate the operative masons. And it is pleasant enough, to see sixty or seventy able men about a little Lewis and capstan &c. erected upon a mahogany platform (purchased at an extravagant price) all employed in raising a little square piece of marble, which the weakest man in company could take between his finger and thumb and throw it over the house.

I have the greatest veneration for such implements as are truly emblematical or useful in refining our moral notions, and I am well convinced that the custom and use of them in lodges are both antient and instructive, but at the same time I abhor and detest the unconstitutional fopperies of cunning avaricious tradesmen, invented and introduced amongst the moderns with no other design but to extract large sums of money, which ought to be applied to more noble and charitable uses. There is now in my neighbourhood a large piece of

---

*   The operative or stone masons are the 30th company in London, they were incorporated by Charles the second, and have a hall in Basinghall street, the number of their livery men about seventy, and the livery fine five pounds.

iron scrole work, ornamented with foliage *&c.* painted and gilt (the whole at an incredible expence) and placed before the master's chair, with a gigantic sword fixed therein, during the communication / of the members, a thing contrary to all the private and public rules of masonry: all implements of war and blood-shed being confined to the lodge door, from the day that the flaming sword was placed in the East of the garden of Eden, to the day that the sagacious modern placed his grand sword of State in the midst of his lodge.[9] Nor is it uncommon for a tyler[10] to receive ten or twelve shillings for drawing two sign posts with chalk *&c.* and writing Jamaica rum upon one, and Barbadoes[11] rum upon the other, and all this (I suppose) for no other use, than to distinguish where these liquors are to be placed in the lodge.

There are many other unconstitutional proceedings, which (to avoid giving offence) I pass over in silence. And hope, that I shall live to see a general conformity and universal unity between the worthy masons of all denominations. This is the most earnest wishes and ardent prayers of,

GENTLEMEN and BRETHREN,
> *Your most sincere friend,*
> > *Obedient servant,*
> > > *and faithful brother,*

LAURENCE DERMOTT, SECRETARY.

[ANON.], *A DEFENCE OF FREE-MASONRY, AS PRACTICED IN THE REGULAR LODGES, BOTH FOREIGN AND DOMESTIC UNDER THE CONSTITUTION OF THE ENGLISH GRAND MASTER* (1765)

[Anon.], *A Defence of Free-Masonry as Practiced in the Regular Lodges, both Foreign and Domestic under the Constitution of the English Grand Master* (London: Printed for the Author and sold by W. Flexney, near Gray's Inn Gate, Holborn, 1765), pp. 1–43.[1]

The author of *A Defence of Freemasonry* is unknown but was probably a senior member of the Moderns' English Grand Lodge, possibly the Grand Secretary. Henry Sadler suggested that it was written either by Samuel Spencer,[2] who was known for his anti-Antients polemics, or his predecessor, John Revis. Spencer may be the more likely candidate. In 1759, responding to a request for charity from an Irish Freemason, Spencer refused, noting that 'our Society is neither Arch, Royal Arch or Antient'.[3]

The pamphlet argues in favour of the practices of the Grand Lodge of England – the Moderns – and against Laurence Dermott's 'Antients' Freemasonry as described in *Ahiman Rezon*.[4] It adopts a counterfactual approach, making a series of points including some designed to demonstrate the accuracy of Anderson's history of Freemasonry.[5] The exercise may have been largely self-defeating. In common with similar historical passages in the Old Charges,[6] Anderson's faux history in his *Constitutions* aimed to set a literary context for Freemasonry. By positioning it as ancient, the narrative afforded the Craft legitimacy and gave it an antiquarian aura and attraction that a more recently formed organization would have found difficult to attain. Dermott's dismissive categorization of the Grand Lodge of England as 'Moderns' and the adoption of the title 'Antients' gives the argument substance. As in previous centuries, Freemasonry's perceived longevity offered an element of protection in a society that remained tradition-based. Nonetheless, it can be viewed as falling within a literary tradition of legend and hyperbole.

This was not always the case and the author of *A Defence* took a more literal view. The statements that 'free and operative masonry received the greatest improvement under King Solomon, Hiram king of Tyre and Hiram Abbif' and 'connecting the history of one with the progress of the other' are meant to be taken factually. However, they fail to counter Dermott's irony, epitomized by his rhetorical question whether 'histories are of any use to the Craft'.

Worse, the assertions that the 'Grand Master of Ireland refused to countenance' the Antients and that although 'a certain noble peer permits them occasionally to make use of his name ... he never presides in any of their assemblies', were at least partly incorrect. The Grand Lodge of Ireland had ceased fraternal communications with the Moderns in 1758 and entered into a mutual recognition pact with the Antients. Moreover, that the Earl of Blessington, described by Dermott as 'a father to the fraternity', did not attend any meetings of the Antients Grand Lodge misses the point. The Antients had sought aristocratic patronage; they did not expect Blessington to make any contribution to the day-to-day management of the lodges, nor would he have intended or expected to do so. Blessington's appeal to the Irish émigrés in London was the imprimatur that an affluent and well-regarded aristocrat provided. And it went further. Blessington commanded a flattering reputation for charitable benevolence and as Lord Mountjoy, while Grand Master of Ireland in 1738–40, had led fund raising and food distribution efforts to support the poor and relieve the famine.[7] His actions became part of working class Irish folklore and were remembered as much as three decades later.[8]

Recognition by Blessington and Irish Grand Lodge gave the Antients an imprimatur the Moderns found hard to counter. Even a century later, Blessington's decision was regarded with incredulity and Moderns' apologists, Gould, for example, wrote that it was 'singular that Dermott secured the services as titular Grand Master [of a] nobleman under whose presidency the Grand Lodge of Ireland conformed to the laws and regulations enacted by the Regular or Original Grand Lodge of England'.[9]

The Modern's core problem with the Antients is revealed towards the end of the pamphlet with a diatribe against the Irish who constituted the majority of Antients Freemasons. The author condescendingly details a three-hour lecture by 'a red hot hibernian' followed by the initiation of a chairman who, too poor to disburse the full lodge fee, pays five shillings in cash and five by way of a note. The author's disdain for the Antients 'customs and ceremonies' and their social standing is epitomized by the 'disgrace to society' represented by their funeral processions, populated by 'some with scarcely a coat or shirt to their backs ... having sat in ale houses ... hooting and hollooing ... they required almost as much supporting as their deceased brother'.

Advertisements for *A Defence* noted that it contained 'a refutation of Mr Dermott's ridiculous account of that ancient society in his book entitled

Ahiman Rezon.[10] The pamphlet also sought to assert the superiority (or at least not inferiority) of Moderns ritual. In the event, it was largely ineffective on both counts. The combination of vilification and earnest semi-facts were substantially useless against Dermott's wry wit and failed to prevent the growing influence of the Antients.

A Defence was an integral component of the rivalry in English Freemasonry in the second half of the eighteenth century. It also demonstrates clearly the prejudice of London's Moderns towards the Irish and English lower middling and working class.

The associational culture of the early eighteenth century had generally been restricted to the upper and professional classes. Within Freemasonry, the Antients altered the paradigm and by the early 1800s, around a third of England's Masonic lodges were Antients with a lower middling membership. Although competition spurred the Moderns to retaliate and reverse their mid-century decline, Antients Freemasonry remained a threat as it became increasingly dominant in Britain's new industrial towns and overseas, especially in America. After Dermott's death, the two rival grand lodges began to cease their mutual hostilities and move towards amalgamation; but this did not occur until 1813 and only after the intervention of the British Crown in the form of the Duke of Sussex and his brother, the Duke of Kent, the younger sons of George III.

No original copy of *A Defence* survives and the reproduction is that of Henry Sadler's facsimile reprint.[11] For reasons of space, the twenty pages of masonic songs and odes at the end of the document have not been reproduced.

Notes
1. This headnote was written by Ric Berman.
2. Grand Secretary of the Moderns from 1757 to 1767. John Revis, his predecessor, held the office from 1729 to 1756 and was subsequently appointed Deputy Grand Master 1757–61.
3. See *Schism*, p. 44. Also, H. Sadler, *Masonic Facts and Fictions* (1887; Whitefish, MT: Kessinger, 2003).
4. L. Dermott, *Ahiman Rezon* (London, 1756). See previous headnote.
5. See J. Anderson, *Constitutions* (1723 and 1738).
6. The first written evidence of early English Freemasonry. They detail the internal rules and regulations under which stone masonry was managed and set out an operating structure for the guild. They reflect the contemporary political and economic conditions prevalent at the time of writing and contain a faux history of Freemasonry dating back to St Athelstan, St Alban, or even earlier. See *Schism*, Appendix II.
7. See *Schism*, esp. pp. 39–41.
8. *Gazetteer and New Daily Advertiser*, 23 September 1766, issue 11.
9. R. F. Gould, *Gould's Freemasonry throughout the World*, rev. D. Wright, 6 vols (New York: Charles Scribener's Sons, 1936), vol. 2, p. 168.
10. *Gazetteer and New Daily Advertiser*, 21 September 1765, issue 11397.
11. H. Sadler, *Masonic Reprints and Historical Revelations including Original Notes and Additions* (London: George Kenning, 1898), pp. xxxvii–xlv.

[Anon.], *A Defence of Free-Masonry, as Practiced in the Regular Lodges, both Foreign and Domestic under the Constitution of the English Grand Master* (1765)

A

DEFENCE

OF

FREE-MASONRY,

As practised in the

REGULAR LODGES,

Both FOREIGN and DOMESTIC,

Under the *Constitution* of the

ENGLISH GRAND-MASTER.

In which is contained.

A REFUTATION of Mr. *Dermott*'s[1] absurd and ridiculous Account of FREE-MASONRY, in his Book, entitled AHIMAN REZON;[2] and the several *Queries* therein, reflecting on the *Regular* MASONS,[3] briefly considered, and answered.

What shall be given unto thee? or what shall be done unto thee, thou false Tongue? PSALM 120, *v.* 3.

To the above Defence is added,

A Collection of Masons ODES and SONGS, most of them entirely new, and never before printed.

LONDON:

Printed for the AUTHOR, and sold by W. FLEXNEY, near *Gray's-Inn Gate, Holborn*; and E. HOOD, near *Stationers-Hall, Ludgate-Street.* 1765.

[Price One Shilling.] /

A
DEFENCE
OF
FREE-MASONRY.

THE Reason for the following *Pamphlet* appearing in Print, proceeds entirely from the *hearty good Wishes and Love* I bear to the *Right Worshipful Fraternity* of FREE and ACCEPTED MASONS, and not from any lucrative or sinister Motives; the Truth of which, I hope will appear to the Satisfaction of every Brother, who will take an impartial View of what is here offered in Defence of the REGULAR LODGES.

A Book, entitled AHIMAN REZON (a new Edition of which was printed last Year) very lately fell into my Hands, and the Perusal of it (though an old MASON, who / had neglected the *Lodges* several Years) rouzed my just Resentment, and I determined to take up my *Pen* (though in no Respect equal to the Talk) in Defence of this ANCIENT and HONOURABLE BROTHERHOOD, which is most scandalously *traduced*, by the malevolent *Author* of that *Book*.

My Intention is not to scrutinize into every Part of his *new-coined Constitution-Book*, especially the ridiculous Story of the sh-tt-n End of * *Daniel Tadpole*, the *Author* of *The three distinct Knocks*, and one of his *Ancient Brethren*.

As a *Mason*, I do not wish Mr. *Dermott* so wretched and untimely an End as poor *Tadpole*, notwithstanding he may think him justly rewarded for his Publication; but when *he* dies (were I to have the ordering of his *Funeral*) he should be buried thus. /

Previous to the Interment, a capacious *Pit* should be dug, in an extensive *Valley* (or in the *Valley* of *Jebosophat*, if in his Life-time he should prefer that Place to any other) and I would have his *Corpse* preceded by *Ancient Masons*, of the following Professions or Callings, *viz. Scavengers* and *Nightmen*, who should bear upon their Poles the *Ensigns* of his *Order, viz.* the *Cross Pens*, pendant, in green, red, or yellow *Ribbands*, or any other† *tawdry* Colour he is now most fond of, and a dirty Leather Apron, lined and bordered with the same Colour, on which may be wrote, in as legible Characters as possible, AHIMAN REZON. The *Deacons* Rods to be carried by two *Chimney-Sweepers*, and the *Columns* by a walking Poulterer, who retails Rabbits, *&c.* in the Streets, and a brawny Chairman, all

---

* He says that Tadpole being pursued by Bailiffs, escaped into Whitechapel-Fields, and hid himself in a Sand, or Clay Pit, where he slept till Night, when a Nightman came with a Cart full of Human Ordure, and emptied it upon him, which smothered him to Death.

† The Grand Lodge of English Masons, have ordered, for Distinction sake, that none but the Grand Officers, shall ever wear Jewels of Gold-pendant to blue Ribbands. But Mr. Dermott, in Opposition to that Law, asserts, that every Member of the Grand Lodge has a Right to wear blue, or any other Colour. Happy are the Regular Masons, that they have no such refractory Members, to dispute the Authority of the Grand Lodge, and set up Opinions of their own.

of the same Country, and likewise *Ancient Masons*. Immediately / preceding the *Hearse*, instead of a Number of pampered *Churchmen*, chanting a *solemn Dirge*, I would have a *dead March*, played by some Rabble, on *ancient British, and Hibernian Instruments, viz.* the *Salt-box; and Rolling-pin, Wooden Spoons, Marrow-bones and Cleavers, Hurdy-gurdys, Frying-pans and Iron Skewers, &c. &c. &c.* Then the *Corpse*, properly habited as an *Ancient Mason* (with the last *Edition* of his *Book* in his Left Hand, and a *Pen* in his Right) borne on an open *Hearse, i.e.* a *Cart*, on which they usually carry dead *Horses*, and sometimes *Asses*, that the Public may have a distinct View of the Figure of a Man, so eminent for Scandal, Defamation, *&c.* and to put them in Mind (if he thinks it will be of any real Service to him) to offer up an Ejaculation for the Repose of his *Soul.* The *Hearse* to be followed, not by his *Relations*, but by as many *Nightmen* as there were Builders in *Solomon's Temple*, every one with a *Cart* loaded with their usual *Commodity*; and after his *Remains* are deposited in the *Pit*, every Man should empty his *Cart* upon him; so large a Quantity being doubtless due to his great Merit. There will be no occasion for *Cassia, Spikenard, Myrrh*, or any other Perfumes used in embalming / the Dead, as that will yield a sufficient Odour, and will not only save Time, Labour and Expence, in building a Monument of Stone, but will also transmit his Memory to Posterity, more than AHIMAN REZON can be expected, or even a *Mausoleum* as large as that built for the *King* of *Caria*,[4] which was usually reckoned the fourth Wonder of the World. After the Funeral is over, his *Friends* (if he has any) may surround the *Valley*, sing *Mass*, and set up a *Howl*, according to the Custom of their Country.

But to return to my Subject, I shall only speak of such Parts of his *wonderful* Publication, which he has compiled for the Use of *Ancient Masons*; at the Beginning of which, "*he solemnly declares, before God and Man, that he has not the least Antipathy against the Gentlemen Members of the modern Society of Masons,*" as he is pleased to call them (Thanks to him for the Appellation.) How far this be true, let the candid Reader judge.

This *Genius* (if I may so call him) begins his Remarks on the *History* of MASONRY, / which was compiled from the ancient Records, and Manuscripts of FREE-MASONS, of *Italy, Scotland*, and many in the Hands of private Brethren, in different Parts of *England*; and because he is, beyond Doubt, incapable of writing an *History* of it himself, he attacks *that* which hath received the Approbation of both the *Great* and the *Learned*, and (under the Similitude of a Dream)* with

---

* He tells us, that when he had sat down, with Intention to write an *History* of *Masonry*, he fell into a Slumber, and dreamt that SHALLUM, AKKUB, TALMON and AHIMON, who were the four principal *Porters* in Solomon's Temple, appeared to him, and told him, that all Accounts of the Temple were imperfect, except those of the Prophets *Jeremiah, Ezekiel* and *Ezra*, and also *Josephus*. That even all *their* Works put together would not be sufficient for a Preface to the *History* of *Masonry*, and that all other Writers thereof knew nothing of the Matter. [Despite the author's comment on this point, Dermott recognized the value of history and tradition explicitly, most especially its

an Effrontery peculiar to his *Country*, ridicules both the *History*, and the *Compilers* of it, some of whom were as great Men, perhaps, as ever employed their Pens on that, or any other Subject.

Though MASONRY may be, and is with great Propriety traced from the Creation, yet the FREE-MASONS Faculty, and ancient universal Practice of conversing without / speaking, and of knowing each other by *Signs* and *Tokens* (which, says an old Tradition, they settled upon the *Dispersion*, or *Migration)* certainly took its Rise from the Confusion of Dialects at the Building of *Babel*; and this Tradition was always firmly believed by the MASONS, the Assertions of this *visionary* Writer to the contrary notwithstanding: Besides, it is recorded of *Nimrod*[*5] or *Belus*, that he was the first who reduced Men into Society and Union, which is an additional Argument in favour of the said Tradition. It is likewise very evident, that FREE-MASONRY has always gone Hand in Hand with the Arts and Sciences, particularly with *Geometry* and *Architecture*, and wherever *they* flourished most, *there* the CRAFT received the most Encouragement, as well as the greatest Improvement.

That FREE-MASONRY took its Name at the building of *Solomon's Temple*, I believe none but our *dreaming* Author will assert, as some Traditions affirm, that the Word *Free* was added, because the *Masons* taught their / *Art* to the *Free-born* only, which was their constant Practice more than nine Centuries before that Period.

It is however certain that both FREE and OPERATIVE MASONRY, received the greatest Improvements under King *Solomon, Hiram* King of *Tyre, Hiram Abbif,* the greatest *Cabalists*, as well as the greatest *Architects*, then in the World; and since then, there has been scarcely a Building of any Consequence carried on, in any Country, but such of the Workmen concerned therein, as were FREE-MASONS, constantly held a Lodge in, or near it.

---

potential emotional impact on prospective recruits. It was a mark of his intelligence that he was willing to satirize masonic historiography. In *Ahiman Rezon*, in his editor's note, Dermott wrote that he had determined to publish a history of Freemasonry and 'purchased all or most of the histories, constitutions, pocket companions and other pieces (on that subject) now extant in the English tongue' (p. vi). But having furnished himself with pens, ink and paper, and surrounded himself with the relevant compositions and started work, he 'fell to dreaming', only to be woken some time later as 'a young puppy that got into the room while I slept, and seizing my papers, ate a great part of them, and was then (between my legs) shaking and tearing the last sheet' (pp. xv–xvi). Dermott's irony was deliberately at odds with the more precious style adopted by previous masonic chroniclers and his conversational introduction and relaxed style epitomized the Antients' accessibility and attraction to the lower middling and working class. See *Schism*, chs 2, 3.]

*   Belus signifies Lord, and Nimrod was a Name given him by the *Israelites*, by way of Invective.

An old Record relates, that "*Euclid* the famous *Geometer* of *Tyre*, came to the Court of *Ptolomy Soter*, and was by him encouraged to teach *Geometry*, particularly to the Children of the great *Lords* of the Realm, who by continual Wars, and Decay of the Sciences in former Reigns, were reduced to great Necessities to get a competent and honourable Livelihood. And having received Commission, he taught such as were committed to his Charge, the Science of *Geometry*, and to / work in Stone, all Manner of Buildings, such as *Temples, Altars, Towers, &c.* and gave them Charge to this Purpose, *viz.* To be true to their *King*, and to the Lord they served, as well as to the *Fellowship* whereof they were admitted: To be true, and love one another, and call each other *Fellow* or *Brother*."

"That they should appoint the Wisest of them to be *Master* of the Work; that the *Lord* should be well served, and *they* not ashamed; and many other Charges he gave them, too long to be inserted, to which he made them swear a great *Oath*, which they used at that Time. Thus was the CRAFT grounded there; and *Euclid* gave it the Name of *Geometry*, which is now called MASONRY."

Hence it appears that FREE-MASONRY is derived from operative MASONRY, and therefore wherever the History mentions the Building of any great Edifice, we have generally some Account of the Progress and Success of FREE-MASONRY, which sufficiently shews the Utility, as well as Necessity of connecting the History of one with the / Progress of the other, notwithstanding Mr. *Dermott*'s Query, *Whether such Histories are of any real Use to the Craft?*

I shall say no more in Defence of the Utility and Authenticity of the *History* of MASONRY, but shall only add the Approbation which is subjoined to the first *Book* of CONSTITUTIONS ever printed in this (or any other) Kingdom, in vulgar Year of MASONRY 5723.

APPROBATION.

WHEREAS by the Confusions occasioned in the *Saxon, Danish*, and *Norman* Wars, the Records of *Masons* have been much vitiated, the FREE-MASONS of *England* twice thought it necessary to correct their *Constitutions, Charges*, and *Regulations*; first in the Reign of King *Athelstan* the *Saxon*, and long after in the Reign of King *Edward* IV. the *Norman*: And whereas the old *Constitutions* in *England*, have been much interpolated, mangled, and miserably corrupted, not only with *false* Spelling, but even with many *false* Facts, and gross Errors in History and Chronology, through Length of Time, and the Ignorance of Transcribers, in the dark and illiterate Ages, before the Rivival of *Geometry* / and ancient *Architecture*, to the great Offence of all learned and judicious Brethren, whereby also the Ignorant have been deceived.

And our late worthy GRAND-MASTER, his Grace the *Duke* of *Montague*,[6] having ordered the Author to peruse, correct, and digest, into a new and better Method, the *History, Charges,* and *Regulations* of the ancient *Fraternity*; he has accordingly examined several Copies from *Italy* and *Scotland*, and sundry Parts of *England*, and from thence (though in many things erroneous) and from several other ancient *Records* of *Masons*, he has drawn forth the above written new *Constitutions*, with the *Charges*, and general *Regulations*. And the Author having submitted the whole to the Perusal and Corrections of the late and present *Deputy Grand-Masters*, and of other learned Brethren, and also of the *Masters* and *Wardens* of particular *Lodges*, at their *Quarterly Communication*: He did regularly deliver them to the late GRAND-MASTER himself, the said Duke of *Montague*, for his Examination, Correction and Approbation; and his *Grace*, by the Advice of several *Brethren*, ordered the same to be / handsomely printed for the Use of the *Lodges*, though they were not quite ready for the Press during his *Mastership*.

Therefore *We*, the present GRAND-MASTER of the *Right Worshipful* and *most ancient Fraternity* of FREE and ACCEPTED MASONS, the *Deputy Grand-Master*, the *Grand-Wardens*, the *Masters* and *Wardens* of particular *Lodges* (with the Consent of the *Brethren* and *Fellows*, in and about the Cities of *London* and *Westminster*) having also perused this Performance, do join our laudable *Predecessors* in our solemn *Approbation* thereof, as what we believe will fully answer the End proposed; all the valuable *Things* of the old *Records* being retained, the Errors in *History* and *Chronology* corrected, the *false* Facts, and the *improper* Words omitted, and the Whole digested in a *new* and *better* Method.

And we ordain that These be received in every particular *Lodge*, under our Cognizance, as the only *Constitutions* of FREE and ACCEPTED MASONS amongst us, to be read at the making of new *Brethren*, or / when the *Master* shall think fit; and which the new *Brethren* should peruse before they are *made*.

Sign'd,

PHILIP DUKE OF WHARTON,[7]

GRAND-MASTER.

J. T. DESAGULIERS,[8] L.L.D. and F.R.S.

DEPUTY *Grand-Master*.

JOSHUA TIMSON,[9] ⎫
WILLIAM HAWKINS,[10] ⎬ *Grand-Wardens*.

And the *Masters* and *Wardens* of 20 *Lodges*.

Since which the Time the *Constitution-Book* has been twice corrected and reprinted, first by Dr. *Anderson*,[11] in the *Earl* of *Darnley's Grand-Mastership*; and lastly by the Reverend Mr. *Entick*,[12] in the *Grand-Mastership* of the *Marquis* of *Carnarvan*,[13] both which times it was inspected by a *Committee* of *worthy* and *learned* Brethren.

Mr. *Dermott* in the next Place attempts to prove the *Authenticity* of (what he stiles) *Ancient Masonry*, and would feign insinuate that FREE-MASONRY, as practised in the Lodges under the *English Constitution* (of / which there are near 340) is of modern Invention. He tells us, by Way of Question and Answer, that *Ancient Masonry* is universal, and that *Modern Masonry* is not so.

To which I answer, that our List of *Lodges* is sufficient to prove the contrary, as *that* contains, by far, a greater Number, regularly constituted by the *English* GRAND-MASTER, than there are by any other GRAND-MASTER whatever; together with a great many *Lodges* in different foreign Parts, which are also constituted and governed by *Provincial Grand-Masters*, under our Constitution, which is certainly an evident Proof of the Universality of *English Masonry*.

He then asserts, that an *Ancient Mason* can discover his very Thoughts to a Brother, in the Presence of a *Modern*, without *his* being able to distinguish that either of them are MASONS.

This may pass for Truth with a *Novice* in the Art, or with an entire *Stranger* to it, but an intelligent MASON will laugh at such an idle Assertion. But I suppose he wrote this with a View to draw in the Credulous and Unweary into their *Lodges*. /

With Regard to the Difference between *Ancient* and *Modern* MASONS, there is certainly a great deal, the former being as remarkable for their *Tautology* and *Prolixity*, as the latter are for their *Brevity;* as the one like a *Methodist* Teacher, who attempts to preach extempore, will engross the whole Evening, in spinning out a *tedious* Lecture, while the other, like an *orthodox* Divine, delivers the Substance of the same Lecture (which fully answers the Purpose, and renders it much more agreeable) in less than an Hour. And I believe every sensible MASON will allow this to be the most material Difference, notwithstanding Mr. *Dermott's* Assertion to the contrary.

He then tells us that a *Modern* MASON may with Safety communicate all his *Secrets* to an *Antient*, but an *Ancient* cannot do so to a *Modern*, without further *Ceremonies*.

It is true, an *English* MASON may safely communicate all his Secrets to either *Scotch* or *Irish* MASONS, provided they have been made in Lodges *regularly* constituted by their respective GRAND- MASTERS, and so, *vise versa;* for as MASONRY is universal, there / is nothing in it, which one *regular* MASON ought to conceal from another; but the *English* MASONS should be cautious with whom *they* converse, as there are many *irregular* MASONS, i.e. made in *Lodges* under the Title of *Ancient*, or *York*, who some time ago pretended to be *constituted* or *authorized* by the GRAND- MASTER or *Ireland*, who (by the bye) I am credibly informed, refused to countenance them, as it would be highly absurd for one GRAND-MASTER to constitute *Lodges* in the Territories of *another*. However it is said that a certain *noble* Peer[14] permits them occasionally to make use of his Name, though he never presides in any of their Assemblies.

The next thing which he affirms is, that the Number of *Ancient Masons*, compared with the *Moderns*, are as ninety to one, which (according to his Assertion) proves the Universality of the *old* Order.

I have already observed, that the Number of *Lodges*, under the *English Constitution*, by far exceeds those of any other, consequently the Number of MASONS must be so in Proportion, which must also set his boasted *Universality* aside. /

Again, he informs us that Sir-*Christopher Wren*[15] having served the Crown fifty Years, was at last displaced at the Age of ninety, in favour of another, which was the Cause of his neglecting the *Lodges*, and as the MASONS refused to hold any *Communication* under his *Successor*, they in Time had almost forgot their Lesson, and that (*Masonry* as now practised in the *Ancient Lodges*, was preserved in the *Lodges* at *York*, without Alteration or Addition; but) about the Year 1717, being desirous of reviving the *Order*, they again assembled, and being very *rusty*, they determined to make up the Deficiency with a new *Composition*, and to render the Whole more pliable to the Humours of the Times; in order to which (among other things equally *scandalous* and *ridiculous*, he says, that) they agreed, that every Person during the Time of his *Initiation*, should wear *Boots, Spurs*, a *Sword* and *Spectacles*. That they should likewise wear their *Aprons* reversed, *i. e.* the lower Part being fastened round the *Abdomen*, or *Paunch*, with the *Bib* and *Strings* dangling downwards, to prevent the *Gentlemen* from looking like so many *Mechanicks*, and to convince the Spectators, that there was not a *working Mason* among them. /

It has been the constant Practice of all *good Masons* to bridle that unruly Member, the *Tongue*, and never to suffer it *to lye against a Brother, but rather to let it hang in his Defence*; but this *ungenerous* Brother, contrary to all the Laws of *Masonry*, is determined, (if possible) to bring Disgrace upon the whole *Fraternity*, and is as profuse with his *very* little Stock of Wit, as a young Spendthrift *Heir* of a large *Estate*.

What he says concerning Sir *Christopher Wren*, I beg Leave to contradict, by observing, that his Age and Infirmities prevented his Attendance on that extraordinary Occasion of laying the last Stone on the Top of the *Lantern* of St. *Paul's Cathedral*, which obliged him to depute his Son *Christopher Wren*, Esq; to perform that Office for him, in the Presence of Mr. *Strong*,[16] and his *Son*,[17] *Grand-Wardens*, as also the *Fellow Crafts*, chiefly employed in the building of that Edifice; by which it appears, that Sir *Christopher* did not neglect the *Craft*, on account of his being displaced, but by reason of his Infirmities and great Age only: For it is reasonable to suppose, that a Man of his Years could not attend *That*, or any other, Society, / so frequently as when younger. Neither was it ever known, that his Successor Mr. *Benson*,[18] was proposed to succeed him as GRAND-MASTERS, nor did the *Masons* continue a great while without one, for the *Cathedral* of St. *Paul* was finished in the Year 1710, and though, through his Disability, he did not attend the Lodges, he was, nevertheless, acknowledged their GRAND-MASTER for some Time after,* till the *Craft* observing that the *Lodges* suffered greatly for want of his Presence, as usual, in visiting and regulating their *Meetings*, they then thought it necessary to cement under a new GRAND-MASTER. For this Purpose (as the *History* of the *Craft* informs us) the *Lodges*,

1. *At the Goose and Gridiron, in St. Paul's Church-yard.*

2. *At the Crown in Parker's-lane, near Drury-lane.* /

3. *At the Apple Tree Tavern, in Charles-street, Covent-garden.*

4. *At the Rummer and Grapes Tavern, in Channel-row, Westminster.*

And some *old Brothers* met at the said *Apple Tree*; and having (as usual on such Occasions) put into the Chair the oldest *Master-Mason* (being the Master of a Lodge) they *constituted* themselves a GRAND-LODGE *pro Tempore*, in due Form, and forthwith revived the *Quarterly Communication* of the Officers of *Lodges* (called the GRAND-LODGE) resolved to hold the *Annual* ASSEMBLY and FEAST, and then to chuse a GRAND-MASTER from among themselves, till they should have the Honour of a NOBLE *Brother* at their Head.

Accordingly,

On St. JOHN BAPTIST's Day, in the third Year of King GEORGE I. A. D. 1717, the ASSEMBLY and FEAST of the FREE and ACCEPTED MASONS, was held at the aforesaid *Goose and Gridiron*; now removed to the *Queen's Arms* Tavern in St. *Paul's Church-yard.* /

Before Dinner, the *oldest Master Mason* (being the *Master* of a *Lodge*) in the Chair, proposed a List of proper Candidates, and the Brethren, by a Majority of Hands, elected.

Mr. ANTHONY SAYER,[19] *Gentleman*, GRAND-MASTER of MASONS, who being forthwith invested with the Badges of Office and Power, by the said *oldest Master*, and installed, was duly congratulated, and homaged by the Assembly.

Mr. *Jacob Lamball*,[20] Carpenter, } *Grand-Wardens.*
Capt. *Joseph Elliot*,[21]

And on St. *John's Day*, 1718, GEORGE PAYNE, Esq;[22] was elected GRAND-MASTER, at whose Request several old Manuscripts of the GOTHIC *Constitutions* were produced and collated.

The GRAND FEAST was again held *June* 2, 1719, when JOHN THEOPHILUS DESAGULIERS, L.L.D. and E.R.S. was proclaimed GRAND-MASTER, who revived several *ancient* Usages. In this *Grand-Mastership*, / several *Noblemen* were admitted into the *Craft*, and several *new Lodges* were *constituted*.

---

*   I wonder he has not the Confidence to affirm, that they had almost forgot their Lesson a second time, during the five Years *Grand-Mastership* of a noble Lord, about twelve Years since; who, though he seldom attended the *Quarterly Communications*, the Business thereof was conducted by his *Deputy*, and Wardens, and the particular Lodges continued their Meetings as usual.

At the ensuing FEAST, *June* 24, 1720, GEORGE PAYNE, Esq; was again proclaimed GRAND-MASTER. This Year several very valuable *Manuscripts* were produced (for they had nothing yet in print) concerning *Lodges, Regulations, Charges, Secrets,* and *Usages,* particularly one written by Mr. *Nicholas Stone,*[23] the Warden of *Inigo Jones,*[24] some of which were too hastily burnt, to prevent their falling into *strange* Hands.

And on *Lady-Day,* 1721, GRAND-MASTER PAYNE proposed for his Successor, our most *Noble Brother* JOHN *Duke* of *Montague, Master* of a *Lodge;* who, on the 24th of *June* following (when the GRAND FEAST, for the first time was held at *Stationers-Hall*) was proclaimed GRAND-MASTER, on which Day the noble PHILIP *Lord Stanhope*[25] was made a MASON.

Thus by the *Fervency* and *Zeal* of GRAND MASTER PAYNE, the *Freedom* of this Society has been fixed upon a noble and solid / *Basis,* having this Year produced the *General Regulations,* which he had compiled from the ancient *Usages* and *Records* of the *Fraternity,* and by whose Means a Series of such *noble Personages* have presided at their Head, which no *Age, Society,* or *Nation,* could ever boast of.

From hence it appears, that the CRAFT was not in that State of Inactivity, as this *pretended Ancient Mason* would insinuate, neither is it to be supposed, that MASONRY was so much forgotten as to render it necessary to substitute any thing *new* in its stead, as the *London Lodges* (which were never reduced to a less Number than four) still continued their Meetings, and though they were a little Time without an *acting* GRAND-MASTER, I suppose they were as capable of preserving the ancient *Traditions,* &c. of the CRAFT, as the Brethren at* *York,* whose Numbers were certainly excelled by those at *London,* as the building of such a noble *Edifice* as St. *Paul's,* and other great Works carrying on at that Time, brought MASONS, not only from most Parts of *England,* but from several foreign *Countries.* /

And it is certain, that the *Lodges* at *York* approved the Conduct of those at *London,* in the Choice of a GRAND-MASTER, &c. since we have no Account of *their* choosing one, neither have we heard of their having a GRAND-MASTER of their own, till of late Years, when some Brethren of *Ireland,* who affect Singularity, being refused the Countenance of their own GRAND-MASTER, and for other Reasons too well known, were glad to assume the Title of *Ancient York Masons,* and under that Character, have influenced some *Noble* Brethren (whom we may reasonably conclude have taken no Pains to examine into these Particulars) to preside over them; it is however very clear, that those *Noblemen,* have been acknowledged as GRAND-MASTERS, under the *Rose* only, to prevent giving Offence to the GRAND-MASTER of *England,* for Mr. *Dermott* has dedicated

---

*   I should be glad to know how many Lodges there were then at York.

the first Edition of his *pirated Constitution-Book* to the *Earl* of *Blessington*, not as Grand-Master of *Ancient, York, Scotch*, or *Irish Masons* (but as to a *Noble* Brother only) which he would certainly have done (as it would have been a great Honor to them) had he been permitted. /

And notwithstanding his Assertion, that the *Lodges* in the Country, particularly in *Scotland* and at *York*, kept up their ancient Formalities, Customs and Usages, without Alteration, Adding, or Diminishing, to this Hour (from whence he concludes them to be the *most* Ancient.) It must be acknowledged, that as Masonry must not be written, and has been handed down by *oral* Tradition only, for so many Ages, that it doubtless has received several Alterations, according to the *Customs* and *Manners* of the several *Countries* it has passed through, and I am sure, that every ingenuous Mason, both *Ancient* and *Modern* (Terms which I am obliged to use to be understood) will likewise acknowledge that Masonry in general has received no little Alteration within these twenty Years, though the old *Landmarks* are nevertheless preserved.

The *London* Masons are much beholden to this *faithful* Brother (as he is pleased to call himself) for his *curious* Account of *his*, and *their Society*, particularly of the *modern* Manner of making *Masons*, with *Boots, Spurs, Sword* and *Spectacles* on, and their *Aprons* reversed; but as the contrary is notoriously / known, by Masons of all Denominations, it requires no Answer.

His next Assertion is, that they seized on the Company of *operative Masons* Arms, and used them as their own. In Opposition to which, I shall insert a Paragraph from an *old Record of Masons*, which says, "The Company of Masons, otherwise termed Free-Masons, of auncient Staunding, and good Reckonning, by Means of affable and kind Meetings diverse Tymes, and as a loving Brotherhood should use to doe, did frequent this mutual *Assembly* in the Tyme of King *Henry* the *fifth*, the 12th Year of his *most gracious* Reign." And as the said Record describes a *Coat* of *Arms*, much the same with *That* of the London Company of Masons, it is generally believed that the said *Company* is descended from the ancient *Fraternity;* and consequently bore the same Arms; and that in former Times no Man was made *Free* of that *Company*, till he was made a Free and Accepted Mason, as a necessary Qualification. This, I presume, will sufficiently prove, that the *modern* Masons (as he calls them) did not *seize* on the *operative Masons* Arms (which *he* says is one of / the Innovations they made) in the Reign of King *George* the *first*.

But this is done with a View to create a Belief, that the Arms in the upper Part of the Frontispiece of his *Book*, is the *Arms* of the *Fraternity*, and in order to acquaint us that he has some Knowledge of *Heraldry*, he has described them in the following manner. "In the first Quarter *Azure* a *Lion* rampant *Or;* in the second Quarter *Or*, an *Ox* passant *sable;* in the third Quarter *Or*, a *Man* with his *Hands* erect, proper robed, *Crimson* and *Ermin;* in the fourth Quarter *Azure*, an *Eagle* display'd, *Or. Crest*, the holy *Ark* of the *Covenant*, proper, supported by *Cherubims*. Motto, *Kodes læ Adonai, i. e. Holiness to the Lord.*" And having told us what the Prophet *Ezekiel*, the learned *Spencer*, and *Bochart*, say concerning them, he tells us that they were found in the Collection of the learned *Hebrewist Architect* and *Brother*, Rabi *Jacob Jebudab Leon*, who had formed a *Model* of *Solomon's Temple*, at the Request of the *States* of *Holland*, in order to build a *Temple* there, but the Expence being thought too great, it was laid aside. The *Model*, he says, was afterwards / exhibited to publick View at *Paris* and *Vienna*, and afterwards in *London;* when *That* Rabbi published a Description of the *Tabernacle* and *Temple*, and dedicated it to King *Charles* the *Second;* and in the Years 1759 and 1760, he tells us that *he* examined both those Curiosities. This is, to be sure, an *amazing Proof* of the Authenticity of those *Arms!* but it is still more wonderful, that those *very Ancient Masons*, who are said to be so *extraordinary* cunning, should have no Account of them, till Mr. *Dermott* produced them in Print!

Our *Ancient Mason* seems highly displeased at a *great* Sword, which, he says, is placed before the *Master's* Chair in a Lodge, in his Neighbourhood.

This I shall likewise venture to pronounce a notorious Falsehood, unless he means the *Quarterly Communication*, or GRAND-LODGE, where a very superb* SWORD of *State* is / always carried before, and placed by the GRAND-MASTER, as a Token of his great *Authority* and *Power*, and not as an Instrument of *War* and *Bloodshed*, as *he* insinuates, as *that* is always confined to the Door of the GRAND, as well as of the *particular* Lodges. But the Word GRAND stuck in our Author's Throat, and the bringing it out would have been too great an Acknowledgment for him who is *called* GRAND-SECRETARY to *that* Society, which (*he says*) is *more* Ancient than *that* which has ever been acknowledged to be the *most* Ancient.

The *little* Piece of *Wit*, concerning the *Tyler's* drawing two *Sign-Posts*, and writing *Jamaica* Rum upon one, and *Barbadoes* Rum upon the other, is (like

---

*   The present SWORD of *State* was a Present from his Grace the Duke of *Norfolk*, [Thomas Howard, eighth Duke of Norfolk (1693–1761), Grand Master of Grand Lodge in 1730. Largely absent during his term of office, he donated the Grand Sword of State. See *Minutes 1723–1739* pp. 112, 118–9, 138.] while he was GRAND MASTER, in the Year 1731, being then at *Venice*. It had been the *Old Trusty* SWORD of GUSTAVUS ADOLPHUS, [King of Sweden (1594–1632), credited as founding Sweden as a great power. See M. Roberts, *Gustavus Adolphus and the Rise of Sweden* (London: English Universities Press, 1973).] King of *Sweden*, and was likewise wore by his Successor in War, the brave BERNARD, Duke of *Sax-weimar*, [a German prince (1604–39) and a general in the Thirty Years' War. See Sir E. Cust, *Lives of the Warriors of the Thirty Years' War – Warriors of the 17th century, Part II* (London: J. Murray, 1865), pp. 307–42.] and has both their Names on the Blade. The Scabbard is richly adorned with the Arms of Norfolk, and the MASONS *Arms*, in Silver gilt, and several Hieroglyphics in *Masonry*. The Cross at the Hilt represents two Columns of the *Corinthian Order*, made of massy Silver, and richly gilt.

many other of his *ridiculous* Criticisms, which I have purposely omitted) beneath my Notice. But after his having deviated from the Character of a *Gentleman*, and a MASON, by traducing and / treating with all the *Ridicule* and *Contempt he* is Master of, the most *respectable Society* perhaps existing, he says, that there are several other *unconstitutional* Proceedings among them, which he passes over in Silence, to avoid giving Offence; by which, some would think, that his *Modesty* had got the better of his *Intentions*, but as *that* is an *Ingredient* which is not to be found in his *Composition*, we will rather suppose that he had already advanced more than he could well support, and was therefore unwilling to subject himself to any further *Censure*.

Thus we see how much we are beholden to (*him* who concludes himself)
Our most sincere Friend,
Obedient Servant,
And faithful Brother.
LAURENCE DERMOTT.

Notwithstanding his *Sneers* on the *History* of MASONRY, he has quoted some things which require a regular *Historical Account*, to set them in a clear Light; and though he has contemptuously treated, and refused / the Assistance of several *Authors* who have wrote on the Subject of *Masonry*, he has neverthe-less thought proper to quote Dr. *D'Assigny*[26] (which was one of them) in Defence of the *Royal Arch Masons*.

He has likewise (to use his own Expression) *seized* on the *English* MASONS *Old Charges*, their *short Charge*, their manner of *constituting a Lodge*, and their *General Regulations*, both *old* and *new*, and has inserted them in his Book almost verbatim, except a few Words, and Expressions, which he has altered, in order to bring them nearer his own Design. To which he has added the *Regulations* of the *Committee* of *Charity*, as practised by the *Grand Lodge* in *Ireland* since the Year 1738, and also the *Regulations* of the *York*, or *Ancient Masons Com-mittee* of *Charity*, as practised by them since the Year 1751. With these, and a great Number of *Songs* (which make one Half his *Volume*) he has patched up his *Constitution-Book*, to the great Joy of his *ancient* Brethren, and to *his* (no *small*) Advantage, as it is published for his *own* private Emolument, and not for the Benefit of the *Ancient Masons* Fund, though he is so *seemingly* solicitous about their Welfare. /

If our *Author* should assert that the *old Charges*, the *Manner of Constitut-ing a Lodge*, and the *General Regulations*, which he has published, are likewise the same as practised in *Ireland*, and by the *Ancient* or *York Masons*; let it be replyed, that the Brethren of *Ireland*, having observed, that from the Foundation of *Masonry* in that *Kingdom*, it had continued in a fluctuating *State*, were at last determined (in Imitation of their Brethren of *England*) to choose a *Noble*

GRAND-MASTER, and in the Year 1730, they elected JAMES KING, *Lord Viscount Kingston*,[27] to that Office, who the Year before had been GRAND-MASTER of the *English* MASONS, and who introduced the same *Constitutions*, and *ancient Usages*, to the GRAND-LODGE of *Ireland*, which are recorded in the *English* MASONS *Constitution-Book*.

With Regard to the *ancient* or *York Masons*, we have no *Regulations* of theirs in Print, but what Mr. *Dermott* has produced, and calls by that Name, and *those* of no longer standing than the Year 1751, which was about the Time that those *very ancient Masons* began to be much talked of. From / hence is appears that the MASONS at *York* approved of the *London* MASONS printing the *Constitution-Book*, from the ancient Records of the *Fraternity*, in the Year 1723, by *their* not printing one in Opposition to it; and they doubtless approved of their Choice of Mr. *Sayer*, as GRAND-MASTER, in the Year 1717, in the room of Sir *Christopher Wren*, or they would certainly have chosen one themselves.

I cannot help observing, that Mr. *Dermott* has not compiled his Book for the Use of *Masons* only, but also for such as may be inclined to be initiated into their *Mysteries*, whom he assures (in order to draw them into his *Society*) *that he has made* FREE MASONRY (both *Ancient* and *Modern) his constant Study for twenty Years past*, and therefore they may depend on him as a *faithful Guide*. However, I find that his Memory is very short (from which some would infer that he is a great *Wit*) and that he is as subject to Error as his *Holiness*, for in *Page* 24, he says, that he was made a *Modern Mason* not above 16 or 17 Years ago; and in *Page* 2, he asserts, that *Masonry Dissected*, was published since the first *Edition* of his / *Book*, which I deny, as it is about 40 Years since that *Publication*, and I had the Curiosity to buy one myself, at least 18 Years ago.

Having finished my *Remarks* on AHIMAN REZON, as well as my *Defence* of our MOST ANCIENT and HONOURABLE FRATERNITY; I shall give a brief Account of the *Characters, Principles* and *Practices*, of those who are called *Ancient Masons*, and conclude with a *Word* of *Advice* to those who are stigmatized with the Name of *Moderns*.

Though there are several Persons of Character and Ability among the *Ancient Masons*, the greater Part of them are a set of *illiterate* and *mean* Persons, such as *Chairmen, Porters, Walking Poulterers*, and the like, chiefly Natives of *Ireland*, who finding it not *convenient* to stay in their own Country, have fled hither to get an HONEST Livelihood; they herd together at Hedge-Alehouses, and because they know the *English* GRAND-LODGE will not authorize their *illicit* and *ignorant* Proceedings, and that the GRAND-MASTER of *Ireland* will not countenance / them *here*, they have, with the Assistance of some HONEST *Yorkshire-Men*, who have come to *London* on the same Account, trumpt up what *they* call *Ancient* or *York Masonry*, and under the specious Pretence of being the *most* Ancient, have drawn in several *well meaning* and *worthy* Persons, by whose

Assistance and Application, a noble *Peer*[28] has condescended to permit them to make use of his Name, as their *Grand-Master*, though (as I observed before) he seldom, if ever, presides in any of their *Assemblies*.

Their Initiation *Fee* is, in general, small, *viz.* ten *Shillings*,[29] and I can safely declare, on the WORD of a MASON (which Expression I shall ever hold sacred) that I have known their *Masters* of *Lodges*, many times, to take Notes of Hand, of the new *Members*, for Half that *Fee*, on Account of their extreme Poverty; notwithstanding Mr. *Dermott's* Assertion, that their *Fee* is never less than two *Guineas*; and it is no uncommon thing for many of them to come to their *Lodges*, without a Farthing in their *Pockets*, and to borrow as much as will make up a *Six-penny* Reckoning of three or four different *Members*. Nay, they go still farther, for if any of / them happen to be *Pennyless*, as they walk the Street, which (I presume) is often the Case, they, without any Ceremony, give the *Sign* or *Signal* of Distress to the first *Brother* they chance to meet, who is obliged to answer, and assist them, or be deemed unworthy their *Vocation*.

Their Contributions to their *Charity* are not *voluntary*, but *obligatory*, and every *Member* of a *Lodge* is obliged to contribute monthly or weekly, a small Sum, after the manner of a *petty Box-Club*, or the *Ancient-Masons* can have no *Charity* for *them*.

The manner of their *working* the *Lodge* is as absurd, as it is prolix. The first time I ever went among them was out of Curiosity, and a *Friend* of mine introduced me, without paying any Regard to that *idle* Distinction between *Ancient* and *Modern*. My *Friend*, and two or three more of the Company were reputable *Tradesmen*, the rest were chiefly such *Persons* as before mentioned. I patiently sat near three Hours, while a red hot *Hibernian* in the *Chair*, was delivering the first *Lecture* (happy was it for him that my Friend *George Alexander Stevens*[30] was / not there, as his *Worship's* Head would certainly have been *Lectured* on at the *Hay-Market*, and I am of Opinion, that it would have afforded as much *humourous* Matter as any Head in *Stephens's* Collection.)

Having sat a great While without opening my Lips, except now and then to moisten them with a little *Porter*, which is their constant, and favourite *Liquor*, I at last was Witness to *their* Form of *initiating* a *Member*, who was by Profession a *Chairman*. This Man paid five *Shillings*, and gave a Note of Hand to the *Master* for five more.

I could not help, though a *Stranger*, expressing my Abhorrence of such ridiculous, mean, and scandalous *Practices*, but my *Mouth* was soon stopt by the *Master*, who said, "*Upon my Shoul now, but I believe he is a Modern!*" then turning to me with an Air of *vast* Consequence, but seemingly much vext, "*Sir*, said he, *the Devil burn me, but I believe you are a Modern-Mason, and that's as good as being no Mason at all!*" Having uttered this, they all cried out, with Voices hoarse as *Thunder*, for the Space of five Minutes, *Hobligate him, Hobligate him*;

which *Ceremony* I was obliged to submit to, / as I now began to think my *Life* in Danger, and glad was I, when I had got out of the *House*. But I have since that, gained Admittance into several of their *Lodges*, from the same Motive of Curiosity, and shall ever be ready to acquaint any regular *Mason* with their *Customs* and *Ceremonies*.

The manner of their *Funeral Processions* is a Disgrace to *Society*. I once saw one which went from *Tower-hill* to *St. Pancras*;[31] the *Corpse* was borne all the Way by sturdy *Chairmen*, who now and then stopt, while others took their Places; about 200 *Persons*, cloathed as *Masons*, attended, some in *laced* Waistcoats, some in *Military* Uniforms, and others with scarcely a *Coat* or *Shirt* to their *Backs*; who having sat in *Ale-houses* adjacent to where the *Corpse* lay, for three or four Hours before, hooting and hollooing with the Windows open, to the great Disturbance of the Neighbourhood, and the Scandal of Masonry; many of them were at last so inebriated, that they required almost as much supporting as their deceased Brother; and Countryman, which afforded much Sport and Diversion to several Hundreds of *Spectators*, who had assembled on that Occasion. /

To the regular Masons of England.

Dear Brethren,

HAving given you a true *Portrait* of those *Deceivers*, and false *Brethren*, I hope you will use your utmost Endeavours to guard against all their *Innovations*, illicit, irregular, and ridiculous *Forms* and *Ceremonies, holding fast the Form of sound Words, without wavering.* Let not the *Masters* of *Lodges* suffer any of their *Brethren* to become Members with those *sham* Ancients, as their *Lodges, &c.* are deemed *irregular* by our Laws, and all who assist at *Makings* in *irregular Lodges*, or attend *Masons* Funerals, *cloathed* as such, without a special Licence, are subject to the following Censure of the GRAND LODGE, *viz.* That they shall not be *Grand-Officers*, or *Officers of particular Lodges*, nor admitted into *Lodges*, even as *Visitors*. They shall likewise be rendered incapable of *Tyling*, or attending on a *Lodge*, or partaking of the *general Charity*, if they come to want it.

If any Person, whom these pretended *Ancients* have drawn in, finds that he is imposed / on, and applies to a *regular Lodge* to be *initiated*, I think there can be no Harm in *re-making* him *gratis*, provided he is a Person of *Character*, and has paid the accustomed *Fee* before, and will faithfully promise not to attend such *irregular Meetings* again. This Opinion however, is submitted to the Sense of the GRAND LODGE.

It were much to be wished, that the *Masters* of *Lodges* were more *brief* in their Instructions than they commonly are, especially when there is *Business* of another Nature, which takes up much Time; as by keeping the *Lodge* open too long, the *Brethren* are detained from their *Families*, which brings Disgrace upon the *Fraternity*; for, a *Lodge* is a Place of pleasant Relaxation from intense *Study*, or Hurry of *Business*, and therefore Prolixity should be avoided; besides, every one who is made a *Mason*, has not a Memory to retain every Particular contained in long *Lectures*, and therefore despair of ever making any tolerable Figure in the *Craft*, and often neglect the *Fraternity* for ever after on that Account. /

As *Ignorance* and *Immorality* are the greatest Enemies to every well regulated *Society*, it is hoped that the MASONS will be particularly careful that the Persons they admit, are such as our excellent *Constitutions* require, for the Preservation of *Harmony* within the *Lodges*, as well as their *Reputation* without.

If what I have written proves of the least Service to that Society, of which I have long been an unworthy Member, my Expectations will be sufficiently answered. And as I commenced *Author* merely by Accident, and drew my *Pen* in a good *Cause*, I hope the candid and judicious *Brethren*, will excuse whatever *Inaccuracies* and *Improprieties* may appear, for I can assure them (*on the Word of a Mason*) that I desire the Reputation of an *Author*, as little as I merit it.

[ANON.], *MASONRY THE WAY TO HELL* (1768)

[Anon.], *Masonry the Way to Hell, a Sermon: Wherein is Clearly Proved, Both from Reason and Scripture, That All who Profess These Mysteries are in a State of Damnation* (London: Printed for Robinson and Roberts at No. 25, in Pater-Noster-Row, MDCCLXVIII [1768])[1]

This anonymous pamphlet is the most virulent attack on English Freemasonry that was published in England in the second half of the eighteenth century. The popularity of this 'celebrated Sermon' is illustrated by the fact that it was reprinted four times in 1768 and brought forth five different masonic responses within a few months.[2] Both the anti-masonic sermon and one of the replies were translated into other European languages. The sheer number of editions – both of the attack and the vindications – shows that they must have been extensively distributed and widely read.

The first edition, which is reproduced as follows, appeared in January or February in 1768.[3] The second edition, which was also printed by Robison and Roberts at no. 25 in Pater-Noster Row and sold by R. Goadby in Sherborne, appeared on 2 May.[4] There is an edition which was published in both London and Dublin, where it was reprinted by W. G. Jones and J. Millikin in the same year. Another London edition with a slightly different title (*Free Masonry The High-Way to Hell, a Sermon, wherein is Clearly Proved, both from Reason and Scripture*) and pagination but with exactly the same content was also published in 1768.[5] A German translation was published in Brunswick in 1768 and the second edition in 1770.[6] A French translation of the German translation was issued in Frankfurt in 1769.[7]

Although *Masonry the Way to Hell* was written in the form of a sermon, its immoderate language makes it unlikely that it was ever preached in a church. One of the reasons why the author chose this genre was to reach the widest audience, including English Catholics. The sermon, as an important means of communication and instruction, was a highly popular genre in the eighteenth century. Religious writings like sermons were regarded as reliable sellers and thus formed a considerable part of the book trade.[8]

The author is unknown. We can infer from the argument that the anonymous writer was either a Roman Catholic or sympathetic to Catholicism. He must have found the rapid growth of English masonic lodges in the 1760s dangerous.[9] John Thompson, who wrote one of the replies to the *Masonry the Way to Hell*, suggests that the author was a Jesuit. He calls him a 'Jesuitical Sophister' who is ignorant of the mysteries of Freemasonry.[10] Thompson asks, 'is it not expedient to enact others to prevent the *Jesuitical* Harpies from entering this Kingdom, and seducing the unwary by their insidious Writings?'[11] It may be noted that after the Jesuits were expelled from France (1764) and Spain (1767), many of them settled in England.[12]

The references to masonic ceremonies – such as the words of the different degrees – in the sermon suggest that the author must have consulted one or more of the 'exposures' that were published in the 1760s. They include *The Master-Key* (1760), *Three Distinct Knocks* (1760), *Jachin and Boaz* (1762), *Hiram* (1764), *Mystery of Freemasonry Explained* (1765), *Shibboleth* (1765), *Mahhabone* (1766) and *Solomon in All His Glory* (1766).[13] The author certainly used the latter, from which he quotes verbatim several times. *Solomon in All His Glory* was a translation of a French exposure, *Le Maçon démasqué* (1751), probably written by George Smith (*c*.1728–*c*.1785).[14] In the annotations of this text, the borrowings from the *Solomon in All His Glory* (1768) are highlighted, a later edition of which is reprinted in volume 2. Some references to masonic ceremonies in the sermon are clearly the products of the author's imagination.

The language of the sermon, which tries to condemn Freemasonry with the help of reason and revelation, is violent and coarse. The author ridicules the mysteries of Freemasonry and charges the members of lodges with blasphemy, impiety, drunkenness and 'abominable actions'.[15] Although the anti-Catholic sentiment of the English population decreased after the failure of the Jacobite cause, this sermon clearly mirrors the sharp religious divisions between Catholics and Protestants in mid-eighteenth century England.

The publishers were George Robinson (d. 1801) and J. Roberts. Robinson was a printer and 'one of the most eminent booksellers of his time', who paid his authors well. He worked in London, Addison's Head, 25 Paternoster Row between 1764 and 1801. He started his career as a 'wholesale bookseller in partnership with J. Roberts, who died about the year 1776'.[16] Their many publications include *The Critical Review, or, Annals of Literature*, which issued a brief review of this pamphlet in March 1768. They also printed two editions of *Solomon in All His Glory*, a translation of a French masonic exposure, in 1766 and 1768.[17] The type of printing and lay-out of these editions are very similar to those of *Masonry the Way to Hell*. Very few printed copies of this anti-masonic tract survive. The text below is based on the first edition available in the Library and Museum of Freemasonry in London.

Notes

1.   This headnote was written by Róbert Péter.
2.   *Critical Review, or, Annals of Literature*, 25 (May 1768), p. 395.
3.   *Monthly Review*, 38 (February 1768), p. 160. *Critical Review, or, Annals of Literature*, 25 (March 1768), p. 239. These short pieces with comments on the book in question are reproduced in volume 5. *Scots Magazine*, 30 (March 1768), p. 147.
4.   *Western Flying Post of Sherborne and Yeovil Mercury and General Advertiser* (2 May 1768), quoted in W. Hammond, 'Two Pamphlets', *AQC*, 10 (1897), p. 158.
5.   *Free Masonry The High-Way to Hell, a Sermon, wherein is Clearly Proved, both from Reason and Scripture: That All who Possess these Mysteries are in a State of Eternal Damnation* (London, 1768). This edition is reprinted in J. T. Thorp (ed), *Reproductions of Masonic Manuscripts, Books and Pamphlets with Notes, Masonic Reprints*, Vol. 5 (Leicester: Printed by Bros. Johnson, Wykes and Paine, 1922), pp. 30–52. Because of the very harsh attack on Freemasonry, Thorp noted that 'some of the Brethren may be inclined to criticize its reproduction' (p. 7). The reproductions in Thorp's *Masonic Reprints* are incomplete as he left out words from the original works that appeared in the rituals of his time and were then regarded by English Freemasons as not to be disclosed.
6.   *Die Freimäurerei, der Weg zu Hölle: ein Predigt, worinn deutlich aus Schrift und Vernunft gezeiget wird, dass alle, die zu diesem Orden gehören, in einem Stande der Verdammniss sind* (Braunschweig, 1768). There is a copy of the German translation in the LMFL.
7.   *La Franche-Maçonnerie n'est que le chemin de l'enfer*, trad. de l'allemand de Meyer (Frankfurt, 1769).
8.   K. Olsen, *Daily Life in 18th-Century England* (Westport: Greenwood, 1999), p. 289. B. Harris, 'Print Culture', in H. T. Dickinson (ed.), *A Companion to Eighteenth-Century Britain* (Oxford: Blackwell, 2002), pp. 283–93, on p. 283. J. V. Eijnatten, 'Reaching Audiences: Sermons and Oratory in Europe,' in S. J. Brown and T. Tackett (eds), *Enlightenment, Reawakening and Revolution 1660–1815. Vol. 7* (Cambridge: Cambridge University Press, 2006), pp. 128–46, on p. 130.
9.   As for the register list of the Moderns Grand Lodge – there were ninety-nine London and ninety-eight country lodges in 1760, whereas in 1768 146 London and 157 country lodges were registered. As for the Antients Grand Lodge – thirty-two London and eighteen country lodges existed in 1760; there were twenty-nine London and forty-six country lodges at the time of the publication of the sermon. J. Lane, *A Handy Book to the Study of the Engraved, Printed, and Manuscript Lists of Lodges of Ancient Free & Accepted Masons of England, from 1728 to 1814* (London: George Kenning, 1889), pp. 158, 160.
10. J. Thompson, *Remarks on a Sermon Lately Published; Entitled, Masonry the Way to Hell. Being a Defence of that Antient and Honourable Order, against the Jesuitical Sophistry and False Calumny of the Author* (London: Printed by S. Axtell and H. Hardy, for T. Evans, at No. 20, in Pater-Noster Row, 1768), pp. 10; 6, 8, 19, 27, 29, 34.
11. Thompson, *Remarks on a Sermon Lately Published*, p. 30.
12. C. Haydon, 'Religious Minorities in England', in H. T. Dickinson (ed.), *A Companion to Eighteenth-Century Britain* (Oxford: Blackwell Publishing, 2002), pp. 241–51, on p. 244.

13.   Of those, editions of *The Master-Key, Hiram* and *Solomon in All His Glory* are reproduced in volume 2. See A. C. F. Jackson, *English Masonic Exposures, 1760–69* (London: Lewis Masonic, 1986).

14.   See *MMLDP*, vol. 3, pp. 2562–6.

15.   See p. 163.

16.   H. R. Plomer, G. H. Bushnell and McC. Dix (eds), *A Dictionary of the Printers and Booksellers who were at Work in England, Scotland and Ireland from 1726 to 1775* (n. p.: Oxford University Press for the Bibliographical Society, 1932), p. 215.

17.   T. Wilson, master of the Swan Tavern Lodge, *Solomon in all His Glory: Or, the Master-Mason. being a True Guide to the Inmost Recesses of Free-Masonry, both Ancient and Modern. ... by T. W. ... Translated from the French Original Published at Berlin* (London: printed for G. Robinson and J. Roberts, 1766). T. Wilson, *Solomon in all His Glory: Or, the Master-Mason. being a True Guide to the Inmost Recesses of Free-Masonry, both Ancient and Modern. ... Illustrated with several Elegant Copper-Plates, Exhibiting the Different Lodges, Free-Masons Cyphers, &c. to which is Added, a Complete List of all the English Regular Lodges in the World, ... by T. W. ... the Second Edition, with the Addition of Two Beautiful Copper-Plates. Translated from the French Original Published at Berlin* (London: printed for Robinson and Roberts, 1768).

[Anon.], *Masonry the Way to Hell, a Sermon* (1768)

MASONRY
THE WAY TO HELL,
A
SERMON:
Wherein is clearly proved,
Both from REASON and SCRIPTURE, That all who profess these MYSTERIES
are in a State of DAMNATION.
Mystery, the Whore of Babylon, &c. Revel.
LONDON:
Printed for ROBINSON and ROBERTS at No. 25, in PATER-NOSTER-ROW.
MDCCLXVIII. /

REVEL[ATION]. XVII. 5.
*And upon her forehead was a name written, Mystery, Babylon the Great, the
Mother of Harlots, and Abominations of the Earth.*

I HAVE been induced to make choice of this text, to rectify the gross misappre-
hension of commentators in regard to its true interpretation. By protestant divines
this portion of sacred writ has generally been applied to the church of Rome; and
for no other reason I can think of, than that the city of that name is built upon
seven hills, and that it is said of the whore of Babylon, that she sitteth on seven
mountains. It is surprising that an analogy so remote, so partial, and so capricious,
could ever be made the foundation of an opinion so repugnant to common sense,
and withal so ridiculous as scarcely to admit of a serious refutation. With / what
justice can the church of Rome be called the mother of harlots, when it is well
known that, in popish countries, a great part of the female sex take upon them
vows of virginity? As to the application of the text to the pope of Rome, who is
the head of that church, it is still more ridiculous: for, is it possible that an old
man should be a whore? Or, can he be said to sit upon seven mountains, when we
are certain that he occupies no more space than any ordinary man? Besides, why
should it be imagined that by the city of Babylon is understood Rome, when they
have no more connection with each other than with London or Constantinople?

From the force of these arguments, I think it must be concluded that something else than the church of Rome, or the pope, is understood in the words of the text. But before I unfold the explanation, let me observe, that there is not any passage in scripture where the meaning is more clearly expressed, or of which the application intended will appear so obvious and unquestionable, that it is amazing how it has hitherto escaped the notice of commentators. /

The words of the text, then, relate entirely to Masonry. If it should be wondered at, that a great part of the sacred writings is employed upon that subject, let it be remembered, that though these pretended mysteries are the most ridiculous nonsense that ever engaged the attention of any rational beings, they are rendered of importance in the eyes of religion, by their malignant influence on the morals of mankind; and on that account only they can lay claim to the smallest regard. The societies of Free Masons are now so well known, and so notoriously infamous, that it is needless to give any definition of them: for there scarcely is one contemptible fellow in the kingdom who is not a member of these fraternities.[1] I shall, therefore, without any farther preamble, enter upon the explanation of the text: in discoursing from which, I propose the following method:

First, I shall clearly prove, both from reason and revelation, that by the title Babylon, is understood Masonry.

Secondly, I shall take a general view of the subject of Masonry; expose the impiety and absurdity of its mysteries, and the / wickedness of those who profess them; pointing out, at the same time, the malignant influence of this institution on society.

Thirdly, I shall expostulate a little with some of those who adhere to the abominations of Masonry: and

Fourthly, shew that all they who adhere to them will be damned.

In the first place then, I shall prove that by the term Babylon, is understood Masonry. The truth of this proposition is evident from the beginning of the text, where it is said, *And upon her forehead was a name written, Mystery*. It is certain that nothing can more properly be called mystery, than the arcana I have mentioned: though, at the same time, they are the most ridiculous absurdities that ever were imposed upon mankind; for they are maintained to be unsearchable, and are always communicated under the sanction of an oath. But the woman upon whom the inscription was written is called Babylon. It is generally allowed that the city Babylon stood in the same plains where the famous tower of Babel[2] was built; and / what could be a more natural appellation for Masonry than a name which will perpetuate the audacious insolence of the trade of builders? She is called Babylon the Great, not only from the vast height to which that tower was carried before its destruction, but likewise in allusion to the amazing number of persons who have been initiated in these mysteries; many of whom, to the disgrace of their dignity, were such as, in the estimation of the world, had been reckoned great, as princes, lords, &c. In conformity to this observation, we are told in the same chapter, that *the kings of the earth had committed abomination with her.*

She is called *the mother of harlots*; a name which is to be interpreted in a figurative sense, alluding, without doubt, to the vices and infamy of these societies. Nothing can be more applicable to Masonry, by which are understood all Free Masons, than the denomination of harlots: for as women of that character affect to inspire men with the warmest ideas of pleasure, until they allure them into their baneful embraces, so the Free Masons, or male harlots,[xviii] / (as they may be emphatically called) practise upon others their deceitful arts, to inveigle them to be initiated in their mysteries. When we consider the closeness of this comparison in every point, we cannot enough admire the propriety of the metaphor which the apostle has here made use of. For to carry the resemblance one step further, what can more strongly denote the vileness and inanity of these contemptible mysteries, which are participated [in] by almost all the meanest, most ignorant, and infamous wretches in the kingdom, than to find them likened to the enjoyment of a common prostitute?

The epithet of *the mother of harlots*, is also wonderfully applicable to the subject: for it is usual with the fools of Masonry to pay a particular regard to one certain place where they celebrate their orgies, in respect of which they look upon all others of the same sort as inferior and dependent, and for that reason call it the mother-lodge. Besides, Masonry, supporting a constant succession of members, who in their own stile are called brethren, may claim the denomination of a parent. /

It is added, *and abominations of the earth*. By the word abominations is intended every species of wickedness, and whatever is contrary to the dictates of reason and religion: now it is certain that there is no set of people in the world more addicted to abominations, and these of the vilest and most enormous nature, than the societies of Free Masons: but of this I shall have occasion to speak afterwards. At present let us only trace the conformity of the application in one circumstance more. It is said in verse third of the chapter from which I have taken my text, that the woman (Babylon) has seven heads; and in verse the ninth, *the seven heads are seven mountains, on which the woman sitteth.* This description alludes plainly to the seven steps which these impostors chalk upon the floor of the lodge[3] at the reception of a brother, and on which they make him tread, persuading him in the mean time that he is ascending into the temple of Solomon. Or, it may likewise refer to the number of the constituent members of a perfect lodge, which are always seven, viz. / the master, two wardens, two fellow-craft, and two apprentices.[4]

Having thus explained the sense of the text in as few words as possible, I think it must appear evident to every unprejudiced person that by the term

Babylon, nothing else is intended than Masonry. I come now to the second head proposed, which was, to take a general view of the subject of Masonry; expose the impiety and absurdity of its mysteries, and the wickedness of those who profess them; pointing out at the same time the malignant influence of this institution on society. I am well aware of the great disadvantages under which I must labour in treating a subject of this kind. My veracity may be questioned even among the disinterested part of mankind; for it will scarcely be credited that any human creatures could employ themselves in such ridiculous mysteries: and to this opinion only it is owing that the nature of Masonry is still generally regarded as secret, though in reality it has been often and ingenuously exposed to the world. But whatever reception my present undertaking may meet with from / readers of sense and candour, I may expect that it will be most virulently calumniated by all those who are inclined to support the reputation of Masonry: for should the reality of such facts as I shall mention be acknowledged by them, they would be for ever deprived of any opportunity of gormandizing upon the spoils of a new-inveigled brother; and they will sooner sell themselves, both soul and body, to the devil, than relinquish an occasion so extremely favourable to the indulgence of all their carnal, and inordinate lusts and appetites. On this account, however much these people may deny the real conviction they feel, I shall draw this advantage from their dissimulation, that their strongest opposition, or affected contempt, will equally be regarded by others as corroborating proofs of my veracity.

In hopes, therefore, that my attempt may be productive of some advantage to the public, I shall here give such a general account of Masonry as is consistent with the nature of this discourse. But I must premise that as Free Masons are sworn not to reveal their secrets, neither by writing, / engraving, carving, nor any other method whatever, and it is by means of oral tradition only that even the initiated are taught them, there is considerable diversity both in the words and ceremonies made use of in different countries. The practice of a regular lodge in France is somewhat different from that in England, as some customs of both these are from the practice of the lodges in Scotland. Besides these capricious variations, a total change of some things has been universally adopted. Of this we have an instance in the master's word, which, originally, was no less than the name of the great Jehovah; but in process of time was changed into Macbenac, a word signifying stink, or putrefaction.[5]

The only important, though not the first step in celebrating the mysteries of Masonry, is an open violation of the great commandment, *Thou shalt not take the name of the Lord thy God in vain:*[6] for an oath of secrecy, the most execrable and tremendous that ever was invented, is administered in the course of their ceremonies. The form of this oath is various; but, in general, they swear not to reveal the secrets of Masonry / directly or indirectly, denouncing upon themselves the most horrid imprecations, if they break this engagement.[7] As the very existence of Masonry depends greatly upon the degree of regard which is paid to this impious oath, it may be worth while to enquire a little into its validity, and examine how far it is entitled in a religious or moral light to the force of obligation. It is universally allowed necessary to the obligation of an oath, that it be voluntary, and not taken through compulsion. The force of every sacramental engagement is founded upon freedom of action: for an oath is no more than a solemn renunciation of the liberty of acting contrary to any stipulated compact. This liberty, therefore, must have remained entire at the time when the engagement was entered into. If it did not, but was overawed by violence or superior power, the assent so procured is void, and of no obligation. Let us now take a view of the reception of a Free Mason apprentice, and enquire whether or not he can be considered as a free agent at the time when the oath is administered to him. /

The poor deluded candidate is conducted into a dark apartment, where, in order to excite the more terrible apprehensions, his eyes are blindfolded with a handkerchief.[8] From this purgatory he is led into the assembly of Masons, which ceremony is performed in some lodges with a halter put round his neck. A dread and portentous silence is held for some time, till of a sudden his ears are assailed either with a hideous rattling of aprons, or the clashing of swords over his head; or perhaps he is accosted in such terms as these: *Rash profane, dare you tread this ground? Tremble, profane, at what this temerity of yours may cost you.* It may be that he is then made to travel under the iron vault, as they call it, frequently running his head against a naked sword, which is held by some worshipful brother, or striking his feet against obstacles purposely placed in his way; while at every step he makes, the frantic assembly is pouring forth the most alarming exclamations. This unaccountable prelude being acted, the culprit is placed in the posture for receiving the oath; when it is reasonable to suppose that he is in such a situation, both / of body and mind, as scarcely to know what he is doing. And in fact, that in many people there is a violent perturbation of the animal œconomy, is evident from the sudden and involuntary discharges which frequently happen at this time. It is the practice in many of these purlieus of Masonry, to receive the oath blindfolded; and lest the poor candidate's resolution should be staggered at the tremendous imprecations to be pronounced, sharp pointed weapons are presented to his breast. In others, the oath is taken with the eyes open; but if the handkerchief is removed, it is only to present to the sight a scene of yet greater horror. The amazed victim beholds now on his right and left a croud of fanatic wretches with naked swords in their hands, presenting the points towards him with menacing looks, and the venerable master holding up a large mallet, as if ready to sacrifice him. In this crisis the oath is administered.

I shall appeal to any reasonable person, whether an oath imposed in these circumstances, where a man is surrounded with such objects as naturally awake the strongest / apprehensions of danger, and his life is apparently threatened, can be reckoned a free and voluntary engagement. On the contrary, is it not in the highest degree compulsive? It can never be urged that the oath is voluntary, because at the beginning of the ceremonies, when the candidate was asked whether he was willing to submit to it, he replied in the affirmative. He received not the smallest suggestion of the terrifying scene which would accompany the administration of it. If these impostors should alledge in their own defence, that this formidable tumult and apparatus was no more than a farce, they must grant, by a parity of reason, that the oath is the same, or incur the sacrilegious guilt of mixing things profane with those which are most sacred and inviolable. In short, whether we consider this strange affair in the light either of a serious or ludicrous transaction, the administration of the oath is equally impious, and the notion of its validity must be spurned at, and exploded, by every friend of reason and religion. The purposes for which this oath is prostituted afford likewise the strongest arguments against its / obligation; for the intention of it here is not like that in all other cases, to confirm some important truth, to maintain justice, or to secure the public tranquility: but it is to keep secret certain words and ceremonies, which consciousness of their futility, and the shame of acknowledging a disappointment, afford sufficient inducement to conceal, and which, so far from being of advantage, are absolutely of the greatest detriment to the interest and happiness of society, as shall afterwards be made to appear. A regard, therefore, to such an oath, is not only weak, but criminal; for while we conceal an infamous artifice which was imposed upon ourselves, and we know to be currently practised, we are actually guilty of imposing that artifice upon others. Let it not be imagined from what is here said, that I mean in the least to invalidate the obligation of oaths in general: on the contrary, I affirm, that of all human regards there is nothing more sacred and inviolable. Even the heathens were so sensible of the moral obligation of oaths, that they fabled the gods themselves to be restrained by them: and certainly the infringement / of them when properly taken, can never be countenanced upon the principles of our holy religion: but what impious, what horrible doctrines, might not be derived from that religion, should we allow it to be rendered subservient to the purposes of iniquity and imposture? Can a more audacious insult be offered to the majesty of almighty God, than to call him solemnly to witness the most ridiculous words and ceremonies, and the extinction of that divine light of reason, which was given us for the direction of our conduct? And shall the mere outward form of a constrained oath, wherein every requisite circumstance of an obligatory engagement is wanting, and every other attending it is founded upon the most flagrant impiety, can such a form, I say, be ever regarded as a ratification of religious and inviolable authority? Adieu religion! adieu morality! farewel, ye deceitful phantoms! and all distinction of right and wrong, if ye assert the validity of a sanction which violence constrained you to yield.

I thought it necessary to insist the more upon this subject, as there is ground to / imagine that the secrecy of many who have been initiated in these ridiculous mysteries has been greatly owing to a mistaken opinion of the obligation of an impious and sacrilegious oath.

After the solemn administration of the oath we have mentioned, who would not conclude that the secrets about to be communicated were of the greatest and most extensive influence on human felicity? But hear, O heaven! and give ear, O earth! these important mysteries, these inestimable arcana, which the name of the most high God was prostituted to conceal, are no more than *Boaz*.[9] Hail sacred and ineffable mysteries! worthy to be concealed in eternal oblivion.

Was ever any farce so ridiculous? Let us imagine we behold a number of men assembled in all the dignity of the Roman senate; around their necks hang the rule, the compass, the plumb-line, and various ensigns of masonry: upon the floor before them are drawn some figures in chalk. Every thing is conducted with an air of solemnity and importance, as if they were ready to carry into execution the proposition / of Archimedes, of moving the world out of its place, or rectifying some fault of the creation. During this scene a person is introduced, who is desirous of being initiated in their important mysteries; in order to which he must be stripped of all metal.[10] It is abominable and the root of all evil. Should even the vestment which covers his nakedness be fastened with a nail, the accursed thing must be extracted; himself must be blindfolded, and every method of terror made use of to inspire him with awe. To secure him sufficiently to themselves, he is then bound by an oath of secrecy. The solemn scene is now over, and while the poor novice is gaping with astonishment and impatience to receive the mighty secret, he is informed it is to make a sign with the hand, or pronounce the word BOAZ. He is then saluted by the worshipful brethren, and congratulated on the prodigious advancement he has made in the mysteries of Masonry. It would be endless, as well as foreign to my purpose, to recount the various absurdities in conversation and behaviour which are solemnly practised in these societies. To point the fingers to the throat; / to form a rule or angle with the knife and fork, and such unmanly tricks, are extremely important actions in the eyes of these harlequins. Should we take a view of them in respect of scientifical accomplishments, we shall find them most deplorably ignorant. They tell us that a lodge has three doors,[11] one to the east, another to the west, and a third to the south, but none to the north. For what reason? Because, say they, the sun never shines in that quarter. They know not that beyond the tropic of Capricorn, the sun shines from the north, as much as it shines from the south on this side the tropic of Cancer.[12] Another instance of their ignorance is still more remarkable, as it relates to one of the most simple facts in mensuration. They say that the circumference of the pillars of the temple were twelve cubits, and their thickness four fingers, by which they would make the circumstance of a circle to be a hundred times greater than its diameter; though it is well known that the proportion is no more than nearly three to one.[13]

How intelligible their conversation is, we may judge by an example from their catechism.[14] /

Q. If you were in danger, what would you do?

A. I would put my hand upon my head, and cry out, The widow's children are mine.

This is the consequence of the confusion of languages which was brought upon the world at the destruction of Babel, and still subsists in these societies. The apprentice knows not the jargon of the fellow-craft, nor the fellow-craft that of the master. Hence arises a necessity for various signs and tokens, to make their meaning known to each other: but so few are the ideas they have to communicate, that this mute intercourse is seldom or never employed but to discover a Free Mason. And what is a Free Mason? If we take the account of him from their own catechism, he answers to the following description. He is an animal which comes from the valley of Jehosaphat: he lives generally to the same age with men; but never will allow that he is older than five years and an half. The foundation of his lodge reaches from the surface to the center of the earth: he keeps the key of it / under the root of his tongue; and his heart may be opened with a key of ivory. He is always to be found betwixt the rule and the compass. When he opens his mouth, it is generally in some absurdity; and he seems to be so sensible of his incapacity for conversation, that he endeavours to make his meaning understood by various odd gestures. He is ever a griping to distinguish his own species.[15]

Such are the words and ceremonies, the tenets and practices of Masonry; a mass of absurdity and extravagance, which all the legends in the universe cannot equal, and so flagrant an imposition, that a council learned in the law would make it out to be clearly comprehended under the act relative to procuring money by fraudulent and false pretences. We suppress brothels, we prohibit by penal laws the religious convention of heretics, while in reality there are no places where impiety and enthusiasm are so effectually propagated, as in the holy lodge of St. John, and no set of people so deserving of prosecution, as they who not only pervert the doctrines of revelation, but extinguish reason itself. / The lodges of Masonry are sinks of all human depravity: and as our blessed Lord told his disciples, that *wherever two or three of them are met together in his name, there he was in the midst of them to bless them*; so it may be said, in contradistinction, that wherever two or three Masons are met together to celebrate their mysteries, there the devil is essentially in the midst of them, to rejoice over them. This will appear incontestible from the account I am now to exhibit of the wickedness of these men.

That they are familiar with blasphemy and impiety in the repeated administration of the most execrable and tremendous oath, I have shewn above: that they are professed liars is evident from their very catechism; for at the admission of a Free Mason apprentice, when the question is put, *whence came you?* he must answer, forsooth, *from the lodge of St. John*.[16] What faith is to be placed in the veracity of a people who make a practice of lying in such frivolous matters? It is likewise a maxim among them, that if one is asked by a brother, *how old are you?* he shall answer, / *five years and an half*;[17] though he be conscious that he is really turned of fifty, or perhaps in his grand climacteric. And yet they dare to establish this absurdity upon an impious allusion to the words of our blessed Saviour, Matt. xviii. 3. *Except ye be converted, and become as little children, ye shall not enter into the kingdom of heaven*; or, as they mean, into the lodge. It is certain, however, that they have a just enough pretension to the title of children, in a metaphorical sense; for their questions and answers, their signs and tokens, are a collection of the most foolish and nonsensical puerilities that ever entered into the head of a bedlamite, and so ridiculously childish, that a boy of five years old would deserve flagellation for repeating them. Among the catalogue of their vices we may likewise reckon a strong propensity to the unnatural crime of murder: for every person who is initiated in their mysteries is bound by the most horrid oath, to submit to have his heart taken out, if he devulge their secrets.[18] By these means they hope to secure to themselves either the close enjoyment of an associate, or the blood / of the delinquent. Nay, so far has the thirst of human blood been indulged among them, even from their own tradition, that, at building the temple of Solomon, the fellow-craft imbrued their rebellious hands in that of their master Adoniram or Hiram[19] (as some of them call him) not on account of betraying their secrets, but because he would not betray them for their profit. Let us examine their conduct in other particulars: Do they propagate either sobriety or industry? Do they cherish among their members the natural affection and attention to the welfare of their respective families? Instead of sobriety, do they not indulge in drunkenness? Instead of industry, riot in dissipation and idleness? Instead of love for their wives and children, do they not give too much ground to admit the suspicion which is entertained of them by many women? Would not good men think it their duty to avoid all appearance of evil? And to say the truth, what abominable actions may not be supposed to be committed amongst them, when their passions are inflamed with drink, and their hearts burn with enthusiastic affection to each other? Then is / the season of every evil concupiscence. Add to this, that their assemblies are held at such hours as are most suitable to the works of darkness; and that the most enormous crimes may be perpetrated by them with impunity, under the inviolable secrecy they enjoin, nay, under the very pretext of their being the mysteries of Masonry. *Wo unto you*, Masons, *hypocrites! It shall be more tolerable for Tyre and Sidon at the day of judgment, than for you.*[20] *Wo unto them that seek deep to hide their counsel from the Lord, and their works are in the dark, and they say, who seeth us? and who knoweth us?*[21]

To this terrible charge may be added a strong attachment to the diabolical art of necromancy, which is apparent from their extraordinary veneration for three, five, and seven, the cabalistic, or Babylonian numbers.[22]

To compensate for all these enormities, they affect to persuade us of their charity. We are told indeed that charity hides a multitude of sins: but let us examine upon what foundation they pretend to this virtue. If, say they, a member of their society should be reduced to indigence, they / contribute to maintain him. I shall not dispute the truth of some such facts; for it is well known that in several institutions among us, which are founded entirely upon charity, the contributions are very inconsiderable, till the members hearts are sufficiently warmed by eating a hearty dinner: and as Masons have more frequent meetings than other societies, and are generally addicted to drinking and gormandizing, it would be strange if an ostentatious act of false charity did not sometimes break forth amongst them. But is it charity to confine our munificence to those only who are connected with us in wickedness? To withhold the sustenance of life from an indigent person of good character, in order to bestow it upon one of the most worthless of mankind? Does not real charity comprehend within its regard every object of compassion, of whatever different class or denomination? It is plain their benefactions are so far from being charity, that they are really the wages of iniquity.

Upon the whole, it appears evident from the history of Free Masons, from their vices and follies, from their rioting / and excesses, from their open contempt, or secret profanation of religion, and from the abuse of reason, on the total prostration of which all their mysteries are founded, that they are both the most weak and most wicked of mankind, and (as I formerly said) that the character of being the *mother of abominations* is in all respects most applicable to Masonry.

If Masons could justly lay claim to any species of virtue, humility would seem that to which they had the most plausible pretensions; for they profess at their meetings to acknowledge no distinction of character. The prince and the porter, the lord and the lackey, are all upon equality: all are united by the friendly gripe. But whatever humility might be inferred from this condescension of the most conspicuous members, the true motive to their conduct is a propensity to low and illiberal gratifications; or pride itself, that very passion of which they would seem destitute, preposterous and disguised pride, may be the source of their conduct. For they who are not qualified to distinguish themselves in legislative or judicial assemblies, may / have their vanity in being regarded as somewhat eminent among low mechanics.

But while the conduct of one part of the fraternity proceeds from sordid pleasure, mean pride, or false humility, that of the other is certainly misguided by a pernicious and delusive ambition; which leads me to consider the malignant influence of this institution on society. People of the lower classes in life are charmed with the flattering idea of being called the brethren of men of rank and fortune. Sometimes, indeed, interest is more their motive than vanity, and they are desirous of cultivating acquaintance with their superiors, from the advantages in point of business which they think may accrue from it; but whatever familiarities are indulged at their nocturnal meetings, I believe it is pretty certain, that for one tradesman who has reaped any advantage from an acquaintance contracted in the lodge, with a person of rank and fortune, a thousand have ruined themselves,[xix] by the extravagant courses into which they have run to obtain it. Say, ye deluded mortals! will any of your noble brethren visit you in the time of your / sickness? will they relieve you out of prison? will they promote you to any post of profit which they have at disposal? Such were the visionary expectations of Sporado,[23] an unfortunate convict, who, after a long but fruitless acquaintance with many of the nobility, ended his days at Tyburn, a victim to Masonry, and a warning to all who profess it.

Sporado was a lamp-lighter in the parish of St. Giles: about the age of thirty he entered into the society of Free Masons, by whom (as he used afterwards to boast) he was received with greater marks of friendship than ever he had met with from any other people in his life. From the time he was initiated, he diligently attended all the meetings of his brethren, and was soon reckoned the best mason in the lodge. On this account it was common for every brother of distinction to place himself near Sporado, whom they all caressed in the warmest manner. Now would he teach them to point their fingers to their throats: now he would review the discipline of bending the arm: then he would instruct them when to say Macbenac,[24] / while betwixt every subject they united in a friendly gripe. So hearty and unreserved were the squeezes which passed on these occasions, that Sporado began to entertain no small hopes of being soon rendered independent, through the interest of his noble brethren. In the mean time, however, the profit which he drew from his business being insufficient to support the expence of such frequent meetings, he resolved to be take himself to house-breaking. For three years he continued his depredations in that capacity, from the connivance of some watchmen, who were brother Masons, and pimps. But being at length apprehended, he was capitally convicted. During the whole time of his imprisonment, he remained confident of procuring a pardon, asserted impudently that the sovereign was his brother, and therefore, that an order for his execution would never be signed by his majesty. However, by the persuasion of some of the fraternity, who had come to condole with him, he employed a person to write in his name (being unable himself) to a noble lord at court, on whose interest he / much depended, to make application in his behalf; adjuring his lordship, by the tender relation of brotherhood in which they were connected, and the many cordial declarations of friendship which had passed between them in the lodge. In vain was all sollicitation. The voice of justice cried aloud for the life of the delinquent. On the fatal day he was drawn to the place of execution, where he solemnly renounced the abominations of Masonry, and sincerely regretted that ever he had cultivated any acquaintance with the nobility, who deserted him in the misfortunes in which he had been involved from the foolish desire of maintaining his connections with them.

Ye partizans of Masonry, behold in this example the result of all your pursuits! Behold the great advantages; behold the faithful friendship ye expect! Yet still intoxicated with the gay delusion, ye dress, ye feast, ye drink, while your miserable wives and children are starved to support your extravagance. Let us now take a view of the habitation of a Free Mason on the / night of his solemn festival. Alas! no festival is there. How desolate! no candle to give light! no fire to bestow its comforting warmth in the rigour of the season! There sits the once beloved wife of his bosom all bathed in tears. A thousand anxious thoughts perplex her mind, concerning the nature, concerning the consequence of that infernal secret, which seems to involve in its fascinating mysteries the fate of all that she holds dear. Her feeble arms, exhausted with fasting, scarce able to support the tender infant which hangs at her breast: her children implore her for the sustenance of nature, which she knows not how to procure. While your husband, O afflicted mother! is now sollacing himself in the mansion of riot, in company with the sons of Belial,[25] and triumphing in the honour of calling a lord his brother, you are lamenting your helpless little children in the house of mourning. Scene of horror! Yet these are the works of men who wear the rule and compass, as emblems of circumspection and prudence in their conduct. /

Having thus briefly pointed out the unparalleled futility of Masonry, and its malignant influence on society, I come now to the third head proposed, namely, to expostulate a little with some of those who adhere to the abominations of it.

Ye legislators, who sit in the great council of the nation, and whose ruling passion ought to be, to promote the good and happiness of the public, what is your motive to encourage a society whose foundation is in deceit, and whose intemperance is supported upon the ruin of a thousand indigent families? If ye are not capable of rendering service to your country by political abilities, pray act not so inconsistent with your duty, as to give sanction to dissipation and drunkenness. Is it not utterly repugnant to all the maxims of good policy, to countenance the meetings of such a numerous association of men, who, from the privacy of their transactions, and the attachment they profess to each other, ought to be regarded with a jealous attention by the guardians of public liberty? Or what confidence is to be placed in the loyalty of enthusiasts, who / represent their venerable master by the same symbol with almighty God? Is it to this honour ye aspire? Go, then, with your great ambition, and preside in the lodges of Masonry; but know, when your applauses resound, they proclaim that folly is of all denominations!

Ye worshipful magistrates, who preside over the peace and morals of the community, what apology can ye plead for entering into these assemblies? I can ascribe your conduct to no other principle than the scandalous love of feasting, for which ye are almost all so remarkable. How unlike the magistrates whose virtuous example gave force to the sumptuary laws of the temperate Spartans! When shall the time come, that an English alderman, like a Roman citizen, shall be contented with his frugal mess of turnips, ready to sacrifice his life for the good of his country, not the interest of his country to his belly!

Ye generals of armies, shall the manly soul of the soldier submit to a discipline too mean even for the diversion of children? Ye who have trodden the glorious fields of war, what pleasure can ye enjoy / in stepping over the lines of chalk which are drawn upon the floor of the lodge? do ye indulge the fancy that ye are then forcing the trenches of an enemy? or, when they tell you ye are mounting into the temple of Solomon, do ye triumph in the imagination of having bravely stormed a fortress? Peace to the temple of Solomon! but be yours the temple of fame, the lodge of illustrious heroes. Far other atchievements must entitle you to that society. Never were the branches of acacia wreathed with the laurel crown.

Ye reverend preachers of the gospel, ye too must have your commerce with the mystical whore of Babylon! Are ye not sensible of what dishonour ye reflect upon religion and the sacerdotal character by entering these infamous assemblies? The ceremonies of bending the knee at the altar of Masonry, and pulling off your shoe, because the floor of the lodge, forsooth, is holy; these ceremonies, are they not a profanation of the passages of scripture to which they are acknowledged to allude; and shall ye give your sanction to such abominations? Ye panders of voluptuousness! / renounce them for ever; or confess that ye hunger and thirst after the elements of this world more than after righteousness.

I come now to the last part of my subject, which is to shew that all those who adhere to the abominations of Masonry will be damned.

This is so certain, that no human catastrophe is more frequently mentioned in scripture, than the final destruction of Babylon. In short, it is the burden of great part of the prophets; and to render the meaning of these threats as evident as possible to our apprehensions, it is remarkable that they are always spoken of in a stile peculiar to the subject of Masonry. Thus in Isaiah, xxviii. 17. *Judgment also will I lay to the line, and righteousness to the plummet*: and the accomplishment of its ruin is mentioned in the same strain by the prophet Jeremiah: *How is the hammer of the whole earth cut asunder, and broken! how is Babylon become a desolation among the nations!* Jer. 1. 23. and in Revel. xviii. 2. *Babylon the Great is fallen, is fallen, and is become the habitation of devils, and the hold of every soul spirit, / and a cage of every unclean and hateful bird.* And in the end of the same chapter, from which I have taken my text, it is declared that she *shall be burned with fire.* This doctrine of eternal damnation is conformable to the whole tenour of the word of God; for we are told, that *the Lord will not hold him guiltless that taketh his name in vain;*[26] and that *the sinner who repenteth not, shall perish.*[27]

I have now finished the subject proposed: I have proved beyond all question, that by the whore of Babylon the Abominations of Masonry are understood; that from the nature of the horrible oath made use of by Free Masons, and the circumstances in which it is administered, it is impious, sacrilegious, and invalid; and that, so far from its being entitled to the least observance, it is the duty of every man, as a christian, and member of society, to disclaim and renounce its obligation. I have endeavoured to expose a little the futility and absurdity of the ridiculous mysteries of Masonry, and the wickedness of those who profess them; have shewn the horrible consequences of which they are productive / to society, and, lastly, the tremendous and eternal punishment, in which those who adhere to them will be involved. It now remains that I should address myself to all who are guilty of these abominations, But by what compellation shall I do it? Shall I call them friends, who are, in reality, the greatest enemies of public happiness? Shall I call them brethren? I abhor it: for what relation have the children of God with the sons of Belial? Shall I call them men? It would disgrace the dignity of human nature: besides, by their own accounts they are no more than five years and an half old: such little children, however, of whom is not *the kingdom of heaven.* Listen then, O Free Masons! (for by that opprobrious name only shall I call you) *ye have hewed you out cisterns, yea, broken cisterns, which can hold no water.*[28] I adjure you in the name of the Lord God to consider your ways. Abandon your infamous society. Renounce the impious oath by which ye have sworn to conceal your abominations. Be not any longer the wicked instruments of / bringing upon children yet unborn the horrors of temporal, and upon their deluded fathers, eternal misery. If ye would shew yourselves to be actuated by true brotherly affection, exhort one another to this undertaking. It is a sacrifice ye owe to yourselves, your salvation, and to mankind; and by performing it ye will dissolve an institution which is detestable to God, pernicious to society, and disgraceful to yourselves.

FINIS.

[ANON.], *MASONRY VINDICATED: A SERMON. WHEREIN IS CLEARLY AND DEMONSTRATIVELY PROVED, THAT A SERMON, LATELY PUBLISHED, 'INTITLED MASONRY THE WAY TO HELL', IS AN INTIRE PIECE OF THE UTMOST WEAKNESS, AND ABSURDITY* (1768)

[Anon.], *Masonry Vindicated: a Sermon. Wherein is Clearly and Demonstratively Proved, that a Sermon, lately Published, 'Intitled Masonry the way to Hell,' is an Intire Piece of the Utmost Weakness, and Absurdity; at the Same Time Plainly Shewing to All Mankind, that Masonry, if Properly Applied, is of the Greatest Utility, not only to Individuals, but to Society and the Public in General: And is Impartially Recommended to the Perusal, as well as to Clear up, and Obviate all the Doubts Entertain'd, of those who are not Masons; and to the Fair-Sex in Particular* (London: Printed for J. Hinton, at the King's-Arms, in Pater-noster Row, 1768).[1]

The publication of *Masonry the Way to Hell* generated an unprecedented pamphlet war in 1768. Five different refutations of this anti-masonic sermon appeared within a few months of its first publication, one of which was translated into German. R. Goadby's bookshop must have played a key role in disseminating the pamphlets – the attack and two defences were sold in his shop (see items 2 and 6 below). The number of defences is unusual and not characteristic of masonic apologetics of the period. It also underlines the significance of this hot debate, the analysis of which has so far been largely ignored in scholarship. Apart from the anonymous *Masonry Vindicated* (1), which is probably the earliest refutation (published in March),[2] the following defences were printed:

(2) *Masonry the Turnpike-Road to Happiness in this Life, and Eternal Happiness Hereafter* (London: Printed for S. Bladon in Pater-Noster Row and sold by R. Goadby in Sherborne, published 18 April 1768).[3] No copy of this edition, which is not listed in the English Short Title Catalogue, seems to survive.

(3) *Masonry the Turnpike-Road to Happiness in this Life, and Eternal Happiness Hereafter* (Dublin: printed by James Hoey, senior, at the Mercury in Skinner-Row, [1768]). Hans Karl Baumann translated either the London or the Dublin edition into German in 1769, the authorship of which is wrongly attributed to J. Thompson in the British Library catalogue.[4]

(4) John Thompson, *Remarks on a Sermon Lately Published; Entitled, Masonry the Way to Hell. Being a Defence of that Antient and Honourable Order, against the Jesuitical Sophistry and False Calumny of the Author* (London: Printed by S. Axtell and H. Hardy, for T. Evans, at No. 20, in Pater-Noster Row, 1768). This was published in April.[5]

(5) I[saac] Head, *A Confutation of a Pamphlet Entitled 'Masonry the Way to Hell', to which are Added; 'A Charge to a Lodge', 1754, and; A Charge Delivered at Scilly, 1766 etc.* (n. p., 1768). This refutation has been unknown to masonic bibliographers. Only one copy of this edition has been identified in the Library and Museum of Freemasonry in London. The author, Isaac Head, was appointed as the first provincial Grand Master of the Scilly Islands in 1755.[6] It was republished with the following, more elaborate title in 1769:

(6) I[Isaac]Head, *A Confutation of the Observations on Free Masonry by an Anonymous Author of a Pamphlet, Entitled Masonry the Way to Hell. Wherein is Plainly Pointed out, to the Candid and Impartial Reader, That he has Grosly, and in the most Disingenuous, Unchristian, and Scandalous, Manner, Misrepresented Free Masonry: That he has Entirely Perverted the Sense and Meaning of the Sacred Text; and that He has neither Candour, Integrity, nor Honour. By a Member of the Most Ancient and Honourable Order of Free and Accepted Masons, I. Head, P. G. M. S.* (Exeter: printed (for the author) by A. Brice and B. Thorn, and sold by Messrs Hawes, Clarke, and Collins, Pater-Noster-Row, and Mr Johnson, in Ludgate Street, London; Mr Goadby, Sherborne; Mr Furseman and one each in Ashburton; Mr Furseman, Ashburton; Messrs Haydon and Whitfield, Plymouth; Messrs Manning and Martin, Launceston; Mr Allison, Falmouth; Mr Rogers, Helstone; Mr Hewitt, Penzance; Mrs Manning, Bideford; Mr Thorn, Exeter; and by the Author, at St Mary's Island, Scilly, [1769]).

(7) John Jackson, Philanthropos, *An Answer to a Certain Pamphlet Lately Published under the Solemn Title of 'A Sermon, or Masonry the Way to Hell'* (1768). No copy of this tract, which was published in May 1768 is known.

The reviewer of John Jackson's refutation in the *Critical Review, or Annals of Literature* suspects that the author of the *Masonry Vindicated: a Sermon* was also John Jackson because of the similarities between the style and manner of the two pamphlets.[7] Because his name is so common, it is not possible to identify the author of the tract(s) with absolute certainty.[8] He might be identical with John Jackson, who was Grand Warden of the Antients Grand Lodge in 1755. He was a tailor in Angel Alley, Houndsditch and a member of Lodge No. 5.[9]

His masonic song was published in the *Constitution* of the Antient Grand Lodge in 1756 to which he subscribed.[10]

We can infer from the date of the publication and the reference to the pagination of *Masonry the Way to Hell* that the author of *Masonry Vindicated* used the first London edition of the pamphlet.

The *Critical Review, or Annals of Literature* had a low opinion of *Masonry Vindicated*: 'This is a weak, injurious, and contemptible vindication, composed of a false title page, unfair quotations, and absurd reasoning; and it is more fit to expose the inability of the author than serve the cause of masonry.'[11]

The sermon was published by John Hinton (d. 1781), who worked as a printer and bookseller in London between 1739 and 1781.[12] His publications include the *Universal Magazine*, one of the most successful early magazines,[13] which listed two of the aforementioned works (2 and 4) among the books published in April 1768.

Besides being the first published refutation of *Masonry the Way to Hell*, the main reason for reproducing this reply is its rarity. It is not listed in the English Short Title Catalogue or in standard masonic bibliographies. Apart from John Jackson's defence, which seems to be lost, the other defences are more easily available in digital archives such as the Eighteenth Century Collections Online.

Notes

1.   This headnote was written by Róbert Péter.
2.   *Critical Review, or, Annals of Literature*, 25 (March 1768), p. 240.
3.   *Universal Magazine*, 42 (April 1768), p. 223. *Monthly Review*, 38 (April 1768), p. 323. The latter with a brief remark on the book is published in volume 5. See vol. 5, p. 162.
4.   *Die Freimäurerei der gerade Weg zur Glückseligkeit: zur Beantwortung der Schrift: 'Die Freimäurerei der Weg zur Hölle': aus dem Englischen übersetzt* (Franfurt und Leipzig, 1769).
5.   *Monthly Review*, 38 (April 1768), p. 323. A comment on this book is reprinted in volume 5.
6.   I. Head also wrote *A Charge Delivered at the Kings-Arms, in Helston, Cornwall, on Tuesday, April 21, 1752*, which was published in J. Entick, *The Pocket Companion and History of Free-Masons: Containing their Origine, Progress, and Present State: An Abstract of their Laws, ... A Confutation of Dr. Plot's False Insinuations: ... and a Collection of Songs*, 2nd edn, revised, corrected and greatly enlarged throughout, and continued down to this time in all its parts (London: Printed for R. Baldwin, ... P. Davey and B. Law, ... and J. Scott, ..., 1759), pp. 325–31.
7.   *Critical Review, or, Annals of Literature*, 25 (May 1768), p. 395.
8.   The records of the Antients Grand Lodge alone in the 1750s mention two John Jacksons – one being a tailor, the other a victualler.
9.   *Schism*, p. 53, 87–8, 193. His name is mentioned in the minutes of the Antients several times. *Antient Grand Lodge Minutes*, 17 September 1755. Quoted in *Schism*, p. 53.
10. L. Dermott, *Ahiman Rezon or, A Help to a Brother; Shewing the Excellency of Secrecy ... The Ancient Manner of Constituting New Lodges ... Also the Old and New Regulations ... To which is Added, the Greatest Collection of Masons Songs ... Together with Solomon's*

Temple an Oratorio ... (London: printed for the editor; sold by Brother James Bedford, 1756), p. 186. Jackson's song was reprinted in subsequent editions of the *Ahiman Rezon*.

11   *Critical Review, or, Annals of Literature*, 25 (March 1768), p. 240. The summary of the criticism is repeated in *Scots Magazine*, 30 (March 1768), p. 147. It may be noted that a later review in this periodical misquoted the original comment on the book – we find 'mean' instead of 'weak' in the following review: *Critical Review, or, Annals of Literature*, 25 (May 1768), p. 395.

12   The publishers of the *Craftsman* issued a warning advertisement about the publication of a bogus *Craftsman* issue in the *London Evening Post* of January, 9–11, 1738/9. The advertisement claimed that it was printed by 'one Hinton' in Bow Street, Covent Garden. But it is not clear to which one they refer since at that time there were at least two Hintons in London.

13   H. R. Plomer, G. H. Bushnell and McC. Dix (eds), *A Dictionary of the Printers and Booksellers who were at Work in England, Scotland and Ireland from 1726 to 1775* (n. p.: Oxford University Press for the Bibliographical Society, 1932), p. 126.

[Anon.], *Masonry Vindicated: A Sermon. Wherein is Clearly and Demonstratively Proved, that a Sermon, Lately Published, 'Intitled Masonry the way to Hell', is an Intire Piece of the Utmost Weakness, and Absurdity* (1768)

Masonry Vindicated:

A

SERMON.

Wherein is clearly and demonstratively proved, that a Sermon, lately published, 'Intitled Masonry the way to Hell', is an intire piece of the utmost weakness, and absurdity; at the same time plainly shewing to all mankind, that MASONRY, if properly applied, is of the greatest utility, not only to individuals, but to society and the public in general: And is impartially recommended to the perusal, as well as to clear up, and obviate all the Doubts entertain'd, of those who are not Masons; and to the Fair-Sex in particular.[1]

Will they not say that ye are mad? Corin.

LONDON:
Printed for J. HINTON, at the King's-Arms, in Pater-noster Row.
MDCCLXVIII. /

I CORINTHIANS, XIV. 23.
Will they not say that ye are mad?

I SHOULD not wonder, if the reader was somewhat surprised at my making Choice of this Text, but when it is considered, as an Answer to the mad Sermon lately published, entitled '*Masonry the Way to Hell*, &c.' by an anonymous but I think not a Rev. Gentleman, (who cannot be supposed to be in his right Senses at the time of writing so confused, ridiculous, and scandalous / a Bundle of Jargon, and Nonsense,) shewing, as he therein madly pretends, that 'Masonry was the way to Hell,' and, that all who professed 'these mysteries were in a State of Damnation.' and then he takes a Text of Scripture out of the Revelation of St. John to prove it, and impiously and impudently says, 'that Text relates intirely to Masonry,' notwithstanding so many of our worthy Commentators on the New Testament, have undoubtedly given us a much more intelligible, and agreeable to reason, as well as our Holy Religion, a better and perfecter, as well as clearer Interpretation of that Text; and yet, according to his Account, all those Revd. Gentlemen, are lyars and fools, because, says / he, 'their Commentations are repugnant to common sense:' but let me observe, it may be so to him, yet, not so to the rest of the World; for it will be found (in my Opinion) that all those, who impartially read his said Sermon over, must naturally conclude with me, that such, (his) common sense, is little better than madness. *Will they not say that ye are mad?* – I therefore shall endeavour, to prove by plain Argument, founded intirely on Reason, and Scripture, first, that so far from the word Babylon relating intirely to Masonry, that it bears no relation or affinity thereto, in any respect whatever.

Secondly, Shall take an opportunity / to convince, beyond any doubt, the impartial reader, that his general view of Masonry, is altogether a piece, of the utmost weakness and absurdity.

Thirdly. Shall expostulate a little with those, who know little or nothing of Masonry, and prove the Utility thereof, to Society and Individuals as well as the Public in General, pointing to those in particular, whose weak minds may in any wise be prejudiced, against that most noble and excellent order among men, not doubting, but the sensible part of mankind, will plainly perceive, that his whole Book, is what I have already advanced, a bundle of Grubstreet Jargon, and Nonsense,[2] and / therefore, they, if no masons, will pay that regard to it, it so justly deserves, (i.e.) they must freely acknowledge, that the only motive in its publication, is purely *a Catch-penny*. (I need not observe in what light every good mason will look upon it, because they, when they have it, will at once see, that he knows, or at least has said nothing of the matter, and that what he has advanced, is equally false, as ridiculous and absurd.

Lastly. Shall draw some Inferences from the whole, and thereby endeavour to clear and obviate the scandalous aspersions he has aimed to stigmatise with a Set of People, whose characters / in life, as a public body, always was, and still is, unquestionably good, and whether in his own innate principle he is not far short of the Sporado[3] he mentions? For this Sporado certainly is only an inventive proof of his argument, though a weak one indeed, he giving no reference where, or how the Story is to be found, to prove the certainty thereof, and therefore at present must think it a falshood of his own Invention; which must not be wondered at, that being not the only one in that ridiculous Book, by many.

In the first place then, I am to prove, that so far from the word Babylon relating intirely to masonry, that it bears no / relation or affinity thereto in any respect whatever: The truth of this is evident to any one, who has ever read the Word of God. He says that it is generally allow'd, that the city Babylon stood in the same plains, where the famous Tower of Babel was built; from hence we may infer, that the City Babylon took its name from Babel, which signifies Confusion, and which may properly be apply'd to the word Babylon, that City for the iniquity thereof being brought to confusion and destruction. Babylon, from its extensive Trade and Commerce with almost the World in general, was a great, powerful, and rich City in its time, and, as is too often the case, that riches produce vices of every kind, so the inhabitants thereof had / waxen exceeding wicked before the face of the Lord, when they, not contented with the enormous wickednesses already committed, but, to aggravate a just and jealous God, still more, to hasten their destruction, made them a Molten or Carved Image (see Daniel iii.) to fall down to, and worship, instead of the only true and everlasting God; there might be mentioned, also, many other instances which Sacred Writ furnishes us with, of destruction following idolatry, and in none where the[xx] Lord did not, in a striking manner, shew his dislike to such abominations.

And whenever a City is drunken, with the baneful lust of idolatry, they / take a pleasure to persecute, and destroy, the true worshippers of the Lord of Life, for in Revel. xvii. 6. it says, *I saw the woman drunken with the blood of the Saints, and with the blood of the Martyrs of Jesus*; and also xviii. 24. it says, *and in her was found the blood of Prophets, and of Saints*. We have seen, and heard of, and know the same, to have been done, even in late Days. Witness Smithfield, and in many other places where idolatrous worshippers have had the pre-eminence, or sway, to rule and govern, so obvious, and well known, that they need not a repetition; when if they can spill the blood, of Christ's Disciples, they think they are doing God service.

This woman *upon whose Forehead was / a name written Mystery, Babylon the Great, the mother of Harlots, and Abominations of the Earth*. Rev. xvii. 5. must imply an Image made by the hands of men, and alludes to that spoken of, by Daniel the Prophet, iii. Chap. which Nebuchadnezzar, the then mighty King of Babylon, set or caused to be set up, at the same time commanding, not only his own nation, but all nations, languages, people, and tongues, to fall down, and worship; from hence we may conclude, that from the King's extream pride, this woman image, or Nebuchadnezzar's God, was dressed in the most costly manner they were able to procure, as in Rev. xvii. 4. it says, *And the woman was arrayed in purple, and scarlet colour, and deck'd / with gold, and precious stone, and pearls, having a Golden Cup in her hand, full of abominations, and filthiness of her fornication*, and placed on the Beast, or in other words, on an Eminence in the City of Babylon, there to be worshipped, instead of the true and everlasting God; such worshipping also implies, Mystery, (not only in that City but in every idolatrous City in the World,) for the people or worshippers thereof, do not know nor can they give any reason for their paying this Adoration, to these Idols; and this word

Mystery, was written in her forehead, which plainly indicates, (from its openness to be seen,) 'twas not understood, by the people, but by the priests alone, because it is well known, the priests pray / and preach in an unknown tongue, consequently it must be Mysterious, to all the hearers, for which St. Paul calls them, Barbarians. The Word of God expressly forbids any one to preach in an unknown tongue. From the foregoing I hope the word Mystery is fully made clear.

In a spiritual sense, this woman or Idol being thus worshipped, and thereby making the Children of men run after such strange Gods, they know not of, may spiritually and justly be call'd, the *Mother of Harlots*, for it is written, they have forsaken the Lord, and worshipped strange Gods, they know not of, and go a whoring after their own inventions, / that is, worship the Gods or Idols, they themselves have made, and invented; admit this, and then follows beyond all doubt, that such Doctrines or Mysteries in the Babylonians Religion, are, '*Abominations of the Earth*' for which the wrath of God, will ever be kindled against such idolaters, who commit whoredom by running after strange Gods, and which was the consequence of this great City Babylon; wherefore the Lord in his just wrath, saith, in Rev. xviii. 2. '*with a strong voice, that Babylon the Great is fallen! is fallen! and is become the habitation of Devils, and the hold of every foul spirit, and a cage of every unclean and hateful bird.* This was foretold by the prophet Isaiah in xiv. 4. *That thou shalt / take up this proverb against the King of Babylon, and say, how hath the Oppressor ceased? the golden city ceased?*

The word Babylon, may justly be apply'd to that exceeding idolatrous and ancient city, Rome, for the very reasons I have already given of Babylon itself, notwithstanding what that Anonymous Gentlemen has said, or may say, to the Contrary, for tho' their situations are so remote, yet their superstitions in respect to religion are similar, and tho' we cannot say by the City of Rome, as is said by Babylon, 'is fallen? Is fallen,' yet we may justly say that its strength, and power, are a falling, and decreasing, every day, more and more, and in due / time as God shall think fit, will be as the Great City Babylon, except it leaves off idolatry, and turns to the true and eternal God, worshipping him only in spirit and in truth.

The King of Babylon could not take upon him more supremacy, and arrogancy, than the Pope of Rome has done, and which is well known, has been, and still is accompanied with so many grievous Burdens, too heavy for the people to bear, that they are endeavouring every day to diminish, and lessen them, 'till by degrees they will conquer, and overcome them, and him, and thereby entirely shake off that heavy Yoke which hath so long Oppressed them. /

Thus I think I have proved sufficiently from reason as well as Scripture, to every impartial person, whether Mason or not, that the word Babylon bears no relation or affinity to Masonry in any respect whatever.

I come therefore now, to the second thing proposed, to convince, beyond any doubt, that his general view of Masonry is altogether a piece of the utmost weakness and absurdity. –

The first thing then I shall take notice of is in folio 5, where he is mentioning the initiation of Masons, he says, 'many of whom, to the disgrace of their dignity, were such as in the estimation of the world, has been reckon'd great,[xxi] as Princes, Lords, &c.' and in folio 6 he gives you this plain contradiction, 'that almost all the meanest, most ignorant and infamous wretches in the kingdom, have participated of the mysteries (as he calls them) of masonry.' I think this carries with it a sufficient proof of its absurdity, but to prove this still more so, he then goes on, and gives you an account of the oath or obligation, and says, 'it is an open violation of the third Commandment;' this cannot admit even of a Supposition, for every man who is sworn to Secrecy of any kind, and keeps that Secret inviolable, it cannot be said in that case, that / he has taken the name of God in vain, but on the contrary; and as he observes that free masons are sworn not to reveal their secrets, neither by writing, engraving, &c. &c.' if he has been admitted a mason, and taken the oath upon him, to reveal none of the Secrets thereof, in what light must every good man conceive of his principles, as he has not only ignorantly pretended to write them, but also brands the members thereof with the most infamous epithets that could be supposed to be uttered by a hibernian coalheaver, or carman, or hackney-coachman; certainly he might have paid that regard to decency, in respect to his Cloth (if a Clergyman,) as well as religion, to have exposed / their impieties (if any) in a genteeler, and more decent manner, and which he might have done full as convincing to the sensible part of mankind, who must acknowledge him, on a mature consideration, in the light of my text.

He then says, 'Let us take a View of the Reception of a free mason Apprentice, and enquire whether or not he can be considered as a free Agent at the time the oath is administered him.' This is equally as absurd, for no man was ever forced to take upon him the Obligation of masonry, which I aver, but always is at his own Option, whether he will or not; in that case it must / be allow'd he is a free agent, and likewise he must be well recommended by a Brother, to be a person of sober life and Conversation, &c. ere he can be: For these Reasons, and on these circumstances only, he is admitted a member thereof, consequently it is done of his own free will and accord, and must be, beyond any doubt, a free agent.

It would make me appear as mad as himself to take any notice of the method in which he sets forth the manner and form the apprentice is entered, that being so weak and simple of itself, and carries with it so great a conviction of its absurdity, as needs no further explanation. /

Notwithstanding all the precaution any public Body (as masons are) may take, yet it is well known, that sometimes there will creep in, unperceived, a wolf in sheep's clothing, even in other societies as well as this; sometimes it may happen, that a man may be worthy of a good recommendation at his first entering of any public society, and yet by intemperance, and the like, after a time, may deviate much from that character; but is the whole body to be accused and stigmatised in a ridiculous manner because it has one bad member? There are but few flocks where there is not one that's marr'd.

In another place he says, 'that the / seven heads are seven mountains on which the woman sitteth.' and that it refers to the number of the constituent members of a perfect Lodge:[4] This is equally false; as every free mason knows, there are more constituent members to make a perfect Lodge, which is not in my place to particularise here, every free mason being sufficiently acquainted therewith.

Also he says when a brother is asked how old he is, he is to answer 'five years and an half,'[5] was there ever such a madman? To impose on the world such base and plain absurdities, and to crown the impiety thereof, declares it to be in allusion to the words of our / Blessed Saviour. O! Impiety, how dost thou come forth from the venal *PEN* of one, whose place and office it is to detect thee wherever thou art found, and root thee out (if possible) from the land of the living; instead of nourishing thee within himself, and sending thee forth among mankind, to make them as bad as him: May every good Christian who reads his impious epistle, conclude it with the prayer of the Psalmist: *Deliver my soul, O Lord, from lying lips, and from a deceitful Tongue. Psalm* cxx. 2.

Thus I think I have proved, beyond a Doubt, to every impartial and unprejudiced mind, without enlarging any more / than the foregoing, that his general View of Masonry is altogether an entire piece of the utmost weakness and absurdity, and therefore shall proceed on to my third Head proposed, viz. to expostulate a little with those who know little or nothing of Masonry, and prove the utility thereof to society and individuals, as well as the public in general. And

First then, let me premise, that Masonry is of a long series of years standing, and has inviolably stood the attempts and contempt of all its adversaries, in every age, with unshaken firmness; and the venal efforts of its weak enemies have had little or no weight upon mankind in general, but is universally / allowed in every country, (there are very few, if any, where it does not flourish) and esteem'd as a valuable and good Order among men.

The meetings of masons in most Lodges in England,[6] are twice a month, for which each member pays the quarterly sum of six or seven shillings, or thereabouts; some few meet only once a month, yet then their expences are much the same: Well, in this case, how are the members to gormandise upon so small a pittance? I appeal to all mankind, who are not masons, and who belong to clubs or societies of different kinds, if they can meet their friends and sociable companions to spend an evening / at a less expence; for it must be allowed, and is certain, that an extra expence is seldom or ever met with in any one Lodge.

I cannot but think it incumbent on me to answer his most infamous and scandalous insinuation, 'Do they not 'give too much Ground to admit the suspicion which is entertained of them by many women.' Vide page 24. In answer to which, though I think it too low almost as a man, much more so as a Christian, to refute. Notwithstanding,

As to their meeting on an Evening (which this romancer makes so vile a handle of) is justly accounted for, most / men having a leisure hour to spare then, when they could not spare that time from the business of the day: Then for what reason are masons to be particularly pointed at for having their meetings on an evening? Do not all other societies the same? And if the expence attending the masons meetings be true, (as mentioned before) how are they to gormandise? as he impudently asserts, not from that small expence, that cannot be; therefore it must then follow, that they cannot be guilty of extravagant living of any kind.

Does he know, that there are many respectable worthy clergymen of the church of England, who think it no / disgrace to associate among masons? Surely, had there been so much impiety in the order of Masonry, and every one professing these mysteries (as he calls them, which can't be understood as such, because every man of good character has a right, and may be entered among them, and know all the arcana thereto belonging,) was in a state of damnation, they would, 'ere now, most certainly have pointed this great danger out to the rest of their brethren, as well as to mankind in general, and would have endeavoured to root out so great an evil to the souls of thousands in this metropolis, as well as other places; besides, a growing evil of this kind would have merited a legislature's notice, and / the great council of this nation would have taken it into consideration, 'ere now, and have stopped the growth of it, for they are not ignorant of the order of Masonry, because many of them, 'tis well known, are masons themselves; consequently know the true meaning and intent thereof.

There are likewise many well-disposed good living, and serious well-inclined christians, who not only applaud it, but take a pleasure in associating with the members of this noble order; and, as a proof of their esteem for it, they recommend their own sons to become members thereof: Could they see so great an evil in it, they certainly would / not recommend the offspring of their own bodies to partake of Damnation, that would be wicked indeed; but, in my opinion, it carries such a weighty negative with it, as to admit of no doubt.

Charitable they are, it is well known, thousands of pounds having been distributed in this metropolis, among their distressed brothers, in proportion to the distress of such brother, and the sum they have got to dispose of, always paying a particular regard to the character of such a brother, for he must be well recommended 'ere he can participate. /

From hence, can it be inferred, that any person (a brother) who lives a scandalous and infamous life, or distresses his family, can be recommended as a proper object to partake of their charity?

They have likewise not been found wanting to contribute, as much as their ability would afford, to the assistance of public calamities, but have stretched forth a bountiful and charitable hand to the relief thereof: Witness a late dreadful fire. Besides all this, a good mason, by having a proper certificate from the Lodge he belongs to in England, when abroad in a foreign clime, is sure to meet with good friends and assistance if he wants it, without exposing / his calamities to a merciless world, who perhaps would afford him no relief. Is not this of great utility to individuals: To prove which, I will relate one instance, which is a real fact.

A free mason was on board a ship bound to the West Indies, but was unfortunately wrecked, and only he, with three more, were saved, by getting upon part of the wreck, when providentially for them, they were taken up by another ship's company, who found them in that distress, and gave them that kind assistance their ship was able to afford; but their kind benefactors not being English, and bound to a foreign part of the world, they could only set them on / shore at the first port they made, which was Lisbon. When they landed, they knew nothing of the place, or the language of the inhabitants, but remain'd there 'till their treasure given them by the ships company, who set them on shore, was quite exhausted; they were consulting then what to do, and in the interim comes by a person who appeared by his habit to be not of the inferior sort of the people; the English Mason (for there was only one of them masons,) made signs to him which he well understood, when he procured an interpreter, to whom the Mason made their case known, and for his own sake they were all caress'd and taken care of; he was esteem'd, and admitted into a Lodge of Masons, and the whole expence attending / them while there, was defrayed entirely by the members of that Lodge, and the first ship that was going for England, they were put on board, and money in their pockets towards defraying the expenses thereof. Can this babbler deny this to be a good act, and one singular advantage attending Masonry; he may as well deny this, and his very existence, as to say I have not proved his whole book, jargon, contradiction and nonsense, and also that it is only calculated purely for a catch-penny; that so far from Masons being in a state of damnation more than other men, merely because they profess Masonry, I think I have clearly and demonstratively proved the contrary, and that Masonry properly apply'd, is of the greatest advantage to society from / the great order, decency, and regularity of the Lodges when the Brethren are assembled. To Individuals, from the close acquaintance and good friendship with the brethren of his Lodge, which encreases his trade, they making a point of employing a brother. – To the public in general, by having so many regular Lodges kept up with the greatest decorum, where every brother may spend an agreeable innocent hour much to his improvement in morality, &c. and any Gentleman, who chuses to be made, has frequent opportunities to be admitted into the most noble, best, and amiablest society that exists among men, *Masonry*.

FINIS.

GEORGE SMITH, 'ANCIENT AND MODERN REASONS WHY THE LADIES HAVE NEVER BEEN ADMITTED INTO THE SOCIETY OF FREEMASONS', IN *THE USE AND ABUSE OF FREE-MASONRY* (1783)

George Smith, *The Use and Abuse of Free-Masonry; a Work of the Greatest Utility to the Brethren of the Society, to Mankind in General, and to the Ladies in Particular* (London: Printed for the author, 1783), pp. 349–67.[1]

In response to these mockeries and anti-masonic writings which attacked the lodges, *inter alia*, for excluding women, Freemasons had to develop justifications for their all-male, gender-exclusive organization. This theme formed a continuing part of masonic apologetics from the 1720s onwards.[2]

'Why we don't admit Women, as well as Taylors, into our Lodges?', asked Aaron Hill (1685–1750),[3] a self-designated Freemason as early as 1724, in *The Plain Dealer*. His answer, which appeared frequently in later defences, was the following: 'I have some Reasons to fear, that our Secrets are in danger of being expos'd.'[4] This was further elaborated by other masonic pamphlets, which argued that women were incapable of keeping secrets. By using the rhetoric of male power and privilege in the cult of the female domesticity of the eighteenth century, these masonic writings primarily reinforced the existing socially constructed gender stereotypes.

The chapter reprinted from George Smith's *The Use and Abuse of Free-Masonry*, which provided the most elaborate explanation of why women were not admitted into masonic lodges, contradicted several arguments of the previous masonic apologetic tracts on the subject in many ways. For example, Smith does not accept well-known Biblical stories, especially the narrative of Samson and Delilah (Judges 16), as a support to exclude women from lodges. Not only did he argue that 'some men are equally as unqualified to keep a secret' but, unlike many of his contemporaries, including women, in accordance with the contemporary medical definitions of male and female bodies,[5] claimed that 'female minds are certainly as capable of improvement as those of the other sex'. What is more, Smith, along with William Dodd (1729–77),[6] regarded the non-admission of women 'a very great misfortune' offending the women and argued for the elimination of that ancient custom that barred women from lodges.[7] According to Smith, it is beyond dispute that women have an 'undoubted right' to become members of masonic lodges. Furthermore, Freemasons who assist the women in forming female lodges do not violate their masonic obligations.[8]

The publication of Smith's book was so influential that 'Several ladies of the highest rank, determined to form a Lodge of Freemasons upon the plan which Captain Smith has given in his new work', according to the correspondent of the *Morning Chronicle and London Advertiser* in 1783.[9] The correspondent had no doubt that they would keep the secret as inviolably as men. If the account of the journalist is authentic, this is the first reference to an all-female lodge in England.

Smith's radical vision of the involvement of women in Freemasonry must reflect the fact that women of the period played an increasingly important role in bodies such as the Blue Stocking Society, female benefit clubs, philanthropic societies and the London debating societies.[10]

The Use and Abuse of Free-Masonry relies considerably on, often verbatim, Wellins Calcott's *A Candid Disquisition of the Principles and Practices of the Most Antient and Honourable Society of Free and Accepted Masons* (1772) and William Hutchinson's [11] *The Spirit of Masonry in Moral and Elucidatory Lectures* (1775).[12] Having considered Smith's request, on the proposal of James Heseltine, Grand Secretary, the Grand Lodge of the Moderns decided not to sanction his publication.[13]

George Smith (*c.* 1722–*c.* 1785)[14] had a controversial private and masonic life, which mirrors his liberal views that can be detected in the following writing.[15] He joined the Prussian Army under Frederick the Great. On 12 October 1742 he was initiated into Freemasonry in the lodge 'Aux trois Compas' (today 'Minerva zu den drei Palmen') in Leipzig (Germany).[16] After the war he moved to the Netherlands, where he founded a lodge affiliated with the Grand Lodge of England. However, it was not recognized by the Grand Lodge of the Netherlands because Smith acted against the fraternity. It is probable that the Grand Lodge accused Smith of publishing an exposure of masonic rituals entitled *Le Maçon Démasqué, ou le vrai secret des Francs Maçons* under the name of Thomas Wolson in 1751. It was translated into English as *Solomon in All his Glory* in 1766, a later edition of which is reprinted in volume 2.[17] He was not only accused of atheism but also of bigamy on the Continent, and it is ironic that he praises the commitment of Freemasons to marriage in his book.[18] Having returned to England, he worked as an Inspector of the Military Academy at Woolwich between 1772 and 1783. He published several books on military subjects. He was appointed Provincial Grand Master of Kent in 1777 and Junior Grand Warden in 1780. In

1783 Smith held a lodge in the King's Bench Prison, where they conferred the three degrees on some prisoners. The Grand Lodge reprehended him since 'it is inconsistent with the principles of Freemasonry for any Freemason's Lodge to be held in any prison or place of confinement'.[19] In 1785 he was expelled from the Grand Lodge because he forged certificates to help two poor Freemasons.[20]

Notes
1. This headnote was written by Róbert Péter.
2. For the relationship between women and eighteenth-century Freemasonry see M. M. Roberts, 'Masonics, Metaphor and Misogyny: A Discourse of Marginality', in P. Burke and R. Porter (eds), *Languages and Jargons* (Cambridge: Polity, 1998), pp. 133–54; C. Révauger, 'Women Barred from Masonic "Work": A British Phenomenon', in I. Baudino, J. Carré and C. Révauger (eds), *The Invisible Woman: Aspects of Women's Work in Eighteenth-Century Britain* (Aldershot: Ashgate, 2005), pp. 117–27; R. Péter, '"The Fair Sex" in a "Male Sect": Gendering the Role of Women in Eighteenth-Century English Freemasonry', in M. Cross (ed.), *Gender and Fraternal Orders in Europe from 1200 until the Present* (Basingstoke: Palgrave, 2010), pp. 133–55. J. A. M. Snoek, 'Freemasonry and Women', in *Handbook*, pp. 407–21.
3. See *MMLDP*, vol. 2, pp. 1433–4.
4. *The Plain Dealer*, 14 September 1724, issue 51.
5. Medical writers of the period argued that the bodies of men and women were totally different: 'Anatomical studies on women's brains argued that they were of smaller size, and thus conclusively demonstrated women's unfitness for intellectual pursuits'. D. Outram, 'Enlightenment Thinking about Gender', in D. Outram, *The Enlightenment* (Cambridge: Cambridge University Press, 2005), pp. 84–98, on p. 82.
6. William Dodd, an Anglican clergyman, was appointed Grand Chaplain of the Moderns in May 1775. He was expelled from the society in 1777 because he was convicted of capital forgery. For this offence he was executed in June 1777. See *ODNB*, *MMLDP*, vol. 2. pp. 1018–22 and the headnote for the text W. Dodd, *An Oration Delivered at the Dedication of Free-Masons' Hall* (1776) in volume 1.
7. See p. 191.
8. The idea that ladies should form separate lodges was not unique to Smith. For example, Ferenc Kazinczy (1759–1831), the leading Hungarian Enlightenment thinker and Freemason, advocated the same view. See *MMLDP*, vol. 2. pp. 1465–6.
9. *Morning Chronicle and London Advertiser*, 26 June 1783, issue 4402.
10. P. Clark, *British Clubs and Societies 1580–1800: The Origins of an Associational World* (Oxford and New York: Oxford University Press, 2000), pp. 130–1. See also the headnote of the section on Women in volume 5.
11. For William Hutchinson (1732–1814), see *MMLDP*, vol. 2. pp. 1475–6.
12. See J. Stokes, 'Masonic Teachers of the Eighteenth Century (The Prestonian Lecture for 1928)', in H. Carr (ed.), *The Collected 'Prestonian Lectures' 1925–1960* (London, 1967), pp. 63–94.
13. 'No particular objection being stated against the aforementioned work, the natural conclusion is, that a sanction was refused on the general principle, that considering the flourishing state of our lodges, where regular instruction and suitable exercises are ever ready for all brethren who zealously aspire to improve in Masonical knowledge; new publications are unnecesary on a subject which books cannot teach.'

J. Anderson (rev. by J. Noorthouck), *Constitutions of the Free-masons Constitutions of the Antient Fraternity of Free and Accepted Masons, containing their History, Charges, Regulations, &c. First Compiled by Order of the Grand Lodge, from their Old Records, and Traditions, by James Anderson, D.D. A New Edition Revised, Enlarged, and Brought Down to the Year 1784, under the Direction of the Hall Committee, by John Noorthouck* (London: Printed by J. Rozea, Printer to the Society, No. 91, Wardour Street, Soho, MDCCLXXXIV [1784]), p. 347.

14. On George Smith, see O. Werner Förster (ed.), *Matrikel der Freimaurerloge 'Minerva zu den drei Palmen' 1741–1932* (Leipzig, 2004), p. 9. I would like to thank Jan Snoek for this information and for other valuable comments on this text.

15. The following account of Smith's life draws on Jan Snoek's entry on G. Smith in *MMLDP*, vol. 2, pp. 2562–6.

16. Förster (ed.), *Matrikel der Freimaurerloge 'Minerva zu den drei Palmen' 1741–1932*, p. 9.

17. The author of *Masonry the Way to Hell*, reproduced in this volume, also relied on this exposure.

18. I refer to George Smith's book/chapter reprinted in this volume.

19. Anderson (rev. by J. Noorthouck), *Constitutions of the Free-Masons*, p. 349.

20. T. O. Haunch, 'English Craft Certificates', *AQC*, 82 (1969), pp. 169–253, on p. 178.

George Smith, 'Ancient and Modern Reasons Why the Ladies Have Never Been Admitted into the Society of Freemasons', in *The Use and Abuse of Free-Masonry* (1783)

THE
USE AND ABUSE
OF
FREE-MASONRY;
A WORK of the greatest UTILITY
TO THE
BRETHREN OF THE SOCIETY,
TO
MANKIND IN GENERAL,
AND TO THE
LADIES IN PARTICULAR.
BY CAPT. GEORGE SMITH,
Inspector of the Royal Military Academy at Woolwich; Provincial Grand-master for the County of
Kent; and R. A.
LONDON: Printed for the AUTHOR;
And Sold by G. KEARSLEY, No 46, Fleet-street, 1783.
[Price Five Shillings in Boards.] /
[...]

ANCIENT AND MODERN
REASONS
WHY
The LADIES have never been admitted into the Society of *Free-masons**.

ARDUOUS is the task I am now entering upon, and very difficult indeed is it to eradicate opinions which have been so strongly impressed upon the people's minds / (and especially those of the fair sex) for ages past: however, the reasons and arguments that I shall lay down, I hope will remove those grounded opinions, and prove highly satisfactory to my *fair readers*; as I am sure when they consider seriously upon *masonry*, and but for a moment reflect that its institution is for the improvement of the mind and morals of mankind; they will allow them to be just.

In the first instance; and it must be allowed a truth beyond the power of contradiction, that no society, or body of men upon earth, can venerate, adore, and esteem the *fair sex* more than *free-masons* do; we cannot but reckon it a very great misfortune, that the ladies should be offended at their non-admission into this order; and the more so, as they learn with what moderation *free-masons* comport themselves in their assemblies: but without knowing the reasons why they are not admitted, some indeed censure us with all the severity their delicate minds are capable of; others again are as liberal and unrestrained in praise of the society. This we must beg leave to say, is entirely owing to mistaken prejudice, because a little reflection would convince them, that / their not being received into this institution is not in the least singular, as some Masonic authors allege, who say, "They stand in the same predicament with respect to the *priesthood*, and many other societies; the solemn assemblies of the ancients, the *senates* of *Pagan*, and the *conclaves of Papal Rome*, all *national senates* and *ecclesiastical synods, universities*, and *seminaries* of *learning*, &c. &c."[1] with which they might with equal propriety be offended.

OTHERS again assert, that the reason why *ladies* were excluded this society, was to take away all occasion for calumny and reproach, which those shallow geniuses seem to think would have been unavoidable, had they been admitted. And again, that since *women* had in general been always considered as not very

---

*   Doubtful of my own abilities in addressing the most beautiful part of the creation on so important a subject as Free-masonry, though a favourite topic to some, it probably may not be thought so to all. Thus circumstanced, my fair readers, I communicated the manuscript to a lady of great erudition and profound judgment; to one whose heart is susceptible of the most refined friendship, and endowed with every peculiarity that can add worth and dignity to the female mind, and who may with the greatest propriety be called the *British Anna Maria a Scheurman*.[2] This lady was pleased to make some amendments much for the better, and for which I think myself highly honoured. The name alone (had I the liberty to mention it) would add a sanction to the whole.

well qualified to keep a secret*, because the woman of *Tamnath*, whom *Solomon* took to wife, betrayed the secret of the riddle, which he intrusted her with, to the *Philistines*†. Likewise, because *Dalilah*, after repeated stratagems / and art, persuaded *Sampson* to inform her where his great strength lay; which he had no sooner done, but she betrayed him to the *Philistines*, who bound him, and put out both his eyes‡. I think it exceedingly unjust to exclude the *fair sex* from benefiting by our societies on account of *Dalilah*'s behaviour; because it is not known, whether she was a woman of *Israel*, or one of the daughters of the *Philistines*; whether she was *Sampson*'s wife, or only a harlot, sacred history has not told us. However this be, her whole behaviour speaks her a mercenary woman, who would do any thing for money; and accordingly *Josephus* calls her a common prostitute to the *Philistines*§.

My fair readers will please to recollect, that in the most early ages of antiquity, women's minds were not so enlightened as in the present age; that they were only considered in the days of king *Solomon* as handmaids, and not as companions and associates to men employed in so learned, so useful, and so mysterious a society as *masonry*, as there are / many transactions in the *royal art*, which are far beyond that knowledge which women in general attain¶. At the first institution of masonry, it was thought proper to exclude the *fair sex*,[3] and as old customs are but too seldom laid aside, their expulsion has been handed down to us. And as we are such strict observers of its ancient manners and customs, so transmitted to us by our forefathers, these I hope will be sufficient reasons, both ancient as well as modern, why that most amiable part of the creation have hitherto been excluded.

MANY of the *fair sex*, I am truly sensible, would be the greatest ornament to masonry, / and am exceedingly sorry that our pretended laws and institutions exclude them. However, what I shall now advance will be allowed, especially among those of my fair readers that are united in the sacred institution of marriage with *free masons*, who I flatter myself are convinced of its truth. And as

---

*   Some men are equally as unqualified to keep a secret, as the women are here represented to be.

†   Judges, ch. 14.

‡   Judges, chap. 16.

§   Josephus, lib. vii. chap. 10, &c. [Flavius Josephus: *The Antiquities of the Jews* (*c.* AD 94) liber vii chapter 10.]

¶   The most ancient inhabitants of the East were little acquainted with the strongest passions of the soul. They never shewed the least marks of attention or tenderness for that sex so much courted by the modern free-masons. They considered their wives rather in the light of slaves than of companions; they did not even suffer them to eat with them always, and had usurped the right of divorcing them, without permitting the indulgence of marrying again. The women then felt themselves born to obey, and submitted patiently to their fate.

free-masons by the obligations of their order, pay a far greater attention to the moral and social duties of life, than the generality of mankind, they are inspired with a far greater desire and reverence for the most sacred and happy of all institutions, marriage; they of all others best know to love, to cherish, to value the dear companion of their fortunes, who, by her kind participation and affectionate regard, softens and alleviates every distress and worldly care, and adds sweetness and comfort to all the pleasures of life. She is the most pleasing companion in the gay and cheerful hour of prosperity, and his chief friend and adviser in the dark and dismal day of adversity. She is the tender and careful preserver of his health, and the ever-anxious and soothing attendant on his sickness. She is the watchful, cautious and prudent manager of all his domestic concerns. /

> *Nor let the dear maid*
>   *Our mysteries dread,*
> *Or think them repugnant to love;*
>   *To beauty we bend,*
>   *Her empire defend,*
> *An empire deriv'd from above.*[4]

FREE-MASONS declare there is nothing which affords so pleasing a prospect of human nature, as the contemplation of wisdom, virtue, and beauty; the latter is the peculiar gift of heaven, to that *sex* we call *fair*; but wisdom, virtue, and beauty, are attributes too celestial to be frequently found united in one form. We too often find beauty capricious, self-sufficient, negligent of adorning itself with any other ornaments than such as are conveyed by the hands of fashion and folly. If this most beautiful part of the creation would but for a moment consider how much their charms are heightened and their empire preserved, by an accomplished mind and manners, they would neglect no opportunity of obtaining those more lasting charms, which will be engraved on the hearts of their husbands, when the transient flower of beauty will be no more. /

> *And thus the libertine, who builds a name*
> *On the base ruins of a woman's fame,*
> *Shall own the best of human blessings lie,*
> *In the chaste honours of the nuptial tie.*
> *There dwells the homefelt sweet, the dear delight,*
> *There peace reposes, and their joys unite.*
> *And female virtue was by heav'n design'd*
> *To charm, to polish, and to bless mankind.*[5]

FREE-MASONS well know, and weigh the great importance of marriage, both as a sacred and a moral duty; they well know, it is a state that colours all their future days with happiness or misery.

WHEN ever a good *mason's* fancy and judgment has agreed in the choice of a partner for life, he will support the authority and dignity of a husband, with that wisdom, moderation, tenderness, and affection, that shall render him honoured and beloved; for the *mason*, above all others, well knows, that if happiness is not found in the narrow circle of his own home, it will be sought for in vain: in short the *fair sex* will ever find in a *mason*, a warm and passionate admirer, a most sincere friend, an affectionate and tender husband, as well as an indulgent father: they will ever / find a *mason* the protector of innocence, and at all times and situations attentive to every delicacy and decorum, they so justly claim from all mankind, and will more particularly experience from *masons*, who love and adore them.

I MUST further add, that in the most solemn and serious moments of the assembled *free-masons* in open lodge, and at the reception of a brother, the ancients, and even the most part of modern *free-masons*, always present the new initiated brother with two pair of *white gloves*,[6] one pair for himself, and the other pair for a lady, with a strict charge to present them to that female, for whom he has the greatest regard: and even in our hours of relaxation from labour, when innocent mirth abounds, we never forget *Milton's* words, *viz.*

> *Grace was in all her steps, heaven in her eye,*
> *In every gesture dignity and love.*[7]

And in another place,

> ———*so absolute she seems,*
> *And in herself complete, so well to know*
> *Her own, that what she wills to do or say,*
> *Seems wisest, virtuousest, discretest, best;* /
> *All higher knowledge in her presence falls*
> *Degraded, wisdom in discourse with her*
> *Loses, discountenan'd, and like folly shows;*
> *Authority and reason on her wait,*
> *As one intended first, not after made*
> *Occasionally; and to consummate all,*
> *Greatness of mind and nobleness their seat*
> *Build in her loveliest, and create an awe*
> *About her, as a guard angelic plac'd.*[8]

OF the numerous societies which mankind have been led to form for the purposes of mutual advantage, none is of more importance to individuals or the public than that of marriage. The very nature of this society requires it to be perpetual; as indeed it is so among married masons, more than among any other set of people. During the virtuous times of the *Roman* commonwealth, this union was regarded as so inviolable (as it is now with masons) as to give rise to a tradition, that for the first five hundred years not a single example of divorce was known; nor doth the annals of our society mention such a circumstance. Observing what *Milton* enjoins in the praise of women: /

> *O fairest of creation, last and best*
> *Of all God's works, creature in whom excell'd*
> *Whatever can to sight or thought be form'd,*
> *Holy, divine, good, amiable, or sweet.* [9]

AND the famous Dean *Swift*,[10] in his well known masonic song, has this verse, *viz.*

> *We're true and sincere,*
> *And just to the fair,*
> *They'll trust us on any occasion:*
> *No mortals can more*
> *The ladies adore,*
> *Than a Free and an Accepted Mason.*[11]

AN anonimous author of reputation observes, that though men are more reserved, and secret in their friend's concerns than their own; *women* on the contrary keep their own and friend's secrets better than men. Modesty in a *woman* supposes all other virtues; immodesty, all other vices. *Women* generally take greater care of their reputation than men do of theirs: Why then do we account them the weaker sex? Hence, virtue makes a beautiful *woman* appear more beautiful, so beauty makes a virtuous *woman* really more virtuous. /

> *The ladies claim right to come into our light,*
> *Since the apron, we know, is their bearing;*
> *They can subject their will, they can keep their tongues still,*
> *And let talking be changed into hearing.*
> *This difficult task is the least we can ask,*
> *To secure us on sundry occasions;*
> *If with this they'll comply, our utmost we'll try,*
> *To raise lodges for Lady Free-masons.*[12]

ON many occasions of late the *ladies* have been admitted to sundry parts of our ceremonies, *viz.* At laying the foundation stone of Free-mason's Hall; dedication of the same. At Royal-arch processions; private and public Masonic orations, &c. at one of which the ladies were thus addressed by the orator*:

---

*   *Thomas Dunckerley*, esq. provincial grand-master for Essex, Wiltshire and Dorsetshire. [Thomas Dunckerley (1724–1795) was probably the best known English Freemason in the latter half of the eighteenth century. He was an enthusiastic member of the Grand Lodge of the Moderns, where he held high office in several masonic orders. See *MMLDP*, vol. 2, pp. 1051–8. R. Péter, 'Religion and Enlightenment in Thomas Dunckerley's Neglected Writings', in A. Önnerfors and R. Péter (eds), *Researching British Freemasonry, 1717–2017* (Sheffield: University of Sheffield, 2010), pp. 127–57. For

"YOU have heard, *ladies*, our grand principles explained, with the instructions given to the brethren; and I doubt not but at other times you have heard many disrespectful things said of this society. Envy, malice, and uncharitableness will never be at a loss to decry, find fault, and raise objections to what / they do not know. How great then are the objections *you* lay on this lodge*! with what respect, superior esteem, and regard are we to look on every *lady* present, that has done us the honour of her company this evening. To have the sanction of the *fair* is our highest ambition, as our greatest care will be to preserve it. The virtues of humanity are peculiar to *your sex*; and we flatter ourselves, the most splendid ball could not afford *you* greater pleasure, than to see the human heart made happy, and the poor and distressed obtain present relief."[13]

HENCE, as there is no law ancient or modern that forbids the admission of the fair sex amongst the society of Free and Accepted Masons, and custom only has hitherto prevented their initiation; consequently all bad usages and customs ought to be annihilated†, / and *ladies* of merit and reputation admitted into the society; or at least be permitted to form lodges among their own sex, in imitation of those in *Germany* and *France*. This is a plan that the unfortunate Dr. *Dodd*[14] had much at heart, and had so far succeeded in, as to be ripe of execution, had his untimely death not prevented it.

I KNOW there will be many prejudices entertained against the character of *masonic ladies*, and, perhaps, if *ladies lodges* were as numerous as those of the other sex, some inconveniencies might arise from it; but I must own it does not appear to me, that a woman will be rendered less acceptable in the eyes of the world, or worse qualified to perform any part of her duty in it, by employing a small allotment of her time in the cultivation of her / mind by studying *freemasonry*. Time enough will remain, after a few hours in a week spent in the study

---

Dunckerley's attitude towards women see R. Péter, 'Les femmes et la franc-maçonnerie dans le grand dix-huitième siècle', *La Pensée et les Hommes*, 82–3 (2011), pp. 195–219.]

*   Lodge of Concord, N° 400, held at Southampton. [The lodge was warranted on 1 July 1775 (Lane).]

†   I beg leave to insert in the words of the learned matron in *Erasmus*, [Desiderius Erasmus Roterodamus (1466–1536)] *Quid mihi citas vulgum, pessimum rei gerendæ auctorem? Quid mihi consuetudinem, omnium malarum rerum magistram? Optimis assuescendum: ita fiet solitum, quod erat insolitum; et suave fiet, quod erat insuave; fiet decorum, quod videbatur indecorum.* i. e. Why do you tell me of the generality of people, the very worst pattern of conduct? Why do you talk to me of the custom, the teacher of all that is bad? Let us accustom ourselves to that which we know is best. So that will become usual which was unusual; and that will become agreeable which was disagreeable, and that fashionable that appeared unfashionable. [Desiderius Erasmus Roterodamus, *Colloquia*, Lugdunum Batavorum 1643 (Cap. Abbatis et Eruditæ), p. 303. The *Colloquia* appeared originally from 1518 onwards.]

of the *royal art*, for the improvement of the person, for domestic concerns, and the acquisition of the usual accomplishments. With respect to these accomplishments, I will not presume to direct the method of pursuing them; I will not so far intrude on a province which by no means belongs to us. The *ladies* themselves, and their instructors, want no directions in matters of external ornament, the end of which is to please on intuition. However arrogant the men have been in their claims of superiority, they have always allowed the ladies the possession of the most refined and delicate taste in the improvement and perception of all kinds of beauty.

FEMALE minds are certainly as capable of improvement as those of the other sex. The instances that might be brought to prove this, are too well known to admit of citation. The study of masonry will open a new scene for female improvement; their minds, if they have been successful in this course, will have imbibed an elegance, which will naturally diffuse itself over their conversation, address, / and behaviour; and they will ultimately become our instructors in an art we have taken so much pains to hide from their knowledge*. It is well known, that internal beauty contributes much to perfect external grace. I believe it will also be favourable to promote virtue, and will operate greatly in restraining from any conduct grossly indelicate, and obviously improper. Much of the profligacy of female manners has proceeded from a levity occasioned by a want of employment and a suitable education. This the study of masonry will effectually move, for she that has no taste for well-written books, will often be at a loss how to spend her time; and the consequences of such a state are too frequent not to be known, and too fatal not to be avoided.

FROM what has been advanced, not one doubt remains but the ladies may, and have an undoubted right to be admitted as members of the most ancient, and most honourable society of *Free and Accepted Masons*; neither can any brother or set of brethren be accused of violating his or their obligation, in aiding or assisting at the initiation of the ladies, or in forming female lodges. Hence, many advantages will arise to the society in general, and among the rest, that of

---

* He of whom antiquity boasts itself as of the wisest of mortals, was instructed in many elegant and profound subjects of learning by a lady. Ασπασια μευ τοι η σοθη Σωχρατους διδασχαλος των ρητοριχων λογων, i. e. *Aspasia, the learned lady, was the preceptress of Socrates in rhetoric.* ATHENÆUS. ['Aspasia ... associated with the wise Socrates'. Athenaeus, *The Deipnosophists*, 13, p. 589.] And Πατων τον Σωχρατην παρ αυτης φησι μαδειν τα πολετιχα, i. e. Plato says that Socrates learned politics of her. ['Menexenus: And can you remember what Aspasia said? Socrates: I ought to be able, for she taught me ... at some future time I will repeat to you many other excellent political speeches of hers'. Plato, *Menexenus*, ll. 235e–236b; 249e3–5.] HARPOCRATION. [Valerius Harpocration (second century AD), *Lexicon of the Ten Orators*. Smith's text suggests that he took at least the second quotation (if not both) from this source.] /

assisting the widows and orphans of deceased free-masons, to which the grand-lodge of *England* gives no relief.

THEREFORE let all *free-masons* unanimously sing aloud;

Open ye gates, receive the Fair *who shares*
With equal sense our happiness and cares:
Then, charming Females, *there behold*
What massy stores of burnish'd gold,
Yet richer is our art;
Not all the orient gems that shine,
Nor treasures of rich Ophir's *mine,*
Excell the mason's heart; /
True to the Fair, *he honours more*
Than glitt'ring gems, or brightest ore,
The plighted pledge of love;
To ev'ry tie of honour bound,
In love and friendship constant found,
And favoured from above.[15]

[A FRIEND TO TRUTH], *A DEFENCE OF FREE MASONS ETC., IN ANSWER TO PROFESSOR JOHN ROBISON'S PROOFS OF A CONSPIRACY* (1797)

[A Friend to Truth], *A Defence of the Free Masons etc.,*[1] *in Answer to Professor John Robinson's*[2] *Proofs of a Conspiracy etc., By a Friend to Truth* (London: Printed for the Booksellers, 1797).

Conspiracy theories that blamed Freemasons for the French Revolution became increasingly popular in the 1790s. In a strong anti-Jacobin and Gallophobic climate, to defend his countrymen against radical conspirators, John Robison (1739–1805), a professor of natural philosophy at the University of Edinburgh,[3] informed British people about the signs of potential plots, endangering peace and public order in his *Proofs of a Conspiracy against All the Religions and Governments of Europe, Carried on in the Secret Meetings of Free Masons, Illuminati, and Reading Societies.*[4] Like the authors of most Illuminati conspiracy theories, he was a Freemason. In 1770, Admiral Knowles invited Robison to help him reform the Russian navy. During his journey to Russia he was initiated in the *Loge de la Parfaite Intelligence* in Liège. He also visited French lodges in Valenciennes, Brussels, Aachen, Berlin and Königsberg.[5] In St Petersburg he joined the English lodge there, whose activities he enjoyed. However, he resisted encouragement to join the French lodges.[6] Then his 'masonic spirit had evaporated'.[7] He became interested in Freemasonry again in 1795 when he read a volume of the German magazine *Die neuesten Religionsbegebenheiten* discussing controversies and schisms in the fraternity, which inspired him to write his first political work.

The first edition was published around September 1797. Extracts from the book were published in the *General Evening Post* in early October and reviews appeared in the *Analytical Review* and the *British Critic* in the same month, in the *Monthly Review* in December as well as in the *Monthly Magazine* and *Evangelical Magazine* in 1798.[8] The second, corrected edition with a postscript was published in 1797. The third edition appeared in 1798 and the fourth in January 1799. This bestseller was translated into French, Dutch and German. The sheer number of editions within a short time indicates the popularity of Robison's book.

Robison distinguished between 'simple' British Freemasonry, which was only a 'matter of amusement for young men who are glad of any pretext for indulging in conviviality' and its Continental manifestation, many lodges of which had become, according to him, seditious, irreligious and 'seedbeds of public mischief'.[9] Robison wanted to defend the genuine British Freemasonry of the early eighteenth century against the dangerous innovations of the Continental Freemasons. The overtly political French and German lodges were infiltrated by the Illuminati Order[10] founded by Adam Weishaupt (1748–1830), a professor at Ingolstadt University, in 1776.[11] Furthermore, not only were French Freemasons active in the French Revolution but their lodges became 'schools of scepticism and infidelity'.[12] According to Robison,

> Even England, the birth-place of Masonry, has experienced the French innovations;
> and all the repeated injunctions, admonitions, and reproofs of the old Lodges,
> cannot prevent those in different parts of the kingdom from admitting the French
> novelties, full of tinsel and glitter, and high-sounding titles.[13]

He wrongly claimed that there were lodges of the Illuminati in Britain. He warned British people of the potentially subversive activities of such lodges which might conspire to destroy the constitution of Great Britain.[14] Consequently, 'all secret assemblies, which afford opportunities of the disaffected',[15] should be discouraged. Two years later Robison's arguments were used in the parliamentary debate about the legislation against unlawful societies, which almost resulted in the outlawing of British Freemasonry.

Abbé Augustin de Barruel (1741–1821), who did not collaborate with Robison, entertained very similar arguments in his *Mémoires pour servir à l'Histoire du Jacobinisme*, the first two volumes of which were also published in 1797.[16] To strengthen his arguments, Robison added a postscript to the second edition of his book, which contained passages from Barruel's book.[17] Robert Clifford, who translated Barruel's work into English, wrote a pamphlet in which he applied Barruel's conspiracy theory to Britain and Ireland.[18]

In a rampant anti-French atmosphere, many British conservatives, including Edmund Burke, subscribed to this theory. In the United States, George Washington supported many of Robison's arguments though he defended his fellow Freemasons against the accusations of revolutionary conspiracy.[19]

Although neither Robison nor Barruel constructed the masonic conspiracy theory[20], they popularized it from the late 1790s onwards.[21] The spectre of a masonic-Illuminati complot came to haunt many political disputes over the next two decades.[22] Even today both works are still often cited by conspiracy theorists. New editions of Robison's work were published in 2010 and 2014.[23]

Immediately after the publication of Robison's work several critics highlighted its inaccuracies and errors. Abbé Barruel praised the patriotism expressed in the book but also noted that he used the sources that he cited imprecisely.[24] The German classicist and archaeologist Carl August Böttiger (1760–1835) criticized both Robison and Barruel for their attack on German intellectuals and claimed that the conspiracy theorists were paid 'propagandists for the English Ministry'.[25] The French judge Jean-Joseph Mounier (1758–1806), who was involved in the early part of the French Revolution, did not subscribe to the view that the members of the Illuminati, Freemasons and the *philosophes* had caused the French Revolution.[26]

British Freemasons also attacked Robison's conspiracy theory. Apart from the pamphlet reproduced here, John Watkins made an attempt to defend the fraternity in a series of articles in the *Freemasons' Magazine* in 1797 and 1798.[27] The Scot David Brewster also pointed out the fanciful ideas in Robison's book in 1804.[28] However, it seems that masonic defences did not manage to invalidate the arguments in Robison's book, the ideas of which rapidly became popular and widespread.

The British masonic refutations of Robison's work as well as its reviews in the periodicals have been overlooked in the examination of the reception and impact of Robison's conspiracy theory in scholarship.[29]

The anonymous immediate defence was written and published between October and December, 1797 in a hurry, which is indicated by the number of typographical errors, including the name of Robison being misspelt three times. The author must have used the first edition. We have been unable to identify the source(s) of the quotations. Two copies of this very rare pamphlet, which is not listed in the English Short Title Catalogue, are lodged in the Library and Museum of Freemasonry in London but only one is complete. The inscription on the title page of the incomplete edition reads 'R Heron'.

Notes

1. This headnote was written by Róbert Péter.
2. Robinson here should read 'Robison'.
3. J. Robison, *Proofs of a Conspiracy against All the Religions and Governments of Europe, Carried on in the Secret Meetings of Free Masons, Illuminati, and Reading Societies. Collected from Good Authorities by John Robison, A. M. Professor of Natural Philosophy, and Secretary to the Royal Society of Edinburgh* (Edinburgh: Printed for William Creech; and T. Cadell, junior, and W. Davies, London, 1797).
4. J. B. Morrell, 'Professors Robison and Playfair and the Theophobia Gallica: Natural Philosophy, Religion and Politics in Edinburgh, 1789–1815', *Notes and Records of the Royal Society*, 26 (1971), pp. 43–63.
5. Robison, *Proofs of a Conspiracy*, p. 2.

6. See *MMLDP*, pp. 2378–80.

7. Robison, *Proofs of a Conspiracy*, p. 5.

8. *General Evening Post*, 3 October 1797, issue 10132; *British Critic*, 10 (October 1797), pp. 416–24 (reprinted in vol. 5.); *Analytical Review*, 26 (October 1797), pp. 401–7; *Monthly Magazine*, 4 (December 1797), p. 503; *Monthly Review*, 25 (March 1798), pp. 303–15; *Evangelical Magazine*, 6 (1798), pp. 125–8. According to the *Analytical Review*, Robison's work contains 596 pages. It has proved impossible to identify an edition with that number of pages.

9. Robison, *Proofs of a Conspiracy*, pp. 40, 465.

10. Robison writes that 'I have observed these doctrines gradually diffusing and mixing with all the different systems of Free Masonry; till, at last, AN ASSOCIATION [the Illuminati Order] HAS BEEN FORMED for the express purpose of ROOTING OUT ALL THE RELIGIOUS ESTABLISHMENTS, AND OVERTURNING ALL THE EXISTING GOVERNMENTS OF EUROPE'. Robison, *Proofs of a Conspiracy*, p. 11.

11. In Ireland, Robison's work seems to have been distributed to magistrates, one of whom, John Dennis Browne, third Earl of Altamont, depicted the organization of the United Irishmen as 'the Dublin Illuminati'. P. Mirala, *Freemasonry in Ulster 1733–1813: A Social and Political History of the Masonic Brotherhood in the North of Ireland* (Dublin: Fourt Courts Press, 2007), p. 19. See also J. Smyth, 'Freemasonry and the United Irishmen', in D. Dickson, D. Keogh and K. Whelan, *The United Irishmen: Republicanism, Radicalism and Rebellion* (Dublin: Lilliput Press, 1993), pp. 167–75.

12. Robison, *Proofs of a Conspiracy*, p. 32.

13. Robison, *Proofs of a Conspiracy*, p. 9.

14. Robison's worries were not totally unfounded. Although most British Freemasons condemned the French Revolution, recent research has highlighted the signs of radical activities in some English, Scottish and Irish lodges. See the volume introduction and the reprint of the following newspaper articles in the section on Debates and Conflicts in volume 5: *Morning Chronicle*, 20 October 1797, issue 8863 and *True Briton*, 20 March 1798, issue 1634.

15. Robison, *Proofs of a Conspiracy*, p. 486.

16. Barruel's book was translated into English, German, Dutch, Italian, Russian, Swedish, Polish, Portuguese and Spanish.

17. In the third volume of Barruel's *Memoirs*, the author refers to Robison's book as follows: 'That work [Robison's *Proofs of a Conspiracy*] was published just as this Third Volume was going to the press. Its author had not then met with my two first Volumes; but in a second Edition he is pleased to mention them in his Appendix.' A. Barruel, *Memoirs, Illustrating the History of Jacobinism. A Translation from the French of the Abbé Barruel*, Vol. 3. *The Antisocial Conspiracy* (London: Printed for the author, by T. Burton and Co. No. 11, Gate Street, Lincoln's-Inn Fields, 1798), p. xiv.

18. R. Clifford, *Barruel's Memoirs of Jacobinism, to the Secret Societies of Ireland and Great Britain. By the Translator of that Work* (London: Sold by E. Booker, No. 56, New Bond-Street, [1798]).

19. S. Luckert, 'Jesuits, Freemasons, Illuminati, and Jacobins: Conspiracy Theories, Secret Societies, and Politics in Late Eighteenth-Century Germany' (PhD thesis, State University of New York at Binghamton, 1993), pp. 6–7, 630 and C. Oberhauser, *Die verschwörungstheoretische Trias: Barruel-Robison-Starck* (Innsbruck: StudienVerlag, 2013), p. 259.

20. Among its forerunners is the French Catholic Abbé Jacques François Lefranc (1739–92), who observed a direct connection between the modern philosophy, Protestantism

and Freemasonry in 1791. It is clear from his anti-Protestant writings that he detested Freemasons.

21. As Andrew Prescott notes, Barruel's and Robison's arguments were mentioned in a novel, *Filial Indiscretions or the Female Chevalier* (Wakefield, 1799), where the characters have a dispute about the association of Freemasonry with the Jacobins. A. Prescott, 'Freemasonry and Radicalism in Northern England 1789–1799: Some Sidelights', in *Lumières (Franc-maçonnerie et Politique au Siècle des Lumières: Europe-Amériques)* 7 (2006), pp. 123–142, on p. 127.

22. For instance, in the United States the Federalists employed this conspiracy theory to weaken the power of the increasingly influential Jeffersonian movement. See V. Stauffer, *New England and the Bavarian Illuminati* (New York: Russell and Russell, 1918).

23. The fourth edition was republished by Kessinger Publishing in 2010 in Whitefish, Montana. The 2014 edition was printed by Wermod & Wermod in Abergele with a foreword and notes by Alex Kurtagic.

24. Barruel wrote as follows about Robison's work: 'I am much flattered by his approbation, heartily congratulate him on the zeal he has himself shown in combating the public enemy, and am happy to see that he has wrought on the best materials. Without knowing it, we have fought for the same cause with the same arms, and pursued the same course; but the Public are on the eve of seeing our respective quotations, and will observe a remarkable difference between them. I fear lest we should be put in competition with each other, and the cause of truth suffer in the conflict. I entreat the reader to observe, that these differences arise from the different methods followed by him and myself. Mr. Robison has adopted the easiest, though the most hazardous method. He combines together in one paragraph what his memory may have compiled from many, and sometimes makes use of the expressions of the German author when he thinks it necessary. Beside, he has seen much, and read much, and relates it all together in the paragraphs marked by inverted Commas. The warning he has given in his preface will not suffice to remove the objections of some readers. In some passages he has even adopted as truth certain assertions which the correspondence of the Illuminées evidently demonstrate to have been invented by them against their adversaries, and which in my Historical Volume I shall be obliged to treat in an opposite sense. Nor will I pretend to say, that Illuminism drew its origin from Masonry; for it is a fact demonstrated beyond all doubt, that the founder of Illuminism only became a Mason in 1777, and that two years later than that he was wholly unacquainted with the mysteries of Masonry.' Barruel, *Memoirs, Illustrating the History of Jacobinism*, pp. xiv–xv.

25. Luckert, 'Jesuits, Freemasons, Illuminati, and Jacobins', p. 664.

26. J.-J. Mounier, *On the Influence Attributed to Philosophers, Freemasons, and the Illuminati on the Revolution in France* (1801; Delmar, New York, 1974). Luckert, *Jesuits, Freemasons, Illuminati, and Jacobins*, pp. 664–7.

27. J. Watkins, 'An Impartial Examination of a Book Entitled Proofs of a Conspiracy against All the Religions and Governments of Europe', *Scientific Magazine and Freemasons' Repository*, 9 (October 1797), pp. 242–9; 9 (November 1797), pp. 324–7; 10 (January 1798), pp. 36–8; 10 (April 1798), pp. 255–8. Watkins' articles were reprinted in the Scottish *Masonic Mirror* (1797) of which we only know one issue. It may be noted that Watkins begins the article of November 1797 as follows: 'I cannot help noticing the curious circumstance of his retracting, in a public newspaper, an invidious assertion

contained in his book respecting a Minister of the Church of Scotland. Mr Robison frankly acknowledges that his information had been incorrect, and even injurious to the party'. The aforementioned newspaper article has not been identified.

28. D. Brewster, *The History of Freemasonry, Drawn from Authentic Sources of Information, with an Account of the Grand Lodge of Scotland* (Edinburgh: A. Lawrie, 1804), pp. 28–32, 101–10, 141–5. This book is often attributed to Alexander Lawrie, who wrote the dedication and printed the work.

29. For the formation of the conspiracy myth and its reception history, see C. Oberhauser, *Die verschwörungstheoretische Trias: Barruel-Robison-Starck* (2013). I would like to thank Claus Oberhauser and Reinhard Markner for their comments on the editorial of this pamphlet.

[A Friend to Truth], *A Defence of Free Masons etc., in Answer to Professor John Robison's Proofs of a Conspiracy* (1797)

A
DEFENCE
OF THE
FREE MASONS, &c.
IN
ANSWER
TO
PROFESSOR JOHN ROBISON'S[xxii]
PROOFS
OF
A CONSPIRACY, &c.
BY A FRIEND TO TRUTH.

LONDON:
PRINTED FOR THE BOOKSELLERS.
1797. /

A
DEFENCE
OF THE
FREE MASONS, &c.

SIR,

You have been more successful, it seems, in renewing the fever of political suspicion and alarm in this country, than in exciting, among the students at the UNIVERSITY of EDINBURGH, a passion for the study of NATURAL PHILOSO-PHY. Amidst your triumph over that distempered credulity of the British Public, which has eagerly gulped up the dreams of your *hypochondriac* fancy; will you, yet, deign to listen, but for ten minutes, to the not unfriendly expostulations of a *Brother-*MASON? Yet, why should I mention *MASON?* You are, no doubt, ready, with unutterable abhorrence, to reject the name. If the *Brothers* have not yet, with one indignant voice, expelled you from their *communion*; surely, you yourself must, ere this time, have, with horrour, abjured a society which you account so dangerous! I would request you to favour me with your attention, for the sake of that SCIENCE which the mighty mind of / a NEWTON[1] first taught mortal intelligence to grasp, But, alas! what have you now to do with science? – You, whom the vain attempt to teach it, threw into a state of fancied, yet languishing illness, out of which nought but the *vision* of a CONSPIRACY, has had power to restore you!

However, though I know no arts of conjuration, that can enable me to gain your willing ear; there is something within me, that bids me speak. Addresses to which we listen with reluctance, are sometimes more salutary than those of which we catch every accent with the fondest delight. – Nay, should you yourself be neither *pleased* nor edified by the very little more I shall advance; who knows, but somebody else may?

Your book bears the title of PROOFS *of a* CONSPIRACY *against all the* RELIGIONS *and* GOVERNMENTS *of* EUROPE; *collected from good* AUTHORITIES. I will own that, when I first saw it advertised in the Newspapers, my surprize and curiosity were, in a very considerable degree excited. The word PROOFS, in the mouth of a *mathematician and natural philosopher*, carries in it a very strong meaning. Accustomed to accept as PROOFS, nothing but the *demonstration* of *mathematics*, or the *results* of a very accurate and complete *philosophical analysis*; such a man is not apt to dignify with the name of PROOFS, those vague plausibilities which will often command the assent of minds less habituated to rigorous investigation and reasoning. I supposed, therefore, that, if you had been able to express your meaning in language sufficiently perspicuous and popular; there would, assuredly, be no want of certainty of facts, and of close, consecutive reasoning, in your promised work. I was concerned to think, that it should be so; for we have had so / much of plots and parties and insurrections and revolutions in Europe, during these last eight or nine years; that my soul was absolutely sick to death, of the very idea of any new alarm arising to distract men's minds in this way, and to fill them with more of mutual hatred and distrust! – Of part of this anxiety, the perusal of your book itself, soon happily relieved me. It is filled with *allegations* which, to my weak apprehension, appear to deserve any other name, rather than that of PROOFS. If you be a mathematician and a philosopher; it should seem, that, as to judgment and ratiocination, you belong most certainly, to a very different school from that of EUCLID and of NEWTON!

Let us recollect, what it is your book contains? Either I mistake exceedingly, or else its whole substance may be summarily expressed in the following propositions:

I. That the societies of Free-Masons, existing throughout Europe, are of no very ancient origin; have much of frivolity, quackery, and imposture, in the principles of their fraternal union; are subject to be easily infected with the contagion of opinions hostile to religion and civil government; have actually been, in no small degree, contaminated by such opinions; are capable, from the nature of their union and correspondence, to accomplish mischief moral and political, the most extensive, and the most fatal to all that is valuable in social life:

II. That, out of the *Mason*-Lodges, and *Masonic* fraternities, in Germany, have arisen the Order of the ILLUMINATI, a combination of hypocritical miscreants, who, under the pretence of *universal benevolence*, and a plan to accomplish the moral reformation of the world, / had entered into the most diabolical CONSPIRACY, that was ever conceived, against all civil and social order, against all that is honourable or virtuous among mankind:

III. That, by the contagion of the same spirit and principles, – nay, even by derivation from the German ILLUMINATI, – was the first spirit of levelling democratical reform, kindled in France; and that the *Jacobin*-Clubs of the French, were but so many descendants from the Free-Masons of Britain and the *Illuminati* of Germany:

IV. That, even in Britain, our Mason-Lodges have already begun to share the general contamination; that, Societies of ILLUMINATI have begun to be formed here; that, even our Missionary Societies are not less likely to propagate the Creed of Jacobinism, than that of Christianity.

These propositions seem to comprehend the principal substance of your book. Whatever else it contains, appears to be only digression, illustration, and declamation intended for ornament. – I shall follow you through these four summary propositions in succession; and shall very briefly mention such hints as occur to me, in opposition to the truth of your facts, and to the accuracy of your reasonings.

I. I must own, that I could not contemplate, without amazement, that ignorance which you, a *ci-devant* Free-Mason, a Scholar, and a Philosopher, have betrayed in regard to the early history of Free-Masonry, in that part of your work which I have referred to this first division. /

It is true, that, in the popular account of the origin of Free-Masonry which prevails among the Masons themselves; there is not a little of fable, interwoven. But, this fable is just such as that of the Heralds, involving in imaginary splendour, and carrying back to unknown antiquity, the origin of all those great families, whose genealogies they record, and whose armour they emblazon. It is just such as that of the ancient history of almost all nations, which vanity, errour, and reverence, have equally embellished and perplexed. Pretensions which

Free-Masonry shares with so many things else of the most august character, are not, however vain, to be hastily imputed to imposture, so long as we can find any fairer source to which to ascribe their origin. I cannot think so meanly of you as to believe, that you did not think more highly of the order of Free-Masons when you first solicited admission among them, as a Brother; or when you aspired to rise still from one degree in Masonry to another, till you began to find, that your farther elevation was likely to become too troublesome and too expensive.

But, it is not necessary for us to rest in general, although plausible conjecture, in respect to the origin of FREE-MASONRY. In those dark ages which succeeded the æra of the conquest of the Western Roman Empire, by the Northern Barbarians; all the Arts in which there was any refinement, and especially the Art of Architecture, were entirely destroyed. The ministers of taste and luxury, were for a long while, to be sought from Constantinople, and from the eastern shores of the Mediterranean Sea. When foreign Masons and Architects came, from Greece and Asia, to Italy; it was extremely natural for them to associate almost / exclusively with one another, and to reserve many *secrets* of their country, their Art, their conduct, their situation among the strangers who entertained and employed them. Between Architects and Masons exercising one of the most useful and honourable among the Arts of peace, and rude warriours, and dejected, servile hinds; there necessarily subsisted a considerable distinction of manners and character, which had a powerful tendency to divide the former from the latter, and to combine them into one peculiar body. It was the spirit of those rude ages, to distribute men into *Casts*. Soldiers formed one *Cast*; Priests, another; Merchants and Artisans, a third; Hinds and Farmers, a fourth. These several great *Casts* were again arranged into many subdivisions. Ecclesiastics were subdivided into Orders, regular and secular; the regulars into many Orders of Monks and Nuns, – each Order bound by *certain vows*, to observe *one common form* of religious service and discipline. At the same time, while knowledge was not yet communicated by a multiplication and circulation of books, such as we now enjoy; whatever of ingenious art or science, happened to be known to one man, or to one society of men; was, partly of necessity, in part by the natural selfishness of the possessors, concealed from others. Masons and Architects, too, travelling from Italy, over all the Continent of Europe; from the Continent, into our British Isle; found, in the circumstances of their dispersion and travels, new reasons to induce them to a fraternal union, not unlike to that of knighthood, not very dissimilar to that of the religious orders, resembling the modes in which Artists in general concealed the peculiar practice of their respective Arts from all but their Apprentices, having an analogy / also to the manner in which Artists and Merchants were combined in the *Guilds* and *Incorporations* of the free towns.

Thus the combination, the oaths, the secrecy, the brotherly beneficence of the Free-Masons, had their origin, not from accident or caprice, not in wicked

imposture; but in circumstances natural to that period in the progress of refinement and of social institutions at which it took place; and in honest endeavours
for the improvement of Art, and for the relief and protection of destitute
humanity. Many of the most eminent Masons and Architects, who were, in the
middle ages, employed in the construction of castles, convents, and churches,
were ECCLESIASTICS. For these, it was exceedingly natural to extend to their
character as Artists and Artisans, more or less of the same system of ideas which
regulated their condition and manners, as Clergymen. That *Masonry* and
Architecture were, in the fourteenth, the fifteenth, and the sixteenth centuries,
exercised in Scotland in very great perfection of the particular *styles of building* then in fashion; is sufficiently attested by the remains of the noble abbies of
Melross, of Kilwinning, of Crossraguel, of Aberbrothwick, of the cathedrals of
Elgin and Dunblane, of the chapel of Roslin, of the palace of Falkland; and by
innumerable other august though ruinous monuments, which I shall not here
stay to name in detail. In such edifices was then placed, almost the only part
of the incomes of our ancestors, which was to be accumulated for the use of
their posterity. In this illustrious age of Gothic Architecture, did the *Fraternity*
of the FREE MASONS first arise in Scotland. It is extremely probable, that associations similar to those now existing under the denomination of *Lodges*, were
/ formed during the building of more than one or two of those stately edifices
which I have named. But, the only one of which the memory has been very distinctly preserved, is that of KILWINNING, formed, no doubt, while the spacious
buildings of the abbey and conventual church of KILWINNING, were erected or
repaired. The existence of this LODGE has been traced back, by satisfactory documents known to almost every intelligent Scottish Mason, – as far as to the end
of the fifteenth century. Yet *Mr* ROBISON[xxiii], educated at the College of Glasgow, versed in all the complex Masonry of the Continent, once an enthusiast in
the pursuit of Masonic rank and science, who has resided for many years in the
City of Edinburgh, without laying aside his Masonic character, – is, it seems, an
entire stranger to these facts! An admirable specimen this, of his skill as a Mason,
and of his liberal curiosity as a Scholar and a Man of Science! For the very little
which you say concerning the antiquity of Free-Masonry,* is obviously made so
very general, only as the veil of ignorance, or of something worse, in order to
confine the origin of all that is venerable in Masonry within a very recent period!

You honestly profess yourself ignorant of the circumstances which first led
persons who did not actually practise the art of *Masonry*, to solicit admission
into the *Masonic* associations. Those circumstances may easily be understood.
Wherever there is any thing professedly kept a secret; there are always many
persons who feel so strongly the impulse of a vain *curiosity*; as to be willing to
purchase, almost at any rate, the knowledge of that secret. The first *Masonic*

---

*   P. 20, 21, Proofs of a Conspiracy, &c.

fraternities; being surrounded with strangers who, while they admired their / art, were often ready to disturb and harrass them by barbarous violence and oppression; would, in consequence of this circumstance, be induced to invite into brotherly union with them, the most powerful and the most liberal-minded of their *noble* and *princely patrons* and *protectors*. While *Architecture* and *Masonry* were respected, as rising to the dignity of the *fine* and *liberal* Arts; it was natural that many persons who disdained the mere manual practice of them, should aspire to an acquaintance with what were accounted their *scientific mysteries*. To obtain those mutual acts of brotherly kindness, too, which *Masons* engage to perform to one another, – which every *Brother* has a right to demand from the members of any Lodge; many persons would naturally desire to be *accepted* among *Masons*, who did not actually exercise their art. It was *honourable* to associate with *Masons*, when the art of Masonry, was, although so useful, yet rare: And this honour would naturally be courted by numbers who sought nothing more when they solicited the name of *Mason*. Into *all societies*, municipal, literary, &c. *honorary* members are admitted: No wonder, then, that the same principle should be known and acted upon, among Masons. How comes it, Sir, that causes so obvious as these, – giving rise to the custom of persons not actually Masons, yet soliciting admission into their society, – can have escaped the notice of a scholar and a philosopher such as you?

But, it should seem, that you are ambitious to rob *Masonry* of the credit of whatever is venerable in its history, for the purpose of reducing it to a level with the modern *jacobin* and *corresponding, political societies*. I wish, my feelings would allow me to acquit you of the charge of malignant misrepresentation in your prosecution of / this attempt! In direct contradiction to what you alledge, the genuine truth is; that the *mystery* and *brotherhood* of FREE-MASONRY have ever been strictly allied to *loyalty*, and to the faithful discharge of all the duties of good subjects.

So venerably ancient, FREE-MASONRY belongs, in truth, to that *Ancient Order of Things*, which you dread lest modern reformers should subvert. Its just pretensions to antiquity of origin, the interests to which it has ever been subservient, its tendency to preserve in men's minds an attachment to the peaceful duties of life, its exclusion of every thing like excess in convivial enjoyment from the social meetings of its votaries, its aversion from all unseasonable interference in matters of politics or religion; make it, in truth, one of those sure *subsidia* of the existing order of things, which ought to be ever cherished by all who wish well to good government, – by all who desire to see civil life improved – not by political convulsion, but by the continual improvement of private knowledge and private virtue among all the individuals of the human race!

That is *praise, indeed!* which is extorted from the reluctant confessions of an enemy. Such praise of the connexion between FREE-MASONRY and steady loyalty, seems to be implied in your admission; that, amidst the misfortunes of *Charles the First*[2] and his family, during the last century, the FREE-MASONS were among the most secret and constant of their friends. I challenge you to produce *one fact*, satisfactorily *authenticated*, from which it can be inferred; that the Jesuits assumed the guise of *Free-Masons*[3] *Free-Masons: Robison wrote that 'at this time the Jesuits interfered considerably insinuating themselves into the Lodges, and contributing to encrease the religious mysticism that is to be observed in all the ceremonies of the order'. According to Robison, the Jesuits were responsible for introducing the higher degrees and knightly ceremonies, which became very popular among French Freemasons. J. Robison, Proofs of a Conspiracy, p. 22.*, and made use of the principles and the associations of Free-Masonry, in order to accomplish, in the last century, the restoration of the Catholic / religion in England. The *Memoirs* of *Gregorie Panzaini*[4], lately published in English, by the learned and eloquent *Berington*[5]; have, in addition to former sources of information, thrown much new light upon the practices of the Jesuits in England, during that period; yet communicate nothing from which there can be aught inferred, to support your bold and calumnious asseveration.

You would have us to believe, that the *Masons* borrowed from the *Friendly Societies*, the idea of contributing charitably from a common fund to relieve the wants of their *Brother-Masons*. So far is this from being true, that, almost all the *Friendly Societies* in this country, – those societies in which labourers lay up while in health, a common fund, – out of which relief may be administered to them, in sickness, and under the infirmities of old age, – have been *set on foot* by *Free-Masons*, or by other persons expressly imitating the benevolent provisions of the *Mason-Lodges*. The British government has wisely given its sanction to the existence of these *Friendly Societies*. How sensibly, how usefully has their influence been already felt, in diminishing the burthen of the poor's rates, and in alleviating the miseries of the poor in manufacturing cities! Had FREE-MASONRY never contributed another benefit to mankind, than this of suggesting the institution of *Friendly Societies*, in which the poor become the relievers of their own miseries; it had, for this alone, deserved the eternal gratitude and esteem of all good men!

But, its sublime and extensive benevolence seems to furnish in your estimation, the strongest objection against *Free-Masonry*! And is it really your opinion, *Mr Robison*, that the affections of humanity ought to be sacrificed to the factitious relations of politics? Would you have all / mankind detach to themselves into so many petty hordes of *American Indians*, continually hostile to one another, ever lying in wait to thin each other's numbers by the most vigilant cunning and malignity, – to wreak their mutual hatred upon its victims, by the most refined practices of cruelty and torture? What, Sir! is the Christian religion odious to you, because it unites all the saints into one church, – because it enjoins that *universal benevolence*, which is the object of your most fearful and abhorrent suspicions? The abuse of the *best things*, frequently generates the *worst*; but are those *best things* to be, for this, proscribed and abolished? To preserve the existence of a particular form of political society, are we to poison all the *sweets* of social life, and to extinguish all those lights which effuse over it, the lustre of love and joy? It is not from genuine benevolence, however *universal* – let me assure you, – that the established Order of Society in Europe, has aught to fear; but from that *bastard*-benevolence, or rather that *undistinguishing malevolence*, which could prompt to the composition and publication of works such as yours!

You inform us, that the FREE-MASONRY of Britain, transplanted to the Continent, has suffered such deterioration in its passage, as to have become, there, the cloak of every imposture, and the vehicle of every mischief! *Where are your proofs*? Your own *ipse dixit*[6] is not enough. Even the confidential papers of your Russian brother, of which you profess to have made so free an use, will not, unless *properly authenticated*, serve as evidence of what you here assert. I have looked over your book again and again; but no shadow of proof, do I find in it, upon which any person, – even a Judge Jefferys[7] – could be persuaded to believe what you tell of the mischievous / tendency of Continental Masonry, Your whole allegations are a mere gossip's tale. Investigated to the bottom, they turn out to be not better founded, than the story of *the man vomiting the three black crows*![8] For shame! Is it for a philosopher to believe and to affirm upon the credit of mere popular report? Or are innuendoes, anonymous papers, fabrications by avowed enemies, the fictions of newspapers, the vain fancy of conjectural criticism, – are these the proofs which it becomes a philosopher to produce, when it is guilt that he has to impute? But, grant that there may have been some *bad* and *foolish* men occasionally conspicuous among the FREE-MASONS on the Continent: – Is the whole fraternity, with all its discipline and institutions, to be therefore condemned as pernicious to society? As well might we condemn chemistry, on account of the impostures and the wild fancies of the alchemists! As well should we condemn reformed Christianity, on account of the militant Anabaptists who attempted to establish their reign at Munster! As well silence all our pulpits, because Savonarola of Florence[9] , because Mr David Black of St Andrew's[10] preached and prayed sedition from the pulpit! As well explode all mathematics and natural philosophy, because it is not impossible for a natural philosopher to be a dreamer, and for a mathematician to be crazy!

"But the FREE-MASONS, in consequence of the peculiar nature and rules of their Association, possess, at least, the power to do very much mischief." – Not at all. They have power to do – not a little good. But, it is impossible for them to do much mischief. You well know that they are precluded from becoming the confidants of any guilty secrets. Princes, nobles, the great, the wise, and the good, have ever been so intermingled / in the Masonic Associations, as to form a powerful check upon the mean, the turbulent, and the wicked. In the course of the present century, very many of the most respectable characters that have adorned the age, have been *Masons*. Would those men have made themselves accomplices in the crimes and in the guilty machinations of their *Masonic* Brothers, by concealing them? Do we not, at present, number among the FREE-MASONS in Britain, very many of those who have stood forward the most zealous in defence of their King, and of the Constitution? The truth seems to be, that the circumstances of the Masonic Associations, are such as to enable them to do much good, but render it impossible that they should do mischief, without effecting, by the very attempt, a spontaneous and necessary dissolution of the Order.

II. In your account of the Continental FREE-MASONS, you give some very few pretended facts, *without authorities, without evidence,* distorted by a continual but vain labour, to discover imposture and conspiracy in what appears to have been entirely harmless, by the most ridiculous efforts to extract matter for moral and political crimination, out of what must appear to every candid mind, to be subject to no just blame. We know, that it is not difficult for certain spirits, to represent any character, any tenor of conduct, any series of transactions, as wicked, by exhibiting them in colours, often but a very little varied from the original. Interpreting every fact in your own way, you thus contrive to represent even the most innocent and praise-worthy acts, as criminal. But is this the proper conduct of a philosopher, of an honest man? /

You tell us, that the FREE-MASONS of the Continent, went from Britain, perhaps from Scotland. – Even the facts which you yourself relate, seem to evince the contrary. Had the *Free-MASONRY* of the Continent been borrowed, at the very first, from Scotland, the distinction of *Maçon Ecossois* would not have been particularized among the gradations of that *Masonry*. Had the whole been Scottish; it would have been vain to distinguish a part as such. The probability is, – nay, more than the probability; – that FREE-MASONRY has had an existence on the Continent, at least as long as in any part of Britain; – but that innovations have indeed been introduced into that FREE-MASONRY, by Jacobite exiles from the north of Scotland; – and that such innovations persuaded the uninformed and credulous to fancy blindly, that perhaps the whole of *Masonry* might be of Scottish origin.

How could you inconsiderately repeat a very foolish piece of calumny, concerning the transactions of *Voltaire*[11] with *Cramer*[12] the bookseller? The following is the true state of that anecdote. *Voltaire* was absolutely blameless. One of *Voltaire's* works was sold to *Cramer*; and *Cramer* was printing it for publication. In the mean time, the Author, aware, that it would not fail to be surreptitiously reprinted in Holland assoon as it was published; and that neither he nor his bookseller could, by any means in their power, prevent this reprinting; was anxious to hinder a bad, mutilated, or altered edition of his book, from being given by the Dutch booksellers. For this reason, he wished *Cramer* to have communicated the sheets as they were printed, to some particular bookseller in Holland. This *Cramer* declined. *Voltaire* himself, not without *Cramer's* knowledge, nor by any invasion / of *his* interests, sent to a bookseller in Holland, a copy either of the manuscript, or of the printed sheets of that work which he had sold to *Cramer*. – But, he did this, merely because neither he nor *Cramer* could hinder the publication of a Dutch edition; and because his composition must otherwise have been, in such an edition, greatly injured. Nothing could be more laudable. It is evident from your own account, that *Cramer* had been requested to take a part in the business. All that *Voltaire* sought, was, merely to hinder the public from having a bad book imposed upon them under his name. – Such is the act which you represent to have been hainously criminal! Much of a similar nature with this act, are the tales which have been propagated by yourself and a lying Abbè of the name of Barruel[13] , concerning the French Literati in general. I am not at all concerned to vindicate Voltaire. But, imputations so flagrantly unjust, as that which I have here noticed, well deserve refutation.

But, the ILLUMINATI are your grand theme. Here I wish to come into an investigation, somewhat closer, into the nature and authenticity of the facts which you produce.

1. To my astonishment, I find; that your principal authority for the facts of a charge so serious, is the *Religion's Begenbeiten*[14], a German periodical work, of no higher authenticity than any *collection of Newspaper-reports*, or than the common tales of popular scandal. I blush for you and for your friends and admirers – when I find a *soi-disant* philosopher, the friend and associate of other philosophers, capable of relating a series of historical truths, – capable of bringing a charge of / atrocious guilt, – upon evidence, so vague, so suspicious, so inconclusive!

2. It appears, that all the papers which you give, upon *such authority*, have, – at least so far as they tend to criminate the ILLUMINATI, come before the world, through the hands of persons who were hostile to *them*. Now, no impartial Court of Judicature, no discerning estimator of evidence, would ever receive papers of such a nature, in the character of proofs of an accusation, from the hands of those persons by whom the accusation was brought. How is their unaltered genuineness to be ascertained? How do we know, that they are not forgeries? We cannot receive them, as evidence, any farther than their truth and validity are admitted by the parties accused. But, of these papers, the truth and validity have not been admitted by *Weishaupt*[15] and his friends, in any instance, in which they can afford the shadow of accusation against these injured men!

Thus, although we should allow, what cannot be hastily allowed, – the unimpeachable veracity of the *Religion's Begenbeiten*; yet the other papers which you give us from it, have not been proved by you to be authentic, in any instance in which they afford unfavourable representations of the *Illuminati*!

3. Even of these last-mentioned papers, the sense is, for the most part, given by you, only from the conjectural criticism of the enemies of – *Weishaupt* and his friends. The vagueness of such criticism is well known to every scholar. It was *never yet accepted as satisfactory evidence*, in an impartial Court of Judicature, nor by any respectable historical writer. Refuse we to admit your conjectural criticism in the present instance, – and there remains neither guilt nor contrivance to be charged / against the *illuminati*. We must refuse it. I should not expect any man of common sense, and common honesty, to admit it. The letters of *Spartacus* and *Philo*[16], the assertions concerning guilty secrets and private acts of horrible immorality, all the hints and innuendoes with which these are accompanied, – cannot be regarded in any other light, than, as the vain fictions of a *NOVEL*, – except so far as they have been admitted, and satisfactorily explained by the *Illuminati* themselves. They cannot otherwise give any evidence.

4. You pretend to give us something of evidence from the confession of *Baron Knigge*[17] But what is this good for? Who would listen to the railing accusations of a renegado or apostate, against the religion which he has nefariously forsaken? Who would chuse to hear a perjured and apostate Free-Mason, if any such should offer to give evidence against the *Mason-Lodges*? Besides, even Knigge's tales convey no idea of guilt so horrible as that which you strive to impute!

5. You have adopted the two expedients which are always the most zealously employed by persons conscious of having undertaken a bad cause. – You endeavour to disgrace the principles of the ILLUMINATI by holding up to reprobation, the private vices *of individuals* among them; *vices which do not appear to have been originally produced by this ILLUMINATISM*, and which were earnestly discouraged, even according to your own account, as inconsistent with its success. – You indulge, at the same time, in *declamation* much like that of your illustrious and sober-minded brother-professor[18], the passionate admirer of the late Queen of France![19] /

No man would have recourse to such shifts, who had any just confidence in the merits of his cause.

6. Had those crimes which you have alledged against *Weishaupt* and his associates, been satisfactorily proved; it is impossible that these unprotected men could have escaped the most disgraceful of corporal punishments. But, you allow, that Weishaupt's works are still in credit in Germany; you own, that he found an asylum; you ascribe to him, influence amid all his disgraces, sufficient to restore the society of the ILLUMINATI, even after it had been once overthrown.

7. It is indeed impossible in the nature of things, that there should be truth in those wicked schemes which you ascribe to the ILLUMINATI. Their *means* you own to have been in the *first* and *exterior* instances good. Their ends, you also own to have been, *externally* at least – good. There is nothing of evil that you can ascribe to them, save the suspicion of some *interior* and *uncertain* wickedness

which is incapable of direct proof. But, there was never yet an association, who made it their *primary* object to convert all mankind to one system of exterminating wickedness. It is highly remarkable, that the accusations offered against the ILLUMINATI, are very nearly the same as those which were urged, without other proofs than those of malice and suspicion, against the societies of the first Christians, by their Pagan antagonists.

8. You talk, too, of booksellers associated for the purposes of *Masonry* and *Illuminatism*, of a profligate person of the name of *Bahrdt*[20] an agent for the ILLUMINATI, of great efforts made at the fair of Frankfort, in order to circulate one class of books, and to impede the sale of books of another class. /

But the crimes attributed to *Bahrdt*, have not been proved by you.

Although proved, what could they have availed, as matter of accusation against the *Masons* or the ILLUMINATI, among whom he happened to be enrolled? The crimes or vices of an individual, are not to be imputed to the society to which he belongs, – unless it shall appear, that the principles or the general example of that society, have been the *first* or *only* means by which he has been infected with such vices, or driven to perpetrate such crimes.

9. The truth of the whole tale in regard to the ILLUMINATI, seems to be merely this. Some of the German Literati, men of warm, romantic imaginations, had conceived the sublime idea of reducing MASONRY into a noble system of enlarged beneficence, regulated upon philosophical principles. Their notion was too romantic and fanciful, to be practicable. In the mean time, secrecy excited curiosity. Defeated curiosity became malignant suspicion. Rivals of the same and talents of *Weishaupt* and *Nicolai*[21], represented them as engaged in criminal projects which could never be proved. There was a great deal of writing and printing about all this, which attracted the notice of an idly inquisitive public. A mathematician just turning his mind from a theory of the moon, – has attempted to make a fuss about it in Britain. – This is all the mighty CONSPIRACY!

III. The FRENCH REVOLUTION is your next great theme. And, if there be any regular connexion of design, combining together the different parts of your work; it must be your intention to prove, that the *French Revolution* was in a great measure, the work of the ILLUMINATI of Germany. /

But, even by yourself, – in direct contradiction to your own objects, – is it stated, that the first grand steps in the *French Revolution*, had been already taken, before ever the aid of *Free-Masonry* or *Illuminatism*, was called in. You are obliged to confess, that they were other qualities, not merely his *Free-Masonry* nor his *Illuminatism*, which so eminently fitted MIRABEAU[22] for that conspicuous part he acted in the commencing revolution of the government of his country. You have yourself owned that, although one of the *Illuminati*, *Mirabeau* was perfectly fitted by his principles, if his ambition had been less towering, for the service of a court. You alledge, that, in France, *Free-Masonry* was perverted to revolutionary purposes. You tell many anecdotes, but you bring no satisfactory evidence. The general result of all that you relate, is, merely this; that there were few or no *Illuminati* in France about the beginning of the revolution; that *Illuminatism* never operated as a direct cause, in accomplishing that revolution; that the duke of *Orleans*[23] happened to be Grand Master of the Mason-Lodges; that persons who were Free-Masons, happened, notwithstanding the better influence of *Free-Masonry*, to become agitators in the revolution, – just as did many persons who were *priests* and nobles, – notwithstanding the different influence of *religion*, and of the principle of French *honour.* From your own account, the only thing we can reasonably conclude, is; that your kindness for your old friends, the *Continental Free-Masons*, is so great; that you gladly would, if it were possible, represent them as the authors of all the crimes which have been perpetrated on the Continent, since you were last among them. But, whatever your own heated imagination may have conceived; you certainly / have not evinced, that Free-Masonry was any thing at all concerned, in accomplishing the French Revolution, more than any other *Denomination* whatever that is known in Society.

IV. You would gladly persuade us, that the *Free-Masons*, and the *Missionary Societies* among ourselves, are also labouring to break asunder the bands of civil order, and are every where assiduous to abet the cause of democratic revolution.

Here you had it more in your power to learn the truth, than when you were to speak of what passed at a distance, in France and Germany. Here, too, you might expect refutation to be eagerly urged against any falsehoods which you should inconsiderately publish. For these reasons, I should have thought it impossible for you, or *any* other *man in his right senses*, carelessly to set down in such a book, – *as a capital fact*, tending to criminate any person in a very high degree, – an *idle story, reported by some* MISERABLE SPY *or* TELL-*tale*, that watched, with wicked purpose, the free unguarded conversation of a convivial meeting. But, supposing any person to be so *wicked* and so *imprudent*, as to produce facts of this character; was it not to be expected, that he would use extraordinary pains to ascertain the certainty and accuracy of what he came by, in this suspicious manner? Was it to be imagined, that he would ever dare to publish to the world, such aspersions, upon less than the unanimous evidence of a whole company? Certainly not. Yet, you, Mr Robison[xxiv], dared to accuse a very worthy man, of having uttered words of democratic fury, and of diabolical malignity, – upon no other grounds, than the hasty reports, – *surely of some detestable tell-tale*; / and in this accusation have so far deviated from the truth; that strict enquiry has obliged you yourself, publicly to confess the meaning of the gentleman belied – to have been, in the conversation misrepresented by you, directly contrary to what you related it to have been. You have made your apology to the man whom you injured, and have probably obtained his forgiveness. You may have retracted other falsehoods, humbled yourself before others who have been injured by your groundless tales, persuaded these also to forgive you! But, what in the mean time, becomes of your CREDIT with the public? *If you have erred thus notoriously, in regard to the only facts which you could very easily ascertain; what shall we think of the credibility of your tales, concerning parties, characters, and events, in France and Germany; the truth of which you could not, however willing, investigate to the bottom?* Had we no other argument against the credibility of the whole contents of your book; this alone ought to be sufficient to make every man, endowed with shrewd common sense, steadily to reject it.

Produce your facts; produce your evidence; if you have any thing farther to alledge against the members of the *Mason-Lodges*. Do not presume to say, – "I am a friend to the *Government*, and to the *Constitution*. I have my fears, my fancies, my anxieties: Listen to them! Believe them! Act upon them! They are well meant!" – *Truth! Truth! Evidence! Evidence!* shall still be my demand. Give us these; and we may, then, perhaps share your anxieties, and your fears.

Nothing can be more certain, than that the *Great Body* of the FREE-MASONS at present in this country, are, "Men the most respectable for liberal intelligence, for good morals, for virtuous industry, for a / steady and tried attachment to the best interests of religion, and of civil order. Their names, their characters, their respectability, are well known. A person of a notoriously profligate moral character, might as soon hope to escape expulsion from among the Quakers, – as a disloyal subject to hide himself among the *Free-Masons*! I know not, if the exertions of the *Free-Masons* have not contributed more effectually to prevent revolutionary convulsion in this country, than perhaps all the bustle of the Alarmists!"

The societies for the Propagation of the Gospel by means of Missionaries, – come in for a share in your fears, jealousies, and hinted calumnies. "What have they done?" Different societies correspond together for one common purpose of exalted benevolence: and the *Jacobin* societies have corresponded together in a manner not at all dissimilar. "But, *Watt*[24] who was executed for treason, breathed the air while he meditated his treason; and can you, *Mr Robison*, deign to do, in ordinary respiration, as that traitor did? There is a sort of common union and correspondence supposed to be continually, carried on among all Christians; would you not abolish that Christianity in which this takes place? The establishment of the Post-Office presents means but too encouraging to criminal political correspondence; Must we not abolish it also? The *Press* and the *Art of Writing*, – are these not mischievously favourable to a treasonable political correspondence among mankind? Should we not be now entirely free of *Democrats*, if we wanted such engines?" – Ha! ha! ha! Good Mr Robison! pray, tell us what certain political mischief has there as yet resulted from the efforts of Missionaries? — Would it not, / think you, be an admirably wise scheme for the minister, amidst his difficulties about the *ways and means,* to seize for the use of government, all the funds of the *Missionary-Associations?*

But, I am heartily weary of this very unpleasant correspondence. I shall now conclude. I call on you, then, Sir, either to suppress your book, and to make a solemn apology before God and the whole world for having dared to publish it; or else to support every one of those facts which I have challenged by irresistible and completely satisfactory evidence? Are you aware, Sir, what injury you have done to the interests of truth, to the cause of rational, steady loyalty, to the honour of that University of which you are a member, to the respectability of that Society in which you hold the pen of Secretary, by this strange *new-fashioned sort of* NOVEL of yours? Yet, I am inclined to think you rather a mistaken and a wrong-headed, than a bad man! God forgive you, and restore you to yourself again!

A FRIEND TO TRUTH.

[ANON.], *THE INDICTMENT AND TRIAL OF JOHN ANDREW, SHOEMAKER IN MAYBOLE, SOMETIME TEACHER OF A PRIVATE SCHOOL THERE, AND ROBERT RAMSAY, CART WRIGHT THERE, BOTH MEMBERS OF A MASONIC LODGE AT MAYBOLE: CHARGED WITH THE CRIME OF SEDITION, AND ADMINISTERING UNLAWFUL OATHS* (1800)

[Anon.], *The Indictment and Trial of John Andrew, Shoemaker in Maybole, Sometime Teacher of a Private School there, and Robert Ramsay, Cart Wright there, Both Members of a Masonic Lodge at Maybole: Charged with the Crime of Sedition, and Administering Unlawful Oaths – and Stiling Themselves, The Grand Assembly of Knights Templars. Before the Circuit Court of Justiciary at Ayr. On Monday the 17th of September, 1800* (Edinburgh, 1800).[1]

Freemasonry, as it appeared in Europe, was 'first articulated in post-revolutionary Britain' and the 'form of the lodge became one of the many channels that transmitted a new political culture, based upon constitutionalism, which gradually turned against traditional privileges and established, hierarchical authority'.[2] In Europe, Margaret Jacob argues, Freemasonry did play a major role in nurturing and promoting revolutionary ideas. Though built upon the British model, Continental Freemasonry had become politically and socially subversive and posed a clear threat to all forms of organized religion. Furthermore, Jacob argues, 'in a British context lodges were, on the whole, remarkably supportive of established institutions, of church and state. Yet they could also house divisive, or oppositional political practices ... and ... at moments show affiliation with radical interests.'[3]

David Stevenson correctly reasons that frequent misuse of the word 'masonic' to describe 'anything combining radical ideas and secrecy ... was illogical and confusing'.[4] This confusion ultimately allowed detractors of the Masons to formulate conspiracy theories which asserted that 'freemasonry was one of the great causes of the French Revolution'.[5] Although there was little tangible evidence to substantiate such allegations, British Freemasonry became the object of much scrutiny and suspicion.

Two nascent degrees of Freemasonry, the Royal Arch and Knights Templar, had appeared on the West Coast of Scotland in Maybole during the 1790s and at the time were not sanctioned by the Grand Lodge of Scotland as official masonic degrees. The Royal Arch and Knights Templar degrees were extensions of the three sanctioned degrees of Freemasonry – Entered Apprentice, Fellow Craft, Master Mason – and were based upon legends of the Knights of St John and the Holy Royal Arch located in Solomon's Temple in Jerusalem. Members of the Royal Arch and Knights Templar professed an interest in the higher degrees of Masonry, and Elaine McFarland explains that these degrees, 'under a pretended connection with Freemasonry', sought to 'propagate the infidelity of the French Revolution, and to evoke sympathy for the democrats in Ireland'.[6] Peter Clark is correct in arguing that although Royal Arch and Knights Templar ceremonies were introduced in Britain, 'they never developed the baroquely elaborate hierarchy of ritual degrees which became widespread in Germany, France, and other parts of Europe'.[7]

The scepticism surrounding these new degrees would be revisited in Western Scotland during the Maybole Trial of Sedition. McFarland claims that by 1797, a 'contagion [which equated] Irishness with disaffection' had gripped Western Scotland.[8] As such, by 1797 Ayrshire had become one of the 'first strongholds' of Irish influence.[9] Rumours alleging Irish exploitation of masonic lodges for seditious purposes in Scotland existed as early as 1779. David Murray Lyon notes that in that year, a body of Dublin Freemasons existing under the title 'The High Knight Templars of Ireland Lodge', or Knights Templar, applied for and received a charter from Lodge Kilwinning in Ayrshire, Scotland. However, according to Lyon, the 'Irish Brethren subsequently erased from their Charter the word "Lodge" ... and, surreptitiously inserting "Encampment", began the practise of Black Masonry',[10] which eventually became the degree of Knights Templar.[11] Other historians agree, suggesting that Masons serving in Irish regiments towards the end of the eighteenth century contributed to the introduction and practice of higher and unsanctioned degrees within Scottish lodges.

Membership lists from radical clubs and societies offer no definitive evidence that Freemasons in Maybole were members of seditious associations. Masonic historian L. D. Wartski, however, corroborates McFarland's assertions by claiming that 'in 1796 some of the members of Maybole Lodge allied themselves with a few masonic United Irishmen in the formation of an Assembly of Knight Templars, and clandestinely entered upon the work of Royal Arch Masonry and Knight Templars'.[12]

Reprinted below are the trial transcriptions and indictments against Free-masons John Andrew and Robert Ramsay, members of No. 264 Lodge Royal Arch Maybole. This remarkable court battle hinged on the association of No. 264 Lodge Royal Arch Maybole with irregular members and illegally consti-tuted lodges, more specifically the Knights Templar, Royal Arch, possibly the United Irishmen, and the perceived seditious oaths required by these organi-zations.

This case illustrates several important trends. Firstly, the sorts of clashes present within Scottish lodges underwent a noticeable change as a result of the French Revolution and the reactionary legislation passed by the govern-ment in the 1790s, namely the Unlawful Oaths (1797) and Secret Societies (1799) Acts. Ultimately, financial disputes and disagreements among opera-tives (or stonemasons) and speculatives (or non-operative Masons) were overshadowed by endless wrangling over lodge precedence and charges of sedition and treason.

Secondly, the Unlawful Oaths and Secret Societies Acts, though they initially offered a measure of protection to the Freemasons, caused turmoil among the Scottish lodges for several years after their passage. Enacted to eradicate seditious societies, masonic lodges actually used them maliciously against one another; not as a legitimate means to safeguard Scotland against revolution, but rather to pursue political quarrels and personal vendettas against other Freemasons.

The pamphlet was printed and sold in Edinburgh by John Morren, Printer, in East Campbell Close Cowgate. Campbell Close served as the location for Morren's printing business from 1796–1810, after which time he relocated to 145 Cowgate. Morren published many chapbooks, or pamphlets, the earliest of which was published in 1800.[13] Copies exist in the Grand Lodge of Scotland Library in Edinburgh, although this text was keyed based upon copies in the British Library and the National Library of Scotland.

Notes

1. This headnote was written by Mark Wallace.
2. M. Jacob, *Living the Enlightenment* (New York: Oxford University Press, 1991), p. 51.
3. Jacob, *Living the Enlightenment*, p. 51.
4. D. Stevenson, *The Origins of Freemasonry: Scotland's Century 1590–1710* (Cambridge: Cambridge University Press, 1988), pp. 1–12.
5. Jacob, *Living the Enlightenment*, pp. 9–10.
6. E. McFarland, *Ireland and Scotland in the Age of Revolution: Planting the Green Bough* (Edinburgh: Edinburgh University Press, 1994), p. 59.
7. P. Clark, *British Clubs and Societies 1580–1800: The Origins of an Associational World* (Oxford: Oxford University Press, 2000), p. 334.
8. McFarland, *Ireland and Scotland*, p. 157.
9. McFarland, *Ireland and Scotland*, p. 158.

10. R. F. Gould, *Gould's History of Freemasonry Throughout the World*, 6 vols (New York: C. Scribner Son's, 1936), vol. 2, pp. 291–2.

11. D. M. Lyon, *History of the Lodge of Edinburgh (Mary's Chapel), No. 1, Embracing An Account of the Rise and Progress of Freemasonry in Scotland Mary's Chapel* (London: Gresham Publishing Company, 1900), p. 335.

12. L. D. Wartski, 'Freemasonry and the Early Secret Societies Act', Monograph Compiled and Presented by the Author for Private Circulation by the District Grand Lodge of Natal of Antient Free and Accepted Masons of Scotland, p. 64.

13. Information taken from the Scottish Book Trade Index (SBTI).

[Anon.], *The Indictment and Trial of John Andrew, Shoemaker in Maybole, Sometime Teacher of a Private School There, and Robert Ramsay, Cart Wright There, Both Members of a Masonic Lodge at Maybole: Charged with the Crime of Sedition, and Administering Unlawful Oaths* (1800)

THE
INDTICTMENT and TRIAL
OF
JOHN ANDREW,
Shoemaker in MAYBOLE, sometime Teacher
of a private School there,
AND
ROBERT RAMSAY,
CART WRIGHT THERE,

THE MEMBERS OF A MASONIC LODGE AT MAYBOLE;
Charged with the crime of Sedition, and administer-
ing unlawful oaths – and stiling themselves,
The Grand Assembly of Knights Templars.
Before the Circuit Court of Justiciary at AYR,
On Monday the 17th of September, 1800.

EDINBURGH:
PRINTED AND SOLD BY J. MORREN, PRINTER,
EAST CAMPBELL'S CLOSE, COWGATE.
(Price One Penny.) /

TRIAL FOR SEDITION.

THIS day came on the trial of JOHN ANDREW shoemaker in Maybole,[1] sometime teacher of a private school there, and ROBERT RAMSAY, cart-wright[2] there.

The libel charges them as being guilty of the crimes of sedition, and administering unlawful oaths,[3] importing an obligation not to discover crimes which it is the duty of every good citizen and loyal subject to divulge and bring to light, in so far as they did, under the shew and pretence of a meeting for masonry, sometime in the year 1796, at Maybole, along with others their associates, most of them from Ireland, form themselves into an illegal club of association, stiling itself, "*The Grand Assembly of Knights Templars*,"[4] which club, under the pretence of initiating into the ceremonies of masonry, did admit various persons as members, and did at said admission perform various ceremonies, partly with a view to vilify and undermine the established religion, and partly to represent the Government of the country as oppressive and tyrannical, and did, with this view, oblige those who were admitted, to take, and did administer to them an oath, binding them, among other things, "*to conceal the Secrets of the Order of Knights Templars, murder and treason not excepted*," or an oath of such import and tendency; and more particularly, charges them with administering, or causing to be administered, such oath on certain occasions libelled in the year 1796.

Mr CLERK, Counsel for the panels, made no objection to the relevancy of the indictment, upon which / the Court pronounced the usual interlocutor, and the Jury were named and sworn in.

EVIDENCE FOR THE PROSECUTION.

QUINTIN MALCAM, Esq. of Waterside, said he was master of lodge of Free Masons at Maybole, of which the pannels[5] were members, but separated, themselves from it.

He was shown the following papers, one entitled – *Regulations of the Grand Assembly of Knights Templars, held at Maybole,* and a printed copy of *Paine's Age of Reason*, having the name *John Andrew* printed upon it. The above papers being libelled on, were identified by this witness.[6]

WILLIAM HAMILTON, Mason in Maybole, said he was a member of a lodge at Maybole, Royal Arch, No. 264. When he was admitted a member a pistol was fired, and some person called out, *put him in death*. He was blindfolded at first when brought into the room, and the covering being afterwards taken from his eyes, he was shewn a stone jug in the corner of the room, and a bush in the jug, and a candle burning in it. He was told by the pannel Andrew that it was the representation of God Almighty in the midst of the burning bush. Andrew was master of the lodge, and was reading the 3d chapter of Exodus. The witness was desired to *put off his shoes as it was holy ground he stood on*; the covering was put down again on the witness's face, and he was led under an arch, and after passing under the arch, he was desired to find the book of the law; it was taken up by some other person in the lodge, who was called *High Priest*, and who said he would explain it. The witness was desired to put money on the book to pay for explaining it to him; the book, he was told was the Bible, The witness put money on the book as desired, and John Andrew made observations on the chapter as he / read it, but the witness does not positively remember any of them. Recollects that part of the chapter where the children of Israel are said to be in bondage.

The passport for a Royal Arch Mason was, *I am that I am.*

After the above ceremonies, the witness being take out of the room, had his coat taken off, and tied on his shoulders in a bundle, and was then brought in; a carpet with a rent in it was called the *veil of the Temple.* He was led through it, and round the room. A sword was put into his hand, and he was ordered to use it against all who opposed him as a Knight Templar. John Andrew read the 4th chapter of Exodus; the witness was desired to throw down the sword, and was told it was become a *serpent*, after which he was desired to take it up again, and told it was again a *rod.*

Andrew poured ale and porter on the floor, and called it *blood.* He was shewn thirteen *burning candles* one in the middle he was told represented *Jesus Christ*, the others the *Twelve Apostles.* Andrew blew out one of the candles, which he called *Judas, who betrayed his Master*, one of them was dim, and was called *Peter, who denied his Master.* Something on a table under a white cloth being uncovered, was perceived to be a *human skull*, which the witness was desired to take up, and view it, and told it was a real skull of a brother called *Simon Magus.* Porter was poured into the skull, which the witness was desired to drink; he did so, and it was handed round the whole Knights, Andrew put the point of the sword into it, and then touched the witness's head with it, saying – *I dub thee in the name of the Father, Son and Holy Ghost.*

He took an oath to "*keep the secrets of the Knights*" "*Templar, murder and treason* not *excepted*;" the penalty for revealing was that *his body would be runted up like a fir deal.*

John Andrew was master at this admission, and at two others where the witness was present.

The witness's impression was, that the ceremonies used were a scoffing at religion, and, though he cannot say positively, he thought they had a tendency to overturn the Government.

The passage as to relieving the Children the Israel out of bondage was not more commented on than any other in the chapter read.

Cross Questioned. – He said he thought the design of the lodge was against the Government because of the words of the oath. Never heard politics discoursed of in the lodge. He was present at three meetings. It is two twelvemonths ago since he declared this matter.

QUINTIN STEWART, tailor in Maybole, said, he went through some parts of masonry with John Andrew, when he had no charter. He was prepared to be a Royal Arch Mason, and taken to the door, where a man in the inside called out *put him to death,* and a pistol was fired; he was blindfolded and brought into the room, and the covering removed, that he might *see the great sight, the Lord in a flame of fire in the bush, and it not consumed;* this was read by Andrew – He was commanded to *put off his shoes, as the place was holy ground.* He saw a thorn bush in a corner of the room, and a candle in the heart of it burning. Andrew said, *go and deliver the Children of Israel from their bondage and the burthen of their task masters.* He was taken round their royal encampment in the middle of the room, and was then put into what they called a *Dark Vault,* in search of the book of the law, and a book was thrown down on the floor, and afterwards put into his hand; he was asked, to explain it. The *High Priest* came and said he could do it upon being paid for it – The High Priest had a carpet round him; his name was *William Moor,* an / Irishman;[7] witness gave money, and the High Priest explained the law. Thirteen candles were burning on a table, they were called *our Saviour and his Twelve Apostles.*

Witness was taken out of the room to be prepared to be a *Knight Templar.* His coat was tied in a bundle on his back; and a staff put in his hand, to travel through the *sandy deserts*[xxv]. He passed[xxvi] through the *first and second veils of the Temple.* He was ordered to case his staff on the ground, so as it might become *a serpent,* &c. He was taken round their royal assembly two or three times; then to a table where something was lying covered; he was ordered to uncover it, and he found it to be a human skull, which he was told was the head of a brother who once tasted, heard, and smelled as we do now. Andrew poured porter into it, and gave it to the witness to drink: he drank a little of it, as did the rest. Andrew took a sword and put the point of it into the porter, and touched the witness's head with it, and said, "*I dub you, I dub you, I dub you.*"

The witness was shewn thirteen small wands, or rods, in a jug, which they called again our *Saviour* and his *Twelve Apostles.* Andrew the master of the lodge commented a little on them, and then took the witness's obligation to keep his secrecy. The words of the oath were *to keep the secrets of a Knight Templar, murder and high treason not accepted."* To the best of the witness's knowledge, these were the words. Questioned if by this oath he conceived he was bound to conceal murder and treason? Answered he thought so. He was tyler to the lodge for a short time, and left them because he thought no man who professed to be a Christian ought to be witness to their ceremonies. Saw a paper entitled *Regulations.*

Cross Questioned, – Said he left the Lodge from religious / scruples. Does not remember the words, "*murder or high treason.*" in a Master Mason's oath. Does not remember any political conversation in the Lodge, and never heard any thing in the conversation hostile either to church or state. Had the Regulations in his custody, and had no injunction to keep them secret – It was in the month of June last he gave information of the oath to the Lieutenants of the county,

The declarations of the pannels libelled on, were produced and read.

The ADVOCATE-DEPUTE concluded the proof on the part of the prosecution.

EVIDENCE IN EXCULPATION.

JOHN McCLURE, jun. in Kirkland Hill – said he was a member of the Royal Arch Lodge, Maybole ; was admitted a Knight Templar along with Quintin Stewart, and took the oath which was to *conceal the secrets of the Knights Templars, treason and murder ONLY excepted.* John Andrew administered the oath. There was no political conversation in the meetings of the Knights Templars. William Hamilton was under lodge scandal of having a child in adultery, and left the lodge after that. Gave an account of the ceremonies of admission; does not remember of a pistol being fired at his admission, or any pistol fired that night; and nothing was said about putting him to death; saw a bush and a candle burning in it; was desired to look and see the candle burning and the bush not consumed; some piece of Scripture was read, viz. the 3d chapter of Exodus; was led round the room, and after that the obligation was taken.

Question by the Court. – Was any thing done after he was led round the room? *Ans.* A human skull was discovered, and all Knights Templars were to drink out of it. He put it to his lips. He was dubbed in the name of the *Father, Son, and Holy Ghost.* /

JOHN McCLURE, Schoolmaster at Craigenoroy. Said he is a Knight Templar; was made in Maybole, along with seven more; was present at Quintin Stewart's admission. The witness took an oath; remembers little of the obligation in it, and cannot repeat it. Murder and treason were excepted in it, the same as in the Master Mason's oath, that is to conceal the Master Mason's secrets, murder and treason excepted, and that he supposed himself at liberty to reveal murder and treason. He did not think the ceremonies had a tendency to ridicule religion, as the observations were such as a good Christian might make, and he heard nothing hostile to religion or government.

Cross Questioned. – Said he was a Royal Arch *Captain* and *High Priest.*

GILBERT WILSON, Sadler, Maybole, said he was admitted a Knight Templar at Maybole, about three or four years ago. William Hamilton was also admitted, and the witness was present at his admission. The Knights are bound by an oath, but does not remember the words of it. He was bound to conceal a great many things, "*treason and murder* ONLY *excepted.*"

The same oath was given to Hamilton, and he never heard any difference in the oath. Various ceremonies were practiced, but he cannot give an account of them.

Questioned by the Court – Said he does not recollect; he was dub'd in the *name of the Father, Son, and Holy Ghost.*

Cross Questioned. – Said he was Treasurer of the Lodge.

HUGH NIVEN, Mason in Ayr, said he was made a Knight Templar. He objected his oath of secrecy, but was told he must tell the whole truth – He said / he did not recollect the terms of the oath, but that murder and treason were excepted from the obligation of secrecy. He thought the ceremonies of admission had a meaning to good, and were a cement to religion.

On being Questioned by the Court. – He answered that he was dubbed *in the name of the Trinity.* He heard no pistol fired when Stewart was admitted. – The oath of a Master Mason has nothing about murder or treason in it.

DAVID CUMMING, Mason near Bargany, was made a Knight Templar at Maybole. He took an oath to conceal the secrets, but does not properly recollect the terms of it. He was bound for nothing hurtful to the state – Nothing about murder or treason. Murder or treason were not mentioned in the oath.

ROGER McLELLAND, Weaver at Prestwick[xxvii], said, he is a mason Arch Royal Arch and Knight Templars, and there are many such in all lodges. The pannels were made in St James's Lodge, Newton-upon-Ayr, according to the established forms. He was present when Andrew acted as Master of a Lodge at Tarbolton, and admitted Knights Templars according to the established form.

Cross questioned. – Said the oath of the Knight Templar is to keep the secrets of the order, but there is no word of treason or murder in it.

JOHN CRAWFORD, Shoemaker, Maybole, said, that Andrew was his journeyman, and he has a good opinion of him.

Questioned by the Court. – He said, Andrew appeared always to be well affected to the Government, and is a volunteer.

JOHN BAIRD, Shoemaker, Maybole, gave Andrew a good character.

JAMES FULTON, Shoemaker, Maybole, said, he / has know Andrew since he was a boy, and knows nothing that could give him a bad opinion of his character either moral or religious; and has heard him speak in favour of Government, and of Mr Pitt's abilities.

WALTER WILSON, Merchant in Maybole, said, he was acquainted with Ramsey, and he always behaved well so far as he knows.

CHARLES DONALD, Merchant in Maybole, said, as to the character of Ramsay, he thinks, as far as he knows, that he is honest, religious, and well affected to Government.

JAMES BARTRAM, Writer, Edinburgh, Clerk of the Grand Lodge of Scotland, authenticated certain papers shown him by the pannel's Counsel, relative to proceedings before the Grand Lodge concerning the pannels.

Mr OSWALD, Counsel for the prosecution said these papers cannot at all influence this cause, however respectable the Grand Lodge is.

LORD JUSTICE CLERK would not allow any of them to be read.

Here the whole evidence finished.

Mr OSWALD rose, and addressed the Jury on the part of the prosecution; after making some judicious remarks on the nature of sedition, he next adverted to the proceedings and ceremonies which had taken place, as proved by the evidence which had been adduced; these he considered had a tendency to ridicule religion: and as the Jury heard the facts before them, they could therefore well form their conclusions on their import; and as religion is protected by the law, and is a part of the common law, therefore the ridiculing of it is an offence, for which a verdict, must be returned against the pannels, if the Jury are satisfied that they have been guilty of it. The imposing of the oath libelled on is subversive of the administration of / justice, because it tends to prevent the giving of evidence. The oath is dangerous, even taken in the terms sworn to by the exculpatory evidence, and the appearance of some of those witnesses strongly demonstrated the baneful effects of the proceedings of the pannels. These, and many other observations, Mr Oswald stated with great force of reasoning.

Mr CLERK, Counsel for the pannels, rose in reply. He said, he considered this case as a very extraordinary one, as near five years had elapsed since the facts charged were said to be carried on, and the prosecution had originated in a dispute which took place between two Mason Lodges in Maybole. He observed, that an act of Parliament was passed in 1796 against administering unlawful oaths, but no notice was taken of that act in this indictment, because it could not be so. The pannels in their transactions had followed a common error, in which they suspected no harm, as they considered them harmless, and in the common course of masonry. The facts charged are not in the nature of *mulum in re.*[8]

The bulk of the evidence related to neither of the heads of the charge, but to an undefined one, viz. that of using impious ceremonies. It is not a crime at common law to administer an unlawful oath; for the Legislature made the special law which he had just mentioned, enacting penalties against it, which shews their sense that it was not punishable before that period. As to religious allusions, it is well known that they abound in masonic ceremonies, and also occur on other occasions, without being construed as intended to throw any ridicule upon that divine institution, and he could not see that the pannels had any such intention in what they did.

LORD JUSTICE CLERK summed up the whole evidence with great perspicuity and candour. His Lordship / observed, that he could have wished that this prosecution had been brought sooner, but this could not be imputed to the Prosecutor, for it did not appear that he had delayed bringing his action after he got the information. Though this species of crime may not have occurred in our law before, still the law may be applied to remedy it when it does occur. The special law enacted in regard to it does not infringe on the law as it stood before. The oath is not innocent, even as limited by the witnesses for the pannels, and though there is no proof that the pannels had entered into a design of leading the persons they admitted into their society to seditious practices, yet the oath may be employed for that purpose. His Lordship said, he could not believe that any such ceremonies were employed in other Mason Lodges because they are so abominable and impious; it rather appeared that this was a new oath introduced by the pannels, and not in use before in admitting Masons.

VERDICT OF THE JURY.

All in one voice find the facts libelled *not proven*[9]
The pannels were therefore assoilzied[10] and dismissed from the bar.

J. MORREN, Printer.

FINIS.

[ANON.], *PETITION AND COMPLAINT AT BROTHER GIBSON'S INSTANCE AGAINST BROTHER MITCHELL, AND HIS ANSWERS THERETO; WITH THE PROCEDURE OF THE GRAND LODGE THEREON AND PROOF ADDUCED* (1808)

[Anon.], *Petition and Complaint at Brother Gibson's Instance Against Brother Mitchell, and His Answers Thereto; With the Procedure of the Grand Lodge Thereon and Proof Adduced* (Edinburgh: A. Lawrie & Co., 1800).[1]

The Whig presence within the Grand Lodge had forced through the union with Kilwinning[2] and had effectively guaranteed that any Tory candidate nominated for the office of Grand Master would be defeated. Leaving aside the problem of a disgruntled Mary's Chapel, the Grand Lodge of Scotland alone controlled the right to grant charters. Victory, however, was short-lived. During the negotiations, 'a fresh trouble was developing' which became 'commingled with the issues of the Kilwinning business'.[3] As Lindsay argues, the key to this 'fresh trouble is to be found in the particular manner in which politics entered into the daily life of the time.'[4]

The Whig Grand Lodge of Scotland was supported by William Inglis of Middleton, Substitute Grand Master from 1805 to 1828. According to Lindsay, Inglis was a staunch Whig who attended the Bastille Dinner in 1789 and was 'one of the most widely known Scottish Masons of all time ... who weathered one of the worst storms' in the history of Scottish Freemasonry.[5] The Whig faction led by Inglis was 'suddenly confronted by unexpected opposition from the Crown in a matter touching its politics, and the train was laid in Grand Lodge that required some exulting Tory to touch it off'.[6] On 4 May 1807, Dr John Mitchell, Master of the Caledonian Lodge in Edinburgh and a Tory, proposed that a letter of thanks be submitted to the king.

Although a misrepresentation to describe masonic political allegiances at this time as hostile to loyalism, it is likely that some masons – especially within the Grand Lodge – retained a suspicion of the uncritical, slavish adherence to every aspect of the constitution that marked the more purblind Tories. Mitchell's proposed address does not necessarily suggest a Tory conspiracy to undermine Whig sentiments. Masonic addresses to the king were not uncommon and often sent to congratulate the ruling monarch on a variety of issues. However, as Lindsay argues, 'it was a very different matter for a Tory to repeat such a performance, as Dr. Mitchell did, in a Grand Lodge of Scotland under Whig control'.[7]

Mitchell's address also signalled the first rumblings of discontent among the Tories. If the Whigs were to maintain control of the Grand Lodge, any challenges which threatened the balance of power had to be quickly suppressed. Given that the initial proposal was defeated by only one vote, a revote was demanded. Despite strong objections from Inglis, the Grand Lodge approved Mitchell's request for a revote. Led by James Gibson, one of the most 'vehement of Scottish Whigs',[8] the motion to address the king was soundly defeated by a margin of 95–47.[9] Under a strong showing of solidarity, it was quite obvious that the Whigs were well organized and arrayed to suppress perceived threats to their influence and apparent supremacy within the Grand Lodge.

Clearly, political manoeuvring and manipulation had prevented the approval of Mitchell's address to the king. The Grand Lodge must have been aware of a minority Tory presence, but it chose to ignore it. As Wartski says, the

> tendency of governments in power for very long periods is to become arrogant, and to disregard the opposition, which on the other hand veers towards resentment and desperation, so the schism between the parties [becomes] marked by tremendous bitterness and ill-feeling'.[10]

Indeed, the masonic divide between Whig and Tory would increase during the ensuing political feud, ultimately culminating with a much-publicized court trial and accusations of a Tory conspiracy to destroy the Grand Lodge and defame Scottish Freemasonry.[11]

The *Petition and Complaint* is noteworthy as it brings to the surface the smouldering political differences and lodge disagreements over the extent of the Grand Lodge's power. Indeed, it might be argued with much certitude that personal differences and dormant disputes, coupled with an egotism born of stubbornness facilitated the Secession as much as the issue of politics. Significantly, the prominent Whig members of both St Luke's and the Grand Lodge of Scotland did little to positively influence the outcome of the trial. Party politics wavered, and the initial solidarity and strength of the Whig party disintegrated. Although historians have questioned whether or not the Grand Lodge 'hoped to bulldoze its way through in the hope of frightening the Seceders into submission',[12] it is clear that such aggressive tactics and the use of the Secret Societies Act both failed. Inevitably, political ambition conflicted with the age-old pragmatism of James Anderson's *Constitutions* and, not surprisingly, the Secession resulted in the public humiliation of Scottish Freemasons and an embarrassing defeat for the Grand Lodge of Scotland.

The pamphlet was printed and sold in Edinburgh by Alexander Lawrie and Company in Edinburgh, bookseller and deputy Gazette writer. Lawrie became a member of the Edinburgh Bookseller's Society on 19 August 1790, and served as Secretary to the Grand Lodge of Scotland in 1816. Lawrie is not to be confused with Alexander Laurie, printer for the Edinburgh *Gazette*; however, from 1825 to 1826 both Alexander Laurie and Company and Alexander Lawrie appeared to share the same address of 4 North Bank Street.[13] Copies of the text exist in the Grand Lodge of Scotland Library in Edinburgh, although this text was keyed based upon copies in the British Library and the National Library of Scotland.

Notes

1. This headnote was written by Mark Wallace.
2. R. S. Lindsay, *A History of the Mason Lodge of Holyrood House (St Luke's No. 44)* (Edinburgh: T. and A. Constable, Ltd, 1935), p. 299.
3. Lindsay, *A History of the Mason Lodge of Holyrood House*, p. 298.
4. Lindsay, *A History of the Mason Lodge of Holyrood House*, p. 298.
5. Lindsay, *A History of the Mason Lodge of Holyrood House*, pp. 269–70.
6. Lindsay, *A History of the Mason Lodge of Holyrood House*, p. 299.
7. Lindsay, *A History of the Mason Lodge of Holyrood House*, p. 300.
8. Lindsay, *A History of the Mason Lodge of Holyrood House*, p. 253.
9. H. Cockburn, *Memorials of his Time* (Edinburgh: Mercat Press, 1971), p. 84.
10. L. D. Wartski, *Freemasonry and the Early Secret Societies Act*, monograph compiled and presented by the author for private circulation by the District Grand Lodge of Natal of Antient Free and Accepted Masons of Scotland, p. 45.
11. GL of S, 25 May 1808.
12. Wartski, *Freemasonry and the Early Secret Societies Act*, p. 61.
13. Information taken from the Scottish Book Trade Index (SBTI).

[Anon.], *Petition and Complaint at Brother Gibson's Instance Against Brother Mitchell, and His Answers Thereto; With the Procedure of the Grand Lodge Thereon and Proof Adduced* (1808)

PETITION AND COMPLAINT
AT
BROTHER GIBSON'S INSTANCE
AGAINST
BROTHER MITCHELL,
AND
HIS ANSWERS THERETO;
WITH
THE PROCEDURE OF THE GRAND LODGE THEREON,
AND
PROOF ADDUCED.

EDINBURGH:
PRINTED BY ALEX LAWRIE & CO.
1808. / /
January 1, 1808.
UNTO THE MOST WORSHIPFUL
The GRAND MASTER and Other OFFICERS and MEMBERS of the
GRAND LODGE of SCOTLAND,

THE
PETITION AND COMPLAINT
OF

JAMES GIBSON, Proxy-Master of the Lodge of St. Andrew's of Aberdeen, and a Member of the Lodge of St. David's, Edinburgh.

Humbly sheweth,

THAT the petitioner finds himself under the necessity of complaining to the Grand Lodge, of the conduct of John Mitchell, master of the Caledonian Lodge of Edinburgh.

The members of the Grand Lodge will recollect, that for some time past, Brother Mitchell has done every thing in his power to disturb the peace of the Grand Lodge, and of the craft, by printing a libelous pamphlet,[1] and by most disrespectful and improper conduct to the Grand Lodge, insomuch, that at the meeting of the quarterly communication of the Grand Lodge, held in the month of November last, a motion was made and seconded, and generally approved of, to expel him from the Grand Lodge; and his conduct at that meeting was altogether so extraordinary, that the substitute grand master, with the approbation of the members present, was under the necessity of ordering the grand wardens to turn him out of the lodge;[2] but the petitioner, unwilling to carry matters to extremities, prevailed upon the Grand Lodge to allow the motion of expulsion to be withdrawn, and the order for turning him out of the lodge not to be insisted in; trusting that Brother Mitchell would see the impropriety of his conduct, and would not again give occasion to proceedings of so very disagreeable a nature.

The petitioner has reason to regret this interference, as, since that time, Brother Mitchell has conducted himself in a manner totally subversive of the authority of the Grand Lodge of Scotland, and of the principles of the craft, and has shown a determined purpose, as far as in him lay, to break through all those rules which ought to govern the conduct of every brother, particularly of every brother who is appointed to preside over any lodge holding of the Grand Lodge of Scotland.

The petitioner need hardly notice, that every brother, and particularly every master of a lodge holding of the Grand Lodge of Scotland, is bound to show every respect to the grand master, and to the other officers of the Grand Lodge of Scotland, and to give respectful obedience to every order issued by the Grand Lodge.[3] As to the master of a lodge endeavouring so far to mislead the brethren under his charge, as to attempt to induce them to disobey and act in direct contradiction to the orders of the Grand Lodge, to separate themselves from, and to hold meetings independent of, the Grand Lodge, it has been reserved for Brother Mitchell to attempt so extraordinary proceedings.

The petitioner complains to the Grand Lodge, *first*, That a dispute having arisen between the Roman Eagle Lodge of Edinburgh and the Caledonian Lodge, with regard to the latter lodge meeting upon the night in which the Roman Eagle Lodge had formerly been in use to meet, the business came before the Grand Lodge; and the quarterly communications which met in November, found that the Caledonian Lodge had acted improperly, in meeting upon the night on which the Roman Eagle had been in the practice of meeting, and prohibited the Caledonian Lodge from doing so in future.[4]

But, notwithstanding, Brother Mitchell endeavoured to prevail upon the Caledonian Lodge to disregard the order of the Grand Lodge, by continuing their meetings on the day upon which the Grand Lodge had prohibited them to meet.

The petitioner complains, in the *second* place, That Brother Mitchell did, at one or other of the meetings of the Caledonian Lodge, propose that the lodge should make a secession from the Grand Lodge, and hold meetings altogether independent of the Grand Lodge.[5]

The petitioner complains, in the *third* place, That on the last anniversary of St. Andrew's, Brother Mitchell prevailed on the Caledonian lodge not to attend divine service along with the Grand Lodge, master, and all the other brethren who joined in the procession of that evening, but, after walking to the Tron Church[6] with the other brethren, to leave the procession without going to church, and to make a separate procession to Oman's tavern; thereby shewing his disrespect to the grand master elect, his disregard to the orders of the Grand Lodge, and his contempt of the religious services in which the brethren were to be engaged, besides holding out to the world that there was a schism in the craft.

And further, although it had been intimated to him, and to the other masters of lodges, that the grand master elect expected to see deputations of the lodges in the course of that evening, he neither / attended the grand master, nor made any apology for not doing so.

These complaints the petitioner, as a member of the Grand Lodge, now prefers against Brother Mitchell; and as a member of the Grand Lodge, and as a member of the lodge of St. David[xxviii] Edinburgh, he complains,

That although it has always been customary for lodges to receive visits on the festival of St. John the Evangelist,[7] from all the lodges by which deputations may be sent, and to send deputations in return, the said Brother John Mitchell did, on the celebration of the festival of St. John the Evangelist, on the 28th day of December last, in a manner contrary to the invariable custom, and unworthy of the character of a mason, insult the lodge of Edinburgh St. David, and other lodges, by refusing to receive into the Caledonian Lodge deputations sent by them.

The petitioner offers proof of the various articles of complaint charged by him against Brother Mitchell, if he shall be hardy enough to deny them; and he submits, that they are of so very serious a nature, that, if proved, they will shew a spirit so inconsistent with every duty which Brother Mitchell owes to the craft, with that respect and allegiance which he owes to the Grand Lodge, and to the grand master elect, and with that brotherly love which every lodge and every brother is entitled to expect from him as a brother, and particularly as master of a lodge, that the Grand Lodge cannot fail to inflict upon him some very severe punishment, to prevent a repetition by him, or by any other evil disposed person, if such can exist in the craft, of acts so highly improper, and so subversive of the constitution and principles of masonry.

May it therefore please the Grand Lodge to order this petition and complaint to
be served upon Brother Mitchell, and to ordain him to give in answers thereto
within a certain short time; and thereafter, upon considering this petition, with
or without answers, to inflict such punishment upon Brother Mitchell, as, in the
circumstances of the case, may appear to be proper.

     · According to justice, &c.

                                     JAs. GIBSON.

At an EXTRAORDINARY MEETING *of the* GRAND LODGE, *held in the New*
Church-Aisle, January 5, 1808.

The roll being called, and the names taken down, the Substitute Grand Master stated, that he had called this extraordinary / meeting, in consequence of a petition and complaint being lodged with the Grand Clerk, at the instance of Brother James Gibson, proxy-master for the Lodge of St. Andrew's, Aberdeen, and member of St. David's Lodge, Edinburgh, against Right Worshipful Brother John Mitchell, master of the Caledonian Lodge, Edinburgh: that, as the petition itself would best explain the nature of the charges, the Substitute Grand Master proposed that the same be read; which, after a few observations from Brother Osborne Brown, was agreed to, and read accordingly.

The petition having been read and considered, the Substitute Grand Master proposed the following deliverance, which was unanimously agreed to. –

SEE EXCERPT
FROM MINUTE-
BOOK OF
ST. DAVID'S
LODGE, DEC.
28, 1807. No. I,
APPENDIX.

'The Grand Lodge, having taken into consideration the foregoing petition and complaint, appoint it to be immediately served upon the Right Worshipful Brother Mitchell, master of the Caledonian Lodge, by the Grand Clerk's[8] furnishing him with a copy thereof; and ordain the said Brother Mitchell to give in answers in writing thereto, on or before Monday the 18th instant, at 12 o'clock noon; ordain the complainer, Brother James Gibson, to condescend upon the names of the witnesses whom he means to adduce, in support of his complaint, on or before Wednesday the 20th instant, at 12 o'clock noon; and also ordain the respondent, Brother Mitchell, to condescend upon the names of the witnesses whom he means to adduce on his part, on or before the same day and hour; and authorize the Grand Clerk to summon all the said witnesses in the usual Masonic form, requiring them to attend the Grand Lodge, on Thursday the 21st instant, at 7 o'clock in the evening, for examination; to which day and hour the Grand Lodge do hereby adjourn this meeting; and, at which adjourned meeting, the Grand Lodge will proceed, with or without answers, to decide upon the subject matter of the said petition; and appoint the Grand Clerk to furnish each of the said parties with a copy of this deliverance: and further, ordain the master of the St. David's Lodge, to lodge with the Grand Clerk, on or before Monday the 18th instant, the minute-book of that Lodge, in which is contained their resolutions upon the Festival of St. John the Evangelist, relative to the refusal of the deputation on that day by the Caledonian Lodge, and the remit to the Grand Lodge, by the Lodge of St. David, on that subject.

(Signed) 'WILLIAM INGLIS, [9] S.G. M.'

January

ANSWERS

FOR

JOHN MITCHELL, Right Worshipful Master of the Edinburgh Caledonian Lodge;

TO THE

PETITION and COMPLAINT of JAMES GIBSON, Proxy-Master of the Lodge of St. Andrew's of Aberdeen, and a Member of the Lodge of St. David, Edinburgh.

THE respondent, Brother Mitchell, has the misfortune to be accused by Brother Gibson, proxy-master of the lodge of St. Andrew's of Aberdeen, and member of the lodge of St. David's, Edinburgh, of various offences which are specified in the petition. Nothing can be more unpleasant to the respondent's feelings than to be accused by any brother, and brought before the Grand Lodge, as guilty of offences which he would be the first to disapprove, and, he trusts, will be one of the last of the brethren to commit. Conscious of his own innocence, and appealing to the candour and impartiality of his upright brethren, he trusts he will be acquitted from them. But whatever consolation he may derive from that reflection, and however fully convinced he is of the indulgence and forbearance of those to whom he states his defence, he must confess, that this charge has given him most serious concern. So far as he is individually concerned, it must be a matter of very secondary consideration; and whatever hardship, or even injustice, he might be subjected to, he trusts, that if it was likely to promote the welfare, the good order, and prosperity of the brethren, he would bear his own sufferings, whatever they might be, with composure, perhaps without complaint. / Upon the present occasion, however, he feels himself called upon to object most solemnly to the nature of this accusation, and the principles which it would sanction, as altogether destructive of the good temper, the good fellowship, and the harmony which have hitherto subsisted in the lodges of this country. If it is in the power of Brother Gibson, proxy-master of the lodge of St. Andrew's of Aberdeen, and member of the lodge of St. David's, Edinburgh, to make such charges, it must equally be in the power of the member of any other lodge, to bring charges against any other individual. Where a brother receives a personal injury from another, he may be peculiarly entitled to claim redress. But where the offences charged are altogether of a general or a public nature, what right has any individual to constitute himself a public prosecutor, and arraign the conduct of a member of another lodge, to which he does not belong? The cases in which an individual may fancy that another has not conducted himself with perfect regularity, or with perfect propriety, nay, has even been guilty of some offence, must be innumerable. Where the offences alleged have been committed in another lodge, at which the accuser was not present, the false and imperfect account which he may receive of what has been said or done, may make him fancy an offence where none was committed.

The first thing, therefore, to be considered is, Whether Brother Gibson has a right to place himself in the situation of accuser-general, or, if the title will sound better, grand accuser to the Grand Lodge. In this case, he complains of no injury as offered to himself individually. If it had been a personal injury, whether real or fancied, it might have been removed by explanation; and the mildness and forbearance, temper and moderation, which Brother Gibson is known to possess, would doubtless have disposed him to forgive and forget, even if he had been injured. For it surely is an article of Brother Gibson's creed, that though his brother should sin against him, he will not only forgive him 'until seven times, but 'until seventy times seven.'[10] But while the respondent with pleasure pays this small tribute to the mildness, good temper, and other virtues of Brother Gibson, as an individual, he must regret, that either from a desire of distinction, or from a mistaken notion of having offences punished which were never committed, and of promoting the peace and tranquillity of the Grand Lodge, by consuming their time with debates about them, or from some other motive, be it good, bad, or indifferent, he has assumed a station, and arrogated powers, to which he has no right. If / Brother Gibson was at once to be made lord-advocate to the Grand Lodge, or attorney-general for all the lodges in Scotland, he might have such a right. Perhaps, being a man of the law, and very skilful in all the intricacies of that profession, he may, with great propriety, conceive himself well qualified for that situation. Yet, as the respondent knows nothing of law, he has fearful odds to contend with, when he is opposed to him. The fact, however, is certain, that no such appointment has hitherto been made, and it is not likely to be made, without due and mature deliberation. What is now attempted, is, however, far more objectionable; for if Brother Gibson accuses Brother Mitchell to-day, Brother Smith may accuse Brother Thomson to-morrow, and the time of the lodge will be entirely consumed in hearing the charges which the members of one lodge may bring, not against the members of the same lodge, but of some other lodge, against whom they may have some real, or supposed ground of offence.

Although the respondent will not allow himself to suppose it possible, that this accusation from Brother Gibson can proceed from private dislike, individual resentment, or political hatred, yet it must be obvious to the members of the Grand Lodge, that there are many persons, who, not possessing so much of the 'milk of human kindness'[11] as Brother Gibson, may bring forward accusations founded entirely on these motives; and while they pretend to have no other motive, but to promote the good order of the lodge, will search for every sort of accusation with which their own malice, or that of other persons, can supply them, and bring them forward at the most favourable opportunity, with the view of harassing and distressing the accused, and disturbing the harmony and tranquillity of the lodges before whom these accusations are brought. What can be more unwise, than to open a door to such proceedings, and to give any individual an opportunity of indulging his malice, and of disturbing the peace of a brother, and the tranquillity of masonic societies, without even the pretence of a personal injury? There may be persons who will conceal their resentments, and nourish them till they have an opportunity of gratifying them. '*Odia in longum jaciens, guæ recondereret auctaque promeret,*'[12] was a character known in antiquity, which may occur in the present times. If such a person should happen to be a man of the law, who is accustomed to draw up accusations, and to magnify small offences into great ones, he would have an opportunity of venting his malice against his most harmless and innocent brethren, who might have accidentally offended them. Yet no encouragement / can be given to this prosecution, without sanctioning such proceedings; and if you shall sanction this accusation, brought by our worthy Brother Gibson, it is impossible to say, what means can be adopted to stop accusations brought by other brethren, who may happen to be less worthy than himself. Surely, then, the brethren whom the respondent now addresses, however much they may be attached to Brother Gibson, and however convinced of the purity of his motives, will not hesitate to put a stop to proceedings, which are likely to be attended with the very worst consequences, and which tend to destroy the good fellowship and good temper, which has hitherto subsisted among the different members of the masonic order in this country. That spirit, together with the sentiments of charity and moderation, gentleness and brotherly love, it is the great object of the order to promote.

The consequences of such a proceeding do not stop here; all the brethren are anxious that the peace and harmony of their meetings should be uninterrupted, but they must also feel zealous for the honour, character, and reputation of the lodges of their country.

The proceedings of the lodges in Scotland, no doubt excite the attention of members of the order in every part of the world. Scotland has hitherto been considered as the country in which masonry has been carried to the highest perfection, and professed upon the purest principles. But what will lodges at a distance think if they shall hear that one individual, not pretending to be injured, not belonging to the same lodge, was allowed to bring an accusation against a member of another lodge, for offences, by which he does not pretend he was injured? In England, there unfortunately prevails an idea, perhaps a mistaken one, that most things in this country are made a sort of job, and carried on by political intrigue and party violence. That this does not merely prevail in what are usually considered matters of political contention, but that the understrappers of the different parties, more zealous, more violent, and more unprincipled than those who are engaged in the higher departments of politics, carry them into the common affairs of life, and disturb the peace of society with their paltry intrigues. At that distance, the character and virtues of Brother Gibson, proxy-master of the lodge of St. Andrew's of Aberdeen, and a member of the lodge of St. David's, Edinburgh, can only be known to a few; and persons ignorant of them, who know nothing more of Brother Gibson and Brother Mitchell, than the situation in which they each hold in the order; that Brother Gibson is a member of one lodge, and Brother Mitchell a member / of another; that Brother Gibson is a man of the law, and Brother Mitchell altogether unacquainted with it; that Brother Gibson accuses Brother Mitchell of offences from which he does not pretend he suffered any individual injury, and which, if they had been committed, ought to have been complained of by other persons who have not complained at all; – such persons may surmise that there is something more at the bottom of the business. There is no saying what mistakes and misconceptions they may be led to form. They may suppose that Brother Gibson, instead of being that pure and upright character which he is known to be, is a tool of some party in the town of Edinburgh. That he is some unprincipled attorney, who is anxious to cultivate the good graces of his superiors, by shewing his disposition for violence and his aptitude for intrigue. They may suppose, that not having an opportunity of indulging it in any other sphere, or being turned out of some situation in which he might exercise his genius for oppression on a higher scale, he is afraid lest he should get out of practice, and coin these accusations against innocent persons, in order to keep his hand in use. Pardon these suppositions, worshipful brethren. You know the character, and respect the virtues, of Brother Gibson; and where they are known, such suppositions are not likely to be made; but at a distance the most mistaken notions may prevail, and the respondent cannot have it in his power to remove them.

The respondent will now proceed to answer the different charges in the petition. He enters upon them with the confidence that he will be able to give a most satisfactory answer to all of them; such as, without presuming too far on the indulgence of his brethren, will entitle him to be acquitted from them. But he must solemnly beseech his brethren, without considering his case in particular, but the interests of the order itself, to pause before they sanction a proceeding so dangerous to the peace and harmony of the masonic order. If the tranquillity of any lodge is disturbed, any attempt of that nature may be repressed at the time.

If one lodge offends against another, the injured lodge may complain by its proper officers; but if one brother shall be allowed to take up the cudgels for all the other lodges in Scotland, and where a lodge is said to have offended, to single out any individual as the person upon whom he is to heap his vengeance, there will be an end to all peace, good order, fellowship, and brotherly society.

The petition sets out with stating circumstances which seem meant / to aggravate all the other charges, although they are not made a separate ground of charge, and have no connection with the other points of dittay.[13] It is stated, that Brother Mitchell has done every thing in his power to disturb the peace of the Grand Lodge, by printing a libellous pamphlet; and 'that at the meeting of the quarterly communication of the Grand Lodge held in November last, a motion was made and seconded, and generally approved of, to expel him from the Grand Lodge; and his conduct at that meeting was altogether so extraordinary, that the Substitute Grand Master, with the approbation of the members present, was under the necessity of ordering the Grand Wardens[14] to turn him out of the lodge; but the petitioner, unwilling to carry matters to extremities, prevailed upon the Grand Lodge to allow the motion of expulsion to be withdrawn, and the order of turning him out of the lodge not to be insisted in.' Supposing all this to be true, what has it to do with the present question? If Brother Mitchell committed these offences, and they were past over, which seems to be the statement of the petition, why should they be again revived? Brother Gibson is a man of the law, and probably knows it well. Now, the respondent has been told, that even if an insult was committed in a court of justice against judges sitting on the bench, and was passed over by them at the time, it could not afterwards be revived by them, and made a subject of accusation. The respondent has been told that instances have occurred of this: but be that as it may, surely it is contrary to every principle of common sense to revive an incident which happened some time ago, and which was passed over at the time. This consideration would surely guide the proceedings of the brethren, although the statement in the petition were true. But the statement is not true. At that quarterly meeting, Brother Gibson, notwithstanding the general mildness and courteous affability of his demeanour, thought proper to pronounce a violent philippic[15] against the respondent, in which he was pleased to apply to him some epithets by no means flattering, and some similies less agreeable than might have been expected on that occasion. A motion was made for expelling the respondent; and whatever obligation the respondent may be under to Brother Gibson, he certainly did not consider that he was indebted to his friendly and benevolent interposition for the failure of that motion. It was received at the time with the most marked disapprobation, expressed in what may seem a somewhat coarse, but certainly a very unequivocal manner, by a general hissing.[16] It was in consequence of that circumstance / that those who had proposed that motion seemed to think it prudent to abandon it; yet the respondent did not conceive that Brother Gibson joined in that disapprobation of the motion, although, if he had been so inclined, no brother is better qualified.

As the respondent has borne ample testimony to the virtues of Brother Gibson in the course of this paper, he trusts he will be pardoned for differing from him as to this particular instance, which he has chosen of his own tenderness and forbearance towards Brother Mitchell. With regard to the libellous pamphlet, the respondent begs leave to assure the brethren, that he never wrote, printed, or issued any libellous pamphlet, and that he is as innocent of writing or publishing libels, either against individuals or government, as Brother Gibson can possibly be. The circumstance to which he presumes Brother Gibson alludes, is a short statement which the respondent wrote of what had passed at a quarterly communication of the Grand Lodge, held in May 1807, with regard to a motion for an address to his Majesty.[17] On that occasion, the respondent, and many other brethren, conceived that the vote had not been accurately taken down by the clerk, as other brethren, who were present at the same time, formed a very material difference between their reckoning and his. The respondent was therefore anxious that a scrutiny should take place,[18] and with that view he wrote a letter, which seems to be the production alluded to, under the terms of a libellous pamphlet. With the exception of one imperfect proof copy of this circular letter, no other copy was in print or circulation. The scrutiny was refused, and the respondent afterwards considered the letter as altogether suppressed, and at rest; so much so, that he was somewhat surprised on the printer afterwards asking him whether the types should be broke up. He was, at this time, informed by the printer, that a worthy brother and member of the Grand Lodge, had been art and part in pilfering and abstracting copies of that letter from the printing-house. This must surely have proceeded from some mistake on the part of the printer; for the respondent cannot believe that any brother would be guilty of so mean an act, as to pry into printing-offices, and bribe apprentices and journeymen to commit a breach of trust; yet the same charity which induces the respondent to misbelieve what is corroborated by very strong facts, will, he trusts, be extended towards him, and Brother Gibson will learn to be cautious in giving his ear to accusations, or in putting harsh constructions on the conduct of one of his brethren.

The respondent will now proceed to the *first* charge, which is, – First Charge. / 'That a dispute having arisen between the Roman Eagle Lodge of Edinburgh and the Caledonian Lodge, with regard to the latter lodge meeting upon the night on which the Roman Eagle Lodge had formerly been in use to meet, the business came before the Grand Lodge; and the quarterly communication which met in November, found that the Caledonian Lodge had acted improperly in meeting upon the night on which the Roman Eagle had been in the practice of meeting, and prohibited the Caledonian Lodge from doing so in future.'

'But that notwithstanding, Brother Mitchell endeavoured to prevail upon the Caledonian Lodge to disregard the order of the Grand Lodge, by continuing their meetings on the day upon which the Grand Lodge had prohibited them to meet.'

To this the respondent begs leave to answer, 1*st*, that the charge is not true; 2*dly*, that Brother Gibson has no right to complain of it, although it were true.

With regard to the original offence, said to have been committed by the lodge, the respondent must state, for the information of the brethren, that it was found, in consequence of the brethren belonging to the theatre, who contribute much to the conviviality of the meetings of the Caledonian Lodge, being unable to attend on the Wednesdays, that it would be more convenient to appoint some other day. A committee was appointed to consider this subject; and the nature of their deliberations appears from the following minute of their proceedings, of date 26th September 1806.

'The committee next had, for their subject of consideration, a proposal to change the day on which the monthly meetings of the lodge were held. As the meetings were at present held on a Wednesday evening, the lodge was deprived of the company of the brethren of the theatre, who contributed much to the harmony of the evening. This, therefore, with other reasons, made Wednesday rather an improper day. As the theatre was shut on the Tuesdays and Fridays, one of these days should be chosen. Friday, on various accounts, was preferred, and none of the sister lodges meeting on the fourth Friday of the month, the committee therefore appointed it for the day on which their monthly meetings should in future be held, and directed that notice should be immediately given of this in all the public papers.'

It is evident, from this minute, that the committee of the Caledonian Lodge had no conception that the Roman Eagle Lodge met upon that night, viz. the fourth Friday of the month. A new card of intimation / was engraved, and advertisements were made in the newspapers, at considerable expence, in order to notify this change; and it was not until some time afterwards that the right worshipful master of the Roman Eagle Lodge informed the Caledonian Lodge that they had taken his day. On inquiry, it was found that it was not the day on which the Roman Eagle Lodge was accustomed to meet; and the almanacks,[19] if they shall be inspected, will bear evidence that the Roman Eagle Lodge was mentioned as meeting on the first Tuesday of the month. Had the Roman Eagle Lodge been mentioned as meeting on the fourth Friday, they, the Caledonian Lodge, would with pleasure have taken the first Tuesday, viz. the day upon which the Roman Eagle Lodge formerly met. But having no information of this circumstance, the Caledonian Lodge was deprived of the first Tuesday, for this was the day on which the Canongate and Leith began again to hold their meetings. It further appears, from the almanack, that several lodges in town have been in the practice of meeting on the same day. The Caledonian Lodge did not therefore conceive that they were guilty of any great offence in fixing a night which they had no knowledge was occupied by any other lodge, and in continuing to meet after they had intimated their meetings, and fixed them at considerable expence. It was not considered very usual for the Grand Lodge to interfere on such occasions; but, after receiving the communication of the Grand Lodge, a committee of the Caledonian Lodge was appointed to consider the subject, of which the respondent was preses. The following report of the sub-committee, in which the respondent concurred, and of which he was also preses, must afford the most complete answer to the charges which are brought against him.

'Your committee, after due deliberation, and communing together, on the subject of the remit to them, and considering the matter with that attention due to the importance of the subject to the Caledonian Lodge, where the honour of that national lodge is involved, humbly are of opinion, and beg to report, that as it becomes the dignity of a lodge so respected in masonry, both for her liberal actions and members, to do every thing in their power that would promote the prosperity of a sister lodge; and that as the complaint given in to the Grand Lodge, in name of the Roman Eagle Lodge, proceeded upon the narrative that it was detrimental to the interest of that lodge that the Caledonian Lodge should meet on the same evening; and as that lodge is senior to the Caledonian Lodge, it would be proper for the Caledonian Lodge, and becoming that spirit of / true masonry which has always been characteristic to her, and practised within her walls, to choose another night for their monthly meetings, not injuring the welfare of a sister lodge. Your committee would propose of the month for their meetings in future, which would not interfere with their meetings. Your committee, in the hopes that the Caledonian Lodge will approve of the above amicable arrangement, and not being inclined to involve the interest of the lodge with making any report with regard to the powers of the Grand Lodge, as authorizing them to interfere in the manner lately done by them, by interdicting[20] the Caledonian Lodge from meeting on the fourth Friday of the month. Your committee, however, would humbly suggest, that the office-bearers be requested to give in a representation, or remonstrance, against that proceeding in the Grand Lodge, to have the same recalled, as a matter that may, some time hereafter, be detrimental to the interests of the lodge. They humbly think this remonstrance should be accompanied with the solemn assurance of the Caledonian Lodge and its office-bearers, that it never was the intention of the Caledonian Lodge to interfere with the interest of any sister lodge or their night of meeting, but which merely proceeded from a mistake which they were led into from the public almanack; but merely wishing to have such an order cancelled or recalled, as quite unnecessary, and a proceeding unprecedented in the annals of masonry, and improper in itself, to remain in the records of the Grand Lodge. Your committee humbly beg to submit the above as their report, on the remit to them, in the anxious expectation of a confirmation and approval of their proceedings, as the most honourable and brotherly manner of setting aside such a frivolous misunderstanding.'

In answer to the charge, therefore, that the respondent endeavoured to prevail upon the Caledonian Lodge to disregard the order of the Grand Lodge, the respondent must say, that it is altogether false. The respondent must, however, observe, that the charge is of a most vague and extraordinary nature, and if such charges are permitted, no person can be secure for a moment. The respondent is not accused of doing any thing, or proposing any thing, but for *endeavouring* to *prevail* on the lodge to disregard the order of the Grand Lodge. In the course of a free debate, and a general discussion, views may be stated which it may be very easy to give a colouring to, and which might only be suggested, and which a brother might have no serious intention of persisting in; nay, which he may merely state for the sake of illustration, or for / the amusement of the meeting. If there is any impropriety in them, that may be taken notice of and repressed at the time. If no notice is taken of them, and the lodge dissolves in peace and harmony, they cannot afterwards be raked up and made the ground of accusations in another place, before persons who did not hear them, and who cannot judge of their meaning and import, and the relation which they had to the discussion at the time. Surely an inquisition into them would put an end to the free and unreserved discussions that take place on every occasion in masonic meetings, and substitute caution, reserve, and distrust, for the openness, gaiety, and freedom, which has hitherto prevailed. But further, what has Brother Gibson to do with this? Though he may be appointed grand accuser, if that office shall be created, he is not hitherto vested in it. His pure ears could not be sullied with any thing which took place at this meeting. No bad consequence could result from it to the masonic order in general, or to Brother Gibson in particular; for he does not pretend to find fault with the resolutions which were adopted, and in which the respondent concurred.

The same observations will nearly apply to the *second* charge, that the respondent 'did, at one or other of the meetings of the Caledonian Lodge, propose that the lodge should make a secession from the Grand Lodge.'[21] This seems what is called a *fishing* accusation,[22] made with the view of giving Brother Gibson the power of fishing for a charge out of every thing which the respondent ever said or did at any of the meetings of the Caledonian Lodge. If any thing wrong was said, why does not Brother Gibson state it? If any thing wrong was proposed

Second Charge.

in the minutes, why are they not referred to? But it would be erecting the Grand Lodge into an inquisition to allow such charges to be made, and the most inno-cent conversations, pronounced in the most unreserved conviviality of a lodge, inquired into, in order to be made ground of accusation against an individual.

The respondent is therefore unwilling to allude to any thing that had passed in the Caledonian Lodge, as that might seem an acquiescence in a bad prec-edent, and led to inquiries altogether unworthy of the attention of the Grand Lodge. If it is, however, necessary for him to do so, he can prove, that when some members seemed to propose to him seriously to separate from the Grand Lodge, he expressed his decided disapprobation of the idea, and he expressed the same sentiment to many members, whose zeal for the Caledonian / Lodge made them somewhat warm on that occasion. The respondent is, however, surprised, that the having uttered such a sentiment in the Caledonian Lodge, without doing any thing further, should be made a charge against him or any individual. At the quarterly communication of November 1807, when it was in agitation that the Lodge of St. Mary's Chapel should be deprived of their place upon the roll, a member of that lodge said, that a meeting would be called to consider of a seces-sion from the Grand Lodge, and that, if the measure took place, he would vote for it.[23] This was heard in the Grand Lodge without any mark of disapproba-tion; and if the Grand Lodge did not think it necessary to find fault with such an expression, how can it be made a crime against any individual, that he might have expressed himself to that effect?

THIRD
CHARGE.

The petitioner complains, in the *third* place, 'that, on the last anniversary of St. Andrew's, Brother Mitchell prevailed on the Caledonian Lodge not to attend divine service along with the Grand Master, and all the other brethren who joined in the procession of that evening; but after walking to the Tron Church, with the other brethren, to leave the procession without going to church, and to make a separate procession to Oman's tavern, thereby shewing his disrespect to the Grand Master Elect, his disregard to the orders of the Grand Lodge, and his contempt of the religious services in which the brethren were to be engaged, besides holding out to the world that their was a schism in the craft.

'And further, although it had been intimated to him, and to the Masters of Lodges, that the Grand Master Elect expected to see deputations of the lodges in the course of that evening, he neither attended the Grand Master, nor made any apology for not doing so.'

In the midst of the impiety which, unfortunately, prevails too much in the present age, it must give sincere delight to every devout person, to observe Brother Gibson's regard for religious services, more especially those in which the brethren are engaged; and the respondent feels led away from the merits of his own case, in order to contemplate so edifying a spectacle. Even if he was deficient in these respects, either on that or any former occasion, he could not be proof against the good effects of so virtuous an example; and to soothe those feelings which, no doubt, are predominant with Brother Gibson, and which, if they are a little quieted, will dispose him to view the other charges with more composure, Brother Mitchell begs leave to assure Brother Gibson, that he will be at all times happy to accompany him on any religious occasion, and more particularly to be edified / by his countenance and example in those religious exercises in which the brethren are engaged.

Having thus, with the utmost respect, and, as he trusts, thereby somewhat appeased Brother Gibson's pious, though wounded feelings, the respondent trusts Brother Gibson will now patiently listen to the following explanation, which must satisfy Brother Gibson, that the charge, so far as the respondent is concerned, is altogether unfounded.

The Caledonian Lodge attended most punctually in the Parliament house at half past two o'clock, and, if the respondent's recollection is accurate, they were there a considerable time before any other lodge. The Caledonian Lodge had no knowledge what mode of procedure the Grand Lodge wished to adopt; and their dinner was ordered at Oman's, according to custom, at half past 4 o'clock. It is well known that the business in the Parliament house was not over until near six o'clock; and it was understood that the lodges might show their respect for the Grand Lodge by walking in procession from the Parliament house. The respondent used all his influence to detain the members of the Caledonian Lodge for that purpose, against the inclination of many members of the lodge, as they knew that many of the brethren, who, from unavoidable circumstances, could not attend the procession, had been appointed to meet them at Oman's, at half past four. Even then, at the late hour of six o'clock, the respondent repeatedly urged the brethren also to attend divine service, which they opposed in the most strenuous manner, not from any disrespect to the Grand Lodge, or disregard for divine service, but from the powerful influence of hunger, which is not surprising, as dinner had been ordered an hour and a half before that time. To attach any great blame to the Caledonian Lodge on this occasion, would be straining matters very far; but surely, the respondent, who had used every effort to make his brethren disregard so powerful an impulse as that of hunger, ought to stand completely acquitted. Besides, there were other lodges which did not attend divine service. The Canongate Kilwinning Lodge, for instance, although they joined in the procession, went from the Parliament house to the Royal Exchange coffee-house; neither did this lodge go in the evening to pay their respects to the Grand Master Elect; neither did the Journeyman Lodge, or the Royal Arch, perform that ceremony. It was never intimated to the respondent that he was expected to wait upon the Grand Master Elect, nor did he conceive that there was any compulsion in the case, or that he could be found fault with for not doing so. In these points the respondent trusts that his conduct must stand completely / cleared. The accusation itself, when calmly considered, cannot attach much blame to any person, but least of all to the respondent. It is not pretended that any other person ever suggested the propriety of their waiting upon the Grand Master Elect. The members of the lodge were assembled to pass the evening at Oman's, rather on the footing of a private company than of a lodge: yet the respondent is singled out, and it is made a charge against him, that he did not make a visit of ceremony, which nobody ever suggested.

FOURTH   The *next* charge is, 'that the said Brother Mitchell did, on the Festival of St.
CHARGE.   John the Evangelist, on the 28th day of December last, in a manner contrary to the invariable custom, and unworthy the character of a mason, insult the Lodge of Edinburgh St. David's, and other lodges, by refusing to receive into the Caledonian Lodge deputations sent by them.'

When the respondent has explained the facts to which this charge refers, he is confident, that, so far from having had any disposition to insult the deputation from the lodge of St. David's, he was, personally, most anxious to shew them every mark of attention. The Caledonian Lodge has no hall of its own, in which it can assemble; and, from that circumstance, they are obliged to accommodate themselves to the room in which they happen to be. As they met at a tavern, each member, it was agreed, should pay a suitable sum for supper, and, on account of the expence and other circumstances attending their meeting there, a committee of the lodge had previously determined, that the lodge should neither send out nor receive any deputations that evening. As the Caledonian Lodge was the junior lodge, they did not expect any visit from the St. David's Lodge, or any other lodge, according to the rule, that the junior lodge should first wait on the senior lodge. About eleven o'clock, the very time when Mr. Oman was about to set down supper, the respondent was informed, that a deputation from St. David's Lodge, to the amount of eighteen or twenty, had arrived. The respondent was most anxious to receive the deputation, but it must have been attended with great expence to the funds of the Caledonian Lodge. The room, further, was not calculated to receive such a large addition to those who were on the point of sitting down to supper. The respondent, therefore, after consulting with his office-bearers, was obliged to desire one of his wardens to apologize to the deputation, and to explain the circumstances in which the Caledonian Lodge was placed. The respondent is informed, that the deputation was informed of this while they / were at the Thistle Lodge; but nothing can be more unfounded than the supposition, that any insult was intended to the deputation of the St. David's Lodge. The two lodges have always been upon the very best terms, and the respondent has always had the highest regard for Brother Gillon, the master of that lodge. Every explanation has been given, and every attempt made, to remove any misunderstanding; and the respondent trusts, that, in that respect at least, his endeavours have been attended with some success. This complaint is not brought by the master or other officers of that lodge. Brother Gibson, who has thought proper to make it, does not pretend that he even formed a part of the deputation which came upon that occasion; yet the offence was entirely of a public nature, alleged to have been committed by the one lodge against the other; and the respondent can most truly say, that he had not the most distant intention or wish to shew any disrespect to that lodge; on the contrary, he has always been desirous to shew them every respect in his power. The respondent understands, that Brother Gibson was accidentally present in St. David's Lodge when the deputation returned, and that he solemnly declared, while he laid his hand on his breast, that he bore no personal enmity to the respondent, and that, should an apology be given, or an explanation made, he would take no further notice of the matter. This explanation has been given, and Brother Gillon, the right worshipful master of that lodge, has declared that it satisfied him. Why then should Brother Gibson persist, after the declaration he has made? but he least of all has any right to allege that he is offended.

It may be proper to state, that, in the course of the evening, there were two deputations, consisting, as far as the respondent recollects, of three or four each, who came to Oman's, the one from the Thistle Lodge, and another from the Mary's Chapel Lodge. As they were not numerous, and came at a more suitable time of the evening, the Caledonian Lodge was able to receive them without inconvenience; and they would have been equally happy to have received the St. David's deputation, if they could have done so. A deputation from the Royal Arch, the respondent understands, came after twelve; but it had been thought proper to shut the lodge at that time. Although no deputations were sent out, in terms of the determination of the committee, it may be proper to mention, to prevent any mistake, that Brother Clark, with one or two of his friends, went, from motives of personal friendship, to see Brother Adams elected to the / chair of the Thistle Lodge. Surely, throughout the whole business, the respondent was blameless. From motives of personal regard for Brother Gillon, and the mutual interchanges of friendship which has always subsisted between the Caledonian Lodge and that of St. David's, the respondent was most particularly anxious to receive the deputation, and begged of his office-bearers to endeavour to make room for them, and regretted most sincerely that they could not be admitted.

Is there, worshipful brethren, any ground for attaching blame to the Caledonian Lodge, and for singling out the respondent of all persons on that account? The respondent, in any other circumstances, would be most unwilling to trouble the Grand Lodge with any farther remarks upon the subject; yet he owes it to himself, and to the lodge to which he belongs, and by which he has been so much honoured, to say something more.

It is well known to the Grand Lodge, that the respondent has been four successive times unanimously elected to the chair of the Caledonian Lodge. Ever since the first time when he attained this honour, in the midst of a laborious and arduous profession, there has been no exertion on his part spared to do justice to the charge he had undertaken. He has discharged his duty, not only to the Caledonian Lodge itself, but also to the craft in general, by fulfilling all those obligations which the craft expect, and which are solemnly imposed upon those who enter into the honourable and ancient fraternity of free masonry. In the course of these four years, the respondent has attended personally to the initiation of about four hundred brethren. Most of these have been his own friends, brought forward either by himself or by some of his friends. There are few, if any of them, whose situation in life, it is probable, will ever render them a burden on the craft; and, on the other hand, there are few, if any of them, who would be no less ready than they are able, to contribute to the relief of unfortunate and needy brethren. Most of the sister lodges in town also must witness how anxious the respondent has ever been, when favoured by a visit from them, to shew them every manner of attention and kindness; and, in short, to act fully up to the principles which we have all along professed, that of entertaining them according to the principles of Highland hospitality. On the other hand, the same lodges must bear witness how anxious the respondent has ever shewn himself to be on the most friendly footing, and to maintain a brotherly intercourse with them. He has been anxious that the Caledonian Lodge should make and return visits to them frequently; / and on such occasions he has been at the trouble of personally mustering his brethren as numerously as he could; and except on one or two occasions at most, the respondent has always headed them himself. Neither have his exertions been wanting to promote every kind of public charity, and to relieve those individual brethren whose situation in life required help, or to render assistance to those whom the lodge could benefit.[24] He might mention here their subscription for the widows and orphans of the brave heroes who fell in the glorious battle of Trafalgar.[25] He might mention also various collections made in the Caledonian Lodge, as well for needy brethren as for destitute and helpless widows and orphans;[26] nor will it be improper to notice the efforts used in encouraging a class of brethren who have strong claims on the public, but still stronger on the craft, not only as masons, but also as contributing, in no small degree, to that harmony, good humour, and conviviality, which should ever distinguish masonic meetings, viz. the brethren of the Theatre, and other places of public amusement. But besides these things, in which the respondent has participated with the Caledonian Lodge, there are others in which he himself has been solely concerned. To every needy brother he can say, 'He had a tear for pity, and a hand open as day for melting 'charity.'[27] And the mite[28] he could afford them he never did withhold. In short, he can lay his hand upon his breast and say, in words nearly similar to those of Job, that when he could help them, 'a brother did not lodge in the street, but he opened his doors to the 'traveller.'[29] So far also as his professional aid could go to relieve a brother, stretched on the bed of sickness, he has given it; and perhaps there are many amongst you who can bear testimony, that on such occasions his best efforts were always ready to be devoted to their service, without fee or reward.

As to the respondent's conduct, he has had repeated proofs, as well public as private, of the approbation of a class of brethren, whom he has ever looked up to as men, as masons, and as gentlemen, and whose approbation it shall always be more his study to merit, and his pride to possess, even than Brother Gibson's, however much he may respect him. The Caledonian Lodge are the class of persons he alludes to. In the present accusation against him they are all most zealous in his defence. Such has been their kindness to him, that he shall never forget it; and gratefully may he address them in the words of the great Augustan poet:

In freta dum fluvii current, dum montibus umbræ

Lustrabunt convexa, polus dum sidera pascet;

Semper honos, nomenq. tuum, laudesq. manebunt,

Quæ me cunq. vocant terræ[30]. – /

The respondent knows that he addresses brothers who are bound by the most solemn oath to render him justice; nay, to put the most favourable construction on his conduct. He has no doubt, therefore, that the full and particular answer which he has given to the charges brought against him will satisfy their minds; his anxiety to state the matter fully may have led him to trespass too far upon their patience. Humbly confident of an acquittal at their hand, he turns to Brother Gibson, and entreats him not to allow his zeal for his new assumed office of grand accuser, to hurry him too far, and make him persist in an accusation so completely unfounded, and which is so inconsistent with the general mildness and candour of his deportment.

The respondent must recur to poetry, to figure to himself a man who would be obdurate in these circumstances. A man who, 'while he walked, moved like an engine, while the ground shrunk before 'his treading,' 'who talked like a knell,' while his 'hum is a battery,' and 'sits in state as a thing made for Alexander,' might think it becoming his dignity to persist in such an accusation. The tartness of such a 'man's face might sour ripe grapes;' and 'he might no more remember his mother or brother, than an eight year old horse.'[31] Such a picture Shakespeare has drawn of an inexorable and resentful person, and had the respondent to deal with such a man, he would probably find, that there 'was no more mercy in him than there was milk in a male tiger.'[32] But surely Brother Gibson is cast in a very different mould. He has celebrated his own forbearance in his own petition, and he has an easy opportunity of giving an instance of it on this occasion, by dropping an accusation, which is altogether unfounded. Should it be otherwise, the respondent certainly regrets it very much, not only on his own account, but because it might make the respondent and others doubt as to his possessing some of those good qualities which the respondent is so much anxious to attribute to him. But, should it come to the worst, the respondent can only say, in the words of the same excellent poet, – 'God mend thee,' Brother Gibson, 'and put meekness into thy breast, love, charity, obedience, and true duty.'[33]

JOHN MITCHELL,

Right Worshipful Master Edinburgh Caledonian Lodge. /

An an ADJOURNED EXTRAORDINARY MEETING of the GRAND LODGE,
January 21, 1808.

After calling the roll, and taking down the names of the brethren present, but before proceeding to the business of the meeting, the Substitute Grand Master stated, that he considered it his duty to call the attention of the Grand Lodge to, what he conceived to be, extremely improper and irregular, viz. the printing of the petition and complaint against the Right Worshipful Brother Mitchell, and of his answers, without the sanction of the Grand Lodge; and, after some deliberation, it was unanimously resolved, that, in future, none of the proceedings of the Grand Lodge should be printed, without the express consent of the Grand Lodge being first asked and obtained.

After this resolution had passed, Brother Mitchell stated, that, before his answers were submitted to the Grand Lodge, he begged to express his regret for any improper strength of expression contained in these answers, which arose from his feelings at the time, and which he would have softened, had he had more leisure for preparing his answers.

The petition and complaint at the instance of Brother Gibson against Brother Mitchell, and his answers thereto, were then read, when Brother Gibson, in a speech of much eloquence, and at considerable length, made various observations on the style in which the answers for Brother Mitchell were written, and the personal insinuations and invectives which that paper so groundlessly contained against himself; and requested the opinion of the Grand Lodge in the first instance upon this point.

Brother Mitchell was then asked from the Chair, if he had any thing to say in reply; and he having answered that he had nothing to say, Brother Proctor, proxy-master for the Lodge of McDuff, moved as follows, viz. – 'That the charges and insinuations to Brother Gibson's prejudice, contained in Brother Mitchell's answers, are entirely irrelevant to the issue of this question, malicious and scurrilous in themselves, disrespectful to the Grand Lodge, and altogether inconsistent with the principles and conciliatory spirit of true Masonry.' Which motion was seconded by the Right Worshipful Brother Miller, master of St. Luke's Lodge, Edinburgh, and carried without a division.

The question of competency being afterwards discussed at considerable length, the Right Worshipful Brother Miller, master of / St. Luke's, moved, that the following decision should be pronounced, viz. – 'That the Grand Lodge having considered the petition and complaint at the instance of Brother James Gibson against the Right Worshipful Brother John Mitchell, and objection to the competency thereof, contained in the answers given in by the said Brother John Mitchell, find, that it has been invariably the practice of the Grand Lodge to sustain all complaints made by any individual brother, on any matter relating either to the interest or honour of the craft; and therefore repel the objection to the said competency.' Which motion was seconded by Brother Imlach, proxy-warden for Stow Lodge; and thereafter Brother Samuel Cuningham, proxy-warden for Inverness Lodge, moved, that a Committee should be appointed to search for precedents, before coming to any resolution on the point of competency; and which motion was seconded by Brother Osborne Brown, proxy-master of Strathaven Lodge, when a vote being put, Right Worshipful Brother Miller's motion was carried by 102 to 74.

Upon which, Brother Gibson stated, that, at this late hour of the night, he would humbly propose, that this meeting be adjourned to another day, in order to proceed with the proof; and requested liberty to cite some other witnesses, which, in addition to those already cited, he judged it necessary to bring forward. The Grand Lodge, accordingly, adjourn this meeting till Friday the 29th current, at 7 o'clock in the evening; and allow both parties to bring forward what other witnesses they may think necessary, provided they lodge with the Grand Secretary, on or before Wednesday the 27th current, at 12 o'clock noon, a list of such additional witnesses; and authorize the Grand Secretary to summon such additional witnesses, in the usual Masonic form, requesting them to attend the Grand Lodge, on Friday the 29th current, at 7 o'clock in the evening, for examination. The Grand Lodge farther recommend to the Grand Secretary, to issue cards to all the members of the Grand Lodge, requiring their attendance on the above day, and at the above hour.

(Signed) WILLIAM INGLIS, S.G.M.

*AD*JOURNED *EX*TRAORDINARY *M*EETING,
29th January 1808.

The roll being called, and the names of the brethren present taken down, the Substitute Grand Master stated, that, in terms of the minute / of 21st January last, Brother Gibson and Brother Mitchell had both cited some additional witnesses; and that the witnesses for both parties being present, he begged to know if it was the wish of the Grand Lodge that the proof should proceed.

Brother Harrowar, in a speech of some length, proposed, in the event of a vote of the House being necessary, that tellers be appointed to take down the votes, which having been seconded by Brother Osborne Brown, was agreed to.

The question was then discussed, whether or not the witnesses should remain in the room while the proof was going on. Brother Mitchell, and others, contended, that they saw nothing improper in allowing the witnesses to remain; while, on the other hand, Brother Gibson, and others, contended, that it was the practice, in all proofs, whether civil or criminal, for witnesses to be shut up, and could therefore see no difference in the present case. Brother Gibson, therefore, urged the propriety of the witnesses being shut up till after their examination. The Grand Lodge thereupon ordered, that the witnesses should withdraw while the proof was going on, but, so soon as the witnesses had given their evidence, they might remain, and hear the evidence of such witnesses as should afterwards be examined.

The evening being at this time far exhausted, Brother Stenhouse stated, that he was satisfied that the proof could not proceed with any regularity in full Lodge assembled, and therefore moved, that a Committee be appointed to take the proof, and report to the Grand Lodge; which motion was seconded by Brother Osborne Brown, and, after some argument, was adopted by consent of both parties; it being agreed upon, that the Committee should consist of ten Members, each party naming five, the Substitute Grand Master being Preses and Convener. And the following is the Committee named by the parties, viz.

Brother ROBERT PROCTOR, Esquire, W.S. Proxy for McDuff.

Brother WILLIAM LAING, Esquire, Master of Edinburgh St. Andrew's Lodge.

Brother THOMAS H. MILLER, Esquire, Advocate, Proxy-Warden for Dalkeith.

Brother ALEXANDER GIBSON HUNTER, Esquire, W.S. Proxy-Warden for St. Andrew's, Aberdeen.

Brother JAMES DAVIDSON, Esquire, W.S. Proxy for Kilsyth.

Brother ALEXANDER JAFFRAY, Esquire, Writer, Proxy for Lennox Kilwinning, Campsie. /

Brother HARROWAR, Esquire, Advocate, Proxy-Warden for Lennox Kilwinning, Campsie.

Brother OSBORNE BROWN, Esquire, W.S. Proxy for Strathaven Kilwinning.

Brother JOHN LAWSON, Esquire, W.S. Master of Canongate Kilwinning.

Brother FRANCIS M. McNAB, Esquire, Writer, Warden for Commercial Lodge, Oban.

Any six, with the addition of the Substitute Grand Master, to be a quorum; the Committee to meet, and proceed to take the proof to-morrow, at 12 o'clock noon, in St. Luke's Lodge-room, and with power to them to adjourn from time to time, as they may find it necessary; the Committee to report progress at the Quarterly Communication on the 1st of February. The Substitute Grand Master intimated to the witnesses present, that they were expected to attend at the above place and hour, without further notice.

Brother Oshorne Brown stated, that as the Substitute Grand Master was cited as a witness, in order that the Committee might not be deprived of his assistance, he proposed, that the Substitute Grand Master be first examined, and that he should not, like the other witnesses, be obliged to withdraw, which was unanimously agreed to.

(Signed) WILLIAM INGLIS, S.G.M. /

BROTHER GIBSON'S PROOF.
COMMITTEE of the GRAND LODGE of SCOTLAND, EDINBURGH, ST. LUKE'S LODGE-ROOM, January 30, 1808,
PRESENT,
R. W. WILLIAM INGLIS, Esquire, Substitute Grand Master.
R. W. Brother LAING.
R. W. Brother ALEXANDER GIBSON HUNTER.
R. W. Brother JAMES DAVIDSON.
R. W. Brother ALEXANDER JAFFRAY.
R. W. Brother J.O. BROWN.
R. W. Brother JOHN LAWSON.
R. W. Brother FRANCIS M. M^cNAB.
R. W. Brother ROBERT PROCTOR.
R. W. Brother THOMAS H. MILLER.
R. W. Brother HARROWAR.
R. W. Brother GEORGE CARPHIN, Grand Clerk *pro tempore*.[34]
In the complaint, Brother James Gibson against Right Worshipful Brother John Mitchell, the following[xxix] witnesses were adduced on the part of the complainer. –

COMPEARED,[35] the Right Worshipful WILLIAM INGLIS, Esquire, Sub-   APP. No. 2. stitute Grand Master of Scotland, aged 30 and upwards, married, who being solemnly sworn, purged of malice and partial counsel, and examined, depones, That he presided at the Quarterly Communication of the Grand Lodge of Scotland, in the month of November last: That, as far as he recollects, a motion for expelling Right Worshipful Brother Mitchell from the Grand Lodge, was made by Brother Sutherland or Brother Ross. Depones, That, to the best of his recollection, certain improper expressions were used by Brother Mitchell; amongst others, he said he could not obtain justice in the Grand Lodge, and made use of the word 'chicane,'[36] which induced / the deponent[37] to take notice of his conduct, and which, as the deponent thinks, gave rise to the motion for expulsion: That after this, Brother Mitchell continued exceedingly violent, and made use of more violent expressions; at least, his manner was more violent, and which, if the deponent recollects right, produced a general outcry of 'turn him out;' and that the deponent, much against his inclination, thought it necessary, in the situation he then was, to desire the Wardens to do their duty, by turning Brother Mitchell out of the Grand Lodge. And being interrogated, if he recollects what prevented that order from being executed? depones, That in the midst of the commotion which took place, and whilst the Wardens, or at least one of them, rose, as the deponent thinks, to obey the above order, Brother Gibson rose, and proposed something conciliatory, tending, as the deponent thinks, to a proposition, that what Brother Mitchell had done should be passed over, in the hope that such conduct should not be repeated: That the deponent then asked the question from the Chair, whether the above proposition from Brother Gibson should be acceded to? and which the deponent certainly recommended for the sake of peace; which measure seemed to be generally approved of by the Grand Lodge. And being interrogated, If he has any recollection of speaking to Brother Gibson some months ago, on the subject of a pamphlet, in the form of a letter, said to be published by Brother Mitchell? depones, That he does, and that he thinks it was the intention of some of the Members of the Grand Lodge to bring it forward there against Brother Mitchell, as a point of dittay; but the deponent himself gave no opinion on the subject; and that Brother Gibson expressed his sentiments as decidedly[xxx] unfavourable to any notice being taken in the Grand Lodge of the above publication. Being interrogated, If, on St. Andrew's day last, when the Grand Lodge was assembled, he recollects of an intimation being made from the Chair, that the Most Worshipful Grand Master expected to be visited in the evening at Fortune's by the Masters of Lodges, and their Wardens? depones, That he thinks so, but he is not certain; but he knows that it was the deponent's intention to make such intimation from the Chair in the Parliament-house at the election. Depones, That Brother Mitchell was present at the election that evening. Interrogated for Brother Mitchell, depones, That he recollects immediately after the motion for expelling Brother Mitchell was made, in November last, there was some hissing in the room; but the deponent does not think it was general. Depones, That, on the above occasion / he does not recollect Brother Mitchell saying, that the laws were now in that state, that he did not know precisely what was law; nor does he recollect of desiring Brother Mitchell to explain himself on that subject; neither does he recollect of desiring Brother Mitchell to retract his words, though such expressions might not improbably have been made use of. Being interrogated, If he ever saw the letter said to be published by Dr. Mitchell? depones, That he did, but cannot say whether it was a proof copy or not; and thinks that the first person who showed him it was Brother Thomson, a Warden of St. Luke's Lodge. Depones, That he does not recollect of having ordered the Grand Clerk to give intimation to the Masters of Lodges in Edinburgh, that the Grand Master expected visitations from Lodges on St. Andrew's day, though to this the Grand Clerk or Secretary will speak more correctly. Depones, That the pamphlet above alluded to, was shown to him in Brother Lawrie's back-shop, and the deponent inclines to think, that he there saw it in the hands of Brother Black. Depones, That he was impressed with the belief, that any copies of the above pamphlet were got by Messrs. Thomson and Black from the printing-house of Mr. Turnbull. All which is truth, as he shall answer to God.

Brother ALEXANDER STEWART, a member of the Caledonian Lodge, Edinburgh, aged 20 and upwards, who being solemnly sworn, and examined, *ut ante,* depones, That he remembers of being present at a meeting of a committee of the Caledonian Lodge, consisting of about 30 or 40 members, when they were debating upon the subject of an order of the Grand Lodge, relative to some preference, as he understood, which had been given by the Grand Lodge to the Lodge of the Roman Eagle, as to their particular right of meeting, containing a prohibition against the Caledonian Lodge holding their night of meeting upon the same evening with that of the Roman Eagle: That the deponent heard Brother Mitchell, in common with the other members of the committee, express an opinion that they were entitled to meet, if they qualified themselves in terms of the act of Parliament, independently of the Grand Lodge, though they all expressed a wish to make every thing agreeable; and a subcommittee of five was thereupon named, to consider the business, and to report to a meeting of the Caledonian Lodge: That in the course of the debate before referred to, a difference of opinion, however, prevailed, some of the members having considered the order of the Grand Lodge as an insult to the Caledonian Lodge, and so / intended; but the deponent does not recollect the reasons assigned for this expression of sentiment. Interrogated, If he is certain that Brother Mitchell did not say, that it would be a disgrace to the Caledonian Lodge if she paid attention to the prohibition of the Grand Lodge? depones, That he does not recollect Brother Mitchell having made use of such an expression; and the witness, of himself, adds, that he is certain that Brother Mitchell could have carried a motion of secession from the Grand Lodge, if he had proposed such a motion, and wished it to be carried, as the greater number of the brethren present were disposed to accede to any proposition of Brother Mitchell's, though there were a good many of another way of thinking, and, among the rest, the deponent himself, as to the secession; but, in fact, no regular motion was made at that meeting, except for the appointment of a sub-committee before deponed to, which was carried unanimously: That several members, some of whose names he does not know, spoke for and against the proposition of secession from the Grand Lodge: That the debate upon the subject of secession had commenced before the deponent entered the room, and the chief argument turned upon this, whether it would be for the interest and the honour of the Caledonian Lodge to secede or not? That by a secession, the deponent means an absolute separation from the Grand Lodge. Being interrogated, Which side of the argument Brother Mitchell took? depones, That he does not think he did any thing particular; but, in delivering his opinion, he did not seem to consider himself obliged to the Grand Lodge. Interrogated, From what expressions of Brother Mitchell's speech he concluded that he did not consider himself obliged to the Grand Lodge? depones, That he explained the act of Parliament to this effect, that the Caledonian Lodge, by qualifying themselves in terms of it, could meet independently of the Grand Lodge, and said, that there was a prejudice in some of the Members of the Grand Lodge against him, Brother Mitchell, who thought the prohibition of the Grand Lodge was particularly levelled against himself; and several of the other members were of opinion, that it was owing to this prejudice that the Caledonian Lodge had not got a better hearing; and the deponent adds, that some of the members who were inclined to obey the mandate of the Grand Lodge, were also of opinion, that the Caledonian Lodge could meet without the authority of the Grand Lodge: That, indeed, the whole members, including Brother Mitchell, were of that opinion. Interrogated, Whether any proposal was made by any person, and by / whom, to secede from the Grand Lodge, and if any debate took place upon such proposal? depones, That no proposal was made for a secession from the Grand Lodge that night, as those who were for seceding wished first to try whether the Grand Lodge would revoke the prohibition. Depones, That the deponent's opinion was against secession. Depones, That he understood that Brother Mitchell had attended the Grand Lodge, on the part of the Caledonian Lodge, for the purpose of getting the day of their meeting continued, though he had not succeeded in obtaining it. Interrogated by a Member of the Committee, depones, That he does not think that Brother Mitchell recommended a secession from the Grand Lodge at the meeting of the committee of the Caledonian Lodge before deponed to, but he did not dissuade them from the measure, observing, that the Grand Lodge would be the greatest sufferers, as the Caledonian Lodge contributed more to the funds of the Grand Lodge than any other Lodge, except one. Interrogated by Brother Gibson, depones, That he dined with several gentlemen belonging to the Caledonian Lodge on St. Andrew's day last: That they did not meet as a Lodge, but only as private individuals: That Brother Mitchell was in the chair, and the Wardens sat in the situation they would have done had they been acting as Wardens: That some of the gentlemen present were not cloathed,[38] but, in general, they were so. Interrogated, If Brother Mitchell was in general addressed as Right Worshipful, and if, in the course of the evening, the healths of the Officers of the Grand Lodge, or any of them, were drank, or any of them proposed?[39] depones, That Brother

Mitchell was generally addressed on this occasion by the title of Right Worshipful Master, but was often addressed as Dr. Mitchell, and thinks, that the healths of all the Officers of the Grand Lodge were proposed and drank: That the circumstance of some of the gentlemen being in clothing, arose, as the deponent thinks, from a certain number of them having been in the procession, and others who joined the party conceiving that a regular lodge was to be opened. All which is truth, as he shall answer to God.

Brother JAMES HAMILTON, Substitute Master of the Caledonian Lodge, aged 30 and upwards, married, being solemnly sworn, &c. depones, That he was present at a meeting of a committee of the Caledonian Lodge for considering a prohibition issued by the Grand Lodge against their meeting on the same evening with the Lodge of the Roman Eagle: That there might be between 30 and 40 members present; and that the deponent was there from its commencement: That Brother Mitchell opened the / business by stating, that he had received a communication from the Grand Lodge, relative to the Caledonian Lodge meeting on the same evening with the Lodge of the Roman Eagle, and entered into, the witness does not know what well to call it, but he thinks, a strain of invective against the Grand Lodge, for the communication: That Brother Mitchell made a long, and, what appeared to the deponent, a violent speech upon the occasion, declaring, that the Caledonian Lodge would, in his opinion, be disgraced, if they submitted to be trampled on by the Grand Lodge; and proposed to refuse obedience to the Grand Lodge; and conjured them, if they had the spirit of Caledonians, to refuse obedience to the Grand Lodge: That Brother Mitchell was thereupon required to produce the communication he had received from the Grand Lodge, which he did; upon which, an appeal was made to Brother Mitchell, whether it was not a positive interdict by the Grand Lodge; and to state, what would be the consequences of a refusal to comply with that interdict? That Brother Mitchell answered, That he had no doubt that the Grand Lodge would shut their doors against the Caledonian Lodge; when it was remarked by one or other of the brethren, that this was but a secondary consideration, the important question being, whether the Grand Lodge would not shut the doors of the Caledonian Lodge, by withdrawing its charter? That, upon this, Brother Mitchell seemed to encourage the idea that the Caledonian Lodge could meet with as much eclat and effect without a charter from the Grand Lodge: That Brother Mitchell then mentioned, that Canongate Kilwinning Lodge of Edinburgh had already seceded from the Grand Lodge, and that the Lodge of Mary's Chapel had declared their determination of also seceding:[40] That after this had passed, the deponent was called into the next room, to assist at the initiation of a brother, and upon the deponent's returning to the Lodge-room, he was informed, that he had been appointed one of a sub-committee of seven, for the farther consideration of this matter: That the deponent attended a meeting of

the sub-committee, when he pointed out clauses in the charter of the Caledonian Lodge, enjoining their strict obedience to the Grand Lodge; which charter,
the deponent had previously moved, should be submitted to the consideration
of the sub-committee: That after this, nothing further passed upon the subject of secession at said meeting; and that the deponent first saw the report of
the sub-committee in Brother Mitchell's printed answers to Brother Gibson's
complaint; and the deponent, of himself, adds, that he saw two of the members of the sub-committee reading a paper at the side table, upon / which he
moved towards them, in order to examine said paper, but considering that it
might relate to private business, he desisted, and the said paper was not communicated at all to the sub-committee; at least the deponent, who was not out of
the room during the whole night, during the sitting of the sub-committee, never
saw it: That it does not consist with the deponent's knowledge, that the report
quoted in Brother Mitchell's answers ever was laid before a meeting of the Caledonian Lodge. Depones, That the deponent never heard any of the minutes of
the Caledonian Lodge read at any meeting. Depones, That, among other arguments employed by Brother Mitchell to excite the Caledonian Lodge to resist
the orders of the Grand Lodge, stated, that he would rather resign the chair than
preside over brethren who would submit to such an order. Depones, That the
deponent received no intimation of any meeting of the Caledonian Lodge, to
which Brother Mitchell's answers were submitted, previous to their publication;
and, to the best of the deponent's knowledge, there was no such meeting, at least
no public one. Interrogated, If, since the witness was cited to appear before the
Grand Lodge, any application has been made to him by any person to withhold
his attendance as a witnesses? depones, That no direct application to the above
effect has been made to the witness himself; but Brother Mitchell complained to
one of the deponent's relations, of the witness's intention to appear here as an evidence against him: That this was to the deponent's father-in-law, Captain John
Grahame, commander of the late Duchess of Montrose Excise yacht, who mentioned the circumstance of Brother Mitchell having complained of the general
conduct of the witness, by which he understood a reference to his appearance as
a witness in this cause; and, besides, Brother Mitchell remarked to the deponent,
that it was odd for him to appear to give evidence, or to take part against his own
Lodge. Upon the interrogatory of Brother Mitchell, depones, That a written
card, addressed to Brother Cooper, and the witness's name afterwards superinduced,[41] was sent to the deponent, desiring him to accompany Brother Mitchell
to a meeting of counsel, and upon the subject of Brother Gibson's complaint, as
the witness understood, though it was not so expressed in the card, and to which
the deponent verbally replied by the messenger who brought it, that he could
not conveniently attend. Interrogated, If he did not approve of the answers being
printed? depones, That he never saw them till they were printed. Depones, That

he was present at the meeting of the Caledonian Lodge, on St. John's day: That, at the sub-committee above deponed to, it was resolved, that no deputations should be received on the evening of St. John: That, when the deputation from / St. David's Lodge was announced, Brother Mitchell expressed his anxiety to receive it, but was dissuaded by his office-bearers, as there was not room to hold the half of the number of the deputation, which was announced to consist of 18 or 20, and expressed his regret that the deputation could not be admitted. All which is truth, as he shall answer to God.

The Committee adjourn the diet for further proving, till Monday first, at 11 o'clock, and appoint the parties and witnesses then to attend in St. Luke's Lodge-room.

Edinburgh, February 1, 1808.

Before further proceedings, Brother Gibson declared, That he passed from the fourth charge, which he had made with the approbation of the Right Worshipful Master Gillon, and of a most numerous and respectable meeting of the brethren of the Lodge of St. David. It appeared, from Brother Mitchell's answers, that some communication had taken place on the subject between him and Brother Gillon. Neither of these gentlemen had, however, thought proper to hold any communication with Brother Gibson, which, if they had done, might have rendered the charge unnecessary; and Brother Gibson now passed from it in consequence of the deposition on that subject given by Brother Hamilton.

(Signed) JAMES GIBSON.

At an Adjourned Meeting of the COMMITTEE *of the* GRAND LODGE OF SCOT-LAND, *held in* ST. LUKE'S LODGE-ROOM, *the 1st day of February 1808,*
PRESENT,
R. W. WILLIAM INGLIS, Esquire, Substitute Grand Master.
R. W. Brother JOHN LAWSON.
R. W. Brother J.O. BROWN.
R. W. Brother FRANCIS M^cNAB.
R. W. Brother HARROWAR.
R. W. Brother ALEXANDER GIBSON HUNTER.
R. W. Brother THOMAS H. MILLAR.
R. W. Brother GEORGE CARPHIN, Grand Clerk, *p.t.*
COMPEARED Brother COLIN M^cKENZIE of KILCOY, aged 20 and upwards, married, who being solemnly sworn, &c. depones, / That he is a member of the Caledonian Lodge, and was for about two years master of that Lodge: That he received sometime in the course of the month of November last, as he thinks, a card from the secretary of the Caledonian Lodge, desiring him to attend a meeting of a committee of that Lodge, to consider matters nearly connected

with the interest of the Lodge: That he accordingly attended that committee, and there might be about 30 or 40 members of the Lodge present: That soon after entering the Lodge, Brother Mitchell informed the meeting in substance, that they were called together to consider how they were to act relative to some disputes between the Caledonian Lodge and the Roman Eagle Lodge and gave it as his opinion, that the Roman Eagle Lodge was more actuated from party spirit,[42] Than from the true spirit of Masonry; and also, that the committee were called together to consider the conduct of the Grand Lodge, who, as he said, had taken up the cudgels for the Roman Eagle Lodge against the Caledonian Lodge, pretty much from the same spirit: That Brother Mitchell expressed himself with considerable warmth upon this occasion: That Brother Mitchell found great fault with the Grand Lodge for interdicting the Caledonian Lodge from meeting on the same day with the Roman Eagle Lodge, which, he said, they had never done before on any other occasion, and had no right to do, saying, that he considered it an insult to the Caledonian Lodge, and hoped they would not suffer themselves to be tamely insulted; and that if he conceived the Lodge to be dishonoured, he would no longer sit in the chair of the Caledonian Lodge, and, during his speech, signified a wish, that they would come to some definite resolution on the subject: That when Brother Mitchell declared, that he would leave the chair, as before deponed to, the members present signified their regret that he should do so. Depones, That soon after this, Brother Mitchell left the Lodge, when a good deal of desultory conversation took place, as indeed had taken place before; and, in the course of the evening, several questions were put by different members, as to the consequences of not complying with the interdict of the Grand Lodge, when it was generally understood, and admitted, that all that the Grand Lodge had in their power, was to deprive the Caledonian Lodge of their charter: That the deponent cannot positively say, that Brother Mitchell stated this; but he is rather inclined to think he did: That the Lodge of Canongate Kilwinning was mentioned as an example of a Lodge prospering independently of the Grand Lodge: That the deponent afterwards rose, and stated, that he / wished rather to receive than to give information; but expressed an opinion, that if an amicable understanding with the Roman Eagle Lodge could be effected, upon terms honourable to the Caledonian Lodge, he would prefer it; but he would be the last person who would agree to the honour of the Lodge being tarnished: That, not long after, a motion was made by Brother Horne, as the deponent thinks, which was seconded by the deponent, for the appointment of a sub-committee for considering the matters in dispute, and to report to the Caledonian Lodge; and that a supplementary motion was afterwards made for the production of certain papers to be laid before the sub-committee, both which motions were unanimously agreed to, as the deponent thinks: That Brother Mitchell concurred in the motions, and himself suggested the members of the sub-committee, with the assistance of Brother Horne: That the deponent recollects of some question being put by a Brother, whether the Lodge, if deprived of their charter, would not become a mere Masonic club, or words to that purpose? Interrogated, If he recollects Brother Mitchell recommending, or appearing to recommend, that the Lodge should hold meetings independently of the Grand Lodge? depones, That he does not: That during the whole time of the meeting, the deponent sat upon Brother Mitchell's left hand. Interrogated, If he recollects if Brother Mitchell stated to the Caledonian Lodge, that he had refused to plead to the complaint given in by the Roman Eagle Lodge? depones, That he does not recollect. Depones, That he conceived the opinion which Brother Mitchell gave to the Lodge, to be, that they should not submit to the interdict of the Grand Lodge, as the Caledonian Lodge would be thereby dishonoured, and the Grand Lodge had no authority to grant it; and these matters, as he understood, had always been left to be arranged among the different masters. Depones, That he was a member of the sub-committee, but did not attend the meeting, and never saw the report of the sub-committee, but in Brother Mitchell's answers to Brother Gibson's complaint. Interrogated by Brother Mitchell, depones, That he considered the meeting of the committee before deponed to, to consist of those members of the Caledonian Lodge who had the interest of the Lodge at heart, and considered that every member present was entitled freely to deliver his opinion. Depones, That he certainly understood Brother Mitchell to have the interest of the Caledonian Lodge at heart. Interrogated, If, in the course of what Brother Mitchell said, he appeared to be more actuated by a regard to the interests of the Caledonian / Lodge, than by ill-will to the Grand Lodge? depones, That, while Brother Mitchell strongly reprobated the conduct of the Grand Lodge, the deponent was aware, as he has already deponed to, that Brother Mitchell had the interests of the Caledonian Lodge at heart; and thinks that he was freely disposed to do whatever the brethren resolved upon, for the good of the Caledonian Lodge. Interrogated, Whether the deponent thinks it possible, if Brother Mitchell had proposed to hold meetings independently of the Grand Lodge, he, the deponent, could have forgot his having done so? depones, That it is very possible, from the very desultory conversation which took place, that he might have forgot, though it is not likely. Depones, That, to the best of his recollection, he did not hear Brother Mitchell make a motion for secession from the Grand Lodge, or for holding meetings independently of the Grand Lodge. Depones, That he recollects having received a card desiring his attendance at the sub-committee before deponed to, in order to make up their report to the Lodge; and thinks that he made an apology to Brother Mitchell for his not being able to attend it. Interrogated, Whether, if Brother Mitchell had made any motion in the committee of the Caledonian Lodge, before mentioned, the deponent does not think he could have carried it? depones, That this is a matter of opinion, and the deponent thinks it would have depended very much upon the nature of the motion. All which is truth, as he shall answer to God.

The Reverend Brother JOHN HODGSON, a member of the Caledonian Lodge, aged 20 and upwards, not married, who being solemnly sworn, &c. depones, That he recollects of having attended a meeting of a committee of the Caledonian Lodge in November last, for the purpose of considering matters of great importance to that Lodge: That there might be about 30 members present. Depones, That he thinks Brother Mitchell stated the purpose of the meeting, and submitted to the committee, whether the Caledonian Lodge should yield to the order to the Grand Lodge, in the dispute between the Caledonian Lodge and the Roman Eagle Lodge, or used words to this purpose: That, upon this, Brother McKenzie rose, and moved, that the Lodge should rather accommodate the matter, if possible; when Brother Mitchell rose, and seemed to think that the Lodge ought to resist the decision of the Grand Lodge. Interrogated, If Brother Mitchell said any thing about the Lodge being dishonoured, if they submitted to the order of the Grand Lodge? depones, That he cannot recollect the particular expressions, / but that his speech was decidedly to that purpose: That the deponent replied to Brother Mitchell's speech, and signified, that it was his wish, as well as that of many members around him, that matters should be accommodated with the Grand Lodge, as the Caledonian Lodge had nothing to gain by such a dispute, but they had every thing to lose; mentioning particularly, that the Grand Lodge might deprive the Caledonian Lodge of their charter, shut their doors, and take from them their Masonic privileges: That, to this Brother Mitchell replied from the chair, that, by qualifying themselves, and taking the oaths to Government, they might meet independently of the Grand Lodge: That, after some desultory conversation, the matter was referred to a sub-committee. Interrogated for Brother Mitchell, depones, That he thinks Brother Mitchell mentioned from the chair, that the whole business had originated from party motives against him; but the brethren around the deponent seemed to think, that, in whatever way the dispute arose, the Lodge had nothing to do with Brother Mitchell's private quarrels: That some of the brethren around Brother Mitchell's chair seemed to think, that the dispute had originated from party motives, though no speech was made to this effect, but by Brother Mitchell himself; and the general complection of the meeting was against this opinion. Depones, That he attended Brother Mitchell to the Parliament-house on St. Andrew's day, and recollects very well that much impatience was expressed by the brethren of the Caledonian Lodge to go to dinner: That the deponent did not hear Brother Mitchell propose a secession from the Grand Lodge in precise words; but it appeared to the deponent from Brother Mitchell's speeches before the committee, that he wished the Lodge to secede. Depones, upon the interrogatory of Brother Gibson, That he was present at Oman's on St. Andrew's day[43] at dinner, and recollects the Prince of Wales's health being drank as heir-appar-ent,[44] but not with reference, so far as the deponent recollects, to his situation as Grand Master: That the deponent does not recollect the Earl of Moira's health being drunk,[45] nor does he think that Mr. Maule's health was drunk.[46] All which is truth, as he shall answer to God.

> To save trouble, Brother Gibson admits, that it was the general wish of the brethren of the Caledonian Lodge not to go to church on St. Andrew's day; and that no brother of that Lodge was heard to express a wish to attend divine service.

JAMES GIBSON. /

Brother ALEXANDER CLARK, Past-Master of the Caledonian Lodge, aged 30, and married, who being solemnly sworn, &c. depones, That he attended a meeting of members of the Caledonian Lodge in the month of November last, and there might be about 30 or 40 members present: That Brother Mitchell took the chair, and stated the purpose of the meeting to be, to consider the propriety of the interdict by the Grand Lodge, in the question between the Caledonian and Roman Eagle Lodges: That Brother Mitchell gave his opinion, that the Grand Lodge had no right to interfere with the nights of meeting of the Caledonian Lodge, as that power was vested in the masters of Lodges: That he does not recollect Brother Mitchell having said, that the interdict of the Grand Lodge was an insult to the Caledonian Lodge. Interrogated, If the witness recollects Brother Mitchell giving any opinion as to the conduct the Lodge should observe, in obeying or in disregarding the interdict of the Grand Lodge? depones, That he does not recollect whether Brother Mitchell gave any opinion upon the subject or not. Depones, That there were various questions put by different members to Brother Mitchell, and, in particular, the witness put this question to Brother Mitchell, Whether, supposing the Caledonian Lodge continued to hold their meetings on the nights on which the Grand Lodge had interdicted them from doing, it was in the power of the Grand Lodge to take their charter from them? to which Brother Mitchell answered, he believed they could: That the witness then replied, if that be the case, the Caledonian Lodge cannot hold its meetings as a regular Lodge, but merely as a Masonic meeting; and something was said, that, if they did not hold meetings as a regular Lodge, the civil power would interpose, and prevent their meetings. Depones, That Brother Mitchell mentioned, that the Caledonian Lodge could hold meetings independently of the Grand Lodge: and that Brother Mitchell also said, that the Lodge of Mary's Chapel, and, as the deponent thinks, the Canongate Kilwinning, or one of the Kilwinning Lodges, had either seceded from the Grand Lodge, or were on the eve of doing so: That, at the meeting above deponed to, a sub-committee was appointed, of which the deponent was one: That he attended a meeting of the sub-committee, who made a written report, agreeing to change the night of meeting: That, as he thinks, a draft of that report was shown on the evening of the meeting to the deponent by Brother Horne. Depones, That at the meeting of the Lodge on St. Andrew's day, the healths of the Prince of Wales and Lord Moira were, / to the best of the deponent's recollection, drank; but he does not recollect of the health of the Grand Master Elect being drank, nor does he recollect of the healths of the Substitute Grand Master, or the other Grand Officers, being drank. Depones, That he does not think that Brother Mitchell gave any opinion whether the Lodge should continue their meetings on the night on which they had been interdicted to meet, or should hold them upon another night. Depones, That some words were said by Brother Mitchell, that it was an insult to the Caledonian Lodge, for the Grand Lodge to prevent the Caledonian Lodge meeting on the night prohibited, as he understood the Roman Eagle had repeatedly changed their nights of meeting. Depones, That Brother Mitchell said that he would not remain in the chair, after the Lodge had been so degraded by the interdict. Depones, That Brother Mitchell did not mention to the Lodge, that he had not resisted in the Grand Lodge the complaint made by the Roman Eagle Lodge. Interrogated by Brother Mitchell, If it appeared to the witness, that Brother Mitchell had any desire to persist in the meeting, in opposition to the sentiments of his brethren, or in defiance of the rights of the Grand Lodge? depones, That it did not; and that Brother Mitchell seemed to be guided entirely by the opinion of the Lodge. Interrogated, If Brother Mitchell did not always express a readiness to do every thing that appeared to the members for the interest of the Lodge? depones, That it did not; and that Brother Mitchell seemed to be guided entirely by the opinion of the Lodge. Interrogated, If Brother Mitchell did not always express a readiness to do every thing that appeared to the members for the interest of the Lodge? depones, That he did. Interrogated, If it was the deponent's opinion, and that of the brethren near him in the room, that the Caledonian Lodge being interdicted from meeting on the fourth Friday, proceeded from party motives directed against Brother Mitchell? depones, That such was the deponent's opinion, and some of the members near him: That Brother Mitchell did not influence the deponent in that opinion. Being interrogated, If Brother Mitchell said from the chair, that rather than the Caledonian Lodge should suffer on his account, he would resign the chair?[47] depones, He did, and that the brethren expressed their regret that he should think of doing so: That there was no motion made by Brother Mitchell, that the Caledonian Lodge should continue to hold their meetings on the fourth Friday. Interrogated, If the witness supposes, that if, at the meeting alluded to, Brother Mitchell had made a motion for the Lodge meeting on the fourth Friday, though interdicted, he would have carried his motion? depones, That he cannot say.

Depones, That he was present from the commencement of the above meeting, and heard Brother Mitchell open the business, and he does not recollect / of Brother Mitchell making use of any invective against the Grand Lodge. Interrogated. Whether he has had conversations with Brother Mitchell on the subject of the nights of meeting? depones, He has. Interrogated, If, at any of these conversations, Brother Mitchell seemed determined to continue the night of meeting? depones, That he did not. Depones, That he was present at a committee-meeting of the members of the Caledonian Lodge, held at Oman's Tavern, at which there was about 12 present, and it was at their desire that Brother Gibson's complaint, and Brother Mitchell's answers thereto, were printed. Interrogated by Brother Gibson, depones, That the witness was desired to attend a committee-meeting at Oman's Tavern, at which the petition and answers were ordered to be printed; but he does not know whether the members present had been appointed as a committee by the Lodge or not, or if any committee had been appointed upon the subject. Interrogated, as the witness has deponed that, in his opinion, the sentence of the Grand Lodge, in the question between the Roman Eagle and the Caledonian Lodges, had been pronounced against the Caledonian Lodge from party motives, he is requested to state the ground of that opinion? depones, That he founded his opinion upon Brother Mitchell having in the Grand Lodge proposed an address to his Majesty, and that the same had been negatived by the Grand Lodge. Depones, That he has had no conversation with Brother Mitchell upon the subject of the petition and answers, except, having met Brother Mitchell on the street, he said to him, that if he had seen the draft of the answers before being printed, he would have endeavoured to make them more mild. Interrogated, If, at the meeting at Oman's, when the petition and answers were ordered to be printed, a copy of the answers was laid before the meeting? depones, That there was not: That the deponent understood the answers were not then prepared; but the meeting gave orders to print them when prepared. All which is truth, as he shall answer to God.

QUARTERLY COMMUNICATION,

February 1, 1808.

The Substitute Grand Master, as Chairman of the Committee appointed to take the proof in the question between Brother Gibson and Brother Mitchell, stated, that that Committee had proceeded so far with the proof; but as there were still a good number of witnesses / to examine, he proposed, that the Grand Lodge should continue said Committee, and renew their former powers: that in the course of taking the proof, the Committee found it sometimes difficult to make a quorum of seven. The Substitute Grand Master, therefore, proposed, that the quorum should consist of four members, and the Substitute Grand Master, instead of seven members, all of which the Grand Lodge unanimously agreed to.

The Grand Lodge adjourn the meeting to this day fortnight, the 15th instant, to receive the final report of the Committee; when Right Worshipful Brother Miller, master of St. Luke's, moved, and it was unanimously agreed to, that the proof, when concluded, and the proceedings in this case, be printed, under the inspection of the Committee, and thereafter distributed among the members of the Grand Lodge, previous to the adjourned Quarterly Communication, so that the members may be the better able to judge of the import of said proof. It was likewise moved and agreed to, that the whole expenses attending the proof and proceedings in that complaint shall be defrayed mutually by Brother Gibson and Brother Mitchell.

(Signed)WILLIAM INGLIS, S. G. M.

At a COMMITTEE-MEETING of the GRAND LODGE OF SCOTLAND held in ST. LUKE's LODGE-ROOM, 5th February 1808,

PRESENT,

R. W. WILLIAM INGLIS, Esquire, Substitute Grand Master.
R. W. Brother J. O. BROWN.
R. W. Brother WILLIAM LAING.
R. W. Brother JAFFRAY.
R. W. Brother HARROWAR.
R. W. Brother DAVIDSON.
R. W. Brother GEORGE CARPHIN, Grand Clerk, *p. t.*

COMPEARED Right Worshipful Brother WILLIAM LAING, Master of St. Andrew's Lodge, Edinburgh, aged 40 and upwards, married, who being solemnly sworn and examined, *ut ante*, depones, That he remembers of Brother Cunningham of Mary's Chapel stating, at the Quarterly Communication in November last, that he would call a meeting of that Lodge, to consider whether they should not secede, / in consequence of the Grand Lodge having approved of the report submitted to them by the Committee, who had been appointed to adjust the differences with the Mother Kilwinning Lodge in Ayrshire[xxxi]:[48] That the deponent recollects, that the Substitute Grand Master, who was then in the Chair, informed Brother Cunningham, if he made such an attempt, he would shut the doors of his Lodge. Upon the interrogatory of a Member of the Committee, Whether Brother Cunningham was reprimanded for holding such language in the Grand Lodge? depones, That he does not recollect That he was personally reprimanded. Interrogated by Brother Gibson, depones, That though he cannot absolutely say, yet, to the best of his recollection, the Substitute Grand Master announced to the brethren, though not from the Chair, in the Parliament-house, on the 30th November last, that the Grand Master Elect expected to receive deputations from the Masters and Wardens, on that evening, from all the Edinburgh

Lodges: That, when this was so intimated, the deponent believes the Grand Master Elect was himself in the Chair, and the Substitute on his left hand. Upon the interrogatory of a Member of the Committee, depones, That the deponent sat on the left hand of the Junior Grand Warden, at the foot of the Clerk's table, and did not see Brother Mitchell in the room, at the time the Substitute Grand Master gave the above intimation. All which is truth, as he shall answer to God.

COMPEARED Right Worshipful JAMES BARTRAM, Grand Clerk to the Grand Lodge of Scotland, aged 30 and upwards, married, who being solemnly sworn, &c. depones, That he recollects Brother Mitchell threatening, at the meeting of the Grand Lodge, held in the New Church Aisle, in the month of June last, to knock any brother down who should attempt to keep him down, or put him down; and when the deponent turned round, he saw him brandishing a pretty large stick in his hand: That the deponent acted as Grand Clerk at the Quarterly Communication in November last, and that a motion was made at that meeting, for expelling Brother Mitchell from the Grand Lodge: That afterwards the Substitute Grand Master ordered the Wardens to do their duty, by turning Brother Mitchell out of the Grand Lodge: That it appeared to the deponent, that this proposition to turn out Brother Mitchell met with the almost universal approbation of the Grand Lodge. Depones, That Brother Gibson rose, and recommended milder measures to be pursued; and recollects, in consequence of this interference of Brother Gibson's, / the motion to expell, and the order to turn out Brother Mitchell, were not carried into execution. Depones, That he recollects of Brother Cunningham, of Mary's Chapel, saying in the Grand Lodge, at the Quarterly Communication in November last, that the Lodge of Mary's Chapel would or might secede; upon which the Substitute Grand Master told him, if any thing of the kind was attempted, he would shut up their doors. Depones, That immediately after the election on St. Andrew's day last, the Substitute Grand Master said to the brethren, that the Grand Master Elect would expect to see a deputation, consisting of the Master and Wardens of all the Edinburgh Lodges, at Fortune's, in the course of that evening. Depones, That Brother Mitchell was present at that meeting; but whether Brother Mitchell was present at the time the intimation was made, the deponent cannot say: That the above intimation was made in consequence of a report of a Committee of the Grand Lodge, which had been approved of, at an adjourned meeting of the Grand Lodge, on the 23d of November last. Depones, That he remembers Brother Black, master of the Roman Eagle Lodge, requiring Brother Mitchell, at two different meetings of the Quarterly Communication of the Grand Lodge, or adjournments thereof, to remain in the Lodge, until a dispute between the two Lodges, regarding their night of meeting, should be settled: That notwithstanding this requisition, Brother Mitchell went away both nights. Depones,

That Brother Mitchell gave in no defence, nor made any answer to the complaint of Brother Black. Interrogated, by a Member of the Committee, depones, That he did not see any brother attempt to put down Brother Mitchell: That the deponent's back was to that part of the room where Brother Mitchell was sitting; and that on hearing the words used by Brother Mitchell, the deponent turned immediately round in astonishment, having never heard such language in a Mason Lodge before. Upon the interrogatory of Brother Mitchell, depones, That when the deponent turned round, he saw Brother Mitchell brandishing his stick, as in the face of the Chair; and the deponent being desired to say, by a Member of the Committee, Whether he really believes that Brother Mitchell was threatening the Chair when thus brandishing his stick? depones, That he appeared to do so, in defiance of the Chair. Interrogated by Brother Mitchell, If he recollects, when Brother Mitchell brandished his stick, that he had appealed twice to the Chair, to take notice of the conduct of a brother who was forcibly pulling and holding him down, and that if he got no redress, he must be / have as a gentleman, and not allow himself to be thus insulted? depones, That he does not. Being interrogated, depones, That it appears from the Minutes, that Brother Mitchell was not present at the meeting of the Committee of the Grand Lodge, held on the 9th of November, when it was agreed upon, that deputations of the Edinburgh Lodges would be received by the Grand Master Elect, at Fortune's on St. Andrew's day, nor at the Quarterly Communication of the 23d of the same month. Depones, That no cards of intimation to this effect were sent to the Masters of the Edinburgh Lodges, nor to any other brother; neither is it customary to do so, it being understood, that the brethren are to be entirely regulated by the resolutions of their Committee, after they are approved of at an adjourned Quarterly Communication. Depones, That it does not appear from the Minutes, that the Lodges of Canongate Kilwinning, Journeymen, Canongate and Leith, or Royal Arch, sent deputations to wait upon the Grand Master Elect, on the evening of St. Andrew's day. Depones, That there was no copy of the petition and complaint, at the instance of the Roman Eagle Lodge against the Caledonian Lodge, served upon Brother Mitchell by the deponent. Interrogated by a Member of the Committee, Whether Brother Cunningham expressed his own approbation of his Lodge seceding from the Grand Lodge? depones, That so the deponent understood him; and that so far as he recollects, Brother Cunningham was not reprimanded for holding such language, excepting the Substitute Grand Master saying, that he would shut the doors of Mary's Chapel Lodge, if any thing of the kind was attempted. All which is truth, as he shall answer to God.

Brother JAMES DUNDAS, accountant in Edinburgh, a member of the Caledonian Lodge, aged 30 and upwards, not married, who being solemnly sworn and examined, &c. depones, That he remembers of having heard of a meeting of the Caledonian Lodge having been held, to consider an interdict by the

Grand Lodge, against their meeting on the same night with the Roman Eagle Lodge: That he remembers of Brother Mitchell coming into the Excise-office on the morning immediately following the night on which the deponent understood that meeting to have taken place: That the deponent was in his office, and there were several persons present when Brother Mitchell came into him; and the deponent recollects to a certainty, that Brother James Hamilton, a preceding witness, was present upon this occasion: That a good deal of conversation took place between Brother Mitchell and / Brother Hamilton, upon the subject of what had passed in the Caledonian Lodge the preceding evening; and the deponent occasionally joined in the conversation. Depones, That Brother Mitchell mentioned, that the proceedings of the Grand Lodge, upon the subject of the interdict, had been violent, and (as the deponent also thinks) irregular: That Brother Hamilton seemed to differ from Brother Mitchell upon this point. Depones, That a good deal of conversation passed on the subject of the proposals made by Brother Mitchell the preceding evening; and Brother Hamilton advised an acquiescence in the resolutions of the Grand Lodge: That, from the tenor of the conversation, the deponent understood that Brother Hamilton disapproved of the propositions that had been made by Brother Mitchell: That Brother Mitchell expressed no regret for the proposals he had made the preceding evening, but, on the contrary, expressed his determination to persist in them: That the deponent understood, from what passed, that Brother Mitchell's object was a secession of the Caledonian Lodge from the Grand Lodge: That Brother Mitchell appeared to be much agitated, and used rather disrespectful language against the proceedings of the Grand Lodge, and against the Grand Lodge itself: That Brother Mitchell's expressions of disrespect against the Grand Lodge were accompanied with an opinion of the irregularity of their proceedings, and of their having been leveled personally against himself. Interrogated by Brother Mitchell, Whether the witness did not frequently hear him say, upon the above and other occasions, that it was his opinion, that the proceedings of the Grand Lodge, which he conceived to be leveled at himself personally, did proceed from his, Brother Mitchell's, having made a motion in the Grand Lodge to address his Majesty? depones in the affirmative. Depones, That the deponent was present at a meeting of a committee of the Caledonian Lodge, in Oman's Tavern, about the 18th or 19th of December last: That upon this occasion, perfect harmony seemed to prevail; and that the members present expressed, in their conversation, an unanimous determination to comply with the order of the Grand Lodge, by changing their night of meeting, though they did not fix upon the particular night: That Brother Mitchell was in the chair; and the deponent is perfectly certain, that he heard Brother Mitchell concur in the unanimous opinion of the meeting: That the deponent saw in the hands of Brother Alexander Clark, a preceding witness, what the deponent conceived to be the draft of the minutes of the committee, consisting of two or / three sheets of paper closely written, and which the deponent observed Brother Clark altering and correcting; but the deponent only heard a small part of them read: That the deponent was not a member of the committee, and did not, therefore, take any active part in adjusting the minutes, or in attending to their particular tenor: That Brother Hamilton was present at this meeting. Interrogated by Brother Gibson, depones, That after Brother Hamilton had been cited as a witness, the deponent and Brother Hamilton called upon Brother Mitchell, when a good deal of conversation and argument took place between them; Brother Hamilton stating, what he conceived to be, Brother Mitchell's proceedings, which are the subject of the present complaint, and regretting that his evidence would not be favourable to Brother Mitchell; expressing some reluctance to become an evidence against him, though he considered himself bound in honour to attend to the citation; upon which Brother Mitchell endeavoured to convince Brother Hamilton, that his ideas of these proceedings were incorrect: That Brother Mitchell did not express a wish, nor insinuate a desire, that Brother Hamilton should not appear as a witness, so far as the deponent observed, but appeared dissatisfied with the observations which fell from Brother Hamilton upon the subject of the complaint; and when they parted, Brother Mitchell appeared very much hurt; and when Brother Mitchell found that he could not convince Brother Hamilton of the accuracy of his, Brother Mitchell's statement, he appeared much irritated by the words he made use of. Depones, That the deponent understood that Brother Mitchell had called upon Brother Hamilton at the Excise-office that morning, which was the cause of Brother Hamilton calling at Brother Mitchell's house, as before deponed to: That the deponent had sent for Brother Mitchell twice that morning, upon revenue business, to the Excise-office. All which is truth, as he shall answer to God.

The Committee adjourn till to-morrow at one o'clock, and appoint the parties and witnesses them to attend in St. Luke's Lodge. /

At an ADJOURNED MEETING of the COMMITTEE of the GRAND LODGE of SCOTLAND, held in ST. LUKE'S LODGE-ROOM, the 6th day of February 1808,
PRESENT,

R. W. WILLIAM INGLIS, Esquire, Substitute Grand Master.
R. W. Brother LAING.
R. W. Brother JAFFRAY.
R. W. Brother HARROWAR.
R. W. Brother PROCTOR.
R. W. Brother BARTRAM, Grand Clerk.

COMPEARED the Right Worshipful Brother JOSEPH GILLON, Master of the Lodge St. David's, Edinburgh, who being solemnly sworn and examined, &c.

depones, That he was present at a meeting of between 20 and 30 members of the Grand Lodge, who were assembled in the Mary's Chapel Lodge-room, and, as the deponent thinks, on or about the 18th or 19th of June last; which meeting, the deponent knew, was called for the purpose of considering the measures to be taken at the meeting of the Grand Lodge, to be held the following evening, upon the question of scrutiny: That Brothers Mitchell, Brown, of Mary's Chapel, and Douglas, of the Operative Lodge, Dunkeld, were amongst those present upon this occasion: That after the proper business of the evening was over, Brother Mitchell read to the meeting, from, what the deponent understood to be a proof copy, a printed letter, to which his name was annexed as master of the Caledonian Lodge; and a printed letter being shown, the deponent, to the best of his recollection, after having read part of it, he thinks it is a copy of the same pamphlet, as the deponent recognizes several passages in the pamphlet now shown him, which he remembers to be contained in the pamphlet read by Brother Mitchell: That the deponent, before this meeting, saw a copy of the pamphlet in Brother Mitchell's house, and in his own hands, which he read to the deponent, and which, he had no doubt, was the same from which Brother Mitchell read at the said meeting: That the deponent never saw till now any other copy of the pamphlet: That the deponent was in the Parliament-house on St. Andrew's day last, and remembers distinctly, that the Substitute Grand Master intimated, on two different occasions, to / the Master and Wardens present, that the Grand Master Elect would expect deputations of Masters and Wardens of all the Edinburgh Lodges, to wait upon him, at Fortune's, in the course of the evening. Interrogated, If there was any agreement among the masters of any of the Edinburgh Lodges, not to wait upon the Grand Master Elect that evening? depones, That he had several conversations with Brother Mitchell of a loose nature, and, as he thinks, upon the street, relative to their not attending the Grand Master on the evening of St. Andrew's day: That these conversations arose from, what he conceived to be, the politics of the Grand Lodge, and took place before the date of the Quarterly Communication in November, when the Grand Officers were proposed: That from these conversations he did not think that Brother Mitchell had formed the determined resolution not to wait upon the Grand Master Elect that evening, but that he might think better of it: That he understood Brother Mitchell, from these conversations, had formed the resolution of retiring from masonry altogether, and giving up the chair of the Caledonian Lodge. Interrogated, If the witness said to any person whatever, that an agreement had been made between him, Brother Mitchell, Brother Lawson of the Cannongate Kilwinning, Brother Brown of Mary's Chapel, or any of them, not to wait upon the Grand Master Elect on the evening of St. Andrew's day, and what reason the witness assigned for his departing from the agreement he had made? depones, That the deponent does not recollect of having mentioned to any person, that such an agreement had been entered into, nor can he believe, that he ever held such a conversation; because at no time, did he conceive himself to be a party to any agreement of the fort, though the deponent may have expressed to different persons, that he once had some intention of not attending the Grand Master Elect; but he had afterwards altered his determination; but whether that intention, and his change of resolution, were mentioned at the same time, the deponent does not remember. Interrogated, as the deponent has stated, that there was no compact among the brethren before mentioned not to wait upon the Grand Master Elect, so far as the deponent knew, he is requested to state what was the impression upon his mind, Whether these brethren, as masters of the Lodges over which they presided, were or were not to wait upon the Grand Master Elect that evening? depones, That he thought it highly probable that the masters of the Mary's Chapel Lodge and the Caledonian Lodge would not attend the Grand Master upon that occasion; and that this opinion / was occasioned chiefly by the apparent irritation produced by some previous discussions in the Grand Lodge; and also, he conceived that Brother Mitchell might be further induced to absent himself from waiting upon the Grand Master Elect, in order to show his disapprobation of the politics of the Grand Master Elect; and that it is most likely the deponent had conversations with Brother Mitchell himself to this effect, though the deponent cannot positively swear to any particular conversation. Interrogated, If the deponent recollects of coming to Brother Gibson in the Parliament-house, after the complaint, but before the answer was given in, and if so, he was desired to state what passed upon that occasion? depones, That in consequence, partly of a conversation which he had with a brother, whose name he does not remember, and partly from his own wish to have matters accommodated between Brothers Gibson and Mitchell, without bringing the complaint to a decision, he went up, unsolicited, to Brother Gibson in the Outer-house, and mentioned to him his wish that such an accommodation might be effected; and further, he stated, that he the deponent, would gladly embrace any opportunity of proposing to Brother Mitchell some reasonable terms of adjustment, which he thought there was a great probability of Brother Mitchell receiving favourably, on account of his previous friendship and intimacy with the deponent: That upon this occasion, Brother Gibson expressed himself most distinctly, as having no personal ill-will to Brother Mitchell; and that he had no objection to have the matter settled by any explanation from the other party, by which the authority and respectability of the Grand Lodge should be recognized, and an assurance given that no such practices, as those complained of, should be attempted in future; but notwithstanding of what had thus passed, the deponent had no communication with Brother Mitchell on the subject, which he now most sincerely regrets. Depones, That when the Substitute Grand Master gave the intimations in the Parliament-house, with regard to deputations, before deponed to, the deponent thinks, that the one was given immediately after the other, to make it more impressive, as the deponent conceived; and thinks that these intimations closed the proceedings of the Grand Lodge in the Inner-house Depones, That while the business was going forward upon that occasion, he noticed Brother Mitchell oftener than once in the room; but he does not remember to have seen him at the particular time when these notices were given. Interrogated by Dr. Mitchell, depones, That the deponent acted in concert with Brother Mitchell / in calling the meeting in Mary's Chapel, on the night previous to the scrutiny in the Grand Lodge. Interrogated, Whether he expressed his approbation of the pamphlet when it was shown the deponent in Brother Mitchell's house? depones, That he thinks he remarked to Brother Mitchell on that occasion, that the pamphlet contained several passages which appeared to be too strong; but that so far as it stated the result of the vote, as reported by the Grand Clerk, on the 4th of May, and the different result which had been mentioned by other brethren, who were said to have taken down the votes as they were given, Brother Mitchell's statement appeared to be correct; and that the deponent felt it the less necessary to go into particulars, as he distinctly understood that the pamphlet, when transmitted, was meant to be attested by some other masters of Lodges, who would of course have an opportunity of examining the pamphlet before it was circulated: That after the meeting of the Grand Lodge which negatived the scrutiny, the deponent never heard the pamphlet mentioned with any view of being published. Depones, That the impression made upon the deponent's mind at the time the said pamphlet was read to him, was, that the general statement of the *res gesta*[49] of the meeting of the 4th of May was correct, so far as therein stated. Depones, That the deponent took no note himself of the state of the vote, and can only speak to its accuracy from the information he received from the brethren who took down the votes upon that occasion. Depones, That during the whole time that the deponent was present at the meeting in Mary's Chapel, above deponed to, the conduct of Brother Mitchell, as to his proceedings relative to the address, was unanimously approved of: That the deponent has the most perfect conviction, that this meeting was composed of brethren friendly to the address, and, of course, to the scrutiny. Depones, That the deponent was present, and acted as one of the Grand Wardens, at the Quarterly Communication in November last; and that he recollects that, upon that occasion, a motion was made and seconded, for expelling Brother Mitchell, which motion was followed by a very loud, and, as it appeared to the deponent, pretty general acclamation, though there might be some hissing, as the deponent remembers there was a good deal of hissing at different periods in the evening. Interrogated, If he recollects, in some of the conversations that he had with Brother Mitchell, expressing, in common with Brother Mitchell, his disgust at the proceedings of the Grand Lodge,

and declaring his determination to resign the chair of the St. David's Lodge, /
and never set foot in a Mason Lodge again? depones, That the deponent has had
many confidential conversations with Brother Mitchell, upon Masonic subjects,
and particularly upon the proceedings of the Grand Lodge, and very probably
he did express himself to the purpose mentioned in the question, as he certainly
had an intention to withdraw himself from Masonry, and all its branches; but he
rather thinks, that, subsequently to the meeting at which the scrutiny was negatived, his conversations with Brother Mitchell have been very unfrequent.
Depones, upon the interrogatory of Brother Gibson, That, at the Quarterly
Communication in November, an order was given from the Chair, to the Wardens to do their duty, by turning Brother Mitchell out of the room, for improper
behaviour: That this order was given without any vote of the Grand Lodge being
previously asked, and seemed to meet with the approbation of the majority of
the meeting: That the deponent had his baton in his hand, to do his duty, by
turning Brother Mitchell out of the room, but was relieved from the painful
necessity of doing so, by a conciliatory speech from Brother Gibson, entreating
that matters might not be carried to extremities, in the hopes that nothing of the
kind would again occur; in which recommendation of Brother Gibson the
Grand Lodge acquiesced. Interrogated by Brother Mitchell, depones, That he
does not recollect of any immediate cause for the motion of expulsion; but
remembers that the proposition for turning Brother Mitchell out of the Lodge,
arose from some improper expressions he had made use of at the time, and thinks
that these expressions tended to a charge against the Grand Lodge of twisting
their own laws to suit particular purposes, or somewhat to that effect. Interrogated, If, in the course of that evening, and previous to the motion for expulsion,
he saw any improper conduct in Brother Mitchell meriting such a motion?
depones, That he conceived that Brother Mitchell, who did not sit near him, was
a good deal irritated, and, sometimes, did not appear to treat the Grand Lodge
with great respect; although it did appear to the deponent, that turning Brother
Mitchell out of the room was a strong measure; and that there were other brethren who differed in opinion with Brother Mitchell, who were equally warm,
though they used no disrespectful language to the Grand Lodge. Depones, That
he does not recollect of having heard Brother Mitchell make use of any other
offensive language, except that above deponed to, of twisting the laws; though,
in general, he remembers that many of the addresses by Brother Mitchell to the
Lodge, / met with a good deal of disapprobation from the brethren. Interrogated, If he recollects when Brother Mitchell used the expression about twisting
the laws, he was desired by the chair to explain himself, and, when he was
attempting to do so, the Substitute Grand Master prevented him, by ordering
the Wardens to do their duty, and turn him out?[50] depones, That, upon the occasion alluded to, the Substitute Grand Master demanded of Brother Mitchell, in

an authoritative tone, what meaning he affixed to the word twist? and he has also some recollection, that Brother Mitchell was upon his legs to say something, but immediately there was a great acclamation, and some confusion among the brethren, which prevented the deponent from noticing what fell from Brother Mitchell, or whether he said any thing at all. Depones, That, upon one occasion, during that evening on which it had been proposed that Brother Mitchell should be turned out, there was a pretty general appearance of assent, on the part of the meeting, to that proposal; and it certainly did strike the deponent at the time, that the Substitute Grand Master, presuming the acquiescence to be general, had, without a vote, given orders to the Wardens to do their duty. Depones, That the Grand Wardens were only once ordered to do this, and at the above time. Interrogated by Brother Mitchell, If it appeared to the witness, that there was a good deal of party-spirit amongst the brethren present at that Quarterly Communication in November? depones, That ever since the Quarterly Communication in May, and even upon the occasion alluded to in the question, he has had occasion to remark indications of party-spirit but too frequently; and the deponent regrets, that any measure in which he has had a share, may, however unintentionally, have been instrumental in producing that effect: That this party-spirit seemed to pervade most of the Grand Lodge. All which is truth, as the deponent shall answer to God. /

At an ADJOURNED MEETING of the COMMITTEE of the GRAND LODGE, held in ST. LUKE's LODGE-ROOM, the 10th February 1808,
PRESENT,

R. W. WILLIAM INGLIS, Esquire, Substitute Grand Master.
R. W. Brother A. GIBSON HUNTER.
R. W. Brother MᶜNAB.
R. W. Brother JAFFRAY.
R. W. Brother BARTRAM, Grand Clerk.

COMPEARED Right Worshipful Brother ALEXANDER JAFFRAY, late Master of the Canongate Kilwinning Lodge, aged 30 and upwards, married, who, being solemnly sworn and examined, &c. depones, That he does not know that there was any understanding amongst any of the masters of the Edinburgh Lodges, that they should not attend the Grand Master on the evening of St. Andrew's day last. Depones, That to the deponent's best recollection, no body mentioned to the deponent, previous to that day, that such understanding did exist. Depones, That, to the best of his recollection, he did not mention to any person that such an understanding did exist. Interrogated, If he knows there was any intention in any of the masters of the Edinburgh Lodges to absent themselves on that occasion? depones, That he knows one master who previously expressed such determination; and that that master did not attend the Grand Master. Depones, that that master was not Brother Mitchell, but the deponent declines to mention his name. Depones, That it is very probable he expressed his surprize that Brother Gillon attended the Grand Master, considering the part he had taken in the address, which, the deponent has been told, originated with Brother Gillon. Depones further, That he was told by some person, whom the deponent, at this distance of time, cannot recollect, that Brother Gillon, at one time, did not intend to wait upon the Grand Master on the evening alluded to. Interrogated by Brother Mitchell, depones, That he was present at a meeting of the Grand Lodge, when the question of scrutiny was under their consideration. Interrogated, If he recollects what passed on the occasion of Brother Mitchell's raising his stick, at that meeting? depones, That / he recollects of Brother Mitchell rising to address the Chair upon some subject or other, when he observed a brother behind him, who endeavoured to put him down, by pulling him by the coat; on which brother Mitchell turned about, and, upon that occasion, as the deponent thinks, said, that if he attempted to do so again, he would knock him down. Depones, That Brother Mitchell complained to the Chair of the usage he had received; and, about this time, there was a great tumult in the Grand Lodge. Interrogated, Whether the Chair reprimanded the brother whom Brother Mitchell had complained of, or paid any attention to this complaint of Brother Mitchell's? depones, That the deponent has no recollection of the Right Worshipful Master reprimanding the brother alluded to: That, as already deponed to, the tumult in the Grand Lodge was very great at this time, and the Right Worshipful Master endeavoured to enforce, by the mallet,[51] peace and order; and it was not till Brother Gibson began to speak, that order was restored. Interrogated, If he recollects whether Brother Gibson took any notice of the conduct of this brother, in pulling and holding down Brother Mitchell; and whether he does not recollect that, upon the occasion of Brother Mitchell's holding up his stick, he, Brother Gibson, did not rise to move some censure or reprimand against Brother Mitchell from the Chair? depones, That he has no recollection of Brother Gibson disapproving of the conduct of the person alluded to; but he recollects of Brother Gibson finding great fault with the language used by Brother Mitchell, as unbecoming and improper in the Grand Lodge: That Brother Gibson said something on the occasion, but the deponent cannot say, that the import of it was, that Brother Mitchell should be censured from the Chair. Interrogated, If, when Brother Mitchell so held up his stick, he seemed to do so in defiance of, or in the way of, threatening the Chair? depones, That such an idea never entered into the deponent's mind, nor was he anyways impressed that such was Brother Mitchell's meaning. Interrogated by Brother Gibson, depones, That when Brother Mitchell turned round from the brother who had been pulling him down, to address the Right Worshipful Master, as above deponed to, he had his stick a little elevated, but not in a threatening posture. Interrogated, If Brother Mitchell addressed the Chair in a calm and respectful manner? depones, That he was not calm, but, on the contrary, very much agitated; and the deponent was not impressed with the idea that Brother Mitchell, on this occasion, either expressed or conducted himself in a way conveying disrespect / to the Chair. Interrogated, If he heard Brother Mitchell say, if he got no protection from the Chair, he would take redress at his own hands, by knocking down any person who might interfere with him? depones, That the deponent, as he has already sworn, perfectly recollects of Brother Mitchell having said, that he would knock down the brother, if he attempted to do so again; but whether this was before or after Brother Mitchell addressed the Chair, the deponent cannot say, but rather thinks it was before, and at the time formerly deponed to. Depones, That he heard that Brother Mitchell was not to attend the Grand Master on St. Andrew's day last, but does not recollect who gave him that information, nor that any special reason was assigned for his not being to do so. Depones, That, in the deponent's opinion, the tumult above deponed to proceeded from the brother attempting forcibly to pull down Brother Mitchell, on the one hand, and his threat, on the other,; although, had Brother Mitchell not made use of the words above deponed to, the deponent does not think that such a tumult would have taken place. All which is truth, as he shall answer to God.

COMPEARED WILLIAM SUTHERLAND, pressman to Thomas Oliver, printer in Edinburgh, aged 30 and upwards, widower, who being solemnly sworn and examined, &c. depones, That he remembers of his master, Mr. Oliver, printing a pamphlet regarding Masonry, for Brother Mitchell, but the deponent never read it: That the pamphlet on the table appears to be the same, though the deponent thinks it is printed on coarser paper. Depones, That, to the best of the deponent's knowledge, about 20 or 22 copies were printed, and thrown off, at one time, which were cut and stitched, and carried into his master's room, and does not know what became of them. Interrogated, If any other person got copies but Brother Mitchell? depones, That Brother Black, of the Roman Eagle, was attending the deponent's wife, as a surgeon, and the deponent had occasion to go to his shop for some medicines, and Brother Black asked the deponent if his master was printing any paper regarding any of the Lodges in Edinburgh: That the deponent said, it was the last thing he had been doing; and upon Brother Black asking if he had any spoiled sheet of the paper, the deponent, who had some of the make-ready copies in his pocket, gave them to Brother Black; and the deponent thinks, to the best of his judgment, that the copy on the table is one of them. Depones, That Brother Black made use of no improper means to get hold of the / copies. Depones, That Brother Mitchell afterwards learned, that Brother Black had got some of the copies from the deponent: That Brother Mitchell sent for the deponent to his house, and the deponent having gone with Mr. Boyd, the partner of Mr. Oliver, Brother

Mitchell abused the deponent, insisting that Brother Black had bribed him to get the copies; and when the deponent positively denied this, Brother Mitchell called the deponent a thief and scoundrel, and many such names. Depones, That the types had stood for a long time, but the deponent does not know of any more copies of the pamphlet being thrown off than those above deponed to. Depones, That the proof-copies were over and above the 20 or 22 copies above deponed to, given to his master. Interrogated by a Member of the Committee, depones, That in throwing off make-ready impressions, it is absolutely necessary to print both sides of the leaf. Upon the interrogatory of Brother Mitchell, depones, That till the night already deponed to, when the deponent delivered to Brother Black the printed sheets of the pamphlet before-mentioned, he never had any conversation whatever with him upon the subject, nor had he any conversation with any other person, except with the people of the printing-office: That the deponent, previous to putting the copies in question into his pocket, wisped them together, at which time they were damp. Depones, That the pressmen are entitled to make use of the make-ready copies, and they generally take them for lighting their fires, or any other purpose. All which is truth, as he shall answer to God.

COMPEARED Brother JAMES YOUNG, of the Caledonian Lodge, aged 20 and upwards, unmarried, who being solemnly sworn and interrogated, &c. depones, That he recollects of being present at a meeting of a committee of the Caledonian Lodge, held, as he thinks, on the 23d of November last, for the purpose of considering an order of the Grand Lodge, in regard to a dispute between the Caledonian Lodge and Roman Eagle Lodge, about the night of their meeting: That Brother Mitchell was in the chair, and explained the purpose of their meeting. Depones, That Brother Mitchell proposed that the Lodge should, notwithstanding the order of the Grand Lodge, adhere to their former day of meeting; and that it would be humiliating to the spirit of Caledonians to submit to the Roman Eagle Lodge: That Brother Hodgson upon this stated, that, in this business, the Lodge had now to do with the Grand Lodge, and not with the Roman Eagle Lodge: That the consequences of disobeying / the order of the Grand Lodge might be, that the Grand Lodge might shut the door of the Caledonian Lodge, and take their charter from them: That upon this, Brother Mitchell observed, that the Caledonian Lodge could meet independently of the Grand Lodge: That Brother Mitchell farther mentioned, that the Ayr Kilwinning Lodge had formerly seceded from, and had granted charters independent of the Grand Lodge; and that the Canongate Kilwinning Lodge was at that moment in a state of secession: That something was said about the Lodge of Mary's Chapel, but he does not precisely recollect what it was. Depones, That, in his opinion, Brother Mitchell wished the Caledonian Lodge to secede from the Grand Lodge, at least so the deponent concluded, from the expressions before deponed to. Interrogated by Brother Mitchell, depones, That several of the members, but the number he cannot depone to, agreed with Brother Mitchell in opinion, that they should continue their meetings on the fourth Friday, as formerly, notwithstanding the order of the Grand Lodge. Interrogated, If it appeared to the deponent to be a pretty general idea prevailing amongst the members present, that the Caledonian Lodge had been deprived of their night of meeting, in consequence of party-motives in the Grand Lodge, chiefly directed against Brother Mitchell? depones, That he cannot say what might be the general opinion, but certainly he, the deponent, did not think so: That the deponent does not recollect that any brother expressed himself to that effect. Depones, That previous to Brother Hodgson delivering his sentiments, he collected the opinions of some of the brethren round him, and the deponent sat near Brother Hodgson during the evening. Depones, That Brother Mitchell made no motion for a secession of the Caledonian Lodge from the Grand Lodge, or for continuing its meetings on the fourth Friday; but the matter was referred to a sub-committee. Interrogated by Brother Gibson, depones, That he does not recollect that Brother Mitchell spoke with any degree of acrimony against the Grand Lodge: That he threatened to leave the chair of the Caledonian Lodge, if the measure he recommended of continuing to meet on the fourth Friday, was not adopted. All which is truth, as he shall answer to God. /

At an ADJOURNED COMMITTEE of the GRAND LODGE, held this 11th February, 1808,
PRESENT,

R. W. WM. INGLIS, Esquire, Substitute Grand Master.
R. W. Os. BROWN.
R. W. Brother MᶜNAB.
R. W. Brother HUNTER.
R. W. Brother BARTRAM, Grand Clerk.

COMPEARED the Right Worshipful JOHN BROWN, Master of Mary's Chapel Lodge, aged 25 years and upwards, unmarried, who being solemnly sworn and examined, &c. depones, That he had no conversation with any of the masters of the Edinburgh Lodges, previous to St. Andrew's day, about not attending the Grand Master on that occasion; and depones, That he does not recollect of having had any particular conversation since that day with Brother Mitchell, or any of the other of the masters of the Edinburgh Lodges, on that subject. Depones, That he does not know that such was the intention of any of the masters of Edinburgh Lodges; at least, the deponent never heard so officially, though he heard a rumour previous to St. Andrew's day, that the Lodges of Canongate Kilwinning, and the Caledonian Lodge, were not to attend the Grand Master in the evening. Depones, That he does not recollect that any particular reason was specified, for the said Lodges not attending. Depones, That the deponent himself had resolved not to attend in the evening; because it had been intimated to him, that the deputation from the Lodges were to consist of the masters and wardens; and he, the deponent, was of opinion, that, in the absence of these officers, the Lodges could not continue to hold their meetings: That the deponent did accordingly state this to the Lodge of Mary's Chapel, over which he presides, and he was directed by a majority of his brethren to visit the Grand Master, which he thought it his duty to do, as his opinion was thus over-ruled: That one of the deponent's wardens, Brother Weir, attended him upon this occasion, and if he recollects right, Brother Cunningham, the other warden, refused to accompany him: That the order of the Lodge was, that the deponent, as master, and both the wardens, should visit the Grand Master. Depones, That he was present at a meeting in Mary's Chapel Lodge-room, of brethren who were friendly to the scrutiny; / and recollects perfectly of Brother Mitchell having read at that meeting a printed pamphlet; and, to the best of the deponent's knowledge and belief, the pamphlet now shown him is a copy of that so read by Brother Mitchell. Interrogated, If he had any conversation with Brother Mitchell upon the subject of seceding from the Grand Lodge? depones, That he had no official communication with him, as master of a Lodge, upon this subject; but he had conversations with him regarding it, though the deponent conceived, from Brother Mitchell's manner of expression, that he was not serious. Depones, That he does not remember of any particular expression which induced the deponent to be of this opinion, except that, in general, he talked in a laughing manner, that if the Grand Lodge continued to act as they had done, he would consider of seceding. Being interrogated, What the deponent said in answer? depones, and declines answering the question, as, if he were to state what had passed, he might criminate[52] himself, and subject himself to a petition and complaint. Interrogated by Brother Mitchell, depones, That he was one of those who took down the state of the vote upon the proposition for an address, and believes he did so with accuracy: That, so far as he recollects, there were 28 voted for the address, and 25 against it, according to the deponent's statement: That Brother Donald Horne, of the Caledonian Lodge, and Brother Mitchell, took down statements also of the vote; and it appeared to the deponent, that Brother Mitchell was anxious to have the votes correctly taken down; and that, in particular, he heard Brother Mitchell frequently call out to the brethren to repeat their votes, when they were not distinctly heard: That the deponent thinks, that the states of the votes taken by the brethren, before deponed to, tallied with each other. Depones, That he was a good deal surprized when he heard it announced by the Grand Clerk, that the address was negatived: That he acted as one of the Grand Wardens on that night. Interrogated, If he assisted in closing the Lodge? depones, and declines to answer that question. Depones, That, after the deponent left the Warden's chair, no other brother supplied his place. Interrogated, If he saw the

Lodge regularly shut? depones, and declines to answer the question. Depones, That he heard Brother Mitchell appeal to the Chair, and demand a scrutiny, though the noise and confusion were so great, that many things past which he could not hear. Depones, That he heard several other brethren calling out for a scrutiny. Depones, That the Substitute Grand Master peremptorily refused to listen to this demand, and insisted, that the Lodge / should be closed. Depones, That he was in the chair at the meeting before deponed to, which took place in Mary's Chapel Lodge-room. Depones, That the pamphlet before alluded to, when read by Brother Mitchell, seemed to meet with the general approbation of those present; and it appeared to the deponent himself, that the pamphlet contained a fair account of the proceedings which took place in the Grand Lodge. Interrogated, Whether he would have had any objection to have put his name to that pamphlet, and attested the facts it contained? depones, That, although he would have had no objections to have attested the facts, he would have stated the facts in a different form. And all this is truth, as he shall answer to God.

COMPEARED THOMAS OLIVER, Right Worshipful Master of the Royal Arch, aged 30 years and upwards, unmarried, who being solemnly sworn and examined, &c. depones, That he was employed by Brother Mitchell to print the pamphlet, of which a copy is now shown to him, and, to the best of his knowledge, Brother Mitchell got about 20 copies of it. Interrogated by Brother Mitchell, depones, That the pamphlet stood long in the types; he thinks about two or three months: That at first Brother Mitchell only received one or two proof copies, but not more: That the deponent having sent over to Brother Mitchell, at the distance from this time of about two or three months, to know what was to be done with the pamphlet, Brother Mitchell returned for answer, that he only wished a few copies to be thrown off to keep by him, or for his friends, but he did not wish it to be made public. Depones, That he believes Brother Mitchell, in return to the deponent's message, added, that if the types were still standing, he would wish a few copies, as before deponed to, from which the deponent conceived, that Brother Mitchell had not been aware of the types being still standing, till the message was sent him by the deponent. Depones, That he received applications from other persons than Brother Mitchell for copies of this pamphlet: That about a dozen or twenty persons applied for copies; and, in particular, Brother Thomson, one of the wardens of the Lodge of St. Luke, made repeated applications: That the deponent refused to comply with these applications, both because it is not his practice to give copies of a publication in this manner, and that he is certain that Brother Mitchell, upon returning the second proof of the pamphlet, prohibited the deponent from giving any copies out of the office, or from / showing the pamphlet to any person whatever. Depones, That Brother Thomson came into the deponent's office, and put into his hands a copy of the pamphlet, upon which the deponent challenged Sutherland, his pressman, for having given out copies; and he acknowledged that he had given some made-ready sheets to Brother Black, but could not say whether there were one, two, or more copies: That the deponent rather thinks Brother Mitchell had at this time received his copies of the pamphlet. Depones, That Sutherland seemed to admit, that the copy in possession of Brother Thomson had been one of those given to Brother Black, and that it did not appear to the deponent to be a make-ready copy, though it might be so. And all this is truth, as the deponent shall answer to God.

Adjourned Quarterly Communication of Grand Lodge, February 15, 1808.

The Substitute Grand Master reported, that the Committee appointed to take the proof in the question between Brother Gibson and Brother Mitchell, had not yet concluded the same: he therefore proposed, and it was unanimously agreed to, that this meeting be adjourned to this day three weeks, at 6 o'clock in the evening, to receive the final report of the Committee, and to decide upon the complaint and defence: that the powers formerly granted to that Committee be continued; and that the quorum of said Committee be reduced to three, the Substitute Grand Master being one, instead of five, as formerly.

It was likewise unanimously agreed to, that at next adjourned meeting, the standing order of the Grand Lodge be strictly enforced, with regard to the exclusion of all who are not members of the Grand Lodge, and the Substitute Grand Master is requested to issue and carry the necessary orders for that purpose into effect.

It was farther unanimously resolved upon, that as the proceedings in Brother Gibson's complaint, and the proof, are ordered to be printed, and distributed among the members, the reading of the said procedure and proof, by the Grand Clerk, shall be dispensed with at the said meeting, as being rendered unnecessary from the above order; and that three copies of the printed procedure and proof shall be sent to the masters of Edinburgh Lodges, and proxy-masters, for the use of themselves and wardens.

(Signed) William Inglis, S. G. M. /

Edinburgh, 17th February 1808.

PRESENT,

R. W. Brother Inglis, Esquire, Substitute Grand Master.
R. W. Brother William Laing.
R. W. Brother Gibson Hunter.
R. W. Brother Thomas Millar.
R. W. Grand Secretary.
R. W. Grand Clerk.

COMPEARED the Right Worshipful JOHN SLATER, Master of St. James's Lodge, aged 27 years, married, who being solemnly sworn and examined, &c. depones, That he was at the meeting of the Grand Lodge at which Brother Mitchell proposed an address to his Majesty, and that the deponent voted for the address. Depones, That when the Grand Clerk marked the votes, the deponent was standing nearly behind him, and observed, with as much attention as he could, how every member voted, and how every vote was marked by the Grand Clerk. Depones, That, in his opinion, the Grand Clerk marked the votes very correctly; and depones, That he observed the Grand Clerk count the votes that were marked, and, in his opinion, he made a faithful report of the numbers on both sides. Depones, That Brother Mitchell called on the deponent twice, to speak to him on the subject of a demand for a scrutiny; and, on both occasions, the deponent told Brother Mitchell, that, in his opinion, the conduct of the Grand Clerk had been perfectly fair. Depones, That the deponent also told Brother Mitchell, that, in his opinion, he, Brother Mitchell, had omitted to take down, in his state of the vote, three members of the Grand Lodge, whom the deponent mentioned as having been the last to give their votes against the address; and at the time they gave their votes there was a good deal of noise in the Lodge: That the deponent recollects, that the name of one of these brethren was Brother Dobson. Depones, That from these brethren being late of coming in, their names were not in the original sederunt,[53] but they came forward after the calling of the roll, and gave in their names, and voted against the address. Interrogated by Brother Mitchell, depones, That he did not himself count / the markings of the state of the vote which had been made by the Grand Clerk; but, from what he saw, he thought that the Grand Clerk himself did so accurately. Interrogated, Whether, at the time Brother Mitchell had an interview with the deponent, he did not express himself, that it was highly proper a scrutiny should be made into the votes for and against the address? depones, That he does not think that he expressed himself to this effect, and inclines the rather to be of this belief, that he perfectly remembers endeavouring to convince Brother Mitchell, that the state of the votes was accurately reported. Depones, That he attended the meeting of the Grand Lodge, upon the question of scrutiny, when he, the deponent, voted against the scrutiny; because he was satisfied from what he had seen, that the votes for and against the address had been fairly taken down, and reported by the Grand Clerk. Interrogated by Brother Mitchell, Whether, after he, the deponent, had voted in favour of the address, any person had disapproved of his conduct in so doing?

Though the Committee, after deliberation, and the removal of the witness, were unanimously of opinion, that the question is irrelevant; yet, as Brother Mitchell insists on the question being put, they allow it to be done, understanding that it is not to form a precedent in the future proceedings.

During the discussion upon the preceding question, Brother Mitchell accused the members of the Committee present, of gross partiality, of being friends of Brother Gibson, and said, that they would not allow questions to be put that tended to do him justice; and, after some altercation, Brother Mitchell left the room, after the Substitute Grand Master had notified to him, that the Committee must proceed in the exercise of the duty imposed upon them by the Grand Lodge, whether Brother Mitchell remained or not; and upon going away, Brother Mitchell said, that the Committee might do as they pleased.

And the witness being called in, and the question being put, depones, That it is very probable, that some person among his acquaintances might have done so, in a laughing manner; and to the best of the deponent's recollection, the person who did so was Brother Hamilton Dunn. Interrogated by the Committee, If there was any influence used with him in any of the proceedings / with regard to the address, or the scrutiny, or any after proceedings? depones, That previous to the meeting at which the address was moved, Brother Mitchell called upon the deponent repeatedly, and pressed him to support the address; when the deponent objected to the measure, as being of a political nature, and therefore inconsistent with the principles of masonry; but the deponent, on the night that the address was moved, agreed to give his vote in its favour, should it be allowed to be put to the vote; and, with the exception of Brother Mitchell's interference with him as before deponed to, no influence whatever was used, or attempted to be used, with the deponent.

And all this is truth, as the deponent shall answer to God.

COMPEARED GEORGE BOYD, of the Roman Eagle Lodge, aged 24 years, unmarried, who being solemnly sworn and examined, &c. depones, That he is a partner of Brother Oliver's, a preceding witness, and recollects that they were employed to print a pamphlet by Brother Mitchell; and depones, That he thinks the copy now shown to him is the same that was printed by them. Depones, That Brother Mitchell got 20 or 21 copies of the pamphlet. Depones, That it was discovered that Brother Black, of the Roman Eagle, had got a copy or copies of the pamphlet; and after inquiring minutely into the business, the deponent discovered that William Sutherland, one of his pressmen, had called upon Brother Black for medicines to his wife, and having some sheets of the proof copies in his pocket, had laid them down on Brother Black's counter. Depones, That Brother Mitchell requested the deponent to bring Robert Sutherland over to his house, that he might discover whether Brother Black had employed him to get the pamphlet: That Sutherland denied that Brother Black had employed him to procure the pamphlet, and told him of his having given the sheets before deponed to, upon his having called upon Brother Black for medicines, as before mentioned. And all this is truth, as the deponent shall answer to God.

Brother Gibson stated, that at present he had no intention of examining any other witness, but Brother Lawson, master of the Canongate Kilwinning; and that he should not in future examine any other witness, without giving in a condescendence of his name, and of the facts on which he meant to examine him, and he now craved that the Committee would order Brother Mitchell to proceed with his proof. /

The Committee appoint Brother Mitchell, peremptorily, to proceed with his proof on Friday next, the 19th current, at one o'clock, in St. Luke's Lodge-room, reserving to Brother Gibson to examine Brother Lawson, and reserving to the future consideration of the Committee, whether Brother Gibson shall be allowed to examine any other witnesses, upon previously giving in a condescendence in the terms before mentioned; and order intimation of this appointment to be given by the Grand Clerk to Brother Mitchell; and grant warrant for summoning such witnesses as Brother Mitchell shall require, and of whom he shall give in a list to the Grand Clerk; and further, order the Tyler to intimate to the rest of the brethren the next sederunt of the Committee.

(Signed) WILLIAM INGLIS, P. /

BROTHER MITCHELL's PROOF.
EDINBURGH, 19th February 1808.

PRESENT,

R.W. WILLIAM INGLIS, Esquire, Substitute Grand Master.
R.W. Brother PROCTOR.
R.W. Brother GIBSON HUNTER.
R.W. Brother DAVIDSON.
R.W. Brother LAWSON.
R.W. Brother Os. BROWN.
R.W. Brother JAFFRAY.
R.W. Brother HARROWAR.
R.W. Brother BARTRAM, Grand Clerk.

Right Worshipful Brother MITCHELL enters upon the examination of the witnesses he means to bring forward in exculpation, under the solemn protestation, that Brother Gibson shall not be allowed to adduce any additional proof, such a practice being quite contrary to common usage, and highly detrimental to Brother Mitchell's cause. The Right Worshipful Brother Lawson, one of Brother Gibson's witnesses, is excepted.

COMPEARED Brother SAMUEL CUNNINGHAM, of the Lodge of Mary's Chapel, who being solemnly sworn and examined, &c. aged 30 and upwards, married, depones, That he was present at the Quarterly Communication in May last, when Brother Mitchell brought forward a motion for an address to his

Majesty, which was objected to by the Substitute Grand Master in the Chair, on
the ground of its being unmasonic: That he voted in favour of the address, and
soon after left the room: That previous to his leaving the room, there might have
been about 20 or 30 votes given. Depones, That he was present at the Quarterly
Communication in November last; and that he heard Brother Gibson rise, and,
in the course of his speech, throw out some severe reflections upon the conduct of Brother Mitchell; and recollects, in particular, of Brother Gibson having
made use of / this expression, That he presumed Brother Mitchell was desirous
of becoming the Buonaparte[54] of all the Lodges, or words to that effect; and
remembers, and as he thinks, in a subsequent speech, when objecting to a proxy-
commission presented in favour of Brother Mitchell, that he, Brother Gibson,
said, that he supposed Brother Mitchell had got a gentle hint of the intention of
the Caledonian Lodge to deprive him of that chair: That the deponent considered this expression to be made use of by Brother Gibson in a sarcastic manner:
That the deponent was of opinion, that both the speeches of Brother Gibson,
in so far as Brother Mitchell was concerned, exhibited a great deal of violence,
so much so, that the deponent himself, at one time, intended to move a vote of
censure against Brother Gibson. Depones, That no notice, so far as the deponent recollects, was taken of these speeches of Brother Gibson's from the Chair.
Depones, That he perfectly recollects a motion being made that evening, for
the expulsion of Brother Mitchell, on account of some apparent disapprobation
of certain of the brethren present, of some expressions made use of by Brother
Mitchell; but the particulars of which the deponent does not recollect: That
the brother who proposed the expulsion, seemed to be in a considerable degree
of passion, and advised the deponent, who sat near him, not to connect himself
more with Brother Mitchell: That this motion did not appear to the deponent to
meet with general approbation, but the contrary, by expressions of some hissing,
and cries of No, no! That the deponent recollects the Substitute Grand Master
having ordered the Wardens to do their duty, at the moment of Brother Mitchell
having said, 'That the laws of the Grand Lodge were so twisted;' upon which he
was interrupted by the Substitute Grand Master, and the order given to the Wardens, as before expressed, Depones, That, in his opinion, there was no part of
Brother Mitchell's conduct, during that evening, which merited a vote of expulsion. Depones, That he was at first at the time the motion of expulsion was made
sitting very near Brother Mitchell, and he was at no great distance from him any
part of the evening. Depones, that he does not recollect Brother Gibson having
made any conciliatory motion for withdrawing the vote of expulsion, though
the confusion was so great, that he might have done so, without the deponent's
hearing it; and, in the deponent's opinion, the reason for the motion not being
persisted in, was, that it did not meet with general approbation, as it appeared to
the deponent. Depones, That it appeared to the deponent, that the only reason

for turning out Brother Mitchell, was the expression he had made use of relative to the twisting of / the laws. Depones, That he does not recollect Brother Mitchell having used any other expression, in the course of the evening, which could have warranted a motion for turning Brother Mitchell out; and the deponent is himself of opinion, that this expression was not sufficient to warrant the measure. Depones, That there were some expressions previously made use of by Brother Mitchell, which gave offence, and produced the motion for expulsion; but what these were he does not precisely remember. Depones, That when the resolution at that meeting was proposed to be adopted, of depriving the Lodge of Mary's Chapel of her place upon the roll, he recollects of having addressed the Chair, and stated, that such a measure, if carried into effect, might produce a secession, which would not be very agreeable; and added, that a meeting would be certainly called of the brethren of Mary's Chapel, to take the resolution of the Grand Lodge into consideration. Interrogated by Brother Gibson, depones, That he never had any conversation with Brother Mitchell regarding an intended secession of the Caledonian Lodge from the Grand Lodge, nor with regard to the dispute between that Lodge and the Roman Eagle Lodge, relative to their days of meeting. Depones, That he does not know that there was any intention on the part of Brother Mitchell not to attend the Grand Master Elect on the evening of St. Andrew's day. Interrogated by Brother Mitchell, depones, That he was present in the Grand Lodge when the question of scrutiny was brought forward, and recollects of having seen Brother Mitchell raise his stick that evening, and threaten to knock down a brother who sat immediately behind him; and he thinks the words used by Brother Mitchell were, that if any brother behaved to him in that way again, he had a good stick, and that he would certainly make use of it. Depones, That the deponent was sitting close by Brother Mitchell, and knows that the cause of his having raised his stick, and used the expression before deponed to, was owing to that brother having repeatedly pulled Brother Mitchell back by the skirts of his coat, when rising to speak. Depones, That a great ferment took place in the Lodge at this time, in consequence of the expression used by Brother Mitchell, and of his gestures; and there was a cry of several voices to turn him out. Depones, That, after this, Brother Mitchell explained to the Chair the reason of his conduct; but the deponent does not recollect that he demanded redress. Depones, That when Brother Mitchell raised his stick, the deponent is of opinion, that the threat applied solely to the brother who attempted to pull him down, and / not in any shape to the Substitute Grand Master, or any other person. Interrogated, Whether he saw Brother Mitchell threaten the Chair, or any other brother, in the course of that evening? depones, That he does not recollect of his having done so, and does not think he did, with the exception before deponed to; and if Brother Mitchell had used any such threats, the deponent thinks he must have seen him, from his sitting so very near him. Interrogated by a Member of the Committee, If any expression was made use of from the Chair, when the deponent said that the resolution of depriving the Lodge of Mary's Chapel of its place in the roll might produce a secession? depones, That the Substitute Grand Master instantly declared, that if any Lodge attempted such a measure, he would shut its doors. All which is truth, as he shall answer to God.

COMPEARED HOUSTON RIGG BROWN, Member of St. David's Lodge, Edinburgh, aged 30 and upwards, married, who being solemnly sworn and examined, depones, &c. That he was present at the Quarterly Communication in May last, when Brother Mitchell moved for an address to his Majesty, which the deponent seconded: That the Substitute Grand Master objected to the motion, as being informal, and moved the previous question: That the address came to the vote: That he heard objections stated to various of the votes tendered for the address, and does not recollect whether there were any objections made against any of the votes tendered against the address: That the deponent marked down the votes as they were given, and he saw Brother Mitchell, and a brother sitting in one of the Wardens chairs, taking down the votes: That he frequently heard Brother Mitchell call out to the brethren to repeat the vote they gave upon this occasion. Depones, That he does not recollect whether his state of the vote, and Brother Mitchell's, or the other brother's state, who sat in the Warden's chair, tallied or not; but they were all different from the report of the Grand Clerk, and all brought out a majority in favour of the address. Depones, That he recollects Brother Mitchell mentioning, immediately after the meeting was over, that the two markings of the votes before deponed to, other than the deponent's, agreed with each other, and also with the markings of the state of another brother, whom Brother Mitchell said had taken down the votes that evening; but the deponent is led to believe, from the silence of Brother Mitchell with regard to the deponent's state of the votes, that it might be different from the other three. Depones, That his statement brought out either / two or three of majority in favour of the address, the deponent does not recollect which: That he is certain there was no communication between the two brethren before deponed to, or between them and the deponent, during their marking the votes as they were called. Depones, That while the votes were called, and taken down, the deponent does not think that such order and regularity prevailed as ought to have done. Depones, That he recollects Brother Mitchell having demanded a scrutiny, after the Grand Clerk had reported the state of the vote, which was not granted: That the scrutiny was demanded of the Substitute Grand Master by Brother Mitchell: That the Substitute Grand Master insisted upon closing the Lodge. Depones, That he saw, in Brother Mitchell's hands, a letter, stating the proceedings of that evening, and the deponent heard it read by Brother Mitchell; and is of opinion, that the statement of facts therein contained was correct:

That he does not recollect whether the letter was in manuscript or print, though he rather thinks it was in manuscript. Depones, That he was present at a meeting of the Grand Lodge, when the question of scrutiny was determined; and does not think, that, during any part of that evening, Brother Mitchell behaved in a disrespectful manner, or used any threats to the Chair; and the deponent was within one or two of Brother Mitchell the whole evening. All which is truth, as the deponent shall answer to God.

EDINBURGH, 20*th February*, 1808.

PRESENT,

R. W. WILLIAM INGLIS, Esquire, Substitute Grand Master.

R. W. Brother LAWSON.

R. W. Brother JAFFRAY.

R. W. Brother LAING.

R. W. Brother HARROWAR.

R. W. Brother M^cWHIRRTER, Grand Clerk, *p.t.*

COMPEARED JOHN CHRISTIE, of the Lodge of Edinburgh St. Andrew's, aged 25 and upwards, who being solemnly sworn and examined, &c. depones, That he was present at the Quarterly Communication in May last, when Brother Mitchell moved an address / to his Majesty, and the deponent sat during the whole evening immediately behind the Grand Clerk: That he heard a great many objections made by the Clerk to various votes, but whether these votes were for or against the address, the deponent, at this distance of time, cannot recollect: That the deponent himself marked the votes particularly as they were given, and, according to the deponent's statement, the address was carried by a majority of two, there being 28 for and 24 against the address, as taken down by the deponent; but he did not mark the votes of the Grand Secretary and Grand Clerk, not having heard how they voted, although the deponent afterwards learned that they had voted against the address. Depones, That there was no such confusion or noise in the room while the votes were taking down, so as to prevent the deponent from accurately ascertaining how each vote was given. Depones, That he heard Brother Mitchell demand a scrutiny from the Chair, which was not granted. Depones, That he was present at the Quarterly Communication which met on the first Monday of November last, and recollects of a proposition being made by a brother, to turn Brother Mitchell out of the Lodge, which he considered arose from the violence of the brother who made the proposal, and that there was no serious intention of carrying it into execution; and the proposition itself was received with a great degree of clamour, and some hissing, and other marks of disapprobation took place. Depones, That in a question which arose with regard to a proxy-commission which was presented by Brother Mitchell, Brother Gibson spoke against its being received, though he did not conceive Brother Gibson's speech as being personal to Brother Mitchell. Depones, however, That he recollects, in the course of the debate, upon that question, Brother Gibson having made use of an expression, comparing Brother Mitchell to Buonaparte, having used the following words. – 'I suppose Brother Mitchell is desirous of becoming the Buonaparte among free masons.'[55] Depones, That Brother Gibson said, in the course of his speech, and in a taunting manner, That he presumed Brother Mitchell was desirous of securing himself a seat in the Grand Lodge, by presenting the proxy-commission, as he, Brother Gibson, knew well, that Brother Mitchell had got a gentle hint to resign the chair of the Caledonian Lodge. /

MINUTE OF COMMITTEE.
Edinburgh, February 23, 1808.

The Committee of the Grand Lodge being met, the following letter, addressed to the Substitute Grand Master, by Brother Mitchell, was delivered and read, viz. – 'Sir, In consequence of the unpleasant circumstances that have occurred, and which are now become very public, it is quite impossible for me to attend the Committee of the Grand Lodge, so as to go on with my exculpatory proof.

'If any report of the business is to be made to the Grand Lodge, for which I continue to entertain the highest respect, I expect that, in justice to me, a fair statement of the circumstances that occurred before the Committee on Saturday last, shall accompany the depositions already made by the several witnesses.

'I request you will have the goodness to communicate this to the Committee, and to assure them of my respect. And I have the honour to be, Sir, your most obedient humble servant,

Edinburgh, February 23, 1808. (Signed) 'JOHN MITCHELL.'

Addressed – 'William Inglis, Esquire, Substitute Grand Master.'

Brother Mitchell having thus declined to proceed further with his exculpatory evidence, the Committee declare the proof concluded, and appoint the same, with the previous proceedings of the Grand Lodge, to be printed, in terms of the order of the Grand Lodge; and the Committee think it their duty to order the printed pamphlet, alluded to in the deposition of the Substitute Grand Master, to be annexed as an appendix.

And agreeably to Brother Mitchell's request, a statement has been this day made out of what took place at the meeting of the Committee on Saturday the 20th instant, to which recourse may be had, if necessary, but which, the Committee are of opinion, ought not to be printed.

(Signed) WILLIAM INGLIS, P.

JAMES DAVIDSON.

JOHN LAWSON.
THOMAS H. MILLER.
ALEX. G. HUNTER.
RO. PROCTOR.
J. HARROWAR.
FRAS. M. M^CNAB.
WM. LAING.
ALEX. JAFFRAY. /

MINUTE OF COMMITTEE.

February 26, 1808.

PRESENT,
The SUBSTITUTE GRAND MASTER.
Brother HARROWAR.
Brother DAVIDSON.
Brother PROCTOR.
Brother M^CNAB.
Brother MILLER.
Brother LAWSON.
The Grand Clerk.

The Committee are unanimously of opinion, that the petition and complaint at Brother Gibson's instance, with Brother Mitchell's answers thereto, should be printed, and distributed along with the proof and procedure.

(Signed)WILLIAM INGLIS, P. /

APPENDIX.
No. I.

EXCERPT from the MINUTES of ST. DAVID'S LODGE, of date the 28th December 1807.

AT an early period of the evening, the Right Worshipful Master, with the approbation of the brethren, sent Brother Duncan, deputy-master, at the head of a deputation, to visit the Lodges of Journeymen, Thistle, and Caledonian. Upon the return of Brother Duncan, and eleven of the brethren who accompanied him, the Right Worshipful Master desired that he might report the reception he and his brethren of St. David's had met with from the different Lodges. Brother Duncan stated, that in the Journeymen Lodge he had been received with those honours which characterize the social intercourse of masons, and received attentions equally honourable to the Journeymen Lodge, as they were flattering and delightful to the brethren of St. David's: he was informed, that the election of the Lodge had been conducted with the most perfect unanimity, and that

Brother Lorimer had been elected master, and Brothers Somerville and Thomson, wardens. That, in the Thistle Lodge, he and his brethren of St. David's met with the same honours and friendly attentions: in this Lodge, too, he understood the election had been unanimous, Brother Alexander Adam, master, and Brothers Buchan and Barker, wardens. That, in further compliance with the desire of the Right Worshipful Master and his brethren, he had proceeded to Oman's Hotel, where he found the brethren of the Caledonian were assembled in a tyled Lodge.[56] As usual on such occasions, he / had desired that a deputation from St. David's might be announced to the Right Worshipful Master of the Caledonian. After waiting some time in the antichamber, the junior warden appeared, and addressed Brother Duncan nearly in the following words. – 'The Right Worshipful Master of the Caledonian Lodge regrets he cannot receive the deputation from St. David's, owing to the room being already crowded; but wishes to know how the election of St. David's had proceeded.' Brother Duncan desired, in answer, that the junior warden might inform the Right Worshipful Master, he did not consider the place they then were, without the walls of a tyled Lodge, as proper for conferences on the subject to which he had alluded; but that he should leave it to the Right Worshipful Master and brethren of St. David's, assembled in their Lodge-room, to make what answer they might think proper, to the message of the Caledonian Lodge.

The Right Worshipful Master wished to hear the sentiments of the brethren upon this so very extraordinary occurrence.

Brother James Gibson, W.S. then stated, that, as an old member, and sometime master of St. David's Lodge, he could not tamely hear of its deputations being treated with indignity or insult; and that, in his opinion, if such acts of aggression and insolence were to be tolerated, they would at once put an end to those bonds of sociality and harmony, which had for so many centuries endeared the meetings of the craft to the brethren. He therefore moved, that the report of Brother Duncan be recorded, and a copy of it sent to the Secretary of the Grand Lodge. Brother Gibson's motion was warmly seconded, and agreed to unanimously. Extracted on these two pages, from the record of St. David's Lodge, Edinburgh, by

(Signed)JOHN WELSH, *Secretary.* /

No. II.

PAMPHLET referred to in the SUBSTITUTE GRAND MASTER's Deposition.

SIR AND BROTHER,

I THINK it proper, through the medium of a circular letter, to communicate to you some proceedings that took place at the Quarterly Communication of the Grand Lodge, on Monday evening, the 4th instant, in order that you may judge of the conduct of some of the Office-Bearers of the Lodge, and give directions to your Proxy, how he and his Wardens shall vote in the election of Office-Bearers on next St. Andrew's Day. The truth of this statement I pledge my honour for.

On that evening I brought forwards the following motion, and it was regularly seconded by a respectable Brother, H.R. Brown, Esq. Proxy-Master for Jedburgh St. Andrews. The motion was couched in these words:

'That an humble Address be presented to his Majesty by the Grand Lodge of Scotland, expressive of their thankfulness and gratitude for the paternal solicitude for the happiness of his people, which he has been graciously pleased to manifest, in supporting the Established Religion of the Country, and the Principles of the British Constitution.'[57]

This motion I prefaced with but few words. I trusted, I said, that it would be unanimous, as it became the duty of an Order, who had experienced much favour and indulgence from his present Majesty, to express their loyalty and attachment to him on an occasion in which his honour and his conscience were deeply concerned; – that all idea of its being a political question would be laid aside, as, whatever my own ideas of politics were, I was too well aware of the constitution of Masonry, to introduce any political matter into it; – that none, I hoped, would be so disloyal, so base, and so ungrateful, / as to take it up in a political point of view, and to endeavour, by this kind of side-wind, to get quit of it; – and lastly, I again candidly declared, that the sole object of the motion was, to evince our loyalty, our gratitude, and our thankfulness to the best of Sovereigns, as had on many former occasions been done by us.

It was soon seen the decided and determined opposition this motion was doomed to meet with from the Substitute Grand Master, William Inglis, Esquire, then in the chair; for every possible objection was made by him, and the party he and his friends had formed, as to the formality and regularity of the motion. The objections made, however, were so frivolous, that they were immediately overruled, and the matter came of course to be argued. But no sooner had one or two of the Brethren delivered their sentiments on the subject, in which they reprobated all idea of political discussion, and maintained, that the present motion had entirely for its object a renewal of their expressions of loyalty and attachment to his Majesty, than Mr. Inglis, champion-like, took up the cudgels. *He*, as might now have been foreseen, entered widely into the field of politics. We had from him a long dissertation on, and explanation of the Test Act,[58] of the analogy between Roman Catholics and Presbyterians in respect of Episcopalians. He, moreover, talked much of my Lord Howick,[59] and of the views and measures of the late Ministry, &c. In short, his speech was an echo of what 'all the talents' had advanced for themselves in both Houses of Parliament; and as being more fit for such supreme assemblies than within the walls of a Mason Lodge, I shall not attempt to re-echo it here, but refer you to the parliamentary debates on the subject, should you have any wish to gratify your curiosity. Mr. Inglis finally concluded, by conjuring the Meeting, as they regarded him, (forsooth!) as they respected their Acting Grand Master, the Earl of Moira, and as they wished to maintain the principles of Masonry, that they should dismiss the motion; and *he* therefore moved the previous question.

It is unnecessary for me to point out to you how far party-spirit had, on this occasion, carried the Chairman out of the line of his duty. Every one knows, that the Substitute Grand Master, in the same way as the Speaker of the House of Commons, or indeed, as a Chairman elected by any meeting whatever, ought to take no side in a debate. It is only his duty to regulate that debate, and to keep order: and so much is this the case in the present instance, that, by / the laws of the Grand Lodge, the person filling the Chair has no vote, unless upon an equality of voices, when he is allowed to give his casting vote. At any rate, a little moderation and modesty would have become one filling that Chair better than pertness and forwardness; and Mr. Inglis might have had patience to hear what was to be said on both sides of the question; and particularly, he might have had the prudence to have waited, and seen whether any one of his party could not have been found to make the same inflammatory speech that he did, and thus have saved himself from appearing in so awkward and unbecoming a predicament. Be this, however, as it may, his arguments were ably answered; and after a long and keen debate, one side of which he alone attempted to sustain, the matter came to the vote, and the question was put, 'Address,' or 'Not Address.'

Here, in the outset of the business, recourse was had to a measure which, if not unprecedented, was at least unusual. A number of votes were objected to, because the Lodges, the Brethren tendering such votes, represented, were more than two years in arrear to the Grand Lodge. That a law to this purpose does exist, I do not deny, but I maintain that it is not usual to put it in force, and I would almost challenge the time it was put in force. In fact, it has heretofore been considered as obsolete; and, as a proof of this, I may mention, that I have now been a member of the Grand Lodge for about these three years. I have seen questions put to the vote in this time, but never have I seen such a measure resorted to. The books, vouchers, and other papers, too, that could have shewn such arrears, were in the hands of the Clerk and Secretary, Messrs. Bertram and Guthrie. These gentlemen were packed in the party determined to vote against the address, and you will not suppose I am very uncharitable when I assert, and the truth of this assertion indeed was evident at the meeting, that every vote tendered in favour of the address was most *scrupulously* scrutinized in terms of this law, of which many of the Brethren were not in the least aware, and that every other advantage was taken by them that their official situations could yield. I shall not go the length of saying, that any Lodge who voted 'Not Address,' and whose votes were received by the Clerk were actually in arrear; but this I can say and maintain, and it is a curious fact, of which you may have your own ideas, that not one who tendered their votes, 'Not Address,' were declared by the clerk to be in arrear, while almost one half of the votes / tendered for the 'Address' were objected to, and, on this account, not received.

On the subject of the inadmissibility of the votes of Lodges in arrear, I shall here take the liberty of mentioning a case in point, and it is a most glaring one. It will shew you whether party-spirit, or a love of principle, justice, and honour, most influence some people. A few years ago, two candidates started for the office of Grand Clerk. A respectable and most useful Member of the Grand Lodge, Brother Peter Douglas, Proxy-Master for Dunkeld, on that occasion, moved that the law relating to Lodges in arrear should be put in force. The most numerous party, one of the ringleaders of whom was our present Substitute Grand Master, Mr. Inglis, overruled this motion. All present indiscriminately voted, and to such a vote is the present Grand Clerk indebted for his situation at this day.

Before I proceed farther, I shall also take notice of another circumstance. As the present was a motion on which I was anxious there should be unanimity, I waited upon as many of the members of the Grand Lodge as my time would permit, previous to submitting it to the Meeting, in order to explain to them the nature of the address, and hear their sentiments on the subject. All thought it a measure highly proper, and promised their hearty concurrence and support. By one or two, however, it was mentioned to me, that they suspected Mr. Inglis would be against it, and to prevent his forming a party, they hinted the propriety of not making it too public. Not only on this account, but also that I should have been sorry it should reach the public ear, that a loyal and dutiful address had been moved to his Majesty, and rejected in the Grand Lodge of Scotland, while similar addresses were approaching the Throne, from almost every community and incorporated body in the kingdom,[60] I in some degree went into the measure. It was late, however, ere I heard such a thing hinted, and I do not believe there were above half a dozen members that I cautioned to observe any kind of reserve on the matter. For this I have been loudly called out against. I have been reproached with stealing a march upon the Grand Lodge. But let us see what the other party *inter alia*[61] did. One of their number, 'A good portly man, i'faith, and a corpulent; of a cheerful look, and a pleasing eye, and a most noble carriage; and, as I think, his age some fifty, or by'r lady, inclining to three-score; and now I remember me, his name is Falstaff,'[62] planted himself, Cerberus-like,[63] in the door of the Grand Lodge, at the commencement of the meeting. Had / this portly gentleman had as many heads as Horace would persuade us the hell-hound Cerberus had, (and surely Horace would allow a mouth with a set of good canine teeth to each head),[64] he would have collared every Brother that entered, and held all fast till they had promised their negative to the Address.

With a pair of nipperclaws,[65] however, powerful and retentive as those of a huge lobster, and that we may make the complexion suit, let us suppose this lobster par-boiled with heat and rage, many of the Brethren were laid hold of, and in the way of carrying matters *vi et armis*,[66] were favoured with a hearty squeeze of the hand, a squeeze, somewhat more rough, you may believe me, than any of our brotherly grips[xxxii]. Let us, however, leave Cerberus at rest in his dark abodes, or, having metamorphosed him into a par-boiled lobster, permit him to pursue his wonted callings, and cool himself, *'Scopulis lobster monifootus in udis creepat;'*[67] and we shall proceed to the state of the votes, as found not objectionable, but received by the Clerk; and in this place I may fairly say to you,

'Thus bad begins, but worse remains behind.'[68]

Mr. Brown, Master of the Ancient Lodge of Mary's Chapel, Mr. H.R. Brown, Proxy for Jedburgh St. Andrew's, Mr. D. Horne, Warden for   and myself, marked down the votes as they were received by the Clerk. That these gentlemen were accurate, there is every reason to believe, and that I myself was particularly anxious to be so, must have been evident to the whole meeting; for every vote that was given, I called out to the person giving it to repeat it to me, in order that there might be no mistake. When all the votes had been given, I summed them up on each side, and found that for the 'Address' there were 28, and for 'Not Address,' 24. Upon consulting with the other gentlemen taking down the votes, although we had no intercourse with each other, I had the satisfaction to find we all tallied most exactly. No doubt remained, then, of the address having been carried in spite of all the opposition, the unfair opposition, I may say, it had met with. But what was our astonishment? What was the astonishment of the whole meeting, when, upon the Clerk's being desired, from the Chair, to declare the state of the votes, he declared the address was rejected by a majority of 28 to 27? And yet this honest Clerk had not another person to corroborate his statement. A scrutiny was, therefore, immediately demanded, but / this was peremptorily refused from the Chair, and all our efforts to obtain it were drowned in noisy shouts of triumph by the Chairman and his party. The Clerk made his escape *quamprimum*[69] from the room, with all his books, papers, &c. and the Chairman would not hear another word on the subject, but after nearly breaking the table to pieces with his mallet, and in vain attempting to close the Lodge, he left the Chair.

I have since waited upon both Clerk and Secretary, to get a list of the Lodges at the meeting, particularly of those who voted, and the manner of their voting, as also to obtain an inspection of the books, that I might be enabled to scrutinize the votes. This I was denied, but seizing an opportunity, when the Substitute Grand Master and Clerk were together, after much shuffling, I was promised an extract of the minutes of that evening, so soon as they were made up. It is necessary they should be made, and doubtless they will be so with a vengeance. It would seem, however, they are not made up yet, for I have waited now upwards of three weeks, and there is no word of such extract. One would, therefore, suspect the Clerk finds a little tough work about the job. Under such circumstances, the difficulty, you must be aware, of bringing any delinquency that might have taken place to light, is great; but from the labour of going amongst, and inquiring at the Brethren, I have made up the following state of the votes tendered for the Address that night. The votes against the Address, I have not been able, with sufficient accuracy, to ascertain; but there is the less occasion for this, since, even admitting the state of the vote was 28 to 27, it will be seen, the majority was in favour of the Address.

Now Sir, I have delivered to you a round unvarnished tale. It beggars comment, and I shall make none upon it. Of the votes, 'No address,' many, we have since learnt, are objectionable. The vote of Brother David Pitcairn, of the Ceres Lodge, was so, for he was not a member of the Grand Lodge, as his Proxy Commission was never read nor received; besides, he was not in the clothing of the Lodge*. Brother John Ross's vote of Proxy for / is also objectionable, on the following grounds. 1*st*, He was not in proper Clothing, as wanting a Sash; 2*d*, The Clothing he had was not that of his Lodge, but of the Defensive Band; and 3*d*, He gave his Sash to another person to enable him to vote. The vote of the person getting this Sash, was also objectionable on the same grounds. The Grand Clerk voted two for the Peebles Lodge; but the Warden he voted for had not on the Clothing of that Lodge. Many more votes might be objectionable, on the score of their being more than two years in arrear, but this we are precluded from ascertaining. It is a pretty shrewd conjecture, however, that the votes of the two Wardens of the Edinburgh St. Luke's Lodge are in this predicament; for upon inquiring at the Clerk of this Lodge, he informs me, there have been no arrears paid since he came to office, and that is nigh two years since, and previous to that, this Lodge met only for the Election of Office-Bearers, yet there was a necessity for taking out certificates. A certain officious Brother, however, of that Lodge, might have made things all square and even on this matter, either before the voting, or most probably, after it. But it was done without the knowledge of the Master, or any other Brother of the Lodge. At the bottom of this, however, we cannot get; for, as I mentioned before, we are precluded from getting justice done us.

Let us, however, throw all these things out of the question, and let us, even for the sake of argument, admit there was a fair majority against the address, and let us simply consider the conduct of the Office-Bearers concerned, particularly that of the Chairman. Now, was it ever heard, that a Chairman should lead a party? If such is allowed to be the case, then we may bid farewell[xxxiii] to

---

*   Since writing the above, I have learnt, that the vote of Brother Pitcairn's Warden, Brother White, who was exactly in similar circumstances with himself, because he tendered it for the 'Address,' was not received!

all order and regularity. Or was it ever heard, under such circumstances as the present, when four respectable people agreed in the state of the votes, and when only one of an opposite party differed, and that it was likely a mistake, not to give it a worse name, with this solitary gentleman had happened; – I say, was it ever heard, that a scrutiny should be refused? Was it ever again heard, that a Mason Meeting should be broke up without the usual formality of closing the Lodge? And lastly, what title has the Chairman to refuse hearing any Brother who has any thing to offer, previous to the usual time of shutting a Lodge, viz. high twelve?

I have now discharged my duty to the Craft. There have been alteration and controversy enough on this subject, and I have no wish to enter farther into it. The time allowed me by my profession / will not permit it, nor is there occasion, since what I have stated is corroborated by respectable testimony annexed. Besides, I am not versed in 'quiddits, quillets, cases, tenures, or tricks;'[70] and of these, God knows, we have already seen enough. It is for you to prevent them ever sullying the dignity of the Chair of the Grand Lodge of Scotland.

I have only to add, that I subjoin a copy of the intended Address to his Majesty, by which you will see how completely politics were steered clear of. And I have the honour to be affectionately,

SIR AND BROTHER,
Your very humble Servant,
JOHN MITCHELL, M.D.
R. W. M. Edinburgh Caledonian Lodge.
ALEX, LAWRIE, & Co. Printers.

[ANON.], *AN EXPOSITION OF THE CAUSES WHICH HAVE PRODUCED THE LATE DISSENSIONS AMONG THE FREE MASONS OF SCOTLAND* (1808)

[Anon.], *An Exposition of the Causes which Have Produced the Late Dissensions among the Free Masons of Scotland, Addressed to the Brethren of the Order by the Edinburgh Lodges that have found it Necessary to Separate from the Grand Lodge of Scotland* (Edinburgh: C. Stewart, 1808).[1]

L. D. Wartski argues that the majority of the 'misfortunes that befell Scottish Freemasonry in 1807 had their origins in the smouldering discontent which followed the formation in 1736 of the Grand Lodge of Scotland'.[2] Wartski is partially correct in his analysis. However, he fails to underscore the significant impact of masonic and national politics on late-eighteenth and early – nineteenth – century Freemasonry.

It would be too convenient and simplistic to conclude that all Scottish Freemasons were bitterly divided along shades of political loyalty. During the early 1800s, however, a polarization of party allegiances occurred within the Grand Lodge of Scotland which ultimately spilled over into several Edinburgh lodges and resulted in the Masonic Secession of 1808. Peter Clark maintains that the discord which resulted from competing political ideologies during the eighteenth century created a 'need for a neutral arena'.[3] This came in the form of clubs and associations such as the Freemasons, where political discussions were in theory prohibited, although Clark asserts that 'the sound of politics was not so much excluded from ... societies as admitted with the volume turned down'.[4] By 1802, Scottish Freemasonry was 'fragmenting and reforming into contesting structures', due largely to the politicisation of the Grand Lodge.[5] Despite the leadership of distinguished loyalists such as Sir James Stirling[6] and George Gordon, Earl of Aboyne,[7] it is clear that the Grand Lodge was rapidly becoming a Whig body. Indeed, as Clark argues, associations without a clear political agenda

– especially the Freemasons – might easily 'be drawn into political activity during periods of national upheaval'.[8]

A major contributing factor to the Masonic Secession can be traced to the establishment of the Grand Lodge of Scotland in 1736, more specifically the ordering of the lodges on the Grand Roll. The initial ordering of the lodges – based on the sequence of entrance into Mary's Chapel – was overturned one year later, however, when the Grand Lodge resolved that numbering on the Grand Roll would be determined by documents, for example charters, that verified the creation of a particular lodge. In the event, Mary's Chapel was situated at the head of the Grand Roll. After the dispute over precedence in 1737, Kilwinning resumed its independence from the Grand Lodge of Scotland. In doing so, it continued the practice of granting charters to new lodges irrespective of the Grand Lodge's disapproval. These differences, though not a central issue for almost fifty years, resurfaced in 1794, and by 1802, the Grand Lodge renewed its effort to 'compell the Kilwinning Lodge to return to her duty as a Constituent Member of the Grand Lodge and in future to desist from granting Charters and other acts and deeds which none but the Grand Lodge herself is intitled to exercise'.[9]

Ultimately, on 14 October 1807, a conference was held in Glasgow to negotiate the terms of an agreement. In exchange for renouncing its charter - granting privileges, Kilwinning would be placed at the head of the Grand Roll of Scotland. As Stewart's transcription illustrates, the deepening rift among Scottish lodges manifested a growing imbalance of power among the Grand Lodge of Scotland and its constituent lodges, and the inability of the Grand Lodge to adjudicate disputes and effectively maintain some semblance of authority over Scotland's Freemasons. The entire affair, however, had been conducted without the participation of No. 1 Mary's Chapel, and this entire fiasco made it obvious that 'politics were to be dragged into the matter and used to inflame the righteous indignation of the Lodge of Edinburgh over the manner in which it had been treated'.[10] Relegated to the second oldest lodge in Scotland, the members immediately expressed their disapproval over the handling of the situation. Regardless of a warning from Mary's Chapel that it would not cede precedence to Kilwinning and subtly hinted at the creation of a new Grand Lodge, the threats were dismissed as meaningless at best.

It is likely that the text was printed by Charles Stewart, who at the time of its printing housed his printing office at Forrester's Wynd; Stewart died 27 April 1823.[11] Copies of the text exist in the Grand Lodge of Scotland Library in Edinburgh, although this text was keyed based upon copies in the British Library and the National Library of Scotland.

Notes

1.   This headnote was written by Mark Wallace.
2.   L. D. Wartski, 'Freemasonry and the Early Secret Societies Act', monograph compiled and presented by the author for private circulation by the District Grand Lodge of Natal of Antient Free and Accepted Masons of Scotland, p. 43.
3.   P. Clark, *British Clubs and Societies 1580–1800: The Origins of an Associational World* (Oxford: Oxford University Press, 2000), p. 180.
4.   Clark, *British Clubs and Societies 1580–1800*, p. 181.
5.   S. Murdoch, *Network North: Scottish Kin, Commercial and Covert Associations in Northern Europe 1603–1746* (Leiden: Brill Academic Publications, 2006), p. 332.
6.   E. McFarland, *Ireland and Scotland in the Age of Revolution: Planting the Green Bough* (Edinburgh: Edinburgh University Press, 1994), p. 159. Stirling was Lord Provost of Edinburgh from 1790 to 1800 and Grand Master Mason of Scotland from 1798 to 1800.
7.   R. G. Thorne (ed.), *House of Commons: History of the House of Parliament*, 5 vols (London: Haynes Publishing Company, 1986), vol. 4, p. 36.
8.   Clark, *British Clubs*, pp. 461–2.
9.   Manuscripts: Grand Lodge of Scotland Minutes (hereafter GL of S), 3 August 1794.
10. R. S. Lindsay, *A History of the Mason Lodge of Holyrood House (St Luke's No. 44)* (Edinburgh: T. and A. Constable, Ltd, 1935), pp. 296–7.
11. Information taken from the Scottish Book Trade Index (SBTI).

[Anon.], *An Exposition of the Causes Which Have Produced the Late Dissensions Among the Free Masons of Scotland* (1808)

AN
EXPOSITION
OF THE
CAUSES
WHICH HAVE PRODUCED
THE LATE DISSENSIONS
AMONG THE
FREE MASONS OF SCOTLAND,
ADDRESSED
TO THE BRETHREN OF THE ORDER
BY
THE EDINBURGH LODGES THAT HAVE FOUND
IT NECESSARY TO SEPARATE FROM THE
GRAND LODGE OF SCOTLAND.
EDINBURGH:
Printed by C. Stewart,
AND SOLD BY JOHN ANDERSON, ROYAL EXCHANGE.
1808. / /

EXPOSITION &c.

BRETHREN,

WHEN we consider the origin of Free-Masonry,[1] and contemplate the peaceful annals of an order whose professed design is the extinction of every unsocial and malevolent passion, we cannot sufficiently lament the proceedings that in these "later times" have convulsed its foundation.

After outliving, for many centuries, the revolutions that have swept away the nations of antiquity, among which it took its rise – after withstanding the torrent of innumerable persecutions, the denunciations of superstition, and the calumnies of the worthless and profane, this venerable fabric has at last been destined to receive its deepest wounds from the unnatural hands that ought to have sustained and protected it – and,

> – *Oh, lamentable sight!*
> *The labour of whole ages lumbers down,*
> *A hideous and mis-shapen length of ruins!*

Ungracious, indeed, is the task which necessity at length imposes on your fellow brethren to detail the persecutions which have compelled them to flee from their / former sanctuary – a sanctuary now polluted with violence and oppression,[2] and where the arm of power is uplifted to burst asunder those ties which the dearest affections, and the most sacred of obligations have cemented. But ill should they now discharge their duties to you, did they not, at this alarming crisis, endeavour to shed a stream of light on the dark schemes which have for some time past been forming, and which now menace the subversion of the Order.

It has been a current opinion among the brethren less versant in the affairs of Masonry, that the Grand Lodge of Scotland possessed, from the beginning, an absolute controul over every mason residing in this country;[3] that from this Lodge, as from a parent source, all the other Lodges originally emanated; and that thence was derived every privilege they enjoyed as Lodges, or as Members of the Craft.[4] But it now becomes our duty to expose the fallacy of this principle, which, though in former times it was unnecessary to question, has now been rendered the too successful engine of a *faction*, in advancing *the eminence of their party*,[5] Indeed, Whig bodies such as St Luke's and the Grand Lodge of Scotland 'gradually attracted to themselves the more talented and ambitious men of the rising generation, who could not see openings for ability without backing in the dominant party', at the expence of every tie which has hitherto preserved the institution of Masonry. Had your brethren not been too fatally assured that those men who have addressed you under the specious title of your "Masonic Guardians," are, in fact, a *junto*, totally destitute of every consideration for masonry, and solely intent on *political contrivances*, to which they have sacrificed the honour and interests of the craft, your attention would not have been thus seriously called on to prevent that destruction of the Order which is rapidly approaching. With these important views, it therefore becomes necessary to investigate the Constitution of Masonry[6] in Scotland, to / contrast it with those disgraceful proceedings which have been lately introduced by *this unlucky set of men*, and thence to deduce a few conclusions that must come home to the reason of every unprejudiced reader.

For many centuries previous to the erection of the Grand Lodge of Scotland, it is an undoubted fact that the Fraternity of Free-Masons existed, and their Lodges were dispersed over the continents of Asia and Europe. The laws which regulated their "*masonic privileges*," originated in sources long since obscured in the mist of tradition. From authentic documents, however, it appears that, prior to the fifteenth century, these laws had acquired the sanction of immemorial prescription in every Lodge of Masons, at that time existing in the World.[7] Their members were bound by the same ties of universal benevolence and brotherly love that, down to the present times, have distinguished the Fraternity. In their lodges, no one was considered a stranger who could display the tokens of a mason – and within their sacred walls the sound of dissention was never heard.— If through the malice of tyrants who had never tasted of their social delights, the Order was basely traduced, and groundless persecutions raised against it, the brethren had still the inward satisfaction in the midst of all their misfortunes, that they had done nothing to merit the censure of mankind.

Into this great Society, admission was freely opened to every respectable character; and the boasted privilege of a mason always was, that, to whatever quarter of the Universe chance might direct him, he was ever sure of an asylum, and a cordial reception in the lodges and meetings of the craft.[8] No petty jealousy existing among the lodges / had the smallest influence on the conduct of a brother to a brother – it was enough that he retained the character of an honest man, and could display the mystic signs of a mason.

With such principles and such laws, did the lodges of the Order disperse themselves over no inconsiderable portion of the Globe; and, about the commencement of the fifteenth century, are supposed to have found their way into Scotland. At the building of the ancient Abbey of Kilwinning, a number of masons from foreign countries were employed, who formed themselves into a Lodge, now known by the name of "*Mother Kilwinning*," which is generally believed to be the Parent Lodge of Scottish Masonry. From this Ancient Lodge, during the succeeding ages, a great variety of other lodges took their rise, and still retain her name, such as the *Cannongate Kilwinning, Edinburgh Kilwinning, Glasgow Kilwinning*, &c. The Ancient Lodge of Mary's Chapel, whose records reach farther back than those of any other Scottish Lodge, in like manner gave birth to a number of other lodges; and in this way the institution of Masonry was establishd for several centuries before any measure was ever thought of for erecting a Grand Lodge.[9]

The Order being thus constituted, it appears that its members, who consisted in those times almost entirely of operative brethren, became desirous of putting themselves under the protection of some eminent character, in order to confer a degree of respectability on the craft, equivalent to that which their brethren enjoyed in foreign countries. With this view, they made choice of the ancient family of Roslin to represent them in the character of hereditary Grand Master of the Order, by a charter in favour of / William St. Clair, then of Roslin, granted soon after the accession of King James VI. to the English Throne.[10]

By a subsequent Charter, granted in the year 1630, they conferred the same office on Sir William St. Clair of Roslin, his Son, and confirmed all the powers contained in the former charter.

On perusing these charters, it evidently appears that the powers thus conferred on the Grand Master extended no farther than a mere superintendence and jurisdiction over the tradesmen of the craft in their *operative capacity*.[11] With their convivial meetings[12] he had nothing whatever to do, at least there is no mention of any such thing in the charters; and if therefore, he presided at any of these, or issued any directions concerning them, it must have been through courtsey alone that these were regarded by the craft, and not from any right conferred by the charters. It is true that the powers formerly granted by the craft, were afterwards ratified by a Royal charter in the reign of James II. in favour of William St. Clair, Earl of Orkney and Caithness, and Baron of Roslin, but it does not appear that this charter contained any extension of the authority already vested in the Grand Master.

Be this, however, as it may, certain it is, that at no time were the genuine principles of the order more strictly regarded, or its interests more rapidly advanced, than during the administration of the family of Roslin. Their principal annual meetings were held at Kilwinning, for the purpose of issuing charters[13] of erections of new lodges, and transacting the general concerns of the order. But although, during these times, there existed a number of lodges altogether independent of this assembly, there is not even, on / the breath of tradition, a single example handed down of a rigorous or prohibitory measure enacted against them.

From these times downwards to the year 1736, matters remained on the same footing, and the order arrived at a degree of prosperity till then unexampled. Long before that period, the family of Roslin appear to have ceased from taking any active share in the concerns of masonry. The aspect of the fraternity was indeed much changed from what it had been in the days of their predecessors, when scarcely any but operative brethren were admitted into it. The lodges then abounding in every corner of the kingdom, were filled with persons of every profession, and of every rank in society.[14] The institutions which had been formed for regulating the operative practice of the brethren were now no longer applicable to their conduct as a great association, connected by invisible ties, and actuated by principles of an universal nature. It now became expedient to consolidate and preserve these principles in their original purity, amidst the torrent of changes which influences the manners of every civilized state. In order to attain this great object, it was necessary to enact a system of subordination and arrangement among the several lodges, to determine the precedency of each,[15] and to collect a general fund for advancing the interests of the order, and displaying its universal beneficence. To effectuate this noble design, no measure seemed better calculated than the formation of a general committee, consisting of certain representatives from every lodge in Scotland, invested with powers for carrying into execution such plans of public utility as should meet with the approbation of the craft.

William St Clair of Roslin, who then held the office of hereditary Grand Master, deeply sensible of the advantage / which promised to result from this public-spirited design, *magnanimously* resolved on testifying his opinion of the laws which should regulate the brethren, by surrendering *into their own hands* all those rights which their predecessors had conferred on his ancestors, or the royal authority had confirmed. Accordingly, upon the 24th November 1736, he resigned, *into the hands of the brethren at large*, 'all right, claim, or pretence, that he or his heirs had, or anywise might have, claim, or pretend to be patron, protector, judge, or master of the masons of Scotland, in virtue of any deed or deeds made and granted by the said masons, or of any grant or charter made by any of the kings of Scotland, to and in favour of William and Sir William St Clairs of Roslin, his predecessors, or any other manner of way, for then and for ever!'

After the execution of this deed, by which every power that the Grand Master formerly possessed was by him resigned *into the hands of the craft*, it will surely be admitted, that no subsequent dominion over masons in this country could be created in the person of any man or body of men, beyond what the brethren themselves should expressly confer. With them it lay to elect a Grand Master, to form a Committee or Grand Lodge, and to prescribe such rules for the conduct of that assembly as they should see proper. All powers conferred in this way by the craft behoved[16] *to be of their own free consent*, and therefore no act of this assembly, stretching in the slightest degree beyond the express limits of the powers thus conferred, can be legal or valid.

Let us now attend to the manner in which the present Grand Lodge was constituted immediately after the resignation of St Clair of Roslin. *Four* of the Edinburgh lodges, / viz. Mary's Chapel and Canongate Kilwinning (both of which are now addressing you), Canongate and Leith, and the Journeymen Masons of Edinburgh, met together, and constituted that very Grand Lodge, whose nominal rulers have now repaid their exertions with such black ingratitude! Yes, brethren, from these ancient and much injured lodges was derived the whole of that power in which these anti-masonic *politicians* are now exulting. It is in vain that they now attempt to boast of the *supremacy* of that polluted Lodge, and its superiority over those *that made it*, but full soon shall they be taught their real origin – and

    – *who created them, lamenting learn,*
    When who can uncreate them they shall know.[17]

The Grand Lodge being thus constituted on such narrow foundations, it is obvious that their jurisdiction could never have been extended to a single additional lodge, had its rulers at that time been *men of party-politics*, and had taken into their heads the notion of prohibiting individuals from visiting their brethren in the other lodges.

But far otherwise was the conduct of the rising Grand Lodge to those who did not acknowledge its constitution. As these lodges had thought proper not to send any representatives to the Grand Lodge, the latter could in justice do nothing less than prohibit all representatives or deputations from being sent to them; for, though both sets of lodges were sensible that the privileges of a mason were in every quarter of the world identically the same, they did not choose to recognise each other as incorporated bodies. One set of masons acknowledged the newly constituted Grand Lodge, another the ancient Mother Kilwinning, another the lodge of Mary's Chapel, another the ancient lodge of Melrose, &c. which still exist, as their respective heads. Some / there were who paid allegiance to the *ancient* Grand Lodge of England, others to the *modern* lodge of that name,[18] and some acknowledged no masonic superior at all. Yet amidst all this diversity of opinion which then existed and still exists among the Scottish lodges, the question was never once started, whether a brother, initiated in any one of these lodges, did not for ever thereafter possess the power and liberty of visiting any of the rest he pleased. It was a matter of no consequence to a well meaning mason, whose only desire was to participate in the harmony of his brethren, whether their charters flowed from this lodge or from that, or whether they sent representatives to one lodge or to another. – That they were *masons* was enough to him; as a mason he visited them, and as a mason he was entitled to do so.

Fortunately for the interests of masonry, no such destructive ideas as those now acted upon by the present Grand Lodge were ever entertained by any of its former rulers. Indeed it appears evident, from the *very laws* of the Grand Lodge itself, as well as its unvaried practice, that nothing could be more foreign to the nature of its institution. Throughout the whole printed code of these regulations, the most anxious attention appears to have been paid to the very words and forms of expression made use of, lest from these a dubiety might arise in the minds of men ever watchful of their personal liberties and privileges. For this reason the lodges not holding of the Grand Lodge, and thence termed irregular, are not so much as mentioned, excepting in the twelfth chapter of these laws, where the following passage appears:

'That no *lodge*, holding of the Grand Lodge of Scotland, shall have any communication or intercourse with / *any lodge* in Scotland not holding of her, *under the penalty* of being deprived of her charter: And provincial Grand Masters[19] are strictly enjoined not to allow *any lodge* in Scotland, not holding of the Grand Lodge, to attend him at any masonic meeting or procession whatever.'*

---

  *   Vide Laws of the Grand Lodge, Cap. XII.

We would now ask any person of common discernment, who reads this quotation, to say, whether it contains any prohibition against the intercourse of *individuals*. It is the *lodges* that are prohibited, and the penalty of disobedience is the loss of their charter. But, if the law applied to *individuals*, it would follow as a necessary consequence, that for a fault of this kind committed by any one of its members, the lodge to which he belonged behoved to lose her charter, this being the *only penalty* which the law had prescribed, and which at all events fell to be inflicted. Again, since the provincial Grand Masters are '*strictly* enjoined not to allow *any lodge* in Scotland, not holding of the Grand Lodge,' to attend him in masonic processions, why do they not also prohibit from allowing the attendance of any *individual* connected with such lodges? That the law, however, has not the most distant reference to individuals, is evident from its own words; and if a doubt can remain on the point, it must be solved by an appeal to the practice of masons since their first institution in Scotland, whether any instance of such a prohibition was ever heard of? Repeatedly, in the course of the proceedings to be afterwards noticed, have we called upon the present rulers of the Grand Lodge to adduce one solitary example of the kind in justification of their conduct; but this appeal they have always evaded. In one of their late publications, they have indeed ventured to say, that the 'Grand Lodge of / Scotland had always, without objection, exercised a controul *over every individual* of the craft, wherever, from *the commission of masonic offences*, it became necessary to do so.' But this is no answer whatever to the question formerly put to them. Can there be adduced, from the records of the Grand Lodge, or the history of the craft, a single instance of an individual, *who never committed any masonic offence*, being prohibited from going, *as an individual*, to such lodges, meetings, or masonic assemblies, as he thought proper? This is the question which was put to them, and which they have been so unwilling to answer. But let them do it fairly now; let them come forward like men, and either produce such an example of this sort as will satisfy their brethren, that their conduct has been agreeable to the practice and principles of the craft, or confess at once, that it is quite a novelty in the annals of the order, which *they* thought beneficial to introduce.

That the Grand Lodge, however, never dreamed of any such powers being vested in them over the actions of individuals, is not only evident from the words of the law above quoted, and the uniform practice of the craft; but is strongly corroborated by other circumstances. The law alluded to, it will be observed, was not promulgated till the year 1799, and must therefore be held to be declaratory not only of every power which the Grand Lodge imagined itself to have been in the use of exercising, but likewise of the very utmost extremity to which they supposed it could be carried on the greatest emergency. – If ever there was a time when the Grand Lodge had most reason to be circumspect in watching the conduct of its members; if ever there was a time when it had most reason to be suspicious of the bad influence which their attendance on other lodges might / create; if ever there was a time when such a restriction on the liberties of individuals could be at all palliated, it was in the year 1799. – It was in that eventful year, as some personages now in the Grand Lodge may have reason to remember, that the contagious principles of atheism and sedition imbibed from a neighbouring country,[20] had excited the attention of the British Legislature. – It was in societies resembling the fraternity of masons on the continent, that these principles were known to have been cherished, and the finger of suspicion began to point at some of our lodges at home.[21] Surely if ever there was a time when the Grand Lodge was called on to do its utmost in preventing the currency of insinuations so dishonourable to the craft, and to enact every law that might testify its abhorrence of any thing that looked like the shadow of insubordination or dissaffection to established ordinances, it was in the year 1799.

To the records of these times we therefore look back, in quest of some precedent to justify the powers which our *political* masons are now exercising; and, although it be unfair to quadrate that permanent system of legislation which obtains in peaceful times with those strong measures which temporary emergencies may require, yet even upon this unequal ground we will meet them, and defy them to adduce an example in defence of their conduct. On perusing the many anxious provisions which the Grand Lodge at that time enacted to regulate the conduct of her members and preserve the purity of the craft, we observe her more than once declaring her responsibility to government for the good conduct and sound principles of "all lodges holding of her," and who shall follow her injunctions then enacted; and yet we cannot perceive a single syllable to guard against / the dangerous influence which these lodges might imbibe from their individual members frequenting "irregular lodges."[22] From this circumstance alone we are warranted to infer, that the Grand Lodge considered any enactment of this sort as beyond the jurisdiction of a masonic assembly.

It is also worthy of remark, that the Grand Lodge, by the words of its own laws, expressly admits the existence of a number of *lodges in Scotland* who do not acknowledge its authority. Indeed these lodges still exist to speak for themselves, and it is therefore quite absurd in our *political* rulers now to inform us, that *no lodge* can meet in Scotland independent of their authority.

From that unlucky hour when the leaders of this faction got themselves established in office in the Grand Lodge, all harmony among the brethren was at an end. They began their ominous reign by the removal of every office-bearer inimical to their views who had seen the lodge in its 'better days;' verifying the maxim, that when the spirit of innovation is once actuated by political motives, it seldom stops short of overturning the most established and revered institutions.

It has ever been understood as a sure symptom of disease in a body-politic, when those laws which uniformly regulate its operations while in health, are in the slightest degree distorted or their meaning explained away in subleties. If such conduct be in one instance permitted; if the party in power for the time are allowed in one instance to interpret the standing laws into any other meaning, different from that which the words of them would at once convey to the mind of an unprejudiced reader, such party, or rather its leaders, become, in fact, the sole legislators of the community; the written laws are good for nothing; and in the / language of Jack Cade, we may one day be told, 'I have thought upon't, – it shall be so: – Away, burn all the records of the lodge, my mouth shall be the parliament of masons.'[23]

But, to apply this observation to the present case, we have only to look back on the conduct of these men and their adherents in the Grand Lodge, *long before* any cause of offence was given them by the Master of the Caledonian Lodge or any body else. In the eagerness with which this faction hurried on to their darling object of *absolute power*, there was no written law, however express, which could form a barrier to their proceedings. It is particularly enacted, that no member representing a lodge in arrear of its usual contribution to the funds of the Grand Lodge, shall be entitled to vote therein until such arrear is discharged. Accordingly, at a contested election of a Grand Clerk, which happened some years ago, a respectable member of the Grand Lodge (Brother Peter Douglas, proxy master for Dunkeld) moved that, in taking the vote, due attention should be paid to this law. – But the present Substitute Grand Master (*Mr Inglis*)[24] perceiving that this would not suit the designs which he and his party had in view; and being unable to use any conclusive argument against the express words of the law, betook himself to the usual expedient of his associates. A tumultuous outcry was set up by the whole party collected there for the purpose; by their voices the law was instantly repealed; and, by the votes thus obtained, the present Grand Clerk was elected. On the fidelity and gratitude of this gentleman to his benefactors on this occasion, we shall have reason, in the sequel, to pronounce a most ample eulogium.

Upon this head, however, it is but doing justice to all parties to observe, that a good deal was said on the above / occasion as to the law having become obsolete, and upon that ground a number of impartial men, though they voted against the election of that gentleman as clerk, did not insist against the repeal of that antiquated regulation. *Mr Inglis*, therefore, and his associates got every thing their own way; the law was repealed; the vote put, and there the matter ended. But the circumstance is here introduced, in order that it may be kept in view, and contrasted with what is to follow.

It has been said by the rulers of the present Grand Lodge, that the whole disturbance which has arisen in the craft, took place in consequence of the Right Worshipful Master of the Caledonian Lodge, having proposed that the Grand Lodge should present an address to his Majesty, on what they have been pleased to term a *political* subject. That the address was in some degree of a *political* nature cannot be disputed.[25] Neither do the whole brethren who now address you, concur in approbation of that measure. Like yourselves, some of us are of opinion, that the Right Worshipful Brother was in the wrong to bring forward that address, others that he was not. Some of us approve of his conduct in that and in other masonic affairs, and others of us do not; but thus far we are all agreed, that whether he was right or wrong in moving the address, he appears to have done it from the best motives, and not without the decided approbation of many respectable members of the Grand Lodge; and that since *Mr Inglis*, as Sub-stitute Grand Master, did not instantly close the lodge, when he perceived what he considered *politics* about to be introduced, he ought to have allowed the pro-posal, whether right or wrong, the benefit of a fair hearing and a conscientious vote. In the next place, we are of / opinion, that if Brother Mitchell did commit a masonic offence by introducing that address, he ought to have been tried for that offence only, and not for the other imaginary crimes which Mr Gibson laid to his charge, (of which, more particulars hereafter,) and which none of us can perceive supported by the evidence adduced. We are likewise agreed, that, taking Brother Mitchell's conduct all in all in contrast with that of his persecutors, there is much to be said in his defence, as a man most cruelly injured, while, in extenuation of the wanton oppression which they have exercised, not only over him, but over the whole craft, there is nothing whatever can be pled. But whether, in bringing forward this address, he acted properly or not, and whether Mr Gibson, in the accusation against him, was possessed of a sincere desire to promote the interests of masonry and check all innovation, or meant nothing more than a gratification of private pique, and to pave the way for carrying the plan he and his associates had already formed into execution, we have no wish to enquire; it is of the pro-ceedings of the Grand Lodge subsequent to the sentence, that attach to many of the craft who, it is not even pretended, were guilty of a masonic crime, and not of the policy and justice of that sentence itself, we complain.

Patronised as the fraternity has been, in so gracious a manner during the reign of our present beloved Sovereign,[26] it was not unnatural surely to expect, on their part, some demonstration of gratitude for the high favour that had been shewn them. In times of National emergency, and when great events had transpired to call forth a spontaneous expression of those feelings by which every Briton is attached to his King, his country, and its laws, the masons / of Britain were never among the last to evince these patriotic sentiments.[27] Whilst other descrip-tions of his Majesty's subjects were approaching the throne with demonstrations of their loyalty and attachment, it could hardly be imagined that a fraternity who had experienced such distinguished marks of his paternal care, should be backward in joining their voices to those of their fellow-citizens. Accordingly, within these few years, we have seen the present Noble Acting Grand Master of

Scotland presenting, in name of the Grand Lodge of England, an "Address" to his Majesty, wherein permission is requested 'to approach the throne with this *public declaration* of their *political principles.*' 'The times,' they said, 'demanded it of them, and they wished not to be among the last to throw *their* weight, whatever it might be, into the scale. Though written in the institute of their order, that they should not, at their meetings, go into *religious or political discussions, a crisis so unlooked for as the present, justified a relaxation of that rule; their first duty as Britons superseding all other considerations*.'[28]

After so noble an example of the *political* sentiments of their English brethren, and of their present illustrious Acting Grand Master, it could not be supposed that the masons on this side the Tweed were so destitute of emulations as not be fired with the same energy. – No, the subsequent annals of the Grand Lodge of Scotland furnish us with no less than five addresses to the throne on the public events of the day. The victories of Duncan / and Nelson,[29] the failure of two impious attempts on the life of our Sovereign, and other events of the times, all furnished the materials of addresses to the throne, carried by an enthusiastic and unanimous vote. The propriety of such addresses, instead of being questioned, was sanctioned by the loudest acclamations; and it may be safely alleged, that within these fifteen years, there has not been a corporation in the kingdom more eager in manifesting their loyalty and attachment to our most gracious Sovereign than the Grand Lodge of Scotland.

With such examples before their eyes, it cannot be surprising to behold the supporters of this motion led away in some degree from that "*rule*," which prohibits the discussion of "religious and political" subjects in Mason Lodges, especially when the Noble Acting Grand Master of Scotland, and the Grand Lodge of England, had already told them, 'that a crisis so unlooked for as the present, justified a relaxation of that rule.' But it will be said that the "*unlooked for crisis*" of 1793, was somewhat different from "the unlooked for crisis of 1807;" that in the one case we were threatened with the introduction of *Atheism*, while, in the other, we had only to apprehend the introduction of *Popery*:[30] – that, in the one case, we would have our liberties in the hands of men who professed no faith at all; and, in the other, we were only to entrust them to men who professed that no faith should be kept with *us*. Unfortunately, the brethren who voted for the address were not clearsighted enough to perceive these important distinctions; and therefore conceived, that the *crisis* of 1807 was as much "*unlooked for*," and as dangerous, if possible, to the constitution, as that of 1793. In this mistaken view of the / matter, they concluded, that the axiom of the Noble Earl

---

and the Grand Lodge of England applied to the one case as well as to the other, and 'justified a relaxation of the 'rule.'

But the system of party had so far contaminated the bosom of a lodge, once susceptible of more generous feelings, that instead of promoting a loyal and dutiful address to that Sovereign, who had acted so beneficently towards them, it was resolved to wreak their vengeance on the unfortunate brethren who proposed it. The brother, who introduced the motion, did every thing in his power to soothe and conciliate their irritated feelings. He prefaced it with a solemn declaration, 'that he trusted it would be unanimous, as it became the duty of an Order, who had experienced much favour and indulgence from his present Majesty, to express their loyalty and attachment to him, on an occasion in which his honour and his conscience were deeply concerned; – that all idea of its being a political question, would be laid aside, as, whatever his own ideas of politics were, he was too well aware of the constitution of masonry to introduce political matter into it; – that none he hoped would be so disloyal, so base, and so ungrateful, as to take it up in a political point of view, and to endeavour by this kind of side-wind to get quit of it; – and, lastly, he again candidly declared, that the sole object of the motion was, to evince our loyalty, our gratitude, and our thankfulness to the best of Sovereigns, as had on many occasions been done by us.'

After this solemn declaration – after the tenor of the address itself*, than the language of which nothing could / be more mild and conciliating to the sentiments of all the brethren – after the fair, open, and liberal manner in which it had been brought forward, at a general meeting of the Grand Lodge, it was scarcely to be expected, that men would be found so very uncandid, and so far blinded by party prejudice, as to impute sinister designs to the promoters of such a loyal and patriotic measure. Admitting, however, that all their ungenerous argument was just – admitting that the supporters of the address, however pure their motives might be, were in the wrong to propose it – in short, admitting the utmost force of all that can be alleged against its political tendency; why, in the name of all that is sacred among masons, did not Mr Inglis, as Substitute Grand Master, sitting in the chair, the instant that he perceived any discussion, which he thought contrary to the rules of the craft, about to be introduced, put a stop to it at once, by closing the Lodge, or by any other method usual in such cases? What meaning could he and his party have in view in doing otherwise on this occasion, and thereby rendering themselves equally culpable with those that brought forward the measure? If the address was of a political nature, and if politics were unfit to be introduced there, why did Mr Inglis and his friends enter so keenly into that discussion? Why did they not instantly call Dr Mitchell to order, when the first

---

*   Vide Appendix, No. 2.

syllable of his purpose was announced; and if he still persisted in it, why were the usual methods of preserving order in such cases not immediately resorted to?

Since, however, Mr Inglis and his party, for reasons best known to themselves, thought fit on this occasion to join issue with the supporters of this motion, in a debate, the very existence of which in mason lodges, they now tell / us, is contrary to all rule, why, in the name of all that is honourable among men, did they not allow the question thus entered on, to have the benefit of that fair discussion which the laws of every well governed assembly require? Can any excuse be figured for the scene which follows?

After a number of frivolous objections to the formality of the motion had been made and repelled without a division, one or two of the brethren delivered their opinions, that there was nothing of a political nature in the motion then before them, but that its sole object being a renewal of the Grand Lodge's former expressions of affection and loyalty to his Majesty, they thought it their duty to give it their warmest concurrence. The question being thus fairly opened, most people would imagine that the Chairman, after having acquiesced so far in the introduction of it, as a subject of debate, would allow the members to conduct it accordingly. By the laws of the Grand Lodge, the Chairman can have no vote, except in cases of an equal division in the voices of the members present. His duty in this, as in every other meeting of the kind, is well known to be, that of preserving order and regularity among those who are debating, and by no means to act himself the part of a disputant. No sooner, however, had the brethren alluded to, delivered their sentiments in favour of the address, than Mr Inglis, losing sight of the duties of his station, and of all established rule, without waiting to hear another word on either side, entered into a long and keen harangue on the merits of the question. Diving at once into the ocean of politics, he gave the lodge copious extracts from all the parliamentary speeches delivered on the Roman Catholic / bill by the leaders of the opposition; he enlarged on the Test Act,[31] and the differences of Presbyterians and Episcopalians; expatiated in glowing panegyric on the sentiments of Lord Howick,[32] the views and measures of the late ministry, &c.; and winded up his long oration with an earnest entreaty, that the brethren, whose minds he had thus enlightened, should negative the address. Without waiting an instant longer, Mr Inglis then moved the previous question.

The Chairman, thus hurried by his zeal, in a manner altogether unprecedented, into the hottest debate, had however the mortification to see his arguments fully refuted, and the motion set in its true light, disengaged from the labyrinth of politics in which he had striven to involve it. A long discussion ensued, till the question came at last to the vote, 'Address,' or 'Not Address.'[33] Here followed a scene, of which, for the honour of our nation, it is trusted there can be found but few examples in the history of any public assembly of its citizens.

It has already been seen, that the old law, disqualifying the votes of lodges in arrear, which had long been considered obsolete, was finally decided to be so, in a question which occurred as to the election of the present Grand Clerk. It has also been observed, that Mr Inglis himself was the chief instrument in bringing about the repeal of that antiquated regulation. On this occasion, however, he again found it necessary to shift sides, and the law which was formerly repealed, upon a few minutes warning, to answer one design, now underwent a resurrection equally sudden to answer another. By the assistance of this clerk, whose gratitude towards his benefactor we cannot sufficiently / extol, Mr Inglis was enabled to perform the most astonishing feats, and with less than *a third* of the members present, to *outvote* the remaining *two thirds* of the meeting, and turn them all out of doors without the least ceremony, when they ventured to scrutinize the manœuvre.

Having declared the repealed law respecting arrears[34] to be still in force, and being in possession at same time of the books, which alone could instruct the true state of these arrears, it was an easy matter to get things managed to answer their purpose; and, during the preceding days, the gentlemen do not seem to have been idle. So neatly was every thing arranged, that when the vote came to be put, *not one* of those who voted *against* the address was declared by the clerk in arrear, while, on the other hand, almost *one half* of those tendered for the address were objected to, and on this account refused.

Of the votes *against* the address, besides the numbers who must have been in arrear, (the Dalkeith Lodge, for instance, and others, whose arrears were afterwards proved *by the books* not to have been paid till next meeting), were many which, though altogether *inadmissible by the laws of the Grand Lodge*, were gladly received on this occasion. The Grand Clerk, for example, voted two for the Peebles Lodge; but the warden for whom he voted had not on the clothing of that lodge. The vote of Brother David Pitcairn of the Ceres Lodge was admitted, though he was not a member of the Grand Lodge, his proxy commission having never been read nor received, (for, at an after meeting of the Grand Lodge, his vote was refused upon this very ground), and though, besides, he was not in the clothing of that lodge. But the vote of Brother White, his warden, / who was exactly in similar circumstances, being tendered *for* the address, was rejected!

But, notwithstanding all these proceedings, the bare narrative of which must excite disgust, it will be immediately seen, that had the matter rested here, and had the votes, even after all this, been faithfully reported, the address was certainly carried. To insure, as much as possible, an accurate account of the state of the vote, *four* gentlemen then present, viz. Brother Brown, master of Mary's Chapel; Brother H. R. Brown, proxy for Jedburgh St Andrew's; Brother D.

Horne, and Brother Mitchell, took each of them a note of the voices as they were received by the clerk. And that there might be no mistake, at every vote that was given, one of these gentlemen called out to the person giving it, to repeat it. In this way the state of the vote was infallibly ascertained by the exact coincidence of these *four* lists, which, though taken by different persons and in different corners of the room, gave each of them, *for* the address 28, against it 24; being a majority of 4.

No doubt then remained but that the address had been carried in spite of all the unfair opposition it had met with. But, what was the astonishment of the whole meeting on hearing the clerk (after some whispering between him and the chairman) announce the *rejection* of the address by 28 against 27, being a majority of *one* voice!! The brethren present, of all descriptions, were confounded. Not another person in the room had the assurance to corroborate the clerk's statement; and a scrutiny[35] was therefore instantly and loudly demanded from every quarter. This, however, was peremptorily refused from the chair; the war-whoop was immediately set up, and for some minutes not a voice could be heard amid the stentorian acclamations and thundering / applauses of the chairman and his party. In this interval of tumult and confusion, while the whole *pack* was in full cry, the clerk slipt[36] out of the room with all his books and papers; and the chairman, who would not listen to another word on the subject, kept driving on the table with his heavy mallet to increase the uproar, till he found an opportunity of rushing out of doors, leaving the lodge unclosed,[37] and the meeting dissolved in a manner unprecedented among masons.

To offer any comment on these proceedings were an idle and unnecessary task; they speak for themselves in a language which no man can misunderstand. Admitting, as already observed, that the address were an improper measure, why did the chairman suffer it to be at all introduced; and since he did so, was this a reason for his relinquishing the duties of his station by becoming the leader of a party? Was this a reason for making a mockery of the laws of the lodge, by enforcing those which had been abrogated, and trampling on those which were in force? Was this a reason for concealing a state of the arrears, for receiving votes which the laws declared inadmissible, and rejecting others which the practice of the lodge had hitherto sustained? Admitting, in the next place, that the address really had been negatived by a majority of *one* voice, as reported by the clerk, under all the circumstances which have been mentioned, was it unnatural to demand a scrutiny, or was it proper in the chairman to refuse that demand? When *four* respectable brethren agreed exactly in reporting the state of the vote, when only *one* immediately under Mr Inglis's influence, *after whispering some time with him*, brought out a / majority of only *one* vote on the side of the question that Mr Inglis had so keenly supported, was it not reasonable to conclude, that a small *mistake* had occurred in the reckoning of this solitary individual; and was it not necessary for the honour of that individual, for the honour of all his party, that the matter should be thoroughly expiscated?[38] After such proceedings, one would imagine that a man of honour and spirit, placed in Mr Inglis's situation, would have spurned at the very idea of lying under such mean suspicions; and that, however much he felt exasperated against the persons who demanded the scrutiny, an honest pride would impel him to be the most earnest man in the room to enforce this demand, that the world might at once perceive the fairness of his own conduct, and the malevolence of those who could suspect him.[39]

Although by this notable manœuvre the party had contrived to maintain their tottering ascendancy in the Grand Lodge, they dreaded the issue of another meeting, and in this view, set every engine to work in collecting recruits. Proxies were showered in from all quarters, and in order to qualify them to vote, the secretary or clerk are known to have compounded the arrears due by most of them for a mere trifle, while every lodge not specially enlisted under the banner of the faction, was compelled to pay to the uttermost farthing. In this way the doors of the Grand Lodge might be truly said to have been thrown open to all and sundry persons of every description, who were ready to vote with its rulers, while every obstruction was opposed to the entrance of any others. Accordingly at the subsequent meetings there appeared a motley crew, most of whom had never been seen in the lodge before. It was at / once suspected that these men had no right to sit there, and the books, which alone could have thrown a light on these transactions, were earnestly called for, that the matter might be investigated. But, notwithstanding the numerous applications for that purpose, all inspection of the books was peremptorily refused until the gentlemen concerned had leisure to get every thing managed in their own way, and a set of entries inserted, to amuse the public and conceal the extent of the manœuvre.

Having thus introduced into the lodge a troop of underlings, ready to vote with them through thick and thin, the leaders carried every thing before them. As an instance of their usual form of procedure, may be noticed the following. A proxy commission being presented for a brother who was favourable to the address, an insinuation was made as to its not having been actually signed on the day it bore date, and, on this account, the commission was instantly rejected. At a subsequent meeting, a commission was presented for Brother Thin (an adherent of the faction), purporting to have been granted by the Dunbar Castle Lodge. The date of this commission being read, a brother rose and offered *to make oath*, that he had been present from beginning to end of the meeting held of that date by the Dunbar Castle Lodge, and that no such commission was then signed or ever heard of in that lodge. Brother Cunningham reminded the meeting of the commission which had been formerly rejected, on a *bare suspicion* of what in this case was offered to be instantly verified *on oath*, and earnestly conjured them to act consistently, by either recalling their sentence against the former, or / rejecting this commission also; but the party, collected there in great force, on the signal being given, set up the usual howl; the chairman thundered on the table with his mallet, Brother Cunningham was threatened with being immediately turned out; and Mr Thin's commission was sustained amid the loudest acclamations!

After this specimen and three or four more of a description precisely similar, it was but too evident that the power of the party was established on a basis which bade defiance to every law, and that the destruction of our masonic liberties was fast approaching. Hitherto it had been struggling for a bare existence; its leaders had put on the smooth semblance of every masonic virtue, until after gradually undermining and displacing the ancient office-bearers, they found means, to introduce a gang of adherents devoted to serve them in every measure. It was then that they first began to display the cloven foot,[40] and to carry into execution the scheme which, from the beginning, they had planned against the liberties of the fraternity.[xxxiv]

The grand object in view was to convert the whole order of masonry in this country into one great *political party*, and every individual whose sentiments might be repugnant to this measure was to be forthwith expelled from 'all masonic privileges.' To accomplish this revolution, a plan was laid, which, for boldness of design and depth of contrivance, is not to be surpassed in the annals of their political career. When the party got possession of a few seats in the Grand Lodge, their first care, as we have already observed, was to fill the places of the office-bearers with trusty adherents; after which they employed / their whole influence in *regenerating* the country lodges, and such of the Edinburgh lodges as were fit for their purpose, by means of suitable elections to the chairs and proxy deputations of these lodges. All this passed for some time unobserved, and might have done so for a while longer, had not the trying measure of the address precipitated their designs rather quicker than these crafty politicians could have wished. After the narrow escape they had made on that occasion, they were under the necessity, even at the risk of detection of their whole plan, to expedite their *recruiting* system by a sudden levy *en masse*, which they poured into the Grand Lodge all at once from every quarter. We have already seen the manner in which these men were collected, and the first experiments which their leaders appear to have made on them, by way of trial, to see how far their services could be safely relied on. Being found qualified for this purpose beyond expectation, their chiefs now resolved on deferring no longer the execution of their design. To clear the Grand Lodge, and all the other lodges of the capital, of every mason, without exception, who had not embraced their *political creed*, was the first great end to be accomplished. But although, with the assistance of their adherents, they might have carried this measure at once by putting it to the vote, they were too wily not to perceive the propriety of keeping up a shadow of decency, and therefore preferred the more gradual, but no less certain method which they afterwards pursued.

The introducer of the address to his Majesty had, as was naturally to be expected, became an object of aversion to the whole party, and its leaders formed the idea / of rendering him the engine for accomplishing their own designs against the liberties of the craft, and transferring upon his shoulders that very odium which would otherwise have alighted upon themselves. They were fully aware that, if they could any how succeed in getting some degrading and unmerited punishment inflicted upon him, the Caledonian Lodge, whose members were known to be favourable to the address, would withdraw its allegiance, and that by this means they could at once get rid of a multitude of antagonists. This being atchieved, they would have nothing more to do, than to declare the secession of *the lodge* to have been the act 'of some of its individuals' only,[41] whom they would accordingly expel, and bestow the name of 'The Caledonian Lodge' upon any number of their own adherents, however *'few'* or *'obscure,'* that happened to be members of it. One lodge being thus *regenerated*, nothing was more easy than to revolutionise the rest in the following manner. In the first place, after expelling the whole of the original Caledonian Lodge, the remaining Lodges of Edinburgh were to be prohibited from visiting her under the like penalty. This measure, it was thought, would be so exceedingly galling to these lodges as to induce a similar secession, and afford a similar pretence for creating new lodges in their room. But should it happen, contrary to expectation, that the lodges of Edinburgh, out of respect to the memory of what the Grand Lodge once had been, should acquiesce in this tyrannical prohibition, there was still another measure which could not fail to be altogether intolerable, and this was to prohibit *every individual*, on pain of forfeiting 'all masonic privileges,' to visit / his friends of the Caledonian Lodge, on any pretence whatsoever! However congenial the rancour of this sentence might be to the disposition of their own partizans, they were certain that it would never go down with any other description of masons, and that the very odium of such a prohibition would induce many of them to visit the Caledonian Lodge who would not otherwise have thought of doing so. Every one of these was accordingly to be instantly expelled, unless he meanly promised never more to exercise that liberty; and, in selecting the objects of such punishment, care was to be taken to pitch, in the first place, on the office-bearers of the most respectable lodges, in order that the lodges thus insulted in their persons might be driven to resolutions of Secession. By this means, and by the creation of new lodges in the room of each as it dropped off, the whole order of Scottish masonry was to be converted either into the partizans or the slaves of the faction. For, even in those lodges who could not thus be purified by an immediate separation of the chaff from the corn, it would be impossible for any independent spirited man long to remain shut up from the society of those with whom he had been accustomed to associate.

Such is the outline of that conspiracy, which, it is now too evident, was hatched long before the address was heard of. It is quite absurd to imagine that the punishment of the mover of it, let his crime in their eyes have been ever so enormous, was the chief end which these designing politicians had in view, when they pursued such *universal* measures against the brethren at large. It was easy to discern, that *something of greater magnitude* lay at the bottom of all this, and that some extensive revolution was in agitation. / From the domineering character of the party, it was but too plain that this latent design was connected with *politics*, and that to these every other consideration would be necessarily sacrificed. As, however, it was of great importance to them to keep this their regulating move perfectly concealed, until the scheme should be perfected, in all their discourses to the brethren, they not only disavowed such intentions, but with the most consummate dissimulation retorted the charge against those who had detected their secret designs. A hue and cry was set up against the Caledonian Lodge, as endeavouring to introduce *politics* into the order; and the very men who were designing to convert the institution of masonry into a political party subservient to themselves, were the first who began the outcry. But, however well such conduct may be suited to the genius of the party, the minds of men now-a-days are too enlightened to be duped by such artifices. Let us now attend to the history of their subsequent proceedings, and observe the perseverance with which these men laboured to accomplish their project.

The mover of the address, as already observed, was for many reasons the first victim to be immolated. As, unfortunately, the proposal of a *dutiful address to our Sovereign* could not with any shadow of decency be made a crime either civil or masonic *in this country*, the leaders of the faction were forced to conceal their spleen from this *vexatious* circumstance, and to examine the conduct of the Caledonian Lodge for years past, in quest of materials to manufacture some charge or other against its master. Luckily it occurred to their recollection, that, the Caledonian Lodge had, in consequence of a complaint at the instance of the Lodge Roman / Eagle, been prohibited by the Grand Lodge from holding their meetings on the fourth Friday of each month, which the Roman Eagle pretended was *their* day of meeting, although, from every document which had been consulted by the Caledonian Lodge before they pitched on the day in question, it appeared that the Roman Eagle had usually met on *another day*.[42] It was also remembered, that when the Caledonian Lodge received notice of this prohibition (which was issued *immediately* upon the application of the Roman Eagle Lodge, without allowing the former an opportunity of being heard,) the master and some of the brethren expressed their surprise at this proceeding, and hoped that the lodge would concur in remonstrating against it. This was unanimously agreed to; but

in the meantime, the lodge thought itself under the necessity of obeying the prohibition, and did so accordingly. From the circumstances of this transaction, an
ordinary person would think it almost impossible to rear up even the appearance
of a crime. But by a mode of reasoning peculiar to themselves, the leaders of the
Grand Lodge had no great difficulty in making out, from the facts above detailed,
two very serious charges against the master of the Caledonian Lodge; *1st*, that he
endeavoured to prevail with his lodge to disobey the prohibition of the Grand
Lodge; *because* he desired them to consider it, and to pray the Grand Lodge to
recall[xxxv] it; and, *2dly*, that he *proposed* a secession from the Grand Lodge; *because*,
in the course of the strong ferment into which that prohibition had thrown the
minds of the Caledonian Brethren, some indignant expressions had been made
use of by a few of them, which the master did all in his power to repress. /

In entering upon the question to which these charges gave rise, we must once
more caution our readers against the attempts which have been industriously
made, to confound the cause of masonic liberty which we are now supporting,
with the private quarrels of Messrs Gibson and Mitchell. This is the artifice
which the rulers of the Grand Lodge have all along employed to mislead you,
from the general question now at issue. But it is needless to add, that with the
private quarrels of these gentlemen, we have no concern whatever. Our object is,
to point out the manner in which the projectors of this masonic conspiracy contrived to sap the laws of the institution, under the pretext of prosecuting crimes.
Our object is, to shew, that the circumstances founded on in the case of this
individual brother, were insufficient to warrant the sentence which followed;
and that, therefore, the rulers of the Grand Lodge, by insisting in the prosecution, *must have had some secret design in view*, of a nature totally distinct from
what they professed. Keeping this constantly in recollection, we now proceed to
investigate the merits of the case.

On the 1st day of January 1808, (*eight months after* the inexpiable crime
of bringing forward the address), Mr Gibson, writer to the signet,[43] assuming
the office of prosecutor, presented, at the bar of the tribunal, a 'Petition and
Complaint' against the Right Worshipful Brother John Mitchell, Master of the
Caledonian Lodge of Edinburgh, as standing charged with certain high crimes
and misdemeanours, and therefore craving the tribunal 'to inflict such punishment upon Brother Mitchell as in the circumstances of the case might appear to
be proper.' It is perhaps unnecessary to inform the brethren, that although this
complaint / stated no less than *four* separate charges, *two* of them were introduced for no other purpose than that of lengthening the paper, and giving it
a formidable appearance; and were accordingly *passed from by Brother Gibson
himself* in the course of the subsequent procedure. Of these it is therefore unnecessary to take any notice. The only two that remained, and which could be at
all insisted in, were those which, as already observed, had been concocted out

of the long forgotten story of the Roman Eagle. Of the first of these charges the irrelevancy must strike every one; but admitting, for the sake of argument, that an *endeavour* of that kind were a species of offence against the Grand Lodge, it will fall to be considered as incorporated with the *second* charge, namely, the *proposal of a secession*. This charge, therefore, comprehends the meaning of all the ramifications into which, for the sake of ostentation, it was thought proper to divide this complaint. In the sequel, we shall see how far this charge of *proposing a secession*, was instructed by the evidence adduced. But, in the meantime, we must notice a few preliminary considerations, which strongly indicate the design that lay at the bottom of all the procedure thus ostensibly directed against the master of the Caledonian Lodge.

The power which was thus conferred on Mr Gibson of dragging any individual that he thought proper before the bar of the Grand Lodge, to answer for alleged crimes of a nature *entirely public*, must at once strike every person as a circumstance exceedingly suspicious. The considerations on this head, which, before entering at all upon the merits of the case, were laid before the Grand Lodge, were of a nature which no impartial mind could overlook. The most judicious brethren pointed out the ruinous consequences / of permitting Mr Gibson, or any other private individual, to arrogate this public and invidious station; to complain, not on account of any personal injury done to himself, but of offences of a general and public nature, alleged to have been committed in another lodge, where the accuser was not present, by an individual not belonging to the accuser's lodge, nor in any shape connected with it. They shewed, that the false and imperfect accounts which individuals might daily receive of what had been said or done in other places, might lead them to fancy offences where none were committed. And if, upon every such occasion, each of these individuals was indulged with the privilege of coming forward as a public accuser, there could be no end of wrangling and dissention. Every person actuated by private dislike or hatred towards another, might thus, without even alleging a personal injury, search for every sort of public accusation which their own malice, or that of others, could supply, and bring them forward, at the most favourable opportunity, to harass[xxxvi] and distress the accused. Thus, under the specious pretext of promoting good order, the whole time of the Grand Lodge would be consumed, in hearing the charges which the members of one lodge might bring, not against the members of the same lodge, but of some other lodge, against whom they might have some real or supposed ground of offence.

In addition to all these arguments against the competency of the complaint, which were of themselves unanswerable, many of the older masons earnestly conjured their rulers to pause for a little, and before opening a door to such lamentable proceedings, to look back on their own records, and regulate the present case according to the laws which had been observed by their forefathers. /

With such convincing reasons before them, enforced by the most earnest and affecting entreaties, is it to be imagined that the Grand Lodge would have refused to examine the competency of the complaint, or to look back on the records for the satisfaction of the brethren, had there not been some latent design in view, of a nature quite hostile to the pure principles of masonry? If the preservation of these principles had been their object, would they have overlooked the important considerations then laid before them – would they have declared it unnecessary to look for precedents, in a case, where the very foundation of all masonic regularity was endangered, and where measures replete with such disastrous consequences were for the first time introduced into the craft? What then are we to conclude respecting the motives of these men, when we behold them thus trampling on every established rule? Must we not infer that *something* different from masonry was the cause?

The competency of the complaint having been sustained, and the motion for a search of precedents over-ruled, the *merits* of the charges were next considered, and a proof allowed to each party of the *facts* they reciprocally alleged. For this purpose a committee was appointed, Mr Inglis, as Substitute Grand Master, being preses[44] and convener, Mr Gibson, as prosecutor, was allowed in the first place to finish his proof, after which the defender was to have adduced his exculpatory evidence.

These arrangements being made, Mr Gibson began his proof; and during the sittings of the committee for several weeks, enjoyed every advantage and leisure in bringing forward and examining his witnesses. Seventeen were interrogated, and their depositions taken down in writing. / On a question of such general importance to the liberties of the craft, it was surely incumbent on Mr Gibson to make out his charge in the clearest manner, lest (as afterwards turned out to be the case) the decision given here should be interpreted into a precedent for future oppression. Instead of this, however, *not one* of the witnesses could swear to the principal, or rather only charge, that of a *secession*; and Mr Gibson, after raking up every circumstance, from first to last; after taking down the very *thoughts*, *opinions*, and *ideas* of the witnesses, as if these had been matters of *fact*, and after exhausting every talent which nature had granted him, or professional experience improved, was at last constrained, on the 17th of February, to declare his proof at an end.

On a former occasion, in the Grand Lodge, Mr Gibson had accused Dr Mitchell of presenting a *forged* commission of proxy. When, therefore, the latter had begun his proof, and was examining his *third* witness, it was judged adviseable that this indecorous behaviour of Mr Gibson should also be taken notice of in the record. On a question being put to that effect, Mr Gibson cried out, '*I say still the commission is a forgery.*' To endure the reiteration of such a provoking insult, was beyond the patience of any man; and, as might be expected, the other declared the assertion to be '*a lie.*' We could wish to draw a veil over the scene which ensued; but, situated as we now are, to develope the conduct of your present rulers becomes our imperious duty.

Mr Gibson, upon hearing this retort, rushed upon his opponent, seized him by the throat, dashed his head against the wall, and struck a furious blow at one of the members of the committee, who was hastening to prevent farther / violence. Brother Mitchell cried out to the chairman (Mr Inglis) for protection; the members of the committee also appealed to him; but is it to be conceived among masons! – that the Substitute Grand Master of the order – of an order whose very essence consists in the diffusion of brotherly love, should refuse to listen to the cries of a brother in distress, should contemplate the unseemly spectacle then before his eyes, and coolly vindicate the '*punishment*,' as he was pleased to term it! Yes, brethren, to the eternal dishonour of our name, the fact is but too well known in the records of that Criminal Court*, where this shocking affair was afterwards investigated; and for the first time, since the institution of the Grand Lodge, were its sacred walls polluted with blood!

In the meantime, Mr Gibson had grasped a bludgeon which lay near him, and was again hastening towards his victim, when the members of the committee, who had in vain implored the intercession of the Substitute Grand Master, now hurried in a body to Dr Mitchell's assistance, and succeeded in rescuing him. It is needless to add, that after this brutal outrage, the latter found it quite impossible to go on with his proof. He therefore had recourse to the last remedy of a gentleman, placed in this unfortunate situation, and demanded of Mr Gibson that satisfaction *which honourable men are unaccustomed to decline.*

The result is already sufficiently public. It is not, however, our design to attack or wound the feelings of individuals. With the private quarrels of Messrs Gibson and Mitchell, as already observed, we have nothing whatever / to do. Neither must we be understood to animadvert in the slightest degree on the private conduct of Mr Inglis, or any other gentleman concerned in the late masonic proceedings. It is their conduct as *masons* only, the views of their party in the Grand Lodge, and the methods which they took to advance them, that we are now engaged in exposing to the merited reprobation of the craft. In private life they may, for aught that we know, be men of the strictest morality. In *politics*, they may also *mean* well; and, when spurred on by party-zeal, may perhaps imagine that it would be better to sacrifice masonry altogether, if they could not get it converted into an engine to extend the principles of their party. But it is in this respect that every conscientious mason must differ from and condemn them; and without levelling at one individual more than at another, is entitled

---

*   Vide Precognition taken before the Sheriff of Edinburgh.

to expose whatever appears improper in their conduct, as members of the craft. When, therefore, we unfold to the brethren the abominable scene which took place in the committee, we do not mean to attack either Mr Inglis or Mr Gibson; but, we ask you, brethren, after what has been detailed, was the one a fit person to sit as Substitute Grand Master? or, was the other deserving of '*the thanks of the Grand Lodge*,' which were voted to him a few days thereafter?

The day now arrived when the Grand Lodge was to deliver its decision on the merits of the complaint, and the voluminous proof led on the part of Mr Gibson *only*. The nature of that proof, and the extent to which it supported the only relevant charge, we have already had occasion to notice. Of the seventeen witnesses adduced, *not one* could swear that the defender had ever proposed a / secession, or any thing like a secession. On the contrary, every one of them to whom the question was put, expressly swore, *that he never heard any such proposal mentioned by that gentleman.* Where then, it may be asked, lay the evidence upon which he was condemned; since, within the four corners of the proof, *led exclusively by Mr Gibson*, there could not be found a syllable to establish the crime set forth in the complaint? For the information of the brethren, we shall answer the question, and state the very strongest paragraphs of the evidence upon which sentence was pronounced, in the precise words of the witnesses themselves:

1. *Brother Hamilton* said – 'That Brother Mitchell declared the Caledonian Lodge would, in his opinion, be disgraced, if they submitted to be trampled on by the Grand Lodge.'

2. *The same brother* said – 'That Brother Mitchell *seemed to encourage the idea*, that the Caledonian Lodge could meet without a charter from the Grand Lodge.'

3. *Brother Hodgson* said – 'That *it appeared to him*, from Brother Mitchell's speeches in the Committee, *that he wished* the Lodge to secede.'

4. *Brother Dundas* said – 'That he *understood* from what passed, *that Brother Mitchell's object* was a secession.'

5. *Brother Young* said – 'That, *in his opinion*, Brother Mitchell *wished* the Caledonian Lodge to secede.'

In these extracts, our opponents themselves must do us the justice to say, that we have faithfully transcribed *the very strongest* passages of the proof. We appeal to every brother who has read it, and ask him candidly to say, whether / we have omitted any passage stronger than those above selected? If not, we would ask, in the next place, Is there any thing here to prove, 'that Brother Mitchell did, at one or other of the meetings of the Caledonian Lodge, propose that the lodge should make a secession from the Grand Lodge, and hold meetings altogether independent of the Grand Lodge*?'

---

*   Vide Complaint.

But if, from the passages above detailed, nothing whatever can be made out in support of the charge, what will be the opinion of the brethren when they read the following extracts from *the very same proof* which candour obliges us to insert, as well as the former?

1. *Brother McKenzie.* – 'Being interrogated if he recollects Brother Mitchell recommending or *appearing to recommend* that the lodge should hold meetings independently of the Grand Lodge? Depones,[45] *That he does not; and that during the whole time of the meeting the deponent sat on Brother Mitchell's right hand.*

2. *Brother Stewart* swore, – 'That *he is certain* that Brother Mitchell could have carried a motion of secession from the Grand Lodge, if he had proposed such a motion, and wished it to be carried.'

3. *Brother Clark* said, – 'That Brother Mitchell seemed to *be guided entirely* by the opinion of the lodge, and always expressed a readiness to do every thing that appeared to the members for the interest of the lodge.'

4. *Brother Dundas*, speaking of the debate which took place where Brother Mitchell was accused of *endeavouring* to prevail with his lodge to meet on the day prohibited / by the Grand Lodge, swore, – 'That the members present expressed in their conversation an unanimous determination to comply with the order of the Grand Lodge, by changing their night of meeting: That Brother Mitchell was in the chair, and the deponent *is perfectly certain* that he heard Brother Mitchell concur in the unanimous opinion of the meeting.'

Such are the words of Mr Gibson's *own witnesses*; and after the extracts which have been quoted on *both* sides from a proof thus led entirely on *one* side, it remains with the intelligent brethren to say whether there was any crime to warrant the sentence which followed. The language made use of by Dr Mitchell at his table and in his bedroom was anxiously retailed by men who had shared his unsuspecting confidence, and every syllable which he uttered either there or elsewhere was paraphrased in the course of this proof, in many a contradictory version. His *inmost thoughts* and *wishes* were guessed at, and delivered by some of these witnesses as their '*opinions;*' but, notwithstanding all the cruel treatment he had experienced from the inquisitors of the Grand Lodge, and which might have excused the harshest expressions of resentment, it appears from the evidence, that the only offensive words, which ever escaped his lips, were 'a hope that the Caledonian Lodge would not suffer itself to be trampled on.' Even this expression was repeated by a witness, who, under the guise of a friend, had shared his confidence, and participated his domestic cheer.

The proof, such as it was, being printed and distributed, those brethren who had the interest of masonry at heart, were at no loss in forming their opinion. But to / prevent farther dissention, and, at the same time, to humour as far as possible the arbitrary spirit of its rulers, a respectable member of the Grand Lodge proposed the following motion: 'That the farther prosecution of this inquiry, however well meant the motives of the brethren might have been that brought it forward, must be highly prejudicial to the interests of masonry; and that, therefore, without entering upon any discussion, as to the import of the proof, the lodge was of opinion that the Petition and Complaint ought to be dismissed.'

But this conciliatory measure did not suit the designs of the party. One of their chief orators immediately proposed that Dr Mitchell should be 'suspended *sine die*[46] from all masonic privileges;' that his Lodge should be ordained to elect another master, and 'THAT THE LODGES WITHIN SCOTLAND SHOULD BE PROHIBITED FROM ADMITTING OR COMMUNICATING WITH HIM AS A BROTHER, WITH CERTIFICATION, THAT, IF THEY ACTED IN THE CONTRARY, THEY SHOULD BE RESPONSIBLE TO THE GRAND LODGE FOR CONTEMPT OF ITS AUTHORITY.' Against the iniquity, the severity, and the absurdity of this proposal, it was in vain to remonstrate. It was in vain to appeal to the evidence adduced, and enquire if there was any thing there to sanction such unheard of rigour. Every remonstrance was disregarded, every argument over-ruled, every precedent violated, to gratify the views of the party. Many of the brethren, deceived by the plausible reasoning of these men, and the specialties of the case, unsuspicious of the true cause which lay at the bottom of this affair, were induced to acquiesce in the sentence, and thus unknowingly to pave the way for the slavery which was preparing for themselves. Little did they / then foresee, that this sentence was to be twisted into a pretext for depriving themselves of the boasted and valuable privileges of masons. Little did they then imagine, that from the precedent thus established, a system of oppression was to be reared, than which the annals of the Romish Inquisition can furnish nothing more truly detestable, or repugnant to the feelings of a mason. But, of the brethren thus deceived, the number was few in comparison with that of the persons already described, who had been introduced into the Grand Lodge for the purpose of supporting its rulers. By their assistance the nominal votes of 63 lodges were obtained in favour of the sentence to overpower the suffrages of 45, among which were reckoned the most respectable lodges in this city, and the most intelligent brethren of the Order.

No sooner was this decision promulgated in the lodges of Edinburgh, than it excited *the highest detestation.* Every sober thinking brother who might have acquiesced in a lighter punishment, was shocked with the vindictive spirit which appeared to actuate the rulers of the Grand Lodge. The severity of the sentence was loudly condemned by every unprejudiced hearer, and the most respectable lodges in Edinburgh, who of all others had best opportunity of judging of the merits of the case, were disgusted beyond measure.

Meanwhile, the chiefs of the party, instead of feeling any remorse on perceiving the animosities which their conduct had stirred up in the craft, did every thing in their power to foment these divisions into an open rupture. When the Caledonian Lodge (as they had foreseen), justly indignant at the sentence pronounced against their master, had almost unanimously confirmed him in the / chair, and voted a secession from the Grand Lodge; instead of striking that lodge off the roll, they had recourse to the new and unheard of expedient of creating *another lodge* out of *five members*, devoted to their own faction, who had been employed for the purpose of going to the meeting and dissenting from its resolutions. To the mock lodge thus created, and who held their meetings in a tavern, divested of cloathing, insignia, books, funds, or any thing else that distinguishes a lodge of masons, they made a shew of transferring the title of '*The Caledonian Lodge*;' thus rendering the sacred mysteries of the craft a matter of ridicule to every uninterested spectator.

It was impossible that the lodges of Edinburgh could behold these profanations without feeling, as every mason ought to do, the greatest abhorrence at the spirit which obviously inspired them. Still, however, they felt themselves restrained from bursting into action, partly by those long cemented ties that bound them to the Grand Lodge as it stood in the days of their fathers, and partly by a fond and lingering hope, that they might yet weather the storm, till its present inauspicious rulers were overthrown, and those happy days restored. From such considerations, they were induced to yield a mournful obedience to the stern mandate, and 'neither admitted,' nor, as lodges, did 'communicate with Brother Mitchell as a brother.' What more could be required from the injured feelings of masons? What more could these men have desired, than that the lodges of Edinburgh should thus suppress their indignation; should deny admittance to a brother in their opinion unjustly condemned; and should cease to depute[47] visitations to his lodge, although they approved of every measure which that lodge had pursued? What more could be demanded / of them than thus to relinquish a connection which years of the most cordial intercourse had cemented; to forsake their old and stedfast friends, to refuse admission to a master recognized as such by a lodge who had often received and welcomed their deputations, and to bow with submission *as lodges* to the mandates of the Grand Lodge?

But all this submission, however satisfactory it must have been to men actuated solely by *masonic* motives, was inconsistent with the views of the party, so long as *any one individual* belonging to the lodges under them had the audacity to enter another lodge which did not recognize their authority. When, therefore, they perceived, that the prohibition imposed upon *the several lodges*, did not answer the intended purpose of forcing a secession, and enabling them by this means to separate the *black sheep* from the rest of the flock, and form them into new lodges as they had done with the Caledonian, they had recourse to another manœuvre, which they knew could not fail to produce this desireable event.

A meeting of the Grand Lodge was hastily convoked, wherein a law was immediately passed, declaring, that EVERY INDIVIDUAL who should thenceforth be discovered to have been present at any meeting of the Caledonian

Lodge, should be instantly deprived '*of all masonic privileges*,' unless he solemnly promised never to enter that lodge again on any pretence whatsoever. This prohibition was of a nature so degrading, so repugnant to every established rule, as well as to every feeling inherent in the human breast, that the consequence was fully anticipated. The emissaries who attended the subsequent meetings of the Caledonian Lodge for that purpose, appear to have received particular instructions to mark out the office-bearers, and / other most distinguished members of the Edinburgh lodges, who went there as private visitors. These respectable brethren were accordingly denounced at subsequent extraordinary meetings called for that purpose, and suspended from '*all masonic privileges*' and the most insulting mandates sent to their respective lodges, commanding them to elect others in their room.

The party had now arrived at the *ne plus ultra* [48] of their despotism; – beyond this it was impossible to extend masonic tyranny, injustice, and oppression. The ancient lodge of Mary's Chapel, and that of Edinburgh St Andrew, presented the most pathetic remonstrances to their arbitrary rulers, conjuring them, by the dearest ties of brotherhood, and by every masonic obligation, to desist from the fatal and unprincipled measures they were pursuing. Every argument and every entreaty was used which could operate on the souls of masons; but it was no longer with *masons* that your brethren had to deal; it was with men divested of every masonic feeling, with unrelenting *partymen*, who, if their designs could not otherwise be accomplished, had determined on the overthrow of Scottish masonry. Instead of receiving the humble petitions of these much injured lodges, the whole of their office-bearers were denounced *en masse*, and suspended *sine die* from '*all masonic privileges*,' and these lodges were ordained to be revolutionised in the same manner that was done with the Lodge Caledonia!

From these lodges, they afterwards proceeded to dismember the ancient lodges of Canongate Kilwinning, Edinburgh St Davids, and Edinburgh Royal Arch, suspending, denouncing, and expelling, without pity or remorse, / almost the whole of their office-bearers, and their oldest and most respectable members. Ruin was now approaching with rapid strides; the whole fraternity of Scottish masons was menaced with destruction; new societies were starting up every day, dignified with the name of LODGES, but composed exclusively of the partizans of the Grand Lodge. What then, brethren, could we do? What remedy was then left to save the sinking constitution of masonry? When we beheld the maxims of the Tyrant of the Continent realized in miniature by the pretended guardians of our '*masonic privileges*,' and the same ferocious principle that dictated to that gloomy despot the idea of placing whole nations in a state of blockade,[49] so exactly imitated by these men in their new system of 'suspension and expulsion,' we thought it high time to testify our abhorrence of the principle, and the model from which it was copied. We unanimously declared them to have forfeited every right which that Grand Lodge, whose name they usurp, once enjoyed. How far we have been justifiable in so doing, the preceding details will enable you to judge; but, before concluding, we have yet a few facts, and a few general considerations, to which our duty demands us to solicit your attention.

Not contented with the devastation they had already created in the lodges of Edinburgh, in pursuance of their main design, they spread abroad the most insidious and fallacious statements of their proceedings, calculated to deceive the brethren into submission till the yoke could be fastened on their necks. Under the specious pretext of preserving regularity and proper subordination in the craft, these men had the assurance to vindicate the general principle on which they proceeded – on the ground of *necessity*. / '*Necessity, the tyrant's plea*,'[50] – an excuse ever ready in the mouth of an oppressor! However justifiable the plea of '*necessity*' may be to the victims of persecution when driven to *self-defence*, it is a suspicious phrase in the mouth of him who *attacks;* and strong indeed must be the circumstances which can stamp it with the currency of belief. But, admitting the plea of these *necessitarians*, was there any *necessity* for resorting to dishonourable means to carry their schemes into execution?

At the different meetings of the lodges in this city, which were held for the purpose of deliberating on the conduct of the Grand Lodge, there uniformly appeared a gang of 'obscure individuals,' under the direction of this party, who went about from lodge to lodge, pretending themselves *honorary* members, and insisting on the privilege of voting, to counteract the general sense of the meetings. But against such an evil the laws of our fraternity admitted of no remedy; for although most of these hirelings were well known to us, we could not refuse them admission as brethren of the order. Hitherto we have overlooked them as unworthy of our notice; but should they hereafter be expelled from all or any of our lodges, we cannot prevent such of our brethren as choose from still recognizing them *as masons*. Of this characteristic nothing but death can deprive them; for, though unworthy, still *they are masons*; and cruel, indeed, and absurd were the law, which should prevent any brother of the craft from acting towards them as his conscience directed.

With such sentiments, we threw open our doors to the brethren at large, and publicly announced our determination to maintain, as far as in our power, the original principles of masonry. At our respective meetings, convoked for the purpose of declaring to the world our secession from a set of / men whose masonic conduct had become altogether intolerable, free access was opened to all and sundry, and amongst others to the whole detachment of emissaries whom these very men had sent to disturb our deliberations. For this, however, we arrogate no praise. We did nothing more than what the ancient custom of the order enjoined; and whatever violations of the brotherly tie these men had exercised towards us, the laws of the fraternity demanded of us to admit them. But what was their conduct in return? In the Lodge Royal Arch, for example, where a certain fee was in use to be exacted from every honorary member to qualify him for voting, a number of the *party*, whose votes could not otherwise have been obtained, are suspected to have had their expenses defrayed from a common purse raised among the more opulent partizans! Many of them had undergone a mock ceremony of initiation in taverns; and others, by dint of mere effrontery, had their votes received without any title whatever! In this way, they perambulated the different lodges, and by the apparent division which their voices created in the sense of the different meetings, they afforded their employers the usual pretext for creating mock lodges, bearing the names of the most ancient lodges of Scotland, that successively withdrew.

After exhausting every artifice to establish their power, they have at length thrown off the mask, and are beginning to deal forth in the way of *terror.* Not only are those who attempt to remonstrate, deprived of their *masonic* privileges; but as *citizens* too, they are threatened with the vengeance of the *party.* The poorer brethren are terrified by the denunciations of their opulent employers; the loss of their livelihood, the ruin of their trade, the deprivation of their domestic comforts are all held forth in / dread array, to appal and confound the dictates of their judgment. Among other instances of this sort may be noticed the following.

Extract of a Letter from the Secretary of the St Andrew's Lodge of Cumbernauld to their late proxy, Richard Cleghorn, Esq. Solicitor at Law.

'*4th July* 1808.

'R. W. SIR & BROTHER,

'I am truly sorry to inform you, that upon St John's day last, the lodge being met in due form, a petition was presented to the lodge from Mr Robert Hill, writer to the signet, factor for the estate of Cumbernauld, *which request was urged* by the Right Honourable Lord Elphingstone, praying the brethren of the lodge to withdraw from you the proxy commission which you hold of us to the Grand Lodge of Scotland, and give a new commission *to Mr Hamilton,* a member of the Caledonian Lodge Edinburgh*,' (meaning the pretended lodge lately erected under that name); and *after reasoning at great length* on the foresaid petition, the vote being called for, *and, owing to a great number of our members being employed on his Lordship's public works, the majority of votes was in favour of Mr Hamilton*, to be our representative in the Grand Lodge, from and after the date of St John's day last. At same time, the thanks of the lodge were *unanimously* voted to you for the unwearied attention you have shewn to the welfare and interest of our lodge.' /

---

*   Vide p. 41 & 43 [in this edition pp. 328 and 329].

Upon this letter few observations need be made. Its own tenor sufficiently indicates the compulsory means which had been employed by this Noble Lord and his man of business on the occasion. In the first place, Mr Cleghorn, a gentleman of respectability, had enjoyed the commission of the lodge for a period of years, during which his 'attention to its interests and welfare' was admitted on all hands to have been 'unwearied,' and the thanks of the lodge unanimously voted to him on that account. His conduct had been in every respect unexceptionable; and, (what ought to have had some weight even with the party) he was never known to have entered the walls of the Caledonian Lodge or any of the other Edinburgh lodges after their secession. All this, however, was insufficient to protect him from insult. He had once voted on the question with the Master of the Caledonian Lodge, and against depriving him of his privileges. He was therefore *suspected* of being hostile to the measures which the rulers of the Grand Lodge were pursuing. But to effectuate his dismissal from the Grand Lodge required more than *common* assurance; a right honourable peer, with all his influence, was scarcely equal to the *noble* deed. For this purpose *his man of business* was employed; and in a lodge composed chiefly of persons 'employed in his Lordship's works,' and whose meetings were held in the immediate vicinity of his Lordship's dwelling, a *petition* was presented, and *'urged'* by his Lordship. But, notwithstanding all this, it would appear, that the members there assembled had the boldness to dispute the matter, and to *'reason at great length'* on the propriety of what was thus *urged* by his Lordship; and even when the vote was *'called for,'* a division of voices took place, and the *majority* only was obtained, as they say themselves, *'owing to* a great / number of them being employed on his Lordship's works.' But to shew the true sense which they entertained on the question, they *at same time unanimously* voted the thanks of the lodge to Mr Cleghorn, 'for *the unwearied attention* he had shewn to its welfare and interest.'

The lodge Leith and Canongate, Canongate and Leith, was summoned by the master to meet on the 24th June, a circumstance which had never before occurred. At this meeting, about twenty members were present, and the minutes of the Grand Lodge were mumbled over by the master, and a plaudit was obtained from those present, many of whom were totally ignorant of the nature of the minutes, and deemed the affair to be some ordinary business. In a few days, however, the brethren began to understand that the measure was not only irregularly carried, but that it was fraught with disgrace to the lodge, and with ruin to the true interests of the craft.

Some of the members accordingly waited upon the master, requesting him to call a *special meeting*, that the matter might be fairly and fully canvassed, and the brethren have an opportunity of expressing their sentiments after due deliberation. This was refused by the master; but upon the members, who waited upon him, threatening to call a meeting, the master agreed that the minutes of the meeting of the 24th should not be transmitted to the Grand Lodge, *but that things should remain as they were.* For that purpose, he delivered to the Senior Warden of the lodge, an order upon the secretary. The secretary, however, from motives best known to himself, also gave his assurance that the minutes of the meeting should not be transmitted; but the brethren were astonished in a few days to find, that these minutes formed no / inconsiderable figure in another fulmination of the Grand Lodge.

After such conduct, the members of the lodge could remain quiet no longer, and after much altercation they procured a meeting to be called by the master, for the purpose of reconsidering the former vote of approbation.

When the hour of meeting arrived, there appeared amongst them that servile band who had haunted the Edinburgh lodges, singing the high praises of the Grand Lodge, and who now claimed to vote as *honorary* members. Alongst with them appeared others, who had not attended meetings for twenty years, and in the train, the whole members of an infant lodge, who owed their existence to the present Grand Lodge, and who had sworn implicit obedience to its mandates. The vote put was, 'rescind the last minutes' or 'dismiss the motion for that effect.' For rescind, there voted 52 original and independent members of the lodge, and for dismiss 50, composed of the motley crew above mentioned.

The tellers, however, disagreed in their calculation, and one of them (a gentleman who is pro-secretary to the Grand Lodge, and who, it is understood, looks higher), declared the vote of rescind lost by a majority of *one*. In this case, the master took upon himself to vote first in order, and one of the tylers,[51] (a servant of the secretary), who had voted rescind, after several other votes had been taken, and after some *friendly hints* from his master, recanted his vote, and was ranged on the opposite side.

That the vote stood as above stated, can readily be established, and as no minute of the meeting, although frequently demanded, has been made out, the strong presumption / is, that the secretary of the lodge, who would lose no opportunity of announcing a triumph to the Grand Lodge, is convinced that, in this case, no new trophy, was added to the brow of oppression.

But, to detain you with an account of the various scenes of this kind, which took place at the different lodges – the threats which were employed by masters against their clerks and dependents, to compel them to vote at these meetings, and to offer their extorted apologies to the Grand Lodge for having dared to frequent the other Lodges, were an undertaking far beyond the limits of this paper. If, after what has been detailed, instances are still awanting, appeal to any one of the hundreds who have joined us, ask them the history of the late dissentions, and satisfy yourselves not only of the truth of all that we have now told you, but of innumerable other iniquities, which our limits, were they trebly extended, would preclude us from detailing, We wish not, brethren, that you should form any hasty opinion either against us or in our favour. On the contrary, you will see from the sequel, that we wish you may satisfy yourselves, in the first place, as to the true nature of the business at issue; and that you may, in the next place, give such instructions to your representatives as will preserve your masonic respectability either *in* the present Grand Lodge, *or independent of it*, if necessary.

Having thus developed the origin and progress of a scheme unparalleled in the annals of the order, and exposed a set of transactions of which till now you have been artfully kept in profound ignorance, it now remains with you, brethren, to say, whether such men are fit to / preside any longer over the affairs of masonry? Do you really expect that, flushed with the victory they have gained over every established usage of the craft, they will regard your rights as masons any more than they have done ours, or that they will deal more mercifully with you than they have done with us? Do you think, because many of you are at a distance from the scene of the hottest action, your lodges will be better treated than your brethren of the metropolis, of whom so many have already been suspended or expelled, without any trial, or form of trial, or even intimation? If this be your idea, look to the fate of Mr Cleghorn; – he, too, was of that opinion, and thought, perhaps, like you, that by an implicit obedience to every mandate of the Grand Lodge, time might be gained till a better order of things could be established. But he was little aware of the *premeditated system* which had been organised, if he thought that any individual, however inoffensive, however respectable, could escape being marked out, sooner or later, if he had not expressly declared his sentiments to be in unison with the rulers of the party. This, brethren, is the only condition on which you will now be permitted to retain your seats in the present Grand Lodge.

But with an assurance equal to their finesse, these men have lately insulted you with threatening denunciations of their vengeance, under the form of *addresses*, and printed *resolutions*, &c. in case of your daring to think for yourselves, in a question where your masonic liberties are so deeply concerned. They brave you to do your worst, and talk of suppressing *rebellions*, shutting up lodges, making acts of parliament, and delivering you over to the *criminal* tribunals, with the same majesty of language, as if they were already at the head of the whole legislative as well as / the executive power of this country. Amid this lofty strain, they seldom condescend to *reason*; and wherever they deign to make an attempt at argument, the sophistry they employ is too wretched to require an answer.

The great string on which they incessantly harp is '*Politics*,' – this being nearest to their hearts; but, there, they drag forward the master of the Caledonian Lodge, and, right or wrong, insist on making that gentleman the *sole* object of attention, and the *sole* cause of the present secession. But the question on which we have split has no more connection with him than it has with the Great Mogul.[52] It is neither more nor less than this – 'Are we to be allowed, as individual masons, to retain the privilege of going to such lodges as we please, or are we to be deprived of it?' This is the sole question now at issue. The Grand Lodge have told us – 'Gentlemen, henceforth not a mason of you will be allowed to accost a brother mason, but at such times and places as we shall think proper, on pain of forfeiting all the "privileges" of a mason.' Against this interdiction we petitioned in vain; – our petitions were spurned, and our office-bearers who presented them, insulted and expelled. Our lodges, consisting of some hundreds of brethren, of course, withdrew; and the only question is, was it right to drive us to that measure? What influence can the name of any individual have upon this abstract and speculative question? We have all along protested against the brethren being misled, by introducing the mover of the address, for the purpose of confusing and disguising the pure and abstract question of masonic liberty, on which alone we are insisting.

By a most singular mode of reasoning, they make it appear, that in order to inflict this punishment, it was also / *necessary* to deprive us of our natural liberties. This was literally punishing the innocent with the guilty; and it is therefore worth while to examine the only reason adduced by these casuists to reconcile the paradox. 'Had you not been deprived of your liberties,' say they, 'the sentence against the Master of the Caledonian Lodge behoved to 'have been *nugatory*.'[53] Now, admitting this to have been the case, was it not better that the sentence against him had proved *nugatory*, than that the whole order of masonry in this country should be subverted? Surely the escape of *one*, or even of a dozen of the most notorious masonic delinquents that ever existed, could not have produced a tenth part of the destruction which this prohibition has created. The truth however is, that the sentence against the mover of the address, had it not been followed up by this unheard of measure against the liberties of the craft, would, instead of proving *nugatory*, have more than gratified the utmost vengeance of his enemies. Agreeably to the ancient practice, none of the Edinburgh lodges could have ever publicly recognised or interchanged deputations with his lodge; and the same practice would have prevented most, if not all of them, from recognising him when visiting them as the master of a lodge. In these circumstances, his lodge could not long have held out; for, although many of the individual brethren might still chuse to go there occasionally, the first ebullition would soon pass away; and their future visits, instead of being hurtful to the interest of the Grand Lodge, would be much in its favour. For, by means of their intercession operating in calmer moments on their Caledonian brethren, the latter would, in the course of a short time, have begun to wish for a renewal of their public intercourse with their sister lodges, and to regret that any / cause had ever separated them. The consequence is obvious; whatever might have been his feelings, Dr Mitchell, if he still remained at the head of that lodge, behoved to follow such conciliatory measures as the relenting spirit of the brethren should inspire; and thus once more would the lodge be brought under controul of the Grand Lodge.

But, it has already been too clearly seen, that such objects as these, however desireable by *masons*, were totally inconsistent with the views of the party; and that, therefore, instead of any endeavour to conciliate, they did every thing in their power to foment the dissention in the craft, which they themselves had created. They should, therefore, have told us candidly at once, that it was not the fear of the sentence against the mover of the address proving *nugatory*, that induced them to act as they did; but the fear of the craft being too closely united by *masonic ties* to admit of being converted into that *political* seminary which they were so desirous to establish.

To give some farther colour to their plea, they have insinuated, that the Lodge of Canongate Kilwinning had it in contemplation to secede, before the period when they were driven to do so by the measures above detailed. Fortunately, however, the high degree of respectability in which that lodge stands, will be a sufficient proof of the falsehood of this statement, when you are informed, that one and all of her members hereby solemnly abjure it, and declare *upon their honour* that it is utterly destitute of truth. Some members of the Lodge of Mary's Chapel, are also said to have entertained the idea of secession before the present question was agitated; but this idea originated in circumstances *peculiar to that lodge itself*, and quite foreign either to the address, or to the general consideration / of *masonic liberty* in which we are all concerned. It originated in consequence of the present Grand Lodge having thought proper to dispossess the Lodge Mary's Chapel of its place at the head of the Grand Lodge roll, to make room for the 'Mother Kilwinning.'[54] Many of the brethren of Mary's Chapel took this highly amiss; but whether they were justifiable for talking of this among themselves as a reason for secession, is quite foreign to the subject now before us. Neither can the opinions which these brethren entertained about a particular circumstance confined to their own lodge, have the slightest relation to a question in which the whole craft is concerned, and on which many of the most respectable lodges in Edinburgh have come to resolutions of secession. As none of the other seceded lodges excepting these two (Mary's Chapel and Canongate Kilwinning) are said to have entertained any previous ideas of that measure, the argument which is endeavoured to be drawn from this insinuation, falls to the ground. The fact is, that until every principle of masonry had been violated, and till the designs on the liberties of the craft became manifest, not one of the Edinburgh lodges, had the slightest idea of *seceding*, however much disgusted many of the brethren already were, from the preliminary steps which the Grand Lodge had adopted.

Ascending from matters of fact, these subtle politicians enter the field of metaphysical discussion in the keenest hopes of success. But the whole argument they have drawn of this sort, sets out upon a principle manifestly unsound; namely, that there is no difference in the relation of a mason to the Grand Lodge from that of a citizen to the Legislature of the State. From these premises they deduce / as a conclusion, the justification of their late proceedings, in virtue of that *supreme controul* which, like the state, they say they possess over the personal liberty of individuals. But although the legislature of the country possessed a controul over the freedom of its subjects, which the *Grandest Lodge* that the world ever saw could not pretend to equal; the legislature, however, never imagined the idea which, among masons, is now attempted to be realized. We have read the history of our country, but not one instance can we find of a power of this kind exercised over the freedom of individuals; although, doubtless, had the legislature been so inclined, there was nothing that could have prevented it from doing so. Over the whole of its *born* subjects, the state possesses an inherent and perpetual controul – it can at any time call forth their services – levy contributions on their property, and abridge the freedom which some of them enjoy, in order to protect the freedom of the whole. All these powers it exercises not in virtue of a certain stipulation or agreement with *every individual* of the realm, but in virtue of that great political compact, which was originally made between the state and the *whole of the people*, as inhabitants or natives of the soil. Hence there is no room for choice on the part of any individual; for, the instant he is born, he becomes a subject of the state, and is bound to obey its laws. But, if he thinks these laws oppressive, he is at liberty to go elsewhere, as soon as he pleases, provided he does not appear in open arms against his country; and if, after trying other places, he chuses to return, he enjoys the same privileges as a subject that he did before. It is, no doubt, true, that the legislature might, if it thought proper, restrain either in whole or in part this natural liberty of its subjects; but / we may safely assert, that in no one instance has it ever yet thought proper to do so. But, although it should, the difference in the relation it bears to its subjects from that of the Grand Lodge to the rest of the craft, is so strikingly apparent, as to exclude every resemblance of analogy between the two cases.

Masons are not the *born* subjects of the Grand Lodge; neither are the services which some of their lodges have been in use to render to that body, in the least degree essential to their existence as a fraternity. Many lodges in Scotland have existed altogether independent of the Grand Lodge, and still continue to do so. The fact is, that the Grand Lodge is neither more nor less than a masonic committee, appointed by some of the Scottish lodges for the purpose of presiding over and representing them in public processions, &c. and for managing the distribution of the funds collected for charitable purposes. It has likewise been in the use of settling matters of precedency and masonic etiquette among the several lodges holding under it; but on no occasion till now has it presumed to interfere with the radical rights of individual masons, much less to abridge or curtail them. A mason when he enters the fraternity parts with none of his natural liberties, nor is there any thing in the obligation which he comes under that could involve such a monstrous proposition. On the contrary, he expressly stipulates for certain *additional* privileges. These are his sole inducement for becoming a member of the fraternity; and a contract is accordingly entered into by *every individual* at his initiation with his mother lodge,[55] whereby she, on the one part, gives him the power of going into that or any other lodge or meeting of the craft throughout the world *in all time to come*; and he, on the other part, / *in consideration* of this privilege, agrees to be faithful to her interests so far as consistent with his own.

So standing the bargain, which *every individual* expressly stipulated, is the Grand Lodge at liberty to break faith with any of these individuals, to deprive him of the privilege for which he covenanted, on pretence that he can no longer exercise it without seeming to *contemn* her authority; and at same time to insist on his performing the other part of this violated agreement?

Yet we are told, in their late address, that unless their doctrine be received, 'a person once admitted a brother, although afterwards found guilty of the most infamous crimes, must remain a brother to the end of his life;' and then they enlarge on the necessity of preserving order and inflicting suitable punishments on such delinquents. As the arguments which they have used in this view of the question, appear at first sight somewhat plausible, and have misled many of the brethren in forming their opinions, we shall take the pains to examine them deliberately, and point out their specious sophistry.

The original obligation of a mason, in so far as regards his *duties* to his brethren, is no part of the secrets of the craft. It is known universally to be neither more nor less than this: that a mason shall associate with every brother, in so far as he is allowed by the laws of his country, and is justified by his conscience. Of the merits or demerits of a brother in such circumstances, it is the privilege, nay it is the *bounden duty* of every mason to judge, not according to the opinion of others, but *according to his own conscience*. By its dictates he must square his conduct, as a man and as a mason. In corporations or societies of men, the same rule of action ought uniformly to obtain, but from the imperfections / of human nature, it frequently happens, that men thus assembled differ from each other in opinion on speculative points, and the more strictly conscientious each of them is, the more differences frequently will arise. In such circumstances, it would be absurd to expect, and glaringly so to compel people who thought differently from ourselves to act in opposition to their conscience, and to adopt our sentiments as the rule of their private life. But, on the other hand, it is *absolutely necessary* in human affairs that *corporations as collective bodies*, should be able to form opinions and come to definitive resolutions as well as the individuals who compose them; something must be said or done, as the resolve of the whole body and in its name, whether a difference of opinion exists among its members or not. Unanimity is at all times desireable; but where this cannot be had, there is *an absolute necessity* for the corporation acting according to the sense of the majority; otherwise it would cease to exist as a corporate body. But although the corporation, in its collective capacity, may be thus said to be a *necessary agent* in all its public acts, the members who compose it are left to the freedom of their own will and the dictates of conscience in their private actions as individuals.

But since the Grand Lodge has ventured to tax us with *perjury*, when we threw off its intolerable yoke, the foregoing considerations open up another view of the subject. In the first place, we would ask these gentlemen, Whether, when they broke faith with us, by depriving us of the privilege which one and all of us bargained for, when we were made masons, and in consideration of which, the obligation alluded to, was come under, they did not *absolve* us from that part of the oath as completely as *their friend*, the Pope, could have done, had the Roman Catholic / religion been re-established *last* year in the country? But, perhaps, they thought, that *no faith should be kept with us*; and, if this be the case, they surely cannot seriously blame us for endeavouring to get out of their way as fast as possible. Since, however, they have attacked us with their casuistry, we shall, in the next place, endeavour to point out to our brethren, *where*, in our opinion, the true guilt of this *perjury* lies, leaving it for them to decide, which party has had most reason to complain.

If the distinction above explained, betwixt the duties of men as individuals, and their duties as members of a public body be evident, it must appear doubly so in the situation of a mason, the dictates of whose conscience are so strongly enforced by the remembrance of the sacred obligation he has come under. What, in another man, might be only a temporary suppression of opinion, is *perjury* in a mason. When we behold a brother groaning under the weight of an unmerited punishment, and exposed with many of his brethren to a fierce persecution, ought we not, like brethren, to visit and support them? But, how strongly is this duty incumbent on a *mason*, if, as an individual, he has already sworn fidelity to the lodge thus cruelly treated. He is barred, it is true, from going there as a representative of his mother lodge; but is he barred from going *as a mason*? It was not as a representative of any lodge, but *as a mason* that he swore to be faithful, when admitted a member of the persecuted lodge. What then can excuse him from performing this sacred duty – is it the paltry artifice resorted to, of creating mock lodges in name of those to which the faith of the brethren has been pledged? Such brethren as *really believe* in this creed, are indeed innocent of any *crime*, while they withhold / those duties which it would otherwise 'SUIT THEIR CONVENIENCE' to perform – but let those who are more intelligent – beware! We are insultingly told, that we cannot perform this duty to God and our consciences, without incurring their displeasure; for, adding blasphemy to their insults, they have sneeringly said, 'Thou canst not serve *God* and mammon.'[56] – Too well are we now convinced of the truth of these words!

The measures lately pursued, are in the next place, attempted to be justified by alledging that the expelled brethren had 'determined, by every means in their power, 'to overthrow the authority of *the Grand Lodge*,' and that they were actually engaged in this design at the time of their expulsion. – Than such an assertion, nothing can be more unfounded. It is indeed perfectly true, that at the period in question these members were 'determined,' by every constitutional means, to root out *the present* Rulers; and, in doing so, they could not have rendered *the Grand Lodge* and the craft a more essential service. Had this been effected we should not have had the anguish to behold the degradation of our Ancient Order, and the humiliating spectacle of a Grand Lodge in ruins. Had these men been hurled from their seats when they first began to display the *cloven foot*, the Grand Lodge of Scotland would have been restored to her pristine dignity, and we, who are now addressing you, would have been the first and most devoted of her adherents. To attack the *Grand Lodge* of Scotland never was our design, while a hope remained of our being suffered to enjoy, under her authority, the privileges of *masons*; but when deprived of a portion of these privileges, and when every hope of regaining them was cut off, it was then, and not till then, that we thought / of secession. But to convince the world of the sincerity of our plea, we hereby repeat the offer we have often before made. Let the Grand Lodge rescind all their late sentences of suspension and expulsion – let them do away the mock-lodges which they have created, in order to furnish representatives for supporting the power of their present officers – let them produce the books of the lodge, that the names of all the informal proxies, and those who had their arrears privately compounded, may be erased from the list of voters – and, above all things, let it be solemnly enacted, that on no pretence whatever shall the liberties of *individual masons* be in future interfered with – Let them do this, and then we shall throw down our arms, and hasten in a body to manifest our attachment to the Grand Lodge, for which in former times we had the fondest regard. But if we should be driven by her present rulers to the last resolution of erecting ourselves into another Grand Lodge, still we shall respect her – and our doors shall be open for the reception of her persecuted children – With us they shall find a secure asylum, till a change of system shall take place, when we shall all again unite in harmony and brotherly love. But, till that happy period shall arrive, the ASSOCIATED LODGES are more than sufficient to brave their utmost vengeance.[57] The antiquity of our names, the preservation of all our ancient insignia, books, and funds; the opulence, the respectability, and the numbers of our brethren, which are daily increasing, will enable us to maintain those seats where our forefathers held their mystic rites, and keep alive in the metropolis of Scotland, the same generous principles that have characterised the fraternity for six thousand years. We despise the threats of these rulers as much as we execrate their measures; and / should the present Grand Lodge continue deaf to all terms of accommodation, we are fully able to constitute another in her room, where the genuine principles of masonry will be preserved and respected.

Besides endeavouring to keep you in the dark as to the true nature and extent of the present secession, these men have retorted upon us the accusation which applies exclusively to themselves, namely, that our meetings are held for the purpose of discussing *politics*. This, however, scarcely requires a refutation. The doors of our lodges are open to all; – let every mason that chooses come in and satisfy himself of the fact. We do not even prevent the most furious of our enemies in the Grand Lodge from doing so as often as they please, although they have shut their doors against us. We have taken the same oaths to government that they have, and we enjoy the like toleration from the civil power that these boasted chiefs themselves possess. And if any suspicion should ever occur to induce that power to interdict one or other of these sets of lodges, whether is it more likely that this suspicion would fall upon lodges whose doors are open *to every mason whatever*, or upon those which are shut to all except to those of *a certain description*? In which of the two places is it most likely that *politics* would be discussed?

In the last place, they have endeavoured to make the brethren believe, that the act of the 39th of his Majesty positively prohibits the meeting of any lodge not holding of the present Grand Lodge! But how will the brethren be astonished at this assertion, when they are informed, that, within the four corners of the act, *the name of a Grand Lodge is not so much as mentioned, nor / the most distant allusion made to the existence of any such body*!! On the contrary, the act expressly tolerates all 'lodges,' or even '*meetings,*' which have been in use to be held '*in conformity to the rules prevailing among the societies or lodges of freemasons in this kingdom.*' * Catching at these expressions of the statute, we are told, that the 'rules prevailing among the free-masons in this kingdom,' imply their subjection to the present Grand Lodge of Scotland. And this indulgence, they say, 'was at that time granted to the craft, *under the assurance*[xxxvii] that the Grand Lodge would superintend the conduct of *all* the lodges in Scotland.'

When one of their fiercest orators first knocked us speechless with the intelligence of 'an act of parliament having been passed prohibiting the meeting of every lodge in Scotland that did not acknowledge the authority of the present Grand Lodge,' you may judge how we were confounded. In these moments of consternation, some of the brethren present happened to inquire when this act of parliament was passed? It then turned out, to our no small relief and astonishment, that the act alluded to was no other than that of the 39th of his Majesty.

* Sect. 39. Geo. III, c. 79.

A copy of the act was instantly produced, and handed to the orator, with an earnest request, that he would point out that section of it where the Grand Lodge, or any other lodge of the kind, was mentioned, and where we were commanded to obey it? His embarrassment on this occasion, and the ridicule which ensued, may be more easily conceived than described. At length he read aloud the passage of the act above quoted, and told the same story of the Grand Lodge having / procured for us the privilege of meeting, &c. that is now laid before you.

Two questions were then put, which seemed to puzzle him a good deal. The first was, how it came to pass that there were then, and still are, a number of lodges in Scotland who never acknowledged a Grand Lodge at all, and many who seceded from it, and who yet, after all, have uniformly enjoyed the protection of a clause, which the Grand Lodge of Scotland had thus procured the legislature to insert in the act in favour of her own vassals only? The second was, how it happened that this Grand Lodge, whose interest in parliament was so great as to procure this exemption, entirely upon her own high responsibility, should not be so much as taken notice of, or even hinted at, from one end of the statute to the other? Surely if the legislature had meant to qualify the exemption they granted us, with the condition of obedience to the Grand Lodge, they would have told us so in as many words. But when, instead of this, we perceive the legislature recognizing the existence of 'the societies or lodges of free-masons in this kingdom,' as so many distinct and separate bodies, and prescribing the forms which *each* of them must observe in qualifying themselves to enjoy the privilege of meeting; and when, on the other hand, we cannot find the most distant allusion to the existence of a Grand Lodge, what are we to conclude from all this? What else, than that the Grand Lodge is in the eye of the law no greater than any other lodge, and that each of them has a right to meet independent of it, on observing the forms of qualifying, in terms of the act, which are applicable to all lodges, without discrimination or distinction. /

What then, it may be asked, could the legislature mean by '*the rules prevailing among the lodges of free masons in this "kingdom?"*' Doubtless nothing else than the following; 1*st,* That the meeting shall be held purely for masonic purposes. 2*dly,* That nothing disloyal to the government and constitution of the country shall be there suffered for a moment to be introduced. 3*dly,* That nothing immoral or indecent shall disgrace the conversation of the brethren; and *lastly,* That the doors of the lodge shall be open to every person of respectable character that can display the tokens of a mason.

These are the '*rules*' which prevail among the lodges 'of free masons in *this kingdom,*' and which have ever distinguished them from the corrupt lodges of the *neighbouring kingdom* of France, which the legislature had so much in its eye at the time of passing this act. To give any other meaning than this to the words of the statute, is quite unwarranted; and the interpretation which we have given is put beyond the reach of doubt, by the uniform toleration of lodges which never acknowledged a Grand Lodge at all.

As a last resource, and as an answer to this fair and obvious interpretation of the statute, they tell us that it is no doubt true, that, at the date of passing the act, a number of lodges were accustomed to hold meetings independent of the Grand Lodge, and therefore, this was the *'rule'* which regulated *them;* but the *'rules'* which regulated the vassals of the Grand Lodge were different, and as their meetings were only tolerated so long as they continued to abide by their *respective rules,* it followed, as a matter of course, that, if any lodge should afterwards secede from the Grand Lodge, it would, in consequence of changing its *rules,* be excluded from the benefit of the act. / Without enlarging on the absurdity to which this doctrine would lead, by preventing lodges at that time *in a state of secession* from changing their *rules* and returning to the Grand Lodge, we shall only observe, that the *'rules'* which the statute mentions, were not the rules which prevailed in *each* lodge but the rules which prevailed *among* the lodges. Now, these *rules* behoved of necessity to be of an universal nature, and identically the same in every lodge to which the indulgence of the act extended. But the *rule* of adherence to the Grand Lodge could not be the *universal rule* alluded to in the act, otherwise it would follow, as a consequence, that no lodge holding another *rule* could enjoy the benefit of the statute. But we have already bestowed a great deal more time in the exposure of these sophistries than their importance deserved.

Lest, however, the leaders of the party should still persist in thus endeavouring to blindfold and terrify the brethren, by talking of 'acts of Parliament,' the 'authority of the civil magistrate,' and other high sounding words with which their papers are filled, the masters of the Associated Lodges thought it their duty to lay the matter before the Professor of Scots Law, that by his opinion the whole craft might receive the assurance that there was nothing to be dreaded from all this empty boasting. This they did, not from any doubt which they themselves entertained on the point, but merely to satisfy the brethren at large, who have not the same means of information. It is perhaps needless to add, that the opinion of the Professor was given without hesitation; that allegiance to the present Grand Lodge was no part of the requisites prescribed by the act of Parliament. /

WE have now arrived at the conclusion of our labours. You have laid before you, brethren, a full and distinct exposition of the motives, the history, and the extent of the present secession. The constitution and powers of the Grand Lodge have been also fully explained, and the designs of its present rulers unfolded in the history of their transactions. The question on which you are now to determine, is, whether it be for the interest of the masonic fraternity in Scotland that these men should continue any longer at the head of affairs in the Grand Lodge. If, like us, you are sensible, that their continuance would produce the destruction of every tie which has hitherto preserved the existence of masonry, it becomes you seriously to consider what steps your own security requires. As for us, although we do not stand in need of your assistance, we cannot contemplate the wretched condition to which the affairs of masonry have been reduced by these men, without endeavouring to open your eyes to the extent of the disasters they have occasioned, and conjuring you by every sacred tie, to put an end to their power ere it be too late, and save your own lodges from the destruction that is approaching. We will be most willing to co-operate with you in any measure that may be conducive to attain this much to be wished for end, whether we are to remain as independent lodges, or to follow the example of our brethren in the sister kingdom, and erect a new Grand Lodge where the pure principles of masonry shall be maintained, unsullied by any of those party views that have actuated your present rulers; – a LODGE, –

—————— *Quod nec Jovis ira, nec ignis,*
Nec poterit ferrum, nec edax abolere vetustas.[58]

FINIS. /

APPENDIX.
No. I.

TO THE
KING'S MOST EXCELLENT MAJESTY,
The Humble ADDRESS of the Grand Lodge of the Ancient Fraternity of Free and Accepted Masons, under the constitution of England.

Most Gracious Sovereign,

AT a time when nearly the whole mass of the people anxiously press forward, and offer with one heart, and one voice, the most animated testimonies of their attachment to your Majesty's person and government, and of their unabated zeal, at this period of innovation and anarchy in other countries, for the unequalled constitution of their own, permit a body of men, Sire, which, though not known to the laws, has been ever obedient to them, men who do not yield to any description of your Majesty's subjects, in the love of their country, in true allegiance to their sovereign, or in any other of the duties of a good citizen, to approach you *with this public declaration of their / political principles.* The times, they think, demand it of them; and they wish not to be among the last, in such times, to throw *their* weight, whatever that may be, into the scale of order, subordination and good government.

It is written, Sire, in the institute of our Order, that we shall not, at our meetings, go into *religious* or *political* discussions: because, composed, as our fraternity is, of men of various nations, professing different rules of faith, and attached to opposite systems of government, such discussions sharpening the mind of man against his brother, might offend and disunite. *A crisis, however, so unlooked for as the present, justifies to our judgement a relaxation of that rule, and our first duty as Britons superseding all other considerations*, we add, without farther pause, our voice to that of our fellow subjects, in declaring one common and fervent attachment to a government by King, Lords and Commons, as established by the glorious revolution of 1688.[59]

The excellence of all human institutions is comparative and fleeting: positive perfection, or unchanging aptitude to its object, we know, belongs not to the work of men: But when we view the principles of government, which have recently obtained in other nations, and then look upon our own, we exult in possessing at this time, the wisest and best poised system the world has ever known. A system which affords equal protection, (the only equality we look for, or that is indeed practicable), and impartial justice to all.

It may be thought, that, being what we are, a private society of men, connected by invisible ties, professing secrecy, mysterious in our meetings, stamped by no act of / prerogative, and acknowledged by no law; We assume a port, and hold a language upon this occasion, to which we can urge no legal or admitted right. We are the free citizens, Sire, of a free state, and number many thousands of one body. The Heir-apparent is our chief; we fraternise for the purposes of social intercourse, of mutual assistance, of charity to the distressed, and goodwill to all; and fidelity to a trust, reverence to the magistrate, and obedience to the laws, are sculptured in capitals upon the pediment of our institution; and let us add, that pervading, as we do, every class of the community, and every walk of life, and disseminating our principles wherever we strike root, this address may be considered, as speaking in epitome, the sentiments of a people.

Having thus attested our principles, we have only to implore the Supreme Architect of the Universe, whose almighty hand hath laid in the deep the firm foundation of this country's greatness, that he will continue to shelter and sustain her. May her sons be contented, and her daughters happy; and may your Majesty, the immediate instrument of her present prosperity and power, to whom unbiassed posterity shall thus inscribe the column –

TO

GEORGE,

The Friend of the People,

and

Patron of the Arts

Which brighten and embellish Life,

With your amiable Queen and your royal Progeny, long, long continue to be the blessing and the boast of a grateful, happy, and united people. /

Given *unanimously* in Grand Lodge, at Free-Masons Hall, this sixth day of February 1793. (Signed)

RAWDON, A. G. M.

PETER PARKER, D. G. M.

Countersigned

WILLIAM WHITE, G. S.

Nota. – The above Address is copied from the Free-Masons Magazine, for June 1793. There also follows it (in the same Magazine) an Address to his Royal Highness he Prince of Wales, from the Grand Lodge of England, for his condescension in presenting the above. /

No. II.

TO THE

KING'S MOST EXCELLENT MAJESTY,

The ADDRESS of the Office-Bearers of the Grand Lodge of Free and Accepted Masons of Scotland, of the Masters, Proxy-Masters, Wardens, and Proxy-Wardens, of Lodges holding of, and composing the said Grand Lodge, assembled at a Quarterly Communication, at Edinburgh, this 4th of May 1807.

May it please your Majesty,

WE, the office-bearers and members of the Grand Lodge of Free and Accepted Masons of Scotland, humbly beg leave, at the present time, to approach your Majesty, and to express our unfeigned sentiments of heartfelt gratitude and thankfulness for the paternal solicitude for the prosperity and happiness of your people, that your Majesty has been graciously pleased to manifest in support of the established religion of the country, and of the principles of the British constitution.

Ever sensible of the blessings[xxxviii] which, through Divine Providence, we have enjoyed under the best of Kings, it becomes us, as brethren of an order, the object of whose institution is the peace and happiness of mankind, to avail ourselves of this opportunity of congratulating our fellow-subjects, / that we have a King whose happiness is the happiness of his people, and whose care has ever been to maintain, and transmit down unimpaired to posterity, a religion that preaches peace and good-will amongst men, and a constitution that the wisdom of our forefathers has reared, and whose perfection is the admiration of the world.

No reign that history records to us has ever been more distinguished for liberality and freedom of opinion than the present; and while every one may enjoy himself quietly under his own vine and his own fig-tree, we trust, those principles that happily placed the illustrious House of Hanover on the Throne shall never be infringed.

That your Majesty may long live happy in the hearts of a free and loyal people, that success may attend, and glory crown your Majesty's arms by land and by sea, and that, when it is the will of the Great Architect of the universe you shall be called from an earthly crown, you may find a crown of glory that will last to eternity, shall ever be our earnest prayer and wish.

[ANON.] *AN ENQUIRY INTO THE LATE DISPUTES AMONG THE FREE-MASONS OF IRELAND; WHEREIN IS DETAILED A FREE AND IMPORTANT ACCOUNT OF THE DIFFERENT TRANSACTIONS WHICH GAVE RISE TO, AND CONTINUED THE CONTROVERSY, FROM THE COMMENCEMENT TO THE ESTABLISHMENT OF THE GRAND LODGE OF ULSTER* (1812)

[Anon.], *An Enquiry into the Late Disputes among the Free-masons of Ireland; wherein is Detailed A Free and Important Account of the Different Transactions which Gave Rise to, and Continued the Controversy, from the Commencement to the Establishment of the Grand Lodge of Ulster; And wherein is Given a Summary History of the Order, from the Earliest Account to the Establishment of the Grand Lodge of Ireland in 1730. The Whole Being Written with a View towards Conciliating the Jarring Parties, Restoring Harmony to a Highly Respectable Community, Particular Attention has been Paid that No Terms should be Used Injurious to the Feelings of Those whose Conduct Proceeded from an Error in Judgment, or Want of Information; it is therefore Confidently Hoped that Such as may not be Convinced by the Arguments, will not be Offended by the Language. To which is Added: An Appendix; Containing, the Reasons of the Union Lodge, 684, from Withdrawing from the Grand Lodge of Dublin, and Adhering to the Grand Lodge of Ulster* (Belfast: Printed by Joseph Smyth, 1812), pp. 37–83 and the Appendix.[1]

In a brief note written in 1897 W. J. Chetwode Crawley announced the discovery of this rare pamphlet, which existed in two copies at that time.[2] Although Francis C. Crossle and his son Philip – both masonic historians of Irish Freemasonry – transcribed this document,[3] they failed to mention it and incorporate its evidence and arguments in their own writings on the same subject[4] despite the fact that it is the only contemporary volume that provides a comprehensive – though largely one-sided – account of the early nineteenth-century rivalries in Irish Freemasonry. Crawley, who possessed one of the copies, described the essay as 'an unscrupulous polemic against the Grand Lodge of Ireland, and the publication was one of the flickers of the flame that Alexander Seton had lighted'.[5] Crawley, the Crosses and most masonic historians in their footsteps – if they bothered to mention this matter at all[6] – provided a distorted picture of the history of this dispute which tore apart Irish Freemasonry at the time. For instance, in their *The Pocket History of Freemasonry*, F. L. Pick and G. N. Knight summarize the beginning of the conflict as follows:

> The story of this discreditable episode, which culminated in a violent struggle between two rival parties in Grand Lodge and eventually in the (temporary) formation of a separate Grand Lodge in Ulster [1808–13], can be told quite simply. In 1801 D'Arcy Irvine, the Grand Secretary, had appointed as his Deputy his friend, Alexander Seton, an able and energetic but dishonest Barrister. This Seton was the villain of the piece. As soon as he was appointed, he went to the house of his predecessor and carried off a 'hackney coach full' of books, MSS and other articles belonging to Grand Lodge some of which have never since been recovered.[7]

Pick and Knight fail to mention though that Thomas Corker, Seton's predecessor, left the financial affairs of the Grand Lodge in a chaotic state characterized by many irregularities.

The aforementioned masonic historians put all the blame on the Ulstermen, primarily on Alexander Seton and Gorges D'Arcy Irvine. The pamphlet refines and questions their interpretations and sheds new light on these feuds from the perspective of the Ulster Grand Lodge. It demonstrates that the followers of Crossle belittled the 'highly unmasonic, arbitrary and unjust' practices of the contemporary Grand Lodge of Ireland. For example this was manifested in the exclusion of Ulster masons from the charitable fund, its use for uncharitable purposes, the innovations of new financial rules concerning the higher degrees and violating the rule of majority during the decision making of the Grand Lodge. These problems were also highlighted in the following works: A Brother, *An Address to the Right Honourable and Right Worshipful, the Worthy Fraternity of Free and Accepted Masons in Ireland, on the State of their Funds, its Application, and Use* (Dublin, 1801) and A. Seton, *Audi alteram partem. Two Letters, in Reply, to Certain Letters and Observations, Published by Direction of the Right Honourable the Earl of Donoughmore, once Grand Master, of All the Lodges of Freemasons in Ireland* (Dublin: John King, 1809).[8]

Of course, the members of the Grand Lodge of Ulster that included Seton, who horsewhipped John Boardman, the Grand Treasurer, after a Grand Lodge meeting on 1 May 1801, were not saints either. They appointed Grand Officers such as Lord Blayney as Senior Grand Warden without their consent, of which the Grand Lodge of Dublin took advantage in their fight against the Ulster Masons. Although the Grand Lodge of Ulster ceased to exist after 1813, the expensive legal suit between Seton and the Grand Lodge continued until at least

1823. Daniel O'Connell, a member of Lodge No. 189 in Dublin, represented the Grand Lodge in the legal case against Seton.[9]

The pamphlet also contributes to the study of masonic jurisprudence, as it addresses who can establish a Grand Lodge and under what circumstances. To justify the creation of the Ulster Grand Lodge, the author refers to the establishment of the Grand Lodge of England and the Grand Lodge South of the River Trent as precedents.[10] Even though the Ulster Grand Lodge styled itself as the 'Ancient Grand Lodge of Ireland',[11] in his argument the author does not use the reasons why the Antients Grand Lodge was established in London by Irish Freemasons in 1751. The possible reason for this omission is that after September 1807 the Dublin Grand Lodge, dominated by Boardman and Alexander Jaffrey as Deputy Grand Master, enjoyed the support of the Grand Lodge of the Antients in England.[12] They did not intend to get involved in a new conflict with either the Grand Lodge of the Moderns or the Grand Lodge of Scotland, which also expressed their support of the Jaffrey-Boardman faction against the Ulster Freemasons. They worried about 'the mischief which must arise to the Craft as well as the danger to the State, if masonic Lodges can be permitted to assume an independence of the Grand Lodge'.[13] This rivalry created a negative image of Freemasonry in society as the conflicts were reported in the press.

According to the title page, the author of the pamphlet belonged to the Union Lodge No. 684 in Belfast, which worked under the jurisdiction of the Grand Lodge of Ulster at the time of its publication. The membership returns of this lodge for 1812 are not extant in the Library of Freemasonry in Dublin.[14] However, in the Grand Lodge of Ireland Membership Register there is a list of members of this lodge containing ninety-four names from 17 April 1788, when it was warranted, to its cancellation on 6 January 1814.[15] Based upon this record it is not possible to reconstruct who the members of the lodge were in 1812 since, according to Rebecca Hayes, the dates by the names indicate when the members received the third degree as well as the dates of their certificates. It is also possible that the 'Member of 684' is a pen name for an influential Ulster Freemason such as Seton.[16]

The Grand Lodge of Ulster accepted a resolution on 3 June 1812 according to which three Freemasons of this lodge – namely Alexander Barr, Hugh Fisher and Thomas Welsh – were appointed, amongst others, as members of 'a Committee for the purpose of collecting subscriptions in the town of Belfast'.[17] They must have been committed and active Freemasons of Lodge No. 684, and thus are among the possible candidates as authors of the pamphlet.

The essay was published in the first half of 1812 and at least 200 copies were printed. According to the minutes of the Grand Lodge of Ulster, they accepted the following resolution on 3 June 1812: 'That the Grand Lodge take 200 copies of a Book, entitled "An Enquiry into the late disputes among Free Masons in Ireland;" and that the several Brethren of the Grand Lodge be requested to endeavour to dispose of them for the benefit of the fund.'[18]

To avoid further conflicts the pamphlet was suppressed by Lodge No. 825 in Larne in County of Antrim at the end of the dispute between the Ulster Grand Lodge and the Grand Lodge of England. On 26 August 1812 this lodge, which seemed to remain loyal to the Grand Lodge of Ireland, accepted a resolution: 'That the said pamphlet be locked in the chair of the lodge for the perusal of the brethren and any brother known to carry such book in future publicly shall be liable to the censure of the lodge.'[19]

Joseph Smyth was a leading publisher of popular works including almanacs and directories in Belfast in the early nineteenth century.[20]

The pamphlet here reproduced is based upon the only known copy in the Library of Freemasonry in Dublin.[21] For reasons of space, the first part of the pseudo-masonic history, largely drawing on Anderson's *Constitutions* (1738) has been omitted. This reprint begins with the section of the legendary history dealing with Ireland.

Notes

1. This headnote was written by Róbert Péter.
2. W. J. C. Crawley, 'Notes on Dr. Barlow's Paper, "A Curious Historical Error"', *AQC*, 10 (1897), pp. 58–9.
3. For F. C. Crossle's transcript, see *CMN*, vol. 6, p. 394–455, Library of Freemasons' Hall, Dublin. Philip Crossle's transcript is the last document transcribed in his *Common Place Book MS*, LMFL. These volumes, along with volume 24 of the *CMN*, contain the transcripts of numerous circulars, accounts and lodge minutes related to this dispute. The *Common Place Book MS* heavily relies on vol. 24 of the *CMN*. Often the only slight difference is that there are page numbers in the brackets on the top right corner in the London version, which are blank in the Dublin copy.
4. F. C. Crossle, 'The Grand East of Ulster', *The Freemason* (21 December 1892), pp. 9–13. *GLFI*, pp. 321–406.
5. Crawley, 'Notes on Dr. Barlow's Paper, "A Curious Historical Error"', p. 58.
6. Gould does not refer to this event in his voluminous history of Freemasonry. To the best of my knowledge, the only book that mentions this pamphlet was written by a German academic historian of British and Irish Freemasonry, see G. E. W. Begemann, *Vorgeschichte und Anfänge der Freimaurerei in Irland* (Berlin: E.S. Mittler und Sohn, 1911), p. 108. He took the reference from Crawley. The findings of this book have not been integrated in either academic or masonic studies on Irish Freemasonry. Petri Mirala, a Finnish historian, provides the only scholarly analysis of the Grand Lodge split. P. Mirala, *Freemasonry in Ulster, 1733–1813: A Social and Political History of the Masonic Brotherhood in the North of Ireland* (Dublin: Four Courts Press, 2007), pp. 258–71.
7. F. L. Pick and G. N. Knight, *The Pocket History of Freemasonry* (London: [n. p.], 1954), p. 151.
8. The transcript of the pamphlet can be found in 'While at Dungannon' chapter, pp. 23–47, *IMR*. See also *GLFI*, p. 366.

9.   See W. J. C. Crawley, *Legal Episodes in the History of Freemasonry* (London: George Kenning, 1899). For O'Connell's masonic membership, which probably helped his legal and political career, see P. Fagan, *Catholics in a Protestant Country. The Papist Constituency in Eighteenth-century Dublin* (Dublin: Four Courts Press, 1998), pp. 144–55 (chapter 5, Catholic Involvement in Freemasonry).

10. It does not make a mention of the establishment of North American Grand Lodges between 1778 and 1790. The Grand Lodge of Delaware was formed in the midst of the Irish contest in June 1806. Mirala, *Freemasonry in Ulster*, p. 263 and *GLFI*, pp. 403–5.

11. For example see *Belfast News-letter* (4 July 1809) transcribed in *CMN*, vol. 7, p. 65. Following the model of the Grand Orient of France, the Grand Lodge of Ulster was also dubbed as the Grand East of Ulster.

12. J. Belton, *The English Masonic Union of 1813* (Suffolk: Arima, 2012), p. 69.

13. The Earl of Moira's letter, representing the views of the Moderns and the Grand Lodge of Scotland can be found in the Grand Lodge of Ireland Minute books. It is cited in *GLFI*, p. 382 and Belton, *The English Masonic Union of 1813*, p. 71. The Ulster Masons also realized that the 'disunion [was] highly dangerous and prejudicial to the interests of the Craft' and accordingly made a number of attempts towards reconciliation, which were rejected by the superior Grand Lodge of Ireland. Drawing on Crossle, Belton expresses his sympathy with Boardman rather than Seton sadly without examining the primary sources related to this dispute.

14. According to Rebecca Hayes, they have only survived from the 1820s.

15. Grand Lodge of Ireland Membership Register, Series I, Volume III. It is possible that errors were made in the compilation of the register and that some names never made it to Dublin. The following names are listed in the register: Alex[ander] Sutherland, Geo[rge] Warnock, Arch[ibal]d J[oh]nston Young, Tho[ma]s McCabe, Arth[u]r Darley, J[oh]n Shaw, Ja[me]s Kenley, Sam[ue]l McMurray, Abel Hadskis, W[illia]m Potter, Rich[ar]d Shaw, J[oh]n Maziere, J[oh]n Gordon, W[illia]m Mitchell Junior, W[illia]m Mitchell Senior, Tho[ma]s Stewart Eldor, Tho[ma]s Charles Atkinson, Tho[ma]s Potts, Tho[ma]s Ireland, W[illia]m McClenahan, Edw[ar]d McClure, J[oh]n Martin, W[illia]m Kelly, Rob[er]t Halliday, David Wallace, Sam[ue]l Hadskis, W[illia]m Steele, Ja[me]s Mason, Hugh Fisher, W[illia]m McMorran, Tho[ma]s McQuoid, Ja[me]s Neill, Ja[me]s Quail, Tho[ma]s Whitaker, H. B. Bryso, W[illia]m Davison, W[illia]m Hamilton, Tho[ma]s Lowry, J[oh]n McGaul, Alex[ander] Stuart, W[illia]m Boyd, Ja[me]s Still, Willliam Mulholland, J[oh]n Bell, Murdoch McCloud, W[illia]m J[oh]nson, Sam[ue]l Moore, J[oh]n Potts, Ja[me]s Neill, Hen[r]y Hammond, Henry Boyle, J[oh]n McAllister, Ja[me]s J[oh]nston, W[illia]m Watt, Rob[er]t Greenfeild, John Sprist Dumont, James Leatham, William Clark, James Campbell, Prof[esso]r Millikin, Henry Arthur, Thomas Day, W[illia]m Aughinleck, W[illia]m Jennett, Ja[me]s Dunlop, Tho[ma]s Walsh, John Mayne, Stephen Wall, Rob[ert]Ferguson, Geo[rge] McAdam, Alex[ande]r Barr, Alex[ande]r Graham, Sam[uel] Tennent, John McGibbon, Hen[ry]Kirk, John Nelson, Brice Chambers, Fra[nci]s Johnston, John Palmer, Alex[ande]r Montgomery, Rob[ert]Telfair, Alex[ande]r Robinson, W[illia]m McKee, Neil McMillan, Neil Kindsey, Ian Howland, Tho[ma]s Gordon, Gilbert Vaner, Jens Thornsin, Sam[uel] Longfellow, Elijah Kempton, Arch[ibal]d Hyndman, Hen[r]y McDowell, Sam[uel] Fitzsimons. My thanks go to Csaba Maczelka, Christopher Powell and John Acaster for their help in transcribing the register.

16. I thank Petri Mirala for this comment.

17. *CMN*, vol. 8, p. 77.

18.   P. Crossle, *Common Place Book MS*. No pagination. The transcript of this resolution, along with the appointment of the Grand Officers, can be found at the end of the manuscript, before the transcript of the pamphlet reproduced here.

19.   *CMN*, vol. 24, refs 85 and 88.

20.   J. R. R. Adams, 'Belfast Almanacs and Directories of Joseph Smyth', *Linen Hall Review*, 8 (1991), pp. 14–15.

21.   Other copies might exist in the archives of Ulster lodges. The Bookmaps online library catalogue lists a misdated copy but it does not state its location: http://lat.bookmaps.org/a/n/ane_25.html [accessed 10 July 2014].

[Anon.] *An Enquiry into the Late Disputes among the Free-Masons of Ireland; Wherein is Detailed a Free and Important Account of the Different Transactions which Gave Rise to, and Continued the Controversy, from the Commencement to the Establishment of the Grand Lodge of Ulster* (1812)

AN ENQUIRY
INTO THE LATE DISPUTES AMONG
THE FREE-MASONS OF IRELAND;

WHEREIN IS DETAILED
*A free and impartial Account of the different Transactions which gave rise to,
and continued the Controversy, from the commencement to the Establishment
of the*
GRAND LODGE OF ULSTER;
AND

Wherein is given a summary History of the Order, from the earliest accounts to the establishment of the Grand Lodge of Ireland, in 1730.

The whole being written with a view towards conciliating the jarring parties, and restoring harmony to a highly respectable community; particular attention has been paid that no terms should be used injurious to the feelings of those whose conduct proceeded from an error in judgment, or want of information; it is therefore confidently hoped, that such as may not be convinced by the Arguments, will not be offended by the Language.

TO WHICH IS ADDED:
AN APPENDIX;
Containing the Reasons of the Union Lodge, 684, for withdrawing from the Grand Lodge of Dublin, and adhering to the Grand Lodge of Ulster.

BY A MEMBER OF 684.

Belfast:
Printed by Joseph Smyth
115, HIGH-STEET.
1812.
[...]

That Masonry had as ancient an origin in Ireland as in Britain, is highly probable. Colonies from Phœnicia having settled here in the year of the world 2736, or 1264 years before the Christian era. When Heber and Heremon, the sons of Milesius* arrived here, / and after many sanguinary conflicts with the princes of the Danaans, conquered the kingdom, and divided it between them. Heber, the elder, taking the southern division for his share, and Heremon, the younger, the northern for his. Shortly after, however, some differences arising between the brothers, the dispute came to blows, and Heber was slain in the contest, and the whole country fell into the possession of the younger brother, Heremon.

The Phœnicians being famous for planting colonies in distant parts for the benefit of trade, and for introducing their manners and customs into all their colonies, and endeavouring to improve the countries with which they held intercourse, it is most probable that Masonry would be among the first of the arts they would / teach their new associates in Ireland. This conjecture is not a little strengthened by the existence of the Round Towers in Ireland, which resemble no species of building in any of the northern countries, but are more similar to those Towers in the East, called Minarets. Some antiquaries have contended that those towers were built by the Danes, and that no stone buildings were erected in Ireland previous to their conquest of the country. None of those authors, however, can take on them to assert that towers such as we have in

---

*   From this period Ireland continued advancing for some centuries to an eminence among the nations of the earth. –

But it was about 930 years before Christ, that the kingdom seemed to have arrived at a high pitch of national policy. – Eochaidh, a descendant of Ir, a younger son of Milesius, having acceded to the throne, he brought about a very important reformation in the constitution and making a variety of useful ordinances, nothing but their strict observance was required to make the country as great and as happy as any nation on earth.

It was this prince that established the great triennial meeting of the states at Tarah, in Meath, for making laws, regulating government, and arranging the national records. He was a prince of great erudition, and was called by way of eminence, Ollamh Fodhlah, or the learned Doctor. A regular communication was no doubt kept up between the mother country and this colony in Ireland, till the final subjugation of the former, by Alexander the Great; and there is every reason to suppose, that the science of Masonry was introduced into Ireland along with other arts of civilization. /

Ireland are to be found in the countries from whence that people migrated. The round towers in Ireland are by those very antiquaries allowed to have been built for religious purposes. Now, had the Danes been the builders of them, there would be every reason to expect that similar buildings should be found in their own country, as we have always found that the hordes of Northern invaders which spread themselves over the Southern parts of Europe had a strong predilection towards establishing their own religion in those countries; it is therefore, more probable that they would have imitated the buildings they left behind them, than that they should have erected structures different from those of their own country.

It does not appear that any of our antiquaries conceive the round towers to have been built for places of strength or fortification; and there is little reason to suppose them built for watch towers, as from the variety of their situation, some in vallies, and others on hills, it does not appear that that could have been the intention. Had they been uniformly built on low ground, and within view of each other, this conjecture might be hazarded; but this not being the / case, many of them being situate on very high ground, as that one at Drumbo, where a most extensive prospect is commanded, without the assistance of a high building, and not one within view of it, there is no reason to suppose they were built for that purpose. – The probable conjecture, therefore, is, that the round towers had a religious origin, and that Pagan; built by the Phoenicians, or the native Irish, long prior to the invasion of the country by the Danes. A people who appear to have very little knowledge of architecture, but such as they applied in constructing their earthen Forts, or Mounds, commonly called Danish Raths.

Ireland was famed in antiquity for a learned nation, and many extensive seminaries of learning were established through the country. Numbers of students arriving here from the Continent for education. Now, the Phœnicians being also much celebrated for learning, having first invented the alphabet and cultivated the arts and sciences – there is strong ground for supposing that learning had been introduced into Ireland by a colony from that country; for how otherwise account for Ireland, at an outer corner of Europe having such a character for education, while the Continent and other Isles on its western coasts were so involved in darkness and ignorance. Provided, therefore, that Ireland is allowed to have been a learned nation in times of high antiquity, it may reasonably be inferred, that the science of Masonry, and the art of Architecture, would at the same time be in a flourishing state.

That Ireland, however, should stand without records to that effect, or monuments to prove (the round Towers excepted) that Architecture, ever in early times had flourished in the country, may easily / and rationally be accounted for. When she became the victim of intestine feuds and invasions from abroad, the science of Masonry must have greatly declined; and many buildings which might have given evidence of former opulence, were, by the invaders, destroyed. The Danes were an ignorant and barbarous race; and wherever they conquered, they levelled to the ground any buildings that might in future have become a shelter, or place of refuge to the natives – And finally, on their expulsion by Brian Boromh, they either carried away or destroyed such records as had remained in the country. To that circumstance it is owing that the history of Irish antiquity is so much involved in darkness, as there was no records left, but such traditions as were preserved by the bards, whose business it was to repeat orally the history and transactions of their great men and heroes.

The round Towers, however, escaped their fury, not being well calculated either for places of strength, or for shelter to the wretched inhabitants – they were therefore, suffered to remain, and are the only existing proof that Masonry had been introduced into Ireland at an early period of the world. – As to ancient records throwing any light on the subject, the reason above assigned must be considered sufficient.

But though the enemies of our country have from time to time deprived us in a great measure of national records, yet many proofs of former greatness appear in the records of other nations; and those notices must be looked on with even greater confidence in their truth, than if they had been found among ourselves; as we are not to expect that the historians of other countries should flatter the vanity / of Irishmen at the expence of veracity, however we might suspect our own writers of doing so. A quotation from one of those is given below as being corroborative of the opinions hazarded above, and applicable to the subject in hand, in respect of Masonry.

In a letter written to Charles the Bald, King of France, about the middle of the ninth century, by one Eric, a philosopher, of Auxerre, the writer expresses himself thus: – 'Why do I speak of Ireland? That whole nation, almost despising the dangers of the sea, resort to our coasts with a numerous train of philosophers, of whom the most celebrated quitting their native soil, account themselves happy under your protection, as the servants of the wise Solomon.' – And in another place he tells us that Charles, the great patron of learned men, and the encourager of improvement among his people, drew Greeks and Irish in flocks for the instruction of his countrymen.

In the history of Masonry in England, it is mentioned that Alfred the Great was the friend and patron of Masons; and that he appropriated great part of his revenue to building and improvements in architecture. Now it appears that Alfred had his education here: as he, according to Bede, imbibed in Ireland[1] that wisdom and piety which distinguished him above his contemporaries. Having studied in the College founded in Mayo, for the converted Saxons, called to this day Mayo of the Saxons and from this country he procured professors for his newly erected College at Oxford. These two circumstances taken together, that is the expression of Eric the French writer, that 'the most celebrated of the Irish philosophers considered / themselves as servants of Solomon;' and that of Alfred receiving his education in an Irish seminary; and afterwards in his own kingdom becoming the zealous patronizer and encourager of Masons, give a strong feature to the conjecture that Masonry had been encouraged and deeply studied in Ireland at this early period.[2]

From the repeated inroads made upon Ireland[xxxix] by the Danes or Normans, commencing in the year 797, and the internal wars carried on by the rival Princes of the country, it is not reasonable to expect that Masonry, which always flourishes most in peacable times, could rise to that degree of eminence in Ireland that it might, in more quiet days. Nor does it appear that the country, even so low down as Henry II's time, made any great show with regard to magnificent buildings, if we are to believe the Welsh[xl] historian, Giraldus Cambrensis, whose remarks on Ireland in his days are not very flattering – but we should believe with caution the story of an enemy. As we have good reason in our own times to observe that British Historians are very unwilling to turn up the bright side of the picture when they treat of Irish affairs – and too many of our own countrymen are willing to follow the example.

Still there remain the ruins of many magnificent structures even to this day, which shew evident marks of great antiquity, and of no common elegance. – Such is the town of Kilmallock in the county of Limerick: commonly called the Irish Balbee; the entire town being composed of the ruins of immense buildings of great antiquity. These, with many other ancient buildings which remain entire to this day, and many of the buildings of / which we have the history, but long since destroyed, prove that Masonry had flourished in Ireland, in times of high antiquity. But, from the conquest of Henry II. till the beginning of last century, it does not appear that the science had been much cultivated in Ireland.

The English partizans, amongst whom the country had been divided by its conquerors, appearing to preserve the greatest partiality to their native soil, generally thought themselves safest in England, and leaving their Irish estates in the hands and to the management of their agents, had little thought of improving that country by building which they did not wish to reside in. This, combined with the frequent struggles made by the natives, to recover their liberty and independence, and to throw off the shackles of their task masters, prevented those improvements proceeding, where the genius of Masonry was required: for, as it was only about the beginning of the last century that the privileges of Masonry were communicated to any but to operative Masons, the society could not flourish in a country where few buildings were to be erected.

Some of the English lords it appears, however, had introduced the craft into Ireland, and several noble structures were erected under their patronage. King John employed Launders, Archbishop of Dublin, as Grand-master, in 1210, to build the castle of Dublin. About the same time the priory of Kilkenny was built by William, Earl of Pembroke.

In the reign of Henry III. St. Mary's, Dublin, was built by Felix O'Quadam, Archbishop of Tuam, who covered it with lead. In this reign the famous Hu[gh] De Lacy was Grand Master, or patron of the Craft, / and founded Carrickfergus, the priory of Ards, and the famous Trim Castle. John De Courcy, Earl of Kinsale, having rebuilt the abbey of Downpatrick, about 40 years before that period.

The Craft was interrupted in its progress by the incursions made into the country, by Edward Bruce, until he was defeated and slain, by Mortimer, Earl of March: after which, Masonry revived in the English settlements, and had been introduced into the North, by some Scotch colonists.

Masonry made some progress in Ireland during the reigns of James I. and his son Charles, till the civil wars broke out, which retarded it greatly, till the restoration, when it was revived by the disciples of Inigo Jones, but was again interrupted by the wars of James II. – But, after the country had been settled at the revolution, Masonry flourished under the reigns of William III. Queen Anne, and George I.: and in the third year of the reign of George II. the ancient fraternity of Free and Accepted Masons in Ireland, assembled themselves in Dublin, and in imitation of their Brethren in England, erected a Grand Lodge, and chose a Grand Master – James King,[3] Lord Viscount Kingston, who had the year before served the office of Grand Master of England: and who introduced similar regulations and constitutions to those of the Brethren in England.

This appears to have been the origin of a Grand Lodge in Ireland; for, two years before, viz. 1728, when the foundation stone of the Parliament-House was laid, there was no mention made of any Grand Lodge, or Grand Master, as the following quotation will shew. – /

'Sir Edward Lovet Pearce,[4] the architect of the new magnificent Parliament-House, (far beyond that of England, founded on the 3d February, 1728–9) when Lord Carteret,[5] Lord Lieutenant; the Lords Justices; several Peers and Members of Parliament; some eminent Clergy; with *many Free Masons*, attended by the King's yeomen of guard, with a detachment of horse and foot, made a solemn procession thither. The Lord Lieutenant having, in the King's name, levelled the foot stone at the South side, by giving it three knocks with a mallet; the trumpet sounded; the solemn crowd made joyful acclamation. – A purse of gold was laid on the stone, for the masons who *drank to the King and the Craft*, &c.'

The Lodges of Free Masons at that time spread over the country were very numerous, and had assembled and worked in the same manner that their Brethren of England had done, previous to the establishment of a Grand Lodge, and without any warrant of constitution. Many, or almost all of the Dublin Lodges adhered to the rules and regulations prescribed for them by the Grand Lodge, but numbers of country Lodges refused to acknowledge their superiority, and to take out warrants from that Body. This was productive of much mischief in the country, as those Lodges who had fallen in with the views of the Grand Lodge, reviled the others as irregular Masons, and branded them with the epithet of hedge, or Bush Masons,[6] which created much ill blood between the parties, and many battles ensued at markets, fairs, or such places of public resort. Disputes and quarrels of this nature, have, however, long ceased to disturb the harmony of the Craft, and Masonry, till within these / few years, flourished in Ireland without any discord, until the unhappy differences commenced, which gave rise to the present publication.

This short history of Masonry is given merely to elucidate the subject herein-after to be treated of; and, if the writer can satisfy the scruples of Brethren, who have not had opportunity to give the subject due consideration; or, if he can be the means of restoring that confidence and harmony to the Brethren who have stood aloof from one another, in consequence of the controversy which has agi-tated the Body, he will consider himself well paid for the trouble he has taken in making the researches, and drawing the consequent conclusions: – this much he must say for himself, that he took up the resolution of examining into the con-troversy, in the most impartial manner, and with a spirit of enquiry, dictated by the purest motives, intending nothing but the most candid and liberal decisions, according to such evidence as came before him, so far as his limited abilities could enable him to judge. If, therefore, in the course of his own observations on the subject, he should inadvertently make use of any expression offensive to the feelings of any individual, (such as have been wilfully guilty of improper or unmasonic conduct excepted) he begs and hopes for excuse, as nothing can be farther from his intention, or more opposite to his views than creating the slight-est degree of animosity – An endeavour to place the question in a fair and candid light, and to conciliate those who have unthinkingly, either by want of informa-tion, or by the intrigues of designing men, attached themselves to a party, whose private interest is their guiding motive, being his only object. /

A fair and impartial statement of the origin and progress of this unfortunate contest, he shall therefore give, as far as is consistent with his ability and infor-mation on the subject: in which he pledges himself 'Nothing to extenuate, or aught set down in malice.'

From the original constitution of the Grand Lodge of Ireland in 1730, down to the 1801, the business of the Grand Lodge, as to accounts and financial con-cerns had always been transacted by the Grand Secretary's deputy;[7] and although by one of the original regulations, the Grand Treasurer might, if he thought fit, appoint a clerk or assistant. Such person never had been appointed by any Grand Treasurer till the period above alluded to.

On the death of a much respected Brother,[8] who held the situation of deputy Secretary in the latter end of the year 1800, it appears, that owing to the long sickness and consequent infirmities of that officer, the affairs of the order were in a considerable degree of confusion; it was therefore thought expedient to appoint a person to bring forward and settle the accounts.

A person was selected for that purpose, by the advice and influence, it appears, of the Grand Treasurer,[9] who, being disappointed in having the same person appointed Deputy Grand Secretary, and not content with paying that person, when the business was done, thought proper to use the same influence in getting him appointed his own Deputy, with a salary of 50 guineas per annum, 10 per cent. on the collection of all Grand Lodge dues, up to the St. John's day preceding; and 5 per cent. on all monies that should thereafter be paid into the Treasury of the Grand Lodge. /

This appointment of Deputy Grand Treasurer, gave great offence to many of the Brethren, both in Dublin and in the country; they conceiving that the Deputy Grand Secretary was fully competent to the discharge of the duties of the office.[10] It appearing to them that the funds of the Order in general passing through the hands of that officer, there was no necessity whatever for the appointment of a third person to carry money from him to the Treasurer, as it would only induce another set of accounts to be kept by the Deputy Treasurer, the necessity of which was precluded by suffering the Deputy Secretary alone to account with the Grand Treasurer, by which means a considerable saving would accrue to the Lodge, inasmuch as the money would not be subject to any reduction in its transit from the hands of the one officer, to those of the other.

From the long confinement of the deceased Deputy Grand Secretary, it is highly probable that the funds and accounts of the Order were in considerable confusion without any reflections on the memory of that worthy and respectable Brother, whose merits and worth were not unknown to the writer of this treatise, and it is also probable that some person well versed in accounts was necessary to arrange and settle them, provided it was more than the Deputy Grand Secretary was equal to within the proper time; all that was required however, was to employ a person as his assistant, pay him when the business was completed, and let him be discharged; not to saddle the order with an office which had been hitherto unknown, and an office which must be paid out of the charitable fund alone, as there was no perquisite of office for that / purpose, as in the case of the Deputy Grand Secretary.

In a publication bearing date the December 12, 1805,[11] the Grand Lodge in apologizing for the appointment of Deputy Treasurer, states, that in the year 1768, the fees of the Deputy Grand Secretary were less than half what had been allowed him at different periods since that date. Now if it was, as is by that paper insinuated, in consequence of the two offices being combined, that the fees of that officer were more than doubled, it was only necessary, when the offices were separated, to take from the Deputy Secretary what had been allowed him for his extra trouble, and give that to the Deputy Treasurer as his remuneration, and not tax the fund of charity to pay the Treasurer's Deputy.

On the 19th of August, 1802, at an emergency meeting, the Grand Lodge[12] resolved that all Lodges holding Warrants under it, should pay the sum of £1 2s. 9d. annually, as Grand Lodge dues, being an addition of 11s. 11d. per annum, to the sum ordered in 1768; that all persons entered or accepted as Freemasons, should pay 5s. 5d. to the Grand Treasurer or his Deputy; that an additional sum of £1 2s. 9d. should be paid for each Warrant thereafter to be granted, and that one half the Lodge dues and admission fine, with the additional guinea on the Warrants should be appropriated to the support of the Female Orphan School;[13] this was the next cause of complaint which was greatly increased by the Grand Lodge proposing to take the Royal Arch Chapters and Knights Templars Encampments under its protection, charging each Lodge 2 guineas for those Orders, 2s. 8 ½d. for each registry of different orders, and / 5s. 5d. for each certificate. This attempt was very generally and justly reprobated for several sufficient reasons. In the first place, there was not the shadow of necessity for issuing Warrants for the superior degrees, no instance having in the memory of man occurred of any difference having arisen in those orders which required the controuling power of a Grand Lodge to settle. 2dly, such an arrangement would have invested Masons of the inferior orders with a controul and undue influence over the superior degrees, an anomaly in Masonry not at all to be submitted to. 3dly, Provided the funds of the subordinate Lodges were in general made accountable for the two guineas demanded, Blue Masons would have been taxed for Red and Black Masons,[14] and if the Red and Black Masons alone were chargeable with the two guineas, that money would go into a fund completely under the controul and management of Blue Masons, so that to take that circumstance either ways, injustice is done to one party; but the most forcible and cogent reason is the fourth, namely, that by this arrangement, a sum of upwards of £30,000* would have been levied off / the brethren at large, and put into the hands, and under the management of persons whom there is good reason to think always took great care not to pay themselves worst, and if we are to judge of their future intentions by their past conduct, there is strong reason to believe that the fund of charity would with this vast accumulation of property, have been only nominally benefited thereby.

The Institution proposed to be supported by this large contribution, was not by any means palatable to the generality of the country brethren, who, observing what they considered gross partiality in the distribution of the fund of charity,

---

*   Supposing 1000 Warrants to be in existence, and on an average each Lodge to consist of 20 members, the following calculation will amply justify the assertion in the text: –

1000 Lodges, 2 Warrants each, at 2 guineas, £4550 0[s.] 0[d.]
Do. say 20 Members each, 3 Registries at 2s. 8 ½d.   8125 0[s.] 0[d.]
3 Certificates to each Member, at 5s. 5d.   16250 0[s.] 0[d.]
£28925 0[s.] 0[d.]

Which, with postage, would, no doubt, raise the sum to / more than that mentioned above, not taking into view the additional 11s. 11d. annual subscription.

had no confidence that the management of the Orphan School would be conducted on more liberal or equitable principles.

They were in a great measure justified in this opinion by the illiberal remarks of several Dublin members of the Grand Lodge, who would not admit that any orphan from the country had a right to have admittance to the charity, as the principal support of it was drawn from the brethren of Dublin.

Such an institution, if established on fair and equitable principles, and in such a manner managed as to be equally applicable to the generality of the Order, must be admitted to be highly meritorious and praiseworthy; and ought to be an object of the first and most important consideration with the Order; but that it should be established upon exclusive principles, / and be more open to the reception of one part of the community than another, or to suppose that the orphans of the Dublin Masons should always have a priority of claim, is both absurd, unjust, and by no means sustainable; therefore, the Masons of Ulster had no right either in common sense or in common justice to subscribe to such amount to such an institution, to which local circumstances alone, formed a heavy objection.

The Masons of Dublin, or the province of Leinster, making such an establishment, and supporting it themselves, either in their individual or collective capacities, or by the private donations of individuals, without looking for support from other more distant quarters, would be acting certainly very creditable to themselves. But that the brethren of Ulster should be taxed to such an enormous amount, with no security, or even the probability that any children of theirs might ever be benefited by the institution, and that they would tamely submit to such an imposition, were to suppose them composed of very different materials than they have ever yet exhibited themselves.

Some spirited though respectful remonstrances were made by the Northern Lodges to these proceedings, and many Lodges in Dublin having been better acquainted with the cupidity of the Grand Lodge, entered warmly into a controversy with them on those points. It is, however, to be lamented that the language used on this occasion was much too warm, and in many cases descended into absolute scurrillity on both sides, the contending parties appearing to have intirely lost sight of argument, by / substituting abuse in its room; even those who had the advantage in the controversy, lost it in a great measure by the acrimony and severity of their animadversions.

Truth never can be aided or supported by scurrility, but it may be easily disgraced by unbecoming or acrimonious language; and it is much to be regretted that in the conducting of this controversy, there was great loss of temper on both sides, and indulgence in terms and epithets[xli] highly unbecoming in men, but more so in Masons, whose principles inculcate a brotherly forbearance with the imperfections of one another.

To the honour, however, of our northern brethren, this, in very few, if in any instances, was the case; their language to the Grand Lodge was respectful, but firm and manly; arguments inforced with that becomingness and respect which is always due to a higher power, whether that power is acting right or wrong. Masons ought, and it is their duty to assume that, their Brethren, if they act improperly, are under the influence of error; and it is also their duty, in calm, moderate, and respectful language, to endeavour to convince them of their mistakes, and not hastily to attribute to wicked motives, what may be the effects of an erroneous judgment. If they are unsuccessful in the attempt, and unjustifiable conduct is persisted in, it then becomes the duty of persons aggrieved, to resort to such measures as the laws and usages of the order have provided for their redress, and in such manner did the Masons of Ulster proceed with their brethren in the Grand Lodge; their remonstrances were drawn up with moderation and / good temper, and they expresed their dissent to the objectionable measures in respectful terms, a specimen of which is here quoted, being a memorial to the Grand Lodge, from 18 Lodges, assembled at Belfast, 16th March, 1803.

TO THE
Right Worshipful
THE GRAND LODGE OF IRELAND.

The Memorial of Lodges No. 272, 484, 491, 499, 550, 598, 609, 621, 636, 684, 651, 687, 761, 762, 763, 793, 845, 861, respectfully showeth, That your Memorialists having been favoured with the resolutions of an emergency meeting of the Grand Lodge, held on the 19th of August last, and having considered them in open Lodge, conceive it their duty to communicate to you their sentiments on a subject which seems to interrupt that Masonic harmony which has so happily existed time immemorial. That whilst your Memorialists highly applaud the humane purposes for which the recent augmentation of the Grand Lodge dues is to be levied; yet with great deference, they are unanimously of opinion, that if said resolutions were enforced, they will very much impair our ability to relieve the numerous and pressing applications of distress, which are pouring in from travelling brethren, and also from those who, residing eighty miles and upwards from the metropolis, cannot hope for assistance from that quarter. That though your Memorialists feel the most poignant regret in dissenting from any resolution of the Grand Lodge, yet they cannot but consider themselves bound in Christian duty, to oppose a measure which would exhaust / their resources, and consequently strip their poor of that, to which they have an undoubted rightful claim, and especially to support those of a city, which for commerce, affluence, and respectability, holds the second rank in the empire. That your Memorialists being influenced by no spirit but that of duty, unanimously declare, that the said resolutions, together with the appointment of an extra officer, called Deputy Grand Treasurer, are unnecessary, and a grievous burthen to the order at large, of which we form a part. And that Memorialists look up to you for redress, earnestly praying that you in your wisdom, will be pleased to rescind the said resolutions, and said appointment, which (in our opinion) will restore to our ancient Order, that happy unanimity and social contentment for which it has always been so deservedly admired and beloved.

Signed in the name, and by order of the Meeting, &c.

March 16, 1803.

(A Copy.)

This Memorial, of which the reader has it in his power to form an opinion, on being laid before the Grand Lodge, was treated by many of those persons most conspicuous in that body in a very contemptuous manner, and a motion 'made that it should be scouted as impertinent.'

This intemperate motion was supported by a considerable number of the members present, and was negatived only by a small majority. Such a memorial as the above, and coming from such a quarter, was surely worthy of better treatment. But at this time, some of the members of the Grand Lodge appeared to have / forgotten how to act either as Masons or as men, giving way to the most violent passions, and indulging themselves in nothing but the most intemperate invective. The Masons of Ulster, however, unwilling to give up the cause while the shadow of hope remained of a reconciliation, and willing to heal the breaches made in the order, if, within their power, without compromising the interests thereof, still resorted to lenient measures.

Representatives from 62 Lodges of the counties of Down and Antrim, met at Belfast, and entered into some spirited resolutions, they were couched in respectful manly language, and expressed with energy.

They stated the willingness of the Brethren, whom they represented, still to adhere to and support the Grand Lodge, provided they were restored to their old regulations, under which they had heretofore enjoyed so much harmony and peace, at the same time most solemnly pledging themselves to their Brethren of the superior degrees that they never would acknowledge the innovations lately attempted by the Grand Lodge, and also expressing their strong apprehension that provided such innovations were persisted in, it might be the means of dissolving that connexion which had so long subsisted between the Grand Lodge and the Masons of Ulster. From the reception their former memorial had met with in the Grand Lodge, they despaired of a patient hearing from that body, they therefore most respectfully memorialed the Right Worshipful the Grand Master,[15] at the same time transmitting to him the resolutions above alluded to; they most / earnestly prayed his Lordship's interference in endeavouring to put a stop to the disputes which had done so much injury to the Order, and that he would please to use the well-known influence of his highly exalted character and station to put a final stop to those dissensions, to restore unanimity, tranquillity and love amongst those who had the superintendance of the Craft, and to rescind those novel and pernicious innovations which had a tendency to irritate the feelings of the Brethren throughout the country.

Meetings took place in almost every county in the province, and resolutions were entered into expressive of approbation of the Masons of Down and Antrim, declaring their hostility to the innovations attempted by the Grand Lodge, and uniformly declaring against the appointment of a Deputy Grand Treasurer.

All these resolutions were transmitted to the Right Worshipful Grand Master, accompanied by memorials, containing the sentiments of upwards of 300 Lodges of Masons, of the province of Ulster. Notwithstanding which, the Grand Lodge would not recede one step from the ground it had taken, but persisted in all the obnoxious measures.

On the 24th May, 1806, a meeting of the representatives of 50 Lodges[16] from the county of Antrim, was held in Belfast, when they resolved (as they expressed themselves) that feeling the greatest reluctance to break off from the Grand Lodge, they would make one final attempt towards a reconciliation; by which to show that nothing but injustice and arbitrary measures could ever induce them to withdraw / their allegiance from a Grand Lodge once deservedly loved and honoured.

To effect this desirable object, they proposed to send delegates to represent them in the Grand Lodge, on the 5th of June following,[17] at the same time advising the rest of the Masons of Ulster to do the same; instructing their delegates to have repealed the late election of Grand Officers; to re-elect the former Grand Secretary;[18] to remove the Grand Treasurer,[19] and appoint a person to that office, worthy of their confidence; to abolish the office of Deputy Grand Treasurer,[20] and to rescind all the late transactions, which infringed upon the ancient rights, and Masonic privileges.

That all innovations should be repealed, and that it should be entered on the Grand Lodge Books, that the moment that any party or faction should renew them, or adopt any novel mode to extort money from the country, that moment the Masons of Ulster would establish a Grand Lodge for themselves.

They also formed a committee of nine for the purpose of corresponding with their delegates, while in Dublin, and to report their proceedings to the different Lodges in the country.

The Grand Lodge Meeting took place accordingly, on the 5th of June following, when two resolutions*, according with the wishes of the Northern /

---

*   1 Resolved, that the resolution of the Grand Lodge, of 1st May last, negativing the reading of the addresses from the north of Ireland, be expunged from the books. / 2 Resolved, the several transactions and resolutions respecting Red and Black Masonry, be for ever expunged from the books of the order.

delegates were passed by a large majority, but the Deputy Grand Master[21] taking exceptions to many of the Northern delegates, as not being qualified to vote, precipitately closed the Lodge, in opposition to a large majority of the members present.

The delegates from the Northern Lodges had been previously examined, their powers verified, and were suffered to vote on the two resolutions alluded to without any objection to their qualification.

But the Deputy Grand Master apprehensive that from the complexion of the meeting, such measures were likely to be carried as would not be well relished by the ruling party, took this unwarrantable mode of (as he thought) extinguishing the spirit of the meeting.

On his retiring, however, the meeting conceiving themselves exceedingly ill-treated by such an arbitrary measure, they ordered the regulation of the 7th March, 1799, to be read – viz, 'that the Grand Lodge shall not at any time be closed for a longer period than one month, or adjourned at any meeting, without the consent of a majority of the Brethren present.'[22] On which the meeting resolved, That the Deputy Grand Master had acted in a manner highly arbitrary in closing the Lodge, and in previously refusing to put two several questions which were fully consonant to Masonry, and that his conduct should be represented to the Grand Master.[23] The Meeting then re-opened the Lodge, appointing two respectable / Brethren to the chair, and filling up the places of the senior and junior Grand Wardens.[24]

The meeting then proceeded to pass a string of resolutions, among which were the following: –

Rescinding as much of the proceedings of the last meeting as related to the appointment of Grand Secretary and Grand Treasurer.

Appointing two respectable brethren to these offices.[25]

Abolishing the Office of Deputy Grand Treasurer.

Rescinding resolution of 12th December previous: which had appointed a committee with a power to appropriate 50 guineas to the purpose of finding out and prosecuting some persons said to have wrote libels on some of the officers of the Grand Lodge.

Resolving that from some charges being substantiated against the Grand Treasurer, he had forfeited the confidence of the order, and was then voted to be disqualified to hold any office in the Grand Lodge.

Thus were the Northern Lodges completely foiled in their attempt at reconciliation, and the breach considerably widened, for the Deputy Grand Master and his party continued to hold what they called Grand Lodge meetings, had a new seal cut and certificate plate engraved, gave themselves out as the Grand Lodge, certifying and registering all that made application to them. This party holding the purse of the Order no doubt considering themselves of as much consequence at least, as the other who had but a poor majority, without funds at their backs.

The future meeting of the Grand Lodge being adjourned till the 3d July following,[26] the members / accordingly attended at 8 o'clock in the evening, but found the doors of the hall locked against them, and understood that the keys had been taken from the Grand Tyler.

On their waiting for about an hour, however, the Deputy Grand Master made his appearance, but looking round him, and not being satisfied with the complexion of the meeting, he declared 'he would not open the Lodge that night,' and immediately left the hall, some of his friends desiring the city Lodges to follow their Grand Master. The doors of the Lodgeroom were, however, unlocked by the members present, and in conformity to the rule of 3d November, 1768, providing for the absence of the Grand officers, the Lodge was opened, and business proceeded on, not, however, uninterruptedly, as certain peace officers had been sent by the disappointed party to disperse the meeting as irregular, and contrary to the king's peace.

The Grand Lodge at this meeting ordered its committee to draw up a statement of the conduct of the Deputy Grand Master, at this, and the meeting in June, and with it a memorial to the right Worshipful the Grand Master, praying the removal of his Deputy, and also containing their opinion that the publicly avowed wish of those few Lodges who supported his conduct, to have another Grand Lodge formed in the country, for the country Lodges, to have no connexion with the Grand Lodge in Dublin, was calculated to divide the Order, and consequently to produce a disunion highly dangerous and prejudicial to the interests of the Craft. /

This communication and memorial being unreplied to, a second one was ordered to be drawn up and forwarded in December following;[27] reiterating the complaints against the Deputy Grand Master, and insisting on his removal; to neither of these memorials, however was any answer returned; therefore, the conduct of a large majority of the Grand Lodge evidently appears to have been opposed to any thing friendly to a separation, and that the idea of another Grand Lodge being formed, originated with that party, which, on its establishment, so loudly exclaimed against the measure.

The Grand Lodge being thus split into two parties, and both holding meetings as the Grand Lodge, it was difficult for those at a distance from the scene of action, and unacquainted with the circumstances, to determine which was right, or which wrong.

Those of the northern Lodges who had the opportunity of observing the conduct of the Deputy Grand Master, and those he acted with, execrated that conduct as highly unmasonic, arbitrary, and unjust, and despaired of a reconciliation ever taking place.

The parties at issue were liberal in their abuse of each other; the press teemed with phillipics against this and that party, and publications, appeals, and remonstrances multiplied, scarce a Lodge meeting in the country, but one or more of them were laid before them. Mutual expulsions were thundered out against individuals on both sides, and Masonic anathemas threatened to those adhering to this or that party.

In this manner the remainder of the year 1806 and 1807 passed over, many Lodges in the north withholding their Grand Lodge dues, not knowing which had the best right to receive them, and many / actually looking forward to the appointment of a Grand Lodge for their own province, well knowing that the contest would never have an end so long as there were persons concerned, whose private emolument was the principal cause of quarrel, which was evidently the case.

From the numerous memorials presented to the Right Worshipful the Grand Master, to use his endeavours to put a period to the existing differences, his Lordship, on 26th March, 1808, sent circular letters to the Lodges,[28] signifying his intention of presiding at the next monthly meeting in April, which meeting having taken place on the 7th of that month, the Grand Master on the throne, and a person appointed a secretary,[29] pro tempore, who had not been known to have taken any part in the late disputes.

His Lordship from the chair delivered his sentiments at considerable length strongly recommending as the means of healing the breaches, and adjusting the differences which had so nearly severed the Order into two separate interests, mutual sacrifices on the part of those whose contests had been productive of so much mischief; and above all things he recommended that the offices of Secretary and Deputy Secretary should be put into such hands as to avoid giving the victory to one party or the other; at the same time stating his intention of committing the office of Deputy Grand Master to a person[30] who had not been concerned in any of the late differences, and around whom all the Brethren of the Order, however they might have heretofore differed in opinion might assemble with the surest confidence, and the certainty of / meeting from him the most cordial efforts for a general and complete accommodation.

The Grand Master concluded with proposing the following resolution, which was unanimously adopted: –

Resolved, that it be strongly recommended to the Grand Lodge, when they assemble together on Thursday 5th May next, for the election of Grand Officers for the ensuing year, to bring with them to this place, that spirit of mutual conciliation, friendship, and brotherly love, which alone can heal those wounds by the late unhappy contentions inflicted on the order of Freemasonry in Ireland.

This resolution recommended all that was required; and had the spirit of it been complied with, all would have been settled, and the order restored to that harmony and peace of which it had so long been deprived; but when men are actuated by selfish views, or when personal interest or private emolument is in the case, such recommendations as the above are paid little attention to, as no argument held out to such men, short of a promise of more profit, or a situation of greater emolument would be conclusive; for had the disputes arisen on any other subject than money matters, the probability is, that the Grand Master's advice would have been followed, and that his interference would have settled the contest, but by the proceedings of the following meeting it will be observed that all passed for nothing, and that in place of the breach being closed, it was made wider, and the differences rendered for ever irreconcileable.

On the 5th May following, the Grand Lodge met[31] for the election of officers for the ensuing year. The brother of the Grand Master presiding as his deputy; the Grand / Master, senior and junior Grand Wardens were appointed;[32] but as it were to show how little regard was to be paid to the recommendation of the Right Worshipful Grand Master, and to evince that the old party had dropped none of the spirit of discord with which they had tormented the Order for now nearly 6 years; the very man was proposed and seconded as Grand Treasurer,[33] that had, by the opposite party, been considered to have forfeited the confidence of the Order, and resolved to be incapable of ever holding a situation in the Grand Lodge, in future.

On the question being put, some of the Northern delegates demanded a division. When the Secretary was ordered to call over the registry of every Warrant in Ireland, and to take the votes accordingly, upon which, a number of the members present were objected to, as being incompetent to vote, their Lodges being in arrear to the Grand Lodge; their votes being thus rejected, the Grand Treasurer was appointed, though contrary to the voice of a large majority of the meeting.

This proceeding gave a death's wound to all attempts at conciliation; the party whose votes were rejected, proposed paying off all arrears, provided a proper and confidential person were appointed to receive them; or to pay them into the hands of the Deputy Grand Master; but to the person then proposed as Treasurer, they had insuperable objections to pay any money, as they conceived, and that with good reason, that he had forfeited the confidence of the brethren, by gross misapplication of the funds of the order, that he had lent his sanction to the paying money away in support of suits at law, and for the purpose of discovering / persons who had written libels against himself: – The Deputy grand Master refusing to accede to this reasonable request, of accepting of the dues, and holding them till a proper Treasurer should be appointed, and the Ulster deputies plainly perceiving there was no appearance of any change in the management of the funds of the Order, instantly adopted the resolution of leaving the meeting, and adjourning to another place in the city.

The officers of 79 Lodges therefore, met in the evening of the same day, and came to the resolution of requesting the Grand Master of Ulster[34] to call a Grand Lodge meeting at Dungannon, on the 6th June following, for the purpose of vindicating their rights, and establishing the future meetings of the Grand Lodge, at such times and places as might be there agreed on. In consequence of which, a meeting was called for the day above mentioned, which meeting took place accordingly.

At this meeting delegates from 311 Lodges attended,[35] and they resolved themselves into the Grand Lodge of Ulster; chose their Grand Officers,[36] and transacted such business as necessarily came before them.

On an impartial and dispassionate review of all those various circumstances, it must appear to the unprejudiced reader that the Masons of Ulster acted with all the forbearance, mildness, and good nature that it was possible for men in their circumstances to act with: – that they had received provocation sufficient to raise the passions of any but such as were guided by wisdom and prudence; and that whatever blame is attachable to the persons who raised and cherished the / spirit of discord in the Order; they conducted themselves in a manner deserving of the highest praise. That great blame is due to some individuals, must appear evident from the statement made here, in which care has been most studiously taken not to charge the picture, even to the highest that impartiality and truth could justify, it being not the intention to irritate or inflame, but merely to endeavour to convince those of error who have not been wilfully culpable, having been misled by an overweening fondness for name or character, or from trifling pique attaching themselves to that party, whose conduct must appear highly reprehensible, and unworthy [of] the slightest confidence.

The disturbing the harmony of such a community as the ancient and respectable Fraternity of Freemasons, cannot be looked on with indifference, nor reflected on without exciting feeling of the strongest disapprobation; and the persons capable of agitating and setting together by the ears men who had hitherto lived in friendship, harmony, and good neighbourhood, it must be said have not acted according to the principles of that society to whom they belong, whose foundation is charity and brotherly love.

It is not the least surprizing circumstance in the history of this unfortunate contest, that the mere management and increase of a charitable fund should be the ostensible cause of quarrel; nor is it less surprizing that the man who appeared to have intirely lost the confidence of so large a portion of the persons contributing to that fund, should endeavour to have himself forced on that community, against their consent, as Treasurer.[37] What can be supposed to be his inducement? / There was no salary attached to the place, nor could any gain be expected, provided the fund had been honestly managed; – yet this person, extremely unpopular as he is, obtrudes himself on the body, and whither they are willing or unwilling, he must be treasurer. There can be only two ways of accounting for his conduct; he either wished to throw the apple of discord, for sake of the mischief, or he had some views of an interested nature not perfectly reconcileable to moral rectitude. Most honest men wish to excuse themselves from holding the money of a charitable fund, as there is no possibility of gain to them, and there is risk of loss.

That some intrigue might by some vain men be used for the honour of being chosen to any of the other grand Offices, would not be surprizing, as to them, there is no pecuniary responsibility attached; but that a whole community should be thrown into commotion, on account of an individual being chosen to an office in which, if fidelity is observed, there may be some risk of loss, but no possible hope of gain, certainly excites feelings not much to the honour or advantage of the intentions of the person wishing for the office.

By an account published in December, 1809,[38] it appears that £500 of government debentures had been sold out by the Treasurer, for which he received £492 4[s.] 1[d.], which, with other sums received from June in that year, amounted to £978 3[s.] 0[d.]; of this large sum, there was expended in charity, [£]258 13[s.] 11[d.] The remainder, with the exception of £1 13[s.] 3[d.] due by the Treasurer, amounting to £717 15[s.] 10[d.] was paid away for law costs, printing, rent, &c. Three / prominent items in this account are printing and stationary, £110 13[s.] 11[d.]; Law costs in suing a person, £146 7[s.] 6[d.]; Law costs in defending a person, £325 2[s.] 10[d.], to this may be added the sum of £377 19[s.] 2[d.], paid to Deputy Treasurers, in all, £1095 15[s.] 0[d.], taken from the charitable fund for any purpose but that for which it was intended, by which the fund, from a state of respectability, was reduced to almost nothing, leaving only, in the hands of the Treasurer, £1 13[s.] 3[d.].

By this simple statement it must evidently appear that the managers of the fund have had nothing less at heart than its benefit.

The inconsistency of those persons is remarkable; in November, 1805, a memorial was presented from 17 brethren, soldiers and sailors, confined as prisoners of war in Vallenciennes,[39] when the Grand Treasurer observed, the funds were low, therefore, he moved, that [£]5 should be sent those poor distress'd brethren;[40] they were, however, ordered one guinea each, a wretched pittance indeed, when at the same meeting, the same Treasurer had influence enough to procure a vote of 50 guineas for the purpose of discovering some person who had libelled him; comparing this economical vote of 17 guineas, with the sums paid to printers and lawyers, in 1809, exhibits a degree of gross inconsistency; and is sufficient to lead one to believe that the fund was not intended for charitable purposes.

For the large sums of money expended in law-suits,[41] however, we are offered the consolation that the law has ruled it so that the Grand Lodge may publish the names of persons expelled, with impunity; but useless was this consolation, when the person whose expulsion / was the cause of action, was at a subsequent meeting, restored by a unanimous vote of those who had before expelled him.

Men of Ulster, can you shut your eyes against the light? Could you submit to be governed by such men? Surely you must answer, No!!!

The conduct of the Grand Lodge in suffering this money to be so expended, is highly reprehensible; it is not a sufficient apology that it was for the recovery of the property of the order, as that property may not be worth any thing like the sum which there is danger of losing by an expensive and long protracted Chancery suit. Much better suffer a trifling loss at first, than to go into Chancery with the purse of the poor and the indigent; but how much more culpable are they if the whole of the risk is to the charity, and the gain, if any, to the individual It appears by an authentic document, that 50 guineas had been voted for the purpose of discovering and prosecuting libellers. Where is the apology that can be offered for this gross misapplication of a charitable fund? or who is the person hardy enough to attempt a defence of such conduct? The libels, if such did exist, could not injure the charitable fund, and why make it accountable for the expense of discovering or prosecuting the libeller? the officer libelled was the only person that could suffer, and why not he bear the expense in his own person? Is a man, because he is trustee to a charitable fund, and happens to have something said or written of him, not flattering to his feelings, to take from that fund money sufficient to discover and prosecute the libeller? Suppose on trial it has not turned out to be a libel, and that the person is acquitted, who / is then to bear the expense? the charitable fund of course, and that without the hope of remuneration, for suppose the libeller even to be convicted, the fine levied off him goes to the king, and the expense of prosecution comes out of the fund of charity, without any part of it ever being returned.

Allowing, however, that the general conduct of the Grand Lodge had been correct, and that the officers objected to had been as pure in their motives and actions as it was possible they could be, it was surely highly unbecoming in them to oppose the voice of so large a majority as the Masons of Ulster, and the Lodges coinciding with them amounted to. The appointment of two officers might have been conceded to them who composed the decided majority in the Grand Lodge, there being more than twice the number of Lodges in Ulster, than are in the rest of the kingdom. For the sake of unanimity, the experiment might have been made; provided the objects of their choice had not answered the expectations entertained of them, they were open to censure and liable to be removed at a next election; but that the *minority*, and that a *small* minority should pertinaciously persist in retaining an officer, who by some means had lost the confidence of the majority of the members of the Grand Lodge, was not only absurd in itself, but contrary to all the regulations of the order, which on all occasions, particularly in the appointment of officers, inculcate the principle of deciding by majorities. The retreat made by the ruling party, that the arrears of dues incapacitated the members for voting, was but a shallow apology. Why suffer the same persons to vote for the other Grand Officers? / Why suffer their votes to be taken, or their voices to be heard on the other business of the Lodge, and not go into a scrutiny of the legality of their votes? it appears that so long as they voted with the faction, their votes were considered good; but the moment they opposed any favourite motion, or any officer which that faction approved of, that moment their votes must be set aside. This conduct, it must be admitted, was indefensible, and greatly derogatory to the dignity of a Grand Lodge. Provided there really had been some arrears due by the Lodges, the delegates sent to the Grand Lodge being the trustees of their constituents, would not have been doing their duty, had they paid the money into the hands of a person who they conceived unworthy their confidence, and it was but just and absolutely necessary that the person to be appointed to that office, should meet their approbation, seeing that they were the majority of the meeting, and were against the person proposed as Treasurer.

For the delegates of the northern Lodges to pay money to a Treasurer whom they had every reason, from his past conduct, to suppose would squander it away, as his own folly or caprice might dictate to him; or who could be so completely the tool of a party as to dissipate to annihilation the funds of the order, in support of litigations, advised and promoted by that party, would certainly have been such a derili[c]tion of duty, as to have forfeited any claim on the confidence of their Lodges; and have rendered them very unfit persons to manage the affairs of their constituents. /

The Northern Delegates, it appears, from what their Dublin brethren presumed to denominate aukwardness of dialect and address, had become objects of contempt and ridicule to those gentlemen. This was both unmasonic and ungentlemanlike, far beneath the conduct of Free Masons; very inconsistent indeed with that brotherhood of love and affection which should pervade the Order; Masonry, without distinction, bringing on a level, in a Masonic point of view, the peer and the peasant.

It is now necessary to consider the question of right. Some persons unacquainted with the subject, having entertained doubts that the right to withdraw from the Dublin Grand Lodge, and to erect another, does not exist in the Masons of Ulster; and that they are therefore, as Masons, bound to adhere to that Lodge, whither it is conducted well or ill.

But that such an opinion should be held, there does not appear to be any authority, either in common sense, or in the history of Masonry. In none of the books of constitutions, whether old or new, is there any law or regulation to that effect, nor is there in any of them, an account of how such a body was originally constituted. The summary history of Masonry, given at the beginning of this book, was designedly collated from the best Masonic authorities, to show that Free Masons have an inherent right, according to their laws and constitutions, to choose their own Masonic government.

All offices in Freemason Lodges are elective, the Grand Lodge being composed of the Masters and Wardens of the subordinate Lodges,[42] are dependant for these offices on those who elect them, and bound / to obey their instructions; therefore, the subordinate Lodges have the appointment of the Grand Lodge. And as the laws and constitutions of Masonry are held by prescription, they are superior to any Grand Lodge, being enacted and adhered to by our predecessors, before there was such a body as a Grand Lodge in existence.

The Grand Lodge, when once formed, is the legitimate head or government of such Masons as have elected it, that is, so long as it exercises its functions according to the laws and constitutions of the order, and no longer, or as is said in old constitutions, so long as they preserve the ancient Landmarks.[43] Nor is allegiance due by the constituent body, longer than they are governed according to the laws and usages of Masonry. Allegiance presupposes protection, and where there is no protection, there can be no allegiance due. Now when a Grand Lodge, contrary to the laws and constitutions of Masonry, by factious means, or otherwise violates the rights, infringes on the privileges, and illegally dissipates the funds of its constituents, it must be clear that allegiance is no longer due to that body, and the power reverts back to those who delegated it. The constituent body, therefore, in their new appointment, exercises the inherent right in Masons, to erect a new Grand Lodge. It is a well known axiom in Masonry, that it is not place which constitutes a Lodge, therefore, the constituent body, through its delegates, may order the Grand Lodge to meet in any place most suitable for the general convenience of the body, without regard to the will or caprice of individuals.

It argues an absurdity to suppose that the minority / can bind the majority; that the convenience of the large should be made subservient to that of the small body. Because it was more convenient for some of the officers or members of the Grand Lodge of Ireland to have their meetings in Dublin, it should be imperative upon the Masons of Ulster to send their delegates there also. In the province of Ulster it appears there are near 500 Lodges, and in the rest of the kingdom there are but few above 200, and of this 200, several Lodges in the province of Munster are represented in a Grand Lodge at Cork; there can be no reason therefore, in insisting, that so large a body as the Masons of Ulster compose, so vastly over-proportionate to those of the other parts of the country, should not have themselves represented in a Grand Lodge in their native province, when it conduces so much to their own convenience.

So far common sense and right reason proves the right in Masons to erect or establish a Grand Lodge when and where it best suits their convenience. Let us now see what precedent or custom will do for us.

In the history of Masonry in early times, it does not appear that a Grand Lodge, such as is now known among Masons, was in existence. There was sometimes a general assembly of Masons held at particular seasons, but at those periods, the privileges of Masonry were intirely confined to operative Masons, therefore, the general body was not so large as to require a delegation, and an aggregate meeting was always held when such meeting was deemed necessary.

In the days of Queen Elizabeth, the Masons of England were divided into two governments, the Earl / of Bedford being appointed Grand Master for the north division, and Sir Thomas Gresham Grand Master of the south division.[44] This arrangement took place merely for the sake of conveniency, the southern Grand Master being appointed in consequence of the Masons in and about London, increasing greatly in number. And in 1719, when the Masons of London erected themselves into a Grand Lodge,[45] and resolved to issue warrants of constitution; they made no application to any other body for liberty or authority to do so. They had the sanction and assistance of the four old Lodges at that time in London, to bring their project into effect, but did not apply to the Grand Lodge at York for any warrant to erect or constitute a Grand Lodge,[46] nor is there any rule, law, or regulation in existence directing how to constitute such a body.

In 1730, the Masons of Ireland constituted a Grand Lodge,[47] as is said in history, in *imitation* of their Brethren in London, but there is no account of their having applied to their Brethren in London or in York for a warrant of *authority* so to do, but in *imitation* of the Grand Lodge of London, they adopted similar rules and regulations, choosing for their Grand Master, Lord Viscount Kingston,[48] who had been Grand Master of England the preceding year.

It does not appear that any exceptions were taken by the Grand Lodge of York, when that of London was established, nor that any objections were made by either, when the Grand Lodge of Ireland was formed.

The Grand Lodges of York and London held communications, and corresponded with the greatest cordiality / for many years after the constituting the latter, but it appears they have had their misunderstandings as well as others, as the greatest coolness subsists between them at this day.

A circumstance worthy of note, however, occurred some years ago between the two Lodges, which goes clearly to prove the right in Masons, as acknowledged in England, to erect a Grand Lodge. In the year 1779, the Lodge of Antiquity in London, had some difference with the Grand Lodge of England,[49] and they withdrew their allegiance from that body, and united themselves with the Grand Lodge of all England at York. In 1799, when their differences were adjusted, they again united themselves with the Grand Lodge of England. This shows that they had the right to chuse betwixt the two Grand Lodges, and that they made their election, which seems to have been admitted by both Grand Lodges; as had they not had the right to withdraw themselves from the Grand Lodge of England, they would not have been received by the Grand Lodge at York, nor would they have been readmitted by the Lodge at London. And since they had the right to leave the one and join the other, the right to be one of a number of Lodges who should form a new Grand Lodge, is clearly established.

That nothing was more clearly recognised than the right of Masons to establish Grand Lodges, must appear from the following extract from a book of constitutions published in 1723, which runs thus, all these* foreign / Lodges are under the patronage of our Grand Master of England, but the old Lodge at York city, and the Lodges of Scotland, Ireland, France and Italy, affecting independency, are governed by their own Grand masters, though they have the same constitutions, charges, &c. with their Brethren of England.[50]

Here no complaint is made that these foreign Lodges, in not acknowledging the Grand Lodge, were illegal or unconstitutional, but they were fully recognized by the Grand Lodge of England, as Masons acting under their own Grand Masters, having the same regulations, and a similar constitution with the Grand Lodge of England.

From what has been stated, it must appear evident that the Masons of Ulster had done no more than the necessity of the case not only authorised, but obliged them to do; for had they tamely submitted to the government of a junto who had no other object but to enrich themselves at the expense of the charitable fund, they would neither have done their duty as men or as Masons. They have done, after a considerable lapse of time, and after repeated attempts to bring those in error to right reason, what they would have been fully authorised to do the day after their first remonstrance was treated with such contempt. Their conduct, however, proves that they had not only virtue to withstand the attempts made to impose on them, but they have proved to the world that they have not forgot or neglected their Masonic duty, but with that forbearance becoming them as Brother Masons, they have used every effort to show those infatuated men their errors, and to prevail on them to adopt a just / and rational conduct in their management of the affairs of the Order. Though unsuccessful in that respect, their efforts on the other hand have been crowned with merited success; they have succeeded in establishing a Grand Lodge of their own, of which, a fair, open, and equal representation of the Lodges is the fundamental principle. They have now only to be careful and circumspect, and to take such measures as may

---

*   By foreign Lodges are meant Lodges not resident in the capital, or provincial towns.

prevent such errors creeping into the Grand Lodge of Ulster; let all their affairs be transacted in the most candid and open manner; have no financial secrets, nor suffer any officer or officers to hoodwink them in the application of the funds; suffer no place of emolument to exist in the Lodge, the Deputy Grand Secretary excepted, and that place restricted to a fair and reasonable remuneration for the person filling it, and the whole of the surplus of the fees of that office to be applied to the charitable fund. Masonry never was intended as a trade for individuals to make money by; one of its fundamental principles, which has been inculcated in the charges from time immemorial, is economy in its members, so that they may not prematurely become chargeable to the craft.

They are in those charges enjoined to use all their industry, in their different avocations, for the support of themselves and families, that they may not be a burthen to the order, but that they may have something to spare for the assistance of indigent brethren. To make a trade of Masonry, therefore, for private emolument, and to take more from the funds than is barely sufficient for remuneration for services rendered thereto, is diametrically opposite to the duty of a Mason. Every Brother should, consistently / with his duty, contribute as much as in his power to the funds of the order, and he that cannot give money, if he contribute time or labour, it is the same, but when a positive injury should be the consequence, he is not expected, nor does his duty require him to contribute.

Economy, therefore, in the Grand Lodge, serves a double purpose, it makes what comes into the funds of the order go farther, and acts as a stimulus on the Lodges to contribute liberally; for when men see their contributions fairly and to good advantage laid out, they have confidence in the managers, and it gives them pleasure to pay when they have proofs of their money being applied to good purposes.

The Grand Lodge, by practising economy, is an example also to the subordinate Lodges, where that virtue cannot be too strongly inculcated. The strongest hold the enemies of Masonry have against it, is the excess too often gone into in Lodges. The multitude have not the opportunity of judging of our principles, because we cannot, consistently, explain them all; but they have a good opportunity of observing when we are guilty of any impropriety, and they are very ready to judge of what they do not know by that which they do know. And too many of our Brethren have in this respect given them an advantage over them by unthinkingly giving themselves up to excess, at a time of all others which they ought to be most circumspect, namely, at the meetings of their Lodges. They should not go to the meetings of their Lodges with the sole intention of drinking to excess. They should go for the purpose of meeting with their Brethren, with whom to enjoy social conversation, and to obtain / rational instruction on the business of Masonry; moderate refreshment is by no means to be totally objected to, but that refreshment should not extend to inebriation; and in place of a blessing become a curse, it should be taken with so much moderation, as not to appear on the person in the slightest degree excessive. Masons in general are not aware of the injury they do to the order by their want of attention in this respect, as the cavillers raise the hue and cry against the order for the conduct of individuals, and it is blamed for their folly, and supposed to inculcate on the initiated, those very habits which it advises them strongly against.

The advantages to the Masons of Ulster to be derived from a Grand Lodge in their own vicinity, composed of persons whom they know, and in whom they have confidence, are incalculable. The facility with which they can make their communications, and obtain information on all necessary subjects, and the immediate controul they can have where they are fairly and fully represented, must appear to the most prejudiced person as advantages they never before as Masons enjoyed. Their business was always done heretofore by a few who were strangers to them and their interests, and who never considered that the Masons of Ulster were deserving of the smallest attention or consideration. That part of the funds which they did condescend to apply to charitable purposes, were partially distributed, and small indeed was the share that fell to the lot of the Ulster poor Masons; it has been known that more money has been granted to the requests of one single Lodge in Dublin, in one year, than was given to the whole province of Ulster during / the same period. Such an occurrence as this, under the present circumstances, can never take place, for if any such partiality should be ever attempted, the remedy is at hand. Let every Lodge take care to have itself represented in the Grand Lodge, and let every subject of that nature come openly and fairly before it, and the quantum to be given, decided, allowing of no reference to a committee on such subjects, unless that committee is in the full confidence of all, and is known to be well attended by the Masters of country Lodges. /

ERRATA.

Page 16, line 4 from bottom, for *Henry 2nd*, read *Henry 3d* ... line 11 from bottom, for *Henry 1st*, read *Edward 1st* ... line 8 from bottom, for *Herman* read *Hermer* ... Page 18, line 9 from top, for *vest* read *vested* ... Page 27, line 6 from bottom, for *artis* read *artists* ... Page 37, line 2 from top, for *having* read *have* ... Page 62, line 10 from bottom [p. 371, line 20 from top in this edition], for *with memorial*, read *with a memorial*.

APPENDIX.

Reasons for the Union Lodge, 684,[51] *withdrawing from the Grand Lodge of Dublin, and adhering to the Grand Lodge of Ulster.*

THE Union Lodge, No. 684, having, from the commencement of the contest, which has for some years divided the Fraternity of Free-Masons, declined to declare for either party, while the controversy was carried on with that heat and animosity unbecoming Masons: and observing lately that the Grand Lodge of Ulster was well disposed to act in a manner suitable to the dignity and importance of so respectable a body, taking up the question as the assertors and vindicators of the rights and privileges of Masons, with the avowed determination of protecting and preserving those rights; and of fairly and impartially managing and distributing the funds of the Order; they have therefore resolved to attach themselves to that Grand Lodge: to which they shall adhere so long as the pure principles of Masonry, and the true interest and welfare of the Craft shall continue to be the objects pursued by that body. /

In coming to this resolution, the Union Lodge conceive it to be their duty to lay before the Brethren at large, and those of Ulster in particular, the reasons which have influenced them in making this decision. They can assure their Brethren, that such determination was not finally agreed on without a minute investigation and strict enquiry having been made by them, into the nature, causes, and progress of the contest, and that on the most mature deliberation, they entertain a firm conviction, that it is for the true interest, the honour, the respectability, and convenience of the Masons of Ulster, that a Grand Lodge should meet, and be supported in their native province.

With almost unparallelled patience have they waded through that mass of scurrility and abuse which has been published on both sides the question: and from that mass they have collected so many facts which stand uncontradicted, as to justify them in withdrawing their confidence in, and allegiance to the Grand Lodge in Dublin. From those documents they are convinced that the Body they thus allude to, have acted inconsistently with their duty, as the guardians of the charitable fund, in allowing that fund to be diverted into others than its proper channels; and contrary to the principles of Masonry, in countenancing individuals, who have not hesitated, / from interested motives alone, to involve the Order in disunion and discord – persons who, rather than forego the profits they derived from their situation in that Lodge, would, to use the words of their Grand Master, 'Sever the Order into two separate interests.'

By those publications it also appears that the funds of the Order have not been distributed with that degree of impartiality to be expected among Masons, who should make no distinction of persons. That large sums have been expended, on objects not consistent with the original intention of the fund, and that its very existence has been put to risk, by involving it in expensive suits at law: and that, by the issue of those suits, the fund once respectable, is now completely annihilated.

Not content with the patronage of one lucrative post in the Grand Lodge, a faction thereof has erected and attempted to saddle the Order with another, which was hitherto unknown – a place, the profits of which arose, and was derived from the fund of charity alone, as there were no fees or perquisites of office provided for the payment of the Deputy Treasurer.

This place, it is evident, was erected merely for the purpose of serving the individual, without rendering any permanent advantage to the Order. The Deputy Secretary had hitherto been found perfectly / competent to the duties of the office, and the shadow of utility could not have been derived to the Order by the appointment, or, as one of the publications has it, 'the separating the offices of Deputy Grand Secretary, and Deputy Grand Treasurer;' the publication alluded to, insinuates that the Deputy Secretary, had his perquisites raised, in consequence of his performing the double duty, but the writer of it has forgot to state at what period the places were united. Or when such an Officer as Deputy Grand Treasurer had been before known in the Order, it would indeed have been difficult for him to say at what time such an appointment had been made. As it is well known that a Deputy Treasurer was never appointed till 1810.[52] It is indeed evident that at the time the place was erected, it was not considered the separating of two situations, held by the same person, from the Deputy Secretary, being continued in the receipt of all his perquisites, for had his fees ever been raised in consequence his serving the two offices, why not on the appointment of the Deputy Treasurer, and the successor of the deceased Deputy Secretary,[53] separate the fees as well as the offices, and allow to each those perquisites attached to their several appointments.

Had this been done, and the charitable fund left unaffected, and undiminished by the transaction, no blame could be attached / by the most fastidious; but that an Officer should be appointed to a duty, for doing which, another person fully competent to it, was paid; and that the salary and percentage for that newly created Office, should be taken out of the fund which was exclusively set apart for the assistance of the poor and the indigent, was surely a departure from the Masonic duty of those concerned, either in the giving or receiving, and acting contrary to the character of honest Trustees of a Charitable Fund.

The marked contempt with which the ruling party in the Grand Lodge, treated the Delegates from Ulster, who composed so large a majority of the meetings, their precipitately closing the Lodge, rather than let business proceed in the presence of those Delegates; and their refusing to take into consideration their respectable Memorials, when they were not present, under pretence, that as they had the privilege of sitting in Grand Lodges, no written document from them, in their absence, should be attended to; all these circumstances combined, with the conviction that the Masons of Ulster forming a large majority of the Brethren of Ireland, should have been heard, and their remonstrances attended to, have induced the Union Lodge to declare the conduct of those persons, who, by violent and arbitrary measures, have misgoverned the Order, and from a community / hitherto remarkable for unanimity and concord, have split the Brethren into factions, hostile to each other, many of whom do not understand the nature of the division yet, and being induced from personal attachment, to take this side, or that, they have become violent partisans, and instead of looking on each other as Brethren, view each other with jealousy, discontent, and want of confidence.

On examining the accounts, the Union Lodge have remarked the vast disproportion in the distribution of Donations from the Grand Lodge to their Brethren of Ulster, although much more numerous than those of the rest of Ireland, the petty sums contributed towards the relief of Ulster poor brethren, by the Grand Lodge, bear no proportion to the largesses bestowed upon Dublin Lodges.

As to the question of Right, the Union Lodge are decidedly of the opinion, that there is in Masons an inherent and indefeasible right to choose a Grand Lodge, and to adhere to, or withdraw from that Body, as it acts consistently or inconsistently with the principles and true interests of the Order; as a departure from those principles laid down for the government of the Order, from time immemorial, absolves all Masons from allegiance to a Body who governs not only without law, but against it.

It is therefore the exercise of that right / by which the Union Lodge has withdrawn themselves from the Grand Lodge, sitting in Dublin, and attaching themselves to the Grand Lodge of Ulster. Conceiving that the former has not acted consonantly to the principles of Masonry, but has removed one of the principal ancient Land-marks, in acting contrary to the decision of large majorities; and that the latter appears to be actuated by those principles which has upheld the Order from remote antiquity to the present day. With this conviction, therefore, the Union Lodge has resolved to adhere to the Right Worshipful, the Grand Lodge of Ulster, while that body continues to conduct the affairs of Masonry, according to the true principles of the Craft.

EDITORIAL NOTES

Anon. [signed Philo Lapidarius], *An Answer to the Pope's Bull, with the Character of a Freemason* (1738)

1. *Lord* MOUNTJOY: William Stewart (1709–69), third Viscount Mountjoy and later first Earl of Blessington. Grand Master of Ireland (1738–40) and the first noble Grand Master of Antients Grand Lodge (1756–60). R. Berman, *Schism: The Battle that Forged Freemasonry* (Brighton: Sussex Academic Press, 2013), pp. 230–1.

2. *MASONS* in their private Assemblies draw such Circles, and other strange Lines: This refers to the fact that before masonic rituals Freemasons sketched the symbols of the ceremonies on the floor. One of the reasons for this was to reduce the chances of any secrets or evidence of ritual being discovered. As the ritual and symbolism developed, the drawings required more detail. Therefore, the long and laborious process of sketching and drawing was replaced during the eighteenth century by floor cloths, which were a more permanent way of visualizing the symbols. They are known as tracing boards. See J. S. Curl, *Freemasonry and the Enlightenment: Architecture, Symbols & Influences* (London: Historical Publications, 2011). Jan Snoek drew my attention to the fact that 'actual descriptions or designs of drawn "lodges" usually do not contain circles, other than the sun and maybe the globes on top of the pillars J & B (and in the *Dialogue between Simon and Philip* of ca. 1725 the halo around the G in "the new lodge under the Desaguliers regulation")'. But there are two cases of 'lodges', which themselves are described as circular: (1) the lady who claims to be the author of *La Franc-Maçonne* (1744) describes the drawing made on the floor to have that shape, and (2) the Dalziel MSS describe a 'circular board' as the tracing board, while Schnitger in his comments on the source text of those manuscripts tells about a set of three of them, used in the Old Swalwell Lodge. See A. Dalziel's MSS of 'Old Harodim Lectures' in vol. 3. N. B. Cryer mentions the Swalwell ones in his book *York Mysteries Revealed: Understanding an Old English Masonic Tradition* (Hersham: Ian Allan 2006).

3. *the MASONS are such* Conjurers *as to raise the Devil*: Such a charge does not appear in the papal bull. It may be noted that Lord Rosse (1702–41), Grand Master of Ireland in 1725 and 1730, was supposed to found the Dublin Hell-Fire Club in 1735 and presided over it in 1737. E. Lord, *The Hell-Fire Clubs: Sex, Satanism and Secret Societies* (New Haven, CT: Yale University Press, 2010), p. 62.

4. *the* Pope: Clement XII (1730–40).

5. *blind* Arrogance of Atheism and Deism: In accordance with James Anderson's *Constitutions* of 1723 and 1738, the First Charge of the Irish Constitution also forbade atheists

and libertines to join lodges, but in practice persons who were accused of atheism by contemporaries reached the highest ranks in the masonic hierarchy. They include the Duke of Wharton, Duke of Montagu or Lord Rosse. See *The Constitutions of the Free Masons, Containing the History, Charges, Regulations, &c. of that Most Ancient and Right Worshipful Fraternity, For the Use of the Lodges* (Dublin: Printed by J. Watts, at the Lord Carteret's Head in Dames-Street, for J. Pennell, at the three Blue Bonnets in St. Patrick-Street, 1730), p. 42.

6. *utterly* abhorring any wicked Plots or dark Designs against the State: This is a reference to the Second Charge of the *Constitution*, which declared that 'A Mason is to be a peaceable Subject to the Civil Powers wherever he resides or works, and is never to be concern'd in Plots and Conspiracies against the Peace and Welfare of the Nation'. *The Constitutions of the Free Masons, Containing the History, Charges, Regulations...* (1730), p. 42.

7. *Religion* of Nature: along with 'natural religion', a key and debated phrase in religious discourse. Apart from the deists and the opponents of the Church, many enlightened thinkers used this expression with different meanings. For its interpretations in the context of eighteenth-century English Freemasonry see R. Péter, 'Masonic Religious Rhetoric in England During the Long Eighteenth Century', in T. Stewart (ed.), *Freemasonry and Religion: Many Faiths – One Brotherhood* (London: Canonbury Masonic Research Centre, 2006), *Canonbury Papers*, vol. 3, pp. 167–204.

8. *as the Ministers of the Scotish Assembly did to their* Elders: See the headnote of William Imbrie and William Geddes, *The Poor Man's Complaint* (1754) in this volume.

9. Philo-Lapidarius: a possible translation is Philo, the Stonemason.

Bernard Clarke, *An Answer to the Pope's Bull, with a Vindication of the Real Principles of Free-Masonry* (1751)

1. GEORGE SACKVILLE: Lord George Sackville (1716–85) was Grand Master of Ireland between 1751 and 1752. He was the youngest and favourite son of the Duke of Dorset. In 1751 he became the chief secretary of his father, who was Lord Lieutenant of Ireland between 1750 and 1755. See *Schism*, pp. 37–8, 197, 233. and *HPO*.

2. *Irrefragable*: irrefutable.

3. *BELLARMINE*: Robert Bellarmine (1542–1621) was a Jesuit cardinal.

4. Pope *ADRIAN*: The author must refer to Pope Adrian VI (1459–1523), who was a church reformer. He argued that the head of the Roman Catholic Church can err even in matters of faith, and claimed that many popes including Pope John XXII (1316–34) were heretics.

5. Pope *SIXTUS VI*: There was no pope with such a name. The author should have written Pope Sixtus V (1520–90).

6. *CLEMENT VIII*: Clement VIII (1536–92) was a reforming pope. His reforms included the publication of a revised edition of the Latin Vulgate, which is referred to above.

7. *Doctorr JAMES:* Thomas James (1573–1629) wrote the *Bellum papale, siue, Concordia discors Sixti quinti et Clementis octaui, circa Hieronymianam editionem* (London: G. Bishop R. Newberie & R. Barker, 1600). The cited passage above is a translation from the preface of this work.

8. *Risum teneatis*: 'Can you help laughing?' (Latin). Horace, *Ars Poetica*, v. 5.

9. *Accusent nos mille licet ... Au*: 'Even if thousands accuse us, we still have our mind conscious of rectitude, and this mind never fears the faces of its judges' (Latin).

10. *When* Free Masons *act irregular*: Throughout the eighteenth century, there was a conflict between the Premier Grand Lodge and the independent lodges, which were branded as irregular or unconstituted. Sometimes they used different rituals and were unwilling to pay dues to the London Grand Lodge.

11. Bishop Sanderson: Robert Sanderson (1587–1663), Bishop of Lincoln. See T. Wood, 'A Great English Casuist', *Church Quarterly Review*, 147 (1948), pp. 29–45.

12. pro hic et nunc: literally 'for here and now' (Latin).

13. *both lawful and binding*: It was also quoted in *A Defence of Masonry* (1730) reproduced in *EMC*, p. 213, *The Poor Man's Complaint* (see pp. 43–66) and *Freemasons' Magazine*, 7 (Aug 1796), p. 85 (reprint of *A Defence of Masonry*).

14. Hipparchus: Greek astronomer and mathematician in the second century BC.

15. *De obligatione Juramenti*: The exact bibliographic details of the cited work are *De juramenti promissorii obligatione prælectiones septem. Habitæ in schola theologicà Oxon. termino Michaelis ann. Dom. MDCXLVI. a Roberto Sandersono. S. Theologiæ in Academia Oxoniensi Professore Regio. Præmissa oratione ab eodem habita cum publicam professionem auspicaretur 26. Octob. 1646* (Londini: typis T.R. & E.M. prostat vænale apud O. Pullen & A. Crook, in Cœmeterio S. Pauli, 1647). It was published several times in the seventeenth and the first half of the eighteenth century, including its English translation (1655, 1716).

16. *Clem: Alexand. Strom. 5*: the Church Father Clement of Alexandria, Titus Flavius Clemens, (*c.*150–*c.*215), *Stromata*, Book 5.

17. To vindicate the ways of God to Man: A. Pope, *An Essay on Man*, 1732–38, line I.16, paraphrased by Pope from John Milton's *Paradise Lost* (1667): 'justify the ways of God to Man' (I.26).

18. *TO all who Masonry despise*: The first four stanzas of this song are reprinted in vol. 1. p. 380. It was reprinted several times in the different editions of W. Preston's *Illustrations of Masonry*.

19. *Brother* Edward Spratt's New Book of Constitution: Edward Spratt, the Grand Secretary of Ireland between 1743 and 1755, revised James Anderson's *Constitution* for the Irish uses in 1751, which served as model for Laurence Dermott's *Ahiman Rezon*.

20. *general* Assembly: about the legend of Athelstan and Edwin, see A. Prescott: 'The Old Charges Revisited', *Transactions of the Lodge of Research No. 2429* (2005), pp. 25–38.

21. *Cessante ratione legis, cessat ipsa Lex*: 'The reason for a law ceasing, the law itself ceases'. (Latin). Johannes Gratian, *Concordia discordantium canonum*, also known as *Decretum Gratiani* (*c.*1140).

22. DEPUTATIONS *granted beyond Sea*: This section was taken from *Constitutions* 1738 pp. 194–6.

23. Anderson's Con.: Clarke selectively and not always literally quotes Anderson's *Constitutions*.

24. *The Right Honourable Lord* Kingston: James King, the fourth Lord Kingston (1693–1761), was Grand Master of the Grand Lodge of England in 1729. He served as Grand Master of the Grand Lodge of Ireland in 1731 and 1735. *Schism*, pp. 13, 196.

25. *The Right Honourable Lord* Netterville: Nicholas Netterville, the fifth Viscount (1708–50), Grand Master in 1732. *Schism*, p. 227.

26. *The Rt. Hon.* Henry Barnewall, *Lord* Kingsland: Henry Benedict Barnewall (1708–74), Viscount Barnewall of Kingsland. Deputy Grand Master (1732), Grand Master (1733–4). *Schism*, pp. 196, 229.

27. *The Rt. Hon. Sir* Marcus Beresford, *Earl of* Tyrone: first Viscount Tyrone (1694–1763), was Deputy Grand Master in 1733 and Grand Master in 1736 and 1737. *Schism*, pp. 196, 227.

28. *The Rt. Hon. the Earl of* Blessington: William Stewart, the first Earl of Blessington (1709–69), was Grand Master of Ireland from 1738 to 1739, and Grand Master of the Antients Grand Lodge between 1756 and 1760. *Schism*, pp. 193, 196, 230–1.

29. *The Rt. Hon. Lord* Donerayle: Arthur Mohun St Leger, third Viscount Doneraile (1718–50), was Grand Master of Ireland in 1740. *Schism*, pp. 196, 230.

30. *The Rt. Hon. Lord* Tullamore: Charles Moore, second Lord Tullamore (1712–64), was Grand Master of Ireland from 1741 to 1742 and in 1760 (as Earl of Charleville). *Schism*, pp. 196–7, 232.

31. *The Rt. Hon. Lord* Southwell: Thomas Southwell, second Baron Southwell (1698–1766), was Grand Master of Ireland in 1743. *Schism*, pp. 196, 236.

32. *The Rt. Hon. Lord* Allen: John Allen, third Viscount of Allen (bap. 1708–45), was Grand Master of Ireland from 1744 to 1745. *Schism*, pp. 196, 232.

33. *Sir* Marmaduke Wywill: *Sir Marmaduke Wywill*, sixth Baronet of Constable Burton (1692–1754), was Grand Master of Ireland from 1747 to 1748. *Schism*, pp. 197, 232–3.

34. *Right Honourable Lord* Kingsborough: Robert King, first Baron Kingsborough (1724–55), was Grand Master of Ireland from 1749 to 1750. *Schism*, pp. 197, 233. Edward Spratt's 1751 Irish *Constitutions* were dedicated to him.

35. *Lord George Sackville*: See p. 388, n. 1 above.

36. Roderick Mackenzie: Hon. Roderick Mackenzie (c. 1707– ?), was Junior Grand Warden from 1749 to 1750, then Senior Grand Warden from 1751 to 1752. *Schism*, p. 197; *GLFI*, pp. 180–1.

37. Brinsley Butler: Hon. Brinsley Butler (1728–79), was the Junior Grand Warden of Ireland between 1751 and 1752, then Deputy Grand Master between 1753 and 1756, and Grand Master in 1757 (from 1756 as Lord Newton–Butler). *Schism*, pp. 197, 234.

38. *It has long run in muddy Streams... and the Essential* Pillars *of the* Temple *appear above the Rubbish*: This is similar to the ritual of the first degree of the Strict Observance: 'Q. What is the emblem of the Apprentices? A. A column, with the top broken off, still standing upon the ground, with the inscription: ADHUC STAT ["It thus [or: still] stands"]'. This symbolism is also central to the Scots Master-degree of the same Order.

39. *this School of Reason*: a remarkably early case of this definition of Freemasonry.

40. *By our Art the distant* Chinese ... *with their British Brethren*: That is, if he were a Christian, since in 1751 the only non-Christian Freemasons were a handful of Jews in a small number of lodges. See J. Harland-Jacobs and J. A. M. Snoek, 'Freemasonry and Eastern Religions', in H. Bogdan, and J. A. M. Snoek, *Handbook of Freemasonry* (Leiden-Boston: Brill, 2014), pp. 258–76.

41. *nor can any Man ... unacquainted with Scripture*: This is the reason why non-Christians were, as a rule, not admitted.

42. *the oftner we hear Lessons of* Morality, Brotherly Love*, and Social Virtue ... as well as the Body*: The author is an early example of someone who looks at Freemasonry from a 'Reformation of Manners' perspective.

43. *a fine Woman, excluded from our Art*: See headnote of the chapter on Women in vol. 5.

44. the Women must be covered because of the Angels: This is a paraphrase of 1 Corinthians 11:4–10.

45. *the true I* am: This is a reference to the name of God in the Old Testament. In response to Moses' question God revealed his name as I Am that I Am (אֶהְיֶה אֲשֶׁר אֶהְיֶה), Exodus 3:14.

46. *When a Person ... rejected*: In Continental lodges this process became widely used only in the 1770s; before that time the good reputation of his proposer was generally regarded sufficient guarantee of the quality of the candidate.

47. *A little Learning ... POPE*: the first four lines of Alexander Pope's poem entitled 'A Little Learning'.

48. Interreign *of* Grand-Masters, *which reduced* Free-Masonry *in this Kingdom to a very low* Ebb: for an account of the decline of Irish Freemasonry in the period, see F. D'Assigny, *A Serious and Impartial Enquiry into the Cause of the Present Decay of Freemasonry in Ireland* (Dublin: Printed by Edward Bate, 1744) and *GLFI*, pp. 84–127.

49. Thomas Southwell: See p. 390, n. 31.

50. Roderick Mackenzie, *Esq*: See p. 390, n. 36.

51. Brinsley Butler, *Esq*: See p. 390, n. 37.

52. Edward Martin: He was Grand Warden of the Grand Lodge of Ireland between 1738 and 1743. From 1743 to 1761 he was Grand Treasurer. In 1746 he was appointed as accomptant-general of the General Post Office in Ireland, and in 1747 as secretary to Sir Marmaduke Wyvill, postmaster-general and grand master in 1747. *GLFI*, p. 168.

53. *If every Person ... received among us*: In many Grand Lodges this is precisely the standard procedure today.

54. *St. Paul in his Second Epistle to the* Thessalonians *Chap. iii.*: more precisely, 2 Thessalonians 3:6–15.

55. *Ensample*: 'A precedent which may be followed or imitated; a pattern or model of conduct' (*OED*).

56. *All Persons admitted Members of a* Lodge, ... Servile Ties of any Kind: See *The Constitutions of the Free Masons, containing the History, Charges, Regulations, &c.* (1730), pp. 43–4 (III. Charge).

57. *sells his* Birth Right for a Mess of Pottage: Genesis 25: 29–34.

58. *A* Lodge ... *but of good Report*: Apart from some minor insignificant differences, this and the following quotations are from the charges of a Freemason. See *The Constitutions of the Free Masons, containing the History, Charges, Regulations, &c.* (1730), pp. 43–50.

59. Pennel's Const.: Pennel's *Constitutions*, see pp. 387–8, n. 5.

60. *the City of Dublin*: The plan to build a hall was also advertised in the press – *Belfast News-Letter* – on 15 December 1750. The actual Freemasons' Hall was erected only in the 1860s.

61. *A* PRAYER: This Christian prayer is also cited from *The Constitutions of the Free Masons, containing the History, Charges, Regulations, &c.* (1730), p. 52.

62. M. Pool: Probably Matthew Poole (1624–79). *Annotations upon the Holy Bible* (also known as *Poole's Annotations on the Bible*). After his death it was completed by others and published in two volumes (London, 1683 and 1685).

63. Joseph. *Antiq*:Titus Flavius Josephus, *The Antiquities of the Jews* (20 vols), *c.* 94 AD.

64. *Doctor* Anderson: James Anderson, the author of the *Constitutions* (1723 and 1738).

65. *Doctor* Leslie, *F.R.S.*: In 1751 there existed (according to the complete list of members) no FRS named Leslie. The earliest person of that name to be appointed FRS was Patrick Duguid Leslie (physician, d. 1783), elected 1781. Also Thomas Lashley was elected only in 1768. Maybe Benjamin Laney (1666), Sir Kingsmill Lucy (1668), Gregorio Leti (1681), Edward Lany (1692), Sir Berkeley Lucy (1698) or John Lindsay (1732) is meant.

66. *A SONG*: This masonic song was published later in L. Dermott, *Ahiman Rezon: or, a Help to a Brother; Shewing the Excellency of Secrecy ... Together with Solomon's Temple an Oratorio, as it was Performed for the Benefit of Free-Masons* (London: printed for the editor, and sold by Brother James Bedford, 1756), p. 185.

William Imbrie and William Geddes, *The Poor Man's Complaint against the Whole Unwarrantable Procedure of the Associate Session in Glasgow, Anent him and Others in Seeking a Confession of the Mason and Chapman Oaths* (1754)

1. *anent*: concerning.
2. *a Letter said to come from Mr. GIBB*: for Adam Gib see headnote, pp. 43–6.
3. *compearance*: appearance.
4. *I desired the minute of the synod*: the 1745 Act of the Associate Synod on the mason oath. See headnote, pp. 43–6.
5. *no process is to be commenced*: no legal proceedings are to be begun.
6. *Perdiven's collection of church discipline*: Walter Steuart [Stuart] of Pardovan, *Collections and Observations Methodiz'd; Concerning the Worship, Discipline, and Government of the Church of Scotland* (Edinburgh: Heirs & Successors of Anderson, 1709). Stewart inherited his lands of Pardovan in 1683, and acted frequently as provost (mayor) of the burgh of Linlithgow. He sat in the Scottish Parliament in 1702–7, M. D. Young (ed.), *The Parliaments of Scotland: Burgh and Shire Commissioners*, 2 vols (Edinburgh: Scottish Academic Press, 1993), vol. 2, pp, 670–1.
7. *probation*: proof.
8. *any intention to join in the bond*: The Secession Church had resolved in 1743 to renew the National Covenant of 1638 and the Solemn League and Covenant of 1643, binding itself to impose Presbyterianism throughout Great Britain and Ireland, and had drawn up a bond to that effect to be signed by members. The controversy over the burgess oath had delayed the signing of the bond, but the Antiburgers had now resolved that signing should take place at communion services. A. Gib, *The Present Truth: A Display of the Secession Testimony; in the Three Periods of the Rise, State, and Maintenance of that Testimony*, 2 vols (Edinburgh: R. Fleming & A. Neill, 1774), vol. 1, pp. 220–52, 254–6.
9. *subordinate standards*: documents such as the Confession of Faith and Directory of Public Worship agreed by the Anglo-Scottish 'Westminster Assembly' (1643–9) and regarded as authoritative, though subordinate to the 'supreme standard', the Bible.
10. *who will read Henry thereon*: Matthew Henry (1662–1714) was an English Presbyterian minister, famed for his evangelical work and his commentaries on many of the books of the Bible. Completed by other ministers after his death, these works were frequently reprinted as Henry's *Expositions of the Old and New Testaments*, or as his *Commentary on the Whole Bible*, in several volumes.
11. *seclude me from privileges formerly granted me*: the privilege of being admitted to take communion. Presbyterians usually held communion services only once a year, often at Easter. Elaborate investigations were undertaken beforehand to decide who was, and who was not, worthy of being granted permission to take part.
12. *Mr. Jameson's*: John Jamieson (*c.* 1726–93) was the first minister of the Antiburgher congregation in Glasgow, having been ordained in 1753. D. Small, *History of the Congregations of the United Presbyterian Church from 1733 to 1900*, 2 vols (Edinburgh: David M. Small, 1904), vol. 2, pp. 27–8.
13. *the elder of my proportion*: Members of the congregation were divided into groups, each supervised by an elder.

14. *Mr. Clarkson*: John Clarkson (*c.* 1691–1761), who had become minister of the Antiburgher congregation at Craigmailen (near Linlithgow) in 1741. Small, *History of the Congregations*, vol. 1, pp. 668–9.

15. *William Templeton's affair*: See headnote , pp. 43–6.

16. *the minister*: John Jamieson. See p. 392, n. 12.

17. *going to and from the tables*: the communion tables, around which communicants sat to receive the elements of bread and wine.

18. *served with tokens*: those seeking admission to communion were examined by ministers or elders, and if admitted were issued with metal tokens as entrance tickets.

19. *deacons*: assistant elders. G. D. Henderson, *The Scottish Ruling Elder* (London: James Clarke & Co., [1935]), p. 68.

20. *Mr. Durham*: James Durham (1622–58), was a notable Scottish Presbyterian theologian whose works remained popular in the eighteenth century. His *The Law Unsealed: Or, A Practical Exposition of the Ten Commandments* (Glasgow: Robert Sanders, 1676) was frequently reprinted.

21. *the second command*: the second of the Ten Commandments.

22. *in time of the persecuting periods ... others they tortured*: These references are to the 'covenanter' Presbyterian religious dissidents who were persecuted in 1660–88. The dead bishop was James Sharp, Archbishop of St Andrews, murdered by dissidents in 1679. Bothwell Brig was a skirmish later in the same year which put an end to an attempted rebellion by the dissidents. Conventicles were the illegal meetings they held for worship.

23. *He that offendeth ... never been born*: quotation from M. Henry, *An Exposition of the Five Books of Moses* (London: T. Pankhurst, 1706), on Leviticus 1–5.

24. *I am against papists and their high commission courts*: Two Courts of High Commission had been established in Scotland in 1610, one for each archdiocese (St Andrews and Glasgow). They were established by royal prerogative and were intended to help uphold royal power in ecclesiastical matters. The two were united to form a single court, which was revived in 1634 by Charles I in order to enforce his planned reforms in worship and other church practices. Oposition to these plans led to the revolt against the king that began in 1637, in which the covenanters seized control of both church and state. Though the monarchs who established these courts were Protestants, their opponents often branded their policies as 'papist' (Roman Catholic).

25. *Samuel Rutherford*: Rutherford (*c.* 1600–61), a Scottish theologian and political theorist, was appointed professor of divinity at the University of St Andrews in 1638, having previously been banished from the parish of which he had been minister by the Court of High Commission (see previous note). He was expelled from office after the Restoration of King Charles II in 1660 and his most famous book, *Lex, Rex, or, the Law and the Prince* (London: John Field, 1644), was ordered to be burnt.

26. *Preface to Lex Rex p. 6*: The quotation that follows is from paragraph 12 of the preface of the 1644 edition.

27. *insest*: incest.

28. *Spotswood ... arms of the whore*: In 1638 the General Assembly of the Church of Scotland deposed all the country's bishops, including John Spottiswoode, Archbishop of St Andrews, and Walter Whitford, Bishop of Brechin. Moral charges against them were mainly invented by their enemies. 'P. P.' is an abbreviation of 'popish prelate', one of Rutherford's favourite terms of abuse for bishops.

29. *In regard ... to the synod*: the synod's act of 1745. See headnote, pp. 43–6.

30.   *bishop Sanderson*: Robert Sanderson 1587–1663, was appointed Bishop of Lincoln in 1660. Several of his published works dealt with oaths and matters of conscience.

31.   pro hic et nunc: 'here and now' (Latin).

James Steven, *Blind Zeal Detected: or, A True Representation of the Conduct of the Meeting I was a Member of, and of the Kirk-Session of the Associate Congregation, at Glasgow* (1755)

1.   *the Meeting I was a Member of*: See headnote, pp. 67–9.

2.   *travelling*: travailing or working.

3.   *Put ceremony of preface apart*: Steven means that he is not going to write a formal preface.

4.   *my elder*: Each member of the congregation was assigned to an elder as an adviser.

5.   vain jangling: pointless angry talk.

6.   *I spoke both with minister*: John Jamieson. See p. 392, n. 12.

7.   *sederunt*: a meeting of a court.

8.   *was teazed*: teased, in the sense of being harassed.

9.   *Mr. Durham*: James Durham. See p. 393, n. 20.

10.   *on the third command*: the third of the Ten Commandments.

11.   *in the sea mark*: between the high and low tide lines.

12.   *Tobias Lundie ... before the town-court*: Steven was involved in a civil dispute with Lundie over oaths (and an obscure matter concerning a hired horse) before the Glasgow burgh court, as well as in the ecclesiastical dispute over the mason oath.

13.   *he was to leave his gift at the altar, and be reconciled with his brother*: based on Matthew 5:23–4, which Steven cites specifically.

14.   *allowed him to swear the bond*: a bond to renew the National Covenant and Solemn League and Covenant. See p. 392, n. 8.

15.   *Rutherford's*: Samuel Rutherford. See p. 393, n. 25.

16.   due Right of Presbytery: S. Rutherford, *The Due Right of Presbyteries or, a Peaceable Plea for the Government of the Church of Scotland* (London: Richard Whittaker & Andrew Crook, 1644).

17.   *the learned Gillespie*: George Gillespie (1613–48) was a leading theologian under the covenanters.

18.   Aaron's Rod blossoming: G. Gillespie, *Aaron's Rod Blossoming, or, the Divine Ordinance of Church-Government Vindicated* (London: Richard Whitaker, 1646).

19.   The eldership ... witnesses at the least: cited from the 'Ordinance concerning Church Government' passed in the English House of Lords, 20 October 1645, which was printed as *The Form of Church-Government to be Used in the Church of England and Ireland* (London: John Wright, 1648).

20.   *the sament*: misprint for 'the sacrament'.

21.   *Ante-nicene and Post-nicene*: The Nicene Creed, adopted by a church council held in Nicaea in AD 325 marked the general acceptance of a number of central theological positions that had previously been disputed.

22.   *Athanasius his creed*: the creed (statement of Christian beliefs) traditionally attributed to Athanasius of Alexandria (d. AD 373), though it is now thought that it was compiled some generations after his death.

23.   *Hierom*: St Jerome (AD c. 347–420).

24.   *Montanists*: Montanism, the teachings of Montanus, a second-century AD prophet, later regarded as heretical.

25. Illi ad omne pene delictum obserant fores: Quotation from St Jermome, Letter 41, 'To Marcella', which criticizes montanist ideas: 'they excommunicate and shut out of the church almost at every offence' (Latin).

26. *for the session, in* cumulo: the session, cumulatively – all its actions taken together (part Latin).

27. *the fifth command*: the fifth of the Ten Commandments.

28. *implicite faith*: Faith that is based on acceptance of church authority without investigation by individuals. Such 'blind faith' was attributed by Presbyterians to Roman Catholics, and contrasted with their own 'rational' faith – see reference in the next paragraph to 'the rational religion of Jesus Christ' on p. 80.

29. Ames in his *Cases of Conscience*: William Ames (1576–1633), *Conscience with the Power and Cases thereof Devided into V. Bookes. Translated out of Latine into English, for more Publique Benefit* ([Leyden and London]: [W. Christiaens, E. Griffin, J. Dawson], 1639). Further editions were published in London in 1643.

30. *Dispute of Ceremonies*: G. Gillespie, *A Dispute against the English-Popish Ceremonies, Obtruded vpon the Church of Scotland* ([s.n.], 1637).

31. or make up the hazard of a given offence: risk punishment for an offence (sin).

32. *I must leave them in the quiet and unenvied possession ... which in the wrong*: Steven ends his pamphlet rather obscurely, but evidently hoping to be reconciled with his opponents. He hopes that the kirk session will see him as a 'fondling' (a foolish person – rather than, possibly, a sinner to be cast out) and that both he and/or it will come to new understandings on the issues between them. Alternately, by 'fondling' Steven may have meant 'foundling' (an abandoned baby), which again would deserve care rather than condemnation by those who had accepted responsibility, in this case the Antiburgher Congregation.

[Associate Synod], 'An Act of the Associate Synod Concerning the Mason-Oath' and A, R, 'An Impartial Examination of the Act against Freemasons' (1757) in the Appendix of *The Free Masons Pocket Companion* (1761)

1. *an overture concerning the MASON-OATH*: a proposal for taking action about the oath.

2. *overturing*: proposing.

3. *a particular case ... was before them*: the case of William Templeton, a deacon of the Glasgow Antiburgher session. See headnote to *The Poor Man's Complaint*, pp. 43–6.

4. *they have found others, beside those of the mason craft, to be involved in that oath*: It is hard to believe that at this date, nearly twenty years after the founding of the Grand Lodge of Scotland, members of the synod had really been unaware that men who were not stonemasons were swearing the masonic oath. Probably they were indulging in a pretence of ignorance.

5. *hainous*: heinous, wicked.

6. *particularly 1 Kings vii. 21*: the biblical verse which describes the setting up in the porch of Solomon's Temple of the two pillars called Joachim and Boaz, which have a prominent place in masonic lore.

7. *applying for sealing ordinances*: to be permitted to take communion.

8. *covenanting-work*: in general, work advancing the ends of the covenants, but here specifically taking the 'bond' to re-swear the covenants.

9. *In the year 1738 ... declaration*: the papal bull *In eminenti apostolatus specula*.

10. ipso facto: 'by the fact itself' (Latin).

11. *TREMENDOUS BULL*: By calling the synod's act a bull (Latin, bulla), a papal edict, the writer emphasizes his argument that it had acted as tyrannically as a pope.

12. *communicated to them, it may be presumed, by the same correspondents*: See headnote, pp. 81–4.

13. *must*: most.

14. *the Trier of the reins of the children of men*: trier of the kidneys, or loins, used metaphorically, in a way similar to the reference to the 'hearts of men', immediately above.

15. *Snatch from his hand ... POPE*: quotation from Alexander Pope, 'Essay on Man' (1734), epistle 1, ll. 121–2.

16. *casuists*: studiers of matters of conscience, etc.

17. *Popish Tyranny rendered abortive by the Revolution*: King James II (of England) and VII (of Scotland) had been overthrown, by those believing he intended to re-establish Roman Catholicism, in the so-called 'Glorious' or 'Bloodless' Revolution of 1688–9.

18. *Cromwell ... immediate death*: Thomas Cromwell, the English statesman, was executed in 1540 by King Henry VIII. The French ambassador recorded that the king had later said he regretted putting to death the most faithful servant he had ever had for minor offences. *An Impartial Examination*'s reference may be a garbled allusion to this story.

19. *obtesting God*: calling upon God.

20. *adhibited*: attached.

21. *"Jack," in the Tale of a Tub ... only for his special favourites*: Jonathan Swift's *Tale of the Tub* (1704) is a political and religious satire. Jack is a character used in the work to ridicule Protestant religious excesses , and is named 'Jack' (a diminutive of John) with reference to John Calvin (1509–64), the founder of Calvinism, and also to John of Leyden (*c*. 1509–36), the Anabaptist. Jack believes in a literal interpretation of the Bible as the only source of truth, and often keeps his eyes closed, symbolizing his determination not to be polluted by other influences. As 'Knocking Jack of the North' he represents John Knox (*c*. 1504–72), the Scottish Calvinist reformer.

22. *The FREE MASON*: When 'An Impartial Examination' was published in the *Scots Magazine* in 1757 the author's name was given at the end as 'A FREE-MASON', but here (and at the beginning of the final paragraph on p. 97) he refers to 'himself' as 'the FREE MASON'.

23. *Oaths were* ... Butler: quotation from Samuel Butler, *Hudibras*, Part II (London: [s.n.], 1663).

24. *Enthusiasm*: The word is here used in a derogatory sense, with a meaning similar to 'fanatic'.

25. Edin. Oct 25: In the *Scots Magazine* the place of writing is given as 'Alloa', a town in Stirlingshire, rather than Edinburgh.

26. *R.A. M.T.L.*: In the *Scots Magazine* the author is simply identified as 'A FREE-MA-SON'. The author 'R. A.' has not been identified. 'M. T. L.' is presumably an abbreviation of some office or qualification that he held.

Richard Lewis, *The Free-Masons Advocate. Or, Falsehood Detected* (1760)

1. *best of monarchs... being a Free-Mason*: Masonic monarchs of the period included Francis I (of the Holy Roman Empire) and Frederick the Great of Prussia. George Augustus Frederick (1762–1830), Prince of Wales and later George IV, was the first English monarch who was a Freemason. He was initiated into the order in 1787 in London and became Grand Master in 1790.

2. *Your secrets ... to mens' eyes*: See vol. 2, p. 49.
3. irrefragable: irrefutable.
4. *that when a candidate ... tell him the rest*: See vol. 2, p. 57. Despite the quotation marks, this is not a verbatim quotation from the original.
5. *that the reception ... being learned at it*: See vol. 2, p. 60.
6. *tis unnecessary ... I have just mentioned*: See vol. 2, p. 61.
7. *Grand Master:* In the eighteenth century the term Grand Master (Grand Maître in French) was still used to address the Master of a lodge, both in England and France. Its usage probably pre-dates the Grand Lodge phase when it became reserved for the Master of the Grand Lodge.
8. *that whoever is invested ... stiled Right Worshipful*: See vol. 2, p. 51. This is not quoted verbatim from the original.
9. *that when a brother is fined ... to relieve the poor*: See vol. 2, p. 52.
10. *it is always applied to the relief of the poor*: See vol. 2, p. 62.
11. *this has been always the practice among Free-Masons*: See vol. 2, p. 62.
12. *some keep the Money to spend it in merry meetings*: See vol. 2, p. 62. In the original, 'at merry meetings'.
13. *they are very reserved ... always observed at their entertainments*: See vol. 2, p. 54. For the complex relationship between women and Freemasons, see also the headnote of the section on Women in volume 5.
14. *the pleasures they enjoy ... distinguishes them from all others*: See vol. 2, p. 61.
15. *that they think ... in the greatest obscenity*: See vol. 2, p. 61.
16. *that the Masters have no words to distinguish them from the Fellow-Crafts*: See vol. 2, p. 60.
17. *they ought to have good ones*: Liars ought to have good memories (proverb).
18. *the Masters have not only a word, but a touch and a sign, peculiar to themselves:* See vol. 2, p. 64.
19. *he himself owns in his dedication, that he is not a Free-Mason*: Since *A Master-Key to Free-Masonry* was probably a pseudo-exposure, it is quite likely that its author was a Freemason. See headnote, pp. 99–101.
20. *Out of thine own mouth will I condemn thee, thou wicked liar!*: Luke 19:22. The last word in the Bible verse is servant rather than liar.
21. *Ipse Dixit*: 'He himself said it.' (Latin) An unsupported statement that relies on the authority of the person who makes it.
22. *in propria persona*: in his own person (Latin).
23. *Samuel Prichard*: He was the author of the highly influential exposure of masonic ritual entitled *Masonry Dissected*, which was republished twenty-two times before 1800 in Great Britain. A Scottish reprint of the *Masonry Dissected* is reproduced in volume 2.
24. *miss Wishfor't*: She was an actress who played in Congreve's *Way of the World*. H. Simpson and Ch. Braun, *A Century of Famous Actresses, 1750–1850* (London: Mills and Boon, [n.d.]), p. 356.
25. *Jack Hackney*: not identified.
26. *Religion and Masonry have a close connection with each other*: for the complex relationship between eighteenth-century Freemasonry and religion, see R. Péter, 'The Mysteries of English Freemasonry. Janus-Faced Masonic Ideology and Practice between 1696–1815' (PhD thesis, University of Szeged, 2006). 'The Religious Aspects of Masonic Ideology and Practice' chapter (pp. 191–232) investigates the religious facets of Freemasonry by using Ninian Smart's seven dimensional framework of religion.

27. *Ahiman Reson*: This is the title of the constitution of the Antients Grand Lodge, written by L. Dermott (1720–91). The correct spelling of 'Reson' is Rezon. The first edition was published in London in 1756 and the Dublin edition in 1760, which Lewis might have read. L. Dermott, *Ahiman Rezon: or, a Help to a Brother; Shewing the Excellence of Secrecy, and the First Cause of the Institution of Free-Masonry; ... To which is Added, a Large Collection of Masons Songs, ... and Solomon's Temple: an Oratorio* (Dublin: printed by Dillon Chamberlaine, for the editor, 1760). For further information about *Ahiman Rezon* see the next headnote.

28. *The body politic, and the body natural*: In political theology the king of England had two bodies: a physical or natural body, which is mortal; and an unseen body politic, which, as his office, was constituted for governing the people and managing the public realm. The body politic is not subject to old age, defects and disabilities of the natural body. This dualism is based on the twofold nature of Christ. See also E. H. Kantorowicz, *The King's Two Bodies: a Study in Mediaeval Political Theology* (1957; Princeton, NJ: Princeton University Press, 1997).

29. *Apollo*: son of Zeus, one of the twelve Olympian deities. He was god of, amongst other things, poetry, oracles and knowledge.

Laurence Dermott, *Ahiman Rezon*, 2nd edn, excerpt containing polemic against Moderns Freemasons and in praise of Antients Freemasonry (1764)

1. *AHIMAN REZON*: *Ahiman Rezon: or Help to a Brother* was first published by Dermott in 1756. It was dedicated to the Earl of Blessington, described as 'a father to the fraternity'. Six editions were published in England during Dermott's lifetime and a further six in the two decades to 1813, when the Antients entered into a union and merged with the Moderns. It was also published elsewhere, including Ireland, with over twenty editions, and in the American and Canadian colonies, where it was adopted as the basis for the constitutions of seven grand lodges. See *Schism*, pp. 20–32. The meaning of the title is unclear. Mackey suggested that it was derived from three Hebrew words: *ahim*, meaning brothers; *manah*, meaning to select or choose; and *ratzon*, meaning the will or law: 'the will of selected brethren' or 'the law of a society of men who are selected as brethren'. See A. G. Mackey, *An Encyclopaedia of Freemasonry and its Kindred Sciences* (Philadelphia, PA: Moss & Co., 1874), p. 46. Other interpretations have included 'brother of the right hand secret', an allusion to the pass grip of a master mason; 'the secrets of a prepared brother'; 'royal builder'; and 'worthy brother secretary'. Dermott chose not to clarify the meaning other than in its byline, 'Help to a Brother'.

2. *Lau. Dermott*: Laurence Dermott (1720–91), Grand Secretary of the Antients (1752–70), Deputy Grand Master (1771–7 and 1783–7). Born Roscommon, Ireland, in the Protestant branch of a Catholic family, he lived in Dublin until migrating to England in 1747/8. A succession of marriages to wealthy widows much improved his financial and social standing. The driving force behind the development of Antients Freemasonry from 1752, he led the public vilification of the 'Moderns', the original Grand Lodge of England, established in 1717. See *Schism*, chs 1, 2.

3. ROBERT BLACK: The printer, an Antient Freemason, was entered as number 849 on the list of Antients' members maintained by the Antients Grand Lodge. See *Registers of the Antients Grand Lodge, 1751–55*, vol. A, p. 2.

4.   *Sir Christopher Wren*: architect, mathematician and astronomer (1632–1723). Although referred to as Grand Master of Masons, there is only limited evidence to support the assertion (*ODNB*). See also J. Campbell, 'Was Sir Christoper Wren a Mason?', *AQC*, 125 (2012), pp. 15–60.

5.   *William B–ns–n*: William Benson (1682–1754), an architect and Whig MP for Shaftesbury (1715–18, 1718–19). Benson's political and court connections were rewarded with the reversionary interest in the Auditor of the Imprest, a lucrative position, and appointment as Surveyor of the King's Works, where he displaced Wren. Benson announced that the House of Lords was in imminent danger of collapse and required remedial work. A report from the Master Mason of Works confirmed otherwise. Benson was censured and accused of having 'occasioned a long interruption and delay ... and much expense'. See *Journal of the House of Lords*, vol. 21, 16 March 1719. He was suspended and subsequently dismissed. See R. Sedgwick (ed.), *The History of Parliament: The House of Commons 1715–1754* (Woodbridge: Boydell & Brewer, 1970), p. 567.

6.   *struck with a Lethargy which seemed to threaten the London lodges with a final dissolution*: In explaining the absence of speculative masonic lodges in London in the late seventeenth and early eighteenth centuries, James Anderson noted that 'in the South the Lodges were more and more disused ... and the annual Assembly ... not duly attended' (*Constitutions* 1738, p. 108). But despite an assertion that there were exceptions 'in or near the Places where great Works were carried on', there are no contemporary records that support the statement. There is similarly no evidence that 'the king [William of Orange] was privately made a Free Mason', nor that he 'approved' of the choice of Wren as 'Grand Master'. See *Foundations*, p. 37.

7.   *for the future pass for masonry amongst themselves*: Anderson's *Constitutions* of 1738 states that Grand Lodge was formed on 24 June 1717. Although the statement cannot be verified, there would have been no obvious reason for Anderson to have lied over a matter that would have been within the experience of many in the relevant lodges. Anderson recorded that the four founding lodges convened at the Apple Tree Tavern, each being known by the name of the public house at which it met: the Apple Tree in Charles Street, Covent Garden; the Goose and Gridiron in St Paul's Churchyard; the Crown in Parker's Lane, near Drury Lane; and the Rummer and Grapes in Channel Row, Westminster. Anderson wrote that the lodges resolved to choose a Grand Master from their own number 'until they should have the Honour of a noble brother at their Head' (p. 109).

8.   *Mr. Senex:* John Senex (1678–1740), cartographer, engraver, publisher and printer. Appointed a Grand Warden (1723) and elected a Fellow of the Royal Society (1728). He co-financed and published several of Desaguliers's scientific treaties as well as Anderson's *Constitutions* of 1723 (*ODNB*).

9.   *placed his grand sword of State in the midst of his lodge*: Dermott's comment alludes to the controversy surrounding the St Paul's Head's Lodge. Until 1733, the Master of the St Paul's Head's had carried a sword belonging to the lodge before the Grand Master in formal processions. The privilege was removed after the Duke of Norfolk presented the Grand Lodge with a new sword of state and appointed his own sword-bearer. The event triggered a petition in favour of the status quo ante role, but it was rejected. The Grand Master was affirmed as having an absolute entitlement to appoint his own officers, including a sword-bearer, and no argument to the contrary would be accepted. The allusion is in keeping with Dermott's highlighting of similar Moderns' controversies. See *Schism*, chs 1, 6.

10. *tyler*: The role of tyler or doorkeeper was to safeguard the lodge during its working and to keep out intruders. It also involved setting out the lodge furniture and chalking the necessary floor markings. The job was paid and frequently given to an indigent Mason. Anthony Sayer, for example, was employed as such by the King's Arms Lodge in 1735 until his death in 1742.

11. *Barbadoes*: an allusion to Jachin and Boaz, the two pillars either side of King Solomon's temple.

[Anon.], *A Defence of Free-Masonry, as Practiced in the Regular Lodges, both Foreign and Domestic under the Constitution of the English Grand Master* (1765)

1. *Mr.* Dermott's: Laurence Dermott (1720–91).
2. *Ahiman Rezon*: See p. 398, n. 1.
3. *on the* Regular MASONS: In this context, a 'regular' Mason is one conforming to the laws and regulations of the Grand Lodge of England.
4. *a* Mausoleum *as large as that built for the* King of Caria: It refers to the tomb of Mausolus, king of Caria (d. 353 BC). Hence 'mausoleum' (*OED*).
5. Nimrod: Nimrod, king of Shinar, appears in Genesis and Chronicles as the great-grandson of Noah. He is also known as Belus, or lord of Babel, and associated with the construction of the Tower of Babel. See S. Dalley et al., *The Legacy of Mesopotamia* (Oxford: Oxford University Press, 1998).
6. Duke of Montague: John Montagu, second Duke of Montagu (1690–1749), became Grand Master of the English Grand Lodge in 1721. Wealthy and well-connected, he had a close association with the royal household. His military positions were both honorific and active. He raised and financed regiments of Horse and Foot and was later Captain and Colonel of His Majesty's Own Troop of Horse Guards, later the 1st Life Guards. Montagu was promoted to Major General in 1735 and Lieutenant General in 1739. The following year, he was appointed Master-General of the Ordnance, a Cabinet position with responsibility for the artillery (*ODNB*).
7. PHILIP DUKE OF WHARTON: Philip, first Duke of Wharton (1698–1731), became a Freemason at the age of twenty-two, inspired by the publicity generated by Montagu's installation as Grand Master. He was a mercurial pro-Jacobite and a divisive figure in a largely pro-Hanoverian organization. He dissipated a fortune in gambling, drinking and mischief-making and was bankrupted. Later tried for treason, he died a pauper in Spain.
8. *J. T.* DESAGULIERS: Jean Theophilus Desaguliers, PhD, FRS (1683–1744), was one of the most influential figures in English Freemasonry in the eighteenth century. Brought up in relative poverty in London's Huguenot community, he attended Christ Church, Oxford, as a servitor scholar and studied experimental philosophy under John Keill. An introduction to Newton let to an invitation to become a Fellow of the Royal Society and its demonstrator and curator. Desaguliers also obtained the patronage of the Duke of Chandos and was renowned as the country's foremost scientific lecturer and 'mechanic'.
9. JOSHUA TIMSON: Joshua Timson, appointed Grand Warden in 1722, and one of the few artisan members of the Grand Lodge, was described by Anderson as a blacksmith. He later claimed from the Grand Charity, as did his widow, whose petition was dismissed. See *Minutes 1723–1739*, inter alia, 24 June 1723, 21 April 1730 and 28 August 1730.

10. *WILLIAM HAWKINS*: William Hawkins, Grand Warden in 1722. If, in Anderson's words, he was 'always out of town' (*Constitution*, 1738, p. 115), he may have been the Deputy Chief Justice of the Brecon circuit in South Wales and a member of the Inner Temple (*ODNB*).

11. *Dr.* Anderson: James Anderson, DD (*c.* 1679–1739), a Scottish Presbyterian minister and author of the 1723 and 1738 *Constitutions*. See *Foundations*, pp. 64–8 and D. Stevenson 'James Anderson: Man & Mason', *Heredom*, 10 (2002), pp. 93–138.

12. *Mr.* Entick: John Entick (*c.* 1703–73), a freelance writer and schoolmaster. He is known (masonically) for having edited a revised version of Anderson's *Constitutions*, published in 1756.

13. Marquis of Carnarvan: Henry Brydges, Marquess of Carnarvon (1708–71), Grand Master of English Grand Lodge in 1738 and the only surviving son of the Duke of Chandos. A member of the Prince of Wales's set, Brydges was a Gentleman of the Bedchamber (1728–42) and Groom of the Stole (1742–51). Elected MP for Hereford (1727–34); Steyning (1734–41); and Bishop's Castle (1741–4), he resigned on 9 August on inheriting to take his seat in the Lords. Brydges support for the Prince of Wales against the king led to him reputedly being described by George II as 'a hot-headed, passionate, half-witted coxcomb, with no more sense than his master', J. Hervey, *Lord Hervey's Memoirs*, at http://www.historyofparliamentonline.org/volume/1715–1754/member/hervey-carr-1691–1723 [accessed 4 July 2014]. See also *Foundations*, pp. 48, 51, 61, 175.

14. *a certain* noble *Peer*: The comment refers to Sir William Stewart, third Viscount Mountjoy and first Earl of Blessington (1709–69). Stewart inherited the viscountcy in 1728 and was created Earl Blessington in 1745. He was mentioned as a Freemason in 1731 as a member of Viscount Montagu's Bear and Harrow Lodge in Butcher Row. Stewart was Grand Master of Ireland from 1738 until 1740. He later gave his imprimatur to the Antients, acceding as their first noble Grand Master (1756–60). Stewart was a loyal Hanoverian Protestant who inherited titles and estates in Ireland and England, with town houses in Dublin and London. Appointed Governor of Co. Tyrone (1748), and Governor of Carlisle Castle (1763). See *Schism*, pp. 6, 8, 14, 28–31, 38–41.

15. *Sir*-Christopher Wren: See p. 399, n. 4.

16. *Mr.* Strong: Edward Strong, an operative stonemason and contemporary and colleague of Wren in the construction of St Paul's Cathedral. A member of the Masons' Company of London. See H. Colvin, *A Biographical Dictionary of British Architects, 1600–1840* (New Haven, CT: Yale University Press, 2008), pp. 995–6.

17. *his* Son: Edward Strong, Jr, an operative stonemason and a member of the Swan Tavern Lodge in Greenwich, who cooperated with Nicholas Hawksmoor at Blenheim. See *Foundations*, p. 82, and Howard, *A Biographical Dictionary of British Architects*, pp. 996–7.

18. *Mr.* Benson: William Benson (1682–1754), an architect and Whig MP for Shaftesbury (1715–18, 1718–19). Benson's political and court connections were rewarded with the reversionary interest in the Auditor of the Imprest, a lucrative position, and his appointment as Surveyor of the King's Works, where he displaced Wren. Benson announced that the House of Lords was in imminent danger of collapse and required remedial work. A report from the Master Mason of Works confirmed otherwise. Benson was censured, suspended and later dismissed. See R. Sedgwick (ed.), *The History of Parliament: The House of Commons 1715–1754* (Woodbridge: Boydell & Brewer, 1970), p. 567.

19. *Mr. ANTHONY SAYER*: Anthony Sayer (*c.* 1672–1742), in 1717 the first Grand Master of Grand Lodge. He was subsequently appointed a Grand Warden (1719) under Desaguliers's Grand Mastership. Although described as a gentleman, Sayer was later a beneficiary of masonic charity, petitioning the Grand Charity on three occasions. He also benefited from charity and the paid office of tyler from the wealthy Old King's Arms Lodge. G. Eccleshall, *The Old King's Arms Lodge, 1725–2000* (London: Published privately, 2001), p. 11.

20. Jacob Lamball: Jacob Lamball (or Lambell), a carpenter, Grand Warden in 1717 and acting GW in 1735 and 1738. See *Minutes 1723–1739*, pp. 247, 259, 264, 273, 276.

21. Joseph Elliot: Joseph Elliott, Grand Warden in 1717. See *Minutes 1723–1739*, p. 196.

22. GEORGE PAYNE, *Esq*: George Payne (*c.* 1685–1757), the second and fourth Grand Master of Grand Lodge in 1718 and 1720, subsequently Senior Grand Warden in 1724 and Deputy Grand Master in 1735. Master of lodge number IV and, in 1749, Master of the King's Arms Lodge in the Strand. Collaborated with Desaguliers and compiled the *General Regulations*. See *Minutes 1723–1739*, pp. 5, 23, 58, 61, 62, 129 and *Foundations*, pp. 34, 50, 57–8, 70–5.

23. *Mr.* Nicholas Stone: Nicholas Stone (*c.* 1586–1647), Master Mason at Windsor Castle (1626), King's Master Mason (1632), Master of the London Company of Masons (1632, 1633). An eminent sculptor and architect whose works include the Banqueting House at Whitehall (to Inigo Jones's designs) and Goldsmiths' Hall in the City of London (*ODNB*).

24. Inigo Jones: Inigo Jones (1573–1652), architect and theatre designer. Pioneered the Palladian architectural style in England. Surveyor of the King's Works (1615). See *ODNB*.

25. PHILIP Lord Stanhope: Philip Dormer Stanhope, fourth Earl of Chesterfield (1694–1733), politician and diplomat, Whig MP for St Germans (1715–22) and Lostwithiel (1722–3). Succeeded to the peerage in 1726. Gentleman of the Bedchamber to Prince of Wales (1715–27); Lord of the Bedchamber (1727–30); Captain Yeomen of the Guard (1723–5); Privy Councilor (1728); Ambassador to The Hague (1728–32); Lord Steward of the Household (1730–3); one of the Lords Justices of the realm (1745); Secretary of State, Northern department (1746–1748). A member of the Duke of Richmond's Horn Tavern Lodge (*ODNB*).

26. *Dr.* D'Assigny: Dr Fifield D'Assigny, a Huguenot physician living in Dublin; author of *A Serious and Impartial Inquiry into the Cause of the Present Decay of Freemasonry in the Kingdom of Ireland* (1744). See *Schism*, p. 42.

27. *JAMES KING*, Lord Viscount Kingston: James King, fourth Baron Kingston (1693–1761), Grand Master of Grand Lodge of England (1728/9) and Grand Master of Irish Grand Lodge (1731, 1735, 1745 and 1746). King owned the 100,000-acre Mitchelstown estate in Ireland. Born in France during his father's exile, he petitioned for naturalization as a 'good Protestant'. Although referred to as a Jacobite, there is little substantiating evidence; the family history was one of political realism rather than idealism. King was initiated at the Swan and Rummer on 8 June 1726 and was Grand Master of Munster in 1731, the year he was first appointed Grand Master of Ireland. See *Minutes of the Grand Lodge of England* pp. 90, 94, 96 and *Schism*, pp. 13, 18–9, 126, 224–6.

28. *a noble* Peer: See p. 401, n. 14.

29. *Their Initiation* Fee *is, in general, small,* viz. *ten* Shillings: The ridicule of the low initiation fee and contempt for Irish nationality and the lack of social distinction of many Antients Freemasons highlight the principal difference between the Antients' and Moderns' respective memberships and the disdainful attitude of the Moderns. See *Schism*, chs 1–4.

30. George Alexander Stevens: George Alexander Stevens (1710–84) was the author of *Songs, Comic, and Satyrical* (Oxford: Printed for the author, London, [1772]). He was a member of the Robin Hood Society around 1750. *Gentleman Magazine* (January 1792) quoted in *AQC*, 27 (1914), p. 32.

31. St. Pancras: St Pancras was renowned as a Catholic and non-conformist cemetery. See W. H. Godfrey and W. McB. Marcham (eds), *Survey of London Vol. 24: The Parish of St Pancras, Part 4: King's Cross Neighbourhood* (London: LCC, 1952), pp. 147–51.

[Anon.], *Masonry the Way to Hell, a Sermon* (1768)

1. *there scarcely is one contemptible fellow ... a member of these fraternities*: See the headnote on the increasing number of masonic lodges in England, pp. 152–3.

2. *the famous tower of Babel*: The Tower of Babel was an important symbol used in the Harodim tradition of Freemasonry. On the one hand it functioned as a warning not to trespass the limits set by God, but on the other it counted in this context as one of the Wonders of the World and an example of excellent masonry, while the confusion of languages would have occasioned the communication between Freemasons through signs and symbols. See volume 3 of this edition, pp. xiii, 2–6.

3. *these impostors chalk upon the floor of the lodge*: See p. 387, n. 2.

4. *perfect lodge*: The number of the members of a perfect lodge was in the early eighteenth century still sometimes defined differently in other places. For example, in *The Flying-Post or Post-Master* (11–13 April 1723, issue 4712) it consists of 'A Master, two Wardens, four fellows, five Apprentices.' See also *Daily Journal*, 15 August 1730, issue 2998. *EMC*, pp. 73, 154. By 1760 it had long become standardised to the definition assumed here.

5. *master's word*: for the different versions of the master's word in French and English rituals see J. A. M. Snoek, 'The Evolution of the Hiramic Legend in England and France', *Heredom* 11 (2003), pp. 11–53, on p. 33. 'The old Master's Word was the name of God in Hebrew, the Tetragrammaton, pronounced as Jehovah, which is the same name that appears in the kabbalistic tradition'. H. Bogdan, 'Freemasonry and Western Esotericism', in H. Bogdan and J. A. M. Snoek (eds), *Handbook of Freemasonry* (Leiden: Brill, 2014), pp. 277–305, on p. 299.

6. Thou shalt not take the name of the Lord thy God in vain: It is one of the ten commandments. See Exodus 20:7.

7. *the most horrid imprecations, if they break this engagement*: See T. Wilson, *Solomon in all His Glory: Or, the Master-Mason. Being a True Guide to the Inmost Recesses of Free-Masonry, both Ancient and Modern. ... by T. W. ... Translated from the French Original Published at Berlin* (London: printed for G. Robinson and J. Roberts, 1766), p. 11, 45.

8. *his eyes are blindfolded with a handkerchief*: See Wilson, *Solomon in all His Glory*, pp. 7, 9, 18, 32, 43, and one of the replies to the *Masonry: the Way to Hell, Masonry the Turnpike-Road to Happiness in this Life, and Eternal Happiness Hereafter* (Dublin: printed by James Hoey, senior, at the Mercury in Skinner-Row, [1768]) pp. 8–9. It may be noted that most texts of the rituals mention a kerchief, not a handkerchief, but in *Solomon* the word used is indeed, exceptionally, handkerchief.

9. Boaz: Boaz was the name of a column in Solomon's Temple and – in Continental and 'Moderns' Freemasonry – the word of the Fellow-Craft, and – in 'Antients' Freema-

sonry – of the Apprentice. See 1 Kings 7:21; 2 Chronicles 3:17; Snoek, 'The Evolution of the Hiramic Legend in England and France', p. 13, and Wilson, *Solomon in all His Glory*, pp. 18, 21, 34, 46.

10. *stripped of all metal*: See Wilson, *Solomon in all His Glory*, pp. 4, 7, 9, 31, 43.

11. *a lodge has three doors*: actually windows.

12. *They know not ... the tropic of Cancer*: We can safely assume that they did know it. The author fails to consider that the rituals were designed for the British Isles only.

13. *the circumference of the pillars of the temple ... no more than nearly three to one*: According to the masonic tradition the pillars were hollow and their shell was four fingers thick.

14. *an example from their catechism*: The cited question and answer are literally copied from Wilson, *Solomon in All His Glory*, p. 50. It is a poor translation of the French: 'A moi, A moi, enfants de la veuve!' ['Help me, help me, children of the widow!']

15. *He is ever a griping to distinguish his own species*: The above paragraph exemplifies an extreme, and probably intentional, corruption of the text of *Solomon in All His Glory*.

16. whence came you? ... from the lodge of St. John: Wilson, *Solomon in All His Glory*, p. 41.

17. how old are you? ... five years and an half: Wilson, *Solomon in All His Glory*, p. 41. The following explanation can be found in the footnote on the same page: 'The brothers who are not masters are always under seven years old, because they reckon their age from the time of their reception. These five years and a half are also to signify innocence and candour.'

18. *have his heart taken out, if he devulge their secrets*: See p. 403, n. 7.

19. *Adoniram or Hiram*: the architect of the Temple of Solomon in the Master Mason ritual. Wilson, *Solomon in All His Glory*, p. 49.

20. It shall be more tolerable for Tyre and Sidon: Matthew 11:22.

21. Wo unto them that seek deep to hide: Isaiah 29:15.

22. *their extraordinary veneration for three, five, and seven, the cabalistic, or Babylonian numbers*: for a detailed examination of the cabalistic influence on Freemasonry, see M. K. Schuchard, *Restoring the Temple of Vision: Cabalistic Freemasonry and Stuart Culture* (Leiden: Brill, 2002) and Bogdan, 'Freemasonry and Western Esotericism', pp. 277–305.

23. *Sporado*: He must be the product of the author's imagination. There is no evidence for the story of Sporado.

24. *Macbenac*: Having found the buried body of Hiram, a new master word is revealed during the ritual, which is 'Macbenac'. It supposedly means 'the flesh falls from the bones', referring to the decomposed state of Hiram's corpse See Wilson, *Solomon in All His Glory*, p. 35 and Bogdan, 'Freemasonry and Western Esotericism', p. 297.

25. *Belial*: the personification of evil, or the synonym of Satan. See 2 Corinthians 6:15.

26. the Lord will not hold him guiltless: Exodus 20:7.

27. the sinner who repenteth not, shall perish: 'Nay: but, except ye repent, ye shall all likewise perish' (Luke 13:3).

28. ye have hewed you out cisterns, yea, broken cisterns, which can hold no water: Jeremiah 2:13.

[Anon.], *Masonry Vindicated: a Sermon. Wherein is Clearly and Demonstratively Proved, that a Sermon, Lately Published, 'Intitled Masonry the Way to Hell', is an Intire Piece of the Utmost Weakness, and Absurdity* (1768)

1. *to the Fair-Sex in particular*: about the complex relationship between Freemasonry and women, see the section on Women in volume 5 and the chapter from George Smith's book in this volume.
2. *Grubstreet Jargon and Nonsense*: Grub Street was famous for the publication of popular, sensationalist and simplistic books.
3. *Sporado*: See p. 404, n. 23.
4. *perfect Lodge*: See p. 403, n. 4.
5. *how old he is, he is to answer 'five years and an half.'*: See T. Wilson, *Solomon in all His Glory: Or, the Master-Mason. Being a True Guide to the Inmost Recesses of Free-Masonry, both Ancient and Modern. ... by T. W. ... Translated from the French Original Published at Berlin* (London: printed for G. Robinson and J. Roberts, 1766), p. 8. The answers to this question were different in different 'exposures' and thus in different lodges. Continental lodges (described in *Solomon*) would often differ in their forms from English ones.
6. *The meetings of masons in most Lodges in England*: See the headnote of the section on Admissions and Lodge Meetings in volume 5.

George Smith, 'Ancient and Modern Reasons Why the Ladies Have Never Been Admitted into the Society of Freemasons', in *The Use and Abuse of Free-Masonry* (1783)

1. *They stand in ... seminaries of learning, &c. &c.*: W. Calcott, *A Candid Disquisition of the Principles and Practices of the Most Ancient and Honourable Society of Free and Accepted Masons; together with Some Strictures on the Origin, Nature, and Design of that Institution. Dedicated, by Permission, to the Most Noble and Most Worshipful Henry Duke of Beaufort, &c. &c. Grand Master. By Wellins Calcott, P.M.* (London: Printed for the Author, by Brother James Dixwell, in St. Martins Lane. A. L. 5769. A. D., 1769), p. 38. Smith's quotation of Calcott differs only in one word: 'many other [particular] societies'.
2. *Anna Maria a Scheurman*: Anna Maria van Schurman (1607–78) was the first woman to study at a Dutch university, where she focused on ancient languages and theology. She wrote a treatise defending the education of women and women's ability for scholarship.
3. *to exclude the fair sex*: In general, English craft guilds were never exclusively male, and women were admitted into their ranks form the Middle Ages onwards. See A. Clark, *Working Life of Women in the Seventeenth Century* (1919; London: Routledge, 1992) and M. K. McIntosh, *Working Women in English Society, 1300–1620* (Cambridge: Cambridge University Press, 2005).
4. *Nor let the dear maid ... An empire deriv'd from above*: This masonic song was published in L. Dermott, *Ahiman Rezon*, 2nd edn (1764), p. 198 and W. Preston, *Illustrations of Masonry* (1775), p. 296, and subsequent editions of the latter.
5. *And thus the libertine ... and to bless mankind:* W. Calcott, *A Collection of Thoughts, Moral and Divine, upon Various Subjects, in Prose and Verse. Dedicated, by Permission, to the Right Honourable Earl of Powis, by Wellins Calcott, Gent*, 6th edn (London: Printed for the author, 1766), p. 29.

6. *always present the new initiated brother with two pair of* white gloves: In the eighteenth century it was the custom for Freemasons to present a woman of their choice with gloves. This tradition can be detected in rituals and minute books of lodges. See volume 2 and L. Dermott, *Ahiman Rezon*, 2nd edn, p. xviii.

7. Grace was in all her steps ... dignity and love: J. Milton, *Paradise Lost* (1674), viii, ll. 488–9.

8. so absolute she seems ... as a guard angelic plac'd: Milton, *Paradise Lost* (1674), viii, ll. 547–59.

9. O fairest of creation ... amiable, or sweet: Milton, *Paradise Lost* (1674), ix, ll. 896–9.

10. *Dean Swift*: Jonathan Swift (1667–1745), writer and dean of St Patrick's Cathedral, Dublin. It may be noted that *A Letter from the Grand Mistress of the Female Free Masons to Mr Harding the Printer* (Dublin, 1724) was wrongly attributed to him by masonic historians. See *EMC*, pp. 229–30.

11. We're true and sincere ... Free and an Accepted Mason: George Smith incorrectly attributed this well-known and oft-published masonic song, still used today, to J. Swift. According to John H. Lepper and Philiph Crossle, this verse was written by Springett Penn (1701–31), a wealthy Quaker and grandson of William Penn, who established the Pennsylvania colony. He was a Deputy Grand Master of Munster in 1726 and 1727. He added this stanza to Mathew Birkhead's famous masonic song. *GLFI*, p. 69.

12. The ladies claim right to come into our light ... To raise lodges for Lady Free-masons: an oft-quoted masonic song. For example, see *The Pocket Companion and History of Free-Masons, Containing their Origin, Progress, and Present State: An Abstract of their Laws, Constitutions, Customs, ... a Confutation of Dr. Plot's False Insinuations: ...* (London: Printed for J. Scott; and sold by R. Baldwin, 1754), p. 326. It was reprinted in most editions of *Ahiman Rezon* and Preston's *Illustrations of Masonry*.

13. *YOU have heard*, ladies ... *distressed obtain present relief*: T. Dunckerley, 'A Charge, delivered to the Members of the Lodge of Free and Accepted Masons, held at the Castle-inn, Marlborough, at a Meeting for the Distribution of Charity to twenty-four poor People, at which most of the Ladies in Marlborough were present, Sept. 11, A. L. 5769 [1769]', in W. Martin Leake, *A Sermon Preached at St. Peter's Church in Colchester on Tuesday, June 24, 1777 ... Before the Provincial Grand Master, and the Provincial Grand Lodge, of The ... Masons of Essex. By the Revd. William Martin Leake ... to which is Added a Charge which was Delivered ... at ... Marlborough ... by Thomas Dunckerley* (Colchester: Printed and sold by W. Keymer, 1778), pp. 34–5. Dunckerley's charge is reproduced in volume 1, pp. 107–114.

14. *Dr.* Dodd: William Dodd (1729–77), see p. 183, n. 6.

15. Open ye gates ... favoured from above: This masonic song was often quoted in the second half of the eighteenth century. For example, it can be found in L. Dermott, *Ahiman Rezon*, 2nd edn (1764), p. 223, less the first three lines.

[A Friend to Truth], *A Defence of Free Masons etc., in Answer to Professor John Robison's Proofs of a Conspiracy* (1797)

1. NEWTON: Sir Isaac Newton (1642–1727), natural philosopher and mathematician. His *Principia mathematica* (1687) is often considered as one of the pillars of modern scientific thinking.

2. Charles the First: Charles I, King of England, Scotland and Ireland (r. 1625–49). His reign was characterized by an ever-increasing conflict with Parliament, eventu-

ally resulting in the outbreak of the Civil War, in the course of which he was be-
headed in 1649.

3. *Jesuits assumed the guise of* Free-Masons: Robison wrote that 'at this time the Jesuits
interfered considerably insinuating themselves into the Lodges, and contributing to
encrease the religious mysticism that is to be observed in all the ceremonies of the
order'. According to Robison, the Jesuits were responsible for introducing the higher
degrees and knightly ceremonies, which became very popular among French Freemasons. J. Robison, *Proofs of a Conspiracy*, p. 22.

4. *The* Memoirs of Gregorie Panzaini: The bibliographic details of the work are: *The
Memoirs of Gregorio Panzani; Giving an Account of his Agency in England, in the Years
1634, 1635, 1636. Translated from the Italian Original, and Now First Published. To
which are Added, an Introduction and a Supplement, Exhibiting the State of the English
Catholic Church, and the Conduct of Parties, before and after that Period, to the Present
Times.* By the Revd. Joseph Berington (Birmingham : Printed by Swinney & Walker;
for G. G. J. & J. Robinson, and R. Faulder, London, MDCCXCIII [1793]).

5. Berington: See previous note.

6. ipse dixit: See p. 397, n. 21.

7. *Judge Jefferys*: George Jeffreys, first Baron Jeffreys (1645–89), was an infamous judge
from James II's time, who convicted a multitude of people on dubious evidence during
the Popish Plot (1678–81), and after the Monmouth Rebellion of 1685 (*ODNB*).

8. the three black crows: 'The Three Black Crows' is a poem by John Byrom (1692–
1763).

9. *Savonarolo of Florence*: Girolamo Savonarola (1452–98), Italian Dominican friar, reformer and martyr.

10. *Mr David Black of St Andrew's*: David Black (*c.* 1546–1603), minister in the Church
of Scotland, who was summoned before James VI after having offended him in his
sermons, and denying his authority in spiritual matters (*ODNB*).

11. Voltaire: François-Marie Arouet (1694–1778), French philosopher, writer and Ency-
clopaedist.

12. Cramer: Gabriel (1723–93) and Philibert Cramer (1727–79), the Genevan printers of
what is regarded as the first 'complete works' of Voltaire in 1756.

13. *Abbè of the name of Barruel*: Abbè Augustin de Barruel (1741–1821). Jesuit anti-masonic writer, responsible for the spread of the theory of a masonic-Revolutionary plot.
See *MMLDP*, vol. 1, pp. 256–71 and the headnote of this text, pp. 195–200.

14. Religion's Begenbeiten: The anonymous author misspelled the name of the journal,
which appears in Robison's text as 'Religion's Begebenheiten'. The full and accurate
title of the referred journal is *Die neuesten Religionsbegebenheiten mit unpartheyischen
Anmerkungen*, edited by Heinrich Martin Gottfried Köster, and published in Giessen
between 1778 and 1797. We can clearly observe the influence of Köster's views on Robison's book. See also the headnote of this text, pp. 195–200.

15. Weishaupt: Johann Adam Weishaupt (1748–1830), professor of canon law at the University of Ingolstadt, founder of the Illuminati Order (1776).

16. Spartacus and Philo: Pseudonyms used by the members of the Illuminati in their correspondence; Spartacus refers to Adam Weishaupt, while Philo stands for Adolph Baron
Knigge. Robison reproduced some of their letters, see for example Robison, *Proofs of
Conspiracy*, pp. 134–7, 152–65. For a scholarly edition of the Illuminati correspondence, see R. Markner, M. Neugebauer-Wölk and H. Schüttler (eds), *Die Korrespondenz
des Illuminatenordens* (vol. 1: Tübingen: M. Niemeyer, 2005; vol. 2: Berlin and Boston,

MA: De Gruyter, 2013).

17.　Baron Knigge: Baron Adolph von Knigge (1752–96) joined the Illuminati in 1780, contributing significantly to the development of their degree system as well as the expansion of the organization in Germany.

18.　*your illustrious and sober-minded brother-professor*: Possibly Hans Axel von Fersen (1755–1810).

19.　*the late Queen of France!*: Marie Antoinette, Queen of France and Navarre (r. 1774–92). Daughter of Francis I, Holy Roman Emperor and Maria Theresa of Austria, wife of King Louis XVI of France. She was convicted of treason and executed during the French Revolution in October 1793.

20.　Bahrdt: Carl Friedrich Bahrdt (1741–92), controversial German theologian and founder of a society similar to the Illuminati, the Deutsche Union (1787).

21.　Nicolai: Christoph Friedrich Nicolai (1733–1811), author and publisher in Berlin. Member of the Illuminati. See R. Markner, '"Ihr Nahme war auch darauf", F. Nicolai, J. Joachim Christoph Bode und die Illuminaten', in R. Falk and A. Košenina (eds), *Friedrich Nicolai und die Berliner Aufklärung* (Hannover: Wehrhahn, 2008), pp. 199–225.

22.　MIRABEAU: Honoré-Gabriel Riquetti, Comte de Mirabeau (1749–91), French politician and orator, a prominent figure of the National Assembly governing France in the early phases of the Revolution. A moderate politician, he tried to reconcile monarchy and the Revolution (*EB*). He became an affiliated member of the Paris lodge Les neuf sœurs in 1783. See C. Porset, *Mirabeau franc-maçon* (La Rochelle: Rumeur des Ages, 1996).

23.　*duke of* Orleans: Prince Louis Philippe Joseph, fifth Duke of Orleans (1747–93), supporter of the Revolution as Philippe Égalité. He joined the Jacobins in 1791, and voted for the execution of his own cousin, Louis XVI, but after his son deserted, he was arrested and executed. Robison claims that the Duke was elected Grand Master of France 'about eight years before the Revolution' (Robison, *Proofs of Conspiracy*, p. 381). Robison was mistaken on this point because the duke was installed as a Grand Master in October 1773. See W. K. Firminger, 'The Romances of John Robison and Augustus Barruel', *AQC*, 50 (1937), pp. 31–69, on pp. 34–5.

24.　Watt: Robert Watt, Scottish political radical, who was convicted of high treason and executed in 1794 in Edinburgh.

[Anon.], *The Indictment and Trial of John Andrew, Shoemaker in Maybole, Sometime Teacher of a Private School There, and Robert Ramsay, Cart Wright There, Both Members of a Masonic Lodge at Maybole: Charged with the Crime of Sedition, and Administering Unlawful Oaths* (1800)

1.　*Maybole*: town on the west coast of Scotland, in South Ayrshire. The two masonic lodges represented were No. 14 Maybole Lodge, and No. 264 Maybole Royal Arch.

2.　*cart-wright*: one who makes or repairs carts.

3.　*The libel charges ... unlawful oaths*: Between the years 1792 and 1799, Parliament took the war against radicalism to a new level. Faced with perceived threats from subversive organizations and a dramatic increase of revolutionary sentiments in Britain, the government launched a campaign to eradicate all traces of sedition, treason and sympathies for reformist societies. The Unlawful Oaths Act (1797) was significant, for the swearing of oaths was the basis by which the working class organized successfully and ensured both secrecy and solidarity. Fearing that such assemblies would incite revolutionary activities, the Unlawful Oaths Act stipulated that 'any person is guilty of a felony and liable to heavy punishment who in any manner or form administers or causes to be administered, or aids or assists at, or is present and consents to the administering or taking of any oath or engagement purporting or intended to bind the person taking it to engage in any mutinous or seditious purpose, or to disturb the public peace, or to be of any society formed for such a purpose or to obey the orders of any committee or body not lawfully constituted, or of any commander not having authority by law for that purpose, or not to inform or give evidence against any associate or other person or not to reveal any unlawful combination or any illegal act done or to be done or any illegal oath or engagement or its import, or who takes any such oath without being compelled to do so', from S. Lambert (ed.), *House of Commons Sessional Papers*, Vol. 103 (Scholarly Resources, 1975), pp. 433–5. By July 1799 the government had passed the Secret Societies Act, or 'An act for the more effectual suppression of societies established for seditious and treasonable purposes; and for the better preventing treasonable and seditious practices', which effectively regulated and policed Freemasonry in Scotland. In no uncertain terms, the Act emphatically declared that 'a traitorous conspiracy had long been carried on with the persons from time to time exercising the power of government in France to overturn the laws, constitution and government and that in pursuance of such design, diverse societies had been instituted ... All and every of the said societies [that require] an unlawful oath or engagement ... shall be deemed guilty of an unlawful combination and confederacy', see *House of Commons*, Vol. 120, pp. 365–84.

4. *importing an obligation ... Assembly of Knights Templars*: Two nascent degrees of Freemasonry, the Royal Arch and Knights Templar, appeared on the West Coast of Scotland during the 1790s and at the time were not sanctioned by the Grand Lodge of Scotland as official masonic degrees. The Royal Arch and Knights Templar degrees were extensions of the three sanctioned degrees of Freemasonry – Entered Apprentice, Fellow Craft, Master Mason – and were based upon legends of the Knights of St John and the Holy Royal Arch located in Solomon's Temple in Jerusalem. Members of the Royal Arch and Knights Templar professed an interest in the higher degrees of masonry; Elaine McFarland, in her book *Ireland and Scotland in the Age or Revolution: Planting The Green Bough,* explains that these degrees, 'under a pretended connection with Freemasonry', sought to 'propagate the infidelity of the French Revolution, and to evoke sympathy for the democrats in Ireland', (Edinburgh: Edinburgh University Press, 1994), p. 59. By the early 1790s, allegations had surfaced which connected these higher degrees to the radical United Irishmen. Established in Belfast in 1791, the United Irishmen advocated religious toleration, parliamentary reform and universal manhood suffrage. Indeed, McFarland claims that by 1797, a 'contagion [which equated] Irishness with disaffection' had gripped Western Scotland, and by 1797 Ayrshire had become one of the 'first strongholds' of Irish influence', see McFarland, *Ireland and Scotland*, pp. 157–8.

5. *pannels*: the person or persons indicted before a court (*OED*).

6. *He was shown ... identified by this witness*: The writings of Paine were so invidious to the defenders of British conservatism that the radical leader was tried and convicted of treason, branded as a traitor, and publishers of *Rights of Man* were fined and imprisoned. As Roger Wells notes in his book *Insurrection: The British Experience 1795–1803*

(Gloucester: Allan Sutton Publishing, 1983), p. 2, Paine's writings were dangerous in that they were a 'potent polemic devoted to the notion of the sovereignty of the people, and its essential corollary – universal suffrage', and Paine's literature polarized political thought in Britain and Irish societies, as it 'infused popularism into the debate started by the Revolution'. James Gray argues in *Freemasonry in Maybole, Carrick's Capital: Fact, Fiction and Folks* (Ayr: Alloway Publishing, 1972), pp. 279–87 that 'as 'Masonic ritual was not standarized then as it is today, probably No. 264 members carried out their ceremonies in a different manner to those of No. 14, who being the older lodge, would feel that the young upstart lodge should fall into line and do as their elders and betters did'. If No. 264 was citing Paine – whose text was the symbol of British revolutionary politics – this was an obvious sign of genuine revolutionary views and a very clear attempt by the Maybole Lodge to accuse No. 264 of radical political sentiments.

7.   William Moor, *an / Irishman*: In 1979, Richard Gallin – in his unpublished thesis 'Scottish Radicalism 1792–1794' (PhD thesis, University of Columbia, 1979), p. 251, compiled lists of clubs and societies and members who were suspected of being radicals and members of clubs and societies labelled as treasonous and seditious by the government. His list of radical clubs and reformers includes a William Muir, weaver in Kilmarnock. Although at best a tenuous connection, it does lend further weight to the arguments of McFarland and others that radical Irish dissidents had some influence on masonic lodges in Western Scotland.

8.   mulum in re: misspelling of *malum in re*, Latin for 'wrong in itself'.

9.   not proven: Scots legal verdict returned when evidence is insufficient to convict defendant(s).

10. *assoilzied*: to absolve from sin, grant absolution to, pardon, forgive (*OED*).

[Anon.], *Petition and Complaint at Brother Gibson's Instance Against Brother Mitchell, and His Answers Thereto; With the Procedure of the Grand Lodge Thereon and Proof Adduced* (1808)

1.   *printing a libelous pamphlet*: Having twice defeated the proposed address to the King, it is unclear why the Grand Lodge pursued the matter further. Apparently, it wanted to summarily vindicate itself of any misconduct and, at the same time, blame Mitchell for the entire political discord. Subsequently, he was suspended from all masonic privileges. Lindsay writes 'unfortunately, Dr. Mitchell nor Gibson could leave well alone, and their differences were followed up outside Grand Lodge until 5th January, when Gibson laid before Grand Lodge a Petition against Dr. Mitchell, in which he alleged: (1) That Dr. Mitchell persisted in holding his Monthly Meetings on a date already expressly forbidden to him as belonging to Lodge Roman Eagle; (2) That at one of the Meetings he had suggested secession from Grand Lodge; (3) That when on the way to the annual Masonic Service in the Tron Church on St Andrew's Day, 1807, he had prevailed on his Lodge to leave the procession and to adjourn to Oman's Tavern, and further, though expected by the Acting Grand Master [Hon. William Ramsay Maule], he had sent neither apology nor Deputation to the Grand Festival, showing by these actions contempt for the religious Service in which his Brethren were engaged, disrespect to the Acting Grand Master, and, to the world, that there was a schism in the Fraternity; (4) That contrary to Masonic custom, he had, on 28 December 1807, refused to receive a Deputation from Lodge St David, Edinburgh, of which the Petitioner was

Past Master', Lindsay, *Holyrood House*, pp. 300–1. The actual petition was received by the Grand Lodge of Scotland on 1 January 1808. The petition and complaint asserted that 'Brother Mitchell has done every thing in his power to disturb the peace of the Grand Lodge, and of the craft, by printing a libelous pamphlet, and by most disrespectful and improper conduct to the Grand Lodge, insomuch, that at the meeting of the quarterly communication of the Grand Lodge, held in the month of November last, a motion was made and seconded ... to expel him from the Grand Lodge', Manuscripts, GL of S, 1 January 1808. Mitchell ignored Grand Lodge's edict to discontinue meetings on the same evening as Roman Eagle and challenged James Gibson to a duel, for which he was suspended from all masonic privileges.

2.   *conduct at that meeting ... turn him out of the lodge*: See previous note.

3.   *The petitioner need ... by the Grand Lodge*: Although it had no constitutional authority to hand down punishments of expulsion and could not legally bar Freemasons from communicating with one another, the Grand Lodge was intent on forcing lodges to comply with its demands and imposing its authority on all Scottish Freemasons.

4.   *That a dispute ... in the future*: Roman Eagle Lodge Minute Books detail this conflict, and in February 1807 the following entry was recorded: 'February 1807 The Lodge being regularly constituted agreeable to the rules of the Craft the Right Worshipful Brother Black rose to inform the Lodge that a Letter had been sent to the Right Worshipful Brother Mitchell of the Caledonians complaining of the conduct of that Lodge in usurping the night of meeting used by this night of Roman Eagle, and that the Secretary Brother Drummond had received for answer "That the Committee of the Caledonian Lodge having fixed upon that Night for their meeting for certain obvious reasons Known to themselves, and public notice of same having been given in the Edinburgh Newspapers they could not now retract from it." The Right Worshipful Brother Black therefore proposed that a Memorial and Petition be drawn up by the Monthly Committee of this Lodge and presented to the Grand Lodge of Scotland setting forth the unmasonic conduct of the Caledonians and praying the Grand Lodge of Scotland may give orders that the Caledonians shall alter their night of meeting. This met with the hearty concurrence of all present and the Committee was desired to prepair the Memorial and Petition accordingly', Manuscripts, Roman Eagle Lodge, February 1807.

5.   *The petitioner complains ... the Grand Lodge*: Interestingly, the accusation of secession was made at the Grand Lodge of Scotland on 5 January 1808; however, the minutes of Caledonian Lodge record no motion to secede until 11 March 1808. During the meeting, Lodge Caledonian recorded that 'no proof is adduced to establish that the Right Worshipful Master [Dr. Mitchell] *did make a proposal to secede* from the Grand Lodge', Manuscripts, Roman Eagle Lodge, 11 March 1808. After the apparent fabrication of the secession charges, the members resolved that the 'sentence of the Grand Lodge is particularly offensive to the Caledonian Lodge, as, in the whole of the persecution, originating, as they deem, in party spirit ... and, with a view to avoid further persecution, they discontinue their connection with the present Grand Lodge of Scotland', Manuscripts, Roman Eagle Lodge, 11 March 1808.

6.   *Tron Church*: also the Tron Kirk, built in the seventeenth century following the Scottish Reformation.

7.   *festival of St. John the Evangelist*: Feast Day of St John the Evangelist, or the day on which a celebration is held. The Feast Day of St John occurs on 27 December.

8.   *Grand Clerk's*: The Grand Clerk is the officer who has charge of the records, correspondence and accounts, and superintends the general conduct of its business (*OED*).

9.   WILLIAM INGLIS: The Whig Grand Lodge of Scotland was also supported by William Inglis of Middleton, Substitute Grand Master 1805–28. According to Lindsay, Inglis was a staunch Whig who attended the Bastille Dinner in 1789 and was 'one of the most widely known Scottish Masons of all time ... who weathered one of the worst storms in the history of Scottish freemasonry'. See Lindsay, *Holyrood House*, pp. 269–70. Referring to William Inglis, Lindsay writes that 'after he [Inglis] left [the Master's Chair of St Luke's] in 1805, he dominated the Craft for the next twenty-three years as Substitute Grand Master in a manner unparalleled before or since. He could and did formulate the policy of Grand Lodge throughout his long tenure of office there; but he required for its successful issue a constitutional support on which he could rely. The way had to be prepared amongst the Lodges. Ears and eyes were essential in places where the Substitute Grand Master could only be received in his official capacity ... Inglis, then, needed a spy ... to see what things were on his side and what o' the other. Naturally he chose for the purpose his own Lodge of St Luke, and so long as he governed the Craft he worked in closest cooperation with its Masters and Proxy representatives for other Lodges in Grand Lodge, and they reaped in his time, and after it, the fruits of Grand Office as the reward of the allegiance', Lindsay, *Holyrood House*, p. 280.

10.   *that though his brother ... seventy times seven*: biblical reference, Matthew 6:21–2: 'Then Peter came to Jesus and asked, "Lord, how many times shall I forgive my brother when he sins against me? Up to seven times?" Jesus answered, "I tell you, not seven times, but seventy-seven times"'.

11.   *milk of human kindness*: spoken by Lady Macbeth in William Shakespeare's *The Tragedy of Macbeth*, I.v.15–18: 'Glamis, thou art, and Cawdor, and shalt be / What is promis'd. Yet do I fear thy nature, / It is too full o' th' milk of human kindness / To catch the nearest way'.

12.   'Odia in longum jaciens, quæ recondereret auctaque promeret': Tacitus, 'A man who lays aside his resentment, but stores it up to bring it forward with additional acrimony' (Latin).

13.   *points of dittay*: in Scots Law, the matter of charge or ground of indictment against a person for a criminal offence; also, the formulated indictment (*OED*).

14.   *Grand Wardens*: either of two officers (called the Senior Warden or Junior Warden) in a speculative lodge whose duty it is to assist the Worshipful Master (*OED*).

15.   *violent phillipic*: of the nature of a bitter attack, denunciation, or invective (*OED*).

16.   *hissing*: the utterance of a hiss or hisses as a sign of disapproval or detestation (*OED*).

17.   *The circumstance ... address to his Majesty*: See headnote, p. 229.

18.   *Scrutiny:* the formal taking of individual votes, as a method of electing to an office or dignity, or of deciding some question proposed to a deliberative assembly; an instance of this procedure (*OED*).

19.   *almanacks*: a handbook containing a calendar or calendars. Also, a diary for the keeping of appointments and dates.

20.   *interdicting:* Scots Law, an order of the Court of Session, or of an inferior court, pronounced, on cause shown, for stopping any act or proceedings complained of as illegal or wrongful (*OED*).

21.   '*The same observations ... from the Grand Lodge*': See p. 410, n. 5.

22.   fishing *accusation*: to use artifice to obtain a thing, or elicit an opinion (*OED*).

23.   *At the quarterly communication ... vote for it*: The decision to secede was not confined exclusively to the members of Lodge Caledonian. Other Masons, such as the Senior Warden of Mary's Chapel and the Junior Warden of Edinburgh St Andrew,

also supported the secession. The presence of an officer from Mary's Chapel is important, for it suggests that the lodge, still harbouring resentment over the precedence controversy, was considering separation. Taking advantage of the dispute with Dr Mitchell, Mary's Chapel now had the support of other lodges which were united in their common dislike of the Grand Lodge of Scotland.

24. *Neither have his exertions been wanting ... lodge could benefit*: Despite the attractions of music, drinking and song, Peter Clark asserts that Freemasonry had its greatest impact 'in the area of philanthropy'. A fundamental purpose of lodge funds, charitable activities were multivarious. Although, as Clark has asserted, lodge charity is difficult to quantify, it is clearly evident from minutes and records that a substantial proportion of lodge funds went towards the relief of the poor and indigent. See P. Clark, *British Clubs and Societies 1580–1800: The Origins of an Associational World* (Oxford: Oxford University Press, 2000), p. 337.

25. *Trafalgar*: reference to the Battle of Trafalgar, 21 October 1805, during the Napoleonic Wars. Fought off the coast of Spain near Cadiz, the naval conflict resulted in a victory for the British Royal Navy over the combined force of the French and Spanish. Unfortunately for the British Navy, Admiral Nelson was killed during the battle.

26. *He might mention ... widows and orphans*: Similar to other Scottish lodges, the majority of Grand Lodge charity was designated for the relief of widows, orphans and injured or sick Freemasons. For example, Grand Lodge Minutes record that charity was given to the widow of a poor operative brother in Glasgow 'who had five small children, all at the point of starving', Manuscripts, GL of S, 3 August 1743.

27. *He had a tear ... melting 'charity'*: Spoken by King Henry IV, in William Shakespeare's *2 Henry IV*, IV.iv.30–2: 'For he is gracious if he observ'd, / He hath a tear for pity, and a hand / Open as day for [meting] charity'.

28. *mite:* any small coin of low value; originally applied to a Flemish copper coin, but in English used mainly as a proverbial expression for an extremely small unit of monetary value; used to denote a more specific unit, as a farthing, a half farthing, or (esp. in accounting) some smaller fraction of a farthing (*OED*).

29. *in words nearly ... the 'traveller'*: biblical reference, Job 31:32: 'The alien has not lodged outside, for I have opened my doors to the traveler'.

30. *In freta dum fluvii ... vocant terræ*: from Virgil's *Aeneid*, book 1, ll. 606–10: 'While rivers run into the sea, while shadows move round the convex mountains, while heaven feeds the stars; your honour, name, and praise with me shall ever live, to whatever climes I am called'.

31. *'A man who ... eight year old horse'*: spoken by Menenius, in William Shakespeare's *Coriolanus*, V.iv.16–24: 'So did he me; and he no more remembers his / mother now that an eight-year-old-horse. The tartness / of his face sours ripe grapes. When he walks, he / moves like an engine, and the ground shrinks before / his treading. He is able to pierce a corslet with / his eye, talks like a knell, and his hum is a battery. He / sits in his state, as a thing made for Alexander. What / he bids be done is finish'd with his bidding. He wants / nothing of a god but eternity and a heaven to throne in'.

32. *'was no more ... male tiger'*: spoken by Menenius, in William Shakespeare's *Coriolanus*, V.iv.27–9: 'There is no / more mercy in him than there is milk in a male tiger, / that shall our poor city find'.

33. *'God mend thee ... true duty:'* adaptation of lines spoken by the Duchess of York in William Shakespeare's *Richard III*, II.ii.107: 'God bless thee, and put meekness in they breast'.

34. pro tempore: for the time being, temporarily; provisionally (*OED*).

35. *COMPEARED*: to appear in court, as a party to a cause, either in person or by counsel (*OED*).

36. '*chicane*': to use subterfuges and tricks in litigation, or quibbles, cavils, shifts and petty artifices in debate or action; to quibble, cavil (*OED*).

37. *deponent*: one who deposes or makes a deposition under oath; one who gives written testimony to be used as evidence in a court of justice or for other purpose (*OED*).

38. *That some of the gentlemen present were not cloathed*: reference to the specific clothes, garb, ornaments and jewels proper to a specified masonic officer.

39. *If brother Mitchell ... any of them proposed*: Toasts were an important part of the meeting, as at other gatherings of clubs and societies, attesting to the unity of the members, and they constituted a principal part of masonic meetings, customarily signifying the closing of the lodge. Recipients and the order of toasts varied, acknowledging the Master of the Lodge and his officers, members in attendance, visiting lodges, the Grand Lodges of Scotland and England, and the king.

40. *That Brother Mitchell then mentioned ... also seceding*: As Wartski notes, 'the situation in Grand Lodge had reached the point of near hysteria. Spite and rancour [were] rampant, where fact and discretion might have saved the day. The cavalier handling of the matter of precedence shows a lack of feeling towards the former premier Lodge, which naturally deeply resented its displacement after so many years. One would not have expected this sort of behaviour from Freemasons, let along those entrusted with the government of the Craft. The actions of the Grand Lodge put the final touches to the revolt that followed, which, though it had been brewing, could have been prevented'. See L. D. Wartski, 'Freemasonry and the Early Secret Societies Act', monograph compiled and presented by the author for private circulation by the District Grand Lodge of Natal of Antient Free and Accepted Masons of Scotland, p. 51. David Murran Lyon writes that 'the success of the Associated Lodges [Seceding Lodges] was due in large part to their common resentment of the Grand Lodge ... There were ... common grounds upon which the Secessionists were united, viz., First, a resistance of the aggression upon their rights that was involved in Grand Lodge passing sentences of suspension and expulsion without affording to the Brethren implicated the opportunity of defending themselves in the way provided by its Constitution; second, the vindication of the right to meet as Freemasons, and as such to be recognised by law, independent of Grand Lodge, and in defiance of its alleged authority over them'. See D. M. Lyon, *History of the Lodge of Edinburgh (Mary's Chapel), No. 1, Embracing an Account of the Rise and Progress of Freemasonry in Scotland Mary's Chapel* (London: Gresham Publishing Company, 1900), p. 309.

41. *superinduced*: introduced or induced in addition; brought in or added over and above something (*OED*).

42. *actuated from party spirit*: By 1802, Scottish Freemasonry was also 'fragmenting and re-forming into contesting structures due largely to the politicization of the Grand Lodge'. See S. Murdoch, *Network North: Scottish Kin, Commercial and Covert Associations In Northern Europe 1603–1746* (Leiden: Brill Academic Publications, 2006), p. 332. Certainly, this fragmentation resulted in the emergence of a Whig faction, led by the former Master of St Luke's Lodge No. 44 in Edinburgh, William Inglis. Indeed, the Whig element was intimately connected to another Lodge, No. 44 St Luke's Lodge Holyrood House. According to Lindsay, the connection between No. 44 and the Grand Lodge cannot be understated. Between 1807 and 1860, 'the Whigs of St Luke exerted a preponderating influence there, for the reason that its senior members were the lead-

ers of the Whig party in Scotland'. See R. S. Lindasy, *A History of the Mason Lodge of Holyrood House (St Luke's No. 44)* (Edinburgh: T and A Constable, Ltd, 1935), p. 299. The presence of senior Whig leaders in each of these lodges suggests that although the 'government of the country might be denied to the Whigs, there were many bodies ... where they could get a footing' and 'rapidly acquire control'.

43. *St. Andrews day*: day of celebration on 30 November, in honour of St Andrew, the patron saint of Scotland.

44. *recollects the Prince of Wales's health ... heir-apparent*: reference to Prince of Wales, future George IV, who reigned from 1820 to 1830.

45. *Earl of Moira's health being drunk*: Whig leaders affiliated with the Grand Lodge. Francis Rawdon-Hastings, the Earl of Moira, joined the opposition in 1789 and became a close personal friend of the Prince of Wales. By 1805, he was the Acting Grand Master of both Scotland and England.

46. *nor does ... health was drunk*: Hon. William Ramsay Maule of Panmure, or Whig MP Maule, was known to be the 'ringleader of a group of wild young men addicted to gambling, heavy drinking, destructive horseplay and sexual licence'. After coming into possession of his great-uncle's estates in 1792, Maule became one of the richest men in Scotland. According to Thorne, 'he sustained this extravagant and dissipated lifestyle ... into which he probably fell the more readily in the absence of paternal discipline, to the end of his days, long after more decorous standards of behaviour had become the norm among his peers ... Maule, who joined the Whig Club in 1798, became an enthusiastic Foxite' and 'supported his Whig friends in power'. See R. G. Thorne (ed.), *House of Commons: History of the House of Parliament*, 5 vols (London: Haynes Publishing Company, 1986), vol. 4, pp. 571–2.

47. *resign the chair*: reference to the Master of a masonic lodge stepping down from his office.

48. *who had been ... in Ayrshire*: See headnote, p. 301.

49. res gesta: the facts of a case, especially spoken words admitted as evidence on the grounds that they relate to an action which is itself admissible (*OED*).

50. *turn him out*: to drive out or forth, to expel (*OED*).

51. *by the mallet*: an attempt to restore order to the lodge by the Master; the mallet is a symbolic masonic tool used to open and close lodge meetings.

52. *criminate*: to prove (a person) guilty of a crime; to incriminate (*OED*).

53. *sederunt*: in minutes of deliberative bodies, used (in its Latin sense) to introduce the list of persons present at a meeting (*OED*).

54. *Buonaparte*: Napoleon Bonaparte. French military and political leader who rose to prominence during the latter stages of the French Revolution; self-styled Emperor of France.

55. *I suppose ... among free masons*: See the preceding note.

56. *tyled Lodge*: to protect (a lodge or meeting) from interruption and intrusion, so as to keep its proceedings secret, by placing a tiler before the door (*OED*).

57. *That an humble address ... the Principles of the British Constitution*: See headnote, p. 229.

58. *Test Act*: various acts directed against Roman Catholics and Protestant Nonconformists, more especially the Act of 1673 passed during the reign of King Charles II, which required an oath of allegiance to the Crown and rejection of elements of the Catholic Church including doctrine of transubstantiation.

59. *Lord Howick*: Charles Grey, second Earl Grey, Whig politician and Prime Minister of Britain, 1830–4.

60. *while similar addresses ... In the kingdom*: Masonic loyalism was also conveyed through letter writing. In correspondence, especially to the government and the king, Freemasons expressed their sentiments about a variety of public issues and continually declared their intense support for the Crown. Style and tone were carefully chosen and crafted in such a way as to portray Freemasons as the most reliable supporters of church and state. Letters were even sent to the King congratulating him on the marriage of family members and anniversaries of his accession. Such letters were not exclusive to Freemasons. As Michael Fry notes, many organizations and public societies were 'urged to send in loyal addresses to George III. More than 400 immediately did so, and many continued to at every excuse'. See M. Fry, *The Dundas Despotism* (Edinburgh: John Donald, 2004), p. 168.

61. inter alia: amongst other things (*OED*).

62. *A good portly man ... name is Falstaff*. Spoken by Falstaff, in William Shakespeare's *Henry IV*, II.iv.421–6: 'A good portly man, i' faith, and a corpulent, / of a cheerful look, a pleasing eye, and a most noble / carriage, and as I think, his age some fifty, or, by'r / lady, inclining to threescore; and now I remember / me, his name is Falstaff.'

63. *Cerberus-like*: in Greek and Latin mythology the proper name of the watch-dog which guarded the entrance of the infernal regions, represented as having three heads (*OED*).

64. *Had/this portly ... to each head*: reference to Horace (Quintus Horatius Flaccus, Roman poet during the age of Augustus, who lived from 65 BC–8 BC) and possibly his allusions to Cerberus in *Odes III*.

65. *nipperclaws*: Grasping claw or pincer-like organ of a crustacean or other animal (*OED*).

66. vi et armis: violently, forcibly, by compulsion; specifically in law, causing direct damage to person or property (*OED*).

67. Scopulis ... creepat: a possible translation – 'something is moving through the cliffs, then the many-footed lobster creeps in the waters' (Latin).

68. '*Thus bad begins, but worse remains behind*': spoken by Hamlet, in William Shakespeare's *Hamlet*, III.iv.179: 'This bad begins and worse remains behind.'

69. quamprimum: forthwith; as soon as possible.

70. '*quiddits ... tricks*': variation on lines spoken by Hamlet in William Shakespeare's *Hamlet*, V.i.99–100: 'Where be his quiddities now, his/quillities, his cases, his tenures, his tricks'? Quiddity: A subtlety or nicety in argument; a quibble. In later use also: a witticism; a quip (*OED*); Quillity: quibble; also, Scots for penis (*OED*).

[Anon.], *An Exposition of the Causes Which Have Produced the Late Dissensions Among the Free Masons of Scotland* (1808)

1. *WHEN we consider the origin of Free-Masonry*: Masonic histories are frequently useful not because of their accuracy, but because of their interest. In 1723 (reprinted in 1738), Scottish minister James Anderson published the *Constitutions of the Freemasons*. This volume attempts to synthesize known masonic manuscripts and fragmentary histories to create a wide-ranging, entertaining yet mythologized account of the origins and development of Freemasonry. More recent endeavours, however, have been made to dispel such extraordinary historical narratives. Frances Yates asserts that the 'origin of Freemasonry is one of the most debated, and debatable, subjects in the whole realm of historical inquiry. One has to distinguish between the legendary history of Freemasonry and the problem of when it actually began as an organized institution'.

F. Yates', *The Rosicrucian Enlightenment* (London: Routledge & Kegan Paul, 1972), p. 266. The abundance of unsubstantiated material is problematic, leading historian David Stevenson to lament the 'historical ghetto' into which Freemasonry 'has all too often been consigned by the narrow historical outlook of many masons combined with the unreasoning prejudice of professional historians'. D. Stevenson, *The Origins of Free-masonry: Scotland's Century 1590–1710* (Cambridge: Cambridge University Press, 1988), p. 3. Margaret Jacob raises interesting questions about the origins of the society and how it changed and evolved after its transportation from Britain to Europe. According to Jacob, the richness of these records and minutes 'has led the historian who has worked most extensively with them, David Stevenson, to argue that the Freemasonry bequeathed to the eighteenth century was a Scottish invention'. M. Jacob, *Living the Enlightenment: Freemasonry and Politics in Eighteenth-Century Europe* (Oxford: Oxford University Press, 1991), pp. 35–8.

2. *compelled them to flee ... violence and oppression*: reference to the Associated Lodges, those lodges which seceded from the Grand Lodge of Scotland. In this instance, the 'former sanctuary' is the Grand Lodge of Scotland.

3. *It has been ... in this country*: Such claims were based on the argument that the resignation of William St Clair of Roslin in 1736 as the hereditary Grand Master effectively empowered the Grand Lodge of Scotland to assume complete and full control of all masonic matters. As the patron and overseer of Scottish Freemasonry Roslin, upon resigning as Grand Master, gave all power and authority to the central governing body; therefore, no other lodge in Scotland could legally – according to the Grand Lodge – grant charters.

4. *Grand Lodge of Scotland possessed ... Members of the Craft*: The organization and development of the Scottish Grand Lodge were both modelled after the Grand Lodge of England. In theory, the four lodges that gathered in Edinburgh in 1736 – Mary's Chapel, Canongate Kilwinning, Kilwinning Scots Arms, and Leith Kilwinning – as no doubt did the founding lodges in England – viewed the new Grand Lodge as a conduit for the gradual development and progression of speculative Freemasonry. In practice, however, the specific motivations behind the creation of the Scottish Grand Lodge differed from its English predecessor. Ostensibly, the main contributing factor to the amalgamation of Scottish lodges into a national system of masonic governance was envy over the success of the Grand Lodge of England. However, as Lisa Kahler explains in her article 'The Grand Lodge of Scotland and the Establishment of the Masonic Community', in W. Weisberger (ed.), *Freemasonry on Both Sides of the Atlantic* (New York: Eastern European Monographs, 2002), p. 94, 'it is likely that the introduction of some type of governing board would have been distasteful to the existing lodges, particularly the older, primarily operative lodges'.

5. *in former times ... eminence of their party*: See p. 414, n. 42. Lindsay, *Holyrood House*, pp. 269–70; p. 299.

6. *Constitution of Freemasonry*: Born in Aberdeen in 1679 and educated at Marischal College, Anderson graduated MA in 1698 and subsequently studied theology for four years, suggesting that he was preparing himself for a career in the Presbyterian ministry. David Stevenson, 'James Anderson (1679–1739): Man and Mason', in W. Weisberger (ed.), *Freemasonry on Both Sides of the Atlantic* (New York: Eastern European Monographs, 2002), pp. 199–205. The basic purposes of the *Constitutions* were twofold: to establish a historical account of Freemasonry largely based on the Old Testament of the Bible and to reconstruct an elite masonic lineage. Anderson's work was not only an 'opportune piece of invented tradition from the point of country ideology; it also

bespoke a desire not to move too far away from the Christian past', J. Money, 'Free-masonry and the Fabric of Loyalism in Hanoverian England', in E. Hellmuth (ed.), *The Transformation of Political Culture: England and Germany in the Late Eighteenth Century* (Oxford: Oxford University Press, 1990), pp. 235–69, p. 258. In effect, his im-agination had conjured up an ingenious instance of masonic propaganda which fused constitutional and religious history. Seen in an eighteenth-century masonic context, however, its implications are much clearer. Stevenson reasons that the numerous in-vented passages and false historical claims comprising Anderson's *Constitutions* were intended to convey the impression that Freemasonry offered 'an escape from competi-tive pressures and rivalries into brotherhood, with the legitimacy of having been highly respected from ancient times', Stevenson, 'James Anderson', pp. 219–20.

7. *From authentic documents ... in the World*: See p. 416, n.1.

8. *admission was freely ... meetings of the craft*: Peter Clark writes that the underlying themes of masonic literature were 'improvement and enlightenment, with a stress on merit as the measure of men, education, and the joys of fraternal association; in sum a utopian world detached from political, religious or ascribed social status', P. Clark, *British Clubs and Societies 1580–1800: The Origins of an Associational World* (Oxford: Oxford University Press, 2000), pp. 335–6.

9. *At the building ... erecting a Grand Lodge*: In 1737, The Grand Lodge of Scotland Lodge resolved that 'all the Lodges ... should be enrolled according to their seniority, which should be determined from the authentic documents they produced, and in ac-cordance with this principle', Gould, *Concise History*, p. 276. The questioning of the initial numbering further suggests an imbalance of power and the inability of the core group to enforce judgments and rulings. Ultimately, Mary's Chapel – having produced minutes extant from 1599 – was designated as the oldest lodge in Scotland and Lodge Kilwinning, having supplied records from 1643, was relegated to number two.

10. *ancient family of Roslin ... English throne*: See p. 416, n. 3.

11. operative capacity: A distinction is made between *operative* – or practicing – Freema-sons, and *speculative* Freemasons, those who are not tradesmen and observe symbolic ritual based upon operative practices and customs.

12. *convivial meetings*: Scottish Lodges are often depicted as social clubs epitomized by their conviviality and the incorporation of arcane rituals and ceremonies into lodge meetings. Moreover, minutes detailing lodge banquets, processions, drinking, music, and songs which appear more toward the middle- to late-eighteenth century. Underu-tilized as historical sources, minutes and records from masonic lodges throughout the eighteenth century provide frequent and sometimes candid allusions to the geniality and gaiety of their meetings.

13. *purpose of issuing charters*: For the Grand Lodge of Scotland, the revocation of its charter-granting privileges was perhaps the most important consequence of the Secret Societies Act. Issuing charters was a tangible method of illustrating the popularity of the organization; and symbolically, the ability to grant charters was one of the great powers of Scottish Freemasonry. Taking away such authority thus effectively prevented masonic growth and development. Moreover, all lodges in Scotland – including the Grand Lodge – now possessed the same fundamental abilities.

14. *The lodges then abounding ... rank in society*: Along with its diversity of activities, a key contributing factor to Freemasonry's success was its occupational diversity. Not lim-ited to stonemasons, lodges were composed of men from many different backgrounds, attracting its rank and file from the upper, middle, and occasionally lower classes.

Occupations include: shoemakers, smiths(one who works in iron or other metals), slaters (one who lays slates), shipmasters, sailors, baxters (baker), vintner (wine merchant), writers, clerks, and landed gentry (*OED*).

15. *to determine the precedency of* each: See headnote, p. 301.

16. *behoved*: to have use for or need of (*OED*).

17. who created them ... they shall know: taken from John Milton's *Paradise Lost*, 5.894–5.

18. *the* ancient *Grand Lodge of England ... of that name*: English Freemasonry also was not totally impervious to high profile conflicts and disputes. During the end of the eighteenth century, when the government passed the Unlawful Oaths and Secret Societies Acts and Scottish Freemasons began wrangling over charter-granting privileges, English Freemasons were in the process of restoring order and organization to the fraternity. In 1751, the Grand Lodge of England split into two Grand Lodges – the Moderns Grand Lodge of England and the Antients Grand Lodge of England. Margaret Jacob describes the conflict as the 'taking over of the old masonry of the operatives by gentlemen, and even nobles...By 1751 it appears that some lodges had become battlegrounds where the meaning of equality, as well as the claim to possess the true, ancient constitution, was being adjudicated...In general, the impulse of the ancients was decidedly reformist. Once freed from the discipline of the Grand Lodge, ancient lodges also experimented in new rituals and degrees. To add an air of respectability to these innovations, they were described as "Scottish", Jacob, *Living the Enlightenment*, pp. 60–1. According to the Antients, the Moderns had drifted away from the *Constitutions* of the Freemasons and effectively created a speculative mason. Imbued with power that steadily grew throughout the eighteenth century, the Moderns Grand Lodge – just as the Grand Lodge of Scotland would do almost fifty years later – alienated many lodges, thus causing the Grand Lodge of England to split. Ironically, the legislation passed by parliament prompted the two rival lodges to reconcile their differences.

19. *provincial Grand Masters*: By 1740, the Grand Lodge of Scotland recognized that the geographic distribution of old-established lodges and the inevitable establishment of new lodges required more than just a central governing body in Edinburgh. To properly collect dues and subscription fees, monitor masonic activities, ensure proper operation of lodges, and maintain communication and correspondence among its constituents, the Grand Lodge created several Provincial Districts across Scotland.

20. *neighbouring country*: most likely France with an allusion to the French Revolution although Ireland and Germany cannot be ruled out.

21. *it was in societies ... lodges at home*: In 1797, amid claims of Jacobin lodges in France and seditious and treasonable activities among German Freemasons, John Robison – eminent mechanical philosopher and professor of natural philosophy at the University of Edinburgh – published *Proofs of a Conspiracy Against All the Religions and Governments of Europe, Carried on in the Secret Meetings of the Freemasons, Illuminati, and Reading Societies, Collected from Good Authorities* (Edinburgh: Printed for William Creech; and T. Cadell, junior, and W. Davies, 1797). Convinced that all of Britain stood on the brink of revolution based on the French model, Robison claimed that secret societies throughout Europe were conspiring to overturn governments and inspire social upheaval. See also headnote of *A Defence of Free Masons etc., in answer to Professor John Robison's Proofs of a Conspiracy*, pp. 195–200.

22. *irregular lodges*: or, Black Masonry. As Gould notes, 'it was to their intercourse with Brethren belonging to regiments serving in Ireland towards the end of the last century, that Scotch Lodges owed their acquaintance with Knight Templarism. This order, then

known as Black Masonry, was propagated, to a large extent, through Charters issued by the High Knights Templar of Ireland, Kilwinning – a body of Freemasons in Dublin, who were constituted by Mother Kilwinning [in Scotland] in 1779, for the practice of the Craft Degrees', R. F. Gould, *Gould's History of Freemasonry Throughout the World*, 6 vols (New York: C. Scribner Son's, 1936), vol. 2, pp. 291–2.

23.   '*and in the language of ... parliament of masons*': satirical representation of lines spoken by Jack Cade in William Shakespeare, *2 Henry VI*, IV.vii.13–15: 'I have thought upon it, it shall be so. Away, / burn all the records of the realm: my mouth shall be/the parliament of England'.

24.   Mr. Inglis: See p. 412, n. 9.

25.   *That the address ... be disputed*: See headnote, p. 229.

26.   *present beloved Sovereign*: reference to King George III, King of Britain 1760–1820. He became heir to the throne in 1751, and in 1760 became the third Hanoverian monarch. Although unfit to rule during his final decade – the future George IV ruled as Prince Regent – George III essentially reigned for sixty years, eclipsed only by Queen Victoria and Queen Elizabeth II.

27.   *In times of National emergency ... patriotic sentiments*: This ideological belief and trust in both the King and constitution played a vital role in establishing a political basis for lodges and contributed to a general standardization of laws and regulations. Lodge constitutions, texts, and rituals were all heavily influenced by 'proto-parliamentary themes' such as electing officers by vote, discussing lodge business and issues in debates, imposing fines and penalties on members who violated rules, and keeping detailed minutes of all lodge transactions'. See J. V. H. Melton, *The Rise of the Public In Enlightenment Europe* (Cambridge: Cambridge University Press, 2001), pp. 265–6.

28.   '*Though written in the institute ... all other considerations*': James Anderson's *Constitutions* of 1723 stated that Freemasons should be 'resolv'd against all Politicks, as what never yet conduc'd to the Welfare of the *Lodge*, nor ever will ... no private Piques or Quarrels must be brought within the Door of the *Lodge*, far less Quarrels about *Religion*, or *Nations*, or *State Policy*'. See J. Anderson, *The Constitutions of the Freemasons, Facsimile Edition* (London: Quatuor Coranati Lodge, 1976), p. 54. Lending itself to a more congenial and open-minded atmosphere in which members could meet, Freemasonry's 'prohibition of overt political discussion and its espousal of natural religion and rational tolerance among good men of all persuasions made it an ideal vehicle for diffusing the non-partisan patriotism of Country ideology among the emerging professional and entrepreneurial elements of provincial society'. See Money, 'Freemasonry and the Fabric of Loyalism in Hanoverian England', p. 257.

29.   *The victories of Duncan / and Nelson*: allusions to the Battle of Camperdown, Admiral Adam Duncan's victory over a Dutch fleet on 11 October 1797 during the French Revolution; and (most likely) Admiral Horatio Nelson's defeat of the French fleet at the Battle of the Nile, 1 August 1798.

30.   *But it will be said ... introduction of* Popery: allusions to the French Revolutionary War.

31.   *Test Act*: See p. 415, n. 58.

32.   *expatiated in glowing panegyric ... Lord Howick*: See p. 415, n. 59.

33.   *A long discussion ... 'Not Address'*. See headnote, p. 229.

34.   *arrears*: outstanding liabilities, amounts, or balances; moneys due; debts (*OED*).

35.   *Scrutiny*: See p. 412, n. 18.

36.   *slipt*: misspelling of 'slipped'.

37.   *leaving the lodge unclosed*: in masonic terms, not formally adjourning the stated meeting through proper ceremony and ritual.

38.   *expicated*: to 'fish out'; hence, to find out by scrutiny (*OED*).

39. *would have spurned ... could suspect him*: On 6 June 1807, a letter was read before a Grand Lodge of Edinburgh meeting, the tenor of which addressed the conflict surrounding the proposed address to the King. 'R. Worshipful Sirs, Though I have great doubts of my right to call such a meeting as you require which I rather think is vested in the Grand Master alone and though I continue decidedly of my former opinion that the demand of a Scrutiny is unconstitutional, conceiving that the Grand Clerk as the legal sworn officer of the Craft is the person who is regularly intitled to declare the state of any vote in the Grand Lodge being of course held from his official situation as beyond all suspicion of partiality. Yet notwithstanding the doubt I entertain and the opinion I have expressed the respect which I bear to the subscribers of the letter which I have had the honor of receiving of 3rd induces me to comply with your request of convening the Grand Lodge for submitting the requisition ... To their consideration and in this view I have fixed Friday the 19th for this special purpose. The above letters having been read the Substitute Grand Master stated that in consequence thereof he had called this meeting and having in his letter above quoted stated his opinion on the subject he left it to the Brethren to determine whether a Scrutiny should or should not be granted. Br. Mitchell and others insisted that they were intitled to have a Scrutiny. On the other hand it was contended that a Scrutiny could not now be demanded as they had not at the time taken the proper and regular method to intitle them to such scrutiny. But in order to save time and much altercation Br. James Gibson proposed and it was agreed to that the Sense of the meeting should be taken whether there should be a Scrutiny or not leaving all objections to the legality of the votes to be discussed afterwards. It was then proposed that two Brethren should be named to take down the votes when Br. Cunningham of Mays Chapel [was] appointed for that purpose. The names of the Brethren called over and the question put "Scrutiny" or "No Scrutiny." Br. Cunningham and Br. Thomson declared that there were "95 voted no Scrutiny" and "47 voted Scrutiny" making a majority of 48 against the Scrutiny. Whereupon Br. Brown sated that seeing the sense of the meeting so completely against the Scrutiny he for himself would not agitate the question further. Br. James Gibson then moved the thanks of the Grand Lodge to William Inglis Esq. Substitute Grand Master for his so readily agreeing to call this meeting and likewise for the handsome manner in which he had conducted himself in the Chair throughout this business. This motion having been seconded was unanimously agreed to and the Substitute Grand Master closed the Lodge in proper form', Manuscripts, GL of S, 6 June 1807.

40. *cloven foot:* the divided hoof of ruminant quadrupeds, consisting of the third and fourth phalanges of the typical mammalian foot; ascribed in pagan mythology to the god Pan, and thence in Christian mythology to the Devil, and often used allusively as the indication of Satan, Satanic agency, or temptation (*OED*).

41. *This being atchieved ... only*: See p. 410, n. 1.

42. *Luckily it occurred ...* another day: See p. 411, n. 4.

43. *writer to the signet*: originally, a clerk in the Secretary of State's office, who prepared writs to pass the royal signet; in later use, one of an ancient society of law-agents who conduct cases before the Court of session, and have the exclusive privilege of preparing crown writs, charters, precepts, etc (*OED*),

44. *preses*: the president or chair of a meeting (*OED*).

45. *Depones:* to state or declare upon oath (*OED*).

46. sine die: without any day being specified; indefinitely (*OED*).

47. *Depute:* to appoint, assign, ordain (a person or thing) to or for a particular office, purpose, or function (*OED*).

48. ne plus ultra: 'the perfect or most extreme example of its kind; the ultimate'.

49. *When we behold ... state of blockade*: most likely a reference to Napoleon I and the French naval blockade of Europe, or the Continental Blockade.

50. 'Necessity, the tyrant's plea': from John Milton's *Paradise Lost*, IV.393–4: 'So spake the fiend, and with necessity, / The tyrant's plea, / excused his devilish deeds'.

51. tyler: The doorkeeper who keeps the uninitiated from intruding upon the secrecy of the lodge or meeting (*OED*).

52. *Great Mogul*: largest diamond discovered in India, unearthed in 1750 in the Golconda Mines.

53. nugatory: having little intrinsic value or worth (*OED*).

54. *It originated in consequence ... 'Mother Kilwinning'*: See headnote, p. 301.

55. *mother lodge:* the lodge into which a Freemason is initiated, henceforth called the mason's mother lodde.

56. '*Thou canst ... mammon*': biblical reference, Matthew 6:24: 'No man can serve two masters: for either he will hate the one, and love the other; or else he will hold to the one, and despise the other. You cannot serve God and mammon'.

57. *ASSOCIATED LODGES ... utmost vengeance*: On 13 June 1808, the Grand Lodge of Scotland expelled all Freemasons involved or associated in any manner with Dr. Mitchell. As a result, these masons – who were led by No. 1 Mary's Chapel – officially seceded from the Grand Lodge and formed the Associated Lodges Seceding from the Present Grand Lodge of Scotland. In a politically charged address on 14 February 1809, the Grand Secretary of the Associated Lodges addressed the lodges, stating that 'It has fallen to our lot to live in eventful times – times as eventful in the annals of Masonry, as they are in the history of Modern Europe. We have lived to see a despotism newly akin to the system of a neighbouring Tyrant, attempted to be established among the British Masons. But we have resisted the odious usurpation with a Spirit the Masons of future ages will commemorate...They sought to enslave us, by debarring individual Masons from the privilege of going where they pleased...We spurned the ignoble bondage... [and] most just, my friends, is the punishment which has overtaken the destroyers of the order', Manuscripts, No. 1 Mary's Chapel, 14 February 1809.

58. 'Quod nec jovis...vetustas': '...that neither the wrath of Jove, nor fire, nor sword, nor the consuming tooth of time, shall be able to destroy. The End', Ovid's *Metamorphoses*, XV.871–9.

59. *glorious revolution of 1688*: social and political uprising which ultimately resulted with the overthrow of King James II, and the establishment of William and Mary as joint British monarchs.

[Anon.] *An Enquiry into the Late Disputes among the Free-Masons of Ireland; Wherein is Detailed a Free and Important Account of the Different Transactions which Gave Rise to, and Continued the Controversy, from the Commencement to the Establishment of the Grand Lodge of Ulster* (1812)

1. *Alfred had his education here: as he, according to Bede, imbibed in Ireland*: This is a false statement. Venerable Bede died in AD 735, 114 years before the birth of Alfred the Great in AD 849, so he could not have written about Alfred.

2. *In a letter written to Charles the Bald ... deeply studied in Ireland at this early period*: Michael Furnell, Provincial Grand Master of Munster, as editor of the 1858 edition of

Ahiman Rezon, used these paragraphs containing the historical error mentioned in the previous note in the chapter 'Remarkable Occurrences in Masonry' (p. 182). See W. Barlow, 'A Curious Historical Error', *AQC*, 9 (1896), pp. 153–6 and W. J. C. Crawley, 'Notes on Dr. Barlow's Paper, "A Curious Historical Error"', *AQC*, 10 (1897), pp. 58–9.

3. *James King:* James King, the fourth Lord Kingston (1693–1761), was Grand Master of the Grand Lodge of England in 1729. He served as Grand Master of the Grand Lodge of Ireland in 1731 and 1735. *Schism*, pp. 13, 196.

4. Edward Lovet Pearce: Sir Edward Lovett Pearce (*c.*1699–1733), architect and surveyor general, 1731–3. His niece was the second wife of Richard Parsons, the Grand Master of Ireland in 1725 and 1730. See *GLFI*, pp. 130–2.

5. *Lord Carteret:* John Carteret, second Earl Granville (1690–1763), an English states-man. Because of his vital opposition to Sir Robert Walpole in 1724 he was sent away from London to serve as lord lieutenant of Ireland, from where he returned in 1730 and continued to criticize Walpole's government (*EB*).

6. *hedge, or Bush Masons:* these hedge lodges did not have warrants from the Grand Lodge.

7. *From the original constitution of the Grand Lodge ... the Grand Secretary's deputy:* See *The Constitutions of the Free Masons, Containing the History, Charges, Regulations, &c. of that Most Ancient and Right Worshipful Fraternity, for the Use of the lodges* (Dublin: Printed by J. Watts, at the Lord Carteret's Head in Dames-Street, for J. Pennell, at the three Blue Bonnets in St. Patrick-Street, 1730), pp. 58–9.

8. *much respected Brother:* must refer to Thomas Corker (d. 1801), a Dublin surgeon, who left his profession to become the deputy grand secretary of Ireland between 1768 and 1801. Renowned for his loyal services to the Lodge, he was the only grand officer to survive Lord Donoughmore's election as Grand Master in 1789. See Mirala, p. 228, and *GLFI*, pp. 198–201.

9. *the Grand Treasurer:* John Boardman, Dublin barrister. He served as Grand Treasurer between 1791 and 1814. In February, 1801 Alexander Seton, barrister, was appointed by Grand Secretary Major Gorges D'Arcy Irvine as deputy Grand Secretary (1801–5). Seton was not supported by Boardman, whose candidate was William Semple, who had been working on the accounts left by Corker. 'Seton, as the Treasurer's Deputy had played a considerable part in the recovery of arrears of dues from lodges, and, in recognition of his services, his salary as Deputy Grand Secretary was increased to £300 p.a.' 'Minute Books of the Grand Lodge of Ireland', p. 50, *IMR*. See Mirala, pp. 259–60, and *GLFI*, pp. 322–5.

10. *This appointment of Deputy Grand Treasurer ... Deputy Grand Secretary was fully com-petent to the discharge of the duties of the office:* According to the records of the Grand Lodge of Ireland of 24 June 1801, 'To avoid the difficulties in which the funds and other important concerns of the Order have hitherto been involved, the offices of D. G. Tr. and D. G. Sec. are from henceforth to be separate and distinct. It must afford satisfaction to the Brethren in General to be informed that our worthy Bro. William Semple is appointed, by the G. Tr., Assistant and Deputy to him in that arduous situa-tion; and pursuant to the 28th Section of the Regulations of 1768' in 'Transactions and References up to 6 June, 1806', p. 6, *IMR*. Semple, as deputy Grand Treasurer, received a fixed salary.

11. *In a publication bearing date the December 12, 1805:* This printed circular of the emer-gency meeting of the Grand Lodge of Ireland, discussing Thomas Corker and resolu-tions regarding the Royal Arch & Knight Templars Encampments, was printed by C.

Downes and available in volumes 24 and 6 (pp. 112–24) of *CMN* in the Library of Freemasons' Hall in Dublin.

12. *On the 19th of August, 1802, at an emergency meeting, the Grand Lodge:* The draft minutes of the meeting is in volume 40 of *CMN*.

13. *Female Orphan School:* The school came under the protection of the Grand Lodge of Ireland in January 1798. John Boardman, Grand Treasurer, was a supporter of the school. W. J. C. Crawley, 'The Craft and its Orphans in the 18th Century', *AQC*, 23 (1910), pp. 167–86.

14. *Blue Masons would have been taxed for Red and Black Masons:* Blue Masons were members of the Craft – that is, the first three degrees of Freemasonry. Red Masons refer to those who were 'exalted' in the Royal Arch degree, sometimes termed as the fourth degree. The term Black Masons signifies the Knight Templar.

15. *the Right Worshipful the Grand Master:* Richard Hely-Hutchinson, first Earl of Donoughmore, (1756–1825).

16. *On the 24th May, 1806, a meeting of the representatives of 50 Lodges:* The printed circular is available in volume 24 of the *CMN*.

17. *they proposed to send delegates to represent them in the Grand Lodge:* The transactions of the Grand Lodge of Ireland (5 June 1806) is reproduced in 'The Two Grand Lodges Meeting in Dublin', pp. 1–3, *IMR*.

18. *the former Grand Secretary:* Major Gorges D'Arcy Irvine. See p. 423, n. 9.

19. *the Grand Treasurer:* John Boardman. See p. 423, n. 9.

20. *Deputy Grand Treasurer:* William Francis Graham. He served as Deputy Grand Treasurer between 1803 and 1807 and Deputy Grand Secretary from 1808 to 1826. *GLFI*, p. 439.

21. *the Deputy Grand Master:* The position was filled at the time by Alexander Jaffray Jr, a well-known merchant and a governor of the Bank of Ireland. He was Junior Grand Warden from 1799 to 1800, and Deputy Grand Master from 1801 to 1806. See Mirala, pp. 261–3, and *GLFI*, p. 437.

22. *'that the Grand Lodge ... a majority of the Brethren present':* quoted in 'The Minutes of the Grand Lodge of Ireland', p. 45, *IMR*.

23. *the Grand Master:* Lord Donoughmore, who was absent from these events. Mirala, p. 262.

24. *appointing two respectable Brethren to the chair ... the senior and junior Grand Wardens:* The Rev. Francis Burrowes, Worshipful Master of Lodge No. 662, and William Bateman, Esq. Worshipful Master of Lodge No. 702, took the chair. John Quinton, Senior Warden of Lodge no. 17, acted as Senior Grand Warden and Hugh Duignan, Worshipful Master of Lodge No. 862, as Junior Grand Warden for the night.

25. *Appointing two respectable brethren to these offices:* Gorges D'Arcy Irvine as Grand Secretary and Peter Digges Latouche as Grand Treasurer. Mirala, p. 262, and *GLFI*, pp. 354–5.

26. *The future meeting of the Grand Lodge being adjourned till the 3d July following:* for the proceedings of the meeting see Appendix II in 'While at Dungannon', pp. 43–5, *IMR*.

27. *a second one was ordered to be drawn up and forwarded in December following:* See Appendix III in 'While at Dungannon', pp. 45–6, *IMR*.

28. *his Lordship, on 26th March, 1808, sent circular letters to the Lodges:* It can be found in *CMN*, vol. 24, pp. 236–7.

29. a person appointed a secretary: John Cuthbert, Esq., of the Grand Master's Lodge, acted as secretary for the day. Hughan reproduces the report of the meeting taking

place on 7 April 1808. W. J. Hughan, 'Freemasonry in Ireland', *The Freemason* (1 April 1871), p. 196.

30. *committing the office of Deputy Grand Master to a person:* Abraham Hely-Hutchinson, the brother of the Grand Master. See the previous note.

31. *On the 5th May following, the Grand Lodge met:* The minutes of the meeting is reproduced in 'Extracts from the Minutes and Records of the Grand Lodge of Ireland which are of a general nature together with information from other sources as indicated', pp. 68–71, *IMR*.

32. *the Grand Master, senior and junior Grand Wardens were appointed:* the Earl of Donoughmore was unanimously elected as Grand Master for the ensuing year, as were Lord Hutchinson and the Earl of Belmore, as Senior and Junior Wardens.

33. *Grand Treasurer:* John Boardman.

34. *Grand Master of Ulster:* William Irvine, the provincial Deputy Grand Master, was addressed as Grand Master of Ulster.

35. *delegates from 311 Lodges attended:* The account of the meeting from a printed leaflet in the Archives of the Grand Lodge can be found in 'Extracts from the Minutes and Records of the Grand Lodge of Ireland', pp. 71–2, *IMR*.

36. *their Grand Officers:* William Irvine, Grand Master; John B. O'Neill, Senior Grand Warden, Earl of Gosford, Junior Grand Warden; Gorges D'Arcy Irvine, Esq., Grand Secretary; William Brownlow, Esq., Grand Treasurer.

37. *the man ... as Treasurer:* John Boardman.

38 *By an account published in December, 1809*: This must refer to A. Seton's financial account of 6 December 1809, which is reproduced in *CMN*, vol. 5, pp. 370–1.

39. *17 brethren, soldiers and sailors, confined as prisoners of war in Vallenciennes*: Gould might refer to these Freemasons where he notes that 'A battalion of the 9th Foot was wrecked on the French coast in 1805, and the members of the Lodge (183) solaced the weary hours of their captivity by assembling regularly at Valenciennes until the peace of 1814.' R. F. Gould, *Gould's History of Freemasonry Throughout the World, revised by Dudley Wright*, 6 vols (New York: C. Scribner's Son, 1936), vol. 4, p. 255. During the captivity the lodge met regularly.

40. *the Grand Treasurer ... those poor distress'd brethren:* We can read the following in a footnote of a printed circular signed by 'A. Seton, D. G. S. U.' in June, 1811: 'Grand Lodge Nov. the 7th, 1805. – "A Memorial was read from 17 Brethren, Soldiers and Sailors, prisoners of War in Vallenciennes praying relief" – The G.T. John Boardman moved that they should be sent "£5 as the Charity Funds were low." – He had then £500 in Government Debentures belonging to that Fund in his possession. – The Grant was increased to 17 Guineas. – God knows a paltry sum for 17 brave and loyal fellows, lying in the enemies Dungeons. – In 5 minutes after, the same J. Boardman exerted successfully his eloquence and his interest, and procure "50 Guineas to be vested in a secret Committee to hunt after some anonymous writer" who had pressed hard upon his corns – The money perhaps was not spent – The act is not the less disgraceful because the culprit is caught in the fact and forced to relinquish the Booty', *IMR*.

41. *law-suits*: The Grand Lodge took Seton to court. The legal battle lasted at least until 1823. Mirala, pp. 258, 266. *GLFI*, pp. 355–60, 364, 377.

42. *the Grand Lodge being composed of the Masters and Wardens of the subordinate Lodges:* See *The Constitutions of the Free Masons, Containing the History, Charges, Regulations, &c. of that Most Ancient and Right Worshipful Fraternity, For the Use of the Lodges*

(Dublin: Printed by J. Watts, at the Lord Carteret's Head in Dames-Street, for J. Pennell, at the three Blue Bonnets in St. Patrick-Street, 1730), p. 58 (General Regulation 12).

43. *as is said in old constitutions, so long as they preserve the ancient Landmarks: The Constitutions of the Free Masons, Containing the History, Charges, Regulations, &c. of that Most Ancient and Right Worshipful Fraternity, For the Use of the Lodges* (Dublin: Printed by J. Watts, at the Lord Carteret's Head in Dames-Street, for J. Pennell, at the three Blue Bonnets in St. Patrick-Street, 1730), p. 70 (General Regulation 39).

44. *In the days of Queen Elizabeth ... Grand Master of the south division:* There is no historical evidence for this statement.

45. *And in 1719, when the Masons of London erected themselves into a Grand Lodge:* According to James Anderson, the founding of the Grand Lodge of London and Westminster by four lodges took place in 1717. *Constitutions* 1738, p. 109. The author of this pamphlet heavily relies on Anderson's account in the legendary history of Freemasonry (pp. 35–6 in the original). Hence, the year 1719 must be a typographical error. Jan Snoek argues that 'the traditional founding date of 1717 is a purely artificial one for the commencement of Freemasonry, and that it is impossible to say when Freemasonry as we know it was founded. 1717 is merely the legendary date, claimed for the founding of the Premier Grand Lodge by four existing lodges in London.' J. A. M. Snoek and H. Bogdan, 'The History of Freemasonry: an Overview' in *Handbook*, p. 3.

46. *but did not apply to the Grand Lodge at York for any warrant to erect or constitute a Grand Lodge: For the* history of the Grand Lodge of York, which also styled itself as the 'Grand Lodge of all England' after 1726, see N. B. Cryer, *York Mysteries Revealed (Understanding an Old English Masonic Tradition)* (Hersham: Neville Barker Cryer, 2006), pp. 219–84.

47. *In 1730, the Masons of Ireland constituted a Grand Lodge:* The Grand Lodge of Ireland already existed in 1725. *Dublin Weekly Journal* (26 June 1725), reprinted in volume 5, provides 'the first credible reference to organized freemasonry in Ireland'. Mirala, p. 55. The Grand Lodge of Ireland must have been constituted in 1723-1724. J. A. M. Snoek and H. Bogdan, 'The History of Freemasonry: an Overview' in *Handbook*, p. 18.

48. Lord Viscount Kingston: See p. 423, n. 3.

49. *In the year 1779, the Lodge of Antiquity in London, had some difference with the Grand Lodge of England:* See the headnote of W. Preston's *State of Facts* in volume 1, pp. 241–4.

50. *all these foreign Lodges ... constitutions, charges, [regulations,] &c. [for substance,] with their Brethren of England: Constitutions* 1738, p. 196. The author omitted the words placed in square brackets from the original. The capitalization also slightly differs from the original.

51. *Union Lodge, 684*: The warrant of this lodge was issued on in Belfast on 17 April 1788. For some records of this lodge see the 'Warrants' folder of the *IMR CD*.

52. *Deputy Treasurer was never appointed till 1810*: This must be a typo. The position was created in 1801. See p. 423, n. 10.

53. *the deceased Deputy Secretary*: Thomas Corker. See p. 423, n. 8.

SILENT CORRECTIONS

i.	*Rebllious*] *Rebellious*
ii.	eudeavour] endeavour
iii.	trival] trivial
iv.	*Tarwinter*] *Farwinter.*
v.	to to] to
vi.	*Montigu*] *Montagu*
vii.	*Stratmore*] *Strathmore*
viii.	*Barnwal*] *Barnewall*
ix.	*Kinsland*] *Kingsland*
x.	*Baresford*] *Beresford*
xi.	*Southwel*] *Southwell*
xii.	*Wivil*] *Wywill*
xiii.	*Makenzie*] *Mackenzie*
xiv.	unlimitted] unlimited
xv.	a a] a
xvi.	*indue*] *imbue*
xvii.	SACCKVILE'S] SACKVILLE'S
xviii.	harlots, lots] harlots,
xix.	themselve] themselves
xx.	*the the*] *the*
xxi.	as in the estimation of the world, has been reckon'd great, / as, in the estimation of the world, have been reckoned great] as in the estimation of the world, has been reckon'd great,
xxii.	ROBINSON'S] ROBISON'S
xxiii.	Robinson] Robison,
xxiv.	Robinson] Robison
xxv.	*desarts*] *deserts*
xxvi.	past] passed
xxvii.	Priestwick] Prestwick
xxviii.	Davi d] David
xxix.	folowing] following
xxx.	decidedy] decidedly
xxxi.	Airshire] Ayrshire
xxxii.	gripes] grips
xxxiii.	farewel] farewell
xxxiv.	fraernity] fraternity
xxxv.	recal] recall

xxxvi.	harras] harrass
xxxvii.	*assurnce] assurance*
xxxviii.	blessseings] blessings
xxxix.	Irelend] Ireland
xl.	Welch] Welsh
xli.	epitnets] epithets

LIST OF SOURCES

Text	Source
Anon. [signed Philo Lapidarius], *An Answer to the Pope's Bull, with the Character of a Freemason* (1738)	Library and Museum of Freemasonry, London [hereafter LMFL], A 798 PHI fol. / IL17712
Bernard Clarke, *An Answer to the Pope's Bull, with a Vindication of the Real Principles of Free-Masonry* (1751)	LMFL, A 798 CLA / L14235
William Imbrie and William Geddes, *The Poor Man's Complaint against the Whole Unwarrantable Procedure of the Associate Session in Glasgow, Anent him and Others in Seeking a Confession of the Mason and Chapman Oaths* (1754)	Edinburgh New College Library, Special Collections, A.c.4.4/2.
James Steven, *Blind Zeal Detected: or, A True Representation of the Conduct of the Meeting I was a Member of, and of the Kirk-Session of the Associate Congregation, at Glasgow* (1755)	Edinburgh New College Library, Special Collections, A.c.4.4/3.
[Associate Synod], 'An Act of the Associate Synod Concerning the Mason-Oath' and A, R, 'An Impartial Examination of the Act against Freemasons' (1757) in the Appendix of *The Free Masons Pocket Companion* (1761)	LMFL, BE 98 SCO / L875
Richard Lewis, *The Free-Masons Advocate. Or, Falsehood Detected* (1760)	LMFL, A 798 LEW / L1144
Laurence Dermott, *Ahiman Rezon*, 2nd edn, excerpt containing polemic against Moderns Freemasons and in praise of Antients Freemasonry (1764)	LMFL, BE 94 GRA (ANT) / L14245

[Anon.], *A Defence of Free-Masonry, as Prac-*
ticed in the Regular Lodges, both Foreign and
Domestic under the Constitution of the English
Grand Master (1765)

LMFL, Facsimile reprint in H. Sadler,
Masonic Reprints and Historical
Revelations Including Original Notes and
Additions (London, 1898). B 10 SAD
/ L1030

[Anon.], *Masonry the Way to Hell, a Sermon*
(1768)

LMFL, A 791 FRE / 5508a

[Anon.], *Masonry Vindicated: a Sermon.*
Wherein is Clearly and Demonstratively
Proved, that a Sermon, Lately Published,
'Intitled Masonry the Way to Hell', is an Intire
Piece of the Utmost Weakness, and Absurdity
(1768)

LMFL, A 791 FRE / L5808b

George Smith, 'Ancient and Modern Reasons
Why the Ladies Have Never Been Admitted
into the Society of Freemasons', in *The Use*
and Abuse of Free-Masonry (1783)

LMFL, A 33 SMI / L12208

[A Friend to Truth], *A Defence of Free*
Masons etc., in Answer to Professor John Robi-
son's Proofs of a Conspiracy (1797)

LMFL, A 798 FRI / L60334

[Anon.], *The Indictment and Trial of John*
Andrew, Shoemaker in Maybole, Sometime
Teacher of a Private School There, and Robert
Ramsay, Cart Wright There, Both Members
of a Masonic Lodge at Maybole: Charged with
the Crime of Sedition, and Administering
Unlawful Oaths (1800)

National Library of Scotland, Special
Collections Reading Room, Yule.61(10)

[Anon.], *Petition and Complaint at Brother*
Gibson's Instance Against Brother Mitchell,
and His Answers Thereto; With the Proce-
dure of the Grand Lodge Thereon and Proof
Adduced (1808)

British Library, 4783.ee.21.(20.)

[Anon.], *An Exposition of the Causes which*
Have Produced the Late Dissensions Among
the Free Masons of Scotland (1808)

British Library, 4783.ee.21.(29.)

[Anon.] *An Enquiry into the Late Disputes*
among the Free-Masons of Ireland; Wherein
is Detailed a Free and Important Account of
the Different Transactions which Gave Rise
to, and Continued the Controversy, from the
Commencement to the Establishment of the
Grand Lodge of Ulster (1812)

Library of Freemasons' Hall, Dublin.
Crossle Collection.